W9-DFG-020

HISTORICAL ENCYCLOPEDIA OF
AMERICAN BUSINESS

HISTORICAL ENCYCLOPEDIA OF
AMERICAN BUSINESS

Volume 2

Gould, Jay—Secret Service, U.S.

Edited by

Richard L. Wilson

University of Tennessee, Chattanooga

SALEM PRESS

Pasadena, California   Hackensack, New Jersey

Editorial Director: Christina J. Moose

Acquisitions Editor: Mark Rehn

Development Editor: R. Kent Rasmussen

Project Editor: Rowena Wildin

Manuscript Editor: Andy Perry

Production Editor: Joyce I. Buchea

Layout: Mary Overell

Design and Graphics: James Hutson

Photo Editor: Cynthia Breslin Beres

Editorial Assistant: Dana Garey

Cover photo: Hulton Archive/Getty Images

Library of Congress Cataloging-in-Publication Data

Historical encyclopedia of American business / edited by Richard L. Wilson.

    p. cm.

Includes bibliographical references and index.

    ISBN 978-1-58765-518-0 (set : alk. paper) — ISBN 978-1-58765-519-7 (vol. 1 : alk. paper) — ISBN 978-1-58765-520-3 (vol. 2 : alk. paper) — ISBN 978-1-58765-521-0 (vol. 3 : alk. paper) 1. United States—Commerce—History—Encyclopedias. 2. Industries—United States—History—Encyclopedias. 3. Industrial management—United States—History—Encyclopedias. 4. Business enterprises—United States—History—Encyclopedias. I. Wilson, Richard L., 1944-

    HF3021.H67 2009

    338.097303—dc22

2009002942

PRINTED IN CANADA

Table of Contents

Complete List of Contents

Volume 1

Volume 2

Volume 3

Gould, Jay

IDENTIFICATION: American financier
BORN: May 27, 1836; Roxbury, New York
DIED: December 2, 1892; New York, New York
SIGNIFICANCE: Gould became rich from buying railroad lines and stocks at bargain prices and selling them for huge profits at a time when American financial markets were largely unregulated. He was almost singlehandedly responsible for the Panic of September 24, 1869, known as Black Friday, when his manipulation of gold prices caused a panic in Wall Street financial markets and a precipitous plunge in stock prices.

Jay Gould was probably one of the most notorious among the robber barons of America's Gilded Age during the mid-nineteenth century. Gould worked his way up from poverty on a rural New York farm to fabulous wealth. He was expert at manipulating the businesses he controlled to maximize his own profits, often at the expense of business partners and stockholders. This was facilitated by the laissez-faire system that typified the capitalism of those years.

Gould made the bulk of his vast fortune (he was worth some $77 million at his death in 1892) in railroads, starting with the Erie Railroad. In the process of gaining control, he apparently bribed officials, including state legislators. He soon expanded his reach all over the country, buying up rail lines at bargain prices and artificially driving up stock prices, mainly by making false claims about profits. By the early 1880's, he controlled more rail trackage than anyone else in the United States. Gould even bought a New York City newspaper, in which he published stories that directly aided his business ventures.

Gould made his most notorious maneuver in 1869, when he attempted to manipulate the price of gold to artificially increase its value. This was not

This Currier & Ives print from 1869 shows Jay Gould attempting to corner the gold market, represented by bulls and bears in a cage. (Library of Congress)

done primarily to make a profit in the metal but as an aid to one of his ever-percolating railroad schemes. On September 24, the United States Treasury countered his moves by dumping gold, and its price plummeted, causing a ripple effect on stock prices, which also tumbled. This date has become known as Black Friday, because many people lost much of their wealth in the ensuing panic, including Gould. However, it was not long before he recouped his own fortunes.

He also had some positive accomplishments. Thousands of miles of additional track were added to at least one of his railroads, and shipping rates were reduced on his routes as a consequence of his trying to force competitors out of business. Among Gould's other business ventures were ownership of most of the New York City elevated railroad system and a telegraph company. Undeniably clever, but known for using his great business acumen mainly for self-enrichment, Gould is remembered for being the man who nearly plunged the United States into economic chaos.

Roy Liebman

FURTHER READING
Ackerman, Kenneth. *The Gold Ring: Jim Fisk, Jay Gould and Black Friday, 1869.* New York: Carroll & Graf, 2005.
Klein, Maury. *The Life and Legend of Jay Gould.* Baltimore: Johns Hopkins University Press, 1986.
Renehan, Edward. *Dark Genius of Wall Street: The Misunderstood Life of Jay Gould, King of the Robber Barons.* New York: Basic Books, 2005.

SEE ALSO: Black Friday; Carnegie, Andrew; Railroads; Robber barons; Stanford, Leland; Stock markets; Treasury, U.S. Department of the; Vanderbilt, Cornelius.

Government spending

DEFINITION: Expenditures by federal, state, and local governments
SIGNIFICANCE: In addition to its impact on the entire economy, spending by government provides attractive opportunities and subsidies for numerous businesses. Such spending, however, requires revenue that is acquired either by taxation or borrowing, both of which reduce the funds available for private-sector investments. Taxes, moreover, are levied on businesses' profits and property.

In the United States, government spending occurs at the levels of the national, state, and local governments. As in other modern democracies, public expenditures since the 1930's have grown substantially more rapidly than the economy as a whole. Not unexpectedly, spending has grown the most dramatically in those program areas that have the greatest appeal for the majority of voters, particularly social programs such as Social Security, Medicare, and Medicaid. In the private sector, the incomes of Americans are quite unequal, but in the political arena, where each citizen has one vote, power is somewhat more evenly distributed. Americans possessing great wealth are outnumbered by those with moderate and low incomes, and on election days, there is a strong tendency for people to vote for candidates and issues according to their perceptions of their particular economic interests. These perceptions may be influenced by advertisements and other forms of political speech available only to the wealthy or to collectively wealthy entities.

Although businesses in the private sector usually express a desire for low taxes, they also demand a variety of services. Because businesses have such different interests, they are unable to present a united front on the issue of government spending. A significant number of industries can exist only by selling their goods and services to government. This is particularly true of those that provide products and research for the military-industrial complex, which President Dwight D. Eisenhower helped name in a cautionary speech delivered as he left office. Producers of agricultural products, both family farms and large agribusinesses, constitute a large sector that is heavily dependent on government subsidies. Many construction firms contract with governments to build roads and public buildings. In the movement toward privatization, moreover, private businesses operate prisons in several states, and some even provide quasi-military operations in Iraq and other areas of conflict.

GROWTH IN SPENDING
Because of economic growth and inflation over the years, the most significant indicator of govern-

GOVERNMENT SPENDING, SELECTED AREAS, 1990-2006, IN BILLIONS OF DOLLARS

Area	1990	1995	2000	2003	2004	2005	2006
Total	1,253	1,516	1,789	2,160	2,393	2,472	2,655
Social Security	249	336	409	475	496	523	549
National defense	299	272	294	405	456	495	522
Medicare	98	160	197	249	269	299	330
Education	23	32	34	59	64	75	96
Veterans' benefits	29	38	47	57	60	70	70
Administration of justice	10	17	29	35	46	40	41
Natural resources and environment	17	22	25	30	31	28	33
International development and humanitarian assistance	6	8	7	10	14	18	17
Space flight, research, and supporting activities	12	13	12	13	15	15	15

Source: Data from the *Statistical Abstract of the United States, 2008* (Washington, D.C.: Department of Commerce, Economics and Statistics Administration, Bureau of the Census, Data User Services Division, 2008)

ment spending is its percentage of the gross domestic product (GDP), which refers to the total amount of money spent on goods and services in the country. Official, nonpartisan statistics since 1929 are available from the Bureau of Economic Analysis, an agency of the U.S. Department of Commerce.

For 150 years, from the time of George Washington until the early 1930's, government's share of the economy during peacetime was relatively small and stable. In 1929, spending by the national government was only 2.5 percent of GDP, and total spending by national, state, and local governments totaled about 7.7 percent of GDP. Because the functions of government were very limited, regulatory agencies were few in number, and they did not require large bureaucracies. Although the national government provided modest retirement benefits for veterans, public officials, and civil service employees, it sponsored no general entitlement programs such as Social Security. Americans did not perceive any great threat from abroad, and except for the years of the U.S. Civil War and World War I, the cost of maintaining an army and navy made up a small part of the small national budget.

Government spending, especially at the national level, really began to take off as a result of the Great Depression of the 1930's. Between 1929 and 1932, federal expenditures grew only modestly, from $2.6 billion to $3 billion, but the GDP declined dramati-cally, from $103.4 billion to $58.7 billion. As a result, the federal government's percentage of GDP went from 2.5 percent to 5 percent by the election year of 1932. From 1933 to 1938, Congress enacted a host of New Deal programs aimed at the so-called three R's: relief, recovery, and reform. The programs included public works for the unemployed, subsidies for farmers, numerous business regulations, and entitlements under the Social Security Act. By 1938, the year when the last major New Deal laws were passed, spending by the national government had grown to 8.4 percent of GDP. It was only after 1940, when monthly payments of the Social Security retirement plan began, that the long-term costs of the New Deal really began take effect.

During World War II, defense expenditures exploded, going from 2 percent of GDP in 1940 to almost half of GDP in 1945. As a result, the total national debt increased from 43 percent of GDP in 1940 to about 120 percent in 1946. Following the war, defense spending came down to 7 percent of GDP in 1947. Other spending also declined, but not to prewar levels. In 1947, federal spending made up 15.3 percent of GDP, whereas the total of federal, state, and local spending represented 19.9 percent of GDP. Because of the Cold War, combined with the growth of Social Security and other domestic programs, federal spending by this time was almost equal to the amount spent by state and local governments combined. By the end of the century, federal spending would be almost twice as much as state and local expenditures.

The next big jump in government spending occurred during the 1960's, primarily as a result of Lyndon B. Johnson's Great Society programs, particularly Medicare, Medicaid, and federal subsidies for education. In subsequent years, additional social programs—such as Supplementary Security Income (SSI), the Cost of Living Adjustment (COLA), and the Earned Income Tax Credit (EITC), among others—further expanded spending, especially by the federal government. Thereafter, an increasing percentage of the budget involved the transfer of income from one group to another. In 1929, transfer programs represented only about 3 percent of all government expenditures, but by 2004, they had increased to almost 44 percent. Defense spending, in contrast, sharply declined, falling from 13.8 percent of GDP in 1953 to 6.3 percent in 1988.

Between 1980 and 2007, total government expenditures at all levels remained fairly stable as a percentage of GDP. In 1980, federal spending totaled $591 billion, which constituted 21.6 percent of the GDP (which stood at about $2.8 trillion). In 2007, the federal government spent $2.9 trillion, which represented some 22 percent of GDP (which had grown to $13.8 trillion). Total government spending that year was $4.6 billion, about 33.3 percent of GDP. Because of the aging of the population, however, many financial experts predicted that paying for entitlement commitments, especially Medicare and Medicaid, would become difficult by the third decade of the century.

Government spending is divided into three major types: purchases of goods and services for current use; purchases of goods and services intended to provide future benefits, as in entitlements and research; and transfer payments, as in Social Security and antipoverty programs. Government spending is also separated into discretionary and mandatory spending. Discretionary spending, which makes up about one-third of federal spending, applies to components such as national defense, education, and highway projects. Each year, Congress has the option of determining how much money to spend on these programs. Programs with mandatory spending, which accounts for two-thirds of government spending, are authorized by permanent laws. They include entitlements like Social Security, Medicare, and Medicaid, in which individuals receive benefits based on age, income, or other criteria. Spending levels for these programs depend on how many people qualify for the benefits.

FISCAL POLICY

The federal government's fiscal policies—which include policies governing taxes, expenditures, and borrowing—have a profound impact on the economy. Early each year, the president, working with the Office of Management and Budget (OMB), presents a proposed budget to the Congress, which has the constitutional authority to approve, reject, or change the various proposals. Surpluses, which occur when revenues are greater than expenditures, have been rare since the 1930's. Deficits, which occur when expenditures exceed revenues, become a part of the national debt.

Keynesian economic theory, named after British economist John Maynard Keynes, has been the dominant liberal paradigm since the 1930's. The theory is based on the premise that government can help maintain growth and stability within a mixed capitalistic system. Because the aggregate demand for goods tends to be insufficient in periods of recession or depression, the result is a growth in unemployment and a loss of potential output. Keynes therefore emphasized that government spending, even if it results in a deficit, should be increased during downturns to expand aggregate demand, thereby stimulating economic activity and reducing unemployment. The theory suggests that government spending might be reduced during periods of prosperity. Experience has demonstrated, however, that it is easy for government to increase spending at any time, but that reductions are always difficult to achieve. For this reason, some economics view Keynes's theory on stimulation as a valid guide for periods of slowdown but irrelevant in good times.

A significant number of economists, especially those with conservative tendencies, do not agree with Keynes's theories. Libertarians, distrustful of governmental meddling in the economy, generally advocate minimal public spending under all circumstances. Milton Friedman, the most influential libertarian economist of the second half of the twentieth century, opposed the use of fiscal policy as a tool to manage aggregate demand. His school of economic thought, called monetarism, holds that a stable supply of money is the key to obtaining long-term prosperity. A related theory, called supply-side economics, developed by economist Arthur Laffer, holds that when too much of the nation's income is collected in taxes, the inevitable consequence is too little money left for purchases and investments in the private sector. Although proponents of supply-side theory focus on taxes much more than on spending, experience has forced them to admit that tax reductions will require some restraints in spending to prevent huge deficits.

DEFICITS AND DEBT

Economists sharply disagree about the extent to which deficit spending and the resulting national debt are problems. It is difficult to deny, nevertheless, that large deficits have two negative results: They tend to promote inflation, and paying for the interest on the resulting debt limits the money available for other purposes. The majority of economists, therefore, advocate avoiding deficits, except during periods of economic slowdown.

From the end of World War II until the 1980's, budget deficits were usually less than 2 percent of GDP, and as a result the national debt, as a percentage of the GDP, significantly declined. During the 1980's, however, because of increases in defense spending without comparable reductions in other areas, the deficit rose to between 3 and 5 percent of GDP, so that the national debt, which stood at $909 billion in 1989, grew to $2.87 trillion in 1989. During the early twenty-first century, tax reductions combined with the War on Terrorism again expanded the national debt. By the end of 2007, the national debt, which was slightly more than $9 trillion, equaled 66 percent of GDP. With growing entitlement commitments from retiring baby boomers, some economists predicted that annual federal deficits by the mid-twenty-first century would perhaps grow to 9 percent of GDP.

Thomas Tandy Lewis

FURTHER READING

Bittle, Scott, and Jean Johnson. *Where Does the Money Go? Your Guided Tour to the Federal Budget Crisis.* New York: HarperCollins, 2008. Compelling and straightforward analysis of fiscal policies, warning against the harmful consequences of large deficits.

Konigsberg, Charles. *America's Priorities: How the U.S. Government Raises and Spends $3 Billion.* Bloomington: AuthorHouse, 2008. Clearly written and in-

formed guide to the complexities of the federal budget, finding that the growth rate of entitlement programs must be reduced.

Peterson, Peter G., and Neil Howe. *On Borrowed Time: How the Growth in Entitlement Spending Threatens America's Future.* Washington, D.C.: Resources for the Future, 2004. Warns that if major reductions are not made in entitlement benefits, the nation will face catastrophe in the years after 2018.

Rubin, Irene. *The Politics of Public Budgeting: Getting and Spending, Borrowing and Balancing.* Washington, D.C.: CQ Press, 2005. Considers federal, state, and local budgeting within a comparative framework, with the thesis that short-term partisan goals often trump long-term public interest;

Schick, Allen. *Federal Budget: Politics, Policy, Process.* Washington, D.C.: Brookings Institution Press, 2007. Explains budgeting at each stage of executive and legislative action, and assesses how the budget effects social issues.

Wildavsky, Aaron, and Naomi Caiden. *The New Politics of the Budgetary Process.* 5th ed. New York: Longman, 2004. Standard textbook arguing that budgetary decisions are based on power, with separate chapters on entitlements, defense, reforms, and deficits.

Yarrow, Andrew. *Forgive Us Our Debts: The Intergenerational Dangers of Fiscal Irresponsibility.* New Haven: Yale University Press, 2008. Discussion of how Social Security, Medicare, and other programs have increased the federal debt, warning of harmful effects if spending is not brought under control.

SEE ALSO: Congress, U.S.; Constitution, U.S.; Monetary policy, federal; Presidency, U.S.; Taxation; Treasury, U.S. Department of the.

Granger movement

THE EVENT: Farmers' movement centered on a set of advocacy clubs known collectively as the Grange

DATE: 1867-early 1870's

PLACE: Midwest

SIGNIFICANCE: The Granger movement worked to improve economic conditions for farmers, lobbying for the creation of railroad and warehouse commissions in several midwestern states. Although Supreme Court decisions later undercut the commissions' power, the movement helped pave the way for the passage of the Interstate Commerce Act in 1887.

Originally founded in 1867 by Oliver Hudson Kelley and six others as a fraternal organization for farmers, the National Grange of the Patrons of Husbandry (also known as the Grange) began to engage in political action during the early 1870's. The years immediately following the U.S. Civil War were difficult ones for U.S. farmers, especially in the Midwest. A combination of falling grain prices and high, often discriminatory, rates charged by railroads, grain elevators, and warehouses brought many farmers to the brink of financial ruin. To combat the powerful economic institutions they felt were arrayed against them, members of the Grange and other farm organizations lobbied for the states to regulate them.

The pre-Civil War era had already seen some successful state regulation—as early as 1831 in New York State, for example. The Granger movement brought about far more comprehensive efforts, beginning in Illinois in 1871. In that year, Illinois passed a law establishing a railroad and warehouse commission to regulate rates. Further legislation in 1873 strengthened this regulatory process. The following year, three additional midwestern states—Iowa, Minnesota, and Wisconsin—established similar commissions. These laws came to be known collectively as "Granger laws," although the Grange itself was only a part of the process that led to their enactment.

In 1877, the constitutionality of the Granger laws was upheld in the U.S. Supreme Court decision *Munn v. Illinois*. Nine years later, however, the decision was reversed in *Wabash, St. Louis and Pacific Railway Co. v. Illinois*. This defeat of state regulation contributed to the passage by Congress of the Interstate Commerce Act in 1887, which set the stage for the federal regulation of railroads during the early twentieth century.

The political influence of the Grange, which had peaked in the first half of the 1870's, diminished as the decade progressed, and the organization was superseded during the 1880's by the various regional organizations composing the farmers' alliance movement. In addition to its role in the passage of the "Granger laws," the Grange during the early 1870's inspired a wide range of cooperative en-

A promotional print from about 1873 for Grange members showing scenes of farming and farm life. (Library of Congress)

terprises, including cooperatively owned grain elevators, warehouses, retail stores, and banks that provided assistance to farmers. The majority of these, however, did not survive the decade.

Scott Wright

FURTHER READING
Carstensen, Vernon, ed. *Farmer Discontent, 1865-1900*. New York: John Wiley & Sons, 1974.
Miller, George H. *Railroads and the Granger Laws*. Madison: University of Wisconsin Press, 1971.
Rugh, Susan Sessions. *Our Common Country: Family Farming, Culture, and Community in the Nineteenth-Century Midwest*. Bloomington: Indiana University Press, 2001.

SEE ALSO: Agriculture; Farm labor; Farm protests; Panic of 1873; Railroads; Supreme Court and commerce.

Great Atlantic and Pacific Tea Company

IDENTIFICATION: Supermarket chain
DATE: Founded in 1859
SIGNIFICANCE: The Great Atlantic and Pacific Tea Company (A&P) was America's first retail chain and made a lasting impact on the distribution of food in the United States.

George P. Gilman and George H. Hartford had a new concept for selling tea: direct buying, eliminating all middlemen, and taking only a small profit per pound. Using this concept, the two men started a small tea company in New York City in 1859. Two years later, it was named the Great American Tea Company. They developed the Club Plan, a nationwide mail-order concept that created an incentive for merchants or individuals to band into "clubs" so that they could purchase quality tea below prevailing prices. Another innovation was a money-back guarantee to customers not satisfied with any purchase. Within a few years, the company captured a notable share of the tea market. In 1869, to indicate future plans for expansion, the company was renamed the Great Atlantic and Pacific Tea Company.

By 1871, A&P had opened a store in Chicago, the first store west of New York City. To generate more business, A&P sold tea at wholesale to independent peddlers and subsequently established its own wagon routes, adding an extensive line of condiments and household items. New stores opened as far west as on the Mississippi River, and by 1878, the company had more than one hundred retail stores. During the 1880's, the company added new products, including A&P baking powder and Eight O'Clock coffee. Innovations continued to increase business. In 1912, the company began opening Economy Stores, thus demonstrating that food could be sold at a substantially lower prices by buying in bulk and setting up standardized, no-frills stores. Within fifteen years, the company grew to more than 15,000 stores with an annual sales volume exceeding $1 billion.

In October, 1929, A&P was on top of the food retailing world, apparently unaffected by the Depression. Some competitors went bankrupt; others formed a new method of retailing, and the American supermarket was born. Thinking the supermarket was a fad, A&P ignored an initial downturn in its business. However, it became apparent that supermarkets were the future, and A&P began to convert its operations. By the end of 1950, 15,000 small stores had been converted to more than 4,000 supermarkets. However, competition began to affect A&P's sales, and the company scaled back. In 1979, the Tengelmann Group, a West German food retailer, acquired A&P and restructured the company, selling unprofitable stores and manufacturing plants.

Despite closing all stores west of the Mississippi and selling its Canadian stores, A&P remained a major player in food retailing. It purchased other chains, such as Waldbaum's and Pathmark. As of 2008, A&P had 447 stores, concentrated in the Northeast, and had annual sales of about $9.4 billion.

Marcia B. Dinneen

FURTHER READING
Adamy, Janet. "A&P Narrows Its Loss." *The Wall Street Journal*, May 11, 2005, p. B3.
Walsh, William. *The Rise and Decline of the Great Atlantic and Pacific Tea Company*. Secaucus, N.J.: Lyle Stuart, 1986.

SEE ALSO: Beef industry; Fishing industry; Food-processing industries; Pork industry; Poultry industry; Retail trade industry; United Food and Commercial Workers; Warehouse and discount stores.

Great Depression

THE EVENT: Major, global economic downturn
DATE: 1929-1941
PLACE: United States
SIGNIFICANCE: The most pervasive and sustained event ever to affect American business, the Great Depression brought about the end of the laissez-faire approach that had characterized the American business world from the nineteenth century through the 1920's and paved the way for government intervention in business and finance.

The Great Depression is generally seen as having lasted from the stock market crash of October, 1929, until the entry of the United States into World War II in December, 1941. However, it is a mistake to conclude that the stock market crash itself caused the Depression. An economic depression as deep and sustained as that of the 1930's can be attributed only to a complex of causes that converge to create a business environment poised for disaster. The stock market crash did indeed contribute to the economic instability that marked the Depression, but many other factors were responsible for the Depression, which continued for almost a decade after the stock market reached its bottom and began its slow recovery in June, 1932.

The U.S. economy suffered a number of economic declines and even a few outright panics between the founding of the republic during the late eighteenth century and 1929. The major difference between earlier panics and the one that brought about the Great Depression was that previous panics, like those in 1837 and 1857, played out in approximately one year, after which the economy began to recover and revitalize. It was unprecedented in American history to have an economic panic last for over a decade with little measurable relief.

THE CRISIS IN FARMING

Although the Depression that affected America's business sector began full-fledged in 1929, American farmers had endured an agricultural depression through much of the 1920's. Prices for farm goods increased early in the decade, causing many farmers to invest in more land to raise the crops that commanded favorable prices. Much of what farmers owned was bought on credit, so when overproduction led to a steep decline in the price of agricultural products, many farmers found themselves overextended and unable to pay their debts. Some were able to hang on, renting land that enabled them to continue farming on a more marginal basis. Others gravitated to cities to live with relatives and, they hoped, to find enough work to keep them solvent.

After World War I, American society had completed its swing from an agricultural to an industrial economy. It still depended, however, on farmers to produce the food people needed to survive. During the 1920's, farming became more mechanized. This mechanization allowed farmers to produce more food, and the excellent growing conditions of the early 1930's resulted in even more agricultural production. As a consequence of the resulting overproduction, prices were driven down, and farmers were unable to earn enough to sustain themselves. Many defaulted on their mortgages and were driven from their land. Between 1929 and 1932, farm prices declined by 53 percent, largely because of an oversupply of food. Droughts in much of the Midwest and Southwest in 1934 and 1936 drastically reduced this oversupply, but they also created dust bowls. Fertile topsoil was reduced to dust and blown away with every strong wind, leaving once-productive land impossible to cultivate.

LOOMING ECONOMIC PROBLEMS

Although many sectors of the economy flourished during the 1920's, some industries were as depressed as farming during that decade. The textile industry suffered serious declines, and mining was also becoming an unprofitable enterprise. Between 1920 and 1929, bank failures occurred at the rate of six hundred each year. An estimated twenty thousand other businesses were forced to close annually because of the deteriorating financial situation. As banks failed, more people became distrustful of them and withdrew their savings, creating severe liquidity problems even for strong financial institutions.

The 1920's witnessed significant growth in some sectors of the business world, as people rushed to buy such consumer goods as radios, automobiles, and a variety of electrical appliances being introduced onto the market. A majority of consumers paid for their purchases by signing installment contracts that required a small down payment and regular subsequent payments until the item they bought was fully paid for.

Automobile registration increased from 9 million during the early 1920's to more than 27 million in 1930. Americans went into debt to buy cars and appliances such as refrigerators and washing machines, both of which were novelties during the 1920's. As the job market began to contract, people saddled with installment payments were frequently unable to make their payments, and the banks that had financed their installment purchases suffered huge losses. Between 1929 and 1932, 44 percent of U.S. banks (more than 11,000 institutions) failed.

GOVERNMENT INTERVENTION

Panicky depositors in banks rushed to withdraw their savings, creating severe liquidity problems for financial institutions that often could accommodate their clients' withdrawals only by selling off their assets at severely depressed prices. Once these assets were exhausted, many banks had no recourse but to close their doors.

Herbert Hoover, president of the United States from 1929 until 1933, believed that the government should not intervene in matters that laissez-faire economists considered the responsibility of bankers and financiers. Under Hoover, the Federal Reserve was powerless to help resolve the banks' liquidity crises. Because the United States maintained a fixed exchange rate, the Federal Reserve could not increase the amount of money in circulation. During Hoover's administration, higher interest rates reduced consumer spending, which, in turn, led to increases in unemployment among those who produced consumer goods. The unemployment rate increased from 9 percent in 1930 to a staggering 25 percent in 1933.

The Smoot-Hawley Tariff Act of 1930 imposed high tariffs on imported goods and led to retaliation by other countries, which raised their tariffs on imports from the United States, causing another economic crisis. In this period of widespread unemployment, many youths from middle America left home to seek work in the West, hitching rides on freight trains. Hobo villages grew up along many railroad tracks, populated by young men desperate for work who lived by begging for food or seeking shelter and sustenance from charitable organizations.

Groups of farmers whose property had been foreclosed on congregated in the seedier parts of many cities, where they erected flimsy shelters made largely from cardboard and packing crates. These villages, where whole families often lived for months at a time, were dubbed "Hoovervilles" to direct attention to the president who, in the eyes of those who were dispossessed, made the shantytowns necessary. Despite such conditions, the Hoover admin-

A breadline at McCauley Water Street Mission under Brooklyn Bridge, New York, in the early 1930's. (Library of Congress)

istration continued to believe that it was not the government's role to intervene.

ROOSEVELT AND THE NEW DEAL

The laissez-faire attitudes that long had characterized Republican policies were well entrenched. Between 1860 and 1932, the United States had elected just two presidents who were not Republicans. However, with the economic troubles gripping the nation during the early 1930's, it was clear that ingrained attitudes of the past were not adequate to deal with the looming problems of the Great Depression. In 1932, Franklin D. Roosevelt, a Democrat, was elected president of the United States.

After his inauguration in March, 1933, Roosevelt's first official act was to declare a bank holiday that would remain in effect for two weeks. The governors of many states had declared similar bank holidays in their states in the immediate past, but Roosevelt realized that despite the Republican obsession with states' rights, the growing economic meltdown called for drastic measures. He could not allow the run on banks to continue without jeopardizing every financial institution in the country. Unlike Hoover, Roosevelt considered it the responsibility of government to take positive and decisive action to control the spread of what had developed into a major worldwide depression.

The most immediate need was to provide relief for those in dire straits. The president called Congress into a special session, later called the Hundred Days, to deal urgently with the economic crisis. He urged Congress to devise means of employing vast numbers of the unemployed. In 1933, Congress created numerous government agencies to put the economy back on track. The Federal Emergency Relief Administration funneled government funds directly to individual states to provide assistance to the needy and to subsidize organized charities within those states.

To employ the thousands of young men unable to find work, Congress established the Civilian Conservation Corps, which employed—and often housed and fed—young workers who needed assistance. The Public Works Administration provided funds for projects related to building and maintaining the nation's infrastructure, focusing on bridges and dams. In 1935, the Works Progress Administration, later renamed the Works Projects Administration, was established to facilitate such projects as building or expanding airports, building roads, and constructing hospitals and schools. Even though such agencies provided employment for millions, they could not accommodate everyone who needed work. Millions remained unemployed throughout the 1930's.

Among the many regulatory agencies created during the decade, none had a more lasting effect on the American economy than the Federal Deposit Insurance Corporation, an agency that insures commercial bank deposits up to a specified maximum. This insurance gives bank depositors confidence that the money they deposit in their bank accounts will be safe even if the bank holding their money fails.

THE RECOVERY

World War II erupted in Europe in 1939. With the Japanese bombing of Pearl Harbor on December 7, 1941, the United States was drawn into this conflict. As many of the nation's young men were conscripted into military service, many of the jobs they vacated in the private sector became available. The need to produce war supplies kept American industries working twenty-four hours a day, seven days a week. Women, who, during the Depression, had been discouraged from working, were in great demand to work in defense industries. Many impoverished African Americans from the South, who had experienced great difficulty in finding work, were drawn to northern cities where there was more than enough work to sustain them.

The war helped focus the attention of Americans on unifying a country that had been severely tested by the frustrations of the long depression that beset it. President Roosevelt worked miracles in establishing the New Deal, but it took World War II to bring a decisive end to the worst economic disaster the United States had ever experienced.

R. Baird Shuman

FURTHER READING

Himmelberg, Robert F. *The Great Depression and the New Deal*. Westport, Conn.: Greenwood Press, 2001. Himmelberg's evaluation of the New Deal, to which Chapter 6 is devoted, is particularly relevant. The author considers the political, economic, and social implications of the Depression.
Meltzer, Milton. *Driven from the Land: The Story of the Dust Bowl*. New York: Marshall Cavendish, 2000. Relates anecdotally how sustained droughts and

the ensuing dust bowls wreaked havoc on farmers throughout much of the southwestern United States.

Neal, Steve. *Happy Days Are Here Again: The 1932 Democratic Convention, the Emergence of FDR, and How America Was Changed Forever.* New York: William Morrow, 2004. Written for general audiences, this account of Franklin D. Roosevelt's rise to the presidency and of his response to the Depression is particularly strong in explaining in detail the New Deal that Roosevelt instituted. An essential resource.

Nishi, Dennis. *Life During the Great Depression.* San Diego, Calif.: Lucent Books, 1998. Presents vivid accounts of how the Depression uprooted and altered the lives of those caught in its grips.

Olson, James S., ed. *Historical Dictionary of the Great Depression, 1929-1940.* Westport, Conn.: Greenwood Press, 2001. Thorough resource that makes salient information about the Depression easily available to readers and researchers.

Wheeler, Mark, ed. *The Economics of the Great Depression.* Kalamazoo, Mich.: W. E. Upjohn Institute for Employment Research, 1998. Collects six essays dealing with the most significant aspects of the Great Depression.

SEE ALSO: Depression of 1784; Depression of 1808-1809; Financial crisis of 2008; New Deal programs; Panic of 1819; Panic of 1837; Panic of 1857; Panic of 1873; Panic of 1893; Panic of 1907; Recession of 1937-1938; Stock market crash of 1929; Stock markets.

Great Migration

THE EVENT: Mass movement of African Americans from the southern United States to northern and western urban areas

DATE: 1915-1960

PLACE: United States

SIGNIFICANCE: Driven from the rural South by economic upheavals and drawn to urban areas by their growing manufacturing and service sectors, millions of African Americans fueled a transformation of the American economy that spanned several decades, leading to dramatic changes in the economies of many American cities and to the economic empowerment of African Americans in those cities.

The Great Migration of African Americans both influenced and was influenced by dramatic changes in the American economy during the twentieth century. In the southern United States, cotton crops were destroyed by boll weevil infestations and a series of natural disasters during the early decades of the century. At the same time, agricultural mechanization significantly increased productivity. Thus, the South experienced a surplus of agricultural labor, which the Great Migration relieved.

In turn, the mass movement of African Americans to northern and western cities fueled the burgeoning automobile and defense industries. Most employment opportunities for African Americans were not in these industries but in service jobs vacated by whites for factory employment. These jobs, however, were necessary to sustain the communities growing up around the automobile and defense factories, and they contributed to the economic empowerment of African American migrants. Many of these newly employed migrants found themselves with substantial disposable income for the first time in their lives.

As a result, the Great Migration produced a dramatic increase in the number of black-owned businesses. African American patronage of white businesses outside the South remained limited by customary segregation, discrimination, and an ingrained reluctance of many African Americans to purchase goods and services from whites. Thus, black-owned businesses such as restaurants, barbershops, and insurance companies proliferated in urban areas during the Great Migration, and they thrived as African Americans continued to pour into northern and western cities.

Migrants from rural areas to southern cities also increased the number of black-owned businesses in the segregated South during the first half of the twentieth century. Much of this growth was short-lived, however, as black-owned businesses suffered a significant decline with the integration of American society during the 1960's and 1970's, which broke down many traditional barriers to African American patronage of white businesses. The growth of retail chains further diminished the presence of black-owned businesses during the late twentieth century.

Despite the absence of legal segregation outside the South, segregation by custom relegated most African Americans to specific locations within urban areas, leading to the creation of ghettos as these areas grew increasingly neglected by government officials and property owners. As the urban African American population grew, these blighted areas spread. Many white residents responded by abandoning city life for the growing suburbs, leading to further neglect and deterioration. As a result, many American cities experienced decades of economic decline that in many cases did not begin to reverse until the late twentieth century.

Michael H. Burchett

FURTHER READING

Baldwin, Davarian L. *Chicago's New Negroes: Modernity, the Great Migration, and Black Urban Life.* Chapel Hill: University of North Carolina Press, 2007.

Gregory, James N. *The Southern Diaspora: How the Great Migration of Black and White Southerners Transformed America.* Chapel Hill: University of North Carolina Press, 2005.

McDonald, John F. *Urban America: Growth, Crisis, and Rebirth.* Armonk, N.Y.: M. E. Sharpe, 2008.

SEE ALSO: Agriculture; Arms industry; Automotive industry; Farm labor; Internal migration; Military-industrial complex.

Greenspan, Alan

IDENTIFICATION: Thirteenth chair of the board of governors of the Federal Reserve Bank, 1987-2006

BORN: March 6, 1926; New York, New York

SIGNIFICANCE: The chair of the Federal Reserve is often described as the most powerful person in the United States after the president. In this role, Greenspan guided the nation's monetary policy, helping maintain a stable business environment with relatively low inflation and unemployment.

A man of humble beginnings, Alan Greenspan seemed destined for a career in music rather than as the second longest serving chair of the Federal Reserve. In the fall of 1943, Greenspan was accepted at the prestigious Juilliard School. By early 1944, the chance to play with a jazz band took him on the road. However, that fall, realizing that he would never be a great musician, he left music to study economics at New York University.

In 1954, with a master's degree in economics from New York University and experience gained through his work at the Conference Board, a nonprofit organization that analyzes business activity, Greenspan partnered with William Townsend to form Townsend-Greenspan, which provided economic analyses to businesses. In this role, Greenspan gained an in-depth knowledge of the economy.

During the early 1950's, Greenspan was introduced to novelist and philosopher Ayn Rand and eventually became part of her inner circle. Rand, a proponent of free-market capitalism and distrustful of government involvement in the economy, had a profound influence on Greenspan. As part of her group, in 1966 Greenspan wrote an essay critical of the Federal Reserve, the central bank of the United States, and the role it played in creating inflation; he argued for a strict gold standard to tame the forces leading to inflation.

Ironically, just more than twenty years later, Greenspan was selected by President Ronald Reagan to lead the Federal Reserve. Greenspan had come to the attention of Republicans through one of his former bandmates, Leonard Garment. Gar-

Alan Greenspan. (AP/Wide World Photos)

ment, a law partner of Richard Nixon, brought Greenspan into Nixon's 1968 presidential campaign. Later, Greenspan served as chair of the Council of Economic Advisors in the Ford Administration. By 1987, with his service in government and his experience analyzing the economy, Greenspan was seen as the leading candidate to replace Paul Volcker at the Federal Reserve.

Despite his previous criticisms of the agency, Greenspan was able to show how the Federal Reserve could provide a stable economic environment with low inflation, promoting economic growth and low unemployment. During his nearly nineteen-year tenure, Greenspan garnered much praise for the role he played in helping guide the economy through a number of potentially devastating crises, including the stock market crash in October, 1987, and the dot-com bubble in 2000. Under his leadership, the U.S. economy enjoyed modest growth with only two relatively minor recessions, in 1990-1991 and 2001. His words and actions were able to calm markets and maintain a relatively stable business environment.

During a Congressional hearing in October, 2008, however, Greenspan was harshly criticized for the role that his economic policies may have played in the financial crisis. He admitted being surprised by the depth of the crisis and stated that his belief in deregulation had been shaken. He said he had placed too much faith in the market's powers for self-correction and failed to anticipate the mortgage lenders' self-destructive actions. He still maintained that the changes occurring in the market during the crisis would function as a natural restraint on markets and his only suggestion for regulation was that any company selling mortgage-backed securities be required to hold a specified number of them.

Randall Hannum

FURTHER READING

Fleckenstein, William A., and Frederick Sheehan. *Greenspan's Bubbles: The Age of Ignorance at the Federal Reserve.* New York: McGraw-Hill, 2008.

Greenspan, Alan. *The Age of Turbulence: Adventures in a New World.* New York: Penguin, 2007.

Woodward, Bob. *Maestro: Greenspan's Fed and the American Boom.* New York: Simon & Schuster, 2000.

SEE ALSO: Deregulation of financial institutions; Dot-com bubble; Federal Reserve; Monetary policy, federal; Presidency, U.S.; Stock markets; Wall Street.

Greeting card industry

DEFINITION: Enterprises that manufacture, distribute, and sell cards that are exchanged on holidays, birthdays, and other special occasions

SIGNIFICANCE: The exchange of greeting cards for holidays, birthdays, and other occasions helps to promote retail sales of gift items, and greeting cards themselves have become an important industry. The greeting card industry has become a multibillion-dollar industry, helped by an explosive growth in electronic technology and burgeoning consumer use of the Internet.

The exchange of greeting cards is one of the oldest and most widely accepted holiday customs in the United States. The custom of sending greeting cards can be traced back to the ancient Chinese, who exchanged messages of goodwill to celebrate the New Year, and to the early Egyptians, who conveyed their greetings on papyrus scrolls. By the early fifteenth century, handmade paper greeting cards were being exchanged in Europe. The Germans are known to have printed New Year's greetings from woodcuts as early as 1400, and handmade paper Valentine's Day cards were being exchanged in various parts of Europe during the early to mid-fifteenth century.

From the mid-nineteenth century through much of the twentieth century, most cards published in the United States were designed to celebrate Christmas and other religious holidays, birthdays, weddings, anniversaries, births, and other family events. By the early twenty-first century, however, cards were being published for virtually every imaginable occasion or relationship and were being sold through approximately 100,000 retail outlets around the United States. Greeting cards are especially popular in the United Kingdom, where the average person purchases fifty-five cards per year.

The greeting card industry started as a traditional printing and stationery business during the nineteenth century. The first modern greeting card was actually for Christmas; it appeared in London in 1843, when Sir Henry Cole hired artist John C. Horsley to design a holiday card that he could send to his friends and acquaintances. Although the first known greeting card, a valentine, can be traced back to 1415, it was not until the early nineteenth century and the easy availability of the mail that the

TOP FIVE SELLERS IN THE EVERYDAY AND SEASONAL MARKET

Type of Everyday Card	Percentage of Sales	Type of Seasonal Card	Percentage of Sales
Birthday	60	Christmas	60
Anniversary	8	Valentine's Day	25
Get well	7	Mother's Day	4
Friendship	6	Easter	3
Sympathy	6	Father's Day	3

Source: Data from the Greeting Card Association

buying and sending of greeting cards became popular and affordable. Esther Howland, from Massachusetts, was the first regular publisher of Valentine's Day cards in the United States. She sold her first handmade Valentine's Day card in 1849, eventually establishing a successful publishing firm specializing in the elaborately decorated cards. Between 1855 and 1879, Howland's Valentine's Day cards were one of the most immediately recognized commercially produced symbols and later became highly prized collector's items.

RISE OF THE COMMERCIAL INDUSTRY

By the 1850's, the greeting card had been transformed from a relatively expensive, handmade, and hand-delivered gift to a popular and affordable means of personal communication, largely because of advances in printing and mechanization, as well as the 1840 introduction of the postage stamp. However, Louis Prang, a German immigrant who started a small lithographic business near Boston in 1856, is generally credited with the start of the greeting card industry in the United States. Within ten years, he perfected the color lithographic process; his reproductions of great paintings surpassed those of other graphic artists in both the United States and Great Britain. During the early 1870's, Prang began publishing deluxe editions of Christmas cards, and in 1875, he introduced the first complete line of Christmas cards to the American public. Prang's cards reached the height of their popularity during the early 1890's, when cheap imitative imports began to flood the market. Between 1890 and 1906, there was a marked decline in U.S. greeting card production, but the domestic business climate for greeting cards soon improved. During this time, a

number of the industry's leading publishers were founded. Most of the cards by these fledgling U.S. publishers bore little relation to Prang's elaborate creations. By the early twenty-first century, two American card manufacturers, Hallmark Cards and American Greetings, had become the largest producers of greeting cards in the world.

WORLD WAR II AND BEYOND

During World War II, the industry rallied for the war effort, helping the government sell war bonds and providing cards for the soldiers overseas. This period also marked the beginning of the industry's close relationship with the U.S. Post Office (later the U.S. Postal Service). By the 1950's, the studio card (a long card with a short punch line) appeared on the scene to firmly establish the popularity of humor in American greeting cards.

During the 1980's, alternative cards began to appear that did not honor any particular holiday but rather an event in a person's life, such as a divorce, the beginning or ending of a relationship, or the death of a beloved pet. These cards continue to show the greatest sales growth of all card categories.

During the early twenty-first century, U.S. consumers purchased approximately 7 billion greeting cards each year, generating nearly $7.5 billion in retail sales. More than 90 percent of all U.S. households buy greeting cards, with the average household purchasing thirty individual cards in a year. Women purchase more than 80 percent of all greeting cards. There are an estimated three thousand greeting card publishers in the United States, ranging from small family-run organizations to major corporations.

Martin J. Manning

FURTHER READING

Chase, Ernest Dudley. *The Romance of Greeting Cards: An Historical Account of the Origin, Evolution, and Development of the Christmas Card, Valentine, and Other Forms of Engraved or Printed Greetings from the Earliest Days to the Present Time.* Detroit: Tower Books, 1971. First published in 1926, this is perhaps the first attempt at a full history of greeting cards.

Lavin, Mau, ed. *The Business of Holidays.* New York: Monacelli Press, 2004. Thirty-three essays on topics ranging from Groundhog Day to Christmas explore the American fascination with holidays.

Pleck, Elizabeth Hafkin. *Celebrating the Family: Ethnicity, Consumer Culture, and Family Rituals.* Cambridge, Mass.: Harvard University Press, 2000. Study of the kinds of community and family occasions that have given rise to many lines of greeting cards.

Schmidt, Leigh E. *Consumer Rites: The Buying and Selling of American Holidays.* Princeton, N.J.: Princeton University Press, 1995. Scholarly exploration of the commercialization of the principal holidays for which greeting cards are designed.

Shank, Barry. *A Token of My Affection: Greeting Cards and American Business Culture.* New York: Columbia University Press, 2006. Well-illustrated history of American greeting cards that seeks to place their use within the broader framework of cultural history.

SEE ALSO: Christmas marketing; Postal Service, U.S.; Promotional holidays.

H

Hamilton, Alexander

IDENTIFICATION: First secretary of the Treasury of the United States, 1789-1795
BORN: January 11, 1755; Nevis, British West Indies
DIED: July 12, 1804; New York, New York
SIGNIFICANCE: Hamilton, as the first secretary of the Treasury, helped establish a national economy with durable structures. A Federalist, he advocated centralized institutions to formulate financial and political solutions.

Alexander Hamilton played an important role in the American Revolution, serving as an aide to General George Washington and later leading forces in battle at Yorktown. After the war, he became a lawyer and became deeply and successfully involved in the financial and legal affairs of the state of New York. He criticized the Articles of Confederation as having inherent flaws and advocated the development of a strong, centralized government. In 1784, he established the Bank of New York, which continued to operate into the twenty-first century.

A vocal and continuing critic of the Articles of Confederation, Hamilton was elected to the New York legislature in 1787 and was selected as a delegate to the Philadelphia constitutional convention. His authoritarian philosophy resulted in his call for a president and senate elected for life and for state governors to be appointed by the federal government. Although Hamilton did not prevail on these points, he did support the U.S. Constitution that emerged from the meeting. Along with James Madison and John Jay, Hamilton argued the case in favor of ratification through a series of essays known as *The Federalist* (1787-1788); Hamilton wrote 60 percent of the essays that supported the new constitution, which was adopted.

FIRST SECRETARY OF THE TREASURY
Hamilton served President George Washington as the first secretary of the Treasury from September 11, 1789, until his resignation on January 31, 1795, when he was succeeded by Oliver Wolcott, Jr., of Connecticut, who had served under Hamilton as auditor and controller. Hamilton's achievements as the secretary of the Treasury were foundational.

Although he faced relentless opposition from Secretary of State Thomas Jefferson and Congressman Albert Gallatin of Pennsylvania, he succeeded in the development of a powerful federal agency and clarified its role in national affairs. Hamilton was interested in establishing a solid currency, good credit, and using the Treasury for the economic development of the nation. Unlike Jefferson with his notion of an agrarian society, Hamilton believed in commerce and capitalism and measured a society's status on the basis of its economic power. He initiated a process of submitting reports to the Congress; through these reports on credit, a mint, taxes, and manufacturing, he created a centralized focus for the discussion of the economy. Jefferson and Madison denounced this procedure but could not contain it.

Hamilton's initial problem was the war debt crisis; he was determined to pay the debt incurred by the American Revolution in full. He was criticized as supporting the currency speculators who bought

Alexander Hamilton. (Library of Congress)

much of the debt from soldiers, businesses, and others in anticipation that they would make a windfall profit because his plan resulted in significant profits for these speculators. However, by paying the debt in full, Hamilton established credit and credibility for the United States among the European powers during the difficult and unpredictable years of the French Revolution. Through custom duties and excise taxes, he established a process for repayment and, in 1791, set up the First Bank of the United States as a clearinghouse for receipt and disbursement of funds and to print and circulate paper money.

In 1792, Hamilton proposed the creation of the United States Mint under the jurisdiction of the Treasury department. He was defeated by Jefferson and his emerging anti-Federalist allies; the U.S. Mint was established but placed under Jefferson's Department of State. In 1794, Hamilton supported the suppression of the antitax Whiskey Rebellion in Pennsylvania.

RETURN TO PRIVATE LIFE

During his years as secretary of the Treasury, Hamilton had an affair with Maria Reynolds; this relationship was eventually made public, and Hamilton made a public confession. In late 1794, Hamilton's reputation was in decline because of the affair, and he needed to return to private business to restore his personal finances. At the beginning of the following year, he resigned from the Treasury but remained a trusted confidant and adviser to Washington. After Washington's departure from office, Hamilton was isolated from both the Federalists under John Adams and Jefferson's Anti-Federalists.

William T. Walker

FURTHER READING

Ambrose, Douglas, and Robert Martin. *The Many Faces of Alexander Hamilton: The Life and Legacy of America's Most Elusive Founding Father.* New York: New York University Press, 2007. This study focuses on unraveling the many questions that have been associated with the enigma of Alexander Hamilton.

Chernow, Ron. *Alexander Hamilton.* New York: Penguin Press, 2004. A comprehensive and very reliable biography in which Hamilton's strengths and weaknesses are considered at length.

Harper, John Lamberton. *American Machiavelli: Alexander Hamilton and the Origins of U.S. Foreign Policy.* New York: Cambridge University Press, 2007. Harper advances a sympathetic interpretation of Hamilton as secretary of the Treasury and the influence he had on the formulation of U.S. foreign policy during Washington's presidency.

Knott, Stephen F. *Alexander Hamilton and the Persistence of Myth.* Rev. ed. Lawrence: University Press of Kansas, 2005. A critical and balanced interpretation of Hamilton and his role in establishing the banking and financial system of the United States.

Murray, Joseph A. *Alexander Hamilton: America's Forgotten Founder.* New York: Algora, 2007. Generally a sympathetic analysis of Hamilton's character and contributions in the establishment of the American republic and the formation of early national policies.

Randall, Willard Sterne. *Alexander Hamilton, A Life.* New York: HarperCollins, 2003. Randall advances a heroic portrait of Hamilton who succeeds in and out of office in spite of the opposition of others who are not his intellectual equal.

Wright, Robert E. *Hamilton Unbound: Finance and the Creation of the American Republic.* Westport, Conn.: Greenwood Press, 2002. This is an essential resource in gaining a comprehensive understanding of Hamilton's contributions and impact on banking and finance during the initial years of the American republic.

SEE ALSO: Annapolis Convention; Articles of Confederation; Bank of the United States, First; Clay's American System; Constitution, U.S.; Mint, U.S.; Monetary policy, federal; Revolutionary War; Treasury, U.S. Department of the; Washington, George; Whiskey tax of 1791.

Hawaii annexation

THE EVENT: The incorporation into the United States of the Republic of Hawaii

DATE: August 12, 1898

PLACE: The Hawaiian Islands

SIGNIFICANCE: Hawaii's incorporation into the United States meant that businesses on the mainland could rely on a steady supply of low-cost sugar and profit from an expanded free-trade zone for investment and trade.

In 1795, the Hawaiian Islands were unified under a single monarchy. After the introduction of the sugarcane crop to the fertile volcanic soil of the islands in 1836, five large companies, four of which were run by American citizens, increasingly dominated trade with the kingdom of Hawaii. Pineapple emerged as a second cash crop in 1895.

In 1890, Republican congressman William McKinley persuaded Congress to adopt a tariff of nearly 50 percent on almost all goods imported from other countries. In effect, the tariff shut out trade from Hawaii to the United States. Gravely threatened, business interests in the islands saw no alternative but to seek annexation, particularly when Queen Liliuokalani proposed in 1893 to revise the country's constitution and establish new regulations for foreign-controlled businesses.

Major business interests in the islands soon formed a Committee of Safety to overthrow the queen. Drawing on American sailors in port with

the collusion of the American consul, the committee held the queen prisoner until she abdicated, whereupon a provisional government assumed control and raised the American flag in anticipation of annexation. However, later in 1893, Democratic president Grover Cleveland repudiated the action as contrary to international law and demanded that the American flag be lowered.

The provisional government then proclaimed itself a republic and awaited the election of a Republican president. After Republican McKinley was elected president in 1896, the U.S. Senate rejected a proposed treaty of annexation in 1897, even though the fledgling republic announced its intention to ratify the treaty.

In 1898, after victories in the Spanish-American War (1898) that imposed American control over Cuba, Guam, and the Philippine Islands, Congress responded to the annexation petition by a resolution (not a treaty) passed by the House of Represen-

Annexation ceremonies in front of Hawaii's Iolani Palace on August 12, 1898. (Hawaii State Archives)

tatives on June 15 and by the Senate on July 6. Mc-Kinley signed the resolution on July 7.

The official transfer of sovereignty occurred on August 12, 1898. The Organic Act of 1900 clarified Hawaii's economic status by establishing the islands as the Territory of Hawaii, a legal arrangement similar to prestatehood arrangements then existing for Arizona and New Mexico.

Michael Haas

FURTHER READING

Kent, Noel J. *Hawaii: Islands Under the Influence.* New York: Monthly Review Press, 1983.

Pratt, Julius W. *Expansionists of 1898: The Acquisition of Hawaii and the Spanish Islands.* New York: P. Smith, 1951.

Silva, Noenoe K. *Aloha Betrayed: Native Hawaiian Resistance to American Colonialism.* Durham, N.C.: Duke University Press, 2004.

SEE ALSO: Agribusiness; Agriculture; Alaska purchase; Spanish-American War; Sugar industry; Texas annexation.

Haymarket Riot

THE EVENT: Deadly confrontation between workers and the Chicago police

DATE: May 4, 1886

PLACE: Chicago, Illinois

SIGNIFICANCE: The Haymarket Riot was a conflict between anarchists, who supported Chicago's workers, and business owners, who supported the police. The riot halted the labor movement's campaign for an eight-hour workday and exacerbated the distrust between workers and management.

The Haymarket Riot was the culmination of decades of conflict between labor and manufacturers. Chicago's huge industrial growth during the nineteenth century produced enormous profits for manufacturers and lured thousands of European immigrants, who needed jobs and were willing to work the fifteen-hour workdays demanded by factory owners. However, once employed, factory workers thought twice about such long hours and sought better conditions. Confrontations between labor and manufacturers, often leading to strikes and violence, were common.

For years, labor leaders across the United States had been promoting an eight-hour workday; to this end, a general strike was called to begin on May 1, 1886. In Chicago, more than forty thousand workers left their jobs. City leaders were prepared for the worst, and the Chicago police force, experienced in suppressing demonstrations and breaking strikes, was ready. Violence broke out on May 3 at the gates of the McCormick Reaper Company, when a group of McCormick strikers attacked strikebreakers. Roughly two hundred police officers attacked the strikers, shooting six dead.

August Spies, a labor leader, composed a leaflet denouncing the police action. It was a call to arms, distributed citywide. A public protest was planned for the evening of May 4 in the Haymarket area of the city. Various speakers were scheduled, including the anarchist leader Albert Parsons. Chicago mayor Carter Harrison, Sr., attended the event and described the speakers as "tame." He heard nothing inciting the crowd to violence before he left at 10:00 P.M. By 10:20, only about five hundred people remained, as the speaker Samuel Fielden concluded his remarks. He then noticed an advancing column of police with their guns drawn. The police commander ordered the crowd to "peaceably disperse." Fielden stated, "All right, we will go."

At that moment, someone threw a bomb at the police. The bomb killed one police officer and wounded several others. The police reacted by shooting into the now running crowd. Some of the workers fired back, but it is unknown how many or how effective their fire was. In the darkness, many police officers shot one another by mistake. A total of seven officers died, some from friendly fire. At least three civilians were killed.

No one discovered who threw the bomb, but prominent anarchists were arrested, as the city's leaders cried for vengeance. Eight men were tried, and Judge Joseph Gary instructed the jury to find them guilty of murder, even if the crime was committed by someone who was not charged. All were found guilty. One was sentenced to hard labor, the others to hang. Appeals were rejected by the Illinois Supreme Court. The day before the execution, one of the condemned exploded a dynamite cap in his mouth and died; Illinois governor Richard J. Oglesby, reacting to a clemency petition signed by more than 100,000 Americans, commuted the sentences of two men to life imprisonment. The remaining four were hanged on November 11, 1887, in Cook County Jail. In 1893, Governor John Peter Algeld pardoned the three remaining defendants and declared that the trial of the so-called Haymarket Eight had been unfair and illegal.

Marcia B. Dinneen

Further Reading

Avrich, Paul. *The Haymarket Tragedy*. Princeton, N.J.: Princeton University Press, 1984.

Green, James. *Death in the Haymarket*. New York: Pantheon Books, 2006.

See also: Knights of Labor; Labor history; Labor strikes.

Health care industry

Definition: Professions and services that include medical doctors, nurses, hospitals, pharmaceutical companies, and various public health services

Significance: Health care has become an important business, and contributions for workers' medical insurance are a major expense for many firms.

Medicines and medical practitioners have been part of human society since ancient times. Benjamin Rush, a signer of the Declaration of Independence, was a prominent Philadelphia physician. He persuaded many people that all diseases had a common cause and could be treated by draining blood from the patient—a bizarre notion that became discredited by the 1840's. Many years would pass before the medical profession clearly did more good than harm.

The first hospital in the American colonies, Pennsylvania Hospital, was opened in 1751. Numerous pharmacies in the colonies marketed a wide variety of purported remedies, some of which contained such dangerous components as mercury, alcohol, or opium. By 1800, the United States had four medical schools, which were associated with the University of Pennsylvania, Columbia, Harvard, and Dartmouth. The number of medical schools expanded from five in 1810 to fifty-two by 1850. Some physicians attended formal medical colleges, such as the prestigious Jefferson Medical College in Phil-

adelphia that was established in 1824. However, many medical practitioners learned their profession through apprenticeships or simply began practicing without any training. Massachusetts had delegated licensing to the state medical society, established in 1781, and leaving the matter to state medical societies became commonplace. Nurses and midwives were largely self-appointed. By 1850, there were about 41,000 physicians in the United States. This figure averaged out to about 176 physicians for every 100,000 people—a very high proportion by historical standards. The pay could be very good and it was relatively easy to become a doctor.

Scientific Advances

Medical science did advance, and knowledge of advances spread rapidly. Edward Jenner developed a successful vaccine for smallpox around 1800 in England. Massachusetts was quick to promote vaccination for smallpox, and New Hampshire required it from 1835. Smallpox was virtually wiped out as a result. Quinine was successfully produced in 1822 and became the standard treatment for malaria. Beginning during the early nineteenth century, gases such as ether and nitrous oxide were used as anesthetics; however, they were seldom used during the numerous amputations resulting from battle wounds in the U.S. Civil War. The American Medical Association (AMA) was formed in 1847 after half a century of growth of state and local societies. Some states and cities had similar groups much earlier. Medical journals spread information on treatments.

The discovery of germs (bacteria) and their role in infection and disease by Louis Pasteur in France during the middle of the nineteenth century profoundly improved medical science. Deaths from major infectious diseases such as tuberculosis, diphtheria, and measles accounted for about half of all deaths in the United States before 1880. From that point on, the death rate from infectious diseases began a rapid decline. Techniques of cleansing and sterilization, along with anesthetics, revolutionized surgery during the late nineteenth century.

Public Health

Health improvements in the nineteenth century resulted not so much from the improvement in medical treatment as from a general improvement in nutrition and living standards, and the spread of public health measures. In colonial times, numerous government units created boards of health, concerned with sanitary conditions and contagious diseases. The obvious filth and stench developing in urban slums focused public attention on the need to upgrade water supplies and waste-disposal systems, partly for aesthetic reasons. Very few cities had sanitary sewers before 1880; most constructed them between then and 1910. A filtered water supply was virtually unknown in 1880, but such supplies reached more than 10 million people by 1910, and some areas had introduced chlorination. Major cities established boards of health. Water was inspected for bacteria. Pasteurization of milk became widespread. Following the example of Providence, Rhode Island, in 1880, public health laboratories became widespread by 1914. School districts instituted physical examinations and enforced compulsory vaccinations. The public schools increasingly spread information from the rising field of home economics, stressing the value of cleanliness, diet, and exercise. These public health measures led to the creation of numerous companies devoted to testing for contaminants and producing the equipment needed to improve sanitation.

THE EARLY TWENTIETH CENTURY

The muckraking literature around the beginning of the twentieth century heavily criticized the unhealthy conditions in urban slums (Jacob Riis) and unsanitary conditions in food preparation (Upton Sinclair). A groundbreaking study of American medical schools by Abraham Flexner (1910) found wide variation in quality. At the top, Johns Hopkins University had developed the first really modern medical school (1893). At the bottom, Flexner recommended several schools be closed— and they were. State governments authorized their medical associations to approve medical schools and to examine and license physicians. These reforms greatly upgraded the quality of the medical profession; however, they also made medical education much more lengthy and expensive. There had been 162 medical schools in 1906; ten years later there were only 95, and the number fell further to 80 in 1923. Between 1900 and 1906, more than 5,000 students per year graduated from medical schools. After 1913, the number dropped below 4,000, and did not return to that level until 1927. In 1900-1906, there had been about 157 physicians for every 100,000 people, but this ratio dropped below

130 after 1923 and did not return to the previous level until the 1960's. The shortfall in physician numbers was somewhat offset by the more rapid expansion in the number of professional nurses. Nurses numbered about 50,000 in 1910; this number doubled in 1920 and doubled again in 1930, reaching about 214,000.

Upton Sinclair's novel *The Jungle* (1906), which exposed unsanitary conditions in the meatpacking industry, was a factor leading to passage of a law creating the federal Food and Drug Administration (FDA) in 1906. The same law required that products be accurately labeled and forbade certain dangerous ingredients. The importance of the FDA increased steadily in the following years.

For most of the first half of the twentieth century, American medical practice fell into a simple pattern. Most doctors were family doctors, operating as individual practitioners out of a small office, often in the doctor's home, and seeing patients both in their office and at the patient's home. Diagnostic instruments were simple—a stethoscope, a thermometer, perhaps a blood-pressure cuff, sometimes X-ray equipment.

Medical costs were not high. A visit to the doctor might cost $5. In 1929, Americans spent about $3 billion for medical care. Half of this went for physicians or dentists. About $400 million went to hospitals. The number of hospitals rose rapidly in the first quarter of the twentieth century, then leveled off for a long time at roughly 6,000.

In 1929, another $600 million went for medicines and other purchased medical items. The drugstore was a familiar Main Street establishment— there were about 58,000 of them during the 1920's, often with a soda fountain, a prescription department, and many over-the-counter (OTC) medicines. Notable among these was aspirin, a proven pain reliever with near-miracle properties yet to be discovered. Miles Laboratories was a major supplier of OTC products, including Alka-Seltzer, whose comforting fizz promised relief for headaches or indigestion. Chain drugstores, such as Rexall, became widespread during the 1920's.

WORLD WAR II

The 1940's represented a turning point in the American medical system. The discovery of penicillin and antibiotics generally revolutionized the treatment of infections. New treatments greatly improved survival rates among soldiers wounded in military conflict. The pharmaceutical industry stepped up its efforts in research and development.

Within the federal government, the National Institutes of Health (NIH), which had been operating on a modest scale since the 1930's, experienced a rapid rise in its budget. NIH research expenditures rose from $33 million in 1952 to $274 million in 1960 and $893 million in 1969. The federal government created a cabinet-level Department of Health, Education, and Welfare (HEW) in 1953.

The war also set off major changes in the financing of medical expenses. Employers discovered they could bypass wage controls and high income tax rates by paying medical insurance costs for their workers. In 1948, insurance paid about 6 percent of personal health care costs. The insurance share rose rapidly, reaching 27 percent in 1960. As a result, the ultimate consumers became less sensitized to costs. Prices of medical goods and services began to rise more rapidly than other prices. Between 1950 and 1970, consumer prices in general increased by 61 percent, but medical costs rose 125 percent.

MEDICARE AND MEDICAID

The federal government's role in the medical world changed dramatically in 1965 with the cre-

ation of Medicare and Medicaid. Medicare was a system of medical-expense insurance for people aged sixty-five and older. People became eligible either by paying Social Security tax (to which a Medicare premium was added) or by paying premiums directly. The adoption of Medicare had no appreciable effect on the health indicators of the elderly but greatly improved their financial condition. Medicaid covered medical expenses of eligible low-income persons of any age. About half of the people below the poverty line qualified for Medicaid.

The new federal programs encouraged the spread of health maintenance organizations (HMOs). These offered basic medical services to members for a fixed annual premium. In many cases, the HMO would pay its participating physicians a flat amount for each client enrolled. The Health Maintenance Organization Act of 1973 helped expand the scope of HMOs, viewed as an effective method of controlling costs through "managed care."

Several health-related federal agencies were created: the Occupational Safety and Health Administration (OSHA, 1970), the Environmental Protection Agency (EPA, 1970), and the Consumer Product Safety Commission (CPSC, 1972). A symbol

CONSUMER PRICE INDEXES OF MEDICAL CARE PRICES, 1980-2005
(1982-1984 = 100)

Year	Medical Care	Medicare Care Services[a]	Medical Care Commodities[b]	Annual Percentage Change Medical Care	Medical Care Services	Medical Care Commodities
1980	74.9	74.8	75.4	11.0	11.3	9.3
1985	113.5	113.2	115.2	6.3	6.1	7.2
1990	162.8	182.7	163.4	9.0	9.3	8.4
1995	220.5	224.2	204.5	4.5	5.1	1.9
2000	260.8	266.0	238.1	4.1	4.3	3.2
2005	323.2	336.7	276.0	4.2	4.8	2.5

Source: Data from the Statistical Abstract of the United States, 2008 (Washington, D.C.: Department of Commerce, Economics and Statistics Administration, Bureau of the Census, Data User Services Division, 2008)
Note: Indexes are the annual averages of monthly data based on components of the consumer price index for all urban consumers.
[a] Includes professional services, hospital and related services, and other services.
[b] Includes prescription drugs, medical supplies, and other commodities.

of the growing federal role was the creation in 1980 of a new Department of Health and Human Services, spun off from HEW.

With these new programs, the share of personal medical care expenditures in gross domestic product (GDP) moved steadily upward, from about 3.4 percent in 1960 to 6.6 percent in 1980 and 10 percent at the end of the millennium. Rising demand brought a steady increase in the number of medical schools and their graduates. In 1956, 82 medical schools produced about 7,000 graduates. By 1970, 107 medical schools produced almost 9,000 graduates. However, the supply did not keep up with the demand. As a result, physicians immigrated to the United States, and some cost-conscious Americans went to other countries for treatment.

The continued rapid rise in medical costs drove up insurance premiums. Many employers stopped offering health insurance or shifted more costs to employees. The plight of the medically uninsured became a significant political issue. During Bill Clinton's first term as president, his wife, Hillary, tried unsuccessfully to put together a program to expand medical insurance provided by the federal government. In 1997, Congress did create the State Children's Health Insurance Program, which substantially enlarged insurance coverage for children. A complex prescription drug benefit was added to Medicare effective in 2006.

THE NEW MILLENNIUM

By 2000, the United States had developed a very large and diverse health care system. State and federal governments provided public health facilities such as a safe water supply, waste disposal, and inspection of goods, services, housing, and workplaces. Total health service employment was 9.3 million in 1990, increasing to 12.7 million in 2000 and 14.9 million in 2006. The number of physicians increased from 615,000 in 1990 to 814,000 in 2000 and 902,000 in 2005. By 2005, one-fourth of all physicians had attended foreign medical schools. There were 420 HMOs, enrolling about 69 million people. Personal health care expenditures were about $1.7 trillion, of which 85 percent was covered by third-party (chiefly insurance) sources. Fifteen percent of the population was not covered by medical insurance. Medicare covered 42 million people and Medicaid 38 million. Government programs of all kinds accounted for $747 billion of personal health care expenditures, representing about 44 percent of the total.

Major indicators of health showed steady improvement. Life expectancy at birth, which was about forty-seven years in 1900, rose to seventy-four years in 1980 and seventy-seven years in 2003. These figures are strongly influenced by lifestyle factors such as smoking, automobile accidents, and violence. A better indicator of medical effectiveness is the number of years a sixty-year-old person is expected to live, which rose from fifteen years in 1900 to twenty years in 1980 and twenty-two years in 2003. Infant mortality, which was a shocking 100 per thousand in 1915, dropped to 13 in 1980 and 7 in 2003.

Paul B. Trescott

FURTHER READING

Coddington, Dean C., Elizabeth A. Fischer, Keith D. Moore, and Richard L. Clark. *Beyond Managed Care: How Consumers and Technology Are Changing the Future of Health Care.* San Francisco: Jossey-Bass, 2000. Analysis of managed health care focuses primarily on implications for changes in health care policy but also provides a clearly written historical overview of HMOs.

Feldstein, Paul J. *Health Care Economics.* 5th ed. Albany, N.Y.: Delmar Publishers, 1999. This respected textbook has gone through several editions since 1973; the updates give good coverage of developments since that date.

Henderson, James W. *Health Economics and Policy.* 2d ed. Mason, Ohio: South-Western Publishing, 2002. This college-level text provides good coverage of the policy changes and their economic effects in the health care industry.

Meeker, Edward. "Medicine and Public Health." In *Encyclopedia of American Economic History,* edited by Glenn Porter. New York: Charles Scribner's Sons, 1980. Especially good on the evolution and importance of public health programs.

Rejda, George. *Social Insurance and Economic Security.* 6th ed. Upper Saddle River, N.J.: Prentice-Hall, 1999. This text for college undergraduates covers health problems and policies in chapters 7-8.

Shafer, Henry Burnell. *The American Medical Profession, 1783-1850.* New York: Columbia University Press, 1936. Although it is an older work, it is an excellent scholarly study of the late eighteenth and early nineteenth centuries.

Stevens, Rosemary E., Charles E. Rosenberg, and

Lawton R. Burns, eds. *History and Health Policy in the United States: Putting the Past Back In.* New Brunswick, N.J.: Rutgers University Press, 2006. Collection of scholarly essays on the history of American health care policy includes substantial information on the origins of managed care and the role of Nixon in the development of the HMO industry.

SEE ALSO: Chemical industries; Child product safety laws; Food and Drug Administration; HealthSouth scandal; Insurance industry; Kaiser, Henry J.; Medicare and Medicaid; Muckraking journalism; Occupational Safety and Health Act; United Food and Commercial Workers.

HealthSouth scandal

THE EVENT: The prosecution of the chief executive of an Alabama health care firm under the Sarbanes-Oxley Act for his company's fraudulent practices

DATE: 2002-2005

PLACE: Alabama

SIGNIFICANCE: Richard Scrushy, the founder and chief executive officer of HealthSouth, was the first person to be indicted under the Sarbanes-Oxley Act of 2002, which held senior executives responsible for the accuracy and completeness of corporate financial reports. His acquittal, particularly in view of the fifteen guilty pleas by others involved in the scandal, surprised many people.

Richard Scrushy, trained as a respiratory therapist, was in management at Lifemark, a Texas hospital administrative company, before he decided to start his own business. On February 22, 1984, Health-South was incorporated as Amcare, with Scrushy as its CEO and major stockholder. In 1985, the company changed its name to HealthSouth. It went public in 1986 on the NASDAQ stock exchange. Before going public, firms must have an independent auditor examine their books and certify their accuracy. HealthSouth's auditor felt the books were not reliable, so Scrushy fired the firm and found a more compliant auditor, Ernst & Young. In September, 1988, the company was listed on the New York Stock Exchange, and on January 7, 1999, it became part of the Standard and Poor's 500 stock index.

THE RISE OF HEALTHSOUTH

By 1990, HealthSouth had fifty facilities throughout the United States. It then began a rapid expansion through mergers and acquisitions. In 1993, it bought twenty-eight hospitals and forty-five outpatient rehabilitation facilities from National Medical Enterprise for $300 million. In 1994, it bought Re-Life for $180 million. In January, 1995, HealthSouth entered the surgery business by acquiring Surgical Health Corporation for $155 million. In February, 1995, it acquired Novacare's rehabilitation hospital business. In 1996, it expanded into diagnostics by purchasing Health Images. These acquisitions made HealthSouth a major U.S. health care provider, with more than two hundred facilities. At its peak, it recorded $4.4 billion in revenues, employed more than fifty thousand people worldwide, and operated eighty outpatient rehabilitation services and twelve home health agencies.

Scrushy was highly rewarded for expanding HealthSouth. Between 1996 and 2002, he was paid $260 million, mostly through stock options. This provided a great incentive for accounting fraud. HealthSouth added thousands of fictitious items to its assets. Most of these were valued under $5,000, since auditors rarely checked assets with such a low value. HealthSouth also removed expenses from its annual income statements to make its profits appear larger and boost the value of its stock.

SIGNS OF TROUBLE

The first sign of accounting problems arose in late 2002. Scrushy sold $75 million of HealthSouth stock several days before the company announced a large loss. This was on top of the 7.7 million shares that he had sold for $77 million between 1999 and 2001. The Securities and Exchange Commission (SEC) began to investigate whether this sale was related to the loss, which would have violated insider trading laws. HealthSouth chief financial officer William Owens became a government informant, recording his conversations with Scrushy to provide evidence for the government's case. In one recorded conversation, Scrushy told Owens that he would "get killed" if he fixed the financial statements immediately, but that the problems could easily be dealt with over time.

On March 19, 2003, the SEC halted trading of HealthSouth on the New York Stock Exchange, charging that the company inflated its earnings by more than 10 percent and overstated its profits by nearly $2.5 billion between 1999 and 2002. The company was also removed from the Standard and Poor's 500 index. After trading as high as $30.81 in 1998, HealthSouth fell to $3.91 per share when trading was halted. One week later, Owens pleaded guilty to doctoring the company's financial statements.

On March 31, the board of directors fired Scrushy and Owens, as well as its auditor, Ernst & Young. They removed Scrushy's name from the company conference center and hired the restructuring firm Alvarez & Marsal to put the company finances in order and help it avoid bankruptcy. To restore profitability, HealthSouth sold or closed its poorly performing facilities, including its surgery, outpatient, and diagnostic divisions. By late 2006, HealthSouth had completed its recovery, becoming primarily a provider of rehabilitation services, and was relisted on the New York Stock Exchange.

HealthSouth CEO Richard Scrushy (left) speaks to reporters outside the courthouse on June 3, 2005, as his attorney, Art Leach, and his wife, Leslie, watch. (AP/ Wide World Photos)

MORE PROBLEMS FOR SCRUSHY

As HealthSouth began to revive, Scrushy's problems were just beginning. In October, 2003, he was indicted on eighty-five counts, including charges that he falsified accounts at HealthSouth, leading to a $2.7 billion fraud of investors, by reporting fictitious profits. Federal officials charged Scrushy with duping investors into believing that the company met earnings targets to boost the company stock price (which would benefit Scrushy, who owned large amounts of HealthSouth stock) and to support his extravagant lifestyle, which included ownership of a Lamborghini, a 92-foot yacht, a 360-acre farm in Alabama, seven corporate jets, and paintings by Picasso and Renoir.

At the trial (January 25-June 29, 2005), former HealthSouth executives testified that Scrushy had ordered the accounting manipulations. However, these officials had pleaded guilty and agreed to testify against Scrushy to have their sentences reduced; therefore, the possibility existed that they were lying to help themselves. The prosecutors could not produce independent evidence that tied Scrushy to the fraud. After the prosecution made its case, Judge Karen Bowdre dismissed forty-nine of the eighty-five charges against Scrushy. The jury acquitted Scrushy of all remaining counts against him.

Scrushy, however, faced further court action. In 2006, he was convicted of bribery, conspiracy, and mail fraud for his part in a bribery scheme involving Alabama governor Don Siegelman. He was sentenced in 2007 to eighty-two months in federal prison and three years of probation, and ordered to pay a $150,000 fine, $267,000 in restitution, and the costs of his incarceration.

Steven Pressman

FURTHER READING

Cast, William. *Going South.* Chicago: Dearborn, 2005.

Johnson, Gary, and Mary Johnson. "CEOs 1, SOX 0: The Case Against Richard Scrushy and Health-

South." *Journal of Legal, Ethical and Regulatory Issues* 8, no. 1 (2005): 35-41.

Markham, Jerry. *A Financial History of Modern U.S. Corporate Scandals.* Armonk, N.Y.: M. E. Sharpe, 2006.

SEE ALSO: Enron bankruptcy; Health care industry; NASDAQ; Stock markets; WorldCom bankruptcy.

Highways

DEFINITION: Major roads owned and maintained by state and local authorities for public transit, usually linking cities and towns

SIGNIFICANCE: During the early twentieth century, a growing automotive industry demanded better roads, which in turn resulted in enormous increases in the production of motor vehicles. As roads and motor vehicles improved, the shipment of goods in the United States moved from water and rail transport to overland conveyance in trucks. By the last quarter of the century, American industry depended on the national highway system to provide the materials it required to function efficiently and profitably.

Early roads linking the towns and cities in the United States were little more than dirt trails used by farmers to transport goods to market. The first road capable of accommodating the stagecoaches that ran between New York and Boston was completed in 1722. The Lancaster Turnpike, the first hard-surface road in the United States, was finished in 1794 and ran for 62 miles between the Pennsylvania cities of Lancaster and Philadelphia. It was a toll road that charged a set fee per mile depending on the size of the vehicle involved and the number of horses pulling it. The first highway, the Cumberland Road (also known as the National Road), was built from 1811 to 1818 and ran from Cumberland, Maryland, to Wheeling, in what would become West Virginia. It was the first road to use macadam surfacing and eventually was extended to reach 800 miles in length.

MODERN HIGHWAYS

By the beginning of the twentieth century, the United States had more than 2 million miles of thoroughfares, most of them dirt or gravel roads. They were difficult to travel on because they were dusty and rutted. In wet weather, they turned into muddy morasses that were virtually impossible to navigate. Before the twentieth century, which was marked by the mass production of motor vehicles, the nation's roads were minimally useful at best. In 1913, the first transcontinental highway, the Lincoln Highway, was completed between New York and San Francisco. By the mid-1920's, more than 250 highways had come into existence, many of them named after the wagon trails whose routes they followed, such as the Santa Fe Trail. The Federal-Aid Highway Act of 1925 attempted to systemize these roads by creating the U.S. Highway System. This act placed highways under state control, gave them numerical names, and labeled them with a standardized shield.

Growth in the production and registration of motor vehicles between 1905, when there were seventy-eight motor vehicle registrations in the United States, and 1929, when the registration of such vehicles approached twenty-seven million, was meteoric. By 1929, there was about one car for every four residents in the United States. With a 200 percent increase in the number of motor vehicles registered in the decade from 1920 to 1929 alone, a corresponding increase in highways to carry these vehicles safely and efficiently was inevitable.

THE PENNSYLVANIA TURNPIKE

The first superhighway in the United States was the Pennsylvania Turnpike, a toll road that connected eastern Pennsylvania with the western end of the state, running from Newburgh in Cumberland County to a spot 160 miles to the west. Construction of the turnpike began late in 1938, and it was hoped that the road would be open by late May, 1940, a deadline that could not be met, largely because of heavy rains throughout the spring of 1940. Finally the job was finished and the highway was opened officially on October 1, 1940.

The Pennsylvania Turnpike, similar in many respects to the German autobahns, was a superhighway that marked a significant advance in road-building technology. The autobahns and the Pennsylvania Turnpike were designed with long, sweeping, banked curves; limited access; no cross streets or railroad grade crossings; and moderate grades that enabled motorists to cruise safely at high speeds. When motorists using the Pennsylvania Turnpike entered the toll gate, they received a card indicating their starting point. When they exited, they returned the card at another toll gate and were charged for the distance they had driven.

These tolls paid for a major part of the expense of building and maintaining the road, although the federal government had also contributed funds for its construction and had bought many of the construction bonds required to finance the project. Rest areas with toilet facilities, a Howard Johnson restaurant, and an ESSO service station were available in several places along the route so that people could attend to their needs without leaving the turnpike.

THE INTERSTATE HIGHWAY SYSTEM

Shortly before the end of World War II, the United States Congress passed the Federal-Aid Highway Act of 1944, partly to provide evacuation routes should circumstances ever require an evacuation of endangered populations but mostly to extend the scope of American business and commerce. It took another dozen years before the federal government, under the leadership of President Dwight D. Eisenhower, passed the Federal-Aid Highway Act of 1956 (popularly known as the National Interstate and Defense Highways Act), which established the program to fund and construct superhighways that would crisscross the nation by the early 1990's. The federal government absorbed 90 percent of the cost of this monumental effort.

Each superhighway was assigned a two-digit route number. North-south interstates were given odd numbers, and east-west interstates were assigned even numbers. As the system developed, most towns

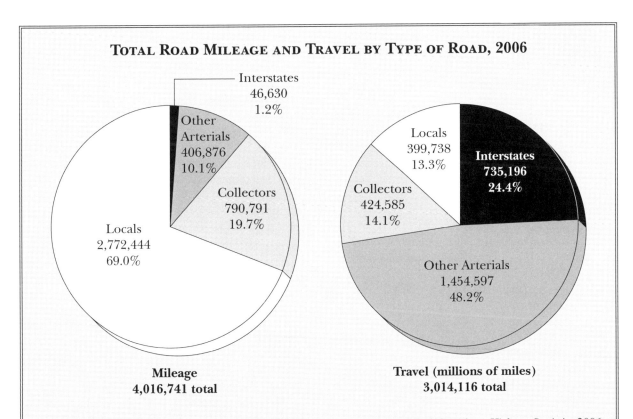

TOTAL ROAD MILEAGE AND TRAVEL BY TYPE OF ROAD, 2006

Interstates
46,630
1.2%

Other Arterials
406,876
10.1%

Collectors
790,791
19.7%

Locals
2,772,444
69.0%

Mileage
4,016,741 total

Locals
399,738
13.3%

Interstates
735,196
24.4%

Collectors
424,585
14.1%

Other Arterials
1,454,597
48.2%

Travel (millions of miles)
3,014,116 total

Source: Data from U.S. Department of Transportation, Federal Highway Administration, *Highway Statistics 2006* (Washington, D.C.: Author, 2007)

Note: Interstates are all designated freeways that meet the standards for high speed and long-distance transportation; arterial roads are limited-access freeways, multilane highways, and other important highways connecting cities and urban areas; collectors are streets linking residential neighborhoods, commercial and industrial areas, and city downtowns, and are built for lower speed and shorter distance travel; locals are streets providing access to land but limited mobility.

or cities in the United States with a population of fifty thousand or more came to be linked by interstate highways.

Interstate highways have at least two lanes in each direction, with some in urban areas having as many as six or eight lanes in each direction. Interchanges provide limited access to these highways at regular intervals and generally connect either with other primary roads and highways or with local, secondary roads.

Superhighways are divided by a median that separates opposing lanes from each other. In some instances, these medians are planted with foliage capable of absorbing energy should errant vehicles run into them. The superhighways have signs at regular intervals indicating route numbers, connecting routes, speed limits, and services available at interchanges. Interstate highways are supported largely through federal funding derived from gasoline and property taxes. They have regular rest areas with toilets, a few vending machines, maps of the region, and, in many cases, picnic tables. The Interstate Highway System (excluding Puerto Rico) contained 46,630 miles of roads as of 2006.

By the end of the twentieth century, the United States had a highway system that comprised some 4 million miles, and Canada had more than 500,000 miles of roads. The aggregate miles that make up these two nations' roadways are sufficient to circle Earth at the equator more than 175 times.

Toll Roads

Despite the growth of the Interstate Highway System (officially the Dwight D. Eisenhower National System of Interstate and Defense Highways), toll roads still exist in many states, particularly in the east and in parts of the Midwest and South. Notable among these are such highways as the West Virginia, Ohio, and New Jersey Turnpikes. In some cases, the toll roads exist side by side with interstate highways.

Often tunnels and bridges also charge tolls, as do all the tunnels and bridges leading into and out of New York City and other large metropolises. These structures usually lead onto toll roads. In the area between Washington, D.C., and the entrance to the New Jersey Turnpike, those using Interstate 95 are charged tolls as they proceed along the course of the highway, and they are also charged a bridge toll where the interstate crosses the Delaware River.

Among the more ambitious undertakings in highway construction is the Chesapeake Bay Bridge-Tunnel that connects southeastern Virginia with its eastern shore. This highway, more than 17.6 miles long, has been called one of the seven engineering wonders of the world. The toll on this structure has always been quite high, but the mileage saved by using it is impressive, and as an added bonus, those who use this scenic thoroughfare have the unique experience of crossing both over and under the Chesapeake Bay.

Jobs and the Highways

The highway system employs literally millions of people and makes jobs unrelated to highways possible for millions more who use highways to get to their places of employment. Among those directly employed by facets of the highway system are those who plan highways, essentially the architects of highways who use highway engineers to bring their plans into being.

Among those who are engaged in the actual construction of highways are all sorts of laborers and operators of the heavy equipment that highway construction requires. The creation of such equipment is a vast enterprise that employs additional millions of workers. Those responsible for highway construction and maintenance also employ staffs of people who identify, locate, and purchase necessary construction materials. Those who haul and supply construction materials also profit from the building of roads. Bookkeepers and accountants keep a sharp eye on spending and make sure that public funds allocated to road construction are expended properly.

Highway patrol officers also hold jobs created by the highway system. Often catering crews are employed to feed construction workers whose work is done away from their homes. Landscape specialists put the finishing touches on highways. These are just a few of the kinds of jobs that highway construction provides.

Impact of Modern Highway Systems

Modern life in the United States would not be possible had the highway system not been developed. In many parts of the United States, the interstate highway system led to the virtual disappearance of small towns in rural areas. Some small towns were bypassed by the superhighways and no longer received as much business from travelers. Others that were near cities found that their residents preferred to shop in the city, easily reached by superhighway.

The interstate highways also allowed people whose jobs in cities had anchored them to the center of those cities to live on the outskirts, where land was cheaper. Commuting relatively long distances to a job was counterbalanced by being able to live in a larger house in a less crowded setting. Quite predictably, suburbs began to spring up. As more people moved to the suburbs, large shopping centers were built in these areas, often easily accessible by superhighway. Large, impersonal chain stores drew people away from the small, independent, neighborhood stores in which previous generations had done much of their shopping. Also, as commutes grew longer, suburb dwellers came home later, to tract houses that had garages where there would have been front porches only a generation before. Many suburban towns failed to develop a sense of community and function as a social center for their residents the way that small towns once had.

R. Baird Shuman

FURTHER READING

Gutfreund, Owen D. *Twentieth Century Sprawl: Highways and the Reshaping of the American Landscape.* New York: Oxford University Press, 2004. Through case studies of Denver, Colorado; Middlebury, Vermont; and Smyrna, Tennessee; the author shows how highways transformed the United States.

Kaszynski, William. *The American Highway: The History and Culture of the Roads in the United States.* Jefferson, N.C.: McFarland, 2000. Especially effective in presenting the sociological and economic implications of developing a road system. Appealing illustrations.

Lewis, Tom. *Divided Highways: Building the Interstate Highways, Transforming American Life.* New York: Viking Penguin, 1997. An extremely thorough book that chronicles the advent of the Interstate Highway System in the United States. Excellent statistics.

Molzahn, Arlene Bourgeois. *Highways and Freeways.* Berkeley Heights, N.J.: Enslow, 2002. Directed to young adult readers, Molzahn's overview is well written and accurate.

Moon, Henry. "The Interstate Highway System." In *Geographical Snapshots of North America,* edited by Donald G. Janelle. New York: Guilford Press, 1992. The best brief account in print on the topic.

SEE ALSO: American Automobile Association; Automotive industry; Bridges; Cumberland Road; Drive-through businesses; Hotel and motel industry; Housing and Urban Development, U.S. Department of; Petroleum industry; Transportation, U.S. Department of; Trucking industry; Turnpikes.

Hoffa, Jimmy

IDENTIFICATION: Labor leader
BORN: February 13, 1913; Brazil, Indiana
DIED: Unknown; disappeared on July 30, 1975; Bloomfield Hills, Michigan
SIGNIFICANCE: Hoffa revived the American labor movement but also became symbolic of corrupt union leadership. Head of the Teamsters union, he worked closely with members of organized crime. He also centralized union leadership, expanded organizing activities, and raised the wages of Teamsters while reducing competition from nonunion drivers.

Jimmy Hoffa began his career in Detroit as a warehouse freight handler for the Kroger food chain. By 1934, he was working full time as an organizer for the International Brotherhood of Teamsters. He became president of his local in 1937 and subsequently obtained help from Detroit gangsters to defeat trade union rivals. In 1946, Hoffa pleaded guilty to extorting small grocers in Detroit to purchase "permits" from the Teamsters to make deliveries with their own trucks. A 1955 Senate investigation into the Teamsters put Hoffa on television and made him a national figure.

Hoffa became the Teamsters' president in 1957. In 1967, he went to federal prison for jury tampering, fraud, and conspiracy in the disposition of union funds. President Richard M. Nixon pardoned Hoffa in 1971, with the provision that he keep out of union affairs until 1980.

Hoffa became one of the most famous missing persons in history when he vanished without a trace on July 30, 1975, after leaving a restaurant in Detroit. The general consensus among biographers is that Hoffa met with foul play, probably at the hands of underworld figures.

Caryn E. Neumann

FURTHER READING

Franco, Joseph, with Richard Hammer. *Hoffa's Man: The Rise and Fall of Jimmy Hoffa as Witnessed by His Strongest Arm.* Englewood Cliffs, N.J.: Prentice Hall, 1987.

Hoffa, James Riddle. *The Trials of Jimmy Hoffa: An Autobiography.* Chicago: Henry Regnery, 1970.

Witwer, David. *Corruption and Reform in the Teamsters Union.* Urbana: University of Illinois Press, 2003.

SEE ALSO: Debs, Eugene V.; Gompers, Samuel; International Brotherhood of Teamsters; Labor history.

Home security. *See* Private security industry

Home Shopping Network

IDENTIFICATION: Interactive retail cable television network

DATE: Begun as a Tampa, Florida, cable channel in July, 1982

SIGNIFICANCE: As television expanded into specialized cable networks during the late 1970's media boom, the Home Shopping Network pioneered the concept of electronic commerce by offering viewers the opportunity to call in live and purchase a wide variety of quality items—predominantly fashion, beauty care accessories, jewelry, electronics, and domestic wares.

In 1977, Lowell W. Paxson, owner of a Clearwater, Florida, easy-listening AM radio station, converted the station's programming to a call-in shopping format to boost sagging audience numbers. He got the idea after a cash-poor advertiser had paid him with 112 can openers, and his on-air personality, in a long-shot attempt to recoup the money, sold them out in two hours. The call-in shopping format was immediately successful, and Paxson envisioned moving to television. He named the program the Home Shopping Club and marketed it to Tampa cable with the financial backing of Roy M. Speer, a lawyer and real estate developer. Again the results were encouraging, and in 1982 the Home Shopping Club was a permanent channel in Tampa, quickly expanding to Ft. Lauderdale and Miami.

In 1985, Paxson and Speer launched the format nationwide. Now called the Home Shopping Network (HSN), it used a sophisticated computer system to handle the volume of call-in orders, as Paxson and Speer recognized that the purchasing process must work smoothly to guarantee return business. Their strategy paid off. The network featured quality items as well as closeouts and overstocks, and it introduced new products. Given its national reach, its impact on sales was unprecedented. The network's policy of guaranteed returns encouraged leery home shoppers. The products were sold live, and because the network did not preview its lineup, audiences watched for extended periods of time, thus creating not merely shoppers but viewers. When the company stock went public in 1986, it was the year's fastest new rising stock. Indeed, the success of HSN encouraged more than a dozen rival shopping networks to debut during the late 1980's.

In June, 2002, twenty-five years after the Home Shopping Network gots its start, telephone operators take orders in Clearwater, Florida. (AP/Wide World Photos)

In the face of competition, HSN maintained its edge. Its on-air personalities developed followings, and the channel featured a variety of celebrities debuting product lines. The network broadcasted year-round, around the clock—except Christmas, when holiday greetings were programmed.

In 1995, HSN was purchased by media mogul Barry Diller, who directed a massive overhaul in network operations and joined it to his vast communications conglomerate IAC/Interactive. In 1999, HSN, recognizing the enormous impact of Internet sales, introduced its own companion Web site. However, HSN remains a vital and robust force in electronic retail. The fourth largest cable television network, it is estimated to reach 70 million households. Its sales have been in excess of $2.5 billion, and it has moved more than 53 million packages. Critical to its success has always been its willingness to engage new technologies: In late 2006, for example, the network introduced a cutting-edge interactive format in which viewers can use their remote control to order products, thus eliminating phoning entirely.

Joseph Dewey

FURTHER READING

Klaffke, Pamela. *Spree: A Cultural History of Shopping.* Vancouver, B.C.: Arsenal Pulp Press, 2003.

Muller, Megan. *Television in the Multi-technical Age: A Brief History of Cable Television.* London: Wiley-Blackwell, 2008.

Parsons, Patrick. *Blue Skies: A History of Cable Television.* Philadelphia: Temple University Press, 2008.

SEE ALSO: Catalog shopping; eBay; Internet; Jewelry industry; Online marketing; Retail trade industry; Television broadcasting industry; Tupperware.

Homeland Security, U.S. Department of

IDENTIFICATION: Federal agency created to provide a unified national response to protect the nation from acts of terrorism, natural disasters, and other emergencies

DATE: Established in 2002

SIGNIFICANCE: A major part of the mission of the U.S. Department of Homeland Security is to enable commerce to take place freely. This is ac-

complished through the safeguarding of the nation's borders, infrastructure, property, and key resources, all of which are vital to the nation's economy.

In response to the terrorist attacks of September 11, 2001, President George W. Bush created a new federal agency to coordinate a comprehensive national strategy to protect the United States from future attacks and other threats both foreign and domestic. The mission of the Department of Homeland Security (DHS) is to prevent and deter terrorist attacks, respond to national disasters, secure the nation's borders, protect critical infrastructure and key resources, and promote the free flow of commerce. The creation of this agency required one of the largest transformations of the federal government in more than fifty years. It transformed and realigned the previous confusing patchwork of government activities into a single department responsible for safeguarding the nation.

OVERVIEW

The DHS and its roughly 200,000 employees encompass twenty-two federal agencies within eighty-seven thousand federal, state, and local government jurisdictions. These include many directorates, services, and agencies that directly and indirectly affect American business. For example, the U.S. Customs and Border Protection service and the Transportation Security Administration regulate the movement of goods, services, and people to and from the United States, with major implications for international commerce. The Federal Emergency Management Agency (FEMA) coordinates disaster relief and the rebuilding of critical infrastructure (electricity, roads, and power) to restore an area's ability to aid citizens and conduct commerce. The Science and Technology directorate protects U.S. energy and agriculture. The National Protection and Programs directorate and the National Cyber Security Center work to secure the nation against terrorist attacks and natural disasters. The U.S. Citizenship and Immigration Services (USCIS) enforce laws regulating citizenship requirements for employment.

INITIATIVES

The DHS has introduced major initiatives that affect American business and that can be broken down into three categories: protecting the nation from dangerous persons; protecting the nation from dangerous goods; and protecting the nation's critical infrastructure. To protect the nation from dangerous persons, the DHS has initiated two programs that also affect business: the Western Hemisphere Travel Initiative (WHTI) and the Real ID requirement. Each is an initiative to secure identification documentation for persons traveling to or within the United States. These initiatives affect American businesses, businesspeople traveling internationally, and foreign nationals doing business in the United States.

The new identification papers and materials procured by business travelers are designed to increase safety. Protecting the nation from dangerous goods includes improving import safety and the Expanded Container Security Initiative. Each of these initiatives is designed to be part of a comprehensive plan to better protect the nation against dangers entering U.S. ports and to enhance the safety of imported goods. This added level of protection means that American business has an additional level of government documentation and bureaucracy to negotiate when importing goods and materials from abroad.

To protect the nation's critical infrastructure, DHS initiatives include increasing cyber security and establishing national standards for security at chemical and power-generating facilities. Federal agencies mandate new, more stringent security measures at facilities that need to be secure to prevent the theft of chemicals or other dangerous materials that could be used as weapons in a terrorist attack. The cost of these new security measures is most likely to be shouldered by private industry, with the costs of such security measures being accounted for as a new cost of doing business.

All Department of Homeland Security programs and initiatives try to balance the protection of America's people, goods, and infrastructure against allowing for the free flow of legitimate commerce. All such programs come with costs that are inevitably passed along and built into the price of the affected goods and services. The security programs and initiatives come with additional costs and time delays for business.

COSTS AND DELAYS

The United States Citizenship and Immigration Service (USCIS) has been backlogged with millions of citizenship applications and requests for work permits. This added delay and expense in the United States' ability to attract and secure people with needed skills has a significant negative impact on American commerce. Further, American business has seen a rise in transportation costs for business travelers as a result of added security fees at airports. Business travelers and their luggage are subjected to longer, more extensive security protocols than ever before. The security programs and initiatives come with additional costs and time delays for business. These costs manifest themselves in additional taxes and fees levied by the government, as well as the additional time required to move goods and people across borders.

Transportation of goods is also more expensive due to security programs. In 2004, the Department of Homeland Security announced the Container Security Initiative. Under this plan, U.S. agents inspect shipping containers at foreign ports before they are cleared for entry into the United States. Transporting goods requires greater paperwork and documentation than it did previously to verify the items being shipped, their country of origin, and the transportation routes followed. All this documentation has to be generated, processed, and verified with appropriate Homeland Security agencies. The costs of these plans are passed on to American business through port fees, taxes, tolls, and levies.

The DHS's mission to protect the United States and secure the free flow of commerce will come with business costs. Each security initiative adds a layer of cost in time and money that American business must take into consideration. The goal of the DHS is to protect and secure the nation while minimizing any interference with American commerce and trade.

Eric Bellone

FURTHER READING

Henderson, H. *Global Terrorism: The Complete Reference Guide.* New York: Checkmark Books, 2001. A general reference resource on international terrorism with a guide for researching terrorism topics.

Hoenig, S. L. *Handbook of Chemical Warfare and Terrorism.* Westport, Conn.: Greenwood Press, 2002. Information on chemicals that can be used as weapons and procedures for preventing and responding to chemical contamination.

Kushner, H. W. *Encyclopedia of Terrorism*. Thousand Oaks, Calif.: Sage, 2003. Three hundred entries covering many aspects of terrorism, including individuals, groups, events, methods, and responses.

Maxwell, B., ed. *Homeland Security: A Documentary History*. Washington, D.C.: CQ Press, 2004. A history of American homeland security up to the formation of the Department of Homeland Security.

The 9/11 Commission Report: Final Report of the National Commission on the Terrorist Attacks upon the United States. New York: W. W. Norton, 2004. The official government report covering the September 11 terrorist attacks.

Roebuck Jarrett, P., comp. *The Department of Homeland Security: A Compilation of Government Documents Relating to Executive Reorganization*. Buffalo, N.Y.: W. S. Hein, 2003. Compilation of main government documents concerning the reorganization of the executive branch of government. Also contains major government Web site addresses.

White, Jonathan R. *Terrorism: An Introduction*. Belmont, Calif.: Wadsworth Thompson Learning, 2002. A general introduction to terrorism.

SEE ALSO: Federal Emergency Management Agency; Secret Service, U.S.; September 11 terrorist attacks; Transportation, U.S. Department of.

Homestead Act of 1862

THE LAW: Federal law making public land free to settlers

DATE: Signed into law on May 20, 1862

SIGNIFICANCE: The Homestead Act encouraged the development of small family farms as important components of agricultural commerce in the still undeveloped American territories. Although East Coast industrial interests expressed concerns that the act would deplete low-cost labor from factories, most of those who took advantage of the free land were already farmers.

The Homestead Act of 1862 was one of a series of laws passed by the federal government during the nineteenth century to encourage the settlement and development of the American West. Previous policies concerning public land distribution re-quired settlers to pay for property that they received from the government. The Homestead Act made a fundamental break with these policies because settlers were provided with up to 160 acres of free land if they agreed to reside there for five years and make improvements to the property.

The passage of the Homestead Act was delayed by two significant business forces. Southern states, representing their constituent slave holders, were concerned that free land would encourage the expansion of nonslave labor and agriculture into the west. Northern industrial interests were concerned about loss of labor and increased costs as workers moved west. Opposition from these business interests dissipated once the South seceded and the U.S. Civil War became the primary concern of the American public. President Abraham Lincoln signed the Homestead Act into law in May, 1862.

The Homestead Act did not lead to a mass migration of urban labor from industrial businesses in the East. Most people taking advantage of the offer of free land were already farmers, many of whom were searching for additional land on behalf of their children. In addition to the costs of moving a family west, many potential homesteaders did not take advantage of the act because they had little money or credit that would allow them to improve and plant on their new land.

The lands available under the Homestead Act were not the most desirable from a business perspective. Farmers who wanted easier access to markets were forced to pay for land that was near railroads, which were given their own land grants from the federal government.

The free-land policy of the Homestead Act lasted approximately seventy-five years and distributed about 30 percent of the public lands in the West. President Franklin D. Roosevelt ended the policy during the mid-1930's by ordering that remaining public lands be permanently retained by the government on behalf of the citizens of the United States.

J. Wesley Leckrone

FURTHER READING

Dick, Everett. *The Lure of the Land: A Social History of the Public Lands from the Articles of Confederation to the New Deal*. Lincoln: University of Nebraska Press, 1970.

Porterfield, Jason. *The Homestead Act of 1862: A Pri-*

mary Source History of the Settlement of the American Heartland in the Late Nineteenth Century. New York: Rosen Publishing Group, 2005.

Shanks, Trina Williams. "The Homestead Act: A Major Asset-Building Policy in American History." In *Inclusion in the American Dream: Assets, Poverty and Public Policy,* edited by Michael Sherraden. New York: Oxford University Press, 2005.

SEE ALSO: Agriculture; Agriculture, U.S. Department of; Congress, U.S.; Immigration; Land laws.

Homestead strike

THE EVENT: Major labor conflict between unionized steelworkers and industrial magnates Andrew Carnegie and Henry Clay Frick

DATE: July, 1892

PLACE: Homestead, Pennsylvania

SIGNIFICANCE: A strike by the Amalgamated Association of Iron and Steel Workers against the Homestead Steel Works Company turned violent when Pinkerton agents and the state militia were sent to break the strike. This strike marked a new level of organization on the part of strikers but also resulted in the destruction of the union and its loss of influence in the Pittsburgh area steel mills.

Homestead, Pennsylvania, is an Allegheny County borough on the southeast border of the city of Pittsburgh along the Monongahela River. Andrew Carnegie's 1883 acquisition of the Homestead Steel Works Company, the industry's most efficient steel plant, increased his almost monopolistic control over steel production in the United States. Carnegie converted Homestead's production to rolling beams and angles to diversify and increase capacity. While Carnegie was acquiring the Homestead works, he was investing in the Henry Clay Frick Coke Company to guarantee a sufficient supply of iron ore and coke for steel production. In 1889 Homestead's craft union of skilled workers, Amalgamated Association of Iron and Steel Workers, held a contract that was about to expire. Carnegie was determined to lower wages by establishing a sliding wage scale. He left the means to a management team and sailed for Europe. The workers went on strike. When more than two thousand locals at-

These engravings from an 1892 Harper's Weekly *show a mob of people assailing the Pinkerton men (top) and the barges burning.* (Library of Congress)

tacked the sheriff and his deputies who arrived to break the strike, the Homestead works manager gave in to the workers' demands for a new three-year contract and official recognition as the plant's bargaining agent in return for the union's acceptance of a sliding wage scale.

When the steelworkers' contract came up for renewal in 1892, Carnegie was determined to take a stronger stand. He hired coke magnate Henry Clay Frick as general manager. Frick was know for his ruthlessness against employees and was regarded as the most antilabor industrialist in the country. Carnegie, who was thinking of retirement, set sail for Europe, leaving Frick in charge. Frick was determined to lower the wage scale and end Amalgamated Association of Iron and Steel Workers' role as a union bargaining agent. He constructed a stockade around the plant equipped with watchtowers, barbed wire, and rifle slits. The Pinkerton National Detective Agency was hired to bring three hundred agents to take control of the Homestead works and to reopen the plant with nonunion workers and workers who had left the union.

The Homestead strike began on July 1, 1892. The Pinkerton agents arrived by river on July 6. When the Homestead workers and residents learned about management's plan to break the strike, they prevented the barges from landing. They poured oil on the river and set it afire. Stranded, the Pinkertons agreed to a truce, which permitted their safe arrival on shore. However, the crowd's anger could not be contained. Nine strikers and seven agents were killed, and many of the rest of the Pinkertons sustained injuries. The Pinkerton agency's reputation was permanently tarnished as antilabor. At the request of management, the governor of Pennsylvania sent the state militia to retake the Homestead borough and plant. On July 23, anarchist Alexander Berkman entered Frick's office and shot and stabbed him, but Frick survived.

The Homestead Strike broke the union and led to Frick's successful removal of unions at the rest of the Carnegie steel plants. Although supportive of Frick's management style, Carnegie regretted the violence; later, he secretly contributed to pensions for some of the strikers and offered a relief fund for former Homestead employees. Carnegie did not retire but instead resumed control over his steel empire and Frick's management of it. Carnegie's reputation as a progressive employer and champion of labor was destroyed. Homestead continued to have sporadic labor problems until 1899, precipitating a steady decline in production at the plant into the next century.

William A. Paquette

FURTHER READING

Krooth, Richard. *A Century Passing: Carnegie, Steel, and the Fate of Homestead.* Lanham, Md.: University Press of America, 2002.

Standiford, Les. *Meet You in Hell: Andrew Carnegie, Henry Clay Frick, and the Bitter Partnership That Transformed America.* New York: Crown Publishers, 2005.

Whitelaw, Nancy. *The Homestead Strike of 1892.* Greensboro, N.C.: Morgan Reynolds, 2006.

SEE ALSO: Carnegie, Andrew; Coal industry; Coal strike of 1902; Labor history; Labor strikes; Steel industry; Steel mill seizure of 1952.

Horses

SIGNIFICANCE: Until the early twentieth century, horses were Americans' primary means of transport for goods and services and enabled commerce to take place over a wider geographical area. Horses also played an important role in building the roads over which they transported merchandise and passengers. Moreover, draft horses working in the fields increased the availability of agricultural products.

Horses were essential to the development of commerce in America. They were the primary means of agricultural production and of transportation of goods until the invention of motorized transportation and mechanized farm equipment. There would have been little movement of either products or people without horses. Dray lines, stagecoaches, and canal boats pulled by horses all contributed to the growth of business in the United States, as they distributed goods and services over a wide area, allowing for increased competition.

Horses were of great significance in the economic development of the western United States. They carried homesteaders into the territories, expanding the nation's agricultural economy. Cattle ranching would have been almost impossible without horses. The quarter horse remains an important member of the workforce on American ranches.

The lives of Native American tribes living on the Great Plains were heavily influenced by horses, which enabled them to hunt buffalo efficiently and increased their mobility. Horses became symbols of wealth for Plains Indians. The animals, however, also brought the settlers and soldiers who usurped the indigenous people's land and changed their way of life, often causing them severe hardships.

Horses continue to affect the U.S. economy. The equestrian sports business generates billions of dollars through the sale of both horses and event tickets. It also provides employment for a large number of workers. The sport of racing requires trainers, jockeys, grooms, owners, and a large staff of employees at the tracks. The thoroughbred, standardbred, and quarter horse racing industry syndicates stallions for millions of dollars every year. Rodeos and horse shows also make a sizeable contribution to the economy.

The horse industry provides a market for a large number of commodities, including tack, equipment, fencing, and agricultural products, as well as real estate such as barns, racetracks, arenas, riding trails, and pastures. Horses, once the nation's primary means of transportation, are now themselves transported in trucks, vans, and airplanes. The need to transport horses further stimulates the economy, as it creates a market for trailers, trucks, and planes specially equipped to accommodate the animals.

Thus, horses have been an important factor in American business from its inception. Although their role and economic significance have changed considerably, they continue to provide a significant stimulus to business activity and to contribute to economic expansion.

Shawncey Webb

FURTHER READING

McShane, Clay, and Joel Tarr. *The Horse in the City: Living Machines in the Nineteenth Century.* Baltimore: Johns Hopkins University Press, 2007.

Walker, Wyman D. *The Wild Horse of the West.* Omaha: University of Nebraska Press, 1962.

SEE ALSO: Agriculture; Native American trade; Pony Express; Postal Service, U.S.; Railroads; Shipping industry.

Hotel and motel industry

DEFINITION: Enterprises formed around multiunit buildings that provide temporary lodging to the general public

SIGNIFICANCE: The lodging industry grew dramatically with the development of national railroad and highway systems, the emergence of a middle class with sufficient leisure time and disposable income to travel, and an increase in business travel. The demand for public lodging also brought about a push toward standardization that ultimately benefited hotel and motel chains at the expense of small, family-owned establishments and older urban hotels.

Catering primarily to travelers, the modern American hotel grew out of the inns and taverns that served as temporary lodging during the colonial period and into the nineteenth century. These establishments typically operated in port cities and along stagecoach roads, often doubling as makeshift meeting halls, courts of law, and convenient locations in which to conduct business deals. Their importance to early American commerce is reflected in a Massachusetts law requiring a tavern in every town.

URBAN HOTELS

The first large urban American hotel, consisting of seventy-three rooms, opened in New York City in 1794, and similar establishments followed in Boston, Baltimore, and Philadelphia. These hotels were often lavish and served as symbols of prosperity and focal points for business activity. In addition, large urban hotels employed substantial numbers of people, contributing to the growth of the service sectors of many American cities.

The emergence of railroad transportation during the mid-nineteenth century brought about an increase in business and recreational travel. Hotels were often among the first buildings to be erected in the towns and cities established along railroad lines. They were vital centers of commercial activity that provided the service and retail establishments of booming downtown areas with steady streams of patrons.

Builders of urban hotels in emerging midwestern and western cities often sought to outdo rival towns by constructing ever-larger and more lavish establishments. As rail travel became more affordable and increasing numbers of middle-class people began to travel, however, other hoteliers began to emphasize cleanliness, affordability, and simple amenities such as private bathrooms and free newspapers. Resort hotels also began operation in many rural areas, offering seclusion and natural beauty for vacationers and health benefits (such as mineral springs and exotic treatments) for seekers of cures for various ailments. The increase in the variety of accommodations available to travelers fueled a burgeoning travel industry that catered both to the growing middle class and to the expanding American business sector.

In addition, hotels of the nineteenth and early twentieth centuries were often laboratories for new technologies such as electric lights, elevators, telephone systems, and air-conditioning. The rapidly changing technological climate of this period rendered many of these modern hotels prematurely obsolete, and the proliferation of hotels frequently led to market saturation, causing many hotels to close or to convert to other uses. Transitions from stagecoach transportation to railroads, railroads to highways, and highways to superhighways produced a constant underlying volatility in the lodging industry throughout the nineteenth and twentieth centuries.

A motel in Helena, Montana, in 1942. (Library of Congress)

ADAPTING TO CHANGE

The arrival of the automobile during the early decades of the twentieth century brought about drastic changes in the American hotel and motel industry. With the development of a system of federal highways and the availability of affordable automobiles such as the Ford Model T, demand increased for inexpensive, convenient lodging catering to motorists. These establishments, known as motor hotels, motels, or motor courts, grew steadily in number as automobile ownership and long-distance travel increased during the pre-World War II era. In this environment, the traditional urban hotels, inconvenient to new highway systems and increasingly located in deteriorating neighborhoods, began to decline both in number and in quality.

The quality of motels also varied widely. Most were locally owned and operated in the absence of industry standards regarding cleanliness, room size, or amenities offered. Many were located inconveniently to restaurants and local attractions and typically charged extra for children. Motel federations such as Travelodge and Best Western established before the 1950's referred customers to member establishments but exercised no control over the operation of such member motels.

THE POSTWAR ERA

The economic boom of the postwar era and the establishment of the Dwight D. Eisenhower National System of Interstate and Defense Highways (also known as the Interstate Highway System) during the 1950's led to the emergence of motel chains and a resultant trend toward standardization. The Holiday Inn chain, conceived by real estate developer Kemmons Wilson during a 1951 family vacation, was established in Memphis, Tennessee, in 1952. Determined to avoid the problems that he and his family had encountered at numerous motels during their vacation, Wilson designed his motels with standard-size rooms, on-site restaurants, and standard amenities such as televisions, swimming pools, air-conditioning, and free stays for children.

To ensure convenient locations, Wilson purchased building sites along the new interstate highways near exits and on the right side of adjoining roads and streets, so patrons would not have to make left turns to reach the motels. As competing motel chains emerged during the 1950's and 1960's, many merely purchased building sites alongside newly constructed Holiday Inns. These motel chains enjoyed a tremendous competitive advantage over locally owned and operated motels, many of which lacked the capital to upgrade their operations or move to more desirable locations.

The standardization of the motel industry increased public trust in motels, as the growing disposable income of Americans and the convenience of interstate highways fueled a steady increase in

WHERE DOMESTIC TRAVELERS STAYED OVERNIGHT, 2005

Type of Lodging	Percentage of Travelers
Hotel, motel, bed and breakfast	53
Private home	34
RV or tent	5
Time share	2
Other	7

Source: Data from the Travel Industry Association
Note: The average stay at a hotel, motel, or bed and breakfast is 3.2 nights.

travel. Newly constructed motel sites along the new superhighways often became magnets for commercial development, attracting retail establishments, restaurants, and other services. As a result, chain motels have sometimes been cited as contributors to the economic decline of downtown business districts and the proliferation of suburban sprawl.

The economic boom of the 1990's and concomitant revitalization efforts in many American cities led to a revival of urban hotels toward the end of the twentieth century, prompting the construction of new downtown hotels and the reopening of many old ones. Urban hotels thus reclaimed their historical status as symbols of vitality and focal points for economic activity. Resort hotels continued to thrive in certain cites such as Las Vegas, and lodging establishments offering a variety of amenities and price ranges remained vital to American transportation and commerce.

Michael H. Burchett

FURTHER READING

Halberstam, David. *The Fifties.* New York: Villard Books, 1993. Charts the effects of the lodging industry on American culture within the context of a study of tumult and change during the 1950's.

Jakle, J. A., et al. *The Motel in America.* Baltimore: Johns Hopkins University Press, 2002. Comprehensive study of the motel industry and its history, including the architecture and design of motels.

Sandoval-Strausz, Andrew K. *Hotel: An American History.* New Haven, Conn.: Yale University Press, 2007. Part social history, part economic history, part political history, this study details the relationship between the hotel industry, capitalism, and the function of public and private space in American culture.

Witzel, Michael K. *The American Motel.* Osceola, Wis.: Motorbooks International, 2000. Copiously illustrated study of U.S. motels, from the early "autocamps" through late twentieth century chains and innovations.

SEE ALSO: American Automobile Association; Automotive industry; Highways; Railroads; Tourism industry.

Housing and Urban Development, U.S. Department of

IDENTIFICATION: Cabinet-level department responsible for aiding citizens in finding housing and stimulating the development of American cities

DATE: Established in 1965

SIGNIFICANCE: Although the official mission of the Department of Housing and Urban Development is to help people find adequate housing and oversee the development of urban areas, it has evolved into the federal agency most helpful to the banking, real estate, and construction industries in the United States.

President Lyndon B. Johnson was very proud of his success in persuading the U.S. Congress to create a cabinet-level department to address the rebuilding of American cities and the needs of American citizens for adequate housing. As a matter of national policy, housing was first addressed in the U.S. Housing Act of 1937 and the Housing and Home Finance Agency of 1949. Johnson was pleased to build on these initiatives developed by two of his heroes, President Franklin D. Roosevelt and President Harry S. Truman. Homes for the elderly were addressed in the Housing Act of 1959. As useful as these earlier pieces of legislation were in addressing some of the problems of housing, it was clear that a cabinet-level department would be helpful in dealing with housing and urban problems by the 1960's. Johnson regarded the creation of the Department of Housing and Urban Development (HUD) as one of the centerpieces of his Great Society initiative.

Improvements in housing policy continued in 1968 with the passage of the Fair Housing Act, which prohibited discrimination in housing. The 1969 Brooke Amendment made it policy for low-income families to be required to pay no more than 25 percent of their income for rent in public housing. The Housing and Community Development Act of 1974 provided for block grants and urban homesteads. The 1977 Housing and Community Act continued aid for elderly and handicapped persons and provided for urban development grants.

A Business Orientation

By the presidency of Ronald Reagan, conservative forces had gradually shifted the emphasis at HUD away from urban development and aid to individual citizens and toward assistance to businesses such as banks, real estate developers, and construction companies. HUD became a helpmate to business. For example, the 1988 Housing and Community Development Act authorized the sale of public housing complexes to resident management corporations. Although the Bill Clinton administration shifted the focus back on the individual citizen to a limited degree with its 1996 Housing Opportunity Program Extension Act, this legislation was most memorable for allowing public housing authorities to bar potential residents who might use drugs or engage in criminal activities that would threaten other residents; it did not provide significant new funding for public housing. By 2007, HUD began a new initiative to assist low-income individuals to purchase homes with as little as $100 down payment. Although this was done in the name of helping individual citizens, it encouraged people to purchase homes that they could not afford and aggravated the subprime mortgage crisis that developed in 2007-2008.

Scandals

During the Reagan administration, HUD developed a reputation for rampant corruption. When the George H. W. Bush administration opened in 1989, his appointments to the agency discovered extensive mortgage fraud that was the product of the previous administration's determination to make the agency friendly to business groups, such as banks, real estate firms, and the construction indus-

try. These efforts were so successful that one staffer testified before Congress that HUD was being run as a "criminal enterprise." Although some improvements were possible during the next decade, problems of inadequate oversight in the housing industry generally were part of the Bush administration, ultimately resulting in the crisis in the subprime mortgage market and the subsequent serious deterioration in the housing industry, although much of the responsibility must fall on Fannie Mae (Federal National Mortgage Association) and Freddie Mac (Federal Home Loan Mortgage Corporation) and not on HUD itself.

Richard L. Wilson

Further Reading

Arnold, Peri E. *Making the Managerial Presidency: Comprehensive Reorganization Planning, 1905-1996.* 2d ed. Lawrence: University Press of Kansas, 1998. A serious academic examination of the efforts to reform the bureaucracy of the national government to improve managerial innovation. Looks at housing related issues.

Cristie, James R., ed. *Fannie Mae and Freddie Mac: Scandal in U.S. Housing.* New York: Novinka Books, 2007. This book examines the scandals in Fannie Mae and Freddie Mac and their impact on housing policy in the United States before the 2008 takeover of both of these dysfunctional agencies.

Kurian, George T., ed. *A Historical Guide to the U.S. Government.* New York: Oxford University Press, 1998. This history of the federal government and bureaucracy provides a thorough understanding of the three branches of government and their relation to economics.

Roessner, Jane. *A Decent Place to Live: From Columbia Point to Harbor Point—A Community History.* Boston: Northeastern University Press, 2000. A case study approach to the problems of housing in one community in the United States, which has important implications for broader housing policy.

Willis, James. *Explorations in Macroeconomics.* 5th ed. Redding, Calif.: North West Publishing, 2002. In this textbook, Willis uses a macroeconomic perspective to explain the effect of taxation on society.

Zinn, Howard. *A People's History of the United States: 1492-Present.* New York: Harper Perennial Modern Classics, 2005. Liberal interpretation of American history that sheds some light on the difficulties in U.S. policies, including housing policies.

SEE ALSO: Construction industry; Mortgage industry; Real estate industry, commercial; Real estate industry, residential; Supreme Court and land law; Zoning, commercial.

How-to-succeed books

DEFINITION: Popular books on financial and business-related topics that offer strategies for achieving financial goals or prosperity and appeal to a wide range of consumers

SIGNIFICANCE: The how-to-succeed genre became an increasingly important and lucrative segment of the book publishing industry from the twentieth into the twenty-first century. It also provided their authors, publishers, and other investors with significant additional revenue through television, radio, films, and the Internet. It exerted an influence on other markets, as consumers made decisions based on the advice they received.

Financial how-to-succeed books are an important segment of a larger genre, self-help books, which also includes books focusing on self-therapy and spirituality, health and weight loss, relationships, and related topics. There is a significant amount of overlap among these subgenres, because self-image, visualization, and human relationships are parts of finance as well as other dimensions of life. The full self-help industry, moreover, exceeds the self-help publishing industry, making it difficult to measure comprehensively. Successful authors leverage their written works to profit from lectures, workshops, training organizations, and media productions.

The first self-help books included financial advice alongside other practical suggestions. One of the earliest authors of these books was Benjamin Franklin, an American business entrepreneur, inventor, and statesman. Franklin's *Poor Richard Improved* (1757; also known as *The Way to Wealth*) was the first American book on personal finance. Originally published as a preface to *Poor Richard's Almanack* (1732-1758), this thirty-page, pocket-sized book established a pattern for subsequent works in the how-to-succeed financial genre and sold millions of copies with numerous printings. Franklin used memorable phrases and couplets to give financial advice about hard work, frugality, debt, and other topics.

Orison Swett Marden, inspired by the self-help writings of Scottish author Samuel Smiles as well as earlier American authors, became a leader of the New Thought movement, and his many books and magazine articles made an important connection between personal cultivation and financial affairs. One of his earliest books, *How to Succeed: Or, Stepping-Stones to Fame and Fortune*, was published in 1896. In 1926, George Samuel Clason published *The Richest Man in Babylon*, a collection of ancient Babylonian parables, each illustrating a simple financial lesson. Stories included "The Camel Trader of Babylon," "Seven Cures For A Lean Purse," and "The Goddess of Good Luck." The book had sold more than 2 million copies by 2004, when Fred Siegel and Rick Crandall published a modern version, *The Richest Man in Babylon for Today: New Secrets for Building Wealth in the Twenty-First Century*.

POPULAR CULTURE

The trend of inspirational authors advocating self-confidence, positive visualization, and good thoughts as prerequisites for success in business grew in the twentieth century, and the genre became an identifiable aspect of American popular culture, as well as a thriving industry. In 1937, Napoleon Hill published *Think and Grow Rich*, a landmark motivational book that has been a consistent best seller. Hill used stories from Andrew Carnegie, Henry Ford, and other wealthy contemporaries to formulate his philosophy of success, which he said was attainable by anyone willing to use the power of the mind. Dale Carnegie, who taught courses in public speaking and related topics, became a renowned writer. His 1937 book, *How to Win Friends and Influence People*, was an overnight success that became one of the most popular how-to-succeed books ever written, with more than 15 million copies sold worldwide. Carnegie believed the key to business and personal success was gaining the support of other people.

The Power of Positive Thinking, by Norman Vincent Peale, was published in 1952, eventually selling 7 million copies. Peale, a minister who had counseled unemployed businessmen during the Great Depression, was active in inspirational radio broadcasts and was a cofounder of *Guideposts* magazine. In the same year, Shepherd Mead's *How to Succeed in Business Without Really Trying* attracted attention by satirizing American corporate culture and the use of instruction manuals to guide careers. Mead's book, which later inspired a successful Broadway musical and a film of the same title, showed the extent to which the self-help book genre had pervaded American society by the middle of the twentieth century.

First published in 1960, Maxwell Maltz's *Psycho-Cybernetics: A New Way to Get More Living Out of Life*, eventually sold more than 30 million copies. Maxwell was a plastic surgeon who was surprised when many of his patients still felt ugly after successful surgery. He came to believe that self-image and human behavior were internal processes controlled by the mind and that positive visualization techniques would lead to happiness and financial success. In 2002, an updated edition, *The New Psycho-Cybernetics: The Original Science of Self-Improvement and Success That Has Changed the Lives of Thirty Million People*, was published.

HOLISTIC APPROACHES

After the cultural changes of the 1960's, large segments of the American public became interested in more expanded notions of self and society. Although traditional self-help and financial how-to-succeed books remained popular, new authors appeared who combined the essentially positive outlook of previous authors with an emphasis on moral and spiritual values, often with insights from other cultural sources.

First published in 1989, *The Seven Habits of Highly Effective People* by Stephen R. Covey sold more than 10 million copies. The book presented a holistic, principle-based approach to personal and professional success. *Your Money or Your Life: Transforming Your Relationship with Money and Achieving Financial Independence* (1992) became a best-selling handbook for a new morality of money management. The authors, Joe Dominquez and Vicki Robin, left successful careers to live more meaningfully and to make better use of their life energy. They advocated frugal living instead of conspicuous consumption, saving the planet while saving money, and a "wholeness" of lifestyle.

Deepak Chopra, an Indian American physician with an interest in meditation, became the author of

Dale Carnegie reads from his best-selling How to Win Friends and Influence People *in 1955.* (AP/Wide World Photos)

more than forty books in which he synthesized insights from Indian philosophy, modern physics, and other fields. A pioneer in the field of mind-body medicine and human potential, Chopra wrote *Creating Affluence: Wealth Consciousness in the Field of All Possibilities* (1993), which suggested simple steps for developing wealth consciousness and attaining what the author saw as a natural state of affluence. In 1994, Chopra published the best-selling *The Seven Spiritual Laws of Success*, which summarized the essence of his teachings in seven principles.

THE NEW REALISM

Avoiding the emphasis on optimism and hope of the mid-century texts and the holistic philosophies of the New Age authors (who also remained popular in their own right), some writers at the end of the twentieth century candidly emphasized wealth as the goal and provided strategies for becoming rich without any spiritual or moral dimension. Many books focused on millionaires and how they became wealthy.

In 1996, Thomas J. Stanley and William D. Danko published *The Millionaire Next Door: The Surprising Secrets of America's Wealthy*, a landmark study that refuted popular beliefs about the wealthy. Based on twenty years of interviews with more than one thousand millionaires, the book asserted that most millionaires were frugal, lived below their means, invested diligently, and had little inherited wealth. They did not have the highest incomes or live in the most expensive neighborhoods. At the same time, many people with high incomes lived extravagantly but had low net worth or actual wealth. Thus, anyone could become a millionaire through hard work, saving, and investing. By 2004, *The Millionaire Next Door* had sold more than 2.5 million copies. In 1999, Stanley and Danko published a second best seller, *The Millionaire Mind*, probing deeper into the secrets of the wealthy.

Entrepreneur and educator Robert Kiyosaki discarded conventional thinking about how to become rich. In his revolutionary best seller, *Rich Dad, Poor Dad: What the Rich Teach Their Kids About Money—That the Poor and Middle Class Do Not!* (1997), Kiyosaki described how his real-life father, the "Poor Dad," saved money and worked hard as an employee all his life but died poor. Instead of depending on wages, his mentor, the "Rich Dad" was a multimillionaire with ample cash flow in the form of passive income from wise investments, real estate, and businesses. *Rich Dad, Poor Dad* sold millions of copies worldwide, and Kiyosaki's financial philosophy led to a series of Rich Dad books, workshops, television appearances, games, and other products.

David Bach became famous for his "Latte Factor" idea that, by avoiding small purchases such as caffe lattes or sodas each day, one could save that money and "finish rich." Bach also argued that saving money had to be automatic to be successful. These ideas formed the basis of his seven consecutive national best sellers. *The Automatic Millionaire* was the number-one business book in 2004. Bach's Finish Rich books were translated into more than fifteen languages, with more

---

NEW YORK TIMES TOP TEN BUSINESS HARDCOVER BEST SELLERS, OCTOBER, 2008

How-to-succeed books continue to hold a fascination for the business reader, even in the midst of the 2008 financial crisis.

1. *Hot, Flat, and Crowded*, by Thomas L. Friedman
   A *New York Times* columnist speaks of American renewal through a green revolution.

2. *The First Billion Is the Hardest*, by T. Boone Pickens
   An oilman describes his career and his thoughts on energy policy.

3. *The Four-Hour Workweek: Escape 9-5, Live Anywhere, and Join the New Rich*, by Timothy Ferris
   A semiautobiographical how-to-succeed book.

4. *Now, Discover Your Strengths*, by Marcus Buckingham and Donald O. Clifton
   Tells managers how to manage themselves and their employees by drawing out their strengths.

5. *Bad Money*, by Kevin Phillips
   A criticism of the financial sector and the government's faith in the efficiency of markets.

6. *The Total Money Makeover*, by Dave Ramsey
   A radio talk-show host discusses how families can reduce debt.

7. *Six Disciplines: Execution, Revolution*, by Gary Harpst
   A step-by-step strategy execution methodology for mid-sized and small businesses.

8. *Debt Cures "They" Don't Want You to Know About*, by Kevin Trudeau
   A criticism of the banking and credit industry that aims to help consumers.

9. *The Gone Fishin' Portfolio*, by Alexander Green
   An insider's view of the investment industry that presents an investment strategy.

10. *Yes!* by Noah J. Godstein, Steve J. Martin, and Robert B. Cialdini
    A guide to improving one's powers of persuasion.

than 5 million copies printed. They include *Smart Couples Finish Rich* (2001) and *Start Late, Finish Rich* (2005).

WOMEN AND WEALTH

Financial and money management books for or written by women became increasingly popular during the late twentieth century. Bach published the best seller *Smart Women Finish Rich: Nine Steps to Achieving Financial Security and Funding Your Dreams* in 1999. Eight years after publishing *The Millionaire Next Door,* Stanley published *Women Millionaires Next Door: The Many Journeys of Successful American Businesswomen.* This significant study portrayed most millionaire women as frugal, hardworking, and very generous.

Kiyosaki's wife, Kim Kiyosaki, used her husband's Rich Dad strategies to become wealthy in her own right and wrote *Rich Woman: A Book on Investing for Women—Because I Hate Being Told What to Do!* (2006) to show women how to become financially independent. Suze Orman, a television celebrity, author, and financial adviser, wrote numerous best-selling how-to-succeed books. These included *The Nine Steps to Financial Freedom* (1997), *The Courage to Be Rich* (1998), *The Money Book for the Young, Fabulous, and Broke* (2005), and *Women and Money: Owning the Power to Control Your Destiny* (2007). Jean Chatzy, a financial coach, television speaker, and magazine editor, has published many popular books, including *Pay It Down! From Debt to Wealth on $10 a Day* (2004) and *Make Money, Not Excuses* (2006). Psychologist Lois P. Frankel applied insights from her field to counsel women in books such as *Nice Girls Don't Get the Corner Office* (2004) and *Nice Girls Don't Get Rich* (2005).

Alice Myers

FURTHER READING

Anker, Roy M. *Self-Help and Popular Religion in Early American Culture: An Interpretive Guide.* Westport, Conn.: Greenwood Press, 1999. Analysis of the role of religion and nineteenth century American culture in shaping self-help and how-to-succeed philosophies and literature.

Archibald, Matthew E. *The Evolution of Self-Help.* New York: Palgrave Macmillan, 2007. Historical study of the self-help movement, focusing particularly on the implications of the movement's institutionalization and the consequences of achieving mainstream legitimacy.

Dolby, Sandra K. *Self-Help Books: Why Americans Keep Reading Them.* Urbana: University of Illinois Press, 2005. Study of the distinctively American character and audience of the self-help genre.

Simonds, Wendy. *Women and Self-Help Culture: Reading Between the Lines.* New Brunswick, N.J.: Rutgers University Press, 1992. Examines the gendering of the self-help genre in general. Useful for understanding the audience of both male- and female-centric how-to-succeed books.

Starker, Steven. *Oracle at the Supermarket: The American Preoccupation With Self-Help Books.* New Brunswick, N.J.: Transaction, 1988. A clinical psychologist studies the social significance of the genre itself, as well as the contents of specific popular self-help books.

SEE ALSO: Book publishing; Franklin, Benjamin; Wages.

Hughes, Howard

IDENTIFICATION: Legendary American aviator and entrepreneur

BORN: December 24, 1905; Houston, Texas

DIED: April 5, 1975; in an airplane en route from Acapulco, Mexico, to Houston, Texas

SIGNIFICANCE: Through much of the twentieth century, Hughes was the embodiment of the American businessman as a larger-than-life adventurer: half-hero and half-outlaw. His most important business contributions were in the field of aeronautics, the film industry, and in investments in Las Vegas casinos and real estate.

Much of Howard Hughes's reputation came not from his enormous success or business talent—he was, for much of his life, one of the wealthiest people on the planet—but from the staggering diversity of his enterprises. From the late 1920's through the 1950's, he was a successful Hollywood producer/director. Throughout the 1930's and 1940's, he gained fame as a daring aviator and test pilot, founding Hughes Aircraft and breaking world records flying airplanes that he had designed himself. He also owned and expanded Trans World Airlines. During the 1950's he founded the Howard Hughes Medical Institute, which soon became one of the country's primary centers of medical research. Other ventures he pursued included automobile and ship design, real estate, and management of hotels, casinos, airlines, and restaurants, many of which were in Las Vegas.

Another source of Hughes's fame was the scandal that accompanied almost every enterprise. During his Hollywood years, tabloids and gossip columns continually linked his name with prominent film stars like Katharine Hepburn and Ava Gardner, and his hit film about Billy the Kid, *The Outlaw* (1942), drew fire from moralists because of the way star Jane Russell's ample bosoms were displayed in an extremely low-cut blouse. After World War II, he was summoned before a congressional committee to account for his failure to deliver the famed *Spruce Goose*, a specially designed fighter plane made pri-

marily of wood, in time to be of help during the war. During the 1970's, his name was linked to the foremost political scandal of that decade—Watergate—when rumors circulated that he had lent a sizable sum of money to President Richard Nixon's brother Donald.

A final factor contributing to Hughes's status as celebrity-businessman is the aura of mystery that surrounded him throughout his life. So much about this successful American entrepreneur remains uncertain, beginning with the date of his birth, Christmas Eve, which may be apocryphal. Also uncertain is the number of his marriages, as he may or may not have been married to film actor Terry Moore from the late 1940's until his death. In addition, his sexual preferences are debatable, as

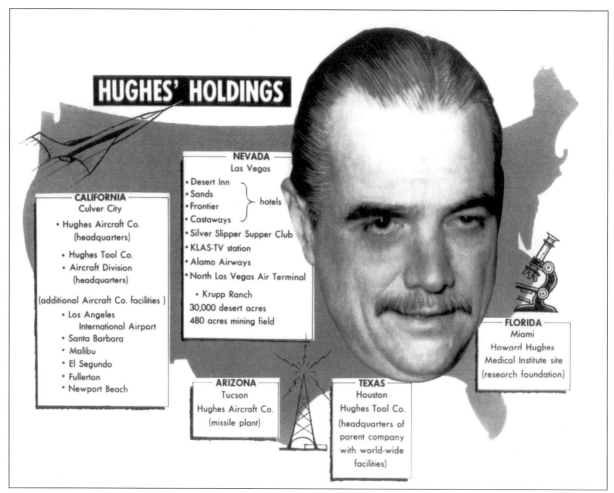

This montage shows Howard Hughes along with charts listing his holdings and properties as of August 18, 1968. (AP/ Wide World Photos)

Hollywood gossip and a popular biography have suggested that he was gay or bisexual. Toward the end of his life, his very sanity was questionable, as he became a hypochondriac, germophobic loner living in rigorously enforced seclusion, in hotels in Las Vegas, Houston, and other locales. This hermetic existence during his final years only heightened his celebrity, as he was spoofed in various television series and celebrated in song by different artists. Not until Donald Trump did another American businessman come close to becoming such a celebrity mogul.

Thomas Du Bose

FURTHER READING

Bartlett, Donald L., and James B. Steele. *Empire.* New York: Norton, 1979.

Higham, Charles. *Howard Hughes.* 1993. Reprint. New York: St. Martin's Press, 2004.

Wildenberg, Thomas, and R. E. G. Davies. *Howard Hughes: An Airman, His Aircraft, and His Great Flights.* McLean, Va.: Paladwr Press, 2006.

SEE ALSO: Air transportation industry; Aircraft industry; Motion-picture industry; Trump, Donald.

Hurricane Katrina

THE EVENT: Category 5 hurricane that struck Louisiana, Mississippi, and Alabama, killing many, displacing more than a million people, and causing widespread flooding

DATE: August 29, 2005

PLACE: Southeastern Louisiana, southern Mississippi, and southern Alabama

SIGNIFICANCE: The most costly storm in U.S. history, Katrina devastated the economy of the Gulf Coast in Louisiana, Mississippi, and Alabama and caused massive damage to New Orleans in particular. The storm had a long-term impact on the national oil and gas industries, the region's tourist and fishing industries, and the shipping operations of one of the country's busiest ports.

On August 29, 2005, Hurricane Katrina made landfall southeast of New Orleans, Louisiana, cutting a swath of destruction through the city and eastward into Mississippi and Alabama. Although the city weathered the storm itself, the levees protecting it were breached, causing massive flooding. The national headlines describing the loss of life and the damage along the northern Gulf Coast and the government's subsequent bungling of rescue and recovery operations often overshadowed accounts of the storm's economic impact both locally and nationally.

Evacuations before and after the storm resulted in more than one million people being displaced, and for weeks businesses in the affected areas were shut down. Although encouraged to rebuild and reopen by a number of hastily passed federal and state tax incentive programs, businesses found that there was a serious shortage of available workers. The heaviest damage in New Orleans had occurred in working-class neighborhoods, making it impossible for thousands to return because their homes were destroyed by flooding. Wages went up almost immediately, as employers tried to attract the limited number of returnees, especially in construction, where thousands of new workers were needed. Additionally, financial backing for business reconstruction was both slow and erratic, as a conservative banking industry in the region and a slow response from the Small Business Administration made it difficult for owners to secure the money necessary to rebuild.

While virtually every business in the area suffered, four industries were especially affected: tourism, fishing, shipping, and energy production. Many New Orleans hotels, restaurants, and tourist attractions suffered serious damage, causing thousands of visitors to stay away and forcing a number of national conventions to relocate to other cities. The same phenomenon occurred in Mississippi, where tourism fueled by legalized gambling along the Gulf Coast was halted because casinos were either destroyed or seriously damaged. Damages to boats, piers, and processing plants caused fishing operations to come to a standstill for weeks or even months.

Because the Port of New Orleans was one of the major hubs for the import and export of goods going by sea, both domestic and foreign trade was seriously disrupted. Most Americans felt the effects of the storm at the gas pumps. The temporary shutdown of drilling operations and refineries along the Gulf Coast caused by Hurricane Katrina and by Hurricane Rita, which hit the region a month later, produced an immediate spike in gasoline prices, with some areas seeing a rise of as much as one dollar per gallon. The final estimates for damages caused by Hurricane Katrina exceeded $100 billion.

Laurence W. Mazzeno

FURTHER READING

Daniels, Ronald, et al., eds. *On Risk and Disaster: Lessons from Hurricane Katrina.* Philadelphia: University of Pennsylvania Press, 2006.

Horne, Joe. *Breach of Faith: Hurricane Katrina and the Near Death of a Great American City.* New York: Random House, 2006.

SEE ALSO: Federal Emergency Management Agency; Fishing industry; Insurance industry; Mississippi and Missouri Rivers; Petroleum industry; Small Business Administration; Tourism industry.

Iacocca, Lee

IDENTIFICATION: Automotive industry executive at Ford and Chrysler who rose to prominence during the 1960's and 1970's

BORN: October 15, 1924; Allentown, Pennsylvania

SIGNIFICANCE: Iacocca led Ford Motor Company during the pinnacle of the American auto industry during the 1960's, and he saved Chrysler Motors from bankruptcy during the 1970's.

Born to immigrant parents in Pennsylvania, Lee Iacocca majored in engineering at Lehigh University, then earned a graduate degree at Princeton. In 1946, he began work at Ford Motor Company. Although he started in the engineering division, he found his job tedious and got transferred to sales. During the 1960's, he led the way in canceling the Ford Cardinal project and promoting a new type of car called the Mustang. The Mustang was an instant sensation and led to a generation of powerful sporty American cars aimed at the youth market. The youth market had previously been dominated by imports and hot rods, and the Mustang model became an icon with tremendous durability.

By the 1970's, Iacocca found his situation at Ford precarious because of frequent clashes with Henry Ford II. In 1978, Ford convinced the corporate board to fire Iacocca. The former Ford employee took a job as head of Chrysler Motors, which was in dire straits. The once excellent engineering division had fallen into neglect. Chrysler had set up partnerships with floundering European automakers that only worsened the position of the American company. The general economic slump of the late 1970's added to the gravity of the situation.

In a controversial move, Iacocca went to the federal government and negotiated an $800 million loan. The request touched off a political firestorm. Opponents blasted it as corporate welfare at a time when services for the poor and unemployed were being slashed. Iacocca succeeded in arranging the loan in 1979 and subsequently turned Chrysler around and repaid the loan by 1983.

Iacocca retired from Chrysler in 1992. In retirement, he remained a corporate celebrity, a role emulated by many but matched by very few executives.

Michael Polley

SEE ALSO: Automotive industry; Chrysler bailout of 1979; Ford, Henry; Ford Motor Company; General Motors.

Lee Iacocca. (AP/Wide World Photos)

IBM. *See* International Business Machines

Identity theft

DEFINITION: Illegal appropriation and use of personal identifying data belonging to other people in order to impersonate them, usually to conduct business transactions in their name

Significance: The criminal act of identity theft costs Americans and American businesses millions of dollars per year in losses, legal fees, and investigations and fosters distrust between consumers and businesses.

Identity theft is the act of one individual stealing another's personal information for the purposes of posing as that person. The most common method of identity theft is credit card fraud, but there are many other variations. There is no official record of the first reported case of identity theft, but incidents can be identified throughout history. In 1863, for example, New York City fell into rioting because of the Union draft. Wealthier citizens who were drafted paid lower-class men to take their identities and report to the Union recruiting centers. The common price was $300 for individuals willing to assume a fraudulent identity for the purpose of being drafted. During those earlier times, victims of identity theft were simply inconvenienced by the need to replace their identification, but as the years progressed, the crimes expanded and the victims multiplied with every offense.

In 1998, the Federal Trade Commission (FTC) was directed to create a repository of all data related to identity crimes. The repository would include the number of victims, cost to the victims, cost to the businesses involved, and length of time to remedy the problem. Within the first year, more than 1,000 crimes were reported, with that number increasing to 31,000 the next year. Each subsequent year, the number of reported crimes doubled from the previous year. By 2004, the number of reported crimes a year climbed to 650,000. The list of offenses had grown from just credit card fraud to include theft of telephone calls, bank accounts, government benefits, and loans, as well as employment-related fraud. Victims were reported from all age groups, including minors. Another survey performed by the FTC in 2006 through telephone interviews found that more than 8 million Americans living at the time had been the victims of some form of identity theft.

Costs

There are many costs resulting from identity theft; the greatest weighs on the consumer. The 2006 FTC survey reported that over 50 percent of all identity theft crimes from the previous year resulted in gains to the thieves of $1,000 or more. One-

quarter of these crimes cost the victims at least $1,000 from their own pockets. In total, from 2001 to 2004, the FTC reported that victims paid out almost $4 billion. These victims also learned that money was not the only thing they lost as a result of these crimes. Some 60 percent of victims spent at least ten hours attempting to resolve the fallout after the incident, with more than half of that number spending forty hours or more.

Not included in the survey were lost wages, legal fees, and other monies directly related to the time spent resolving the problems created by the thefts. On the surface, once money has been repaid and the issue has been handled, everything can slowly go back to normal, but victims quite often continue to have various problems that plague them after the crime has been committed. The paramount complaint is from creditors, because after an identity theft, the victim becomes a greater risk for future attacks. Collection agencies can start to call for charges that the victim never made, banks can refuse to service victims through new loans or opening new accounts. The legal ramifications could be the worst problem of all. Law-enforcement agencies continue to investigate the incident and watch the victim in case they are struck again. The problems that arise after the crime has been resolved may persist for years and, in worst-case scenarios, until the end of the victims' lives.

American businesses as a whole have also suffered greatly. Lost manpower hours hurt any organization, but to a small business, losing an employee for any amount of time can very difficult to work around. The FTC survey also reports that businesses were losing around $197 for every data record lost to identity theft. Businesses can also lose money for the same reasons that individuals do, if they are tied up in legal troubles, as well as developing an inability to trust their client base. Insurance companies spend millions of dollars a year on cases in which their clients have been victimized. The government also spends billions of dollars a year maintaining multiple task forces and organizations that assist in combating identity theft.

Law-Enforcement Efforts

The FTC gathers information on identity thefts. The Department of Justice, Central Intelligence Agency (CIA), Federal Bureau of Investigation (FBI), and Secret Service all get involved in tracking down criminals who commit identity theft. Several of these organizations travel the world, tracking down identity thieves and perpetrators of fraud against American citizens. The President's Task Force on Identity Theft, formed May, 2006, is a co-operative organization that aids the other government agencies by sharing information between them all. The task force was designed to aid the law-enforcement community to track down and prosecute identity theft criminals. It also provides education services to governmental agencies and corporate businesses on how they can help individuals protect themselves against identity predators. As identity theft increases, the need for government response grows, as does the burden on taxpayers. Identity theft affects all citizens, whether they have been victims or not.

Christian V. Glotfelty

FURTHER READING

Abagnale, Frank W. *Stealing Your Life: The Ultimate Identity Theft Prevention Plan.* New York: Broadway Books, 2007. Practical advice on avoiding identity theft from a former master of identify theft.

Collins, Judith M. *Investigating Identity Theft: A Guide for Businesses, Law Enforcement, and Victims.* Hoboken, N.J.: John Wiley & Sons, 2006. Comprehensive survey of identity theft investigations with many case studies.

Cullen, Terri. *The "Wall Street Journal" Complete Identity Theft Guidebook: How to Protect Yourself from the Most Pervasive Crime in America.* New York: Three Rivers Press, 2007. Practical advice on methods to avoid having one's identity stolen.

Hammond, Robert J. *Identity Theft: How to Protect Your Most Valuable Asset.* Franklin Lakes, N.J.: Career Press, 2003. General guide for laypersons focuses on identity theft prevention and awareness.

Hayward, Claudia L., ed. *Identity Theft.* New York: Novinka Books, 2004. Collection of articles on a variety of aspects of identity theft.

Sullivan, Bob. *Your Evil Twin: Behind the Identity Theft Epidemic.* New York: John Wiley & Sons, 2004. Comprehensive exploration of identity theft investigation, prevention, and education.

SEE ALSO: Counterfeiting; Credit card buying; eBay; Insurance industry; Internet; Justice, U.S. Department of; Online marketing; Organized crime; Private security industry; Secret Service, U.S.

ILA. *See* International Longshoremen's Association

ILGWU. *See* International Ladies' Garment Workers' Union

Immigration

DEFINITION: Influx and settlement of people into an area or region from another country

SIGNIFICANCE: Immigration has affected the U.S. economy by increasing the supply of both skilled and unskilled labor, elevating demand for low-cost retail consumer goods and services, and suppressing labor costs. In addition, many immigrant laborers send money back to their country of origin, resulting in significant international cash flows.

Like a number of countries, the United States is largely a nation of immigrants. North America's indigenous peoples were forcibly displaced by European immigrants, mostly from Great Britain, during the colonial period. Following American independence, plantation agriculture gradually took hold in the southern United States, fueling the massive importation of slave laborers from Africa. During the first half of the nineteenth century, successive waves of European immigration continued alongside of the growth of slavery. A great number of Irish people immigrated to the United States during the 1840's-1850's, in large part because of potato crop failures in Ireland. Many Germans immigrated following the political fallout of a failed revolution in 1848.

LATE NINETEENTH CENTURY PATTERNS

African slaves provided labor for plantation agriculture and to a lesser extent for mining. After slavery was abolished in 1865, African Americans worked in agriculture and other manual labor. The newly immigrated Irish and Germans served as domestics and manual laborers in a variety of industries. Chinese immigrants were employed to build the expanding railroad system. These sources of cheap, imported labor are thought to have provided the foundation for industrialization by ensuring that there were enough workers to fill the growing number of factory production jobs. As the industrial economy expanded, the demand for cheap labor grew, paving the way for new waves of immigration. In the second half of the nineteenth century, many immigrants came from southern and eastern European countries such as Italy, Poland, Greece, and Russia, as well as Asian countries such as Japan and China.

A rise in anti-Asian sentiment in the final decades of the nineteenth century led to restrictions being imposed on immigration from Asia, resulting in decades in which much of the immigration was from southern and eastern Europe. At the same time, immigration across the southern border of the United States added to the existing Latino population.

During the early 1920's, the federal government began to enact legislation designed to restrict overall immigration. Until that time, U.S. public opinion had generally favored an open immigration policy as synonymous with the conditions of modern liberty. The shift toward placing federal restrictions on immigration in the form of quotas was in large measure a response to the growing power of U.S. organized labor. Industrial trade unions demanded protection from the threat posed by the influx of immigrant laborers, who were generally willing to work for lower wages. Immigrant laborers not only undercut the ability of trade unions to negotiate higher wages and better working conditions but also were often hired by U.S. business owners as strikebreakers.

WAR AND IMMIGRATION

During World War I and World War II, the combination of U.S. soldiers fighting overseas and factory production running at full capacity created serious labor shortages. In both wars, Washington looked to immigrant labor to solve the problem. Because most of Europe was embroiled in war, most of the immigration was from Mexico. As each war came to an end, however, the slowdown in factory production, coupled with the return of troops, led to sharp rises in unemployment and tight competition for work. This inevita-

bly created the conditions for social conflict and presented new dilemmas for immigration policy makers.

For example, during the intense 1921-1922 recession, Mexican laborers who had come to the United States during World War I quickly were seen as unwelcome by more established American immigrants. The anti-Mexican climate resulted in a large-scale repatriation program that was orchestrated to show government concern for rising unemployment and the economic downturn. Thousands of Mexicans were deported. Although the campaign soon eased along with the recession itself by 1923, the Great Depression that set in at the end of the 1920's would once again lead to a renewed drive to repatriate Mexican immigrant laborers.

For its part, the Mexican government consistently protested aggressive U.S. moves to deport its citizens, often at moments when its own country was experiencing an economic slowdown and a reduced capacity for reabsorbing laborers. Although the Mexican government cooperated with U.S. authorities in facilitating the repatriation of its citizens, it urged Washington to legislate a more orderly institutional arrangement for handling the U.S. demand for foreign immigrant labor. This call went mostly unheeded until the 1940's, when the U.S. moved to formalize a large-scale contract labor program.

As World War II intensified, the stage was set for another critical labor shortage in the United States. When factory production reached full capacity in

---

A CLOSER LOOK AT THE NUMBERS

- The immigrant population in the United States reached a record 37.9 million in 2007.
- About 11.3 million of the immigrant population in 2007 is believed to be illegal immigrants, or nearly 1 in 3 immigrants.
- Some 10.3 milllion immigrants have arrived between 2001 and 2007.
- As of 2007, 1 in 8 residents in the United States is an immigrant, compared with 1 in 13 in 1990, 1 in 16 in 1980, and 1 in 21 in 1970.

Source: Center for Immigration Studies

1942, Washington responded by introducing the Mexican Contract Labor Program, which later became commonly known as the bracero program. Over a three-year period beginning in August, 1942, around 300,000 Mexican laborers were contracted to work in agriculture and railway construction under conditions negotiated with the Mexican government.

The accord was bitterly opposed by Mexican business owners who complained that the program artificially raised the price of labor in Mexico. Throughout the remainder of World War II, the Mexican government asserted its authority by enforcing certain minimal protections of its workers in the United States. For example, the Mexican government enforced a ban on labor contracts with the state of Texas that was in place because of previous abuses in the treatment of Mexican laborers. Mexico resisted pressure from the United States to lift this ban over the life of the program, thus creating a new pattern in which U.S. and Mexican authorities jointly negotiated immigration in accordance with their respective national interests.

Although the bracero program was suspended after World War II, it was resumed during the Korean War and continued to bring hundreds of thousands of mostly Mexican laborers into the United States each year until the program was terminated in 1964. By that time, it had sponsored the entry of more than 4 million Mexican laborers, which in turn had largely shaped the face of modern U.S. agriculture.

CONTROVERSIES AND REGULATIONS

Increased cooperation between Mexican and U.S. authorities failed to alleviate persistent tensions over Mexican immigration. After the Korean War, a rise in unemployment resulted in widespread complaints about Mexican laborers remaining in the United States after their contracts had ended, thus putting renewed pressure on Washington to act. In April, 1954, President Dwight D. Eisenhower authorized a military-like operation designed to deport Mexican laborers. Dubbed "Operation Wetback," the repatriation program rode on the crest of racist sentiments that blamed Mexican immigrants for labor strife and a host of other social problems.

U.S. agricultural producers saw their cheap supply of migrant labor abruptly shrink as federal authorities concerned themselves with reassuring the public that immigration was firmly under their con-

trol. Operation Wetback had a traumatic and stigmatizing effect on Mexican American communities and legal residents, some of whom were mistakenly deported. Although this repatriation program was short-lived, it had the effect of further weakening the already slim protections offered to immigrants under the bracero program.

By the 1960's, U.S. immigration laws and border control policies had emerged as Washington's chief policy instruments to help synchronize the flow of immigrants with the larger business cycle. The federal government sought to exert control over an increasingly globalized labor market with an eye to managing potentially harmful domestic political and social conflicts. New immigration surges beginning during the 1980's saw the influx of Mexicans, Central Americans, and other Latin Americans, along with Caribbean and Asian immigrants. This influx renewed the public debate over how to address the strain on public services posed by both legal and illegal immigrants.

IMPLICATIONS FOR BUSINESS

As the American public became aware that undocumented immigrants were being routinely hired for agricultural and food-processing work, people began to pressure the government to enact sanctions on employers. The Immigration Reform and Control Act (IRCA) of 1986 made it a crime for businesses to knowingly hire illegal immigrants. The new law required employers to demand proof of U.S. citizenship or legal residence before contracting with laborers. Business owners failing to comply and who knowingly hired illegal immigrants faced thousands of dollars in fines and in some cases even possible prison sentences. However, the debate did not end there, nor did illegal immigration. The flow of illegal immigrants into the United States continued, keeping immigration reform in the public spotlight.

In the twenty-first century, the debate about immigration had come to center on undocumented immigrants. In 2005, the number of undocumented workers in the United States was estimated at around 12 million. If these undocumented workers were forced to leave in accordance with the existing law, the U.S. labor force would shrink by 5 percent, and the low-skilled portion of the national labor force would decline by at least 10 percent. About a quarter of all undocumented workers work in agriculture, 17 percent in domestic work, 14 percent in construction, and 12 percent in food preparation industries. Any dramatic change in their availability would have a disproportionately adverse effect on businesses in these areas, as wages for low-skilled laborers would inevitably rise.

In strictly economic terms, the costs of aggressive border control may exceed the costs incurred by illegal immigration. Various cost-benefit studies have shown that the net fiscal drain on public finances caused by illegal immigration remains relatively low, at around 0.07 percent of the gross domestic product, and the cost of measures proposed to heighten control over immigration would be greater, at around 0.1 percent of the gross domestic product. Although analysts and experts disagree, many think that the American business community generally benefits from higher immigration levels (legal or illegal), and organized labor is the most adversely affected.

Also significant has been the rapid growth in the money that many immigrant workers send to their home countries. Since the late 1990's, the steady pace of increase has fueled a thriving industry that handles these financial transactions. Annual family remittances, estimated at more than $20 billion in 2000, had more than doubled by 2008, making it an extremely lucrative market for banks and electronic transfer firms. Abuses caused by unscrupulous practices that take advantage of a vulnerable clientele have led to increased governmental regulations over fees and charges assessed against this high volume of remittance transactions. Some developing countries have come to view these financial inflows as important sources of national finance capital that compensate for the absence of its laborers.

Richard A. Dello Buono

FURTHER READING

Baddour, Ann, and Sonja Danburg. *Creating a Fair Playing Field for Consumers: The Need for Transparency in the U.S. Remittance Market*. Baltimore: Center for Financial Services Innovation, 2005. Offers a good explanation of the role of the remittances sent to foreign countries by immigrants to the United States. Discusses the issue of consumer protection measures as well as other financial and regulatory aspects of the remittance market.

Calavita, Kitty. *Inside the State: The Bracero Program, Immigration, and the INS*. New York: Routledge, 1992. A sociological analysis of U.S. policies aimed at Mexican immigrants and the mechanisms developed by immigration authorities. Particular attention is given to immigration law as a means to regulate the demands presented by U.S. business interests and organized labor.

Cervantes, Esther. "Immigrants and the Labor Market: What Are the Jobs Americans Won't Do?" *Dollars and Sense* (May/June, 2006): 30-32. Written from the perspective of organized labor, the book shows how the U.S. labor market is degraded by abuses of immigrant laborers. It is argued that the best remedy for this problem is increased unionization of the American economy.

Hanson, Gordon H. *The Economic Logic of Illegal Immigration*. New York: Council on Foreign Relations, 2007. An economic analysis of the policy issues and their implications regarding illegal immigration. The author argues that illegal immigration causes little net harm to the U.S. economy, thus making expensive border control proposals counterproductive.

Shanks, Cheryl. *Immigration and the Politics of American Sovereignty, 1890-1990*. Ann Arbor: University of Michigan Press, 2001. An historical overview of changing public conceptions of immigration. The author draws attention to issues of national sovereignty and relates them to immigrant reform issues as viewed from civil society.

SEE ALSO: Bracero program; "Coolie" labor; Farm labor; Food-processing industries; Homeland Security, U.S. Department of; Internal migration; Labor history; Meatpacking industry; Mexican trade with the United States; Wars.

Income tax, corporate

DEFINITION: Tax levied on the net profits (revenue minus costs) of a business corporation

SIGNIFICANCE: Corporate income taxes became an important source of government revenue in the twentieth century and were a major influence on corporate policy, especially financial structure and accounting methods.

Corporations, chiefly in banking and insurance, arose early after the United States won its independence in 1783. From the 1830's, railroads became the first truly big-business corporations. The early corporations were routinely subjected to various taxes although these taxes were not based on their profits. The U.S. Civil War brought the first federal experiments with taxation of income. Although the new tax applied to corporation income as well as personal, corporations found the tax easy to evade. It yielded little revenue and was repealed soon after the war ended in 1865.

The domain of business corporations expanded greatly after the Civil War, extending into manufacturing and trade. Accounting standards were improved, and disclosure of corporate finance became more extensive. Corporations were unpopular and, therefore, a politically suitable object of taxation. The Wilson-Gorman Tariff Act of 1894 imposed a 2 percent tax on personal and corporate income over $4,000. In 1895, the Supreme Court held this income tax to be unconstitutional because it violated the constitutional requirement that any direct tax must be proportional to the population.

THE MODERN TAX

In 1909, Congress imposed a 1 percent tax on corporate net income above $5,000, calling it an excise tax to bypass the constitutional issue. In 1909, some 262,000 corporations filed returns, and the tax yielded about $21 million. The constitutionality issue was soon settled by the adoption of the Sixteenth Amendment, which authorized an income tax. A comprehensive income tax law in 1913 extended the 1 percent tax on corporate profits. By 1913, the corporate income tax accounted for 5 percent of federal government tax revenue, as 317,000 corporations submitted returns and the government received $43 million in revenue. The corporate tax rate was raised to 2 percent in 1916.

The enormous increase in federal spending during World War I brought an increase in the corporate tax, which jumped to 6 percent in October, 1917. In addition, the law imposed an excess-profits tax, levied on profits in excess of those received in 1911-1913. This provision was a huge source of revenue, yielding $2.2 billion in the year ending June, 1918. By comparison, the personal income tax produced $600 million and the regular corporate profits tax only $48 million. Additional tax was applied to undistributed corporate profits, a policy intended to discourage a potential channel for the stockholders to avoid paying personal income tax.

After the war's end, the taxes on excess and undistributed profits were removed. However, the government was confronted by a huge national debt that its leaders were determined to reduce. In February, 1919, the basic corporate tax rate was set at 12 percent for the profits of the previous year and 10 percent for the following years. Combined with increases in the personal income tax, these had a strongly deflationary impact and contributed to the painful depression of 1920-1922. The depression was brief, and the revenue success of the federal tax on profits led to imitation of the federal government by state governments. During the 1920's, the states were receiving about 5 percent of their tax revenue from this source.

Further federal increases yielded an average rate of around 11 percent from 1922 through 1924. By this time, the corporate tax had emerged as the centerpiece of the federal tax system. Federal revenues from the corporate tax exceeded $1 billion each year from 1926 through 1931 and topped personal income tax revenues each year until 1934. Tax paid reached 11 percent of corporate profits in 1922 and moved steadily up to 12.7 percent in 1926. The abundant flow of tax revenues allowed the federal government to run substantial surpluses every year from 1920 through 1930 and significantly reduce the national debt. President Calvin Coolidge and Secretary of the Treasury Andrew Mellon agreed on the desirability of tax reductions to stimulate investment, so corporate rates were reduced and the ratio of tax revenue to profits decreased from 12.7 percent in 1927 to 10.2 percent in 1929.

THE GREAT DEPRESSION

Because of the government's large structural surplus, President Herbert Hoover was able to obtain a reduction in tax rates early in the downswing. In December, 1929, the corporate rate was reduced by one point. However, the continued decline in incomes lowered tax revenues, and surpluses turned to deficits. President Hoover was passionately opposed to deficit spending. In 1932, he pushed through the largest tax increase in U.S. history. On average, corporate tax collections rose from 11 percent of profits in 1930 to nearly 14 percent in 1933-1935. Profits had fallen by three-fourths between 1929 and 1932. The tax increases contributed to an adverse environment for business investment.

President Franklin D. Roosevelt was also opposed to deficit spending. He wanted to increase federal expenditures for relief and recovery, but he tried to match the increases with higher tax rates. However, the effective corporate profits tax remained in the range of 12 to 14 percent. Consistent with the antibusiness thrust of the New Deal, an excess-profits tax was imposed in 1935, but it yielded very little revenue. A tax on undistributed corporate profits was enacted in 1936 but was soon withdrawn.

As defense spending was sharply increased in 1940, the corporate tax rate was increased to 19 percent. The excess-profits tax was sharply raised. The tax base was profit in excess of 95 percent of average earnings in 1936-1939, or the dollar value of a specified percentage of invested capital. The tax rate was a staggering 86 percent. In 1942, the basic corporate rate was raised to 40 percent. The combined burden of the two was capped at 80 percent, and there were generous provisions for treatment of losses.

In World War II, revenue from the tax on excess profits eclipsed the regular corporate tax. Excess-profits tax revenues exceeded $10 billion in 1943 and 1944, at which time the regular corporate tax was yielding slightly over $4 billion. From 1942 through 1945, excess-profit tax revenues were $36.5 billion, more than double the $17.3 billion from ordinary corporate tax. During that period, the combined burden of the two taxes was slightly over half of all corporate profit.

POSTWAR STABILITY

At the war's end in 1945, the excess-profits tax was repealed. However, the regular corporate tax rate was moved up to about one-third of corporate profits, where it stabilized in 1946-1949. With the outbreak of the Korean War in the summer of 1950, corporate rates were moved up again. The excess-profits tax was revived, but its bite was much gentler: Its yield in 1950-1953 was only about 10 percent of the regular corporate tax. In 1951-1953, the two taxes combined took about 48 percent of corporate profits. The end of the Korean War brought some rate reductions. Even so, the corporate income tax took about 42 percent of corporate profits until the 1980's.

Tax reform in 1986 reduced the basic corporate tax rate from 46 percent to 34 percent, after which the rate changed very little. By 2006, the tax generated $454 billion out of total corporate profits of $1,554 billion, for a ratio of 29 percent. Between 1960 and 1980, the share of the corporate tax in total federal tax revenue declined substantially, from 23 percent in 1960 to 13 percent in 1980. The share fell below 10 percent during the early years of the new millennium. However, the surge of profits in 2004-2006 brought the share back to 13 percent by 2006.

TAX STRUCTURE

Because the tax was levied on corporate profits, it has been sensitive to all the complexities of corporate accounting systems. Important issues have concerned those business expenditures that could be treated as costs and thus deducted in computing taxable profits. An example is depreciation. Expenditures for capital assets such as buildings and equipment are not normally treated as costs in the year they occur. Rather the cost is spread over the lifetime of the asset. Accelerated depreciation has allowed firms to reduce tax liability. Beginning with the presidency of John F. Kennedy, the government has periodically relaxed depreciation rules to encourage business investment. In 1981, the tax incorporated the Accelerated Cost Recovery System (ACRS). This grouped most capital assets into three categories, with depreciation lifetimes of three, five, and fifteen years. Most equipment and machinery fell into the five-year category, although vehicles were generally in the three-year component. Property and buildings could be written off over fifteen years. The ACRS guidelines were generally much shorter than the true rate of depreciation. This reduced the effective rate of the tax.

In 1962, the tax code incorporated the investment tax credit. This permitted corporations to take 10 percent of the cost of assets during the tax year as a direct credit against their tax liability. The credit was adopted to stimulate investment for economic growth and business-cycle recovery. It was suspended and reinstated periodically, depending on business-cycle conditions.

Another deductible business expense has been interest paid on borrowed money. However, dividends paid to stockholders have not been a deductible expense for the corporation. Dividends thus are taxed twice, as stockholders pay personal income tax on dividends received. This created a bias in favor of debt financing, which tended to expose corporations to greater risk. The extent of double taxa-

U.S. CORPORATE INCOME TAX, TAX BRACKETS AND RATES, SELECTED YEARS

Year	Taxable Income Brackets	Rates (%)
1909-2/28/1913	Over $5,000	1.00
1932-1935	All taxable income	13.75
1946-1949	First $5,000	21.00
	Next $15,000	23.00
	Next $5,000	25.00
	Next $25,000	53.00
	Over $50,000	38.00
1988-1992	First $50,000	15.00
	Over $50,000-$75,000	25.00
	Over $75,000-$100,000	34.00
	Over $100,000-$335,000	39.00
	Over $335,000	34.00
1993-2004	First $50,000	15.00
	Over $50,000-$75,000	25.00
	Over $75,000-$100,000	34.00
	Over $100,000-$335,000	39.00
	Over $335,000-$10,000,000	34.00
	Over $10,000,000-$15,000,000	35.00
	Over $15,000,000-$18,333,333	38.00
	Over $18,333,333	35.00

Sources: Data from Internal Revenue Service, "Corporate Income Tax Brackets and Rates, 1909-2002," Statistics of Income Bulletin, 2003, and "Appendix, Tax Years, 1909-2004," 2005

Note: Tax rates are the standard tax rates applied to all taxable corporate net income. An additional "declared value" excess profits tax was in effect from 1933 through 1945.

tion was reduced in 2003 when the personal income tax rate on dividends was substantially lowered. As a result, the percentage of profits paid out in dividends increased substantially.

An important deductible expense has been payment of insurance premiums for employee health care. From the 1940's, employer-provided health insurance became the prevailing pattern. This arrangement created a disadvantage for those not receiving employer-paid insurance. Not all employee compensation is deductible; under President George W. Bush, Congress voted to deny deductible status to cash salaries exceeding $1 million per year

to an individual. Corporations that sustain losses are allowed, within limits, to offset these against profits in earlier or later years.

EVALUATING THE TAX

All taxes fall on people. Economists have long disliked the corporate profits tax because it is difficult to determine which people are burdened. A 2008 study by the Organization for Economic Cooperation and Development concluded that corporate taxes were more harmful to economic growth than other types of tax because of adverse effects on investment spending for capital goods. Profit income has been a major source of funds for financing capital expenditures. Also, a high rate of expected profit is a motivator to direct investment into highly productive channels.

In the twenty-first century, increasing attention was directed at the relative level of profits tax in the United States and in European countries. From the late 1980's, European countries steadily reduced their profits tax rates, while those in the United States remained steady. By 2008, rates in the United States were much higher than those in most other countries. Therefore, some American companies moved their home offices overseas or were bought out by foreign interests who could achieve higher overall profitability because of the lower taxes. Because of its complexity, the profits tax has had substantial compliance cost. Hiring tax accountants and tax lawyers cost firms an estimated $40 billion in 2004.

Paul B. Trescott

FURTHER READING

Abrams, Howard E., and Richard L. Doernberg. *Federal Corporate Taxation.* 6th ed. New York: Foundation Press, 2008. A detailed treatment of corporations and taxation that looks at corporation structure and taxation among many other topics.

Bruce, Neil. *Public Finance and the American Economy.* 2d ed. Boston: Addison Wesley, 2001. This college text examines the story of taxation through the twentieth century.

Buchanan, James, and Marilyn Flowers. *The Public Finances.* 6th ed. Homewood, Ill.: Richard D. Irwin, 1987. Nobel-laureate Buchanan presents a lucid overview of public finance. Chapter 25 concentrates on the corporate tax. An examination of the successive editions since 1960 covers a lot of history.

Panteghini, Paolo. *Corporate Taxation in a Dynamic World.* Berlin: Springer, 2007. Focuses on how tax policies affect the choices businesses make, including where they locate their plants and facilities.

Pechman, Joseph A. *Federal Tax Policy.* 5th ed. Washington, D.C.: Brookings Institution, 1987. Chapter 5 deals with the corporate tax, summarizing its current structure and theories of its impact.

Ratner, Sidney. *American Taxation: Its History as a Social Force in Democracy.* New York: W. W. Norton, 1942. An encyclopedic study with much detail on the legislative and judicial developments.

See also: Civil War, U.S.; Income tax, personal; Incorporation laws; Internal Revenue Code; Taxation; Wars; World War I.

Income tax, personal

Definition: Tax levied on an individual's earnings and other income and paid to a government, which uses the money as revenue

Significance: Taxes are an important source of revenue for local, state, and federal governments. Historically, the federal government has used tax policies to promote investment in the American economy. Giving deductions for certain business expenses and tax breaks for small businesses are among the ways that the federal government has used personal income tax laws to promote business.

When the U.S. Constitution was adopted in 1789, the federal government was empowered to collect excise taxes and duties. To pay the debts of the Revolutionary War, the U.S. Congress levied taxes on alcohol, sugar, tobacco, carriages, and property sold at auctions. Collecting taxes, however, was a sensitive issue, as resentment against British taxation had been a primary cause of the Revolutionary War. When the government charged taxes on whiskey, a group of farmers rebelled in 1794. President George Washington had to send in troops to suppress the Whiskey Rebellion. Therefore, until the U.S. Civil War, the early government raised most of its revenue by selling land and charging duties rather than by levying taxes.

Early Tax Efforts

In 1862, as a way to finance the Civil War, the government started collecting personal income taxes. The tax was 3 percent on incomes above $800 per year and was repealed in 1872. This measure created the office of the commissioner of Internal Revenue, the predecessor of the Internal Revenue Service (IRS).

Congress tried to reenact the income tax in 1894, but the Supreme Court found the collection of income taxes to be unconstitutional. In 1913, the ratification of the Sixteenth Amendment and enactment of the Revenue Act allowed the federal government to legally collect income taxes. That same year, Congress adopted an income tax with rates starting at 1 percent on income of $3,000 and rising to 7 percent on incomes of more than $500,000. At the time, less than 1 percent of the American population paid income tax. The first codes allowed for taxation of only lawful income. As a result, people chose to run illegal businesses to avoid taxation until Congress deleted the word "lawful" from the definition of income in 1916.

When the United States entered World War I, the tax rate was raised from 1 to 2 percent, and the top rate was raised to 15 percent. The economy boomed during the 1920's, and Congress decreased taxes, but after the stock market crash, Congress raised taxes because it needed revenue. After World War I, tax rates have both declined and risen depending on the economy and the country's involvement in wars.

Between the end of World War I and 1939, various revenue acts were passed. The Great Depression resulted in the passage of the Social Security Act in 1935, which created a tax shared by the employer and employee. In 1939, the varied personal income tax laws were codified into the Internal Revenue Code.

Taxes on citizens and businesses have increased over time. In 1942, an act was passed that increased income taxes but allowed deductions for medical and investment expenses. In 1943, another act required employers to withhold taxes from employees' wages and remit them quarterly.

By 1945, 43 million Americans were paying income taxes. The tax code went through two modifications in 1954 and 1986. The Tax Reform Act of 1986, with three hundred tax provisions, was the most significant piece of tax legislation passed in thirty years, taking three years to implement.

How the Tax Works

The calculation of income tax starts with an individual's gross income, from ordinary income and capital gains. Ordinary income includes earnings, business profits, dividends, and interest income; capital gains are typically from the sale of investment property. Above-the-line deductions, including moving expenses and alimony payments, are taken from the gross income to create the adjusted gross income. Then taxpayers either take the standard deduction or subtract itemized deductions. This leaves taxable income, which is multiplied by the tax rate to produce the tax due the government. Some taxpayers qualify for tax credits, which are taken from the amount due.

Individuals can have several types of businesses on which they can be taxed, including rental properties, sole proprietorships, and farms. Also, taxpayers who are employees of businesses can take deductions for business-related expenses incurred on the job. Several significant tax provisions affect these taxpayers. These provisions are usually written to stimulate the economy or with the goal of administrative ease.

Taxpayers who own these types of businesses must report total revenues and related expenses. In addition, they are allowed to recover the cost of investments in capital assets. Cost recovery provisions refer to the deductibility of capital expenditures, which are assets with a life longer than one year. This includes vehicles, computers, equipment, furniture, land and leasehold improvements, livestock, and real estate. These different classes of assets have different recovery periods. For example, computers are depreciated over 5 years, furniture over 7 years, and real estate over 29.5 years if residential and 39 years if nonresidential. These cost recovery provisions are subject to change. The Economic Recovery Act of 1981 included provisions to accelerate cost recovery. Businesses were allowed to depreciate equipment at an accelerated rate and were given an investment tax credit to encourage investment in the economy. In 1986, these laws were repealed because they were considered overly generous.

Another cost recovery provision is the deduction allowed by Internal Revenue Code section 179. This provision allows for the immediate write-off of some capital purchases in the year of purchase. The deduction is limited by the amount of business income and amount of assets purchased. This deduction has been increased over the years, again to encourage investment in the economy. In 2002, the section 179 expense was limited to $24,000 but was increased to $250,000 in 2008. The same philosophy pertains to

A group of people fill out tax forms at an Internal Revenue office around 1920. (Library of Congress)

depreciation. In 2004, businesses were allowed bonus depreciation in addition to the regular cost recovery amounts; this benefit ended in 2005 but has been reenacted for 2008.

EXPENSE DEDUCTIONS

The prevailing rule for whether a business expense is deductible is determined by the "ordinary" and "necessary" rules. "Ordinary" means the expense would be considered common for the business, and "necessary" means the expense is helpful and appropriate. In addition, to be deductible, the expense must be "reasonable." This is where subjectivity enters into the picture, because what might be reasonable for one business might not be for another.

Congress has placed some restrictions on the deductibility of certain expenses. Expenses such as speeding tickets, tax penalties, and bribes are not deductible, nor are political contributions and most lobbying expenses. Furthermore, common expenses prone to abuse have become limited in their deductibility. For example, meals are only 50 percent deductible rather than 100 percent as in earlier years, and the depreciation of personal automobiles used for business is also limited. These expenses can be deducted only if backed up by written records. The time, place, and business purpose of the meal must be recorded, and a mileage log must be kept for automobiles.

Businesses generally receive more favorable tax treatment than individuals for the same deductions. For example, theft and casualty losses for individuals are limited to amounts in excess of 10 percent of adjusted gross income and $100 per event, but there is no such limitation for business theft losses. In addition, losses on investments are classified as capital losses (limited to $3,000 per year), but business losses are often treated as ordinary losses, meaning there is no limitation to their deductibility.

Expenses for the investigation of new businesses are also deductible if the individual goes into the

---

THE CANONS OF TAXATION

During the eighteenth century, Adam Smith, the founder of classical economics, wrote the four canons of taxation: equality, convenience, certainty, and economy.

Equality means that all taxpayers should be treated fairly. In the United States, a progressive tax structure has been adopted. This means that the more income an individual earns, the more taxes the person pays. Most citizens consider this system to be fair. As of 2008, the tax rate ranged from 0 to 35 percent, depending on a taxpayer's income level.

Convenience means that taxes should be easy to pay. Employers automatically withhold taxes out of their employees' pay. This, however, places an administrative burden on the employer, who has to calculate the withholdings and submit them to the Internal Revenue Service.

Certainty means that taxpayers should know what their taxes will be and when they are due. Congress rarely passes tax provisions that are retroactive.

Economy means that the cost of collection of taxes by the government should be nominal. The cost of collections in 2008 is about 0.5 percent of the total revenues collected. As a result of this canon, the government often opts for administrative ease in its creation of tax policies.

The canons of taxation still underlie the development of tax policies in the twenty-first century. Debate exists as to the proper application of the canons but not as to their validity. For example, economists debate whether a progressive tax system is really fair or whether all taxpayers should pay the same tax rate (the flat tax).

---

business or already has a business in the same field. If it is a new business, the expenses are deductible only over time, but if it is a continuation of an already existing business, investigation expenses are deductible in the year incurred. The only time investigation expenses are not deductible is if the business is a new venture and the taxpayer does not start the business.

SELF-EMPLOYMENT ISSUES

One area that received media attention in 1993, when the *Commissioner of the Internal Revenue Service vs. Soliman* case was heard by the Supreme Court, is the home office deduction. Whether the taxpayer is an employee of a company or self-employed, the taxpayer may, under certain circumstances, deduct expenses related to the business use of a home office. Typically the office must be used exclusively for business and to meet clients or customers. If the taxpayer is an employee, the office must also be for the convenience of the employer. The Court found that even though Nader Soliman, an anesthesiologist, spent ten to fifteen hours working in his home office, he did not meet patients there; thus his home office deductions were disallowed. As a result of this ruling, many taxpayers, such as plumbers, builders, and restaurant owners, also lost their home office deductions. In 1997, Congress modified the home office tax laws so that if the office is used for administrative or management activities and if there is no other fixed location at which those duties can be conducted, taxpayers may take the home office deduction.

One other major tax provision related to individuals is the self-employment tax. Employees pay 7.65 percent of the social security tax, and employers pays 7.65 percent. Self-employed individuals must pay the entire 15.3 percent themselves. This places an increased tax burden on the self-employed person.

Income taxes affect all income earners, whether employed by a company or self-employed. Although they reduce the amount of money taxpayers have to invest or to spend, they provide important revenue for governments. In 2007, personal income taxes made up 45 percent of federal revenue.

Marsha M. Huber

FURTHER READING

Conable, Barber B., Jr., and A. L. Singleton. *Congress and the Income Tax.* Norman: University of Oklahoma Press, 1989. A history of the role of Congress in the development of tax policy and laws.

Department of Treasury: Internal Revenue Service. *Publication Seventeen: Your Federal Income Tax.* Washington, D.C.: Government Printing Office, 2007. Thorough, annual publication from the IRS on all the basic tax laws dealing with individual tax filing.

Willan, R. *Income Taxes: Concise History and Primer.* Baton Rouge, La.: Clairor's, 1994. The history of tax development and a primer on special topics,

such as capital gain rates, depreciation, investment tax credit, alternative minimum tax, and itemized deductions. Concludes with a discussion on tax simplification and fairness.

Willis, Eugene, William H. Hoffman, David M. Maloney, and William Raabe. *West's Federal Taxation 2008: Comprehensive Volume.* Boston: Southwestern Publishing, 2008. College-level textbook that covers all the basics of tax law.

Witte, J. *The Politics and Development of the Federal Income Tax.* Madison: University of Wisconsin Press, 1985. A thorough history of tax policy changes from the War of 1812 until the administration of Jimmy Carter. The author also discusses tax politics and how taxes are spent.

SEE ALSO: Bush tax cuts of 2001; Income tax, corporate; Internal Revenue Code; Sales taxes; Taxation.

Incorporation laws

DEFINITION: Body of laws that allow for the creation of corporations, or associations of shareholders who use the laws to create separate legal entities that act as artificial but legal persons

SIGNIFICANCE: In the United States, nearly 4 million corporations generate more than 85 percent of the country's gross business receipts. The laws that regulate the formation and operation of corporations affect their efficiency and profitability and thus play a major role in the national economy.

Corporations are owned by shareholders, each of whom owns a percentage of the corporation. Ownership is often represented by shares of stock. The shareholders elect a board of directors, which runs the major operations of the corporation. The board of directors chooses the chief executive officer (CEO), president, treasurer, and other officers of the corporation, who in turn run the day-to-day functions of the corporation.

State laws regulate corporations. Articles of incorporation are the founding documents of corporations. They must include the name of the corporation, the number of shares the corporation is authorized to issue, the name and address of the corporation's registered agent (the main contact of the corporation), and the name and address of each incorporator (the people or entities signing the articles of incorporation). The articles of incorporation have to be filed and approved by the incorporating state government before the corporation can begin doing business.

THE ADVANTAGES

Corporations offer many advantages to American business. One of the most important features of a corporation is that the corporation is a separate legal entity, an artificial but legal person, and therefore separate and distinct from the shareholders. Because corporations are "legal" people, they can do all the things that "real" people do, such as own property, make and receive loans, sue and be sued, and be found liable for violations of the law. Incorporated businesses have distinctive features that separate them from sole proprietorships and partnerships, including limited liability for shareholders, transferability of shares, perpetual existence, and centralized management.

Limited liability means that corporations are responsible for their own debts and responsibilities under contracts but that the shareholders are not. Under corporations, a shareholder's liability is limited to the extent of the money or capital that person has contributed to the corporation, and the shareholder is not personably liable for the corporation's debts or contractual responsibilities. During the Industrial Revolution, limiting the liability of shareholders to their contributions was of great benefit to shareholders, because their personal wealth was not at risk in the corporation. This allowed shareholders to invest in many risky or dangerous enterprises, such as building canals, railroads, or sailing across oceans. If the venture was successful, the corporation often paid shareholders handsomely; if it failed, the shareholder lost only the capital invested. Incorporation laws that limited shareholder liability made it possible for the United States to rapidly grow and prosper.

Free transferability of shares means that shareholders can transfer their shares of stock to other people or entities by sale, gift, or assignment. Most major shares are bought and sold in large security markets, such as the New York Stock Exchange. These large security markets have been created and regulated for the orderly and reliable transfer of shares of stock. Incorporation laws that allow shares to be freely bought and sold allow for appropriate values to be placed on shares of stock. This freedom to buy and sell shares allows people to make their own determination of the value of a corporation's stock. American business has profited greatly from this because strong, healthy businesses are rewarded by attracting the highest prices.

Corporations exist forever unless ended by the shareholders or bankruptcy. Having corporations exist forever allows a corporation to grow and evolve over time and not be threatened by the death or sickness of any one shareholder, corporate officer, or director. Perpetual existence allows for profitable corporations to grow and expand into new areas of business and permits corporations to evolve and migrate into more lucrative areas of business while departing from less profitable enterprises. American business history has many examples of corporations that have done this, including Citigroup and General Electric.

Management of corporations is centralized in the board of directors and the corporate officers. The shareholders elect the board of directors, which has the necessary expertise to oversee the corporation. The board of directors in turn chooses corporate officers that have the requisite business experience to run the daily operations of the corporation. This system allows shareholders to invest in corporations without involving themselves in the corporation's daily operations.

HISTORY

Corporations are a cornerstone of the American business landscape and have roots in British legal tradition. The British king often granted charters of incorporation to select groups of people within the British Empire. These royal corporate charters helped develop the American colonies. The founding of new colonies was both expensive and risky, and royal charters, by selling shares of ownership in the colonies, allowed funds to be raised for these ventures and limited the liability of the shareholders in case of financial failure.

After the United States achieved independence, the states assumed the role of granting corporate charters. New York state was the first jurisdiction to allow incorporation of businesses in 1811. The extent of state authority over corporations was first tested in the case of *Dartmouth College v. Woodward* (1819), in which the U.S. Supreme Court held that the state of New Hampshire could not revoke the college's charter without its consent because the incorporation charter created the college as an "artificial being," independent of its creator, and as such, the college enjoyed constitutional protections.

The federal government limited the extent of corporate power in a series of Supreme Court decisions in first half of the nineteenth century. In *Gibbons v. Ogden* (1824), the Court held that the federal government had the right to regulate commence with foreign nations and between the states. This ruling established that Congress could pass laws affecting the business activities of corporations. In *Charles River Bridge v. Warren Bridge* (1837), the Court restricted the rights of corporations if they conflicted with those of the community in which the corporations were located, and in the *License cases* of 1847, the Supreme Court upheld a state's police power to regulate corporations for the protection of the health of that state's citizens.

After the U.S. Civil War, the adoption of the Fourteenth Amendment, which was intended to protect freed slaves from oppressive state laws that might "deprive any person of life, liberty, or property without due process of law," was quickly used by corporations using their status as "legal persons." This was affirmed by the Supreme Court in *Santa Clara County v. Southern Pacific Railroad* (1886).

In the latter part of the nineteenth century and the early twentieth century, the federal government passed a series of laws that further regulated corporations. In 1887, the federal government established the Interstate Commerce Commission primarily to regulate corporations, and in 1890, Congress passed the Sherman Antitrust Act to further regulate corporations. In 1913, with the passage of the Sixteenth Amendment, allowing the federal government to levy an income tax, corporations were subjected to this new form of taxation. In 1914, Congress further checked the power of American corporations with the establishment of the Federal Trade Commission and the passing of the Clayton Antitrust Act. In 1937, the Supreme Court held that workers had the right to organize into unions in *National Labor Relations Board v. Jones & Laughlin Steel Corp.*, and in 1942, the Court upheld the constitutionality of the Fair Labor Standards Act. The 1937 case and the establishment of the Fair Labor Standards Act cleared the way for laws regulating wages, hours, and working conditions for employees of corporations.

TWENTY-FIRST CENTURY ISSUES

Issues facing corporations in the twenty-first century include deregulation, global competition, and rising costs. The increasingly competitive world market has forced corporations to streamline their operations. The drive for increased corporate efficiency and profitability have put added pressures on corporations to be more aggressive. Aggressive corporate policies often are in danger of running afoul of the law. Scandals at companies such as WorldCom and Enron Corporation have given rise to renewed calls for regulation of American corporations.

Eric Bellone

FURTHER READING

Bock, Betty, et al., eds. *The Impact of the Modern Corporation.* New York: Columbia University Press, 1984. A review of the historical impact of corporatations on the business environment.

Donaldson, T. *The Ethics of International Business.* New York: Oxford University Press, 1989. An overview of the ethical implications of the influence of the modern corporation.

Eisenberg, M. A. *The Structure of the Corporation: A Legal Analysis.* Toronto, Ont.: Little, Brown, 1976. An analysis of the legal history of corporations and the nature of corporate change.

Frederick, W. C. *Values, Nature, and Culture in the American Corporation.* New York: Oxford University Press, 1995. An overview of corporate culture and its impact on societal values.

Kotter, J., and J. Heckett. *Corporate Culture and Performance.* New York: Free Press, 1992. A synopsis of corporate culture and how it has changed over the years.

Micklethwait, J., and A. Wooldridge. *The Company: A Short History of a Revolutionary Idea.* New York: Modern Library, 2003. A good history of corporations, highlighting time lines and basic corporate principles. A solid starting point for understanding incorporation laws and their history.

Nader, R., and M. J. Green, eds. *Corporate Power in America.* New York: Grossman, 1973. A review of the historical impact of corporate power in American business from a liberal perspective.

Williamson, O. E., and S. G. Winter, eds. *The Nature of the Firm: Origins, Evolution, and Development.* New York: Oxford University Press, 1991. An overview of corporate history and development.

SEE ALSO: Enron bankruptcy; New York Stock Exchange; Sherman Antitrust Act; Supreme Court and commerce; Taxation; WorldCom bankruptcy.

Indentured labor

DEFINITION: Work performed under contracts that obligate indenturees to work for stated periods of time in exchange for transportation, lodging, food, and clothing

SIGNIFICANCE: During the colonial period and into the eighteenth century, the system of indentured labor provided a workforce for labor-intensive businesses such as tobacco farming. It also provided a means for individuals, many of whom were already skilled tradesmen but who lacked money, to pay their ship's passage to the United States. These workers played an important role in the building of a prosperous economy.

In the sixteenth and seventeenth centuries, Great Britain and the German principalities had a surplus of labor. There were more skilled artisans, domestics, and general laborers than there were jobs. Moreover, a substantial number of rural workers who farmed as tenants or as small landowners found that they could not make an adequate living. These individuals saw an opportunity in the American colonies but lacked the funds to pay their passage.

The colonies, in contrast, suffered from a shortage of laborers. There was land to clear and cultivate, timber to harvest, agriculture products to be processed, and goods to be manufactured, as well as a thriving fishing industry. Workers were needed to transport these products to markets or points of export. Domestics were needed in the homes of affluent planters and entrepreneurs.

Indentured labor did not resolve the problem of labor shortage indefinitely, because most indentured servants left their masters at the end of seven years, and there was no assurance for the master that another indentured servant would become available. However, the indentured servants who sailed to the American colonies did provide a valuable short-term solution.

REDEMPTIONERS AND CONTRACTS

There were two ways in which payment of ship's passage to the New World could be arranged. A few individuals were able to sign contracts with someone they knew or with whom they were put in contact in America. The majority of those willing to accept indenture in exchange for passage, however, sailed without a prearranged situation. A shipowner or captain advertised the group of people he was bringing, giving details as to the kind of labor for which they were suitable. Colonists needing laborers paid the passage owed. The redemptioner, the person whose passage was paid, signed a contract with the individual who paid the passage. The contracts were regulated by the local government.

The master was required to provide food, lodging, clothing, and other necessities. He typically agreed to give the indentured servant a set of clothes, a gun, and a small tract of land—or tools or a sum of money, depending on the type of work to be performed during the indenture. The indentured servant agreed to work without monetary pay for a specified period of time, usually seven years. The contract was binding, and if the indentured servant left the master before the end of the indenture, the individual was forced to return. An additional period of time was added to the service time. The length of an indenture could also be increased for other reasons. If children were born to the indentured servant, the children were free, but the indenture time increased to provide for the children. Often, indentured servants borrowed money from their masters and agreed to continue their indenture to pay the money back.

Although many people willingly became indentured servants, others had little or no choice in the matter. The transporting of individuals to become indentured servants was a profitable business for shipowners and captains. Thus, it was not uncommon for people, especially women and orphans, to be kidnapped and brought to America. The deportation of convicts also provided large numbers of indentured laborers. A convict with adequate funds to pay the passage could avoid indentured labor and enjoy freedom once in America. This rarely occurred, however.

CONDITION AND CONTRIBUTIONS

The majority of indentured servants were white adults, most often from England, Scotland, or German principalities. The Chesapeake region, Delaware, New Jersey, and Pennsylvania, as well as Virginia and the Upper South, were highly dependent on indentured labor for a healthy functioning of their economy. In the cities of the North, the indentured servants worked as domestics for affluent households or as apprentices for skilled tradesmen. In Pennsylvania, they worked as farmhands, while in the Upper South, they worked in the tobacco fields.

The conditions under which the indentured servants worked varied considerably. Life on the tobacco plantations was harsh, while work for a skilled tradesman provided not only better working conditions but also the opportunity to learn a trade. Some indentured servants actually lived with the families for whom they worked and were treated as members of the family; others, however, were ill treated. Female domestics and children were often at risk of sexual abuse by masters. Theoretically, they had recourse to courts of law, but the majority of them lacked the funds and the social status to bring suits against their masters.

Indentured or contract labor played an important role in the American economy into the early years of the eighteenth century. This type of labor was essential to the development of the American economy, as many of the business activities were labor intensive and required workers who worked long hours at minimal expense for the employers. During the eighteenth century, however, the increasing slave trade brought large numbers of Africans to America, and slaves replaced more and more of the indentured labor force on plantations and farms. Although the colonial system of indentured labor had declined rapidly after the American Revolution, the use of similar types of contract labor continued until the late nineteenth century. In 1885, the Contract Labor Law made it illegal for individuals or companies to bring aliens into the country as contract labor.

Shawncey Webb

FURTHER READING

Ballagh, James Curtis. *White Servitude in the Colony of Virginia: A Study of the System of Indentured Labor in the American Colonies.* Whitefish, Mont.: Kessinger, 2007. Provides details of the establishment of indenture. Bibliography.

Bush, Michael L. *Servitude in Modern Times.* Malden, Mass.: Blackwell, 2000. Portrays indentured labor in relation to other bound labor and to capitalism.

Dubofsky, Melvyn, and Joseph A. McCartin. *American Labor: A Documentary History.* New York: Palgrave Macmillan, 2004. Discusses indentured labor, how it disappeared, and what replaced it.

Northrup, David. *Indentured Labor in the Age of Imperialism, 1834-1922.* New York: Cambridge University Press, 1995. The author examines the indetured laborers from Asia, Africa, and the South Pacific.

Palmer, Colin A., ed. *The Worlds of Unfree Labor: From Indentured Servitude to Slavery.* Brookfield, Vt.: Ashgate Variorum, 1998. Collection of essays that looks at both indentured servitude and slavery.

SEE ALSO: Agriculture; Child labor; Colonial economic systems; Cotton industry; Farm labor; Labor history; Plantation agriculture; Sharecropping; Slave era; Slave trading; Tobacco industry.

Indian removal

THE EVENT: Program of forced removal of the members of several Native American tribes from the eastern United States to lands in the west
DATE: 1830's-1840's
PLACE: Eastern United States and the Indian Territory (now part of Oklahoma, Kansas, and Nebraska)
SIGNIFICANCE: The Indian removal resulted in European American farmers claiming and transforming the Southeast and the Ohio River Valley, instituting intensive agricultural development of those regions and increasing the agricultural production of the nation. Treaties instituting the removal granted Native American tribes ownership in perpetuity of lands that would later become the states of Kansas and Nebraska, once those agreements were broken.

As agricultural development and settlement increased in the Southeast and in the area between the Appalachian Mountains and the Mississippi River, settlers, farmers, and others interested in the economic potential of these lands came to resent the large number of Native Americans still occupying valuable lands in these regions. Political pressures grew to exchange government lands west of the Mississippi for the Indian lands in the East. In 1830, Congress passed the Indian Removal Bill. Under this legislation, the government created the In-

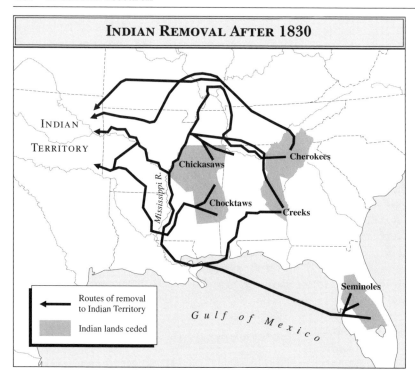

INDIAN REMOVAL AFTER 1830

INDIAN TERRITORY

Mississippi R.

Chickasaws

Chocktaws

Cherokees

Creeks

Seminoles

Gulf of Mexico

→ Routes of removal to Indian Territory

▓ Indian lands ceded

some cases the businessmen involved did not provide nearly enough supplies or equipment to carry out the task, through either ignorance, inattention, or simple fraud.

Although all the tribes moved to the west were at least partly agriculturalists, the non-Indians who replaced them farmed the land more intensively, and the economic production of the vacated lands increased dramatically after removal. In 1854, the Kansas-Nebraska Act opened Kansas and Nebraska to white settlement, and the tribes that had been promised them "forever" were moved again, into present-day Oklahoma, which remained the Indian Territory until 1898.

Mark S. Joy

dian Territory in the west and guaranteed it to Native Americans forever.

Treaties were negotiated under which tribes from the East moved to lands in the central and southern plains. At the time, many believed that white farmers would never settle the semiarid plains. Although many people in the eastern states simply wanted the Indians out of the way, some missionaries and other humanitarians believed that removal was actually in the best interest of the Native Americans because it would allow for their more gradual assimilation into American culture.

Roughly sixty thousand Native Americans were moved from the Southeast into present-day Oklahoma. The so-called Five Civilized Tribes (a term used by whites because these tribes were considered more assimilated than others) included the Cherokee, the Muskogee or Creek, the Choctaw, the Chickasaw, and the Seminole. Approximately ten thousand Native Americans from about twelve smaller tribes in the northern parts of the Ohio River Valley were moved into what is now Kansas. There was much death and suffering involved in these removals. Some of the suffering was caused by the fact that the government contracted with private businesses to carry out the actual removals, and in

FURTHER READING

Joy, Mark S. *American Expansionism, 1783-1860: A Manifest Destiny?* London: Pearson Education, 2003.

Perdue, Theda, and Michael D. Green. *The Cherokee Nation and the Trail of Tears.* New York: Penguin Group, 2007.

Prucha, Francis Paul. *The Great Father: The United States Government and the American Indians.* 2 vols. Lincoln: University of Nebraska Press, 1984.

SEE ALSO: Land laws; Native American trade.

Industrial research

DEFINITION: Corporate research aimed at developing new products, manufacturing techniques, and other sources of increased profit

SIGNIFICANCE: Industrial research has led to the birth of many important American businesses through the development of new products and the improvement of established products. It has played a significant role in the phenomenal industrial growth of the United States since 1900.

Pure scientific research, sometimes called basic or fundamental research, is the study of phenomena through observation and experiment to acquire reliable knowledge about the puzzles or secrets of nature. Industrial research, sometimes called applied or practical research, is the study of natural and other phenomena to discover ideas, processes, and devices of material benefit to humanity. Research and development (R&D) is the process of making scientific and technological knowledge practicable and economically successful in the marketplace.

ORIGINS

Although pure scientific research has had a long history, industrial research had a modern origin. Scientific knowledge had been used to establish such industries as those manufacturing beer, iron, textiles, and various chemicals in the ancient, medieval, and early modern periods, and some scholars have been hesitant to sharply distinguish fundamental from applied research because both were involved in the formation of new industries. Nevertheless, at the end of the nineteenth and the start of the twentieth century, especially with the foundation of industrial research laboratories, industrial research became characterized by laboratories separated from production facilities. In these laboratories experts in scientific disciplines and engineering worked to improve old and create new products and the means to manufacture them.

Some scholars trace the origin of the industrial research laboratory to the German dye companies during the 1870's and 1880's, even though American iron and railroad companies had set up small research laboratories during the 1860's and 1870's. Other scholars state that the research laboratory that Thomas Alva Edison founded at Menlo Park, New Jersey, in 1876 was the world's first industrial research laboratory. Edison hired scientists, engineers, and technicians to help him test his ideas and construct prototypes of various devices. Within a decade, Edison had over five hundred patents, several of which led to the formation of new industries manufacturing such successful products as the phonograph, incandescent lamp, and motion picture. Edison's accomplishments inspired other companies to found research laboratories, although this was truer of science-based industries than traditional ones. For example, the food-production and coal-mining industries did little research whereas the petroleum-refining and pharmaceutical industries did extensive research.

GENERAL ELECTRIC

A landmark institution in the history of industrial research was the General Electric Research Laboratory in Schenectady, New York. In 1892, General Electric (GE) had been formed by the merger of the Edison and Thomson-Houston companies, and in 1900, Willis R. Whitney established and began managing an influential corporate laboratory for GE. By hiring highly trained scientists and engineers, Whitney was able to keep GE competitive in the lightbulb business and to create successful new products. For example, William D. Coolidge, by developing a process for making tungsten wire, enabled GE to manufacture tungsten-filament lamps that were much

George Eastman (left) of Eastman Kodak and Thomas Alva Edison were pioneers in industrial research. (AP/Wide World Photos)

more efficient than carbon-filament lamps. Whitney often called his laboratory GE's life-insurance policy because it enabled the company to grow and prosper. Other companies that founded industrial research laboratories were Du Pont in 1902, Goodyear in 1908, General Motors in 1911, and Eastman Kodak in 1912. These laboratories changed the nature of American invention from individualists, exemplified by Edison, to corporate inventors whose innovations were contractually owned by the company.

THE ROLE OF GOVERNMENT

World War I, through such institutions as the National Research Council, increased the role of the federal government in controlling industrial research for national defense. After the war, many more companies set up industrial research facilities, and some developed ventures with academic institutions such as the Massachusetts Institute of Technology to fund research projects of potential benefit to American businesses. During this time the term "research and development" began to be used to describe the initiatives to derive marketable products from scientific and technological knowledge, for example, Du Pont's cellophane and Kodak's color film. By the early 1930's, more than sixteen hundred companies had industrial laboratories employing more than thirty thousand scientists and technicians. During the Great Depression of the 1930's, many companies reduced their economic distress by curtailing research expenditures, but during World War II, federal funds for industrial research dramatically increased through such institutions as the Office of Scientific Research and Development, blurring further the line between industrial and government research.

By the 1950's, American industrial research had become a massive enterprise, with more than two thousand businesses spending in excess of $2.5 billion annually to support the work of over a hundred thousand scientists. Government and academic involvement in industrial research also continued to increase, despite some scholarly studies indicating that the transformation of scientific research into commercial and military technologies was neither so simple nor so direct as once believed. Despite these studies and President Dwight D. Eisenhower's warning about the creation of a dangerous military-industrial complex, federal expenditures continued to increase during the 1960's, accounting for two-thirds of all research and development. A significant portion of this government investment went into the aerospace and defense industries.

By the 1980's American companies began to spend more on industrial research than the federal government. This was due to increased competition from Europe and Japan and because of the exponential growth of such fields as biotechnology and computer science. The unprecedented growth of these and other science-based industries depended more and more on the inventive skills of researchers to develop new ideas, processes, and products. In the twenty-first century, some analysts predict that the exponential growth experienced by many American companies will continue, but environmentalists have cautioned that natural limits to growth exist and that more research should be directed to funding new products and processes that will foster sustainability rather than untrammeled development.

Robert J. Paradowski

FURTHER READING

Birr, Kendall. *Pioneering in Industrial Research: The Story of General Electric Research Laboratory.* Washington, D.C.: Public Affairs Press, 1957. The author, one of the first historians to study industrial research, uses his account of the origin and development of the pioneering GE Research Laboratory to analyze the successes and problems of scientists engaged in applied corporate research. Notes and index.

Griliches, Zvi, ed. *R&D, Patents, and Productivity.* Chicago: University of Chicago Press, 1984. The contributors to this volume study the relationship between investment in industrial R&D and the market success of products that resulted from various patents. References at the end of each contribution and a subject index.

Holland, Maurice. *Industrial Explorers.* New York: Harper & Brothers, 1928. After an introductory chapter on industrial research, this popular treatment uses narrative accounts of such leaders of American industrial research as Willis R. Whitney, Elmer A. Sperry, L. H. Baekeland, and Arthur D. Little to help readers experience the dramatic discoveries of "industrial explorers." Illustrated with photographs, and an index.

Reich, Leonard S. *The Making of American Industrial*

Research: Science and Business at GE and Bell, 1876-1926. New York: Cambridge University Press, 2002. Intended for scholars and industrial researchers, this comparative historical study examines the origin and evolution of industrial research in two important American companies with a view toward making modern American industrial research more efficient. Forty-three pages of notes and an index.

Wise, George. *Willis R. Whitney, General Electric, and the Origins of U.S. Industrial Research*. New York: Columbia University Press, 1985. According to the author, no one did more to shape American industrial research than Whitney, and this biography traces his life from his birth in upstate New York to his creation and managing of the GE Research Laboratory. Bibliography and index.

SEE ALSO: Aircraft industry; Arms industry; Automotive industry; Bell Labs; Chemical industries; Commerce, U.S. Department of; Computer industry; Genetic engineering; Inventions; Pharmaceutical industry.

Industrial Revolution, American

THE EVENT: Transformation of the U.S. agrarian, handicraft economy into an industrial economy based on the mass production of consumer goods in large factories

DATE: First phase, 1790-1860; second phase, 1860-1914

SIGNIFICANCE: The American Industrial Revolution fostered an increase in the quantity and diversity of consumer goods produced by American businesses, though small businesses employing artisans suffered. In its second phase, the revolution grew to include new businesses mass-producing such items as electric lights, telephones, pharmaceuticals, and automobiles, and by the end of this phase, technological and business supremacy had passed from British to American companies.

For many modern scholars, the use of the term "revolution" to describe disruptively abrupt changes in science, technology, and industries is problematic. Some claim that "Industrial Revolution" is a misnomer, because technological change, with its concomitant socioeconomic influence, has been a grad-ual, cumulative process, rather than sudden and discontinuous. These scholars prefer to speak of an industrial evolution. Even those comfortable with the idea of an industrial revolution often disagree about where, when, and for how long such revolutions occurred.

For example, Lewis Mumford, a social critic and historian of technology, argued in his *Technics and Civilization* (1934) that the first industrial revolution occurred in medieval Europe, when extensive use was made of water and wind power. Others have found fault with the traditional view of the British Industrial Revolution, which several scholars see as extending from 1750 to 1850, for how can "revolution," which implies sudden change, be properly applied to a process that took a century to complete? Indeed, others argue that the process of modern industrialization was not really perfected until well into the twentieth century.

Similar disagreements exist among scholars over the meaning of the American Industrial Revolution. Several analysts associate this revolution with the change from craft technologies, practiced by artisans working on farms and in small businesses, to specialized machines, operated by technicians in large factories. These analysts believe that the transformation occurred largely between 1790 and 1860. Others assert that the American Industrial Revolution encompasses the advent of the system of mass production. They extend the duration of the revolution into the early twentieth century. Those who believe that the revolution was not completed until the mass production system was perfected extend it even further, to 1930 or to World War II.

Those who question the use of "revolution" to describe this American transformation, which took over a century and a half, have a point. However, no one has yet been able to supplant this widely used term, acceptable to ordinary people and to many scholars, to denote the radical transformation of American society from an agrarian nation to one that was increasingly urban and populated by factory workers who mass-produced goods using ever more sophisticated technologies.

FROM 1790 TO THE CIVIL WAR

The timing of the American Industrial Revolution was crucial: It began after the Revolutionary War, when the British Industrial Revolution was already well under way. Thomas Jefferson, who favored an America of self-sufficient farmers, was appalled by the dehumanizing effects of the British Industrial Revolution, but Alexander Hamilton, who favored an America of big businesses and large factories, used his "Report on Manufactures" (1791) to show that Americans were already forming businesses based on new technologies. He urged the federal government to nurture these businesses with protective tariffs.

Despite Hamilton's examples of early American industrialization, scholars have traditionally given the birthplace of the American Industrial Revolution as the Slater mill in Pawtucket, Rhode Island, and its birth date as the early 1790's. Samuel Slater was an immigrant from England, where he had worked in a cotton-spinning factory. He was able to gain entrepreneurial support from Moses Brown, a Quaker merchant, to build a water-powered cotton mill based on machinery that had been invented by the British. With the use of child labor, the Slater mill developed into a very successful business, particularly after Eli Whitney invented the cotton gin in 1793, providing massive amounts of inexpensive raw cotton to New England mills.

The Slater mill's success stimulated the construction of other cotton mills throughout New England, and American inventors adapted British inventions in woolen mills. They also created their own technologies: For example, their water-powered shearing machines accomplished in a single day what it had taken hand shearers three weeks to do. During the early decades of the nineteenth century, water-powered textile technologies spread to the states of New York, New Jersey, Pennsylvania, Maryland, and Delaware. A congressional report in 1816 was significant, because its data indicated that factory-produced cottons and woolens had by then exceeded homespun goods.

An important event in the evolution of American textile industrialization occurred in Lowell, Massachusetts, during the 1820's, when a successful system for turning raw cotton into finished cloth at a single site became operative. Besides pioneering comprehensive integrated industrial systems, the Lowell mills led the way in employing women (in 1836, almost 80 percent of their nearly seven thousand workers were women). The Lowell system spread to other towns where waterpower was available, and by mid-century, American textile businesses had become serious competitors to their British rivals.

The American Industrial Revolution comprised much more than advances in textile manufacturing. Just as iron was replacing wood as a principal material in structures and certain products, steam began to replace waterpower as a principal power source. Although the steam engine had been developed in England, Americans such as Oliver Evans improved it, and entrepreneurs such as Robert Fulton applied it to river transportation. Fulton's steamboat service on the Hudson River was a great financial success, and other businessmen became successful in introducing steamboat service to the Mississippi River, the Great Lakes, and Chesapeake Bay.

John Stevens, who had been a builder of steamboats, became even more well known as a proponent of steam-powered railroad transportation. American inventors found that they had to adapt British locomotives to the diverse and challenging landscapes of the United States. Some of their inventions, such as the T-rail, became the standard for railroads throughout the world, and their swivel truck allowed locomotives readily to navigate sharp curves. On the other hand, different railroad companies used different gauges (separations between the rails), and this lack of a uniform system hampered commerce. Nevertheless, by the time of the U.S. Civil War many more miles of railroad track existed in the United States than in all of Europe. American railroad businesses had become major employers of workers, managers, and technical people.

The success of the railroads also stimulated another American industry, iron and steel manufacturing. This industry experienced a transformation from blacksmith shops and local forges to iron mills and the large-scale factory production of iron and steel products. Some scholars have argued that the transformation of American iron and steel businesses was more by gradual accretion than by revolution, and that its businessmen of the 1850's were not unlike their counterparts of the 1750's. Nonetheless, in cities such as Pittsburgh, which became known as the "Iron City of America," new processes, such as the rolling and puddling systems, revolutionized the refining of iron, and this iron found a ready market with railroad companies and those businesses and federal armories manufacturing military weapons.

Several scholars believe that it was at such armories as those in Springfield, Massachusetts, and

Harpers Ferry, Virginia, that an important event in the American Industrial Revolution took place. John Hall, working at these armories, developed the first system for manufacturing rifles with truly interchangeable parts. Hall's "uniformity system" was based on a division of labor through which trained workers, using precision gauges and sophisticated machines, were able to manufacture a high-quality, consistently unvarying product. This American system of manufacturing spread to such private businesses as Samuel Colt's factory in Hartford, Connecticut, which manufactured his famous revolver, and the Wheeler and Wilson Manufacturing Company, which made sewing machines.

By the time of the Civil War, the United States had more than 140,000 manufacturing businesses worth over $1 billion. These businesses produced nearly $2 billion worth of goods and employed more than one million men and 250,000 women. Although textile businesses were the largest, other companies manufactured shoes, clocks, chemicals, and many other consumer goods. The McCormick steam-powered factory in Chicago produced reapers that helped harvest the crops that fed northern soldiers during the Civil War.

American products such as the McCormick reaper and the Colt revolver won prizes at such international world's fairs as the 1851 London Exhibition (the Crystal Palace), and these international prizes fostered the development of markets for American-made products in European and other countries. American inventors, with their "Yankee ingenuity," were becoming famous for creating such labor-saving devices as apple-peeling machines and eggbeaters. As Hamilton had predicted in his "Report on Manufactures," the United States had overcome its handicap of scarce labor by making increasing use of mechanical power to create a new system of manufacturing.

FROM THE CIVIL WAR TO 1914

During this phase of the American Industrial Revolution, both old and new businesses grew through industrial expansion and systematization into large corporations that used the assembly-line mass production of goods to become the most economically powerful companies in the world. Military necessity during the Civil War goaded both government and private producers to manufacture such new things as ironclad ships, breech-loading ri-

fles, minié bullets, and machine guns. After the Civil War, new inventions continued to foster new businesses, and an expanded and systematized railroad system (which became transcontinental with the linking of the Central Pacific and Union Pacific railroads in 1869) helped various companies and farmers distribute their products to consumers all over the United States.

Some scholars see three major new technologies as fundamental to the second phase of the American Industrial Revolution: the internal-combustion engine; devices for the generation, distribution, and use of electrical power; and the creation of many advanced chemicals, such as dyes and pharmaceuticals. During this period, steam-powered facilities replaced water-powered ones, then steam power began to be replaced by electric power. Some corporations became so powerful that their workers unionized, seeking a remedy for low wages and deleterious working conditions. Certain scholars emphasize the change from the American system of manufacturing to modern mass production as the most important transformation in this phase of the American Industrial Revolution.

Because of the large numbers and great variety of businesses that developed during this period, not all could survive in the increasingly competitive marketplace. Those that were most likely to succeed were those that created products for which there was a significant demand and that they could manufacture efficiently and market effectively. For example, a "bicycle boom" occurred at the end of the nineteenth century, and Albert A. Pope, the founder of the American bicycle industry, was able to adapt methods of the Springfield armory to make high-quality bicycles with interchangeable parts. Alexander Graham Bell, who patented his telephone in 1876, initially thought that it would be primarily a business machine. It proved to be extremely popular with the public, however, and Bell's American Telephone and Telegraph Company became so successful, largely through the creation of an efficient long-distance system, that Bell's patent has often been called the most valuable in American history.

Thomas Alva Edison registered more than one thousand patents. Many of them led to the creation of successful businesses, and Edison became a successful entrepreneur with the formation of the Edison Electric Illuminating Company of New York in 1880. He not only invented the first commercially viable incandescent lamp but also developed the first electricity generating and distribution system in lower Manhattan, which became the model for other cities such as Chicago, Detroit, Boston, and Philadelphia. The Edison company was also successful in expanding to foreign markets.

For many scholars, the culminating figure in the second phase of the American Industrial Revolution was Henry Ford. By establishing methods for making an internal-combustion-engine-powered automobile that was affordable by the growing middle class of the United States, Ford became a very important businessman. He was an advocate of interchangeability, and he devised assembly-line techniques for efficiently putting interchangeable parts together to form a product. He made his first Model T in 1908, and he opened his Highland Park facility in Detroit in 1910 to meet the enormous demand for this automobile.

Because assembly-line workers found their repetitive tasks so boring that they quit their jobs in droves, in 1914, Ford introduced the eight-hour workday and forty-hour workweek, and he increased salaries to $5 per day, far higher than what other businesses offered. So successful was the Ford Motor Company that its techniques rapidly spread to other businesses. In this way, mass production helped foster mass consumption, and Ford established what became a defining business paradigm for the twentieth century.

Robert J. Paradowski

FURTHER READING

Hawke, David Freeman. *Nuts and Bolts of the Past.* New York: Harper & Row, 1989. Traces the evolution of water-driven mills into steam-powered factories through case studies of such businesses as clock-making. Bibliography and index.

Hindle, Brooke, and Steven Lubar. *Engines of Change: The American Industrial Revolution, 1790-1860.* Washington, D.C.: Smithsonian Institution Press, 1986. This extensively illustrated survey explores the forces behind American industrialization. Suggested readings and index.

Hounshell, David A. *From the American System to Mass Production, 1800-1932: The Development of Manufacturing Technology in the United States.* Baltimore: Johns Hopkins University Press, 1984. This book, which won the Dexter Prize of the Society for the History of Technology, emphasizes the evolution

of mass production technologies, particularly as experienced by businessmen, managers, and engineers. Illustrated, with a bibliography and index.

Hunter, Louis C. *A History of Industrial Power in the United States, 1780-1930.* 3 vols. Charlottesville: University Press of Virginia, 1979-1991. Hunter's massive work has been called essential reading for anyone interested in the technological and industrial development of the United States during the two phases of the Industrial Revolution. Each volume contains many maps, illustrations, charts, tables, and appendixes. Extensive notes and indexes.

Kasson, John F. *Civilizing the Machine: Technology and Republican Values in America, 1776-1900.* New ed. New York: Macmillan, 1999. Highly praised work that attempts to integrate technology, business, and culture. Index.

Smith, Merritt Roe. *Harpers Ferry Armory and the New Technology: The Challenge of Change.* Ithaca, N.Y.: Cornell University Press, 1977. The primary source for an understanding of the origin and development of the American system of manufacturing. Well documented, with an index.

SEE ALSO: Agribusiness; Automation in factories; Automotive industry; Cotton gin; Edison, Thomas Alva; Ford Motor Company; Labor history; Labor strikes; Railroads; Steel industry.

Industrial Workers of the World

IDENTIFICATION: International, cross-industry labor organization that holds that all workers should unite as a class

DATE: Founded in June, 1905

SIGNIFICANCE: When the Industrial Workers of the World was founded, it was the only union to welcome African Americans, women, and immigrants. Active in many labor disputes and opposed to war, it has faced strong opposition from company management and the U.S. government.

The Industrial Workers of the World (IWW) emerged in 1905 in the United States as a labor union committed to organizing a wide range of unrepresented workers by using the tactics of direct workplace action. The IWW, whose members are known as the "Wobblies," took as its fundamental premise the reality of sharp and sustained class conflict in American capitalist society. IWW organizers argued for a broad-based multiethnic union to advance the interests of all wage laborers, but especially those workers not included in large craft unions. Initial organizers of the IWW came from already established unions, such as the Western Federation of Miners, the United Metal Workers, the United Brewery Workers, and various socialist and labor rights groups. Wobblies defined their work within the international labor movement as well. In contrast to organizations like the American Federation of Labor (AFL), which emphasized contract negotiations and electoral politics within existing industrial and economic relations, IWW political philosophy called for direct action to build working class power, with the eventual goal of ending the inequities of wage labor and shifting to decentralized worker control across the spectrum of American industry and business.

During its early decades, the IWW used organizing tactics such as strikes, work slowdowns, worker education classes, music, political art, and journalism. This emphasis on cultural work and strikes has made the IWW a very visible presence in American labor organizing, with organizing work in the twenty-first century focused on low-wage, skilled, and semiskilled workers.

The tactics employed by the IWW in its early decades were agitation within agricultural work, domestic service, and the mining, logging, textile, and construction industries. By refusing to focus on contract strategies, IWW organizers brought workers into direct confrontational encounters with owners and managers, on terms set by the union through strikes, slowdowns, and independent journalism. Wobblies pushed the flashpoints in labor politics decidedly to the left.

The IWW also broke through racial, gender, and ethnic barriers to integrate unions around the country, to work for the rights of agricultural and migrant workers, and to propel women into na-

INDUSTRIAL WORKERS OF THE WORLD

These two paragraphs from the preamble to the constitution of the Industrial Workers of the World clearly state the organization's core beliefs.

The working class and the employing class have nothing in common. There can be no peace so long as hunger and want are found among millions of the working people and the few, who make up the employing class, have all the good things of life.

Between these two classes a struggle must go on until the workers of the world organize as a class, take possession of the means of production, abolish the wage system, and live in harmony with the Earth.

tional labor leadership. By prioritizing worker education, music, journalism and cultural creativity (art, cartoons, and the like) the Wobblies expanded public exposure to leftist critiques within American labor relations. Committed to decentralized power, Wobblies also rejected authoritarian and centralized models for socialism or communism as strongly as they rejected the AFL focus on contract negotiations. IWW activity often sparked severe reactions from government and business, including violent suppression of strikes, suppression of free speech, and imprisonment of IWW organizers. These dynamics exposed American labor relations to critical public scrutiny, both domestically and internationally.

Sharon Carson

FURTHER READING

Buhle, Paul, and Nicole Schulman, eds. *Wobblies! A Graphic History of the Industrial Workers of the World.* New York: Verso, 2005.

Dubofsky, Melvyn. *We Shall Be All: A History of the Industrial Workers of the World.* Urbana: University of Illinois Press, 2000.

Kornbluh, Joyce. *Rebel Voices: An IWW Anthology.* Chicago: Charles H. Kerr, 1998.

SEE ALSO: AFL-CIO; Brotherhood of Sleeping Car Porters; Debs, Eugene V.; International Ladies' Garment Workers' Union; Labor history; Labor strikes; Lewis, John L.; Panic of 1873.

Inflation

DEFINITION: Sustained, general increase in prices
SIGNIFICANCE: Inflation temporarily increases business profits, but it distorts business accounting measures; drives up interest rates; augments conflicts with customers, suppliers, debtors, and creditors; and contributes to antibusiness political sentiment.

Before the twentieth century, inflation in the United States generally resulted from government issues of paper money, primarily in wartime. The dollar was linked to gold or silver, and people measured monetary imbalance by deviations between the price of precious metals on the open market and the face value of the paper currency.

Paper money issues were relatively common in the American colonies before the American Revolution. Some resulted from the operation of government loan offices. In other cases, paper money was simply issued to help finance government expenditures. Although not formally redeemable in precious metal, the paper money could be used to pay taxes and to buy government securities. Conflicts arose when debtors attempted to repay private debts originally arranged on the basis of repayment in precious metals. Most colonies used paper money constructively, but significant price increases accompanied currency issues in Rhode Island and North Carolina.

After the American Revolution began in 1775, the Continental Congress began to issue a national paper currency, paid out to soldiers and suppliers. The Continental currency was linked to Spanish milled silver dollar coins (known colloquially as "pieces of eight"), and each specified on its face that it could be exchanged for a specific number of "Spanish milled Dollars, or the value thereof in gold or silver." Before the end of 1776, about $25 million worth of currency had been issued, and prices were rising. By the end of 1779, an estimated 226 million had been issued. The paper currency quickly lost its value against precious metal. In October, 1778, a silver dollar was worth 5 paper dollars. It was worth 30 dollars a year later, 78 dollars in October, 1780, and 168 dollars in April, 1781. Meanwhile, state governments were issuing their own paper money. Governments attempted to fix prices, punish hoarders of goods, and make paper currency legal tender.

The Constitution of 1787 reflected a desire to avoid repetition of the coercive and confiscatory elements of revolutionary inflation. State governments were forbidden to impair the obligation of contracts or make anything but gold or silver legal tender for debts. The remaining Continental currency was accepted at a rate of one hundred to one for new, gilt-edged federal government securities created in 1790. The new federal government did not officially issue paper currency again until the U.S. Civil War. The War of 1812 brought a renewed burst of inflation, most of it resulting from extensive issue of banknotes, as banks bought war bonds from the government. Wholesale prices rose almost 50 percent from 1811 to 1814. The war's end was followed by sharp deflation. By 1820, wholesale prices were below their 1811 levels.

CIVIL WAR INFLATION

The dollar was kept more or less on a stable equivalence to precious metals until the outbreak of the Civil War in 1861. The magnitude of war expenditures led both North and South to repeat the paper money experience of the revolution. In the North, federal expenditures in 1862 were six times those of the 1850's. Rapid expansion of money resulted from bank purchases of government bonds and the creation in 1862 of a new currency—greenbacks. The federal government paid these out to soldiers, civilian workers, and suppliers. In December, 1861, banks ceased redeeming their notes in gold, and the new greenbacks were not linked to precious metals. The new currency retained value, however, in part because it could be exchanged for government bonds on which interest was paid in gold. By the time the war ended in 1865, the money supply had doubled in the North. The cost of living was 75 percent above what it had been in 1860, and wholesale prices at their peak were more than double their prewar levels.

Inflation resulting from paper-money issues was much more severe in the Confederacy. Confederate paper currency issues began in mid-1861, and by early 1862, the money supply of the Confederacy was more than double what it had been a year previous. Between October, 1861, and March, 1864, prices rose at an average rate of 10 percent per month. By 1865, prices had risen almost one hundredfold, and for a brief period there was genuine hyperinflation—that is, price increases of at least

50 percent per month. When the war ended, Confederate currency became worthless—until a collectors' market emerged. Thereafter, prices trended steadily downward until the 1890's, as national output grew faster than the money supply. After 1896, gold discoveries contributed to monetary growth, and prices rose again.

WORLD WAR I AND WORLD WAR II

The Federal Reserve system came into operation in 1914, and just a few months later war broke out in Europe. As the belligerents purchased more U.S. products, U.S. price increases accelerated. The inflation process became severe when the United States entered World War I in 1917. Unlike the situation during the American Revolution and the Civil War, the Treasury did not significantly pay for its purchases with its own currency but instead paid with checking deposits created by the Federal Reserve and by commercial banks. Bank deposits grew rapidly, because the Federal Reserve loaned freely to banks, increasing their reserves and enabling them to purchase more government bonds.

Although by 1918 wholesale prices had risen to approximately double what they had been in 1913, the cost of living rose by only about 50 percent over that period. After 1918, the Federal Reserve continued to promote monetary expansion to aid the Treasury in refinancing war loans. The cost-of-living index in 1920 was at approximately double its 1913 level. Finally, in January, 1920, the Federal Reserve adopted a restrictive monetary policy. This policy quickly put an end to price increases and led instead to brief but severe deflation in 1921 and 1922.

A new bout of inflation emerged as war spread across the world beginning in 1939. After the United States entered World War II in December, 1941, the Federal Reserve once again facilitated rapid expansion of money and credit to help the Treasury sell bonds. The corresponding wartime price increases were far smaller than in World War I, however, and were smaller than the proportional monetary expansion. One reason for this relatively low inflation was that the economy was still recovering from the Great Depression. Many unemployed workers and idle factories were brought back into production to meet the rising demand for wartime labor, and the wages paid to the newly employed workforce reduced the extent to which newly issued currency represented a surplus and therefore an inflationary pressure. Furthermore, people were willing to save a significant proportion of their income, anticipating that the war's end could bring on another serious depression. Extensive controls over prices and wages were imposed, beginning in 1942.

POSTWAR AND THE 1950'S

Consumer prices in 1945, when World War II ended, were only 22 percent higher than they had been in 1941. After the wartime controls were removed in 1946, a powerful upsurge of spending by consumers and businesses triggered a new round of inflation. Consumer prices rose about 10 percent per year between 1945 and 1948. Americans began to realize that there would not be a repeat of the postwar depressions of the past.

The inflation surge ended temporarily when a mild recession in 1949 brought price reductions, but a new inflationary shock erupted with the out-

This 1942 drugstore display reminds customers how price controls help limit inflation and aid the war effort. (Library of Congress)

break of the Korean War in the summer of 1950. Fearing a return to wartime price controls and shortages, consumers and businesses rushed to buy goods, driving up prices by 10 percent in the first twelve months of the war. Tax rates were increased in the latter part of 1950; consequently, the federal government did not engage in large-scale deficit spending. Fiscal policy was aided by the reimposition of price controls in January, 1951.

The buying frenzy of 1950 was financed in part by borrowing from banks, leading to an expansion of money and credit aided by Federal Reserve purchases of bonds from banks. The public's money holdings increased by $6 billion during 1950. Unhappy with this situation, Federal Reserve officials ended their commitment to support government bond prices. Interest rates were thus free to increase, and they did.

The inflation of 1942-1952 resulted from a great expansion of aggregate demand that led to a huge increase in national output, employment, wages, and consumption. Many households held savings accounts and savings bonds with very low interest rates. Inflation reduced the value of these assets, and higher nominal incomes placed many Americans in higher income-tax brackets.

With the end of hostilities in Korea in 1953, most of the government's direct price controls were removed. Defense spending was curtailed. Prices drifted upward gradually between 1951 and 1965, as inflation averaged about 1.4 percent per year. Because of product improvements and innovations, the value of the dollar did not decrease for consumers. A steady rise in interest rates compensated creditors for higher product prices.

THE PEACETIME INFLATION SURGE

Booming business and the increased U.S. involvement in the Vietnam War escalated price increases beginning during the mid-1960's. The government incurred substantial deficits, and the Federal Reserve expanded the money supply rapidly. Demand for goods rose more rapidly than production could expand. Unemployment declined to a very low 3.5 percent of the labor force in 1969. In 1971, President Richard M. Nixon imposed direct controls on wages and prices. Inflationary demand pressures were already slowing, as the United States withdrew from Vietnam. Congress voted in 1972 to index Social Security benefits. After 1974, these ben-

efits increased automatically in step with rising prices, so their real value would not decrease.

The economy was rudely jolted in October, 1973, when members of the Organization of Petroleum Exporting Countries (OPEC) imposed a ban on shipments of petroleum to the United States. The wholesale price of crude oil rose by 27 percent during 1973. The ban was lifted in March, 1974. Largely by coincidence, most wage-price controls were removed the following month—but not those on petroleum products. While the oil crisis developed, the Federal Reserve was generating a rapid increase in the money supply in an effort to reduce unemployment. The combination of a restricted petroleum supply, higher business costs, and expanding demand drove the rate of inflation above 12 percent in 1974.

As oil supplies improved, prices of gas and oil peaked in the summer of 1974 and then slowly began to decrease. The inflation rate receded to 6 percent in 1976. Distressed by rising unemployment, Federal Reserve officials accelerated monetary expansion. This expansion in turn increased the demand for goods and services. In January, 1979, Islamic militants drove the shah of Iran from power, and the new Iranian government stopped oil exports. In two months, Iranian oil prices rose by 30 percent. The shock was quickly transmitted to the U.S. economy. By September, 1979, gasoline prices were 52 percent higher than they had been one year earlier, and heating oil prices were 73 percent higher. The general inflation rate exceeded 13 percent per year in 1979 and 1980.

BusinessWeek commented in May, 1978, that "inflation threatens the fabric of U.S. society." Much of this concern arose from public anxiety. Inflation generated animosity toward labor unions and businesses alike and eroded confidence in the government. The inflation of the 1970's raised nominal wages by nearly the same percentage as it raised consumer prices, so real wages were relatively constant. Under normal circumstances, however, real wages would increase in response to rising productivity, and that did not occur.

Because price increases made people eager to borrow and reluctant to lend, they drove interest rates to unusually high levels. Rates of return on high-grade corporate bonds reached 8 percent in 1970. They fluctuated around this level, then rose to 9.6 percent in 1979 and 12 percent in 1980. Higher costs and higher tax liabilities prevented a rapid rise in corporate profits, which dampened the stock market. Stock prices rose very little from 1969 to 1979, so investors lost real buying power.

Economists struggled to interpret the experience of the 1970's. The unemployment rate, which had averaged less than 4 percent from 1966 to 1969, hovered around 7 percent between 1975 and 1979. The term "stagflation," signifying inflation accompanied by stagnant economic growth, came into common use. Inflation was blamed by some on wage demands of labor unions and by others on the monopoly power of big business, but the chief cause was rapid monetary growth. By 1980, economists generally agreed that market interest rates would rise point-for-point with increases in the expected inflation rate. It became clear that unexpected inflation caused much more harm than did anticipated inflation. Public discontent with inflation, high interest rates, and high unemployment all contributed to the victory of Ronald Reagan over Jimmy Carter in the presidential election of 1980.

AFTER 1980

Encouraged by the election results of fall, 1980, Federal Reserve chief Paul Volcker took steps to reduce the growth rate of the money supply. In the short run, this put the economy through a painful economic recession. The inflation rate quickly receded, falling below 4 percent in each year from 1982 to 1986. The reduction in inflation was aided by declining world oil prices, which helped stabilize household energy prices (which shot up by 30 percent in 1980-1981) and ultimately caused them to decline by 20 percent in 1986. Energy prices were lower in 1986-1989 than they had been in 1981. The reduction in inflation seemed to validate the "monetarist" perspective, according to which inflation is a response to excessive money growth and high interest rates are a response to expectations of high inflation.

Between 1983 and 2007, consumer prices rose at an average annual rate of about 3 percent. This rate was below the public's threshold of pain and panic. The Federal Reserve learned to keep monetary expansion under restraint. Import competition attending the increasing globalization of the U.S. economy helped hold down prices and wages. Because Social Security benefits had been indexed, beneficiaries received higher payments to offset higher living costs. Indexation was extended to the personal income tax during the early 1980's, reducing the tendency for inflation to push people into a higher tax bracket. In 1997, the government began issuing inflation-indexed bonds.

EFFECTS OF INFLATION

Most individual households are harmed by inflation. For the entire economy, however, the negative effects of inflation are questionable. Inflation is commonly the result of strong increases in the demand for goods and services, enabling businesses to obtain higher prices and stimulating greater production. The same inflation that raises product prices also tends to raise wages. When production increases, it is doubtful whether society as a whole is made worse off. When inflation is anticipated, people factor it into their decisions. Wages and interest rates are adjusted. In contrast, unanticipated inflation victimizes creditors who have made long-term commitments. Widespread indexation has reduced inflation vulnerability, partly among the elderly.

Even so, inflation tends to generate anxiety, even among people who appear objectively to benefit from it. This is because most people do not understand the sources of inflation and feel they are being victimized. Such anxiety can lead to harmful scapegoating of businesses and labor unions and to political "remedies" such as price controls that may do more harm than good.

Inflation poses problems for business accounting. Tax laws permit firms to recover tax-free the cost of capital assets, allocated over time by depreciation. However, if the prices of physical assets are rising, the depreciation allowances will not permit recovery of enough money to replace an asset.

By the early twenty-first century, the view that inflation is a result of excessive monetary expansion had become widely accepted. The Federal Reserve and the European Central Bank acted accordingly to anticipate, limit, and mitigate periods of inflation.

Paul B. Trescott

FURTHER READING

"The Great Government Inflation Machine." *BusinessWeek*, May 22, 1978, pp. 106-150. This "report from the battlefield" conveys a sense of the social tension and political unrest of the 1970's.
Mishkin, Frederick S. *The Economics of Money, Banking, and Financial Markets.* 7th ed. New York:

Pearson/Addison Wesley, 2004. This widely used college text analyzes the relative roles of OPEC and the Federal Reserve in the inflation of 1973-1983; also provides analysis of interest rates and foreign-exchange rates.

"Reflections on Monetary Policy Twenty-Five Years After October, 1979." *Federal Reserve Bank of St. Louis Review* 87, no. 2, Part 2 (March/April, 2005). Traces the recognition that inflation is primarily a result of monetary policy and the Federal Reserve's policy adjustments in 1979.

Sargent, Thomas J. *The Conquest of American Inflation.* Princeton, N.J.: Princeton University Press, 1999. Reviews the historical experience of inflation in the United States and how policy makers have learned from it.

Schmukler, Nathan, and Edward Marcus, eds. *Inflation Through the Ages: Economic, Social, Psychological, and Historical Aspects.* New York: Brooklyn College Press, 1983. The fifty-three articles in this collection cover a breathtaking range of topics, including several on U.S. inflation.

SEE ALSO: Civil War, U.S.; Currency; Federal Reserve; Interest rates; Monetary policy, federal; Revolutionary War; Trickle-down theory; Wars; World War I; World War II.

Insider trading

DEFINITION: Transaction in which a person with inside knowledge of a corporation buys or sells securities or advises another to do so based on material information not yet made public

SIGNIFICANCE: Prohibitions against insider trading seek to reassure investors that corporate managers and other with an obligation to the public (that is, those with fiduciary responsibilities) do not act in their own or others' financial interest on the basis of information that is required to be but has not yet been disclosed regarding business developments, such as serious pending financial losses.

The term "insider trading" first was employed in regard to American business during the 1980's, when Congress decreed tough penalties for the practice and the U.S. Department of Justice began to move aggressively against those charged with the behavior. The United States is regarded as having the most stringent laws in the world against insider trading.

The 1980 the U.S. Supreme Court decision in *Chiarella v. United States* clarified the reach of the Securities Act of 1933. Vincent Chiarella worked for a financial printer and was able to profit by discovering the identifies of companies involved in takeovers even though their names were camouflaged in the material with which he worked. He was sentenced to disgorge his takings and to serve a one-year prison sentence, but that verdict was overturned by the Supreme Court on the ground that he was not a corporate insider and therefore not restrained from acting on confidential information.

Insider trading often is difficult to prove because it is essential to show that nonpublic information has spurred a transaction rather than, as the accused is likely to claim, a hunch or some other financial motivation, such as the need for cash. The case of editor and homemaker advocate Martha Stewart put insider trading in the limelight, but it is notable that Stewart was convicted not of that offense but of perjury for lying about what she had been told and what she had done about information from her broker.

Considerable debate exists about the value of prohibitions against insider trading. Some insist that it is economically counterproductive because to permit insider trading would alert others at an early moment about impending developments and allow them to arrange their holdings to cope with such contingencies. Those favoring a tough enforcement stance maintain that in the absence of vigilant oversight to ensure market integrity, the capital necessary to fuel the economy would not be entrusted to the stock markets.

Gilbert Geis

FURTHER READING

Bainbridge, Steven M. *Securities Law: Insider Trading.* New York: Foundation Press, 1999.

Szockyj, Elizabeth. *The Law and Insider Trading: In Search of a Level Playing Field.* Buffalo, N.Y.: William S. Hein, 1993.

Wang, William K. S., and Marc I. Steinberg. *Insider Trading.* New York: Practicing Law Institute, 2005.

SEE ALSO: Black Monday; Business crimes; HealthSouth scandal; Stewart, Martha; Stock market crash of 1929; Stock markets.

Insurance industry

DEFINITION: Business enterprises that indemnify individuals, families, businesses, and other entities against losses caused by specified contingencies and perils.

SIGNIFICANCE: Originating in companies that insured merchant cargoes carried on the high seas, the American insurance business has grown into a complex, multitrillion-dollar industry that protects almost every conceivable asset threatened with possible loss.

A financial device used to manage risk, insurance works on the principle of pooling, which allows members of groups to share the risk of losses to individual members. Insurance allows pooling by collecting relatively small sums, called premiums, from each group member to establish reserves to be used to pay the losses of any member. Payments made after losses are incurred are called indemnities, and the process is called indemnification. Through insurance systems, each covered individual's risk of loss is shared by the group.

Fire insurance illustrates the principle of pooling. If a house is worth $100,000 and there is a one-in-one-thousand chance that it and other houses like it may burn down in any given year, one thousand homeowners who each pay a premium of $100 would collectively cover the costs of rebuilding one home destroyed by fire. Thus, for the payment of a $100 premium each, individual homeowners would avoid the risk of losing the entire value of their homes to fire. However, the actual calculation of risks and the setting of premiums is naturally much more complicated than in this illustration. Insurance companies gather information to make such decisions and invest the premiums. In exchange for their efforts, they earn profits.

Insurance is available for many kinds of risks. For example, life insurance helps reduce the financial consequences of death. Health insurance addresses the risk of injury or disease. Property insurance may cover damages due to windstorms or hail, explosions or riots, and theft or fire. Liability insurance provides a defense and can pay settlements or judgments in the event of lawsuits.

HISTORY

Since the development of the concept of owned property in early human societies, managing risks associated with property ownership has been an issue. Whether that has been the personal ownership of the property and the desire to protect the property from damage, loss, or theft, or materials produced and sold to others that derive a livelihood for a business, some form of guarantee has always been in demand. In early times, those who had the wealth were able to provide assurance to those receiving the goods that they would be delivered as stipulated. To insure was to provide a guarantee to the parties involved that the transaction would take place as agreed upon.

Great Britain, which has long been heavily involved in maritime trade, pioneered commercial insurance and created the types of insurance companies that were established in North American colonies. During the American colonial era, insurance companies were designed to make profits, and many early companies profited at the expense of others by placing many restrictions and barriers for parties to be indemnified for their losses. After the American colonies became independent, churches tended to take over the insurance business in the United States, and the concept of classifying risks began. Insurance companies assessed the possibilities of loss due to fire and other "acts of God," as well as losses to theft or damage. They even began placing values on the loss of life, in the form of life insurance.

During the nineteenth century, many enterprises found it necessary to protect both their employees and their companies against losses due to injuries to workers on the job and against claims of customers who suffered losses because of defective products that were the result of negligence on the part of the companies. Insurance to compensate workers for their losses was created, along with new forms of health, disability, and life insurance. Much of this was offered by fraternal organizations to their members. As risks were identified and defined, insurance policies were developed to cover those risks. Insured parties paid premiums to insurance companies to obtain the protection they desired.

Insurance companies found ways to collect premiums from many parties, while paying out benefits to few. The insurers created the means of underwriting such risks—knowing that some categories of risks and individuals or businesses were more likely to require compensation for losses than others.

PREMIUMS FOR PROPERTY AND CASUALTY INSURANCE, 2000 AND 2005, IN BILLIONS OF DOLLARS

Type of Insurance	2000	2005
Accident and health	14.5	9.6
Automobile, private	120.0	159.7
Automobile, commercial	19.8	26.8
Homeowners' multiple peril	32.7	53.0
Marine, inland and ocean	8.3	11.2
Workers' compensation	26.2	39.7

Source: Data from the *Statistical Abstract of the United States, 2008* (Washington, D.C.: Department of Commerce, Economics and Statistics Administration, Bureau of the Census, Data User Services Division, 2008)

Note: Premiums are net written.

Through analysis of statistics and probability theory, companies determined rate structures that allowed them to collect premiums from large categories of customers, knowing they would not have to pay out the same amount collected to all people within that group. That shared risk philosophy was the beginning of a very lucrative industry.

THE INDUSTRY

The insurance industry is made up of hundreds of companies and thousands of agents who represent the companies. Captive agents may sell policies only for the companies that employ them and their subsidiaries. Independent agents sell policies for multiple companies and may be better placed to offer the insurance that individual parties need. Most agents are multiline providers who sell all types of insurance policies—automobile, home, commercial, life, health, and long-term care. Some agents concentrate on single lines, such as health insurance, life insurance, or a combination of both. Most companies pay their agents salaries, commissions, or combinations of both and typically offer bonus plans tied into company growth, company loss ratios, and retention of customers. Some companies have moved away from commission systems to keep premiums lower. To some extent, this change is a response to the rise of the Internet, which has helped consumers become more knowledgeable about in-surance and made it easier for them to find the best deals.

The key to the construction of insurance is based around indemnification—the restoration of policyholders to the condition they enjoyed before their losses. Many insurance policies are designed to have the insurers act as third parties, taking care of losses after deductible or copayment requirements have been satisfied. Deductible provisions require the insured parties to share risks, thereby reducing the cost of the insurance premiums. Indemnification clauses prevent insured parties from profiting from losses. However, people soon learned that it was difficult to collect when a loss occurred, while many others framed their losses to comply with the policies in place. This would lead to a form of governmental regulation of the insurance industry.

GOVERNMENT INVOLVEMENT

The insurance industry is one of the most regulated businesses in the United States. Government regulation of the industry began in Europe during the nineteenth century. Because insurance policies are legal contracts, their wording is generally very complicated and often must be interpreted by courts. As the main concern of government should be to protect the interests of its citizens, ambiguous language in insurance contracts is generally interpreted against the makers of the contracts and in favor of the policyholders.

Government took on the role of wearing many hats to help better manage the American insurance industry during the early twentieth century. The role of compliance and oversight looked at many areas. These included ensuring that insurance companies have adequate reserves in place to pay possible claims, ensuring that rates being charged are not excessive, and protecting consumers against fraudulent acts of companies and their representatives. The federal government plays a role in public policy and political posturing by insurance companies, but most regulation of the industry occurs at the state level.

Every U.S. state has an insurance commissioner

who seeks continuity and consistency through their National Association of Insurance Commissioners organization. Although the insurance laws vary among the states, insured parties have the comfort of knowing that their policies cover their property, regardless of in which state they may be. As insured parties move from one state to another, companies typically simply transfer coverage from one location to another, charging whatever is the appropriate risk premium for the new location. State-based regulation is seen as the strength of the American insurance industry in many ways.

FEDERAL GOVERNMENT UNDERWRITING

Some insurance policies are underwritten solely by the federal government, although managed and directed through individual agents. A primary example is flood insurance. The federal government's National Flood Insurance Program allows individuals and businesses in flood-prone areas to buy insurance policies that protect them against flood-caused losses.

Other catastrophic perils that may have exclusivity by companies include hurricane and earthquake policies. Because such natural hazards tend to be geographically isolated, it is difficult to spread the risks among many parties: People who live outside hurricane regions do not need to buy hurricane insurance, but people who live within such regions face high risks. Consequently, premiums for such insurance tend to be so high that some people forego insurance coverage. Hurricanes caused about $25 billion in damage in the United States during the year 2004, making that year the worst in U.S. hurricane history. In 2006, only two years later, the Gulf Coast was ravaged by Hurricane Katrina, which caused damage estimated at nearly $100 billion.

INSURING BUSINESSES

Although many people associate insurance primarily with personal and family protection, many insurance companies also protect commercial businesses from the same perils that threaten individuals and also offer additional protection for liability. Many industries have created risk-management divisions that help businesses identify risks that may potentially ruin them and find the means to protect them from possible losses. Although insurance is the main tool used to provide protection from many perils, businesses can also eliminate, transfer, or ab-

sorb portions of such risks to help keep their insurance costs down.

A modern twist in the insurance industry is the use of reinsurance. Reinsurance allows insurance companies to essentially insure themselves through other means of insurance. The reasons for this are many, including transferring their own risks to another, having more funds to dedicate toward catastrophic losses they may incur, and lowering the amounts of capital that are needed to cover possible claims. Part of their goal is to keep their own premium levels down to make their policies more attractive to consumers.

Reinsurance takes one of two forms—proportional or nonproportional. In the proportional construction, it is a shared quota based on a percentage. Insurance companies can have a reinsurance company take on a percentage of any catastrophic loss. For example, if a company incurring tens of millions of dollars in losses from a hurricane were to have a proportional plan of 50 percent, it would be obligated for only 50 percent of those losses. The other 50 percent would be taken on by the reinsurance company. The nonproportional form of reinsurance is similar to a deductible, in which the company's policy would come into a play only after a certain level of losses were reached. For example, if a company with a $3 million reinsurance policy with a $1 million retention were to incur a $2 million loss, it would pay out the first $1 million and its reinsurance company would pay the remaining $1 million.

Throughout its history, the American insurance industry has grown greatly, not only in size but also in complexity. The modern industry now offers many hundreds of types of insurance policies to individuals and businesses. These range from automobile and aviation policies to identity theft and terrorist protection policies. Hundreds of companies and their representatives are licensed and regulated to conduct business in the states in which they operate. These companies work with both federal and state government agencies to provide constantly changing insurance services.

Karel S. Sovak

FURTHER READING

Altman, E. *The Financial Dynamics of the Insurance Industry.* New York: Irwin Professional, 1994. Analysis of the American insurance industry that explores opportunities and challenges from in-solvency to asset allocation.

Harrington, Scott E., and Gregory Niehaus. *Risk Management and Insurance.* 2d ed. Boston: McGraw-Hill, 2004. Textbook on insurance law offering the essential aspects of insurance contracts and the insurance industry while providing a substantial conceptual analysis and attention to business risk management and public policy issues.

Jenkins, David, and Takau Yoneyama. *History of Insurance.* 8 vols. Brookfield, Vt.: Pickering & Chatto, 2000. Collection of primary documents on the history of insurance in Great Britain through the nineteenth century.

Jerry, Robert H., II. *Understanding Insurance Law.* 4th ed. Newark, N.J.: Lexis Nexis/Matthew Bender, 2007. Up-to-date textbook that is an eminently readable book about insurance law.

Keeton, Robert E., and Alan I. Widiss. *Insurance Law: A Guide to Fundamental Principles, Legal Doctrine, and Commercial Practices.* St. Paul: West, 1988. Old but still widely used single-volume reference work on insurance law.

Murray, John F. *Origins of American Health Insurance: A History of Industrial Sickness Funds.* New Haven, Conn.: Yale University Press, 2007. Well-regarded revisionist history of Progressive-era industrial sickness funds, when efforts were made to enact government health insurance.

SEE ALSO: Federal Deposit Insurance Corporation; Health care industry; Medicare and Medicaid; Pension and retirement plans; Social Security system; Triangle Shirtwaist Company fire.

Interest rates

DEFINITION: Rates of payments made for the use of money, expressed as percentages of the sums owed

SIGNIFICANCE: Borrowing at interest is an important source of funds to finance business investment in machinery, buildings, inventories, and general operations. Banks and other financial businesses borrow and lend money as well as pay and receive interest.

Many debt claims, such as bonds and mortgages, are bought and sold among private investors and insti-tutions at prices that vary with supply and demand. The supply of loans comes mainly from savings, while demand for loans, earlier dominated by business borrowing, now comes from households and government as well.

The higher the price of a marketable bond with a fixed-dollar interest payment and redemption value, the lower its yield to an investor who buys it at the higher price. Because many financial claims are close substitutes for each other, debt claims of similar risk and time to maturity tend to have the same yield. Interest rates tend to rise and fall together, although the differentials may change.

Interest rates will tend to be higher on high-risk financial claims. For example, home-mortgage interest rates are higher than corporate bond rates, which are higher than U.S. Treasury bond rates. An increase in the expected rate of inflation tends to lead to a rise in interest rates, as demonstrated by the great rise of the 1970's.

Historically, interest rates have tended to rise and fall over the business cycle. During boom periods, business firms and households have been eager to borrow, driving interest rates up. During business downswings, profit prospects are less attractive, demand for loans falls, and interest rates decline.

EARLY HISTORY

Reliance on debt claims was very widespread in colonial America. Many people borrowed money to buy land. Merchants borrowed money to buy ships and to pay for their inventories of goods for sale. Colonists drew extensively on loans from British sources. A benchmark for interest rates was the national debt of the British government. Yields on British government securities averaged between 3 and 4 percent during much of the eighteenth century.

In the absence of banks in colonial America, some of the individual colony governments opened loan offices to supply credit. Examples include Massachusetts (1711-1714, loans at 5 percent), Pennsylvania (1722, at 5 percent, loans secured by land), and Virginia (1755, at 5 percent).

The American Revolution required heavy borrowing by the newly formed national government and by the states. The national government borrowed from bankers in Paris and Amsterdam at yields of between 4 and 6 percent, but much of the war was financed by issues of paper money. This generated severe inflation. Domestically, governments issued bonds payable in paper money, but because the contractual payments were not met, these fell in price far below par, generating effective yields as high as 40 percent. Financial conditions during the 1780's were chaotic. However, the first banks and insurance companies were established during this period.

After adoption of the Constitution of 1787, the new government redid the funding for the chaotic mass of debt claims previously issued by state and national governments. New government securities were issued in several varieties, paying either 3 or 6 percent. All initially fell below par, reflecting the shaky finances of the new government. By the first decade of the new century, however, yields were once again only slightly over 6 percent. Congress gave high priority to paying interest and redemption as promised. U.S. government securities thus became, as they have been ever since, among the safest and most secure debt claims in the world.

The new nation soon developed banks in major cities. During 1812-1815, war with England drove interest rates up, with government securities yielding as much as 9 percent in 1814. The rise reflected heavy government borrowing to finance the war and the fear of inflation. A postwar slump ended the inflation fear, depressed demand for private credit, and brought yields on federal securities down into the 4 to 5 percent range during the 1820's.

As the population grew and the area under cultivation expanded, the number and activity of banks expanded. Much bank lending was done at 6 percent interest. Often state laws (usury laws) forbade charging higher rates. Savings banks paid about 5 percent on deposits from 1836 through 1867 They generally used these funds to buy mortgages or bonds.

As banks proliferated, the economy was subject to periodic episodes of banking panics and depressions. Bank efforts to borrow to cover panic withdrawals would lead to brief episodes of very high short-term interest rates. Such financial panics occurred in 1819, 1837-1841, and 1857. Interest rates on short-term commercial paper went as high as 36 percent in 1819, 1836, and 1839, and reached 24 percent in 1834 and 1857.

Railroad building commenced on a serious scale during the 1840's and expanded rapidly during the 1850's. Many railroad projects were financed by issuing bonds, often sold to British and other foreign investors. During the late 1850's, such bonds were yielding between 6 and 7 percent on average.

THE CIVIL WAR AND RECONSTRUCTION

During the U.S. Civil War, both the North and the South resorted to bond issues and paper-money issues to finance their large military expenses. The North issued bonds for which interest and redemption were paid in gold. This protected bondholders against inflation and protected foreign investors against foreign-exchange depreciation of the dollar. Yields on such bonds averaged between 4.5 and 6 percent in 1862-1865.

After the war's end in 1865, the country experienced a long period of gradually declining prices—deflation. High-grade railroad bonds yielded an average of 5.7 percent during the 1870's, 4.0 percent during the 1880's, and 3.5 percent during the 1890's. Short-term rates on commercial paper fluctuated much more widely in response to business cycles, going as high as 16 percent in 1873 and 11 percent in 1893. Rates on savings deposits slid down from 6 percent during the 1860's and 1870's to 4 percent during the 1880's and 1890's.

THE TWENTIETH CENTURY

During the 1890's, Yale economist Irving Fisher advanced the later fashionable theory that interest rates would move point for point with changes in inflationary expectations. The grinding deflation following the Civil War led to low interest rates because lenders expected to benefit from the increased purchasing power of their interest and redemption payments. That deflation ended during the 1890's, when gold production expanded. As Fisher predicted, the shift to an inflationary outlook caused interest rates to begin an upward trend.

Bank deposits, which constituted half the money supply in 1865, rose to 90 percent by 1916. The interest received by banks provided the revenues from which deposit-management costs were paid. In 1914, the Federal Reserve System, the central bank of the United States, came into operation, intended to protect the public from disastrous bank panics. The Federal Reserve (known as the Fed) was empowered to lend to banks, and its chief tool was to be the interest charged—the rediscount rate. The Federal Reserve was also authorized to buy and sell government securities. It soon discovered that its purchases tended to reduce interest rates, and sales tended to increase them.

Hardly had the Federal Reserve begun operations, when World War I broke out in Europe. The Federal Reserve Banks began lending to banks at a rediscount rate of 6 or 6.5 percent in late 1914, but lowered the rate to 4 percent or less from 1915 through 1917. After the United States entered World War I in April, 1917, federal expenditures rose rapidly and were financed largely by issuing bonds and other forms of debt. The Federal Reserve aided the Treasury by lending freely to banks to encourage them to buy government securities. The earliest war loans yielded about 3.5 percent to investors, and subsequent loans in 1918 yielded slightly over 4.5 percent. Short-term rates were generally higher—an unusual situation. Commercial paper rates averaged 5 percent in 1917 and 6 percent in 1918.

The easy-money policies of the Federal Reserve contributed to rapid expansion of bank reserves, bank credit, the money supply, and inflation. After the war ended in November, 1918, the Treasury no longer needed to borrow as much. In an effort to curb the inflationary process, the Federal Reserve rapidly raised rediscount rates until by June, 1920, all twelve Federal Reserve Banks were charging 6 or 7 percent for loans to banks. The result was a drastic reduction in Federal Reserve lending to banks and a corresponding upward shock to interest rates.

Inflation soon ceased, giving way to a painful economic depression in 1921-1922. This reduced the demand for loans, particularly by business, and brought lower interest rates. By mid-1922, commercial paper rates were down to 4.1 percent, with government bonds just slightly higher. For the remainder of the decade, long-term rates stabilized between 3 and 4 percent, while short-term rates fluctuated more widely with the business cycle.

The 1920's brought a major transformation in consumer credit, as installment lending became common, particularly for automobile purchases. Because of the greater risks and transaction costs, these loans often involved interest rates substantially above those on corporate bonds or commercial paper.

Boom and Bust: 1927-1933

The late 1920's witnessed an accelerating rise in the prices of corporate stocks. The prospect of stock price increases encouraged many investors to borrow money to speculate, driving up interest rates.

Stock market ninety-day loans fell as low as 4.0 percent in late 1927, then moved steadily upward, passing 7 percent in 1928 and hitting 9 percent just before the market crashed in October, 1929. However, long-term bonds were not much affected. The economy's descent (1929-1933) into the worst economic depression in history thoroughly disrupted the financial world.

A high rate of bank failures reduced the availability of bank loans. Investors sought security, liquidity, and the opportunity to benefit from falling prices of goods and services, stocks, and real estate. They eagerly demanded short-term low-risk debt claims, such as Treasury bills, on which yields fell below 1 percent from 1931 until 1947. High-risk corporate bonds (BAA grade) were hard hit by corporate bankruptcies and loan defaults. As their prices fell dramatically, their yields rose from 6 percent in late 1929 to more than 11 percent in mid-1932.

The Federal Reserve Banks, most of which were lending to banks at 5 percent in 1929, reduced their discount rates at first—the New York rate went as low as 1.5 percent in 1931. However, they believed that higher interest rates were necessary to keep from losing a lot of gold during a panic episode in September of 1931 and raised rates to 3.5 percent, which precipitated a new wave of bank failures.

After the inauguration of President Franklin D. Roosevelt in March, 1933, drastic measures were taken to end financial panic. A variety of federal agencies were established to make loans directly or to insure or guarantee private loans. The Federal Housing Administration used its role in insuring home mortgages to promote long-term amortized mortgages. To protect banks against competition, the government forbade paying interest on demand deposits and imposed (low) ceiling rates on time-deposit interest rates. As the economy experienced a painfully slow recovery, interest rates remained low. High-grade corporate bonds, which had yielded more than 4 percent in 1930-1933, slid down to 2.7 percent in 1940.

World War II and After

After the outbreak of World War II in December, 1941, the U.S. government rapidly escalated military spending. The Treasury was eager to keep interest rates low in the face of its need to borrow heavily. The Federal Reserve Banks kept discount rates low and adopted a policy of "pegging" the prices of marketable government bonds, buying them if their prices appeared to be falling. The pegging policy kept government bond yields at or below 2.5 percent, despite extensive borrowing.

The public was willing to save a lot of money despite interest rates of 2 percent on savings deposits and 2.9 percent on the newly created (and widely popular) U.S. savings bonds. Many people feared

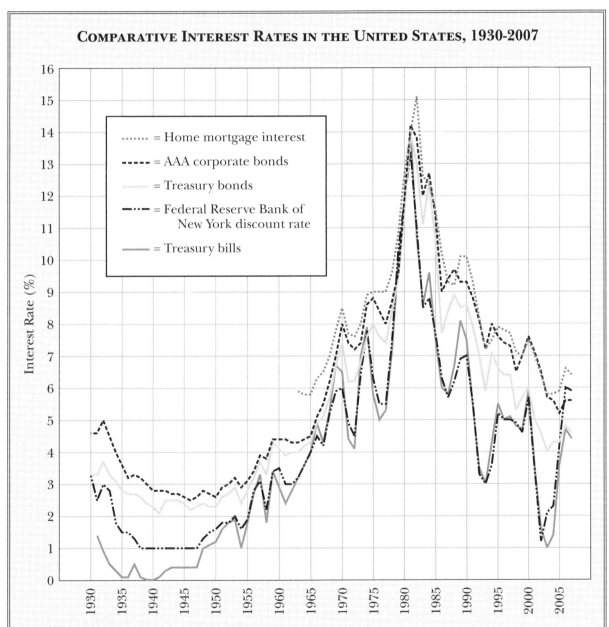

COMPARATIVE INTEREST RATES IN THE UNITED STATES, 1930-2007

Legend:
- .... = Home mortgage interest
- – – – = AAA corporate bonds
- ——— = Treasury bonds
- –··–·· = Federal Reserve Bank of New York discount rate
- ——— = Treasury bills

Y-axis: Interest Rate (%)

Sources: Susan B. Carter, ed., *Historical Statistics of the United States* (New York: Cambridge University Press, 2006); *Economic Report of the President* (Washington, D.C.: U.S. G.P.O., various editions); Board of Governors of the Federal Reserve System, *Annual Statistical Digest* (Washington, D.C.: author, various years), *Banking and Monetary Statistics, 1914-1941,* and *Banking and Monetary Statistics, 1941-1970* (Washington, D.C.: author, 1943, 1976 respectively)

that Depression conditions would return and wanted to accumulate funds for that feared rainy day.

The low-interest policy of the Treasury and Federal Reserve resulted in a large increase in the money supply and increasing inflationary pressure. Wishing to take a more aggressive anti-inflation stance, the Federal Reserve broke off its support of government bond prices in 1951, allowing interest rates to rise. The postwar boom brought a strong demand for loans, and all interest rates migrated upward. Long-term government bond yields passed 3 percent in 1956 and reached 4 percent in 1959. After a slight pause, their increase resumed under pressure from inflation during the early 1960's. The Federal Reserve Banks raised discount rates from the neighborhood of 3 percent in 1961-1962 to nearly 6 percent in 1969-1970. However, they did not slow the rate of monetary growth, and inflation continued to rise. Interest rates on AAA (top-grade) corporate bonds rose from 4.4 percent in 1960 to 8 percent in 1970.

From the late 1960's, credit cards came to play a major role in household borrowing. Explicit interest was charged if the borrower failed to pay the balance in full each month; rates were typically around 17 percent. As household incomes rose, people devoted more of their income to housing and durable goods, expenditures often involving credit. The sum of household mortgage debt and consumer credit rose from 31 percent of personal income in 1950 to 65 percent in 1960 and 117 percent in 2006. Households paid more interest, but they also received more. The rapid expansion of retirement plans in particular contributed to a rising share of interest in people's incomes. Personal interest income was only 4 percent of personal income in 1950 but rose to 10 percent by 2006.

The sharp run-up in international petroleum prices in 1973 accelerated inflation and raised inflation expectations. Interest rates reached peacetime record high levels. From 1974 through 1978, AAA bond yields were between 8 and 9 percent. Restrictive actions by the Federal Reserve sent them into double digits, peaking at 14 percent in 1981. Newly developed money-market mutual funds allowed households to share in receiving high interest. In 1986, most ceiling rates on deposit interest rates were removed. After 1979, the Federal Reserve's actions in slowing money growth brought down the inflation rate, and interest rates gradually returned to more nearly normal levels. In January, 1997, the Treasury began to issue Treasury Inflation Protection Securities (TIPS). The interest and redemption payments were adjusted up or down to compensate investors for changes in the price level.

By the end of the millennium, actual inflation rates and expected inflation rates had reached low levels, and interest rates were correspondingly low, although they continued to rise in cycle booms and decline in slumps. Increasing globalization caused bond prices and long-term interest rates in the United States to be strongly affected by conditions in the international capital markets.

Interest rates were central to the subprime mortgage crisis that surfaced in 2007. Eager to reap large transactions fees, financial institutions developed "securitization," packaging numerous home-mortgage loans together and using them as collateral for bond issues. Many loans were made to borrowers with poor credit ratings and provided for interest rates to rise substantially after an initial period. When home prices ceased rising, many of the loans fell into default.

Paul B. Trescott

FURTHER READING

Fisher, Irving. *The Theory of Interest.* New York: Macmillan, 1930. This classic work by one of America's greatest economists presents extensive history as well as theory.

Friedman, Milton, and Anna J. Schwartz. *A Monetary History of the United States, 1867-1960.* Princeton, N.J.: Princeton University Press, 1963. Numerous references to interest rates are interwoven into American financial history.

Homer, Sydney, and Richard Sylla. *A History of Interest Rates.* 4th ed. New York: John Wiley & Sons, 2005. The definitive historical resource, with information regarding many countries and a time span of many centuries.

Kaufman, Henry. *Interest Rates, the Markets, and the New Financial World.* New York: Times Books, 1986. One of Wall Street's legendary gurus mingles autobiography with sage commentary on the evolution of financial markets.

Mishkin, Frederic S. *The Economics of Money, Banking, and Financial Markets.* 7th ed. New York: Addison Wesley, 2004. This college-level text deals extensively with both the theory and history of interest rates.

SEE ALSO: Banking; Bond industry; Business cycles; Credit card buying; Federal Reserve; Monetary policy, federal; Mortgage industry; Stock markets; Treasury, U.S. Department of the; Wall Street.

Interior, U.S. Department of the

IDENTIFICATION: Cabinet-level department of the federal government controlling most nationally owned land, which totals about one-fifth of all the land in the United States

DATE: Established in 1849

SIGNIFICANCE: Since its inception, the Department of the Interior has handled miscellaneous duties in addition to controlling public lands. With such wide-ranging duties, the department has been difficult to manage and corruption has been rife. Business has both benefited and suffered from the department's control over public lands and natural resources.

The U.S. Department of the Interior (DOI) was created in 1849 by taking the Indian Affairs office from the Department of War, the Patent Office from the State Department, and the General Land Office from the Department of the Treasury. None of these offices had fit well within the cabinet-level departments from which they were removed. By the 1840's, it was clear that a new department to handle these miscellaneous offices was required. This became especially clear after the Mexican War, when a large section of land was added to the United States. From the very inception of the Interior Department, it had the character of the department of miscellany; in the department's official history, it is labeled the "department of everything else."

As of 2008, the Interior Department was in charge of the National Park Service, the U.S. Fish and Wildlife Service, the Bureau of Indian Affairs, the Bureau of Land Management, the Minerals Management Service, the Office of Surface Mining, the U.S. Geological Survey, the Bureau of Reclamation, and the Office of Insular Affairs. American businesses have significant interactions with each of these departments. Given the wide range of activi-

This 1938 poster shows Old Faithful erupting at Yellowstone National Park. Management of national parks is part of the Department of the Interior's duties. (Library of Congress)

ties, it has been difficult for the Interior Department to maintain tight control over its subdivisions. Because each new subdivision had so many ways to enrich various American businesses, the department has been subject to repeated scandals.

Almost from its inception, the Interior Department has been involved in scandals in which it gave some businesses improper advantages over their competition and gave public land and resources belonging to the American people to a handful of people who were willing to pay bribes. Early in its history, the Bureau of Indian Affairs was rife with scandal, which received very little public scrutiny because most of the citizenry did not care much about the Native Americans who were affected.

Throughout the department's history, businesses have sought to use public lands and the natural resources contained in them for private profit. Early in the twentieth century, a major scandal occurred over the management of national forests. During the 1920's, the U.S. strategic petroleum reserve was removed from the control of the Department of the Navy and placed under the control of the Department of the Interior with the deliberate intent that the oil reserves would be accessed by private companies at the expense of the public. This became known as the Teapot Dome scandal. Throughout the twentieth century, many of the public lands have been opened for grazing at little or no cost to ranchers, allowing public resources to be used for private gain.

In 2008, another scandal involving oil resources was uncovered, in which public officials allegedly bartered away billions of dollars in oil royalties for sexual favors and lavish gifts. No other department in American history has been as involved in improperly benefiting selected businesses as the Interior Department.

Richard L. Wilson

FURTHER READING

Arnold, Peri E. *Making the Managerial Presidency: Comprehensive Reorganization Planning, 1905-1996.* 2d ed. Lawrence: University Press of Kansas, 1998. A serious academic examination of the efforts to reform the federal bureaucracy to improve managerial innovation.

Cronin, John, and Robert F. Kennedy, Jr. *The Riverkeepers: Two Activists Fight to Reclaim Our Environment as a Basic Human Right.* New York: Scribner, 1999. A case study of unwise Interior Department practices that threaten rivers. Examines these practices in the context of American environmental policy.

Kennedy, Robert F., Jr. *Crimes Against Nature.* New York: HarperCollins, 2005. Spirited attack on environmental problems, which are exacerbated by Department of Interior policies.

Utley, Robert M., and Barry Mackintosh. *The Department of Everything Else: Highlights of Interior History.* Washington, D.C.: Department of the Interior, 1989. Although this is an official history of the department, it nonetheless contains much useful information.

Zinn, Howard. *A People's History of the United States: 1492-Present.* New York: Harper Perennial Modern Classics, 2005. A liberal interpretation of American history, which sheds some light on the difficulties in U.S. policies, including those involving public land use.

SEE ALSO: Education, U.S. Department of; Environmental Protection Agency; Labor, U.S. Department of; Land laws; Mineral resources; Native American trade; Supreme Court and land law; Teapot Dome scandal.

Internal migration

DEFINITION: Large-scale demographic shifts within America caused by people moving from one region to another

SIGNIFICANCE: The movement of people from rural to urban or suburban communities, as well as racial, age, and other groups moving from one part of the country to another, has significant economic and political consequences. When regions gain or lose workers, consumers, and voting power, their business interests may prosper or decline as a result.

Internal migration began in North America after the earliest immigration of hunters from Siberia across a land bridge into what would become Alaska. Gradually, during the last Ice Age and the centuries that followed it, the peoples who came to be categorized as Native Americans made their way through Alaska and the interior of western Canada or along the Pacific Coast into the middle of North

America. Thousands of years later, other peoples, the Aleuts and the Inuit, crossed the Bering Strait and then migrated to make their homes in western and northern Alaska. Even later, about 400 C.E., Polynesians arrived at the Hawaiian Islands and eventually migrated throughout them.

After the European discovery of America, the greatest internal migration of Europeans and their descendants within the present-day United States came with the expansion of settlement in the thirteen British colonies that eventually emerged on the Atlantic Coast. Traveling often up river valleys and eventually through Appalachian passes, European Americans had made homes for themselves in Tennessee and Kentucky by the time the American Revolution started in 1775. When Britain and the United States formally made peace in 1783, the new nation stretched west to the Mississippi River, and settlers soon filled the land.

A family heads to California from Muskogee, Oklahoma, in 1939. (Library of Congress)

EARLY MOVEMENT

When European Americans moved west, surviving Native Americans often had to move ahead of them. That pattern continued after the Louisiana Purchase in 1803, the Mexican cession in 1848, and other territorial acquisitions by the United States, until most Native Americans in the forty-eight contiguous states were confined to tribal lands much smaller than and often significantly different from the lands their ancestors had hunted or farmed.

Besides Native Americans, the other big group whose members involuntarily migrated consisted of African Americans. After the first African slaves arrived at Jamestown in 1619, slavery eventually spread throughout the thirteen British colonies but was most common on plantations from Maryland to Georgia. When cotton replaced tobacco as the biggest cash crop in the South and European Americans moved westward, slavery spread all the way to Texas. The legal importation of enslaved Africans ended in 1808, but until the American Civil War, the domestic market for slaves and their consequent migration continued in the states where slavery was still legal.

Although people born in the United States were migrating westward, even as far as the Pacific Coast, Chinese people were crossing the Pacific Ocean eastward to San Francisco. Those who did not remain there moved elsewhere in California and other Western states, often building railroads or working in mines. Other Asian immigrants, including the Japanese, would later arrive in the United States and migrate internally.

The biggest influx of immigrants at the time, however, was from Europe. Although some stayed in the Northeastern cities where they had disembarked, many others moved west, becoming part of the mainstream of migration in America. By 1890, there was no more frontier in the United States, except for Alaska, but immigrants kept arriving, most notably during the late nineteenth and early twentieth centuries from southern and eastern Europe. If they did not stay in the cities where they landed, they usually migrated to other industrial cities, because by then America was shifting its employment opportunities from agriculture to industry.

LATER MOVEMENT

By the beginning of the twentieth century, the United States was becoming heavily industrialized, and agriculture was becoming more scientific. The lure of jobs in factories drew Americans away from farms and into cities. For African Americans, opportunities opened during a lull in immigration during World War I, and many of them left the rural South by train for industrial cities, sometimes southern ones but more often ones in the North, where racial segregation was not as solidly embedded in law. European Americans also left farms in the Midwest and the South early in the twentieth century, pushed out by poverty, agricultural efficiency, and the hope of bettering themselves in a city. Although the Great Depression of the 1930's slowed the movement of Americans from farms to cities, a severe drought in the southern Great Plains combined with unwise farming to create the Dust Bowl in the Oklahoma Panhandle and parts of the adjacent states and thus to lead thousands of families to leave their homes in the hope of working in California fields.

With World War II came an end to economic depression, and with peace there came a massive movement of families, mostly European American, from cities proper to their suburbs—a movement made possible by an abundance of automobiles and good roads. There also came eventually, despite notable growth in the population of Alaska, a trend of moving away from areas with cold winters. Thus, for example, partly because of air-conditioning, the populations of Florida and southern Arizona grew enormously. The national population continued to grow into the twenty-first century, in large measure because of massive immigration from Mexico and Central America, sometimes legal but often illegal. Many of those new residents of the United States moved well beyond the Mexican border, thus contributing their part to the long story of American internal migration.

Victor Lindsey

FURTHER READING

Flanders, Stephen A. *Atlas of American Migration*. New York: Facts on File, 1998. With numerous visual aids and statistics, Flanders presents for a general audience both immigration and internal migration from the Stone Age to the late twentieth century.

Gregory, James N. *The Southern Diaspora: How the Great Migrations of Black and White Southerners Transformed America*. Chapel Hill: University of North Carolina Press, 2005. Integrated, thematically organized study of two massive twentieth century migrations from the traditional South and their political, social, and religious effects.

Longino, Charles F., Jr. *Retirement Migration in America*. Houston: Vacation, 1995. Statistically rich study of the movement of elderly Americans after their retirement.

Rodriguez, Marc S., ed. *Repositioning North American Migration History: New Directions in Modern Continental Migration, Citizenship, and Community*. Rochester, N.Y.: University of Rochester Press, 2004. Migrating, building a community, and forming a nation are the ideas linking these scholarly essays.

Turner, Frederick Jackson. *The Frontier in American History*. New York: H. Holt, 1920. The first chapter is a reprint of the classic paper "The Significance of the Frontier in American History," which Turner presented in 1893 at the World's Columbian Exhibition in Chicago.

SEE ALSO: Automotive industry; Bracero program; California gold rush; Dust Bowl; Farm labor; Great Migration; Immigration; Land laws; Railroads; Slave era.

Internal Revenue Code

THE LAW: Main domestic statutory tax law of the United States
DATE: 1986
SIGNIFICANCE: The Internal Revenue Code is so complex that it forces businesses to spend large amounts on tax-related accounting, creating a large negative impact on business in the United States.

Formally known as the Internal Revenue Code of 1986, this law covers the statutory excise taxes, gift taxes, estate taxes, payroll taxes, and income taxes in the United States. The income taxes are divided into corporate and individual taxes and are the largest sources of revenue for the United States. As such they have the greatest impact on the economic aspects of business of any laws in the United States.

Tax laws were not codified prior to 1874. Although revisions occur almost every year, the major comprehensive revisions have occurred in 1926, 1939, 1954, and 1986. The structure of the income tax code in the first decade of the twenty-first century continues to be the 1986 version, an effort made in the administration of President Ronald Reagan. As a result of all these changes, the United States has the most complex tax structure of any country in the world. It is widely acknowledged that the complexity of this code has a major impact on the conduct of business in the United States. Although this complexity has spawned a massive accounting industry in the United States, the main impact on business is negative, no matter what the rate of taxation is.

The federal income tax is categorized as a progressive tax, in which those with higher incomes pay a higher percentage in taxes than those with lower incomes. This is justified on the theory that those with higher incomes are better able to pay the higher taxes. Some economists and most upper-income individuals argue that such higher rates are unfair and act as an impediment to the maximum economic growth of the country. Supporters of the progressive features of the income tax maintain that the drag on economic activity from the progressive features of tax is not significant.

Despite complaints from corporations and upper income individuals that the progressive feature of the income tax is unfair, many corporations and individuals have had such sufficient influence on Congress to have had provisions enacted that enable them to avoid paying tax on a substantial amount of their income. These provisions have produced much of the complexity in the income tax code and have frequently led to calls for reform. However, these calls for reform have so far proved ineffective.

Richard L. Wilson

FURTHER READING

Abrams, Howard E., and Richard L. Doernberg. *Federal Corporate Taxation*. 6th ed. New York: Foundation Press, 2008.

Baiman, Ron, Heather Boushey, and Dawn Saunders. *Political Economy and Contemporary Capitalism*. Armonk, N.Y.: M. E. Sharpe, 2000.

Willis, James. *Explorations in Macroeconomics*. 5th ed. Redding, Calif.: North West Publishing, 2002.

SEE ALSO: 401(k) retirement plans; Income tax, corporate; Income tax, personal; Taxation; Treasury, U.S. Department of the.

International Brotherhood of Teamsters

IDENTIFICATION: Labor union representing truckers and other workers responsible for transporting, storing, and handling goods

DATE: Founded in August, 1903

SIGNIFICANCE: The International Brotherhood of Teamsters has been instrumental in improving working conditions for laborers in numerous sectors of the business community and in standardizing contracts and promoting fair treatment for all workers.

Throughout the nineteenth century and into the early years of the twentieth century, most of the goods and merchandise manufactured and sold were transported in wagons drawn by teams of horses or mules. The drivers of these wagons were known as teamsters. Their work made their lives harsh and financially insecure. The average teamster worked a twelve- to eighteen-hour day and earned on the average $2 for the long day's work. The workweek could easily be seven days. Teamsters were financially responsible for any merchandise that was lost or damaged and also for accounts that were not collectible on delivery.

In 1901, in an effort to improve their working conditions and their lives, a group of teamsters organized the Team Drivers International Union (TDIU). The organization had a membership of seventeen hundred. However, factions developed during the first year. In 1902, part of the membership withdrew from the TDIU and formed the Teamsters National Union. Then, in 1903, under the influence of Samuel Gompers, the leader of the American Federation of Labor, the two rival groups reunited. In August of 1903, the International Brotherhood of Teamsters (better known as the Teamsters) was founded at Niagara Falls, New York. Cornelius Shea was chosen as the first general president.

At the time, there were no labor laws to protect workers. Companies used antitrust laws against unions, arguing that work stoppages and strikes interfered with the free operation of the market and affected the prices that consumers paid. In 1905, the Teamsters supported a strike against Montgomery Ward, based in Chicago. The strike lasted for one hundred days, resulted in twenty-one deaths, and cost $1 million, but Montgomery Ward defeated the strikers. The union leaders realized they needed to change their tactics.

AGGRESSIVE LEADERSHIP AND RECRUITMENT

In 1907, Dan Tobin, a member of the Boston Local 25, was elected general president of the Teamsters. He held the office for forty-five years. Tobin provided the aggressive leadership that the union needed to prosper. He immediately began an active campaign to increase and broaden union membership. Large numbers of teamsters from different sectors of business joined the union, including gravel haulers, beer-wagon drivers, milk-wagon drivers, and bakery delivery drivers. The union faced considerable opposition in its desire to represent beer-wagon drivers. The United Brewery Workers seriously objected to their recruitment by the Teamsters and stopped the recruitment in 1913 by appealing to the American Federation of Labor. It was not until 1933 that the Teamsters gained the right to organize the beer drivers.

During this period, the Teamsters began to make some important gains for their membership. The union won strikes and obtained standardized contracts with reduced hours, increased pay, and benefits. However, the battle for nationwide recognition of the union and equality in negotiating with business firms was not easily won.

MINNEAPOLIS, 1934

In 1934, Minneapolis, Minnesota, one of the major hauling centers in the United States and the major distribution center for the Midwest, had not been effectively organized by the Teamsters. The General Drivers Local 574 undertook the organization. There was intense hostility, especially from the Citizen's Alliance, to the efforts to bring the local workers into the union. In February, Local 574 staged a successful strike at a local coal yard, with the result that several thousand workers joined the union. Many of the companies where the workers were employed refused to recognize the union, however.

On May 16, a general strike was called; demands included recognition of the Teamsters union, the right to represent warehouse and loading bay workers as well as truckers, increased wages and shorter working hours. The Teamsters managed to bring all trucking in Minneapolis to a standstill. The conflict escalated over the next months, reaching its crescendo on July 17, when two union pickets were killed and sixty-five were injured in a conflict with police known as Bloody Friday. Union leaders were arrested on July 31. A protest by almost forty thousand people brought about the release of the leaders. On August 21, the strike ended as the result of mediation. The major union demands were accepted, and the Teamsters union was recognized as the collective bargaining representative of its membership by the business firms.

TRUCKS AND HOFFA

During the early years of Tobin's presidency, the Teamsters were instrumental in advancing the use of "motor trucks" for deliveries. Tobin encouraged horse and wagon companies to train their drivers both to drive and to repair "motor trucks," and he began organizing these drivers. In 1912, Teamsters from the Charles W. Young Company made the first transcontinental delivery of goods by truck. The five-man crew left Philadelphia, Pennsylvania, with three tons of Parrot Brand Olive Soap and drove to Petaluma, California, in ninety-one days.

Although there is evidence that corruption was present in the union almost from its founding, it was particularly during the presidency of Jimmy Hoffa that corruption and links to organized crime became an issue of national importance for the Teamsters. Hoffa stood trial and, after numerous appeals, was convicted and went to prison in 1967. Hoffa was, however, instrumental in winning enactment of the National Master Freight Agreement in 1964. The agreement provided standardized protection and benefits to all Teamsters. The International Brotherhood of Teamsters continues to be a significant force in American business relations, with its workforce, and in American politics.

Shawncey Webb

FURTHER READING

Brody, David. *Workers in Industrial America: Essays on the Twentieth Century Struggle.* New York: Oxford University Press, 1993. Discusses the development of unions, their industrial and political importance, and the Teamsters' interaction with other unions.

International Brotherhood of Teamsters. *One Hundredth Anniversary: A Strong Legacy, a Powerful Future.* Philadelphia: DeLancey, 2003. An official history of the Teamsters that portrays the strengths of the union.

Korth, Philip. *Minneapolis Teamsters Strike of 1934.* East Lansing: Michigan State University Press, 1995. Detailed study of the strike that gained recognition and influence for the Teamsters.

Nicholson, Philip Yale. *Labor's Story in the United States.* Philadelphia: Temple University Press, 2004. Traces the history of labor from revolutionary times and the life of early teamsters as horse drivers; good coverage of late twentieth century Teamster activity. Bibliography, index.

Witwer, David. *Corruption and Reform in the Teamsters Union.* Urbana: University of Illinois Press, 2003. Historical study of how and why the Teamsters were plagued with corruption and efforts to combat it. Numerous perspectives.

SEE ALSO: Hoffa, Jimmy; Labor history; Labor strikes; Organized crime; Trucking industry; United Farm Workers of America; United Food and Commercial Workers; United Mine Workers of America.

International Business Machines

IDENTIFICATION: Information technology company
DATE: Founded in 1896
SIGNIFICANCE: IBM's tabulating machines introduced American business to data processing. In the post-World War II era, IBM helped lead the United States into the computer age.

Herman Hollerith founded the Tabulating Machine Company in 1896 to produce and market punch-card data-processing machines he invented for use by the United States Census Bureau. Numbers encoded by punching holes on rectangular cards at designated positions were read by passing the holes though electric contacts; the cards could then be sorted, counted, and used to calculate various relationships. The 1880 census had taken eight years to complete; his invention permitted the Census Bureau to compile the 1890 census in one year.

In 1911, Hollerith retired and merged his company with one producing scales that calculated the price of items weighed and a second selling employee time clocks, to form the Computing-Tabulating-Recording Corporation. The merger was unprofitable until Thomas J. Watson took over as president in 1914. Watson concentrated the company's efforts on selling punch-card tabulating machines. Watson trained and exhorted his sales force, motivating them to convince corporate leaders that using these machines to store, analyze, and retrieve data would drastically cut their accounting and control costs. Renamed International Business Machines (IBM) in 1924, the company became very profitable. Leasing rather than selling machines, and insisting that only IBM keypunch cards be used, assured the company of continually increasing income during the 1920's.

Always paternalistic toward his workforce, Watson practically guaranteed lifetime employment. He risked bankrupting his company by refusing to fire anyone during the Great Depression. Record-keeping needs generated by the New Deal rescued the firm. Social Security and other governmental agencies leased thousands of machines and bought reams of IBM cards. Companies found they needed the IBM system to record and manage their operations.

During World War II, IBM operated weapons factories. In 1945, left with greatly expanded plants and labor forces, Watson again put his company at risk by retaining all his employees. He set new factories to remodeling punch-card machines returned by the armed forces and directed his salesmen to offer them to small businesses on easy terms, spreading electro-mechanical data processing over yet more of the business world.

COMPUTERS

Although Watson never owned more than 5 percent of the stock in his company, he treated IBM as if it were family property. He assumed his son would follow him as president of the company and made sure that he did. Although reluctant to yield control to Thomas J. Watson, Jr., Watson, Sr., assigned him to oversee the new area of electronics. Watson, Jr., built extensive research facilities and poured billions of dollars into developing computers.

Even before it became a technology leader during the 1960's, IBM outsold its competitors. Watson, Jr., credited his salesforce for his success. Where other companies' representatives often boasted of arcane technical advances to uncomprehending purchasing agents, salespeople trained by Watson, Sr., stressed what computers could do for the buyer.

A woman uses the new IBM personal computer and printer in 1981. IBM was an early leader in the personal computer market. (AP/Wide World Photos)

By the 1960's, IBM had become the dominant manufacturer of mainframe computers, and most of its early competitors had dropped out of the business.

DECLINE AND REVIVAL

The younger Watson suffered a heart attack in 1970 and retired the next year. Although his successors tried to emulate the Watsons' success, the company went into decline. IBM pioneered personal computers in 1981, and the overwhelming majority of personal computers ever built were IBM-PC compatible, but the company fell behind and ultimately abandoned the field.

Company leaders imitated Watson, Sr., without understanding why he did certain things. Even during the 1990's, the company insisted that salespeople wear dark-colored suits and white shirts. During the 1920's, a decade when workmen wore work clothes and only managers wore business suits, salespeople wearing suits could talk as equals with their customers. By the 1990's, however, as casual clothing became prevalent, the IBM salespeople's dress code seemed anachronistic.

By 1993, the company was in distress. More than 100,000 employees were laid off, reversing a policy dating from IBM's beginnings. Its mainframe computers were becoming obsolete, and critics asked whether the company was too big to compete in a fast-changing market. Rumors circulated that the company would be dismantled, with various divisions sold off separately. Instead, in April, 1993, the Board of Directors hired Louis V. Gerstner, Jr., the first chief executive from outside the company. Gerstner had held senior positions at food company RJR Nabisco and American Express; like Watson, he understood how to sell services as well as goods.

Gerstner insisted on keeping the company together and refocusing its activities around its information-technology roots. Layoffs continued in the first years, as he restructured the organization. Research paid off, and IBM reclaimed its position at the leading edge of the computer world. The company got favorable worldwide publicity for its turnaround in 1997, when its "Deep Blue" chess machine, a supercomputer IBM developed using artificial intelligence research, defeated the reigning chess world champion. The champion wanted a rematch, but IBM retired the game-playing machine and concentrated on building business- and research-oriented computers. Like Watson, Gerstner had salespeople emphasize customer service first, technology second. When Gerstner retired in 2002, IBM was once again an outstanding business enterprise and a leader in its field.

Milton Berman

FURTHER READING

Gerstner, Louis V., Jr. *Who Says Elephants Can't Dance?* New York: Harper Collins, 2002. Examination of how IBM declined and then revived.

Maney, Kevin. *The Maverick and His Machine: Thomas Watson, Sr., and the Making of IBM.* New York: John Wiley & Sons, 2003. Using full access to IBM's archives, Maney paints a nuanced picture of IBM under Watson, Sr.

Rodgers, William. *THINK: A Biography of the Watsons and IBM.* New York: Stein and Day, 1969. Unauthorized biography that Watson, Jr. calls the best life of his father.

Tedlow, Richard S. *The Watson Dynasty: The Fiery Reign and Troubled Legacy of IBM's Founding Father and Son.* New York: Harper Business, 2003. Harvard Business School professor analyzes the impact of the Watsons on IBM.

Watson, Thomas J., Jr., and Peter Petre. *Father, Son &*

Co.: My Life at IBM and Beyond. New York: Bantam Books, 1990. Describes his relations with his father and his work at IBM.

See also: Antitrust legislation; Apple; Computer industry; Gates, Bill; Internet.

International economics and trade

Definition: Exchange of commodities and currency among the governments, corporations, and residents of different nations, as well as the economic principles governing that exchange

Significance: With the advent of a national reliance on significant importing and exporting, the changes in international economics and the world trade policy have been important influences on manufacturing, on agriculture, and on employment. As the United States interacts economically with other countries, the monetary systems and policies, the labor standards or lack thereof, and the environmental standards and investment policies of these countries have the potential to affect conditions in the United States and to improve or worsen the domestic economy.

Trade in an international economy offers many advantages to participating countries. International trade makes a wider variety of products available to consumers. It has the potential to increase demand for products, thus increasing production, which creates a greater number of jobs. International trading provides a market for the surplus production of a nation. It is also procompetitive. Trade brings a greater level of competition into the market and eliminates monopolistic control of local markets. In addition, trade may have important effects on the diffusion and development of technology. International trade introduces technological advances into a larger market. This expansion of the market may also serve to stimulate greater research and development of technological advances.

International trade also has financial advantages for the trading partners. Trade stimulates national economies and thereby raises real income that in turn increases levels of savings. This situation then makes a greater amount of funds available for investment.

Although international trade in a free market, international economy provides many benefits to individual nations, there are also areas of concern. International trade enhances interdependency of countries and makes each country more vulnerable to the effects of natural disasters, political upheavals, and financial mismanagement that occur in the other countries. Labor standards and environmental standards are areas of potential problems. Products from countries with lower standards may have much lower prices and be more affordable than those produced in higher-wage environmentally conscious countries. Import of such products without high tariffs may reduce domestic manufacturing and therefore eliminate jobs.

Certain moral considerations also become issues in an international economy. Questions include whether it is morally correct to purchase goods made by exploited workers. Without international safety standards, international trade may pose serious health threats. Proponents of international cooperation and trade have addressed these issues by the creation of international organizations such as the World Trade Organization to police and regulate international trading.

History

International trade has a long history, going back to the early trade routes of the Roman Empire and before. However, until well into the twentieth century, trade was conducted on a country-to-country basis. Each country acted as an independent agent; there were no general trade agreements and no international control of trade. Developed countries imposed high tariffs and quotas on foreign goods and were primarily focused on protecting their domestic economies. Colonization of underdeveloped countries occurred more often than trade between them and developed countries. Countries followed a policy of self-sufficiency and avoided interdependence with other nations.

Until 1934, the United States followed a protectionist trade policy, using high tariffs and quotas. American exports fell significantly as other countries, primarily European, levied high tariffs against American goods in acts of retaliation. In 1934, the Reciprocal Trade Agreements Act (RTAA) was passed, giving the executive branch the power to reduce tariffs for the first time. The agreement lowered tariffs equally with the United States' trading partners. By the early 1940's, the United States had entered into bilateral trading agreements with approximately twenty-five countries, primarily European. These agreements were the first step in an effort of international economic cooperation. After World War II, relations between the United States and Europe moved further in the direction of political and economic cooperation.

THE BRETTON WOODS CONFERENCE

In the years following World War II, a new attitude of alliance and cooperation developed between the United States and its trading neighbors. The war had caused serious devastation and severely affected the economies of many countries. In an effort to speed up the postwar recovery of these nations, delegates from forty-four Allied nations met for the United Nations Monetary and Financial

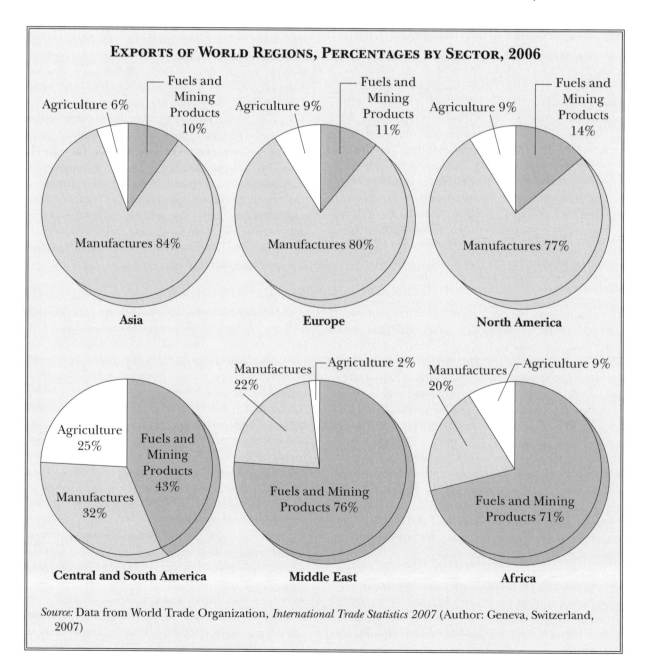

EXPORTS OF WORLD REGIONS, PERCENTAGES BY SECTOR, 2006

Asia: Agriculture 6%, Fuels and Mining Products 10%, Manufactures 84%

Europe: Agriculture 9%, Fuels and Mining Products 11%, Manufactures 80%

North America: Agriculture 9%, Fuels and Mining Products 14%, Manufactures 77%

Central and South America: Agriculture 25%, Fuels and Mining Products 43%, Manufactures 32%

Middle East: Manufactures 22%, Agriculture 2%, Fuels and Mining Products 76%

Africa: Manufactures 20%, Agriculture 9%, Fuels and Mining Products 71%

Source: Data from World Trade Organization, *International Trade Statistics 2007* (Author: Geneva, Switzerland, 2007)

Conference from July 1 to July 22, 1944. The conference was held in Bretton Woods, New Hampshire, and is usually designated as the Bretton Woods Conference. The conference's purpose was to establish international regulation of economic activity. The conference successfully established the International Monetary Fund (IMF) to regulate the international financial system through a set of rules, procedures, and institutions, and the International Bank for Reconstruction and Development (IBRD), later part of the World Bank.

The conference also proposed the creation of the International Trade Organization to institute rules to govern international trade and to regulate trading activity. In March of 1948 at the United Nations Conference on Trade and Employment held in Havana, Cuba, there was agreement to establish the International Trade Organization, but the United States Senate failed to ratify the agreement and the organization was never established.

THE GENERAL AGREEMENT ON TARIFFS AND TRADE

Although the negotiations for the International Trade Organization were taking place, fifteen of the nations began separate negotiations on a treaty to procure more immediate reductions in tariffs. The implementation of the treaty was to become a function of the International Trade Organization. When the attempt to found the International Trade Organization failed, this treaty, the General Agreement on Tariffs and Trade (GATT), was the only mechanism in place to regulate trade. The reduction of all barriers to international trade, including tariffs, quotas, and subsidies, became the goal of GATT. This objective was to be accomplished through a series of agreements.

On January 1, 1948, twenty-three countries had signed the GATT agreement. The treaty was based on the concept of the unconditional most-favored nation. This concept means that any condition used in relation to a most-favored nation, one that has the least restrictions, must be used with all trading nations. The signatory nations of the GATT met at various time intervals in what were referred to as rounds to eliminate further trade barriers and to open the world market. Between 1949 and 1993, there were seven rounds of GATT. The Uruguay Round of 1986-1993 was particularly important for its achievements. In this round, the signatory nations created the Agreement on Agriculture, lowering tariffs and subsidies on agriculture, a trade area that had always been exempted. The round also created the World Trade Organization (WTO).

WORLD TRADE ORGANIZATION

The World Trade Organization was created on January 1, 1995, with seventy-five GATT signatory nations and the European Communities as founding members. During the next two years, the fifty-two remaining GATT signatory nations joined the WTO. The Democratic Republic of the Congo, which became a member in 1997, was the last of the GATT signatories to join. Non-GATT nations subsequently joined the WTO, bringing the membership to 153. This membership accounts for 95 percent of the total world trade. Unlike GATT, which was never an organization but rather a group of treaty signatories operating as a de facto organization, the WTO is an actual organization with a formal structure.

In general, the WTO deals with the rules of trade between nations. The goal of WTO is to improve the well-being of the people of its member countries by lowering trade barriers and making an arena for trade negotiations available. The mission of the WTO is a continual advance toward an ever freer trade environment and an open international market. The WTO watches over approximately sixty different agreements that are classified as international legal texts. Its responsibilities include negotiating and instigating new trade agreements, monitoring the adherence of its members to all of the WTO agreements that have been signed and ratified, and settling trade disputes among members.

The Uruguay Round, in which the WTO was created, also saw the signatory nations sign agreements in a broader range of trade activity. Four new areas of trade issues were addressed by four new agreements. The General Agreement on Trade in Service (GATS) brought the multilateral trading system into the service sector. The Trade Related Aspects of Intellectual Property Rights Agreement (TRIPS) established minimum standards for a considerable number of intellectual property rights. The Sanitary and Phyto-Sanitary Agreement (SPS) set up restrictions on member nations' policies regarding animal and plant health and food safety. The Agreement on Technical Barriers to Trade (TBT) dealt with the elimination of obstacles of trade that might result from technical negotiations and standards. The TRIPS and TBT Agreements entered into force in 1994; the GATS and SPS Agreements did so in 1995.

In 2001, the WTO began a new round of negotiations, the Doha Development Agenda or Doha Round. These negotiations are addressing tariffs, nontariff trade barriers, and agriculture, all traditional areas of trade negotiation, but the round is also focusing on the issues of labor standards, environmental concerns, and patents.

THE UNITED STATES AND TRADE

The United States has been particularly active in encouraging the implementation of free trade and in opening its markets to developing countries. An early effort at opening markets was made during the 1980's with the Caribbean Basin Initiative providing low tariff rates on a number of products from most of the Caribbean Basin nations. In 1991, the Andean Trade Preference Act (ATPA) extended tariff-free access to American markets for a substantial variety of products from Bolivia, Peru, Colombia, and Ecuador. In 1994, the North American Free Trade Agreement (NAFTA) went into effect. The agreement implemented a program for phasing out tariffs on products traded between the United States, Canada, and Mexico.

Shawncey Webb

FURTHER READING

Bergsten, C. Fred, ed. *The United States and the World Economy.* Washington, D.C.: Institute for International Economics, 2005. This excellent collection of essays written by senior staff members of the Institute for International Economics focuses on the changing role of the United States in the world economy and the need for changes in American trade policies. It also treats the impact of world trade on the American domestic economy.

Bernstein, William S. *How Trade Shaped the World.* New York: Atlantic Monthly Press, 2008. Bernstein recounts the history of trade from its primitive beginnings as barter to its complex modern forms. The historical focus adds a cultural aspect to the consideration of trade and broadens the reader's view of trade and its importance.

Dam, Kenneth W. *The Rules of the Global Game: A New Look at U.S. International Economic Policymaking.* Chicago: University of Chicago Press, 2004. This in-depth treatment of U.S. policy making is useful for both students of economics and general readers. Dam explains how international economics operates, how policy is determined, and who makes decisions regarding policy. Chapters on foreign investment, the international monetary system, and foreign markets emphasize the impact of international economics on the United States.

Rivera-Batiz, Luis A., and Maria A. Oliva. *International Trade: Theory, Strategies, and Evidence.* New York: Oxford University Press, 2004. This detailed technical study of international trade is best suited for readers with an understanding of the basics of how international economics works. Chapter 16 is excellent for understanding the benefits and problems related to preferential trade agreements. Part 6 presents a very complete discussion of the role of the World Trade Organization in international trade.

Rosenberg, Emily S. *Spreading the American Dream: American Economic and Cultural Expansion, 1890-1945.* New York: Hill & Wang, 1982. This study is useful for understanding the role of the government in the development of the U.S. domestic market and how the United States extended much of its economic practices and culture throughout the world.

Schott, Jeffrey J., ed. *Free Trade Agreements: U.S. Strategies and Priorities.* Washington, D.C.: Institute for International Economics, 2004. Edited by a member of the U.S. delegation to the Tokyo Round of the GATT agreements, this study is one of the most thorough presentations of the United States' participation in free trade agreements. It elucidates why free trade agreements are replacing tariffs and deals extensively with NAFTA. It also discusses U.S. free trade agreements with Asian and African countries.

SEE ALSO: Asian financial crisis of 1997; Bretton Woods Agreement; Canadian trade with the United States; Chinese trade with the United States; European trade with the United States; Export-Import Bank of the United States; General Agreement on Tariffs and Trade; Japanese trade with the United States; Latin American trade with the United States; Mexican trade with the United States; Multinational corporations; Tariffs; World Trade Organization.

International Ladies' Garment Workers' Union

IDENTIFICATION: Labor union for both male and female workers in the women's garment manufacturing industry
DATE: Founded in 1900
SIGNIFICANCE: The International Ladies' Garment Workers' Union was a workers' union for the women's clothing industry that played a major role in the American labor movement in the twentieth century.

The International Ladies' Garment Workers' Union (ILGWU) was formed in 1900 to represent workers in sweatshops where women's clothes were manufactured. Its members were mainly immigrant women, particularly Jewish and Italian, but also included men. Most of the factories were concentrated in the garment district of New York City, but the union activities were nationwide. The ILGWU began to make significant strides in organizing when the tragic fire at the Triangle Shirtwaist Company in 1911 killed 146 workers.

During the mid-1920's, the union suffered from internal disagreements. David Dubinsky assumed the presidency of the union in 1932, when its dues-paying membership had fallen to 32,000. Dubinsky was a Jewish Russian immigrant, who after being arrested in Russia for belonging to a union, had fled to the United States in 1911, become a cloak maker, and joined the ILGWU. While president, he also served as vice president of the American Federation of Labor (AFL).

After the passage of the National Industrial Recovery Act in 1933, which protected the right of workers to organize, membership in the ILGWU grew, reaching 300,000 at the end of the Great Depression. In 1935, the ILGWU joined the Congress of Industrial Organizations (CIO; originally the Committee for Industrial Organization). However, in 1938, Dubinsky resigned from the CIO over policy differences and led the ILGWU as an independent union for two years before the union rejoined the AFL. The labor leader again became a vice president of the AFL. After the AFL and CIO merged in 1955, Dubinsky served as a member of the executive board of the AFL-CIO, energetically fighting against corruption. During World War II, he was instrumental in helping found the American Labor Party but later left because of its communist influence and formed the Liberal Party.

After World War II, the ILGWU lost much of its membership as manufacturers shifted production overseas, and the union's membership changed from Italians and Jews to Latinos, African Americans, and Asian Americans. However, in the years just after Dubinsky's retirement in 1966, membership was 450,000. In 1995, the union merged with the Amalgamated Clothing and Textile Workers Union (ACTWU) to form the Union of Needletrades, Industrial and Textile Employees (UNITE). In 2004, UNITE merged with the Hotel Employees and Restaurant Employees Union (HERE) to form UNITE HERE.

Frederick B. Chary

FURTHER READING
Daniel, Cletus E. *Culture of Misfortune: An Interpretive History of Textile Unionism in the United States.* Ithaca, N.Y.: ILR Press, 2001.
Parmet, Robert D. *The Master of Seventh Avenue: David Dubinsky and the American Labor Movement.* New York: New York University Press, 2005.
Taylor, Gus. *Look for the Union Label: A History of the International Ladies' Garment Workers' Union.* Armonk, N.Y.: Sharpe, 1995.

SEE ALSO: AFL-CIO; Labor history; Labor strikes; Lewis, John L.; Minimum wage laws; Sewing machines; Triangle Shirtwaist Company fire.

International Longshoremen's Association

IDENTIFICATION: Labor union representing those who load and unload ships' cargoes
DATE: Founded in 1892
SIGNIFICANCE: The work of longshoremen—loading and off-loading ships—plays a vital role in moving goods into the marketplace. The International Longshoremen's Association has helped these workers attain better pay and working conditions.

Daniel Keefe, a tugboat worker from Chicago, formed the first local (chapter) of the Association of Lumber Handlers in 1877. Facing hostility from Chicago industrialists, he worked to improve working conditions and wages for dock workers. Membership in the local grew, and other midwestern locals were organized. In 1892, delegates from eleven ports met in Detroit, adopted the bylaws of the Chicago local, and took the name National Longshoremen's Association of the United States. Because of increasing Canadian membership, the name was changed in 1895 to International Longshoremen's Association (ILA), and that year the union affiliated with the American Federation of Labor (AFL). At the end of the century, the ILA had approximately fifty thousand members, and by 1905, membership had doubled. In 1911, there were more than 307 locals, and more were forming at ports on the East, West, and Gulf Coasts. The ILA actively recruited members and formed locals in the Port of New York City, the largest in the country by cargo handled and number of longshoremen.

As the union grew, power shifted from the Midwest to the Port of New York. Joseph Ryan from New York Local 791 became ILA president. Under Ryan's presidency, the union continued to grow but also experienced major problems. In 1934, West Coast longshoremen revolted against the ILA and formed a new union. Consequently, the ILA lost a significant number of members, as well as its power on the West Coast.

In New York, a wage agreement negotiated by Ryan was not accepted by union members, prompting a walkout. In 1951, Ryan renegotiated a larger wage increase that was also rejected. The resultant strike lasted eleven days. A wage increase above that in Ryan's agreement was one outcome of the strike; the other was an investigation of the ILA. New York governor Thomas Dewey ordered a full investigation of the ILA by the state crime commission. Hear-

The emblem of the International Longshoremen's Association, from around 1901. (Library of Congress)

ings were highly publicized, and the media portrayed the waterfront as being run by criminals. The Oscar-winning film *On the Waterfront* (1954) provided graphic images of gang activity and rampant corruption on the docks. Although the union worked to eliminate the criminal elements, it was suspended from the AFL in August, 1953. The AFL created the International Brotherhood of Longshoremen (IBL) to replace the ILA, but longshoremen voted to stay in the ILA.

When the IBL was dissolved in 1959, the ILA was readmitted to the AFL. During the 1960's and 1970's, union president Thomas "Teddy" Gleeson negotiated a series of contracts that acknowledged the advent of automation and containerization. He developed rules on containers, guaranteed annual income, and job security programs. Although the amount of cargo handled on the docks continues to increase as a result of containers and new technology, the number of union members has decreased. However, in a global economy, technology-enhanced longshoremen remain essential to worldwide commerce.

Marcia B. Dinneen

FURTHER READING

Kimeldorf, Howard. *Battling for American Labor.* Berkeley: University of California Press, 1999.

Nelson, Bruce. *Workers on the Waterfront.* Urbana: University of Illinois Press, 1988.

SEE ALSO: AFL-CIO; International Brotherhood of Teamsters; Labor history; Labor strikes; Shipping industry.

Internet

DEFINITION: Worldwide computer network, driven by shared protocols allowing different systems to exchange information

DATE: Internet protocols published December, 1974; implemented, January, 1983

SIGNIFICANCE: As the Internet has expanded, it has fostered an explosive and self-generating wealth of textual, audio, visual, and multimedia resources that have made possible an exceptional rise in U.S. labor productivity.

At the middle of the twentieth century, computers were large, stand-alone machines for data processing. If connected, however, their productive capacity increased considerably. During the 1960's, efficient and economical means for connecting them emerged using packet switching. Designed by scientists in the United States and Great Britain, this method operated in digital rather than analog mode. A distributed system of nodes transmitted messages that a sender broke down into packets of data-bits and a recipient subsequently reassembled.

Within the U.S. Department of Defense, the Advanced Research Projects Agency (ARPA) operated. It funded a project that by the end of 1969 connected four computers at research centers in California and Utah. Named ARPANET, within a decade the project included nearly two hundred hosts in and outside the United States. This network formed the original backbone of the larger network dubbed the Internet. Further increases in size prompted division of the network into "domains," such as .gov, .edu, .org, and .com. Financial speculation in the latter domain provoked a recession at the end of the twentieth century due to a dot-com bubble.

The most popular feature of ARPANET was its ability to transmit electronic notes or messages, later known as e-mail. Additional networks emerged in the United States and various countries. A commercial network, CompuServe, appeared in 1975 as a publicly traded, timeshare service company. The network was changing fundamentally. From a publicly funded, data-processing operation at specialized institutions, it was becoming a commercial information and communications medium with a mass market.

A new challenge arose, the interconnecting of these networks through an "internetwork." ARPANET developed a set of transmission and reception protocols for such internetworking, beginning operation in 1983. When adapted to "internet" protocols, computers could enter the system and access machines similarly adapted. A vehicle for accessing networked information, "the Internet" came also to mean the totality of this information.

INTERNET ACCESS AND USAGE, 2006

Number of adults who

- Have Internet access at home: 142.1 million
- Have Internet access at work: 80.6 million
- Used the Internet in the last 30 days at home: 123.1 million
- Used the Internet in the last 30 days at work: 69.1 million

Source: Data from the *Statistical Abstract of the United States, 2008* (Washington, D.C.: Department of Commerce, Economics and Statistics Administration, Bureau of the Census, Data User Services Division, 2008)

POPULAR DIFFUSION

The physical attributes of computers radically changed. From large, hugely expensive machines operated by specialists, they became smaller, relatively less costly, and more amenable to a wider number of users. During the late 1970's, microcomputers appeared, often as kits for assembly. In 1977, Apple Computer (later known as Apple) launched a desktop computer with a user friendliness that made it widely popular. The iconic form of a "personal" computer emerged: a television monitor set on a processor, operated by an attached typewriter keyboard. To compete with the growing market for microcomputers, International Business Machines (IBM), a behemoth of the old-style machines, marketed its first PC (personal computer) in 1981.

The creation of smaller computers, inaugurating a radical increase in the number and extent of users and networks, was due to microprocessors. Tiny transistor chips replaced older, cabinet-sized processors. Over three decades, from the early 1970's, the bit capacity of computers doubled every decade, greatly magnifying operating capacity and radically reducing production costs. Intel was a leading innovator in ever-denser chip capacity. Throughout the 1980's, computer production, use, and networking achieved a global reach. The IBM-PC supported further networking, because it used an operating system licensed from Microsoft that penetrated most national and international markets. During this period, commercial Internet service providers, such as Netcom and UUNET, appeared.

GLOBAL PROFUSION

Ever smaller devices (laptop, hand-held) at steadily declining prices expanded the number of computers worldwide to over one billion in the first decade of the twenty-first century. Advanced in developed and developing countries, the Internet achieved a global scale, economic impact, and cultural dimension never imagined. The Internet activated a self-generating wealth of textual, audio, visual, and multimedia resources. Its technologies prompted an exceptional rise in U.S. labor productivity.

A key to this enrichment was the World Wide Web (WWW), released in 1992 by the Geneva-based European Organization for Nuclear Research. Using "markup" language, it created enriched or hypertext documents that embedded various media. Web browsers emerged to find and use such documents. The most prominent browser became Microsoft's Internet Explorer. Search engines indexed Web content, allowing subject keyword searching. Initially, Yahoo! led in this service. However, in 1998, Google improved "hit" accuracy by tracking frequency of site connections rather than text phrasing. A magnet of advertising revenue, the company capitalized more than a billion dollars in its initial public offering.

The Defense Department eventually discontinued its connection with the Internet. In 1990, the National Science Foundation Network (NSFNet) replaced ARPANET as the Internet backbone. The administration of the Internet has remained resolutely noncentralized and emphatically participatory. Open standards develop via deliberations of the Internet Engineering Task Force (IETF), founded in 1985, which is part of the Internet Society, a professional association. The Internet Assigned Numbers Authority (IANA) is managed under contract from the U.S. Department of Commerce by the Internet Corporation for Assigned Names and Numbers (ICANN).

Within a quarter century of its beginnings, the Internet was operating throughout the world. Its speed and economy wrought a socioeconomic impact similar to those of automobiles and electricity. Generating exceptional increases in productivity, the Internet became the lifeblood of globalization. From it has arisen a global culture that emphasizes egalitarian, participatory, and enterprising values.

Edward A. Riedinger

FURTHER READING

Abbate, Janet. *Inventing the Internet.* Cambridge, Mass.: MIT Press, 1999. Narrates technical developments of the Internet and its creators, examining its design and use as a product of varying sociocultural contexts. Includes bibliography.

Burman, Edward. *Shift! The Unfolding Internet: Hype, Hope, and History.* Hoboken, N.J.: John Wiley & Sons, 2003. Views the creation and application of the Internet within the framework of "paradigm shifts" that result from scientific revolutions. The consequences are as penetrating as the development of aviation, wireless communication, cinema, television, and electricity.

Hillstrom, Kevin. *The Internet Revolution.* Detroit: Omnigraphics, 2005. Provides a seven-chapter overview of Internet history followed by biographies of principal personalities involved in its technical development and social diffusion. Includes a chronology, illustrations, and bibliography.

Poole, Hilary W., ed. *The Internet: A Historical Encyclopedia*. Santa Barbara, Calif.: ABC-Clio, 2005. Consists of three volumes comprising, respectively, biographies, issues, and chronology. Includes illustrations, glossary, list of acronyms, and article bibliographies.

Schell, Bernadette H. *The Internet and Society: A Reference Handbook*. Santa Barbara, Calif.: ABC-Clio, 2007. Reference work with entries on technical, socioeconomic, cultural, political, and legal consequences, issues, and controversies related to the Internet. Includes organizations, case histories, and chronology.

SEE ALSO: Apple; Computer industry; Dot-com bubble; eBay; E-mail; Gates, Bill; Google; NASDAQ; Online marketing; Telecommunications industry.

Inventions

DEFINITION: Novel products, devices, materials, processes, or techniques, often meant to improve on existing items or to achieve existing goals in a new or superior fashion

SIGNIFICANCE: Inventions drive many segments of the American economy, especially the technology sector, in which novelty is a significant driver of demand. Moreover, invented manufacturing techniques and tools, such as the use of assembly lines to facilitate the division of labor, have transformed the nature of the economy and of nearly all American businesses.

Dissatisfaction with existing artifacts or methods is at the core of all inventions and their applications—innovations. Initially, some new knowledge may prompt an idea of doing or building something. When someone with such an idea also has the requisite skills to put it into practice, the result may be an invention. One invention may lead to another. For instance, were it not for the earlier invention of the integrated circuit (IC) by Robert Norton Noyce in 1959, the modern computer would not have been possible.

Conversely, although a new or useful object or method may be developed to fulfill a specific purpose, the original idea may never be fully realized as a working invention, perhaps because the concept is in some way unrealistic or impractical. Nor are inventions necessarily achieved in the most useful sequence. For instance, the design of parachutes was worked out before the invention of powered flight. Other inventions solve problems for which there is no significant economic demand.

Inventors many have various motivations. Some work for economic gain or prestige, to satisfy their curiosity, or to fulfil an urge to create. Often they work to fulfil an evident group need, as in the case of medicines, vaccines, and medical procedures. National military needs may also drive invention.

There is frequently an inherent conflict between the interests of an inventor and those of the market or society as a whole. For instance, the introduction of robots in industry may lead to unemployment—at least in the short term. Many useful products constitute threats to the environment, as in the case of plasma television sets, which use more power and thus generate more greenhouse gases than earlier models.

Inventions require a wide range of skills beyond the creation of novelty. These include developing the invention to be a stable manufactured product or a useful process, adapting the invention to particular contexts, creating demand for the invention, and delivering it to its potential users.

The dividing lines among inventions, innovations, and discoveries are not clearly drawn. Generally, innovation is the application of invention, the realization of a product based on an invention, the bringing of a product to market. Discovery implies the previous existence of something now identified or determined. Thus, it is not always easy, even for the U.S. Patent and Trademark Office, to determine when an invention is truly new and unique, because an invention often represents a combination of dozens of separate technological advances or changes.

BUSINESS CYCLES

Scientific and technological inventions and new methods of production have significant effects on the national level of economic activity. Inventions and innovations are vital to economic growth and provide the incentive that business needs to invest in research and development in the hope of reducing costs and increasing profits. Major inventions and innovations—including railroads, nuclear power, and the transistor—have provided important stimuli to economic activity, resulting in significant increases in investments that, in turn, have led to business cycle upswings.

To the extent that inventions and their innovative applications, which may be either capital or labor saving, provide a competitive edge to American businesses in domestic and international trade, they are important to individuals, firms, the economy, and the government. By generating increased demand for American products and processes, they increase profitability for business and tax revenues for government. Social progress also depends on inventions to boost social capital—that is, the education, skills, discipline, and work attitudes of the labor force that in turn enhance productivity.

Inventions that may be subject to legal protection via patents may be initially created by one individual or organization and subsequently developed for the market by others, or the entire process may be carried out by one organization, especially a corporate research laboratory. There may be a lengthy hiatus between invention and profit-yielding innovation. For example, the Wright brothers invented powered aircraft in 1903, but profitable scheduled intercity flights in the United States began only in 1933.

ECONOMICS OF INVENTIONS

Especially since the work of economists Joseph A. Schumpeter and Colin Clark, inventions and innovations have been recognized as underlying economic productivity (or efficiency) and growth. Specifically, Austrian economist Schumpeter—who analyzed the role of inventions and innovations most clearly in economic development, business cycles, and the capitalist process—found that the invariant, undisturbed, circular flow of economic activity without innovation would not lead to progress. That unchanging flow may be disrupted by innovation undertaken by a profit-driven entrepreneur. Successful innovations are then imitated by others, driving progress until they become absorbed into a new stable circular-flow pattern.

To Schumpeter and many other economists since, this process forms the essence of economic growth. Standard textbooks on economic principles, most famously those of Paul A. Samuelson, have given increasing space to the role of technological change in economic growth. Indeed, most of them highlight the role that inventions and innovations play in this process by referring to the quality of scientific and engineering knowledge, managerial (organizational) skill, and the rewards for inventions and innovations. Appropriate public policy—say, in protecting the intellectual property of inventors—also plays an important role in encouraging such technological change and thus economic growth.

Each invention or innovation has a different economic significance. The intensity of scientific knowledge cannot be used as a predictor of the economic significance of an invention or innovation. Over time, the most economically successful inventions are generally those that are most useful rather than those that are simply most novel or based on gimmickry. It may be difficult to predict how the benefits of an invention will be distributed among its inventor, users, and imitators.

Science, technology, and invention, linked as they are, all influence overall human progress, including economic advance. At the level of the individual enterprise, invention and innovation are often tantamount to survival if not economic success. For instance, if a pharmaceutical company wants to stay in business, it must bring new drugs or medical procedures to market. Otherwise, when its proprietary products lose their patent protection, generic versions of those products will drastically reduce their value. This explains why the vast majority of inventions have in the past few decades come from industrial research and development laboratories such as those of International Business Machines (IBM). Inventions also tend to cluster in cycles that are often based on technological breakthroughs, such as the integrated circuit microchip.

ECONOMIC IMPACT

Inventions may have economic, social, and intellectual impacts. The most iconic inventions—such as methods for creating fire, the wheel, the clock, writing, and methods of power generation—have altered every material circumstance of life, work, and leisure. They have made it possible for human societies to evolve. The United States has progressed from comprising agricultural and mining communities to industrial ones to service-driven postindustrial economies as a result of such revolutionary inventions.

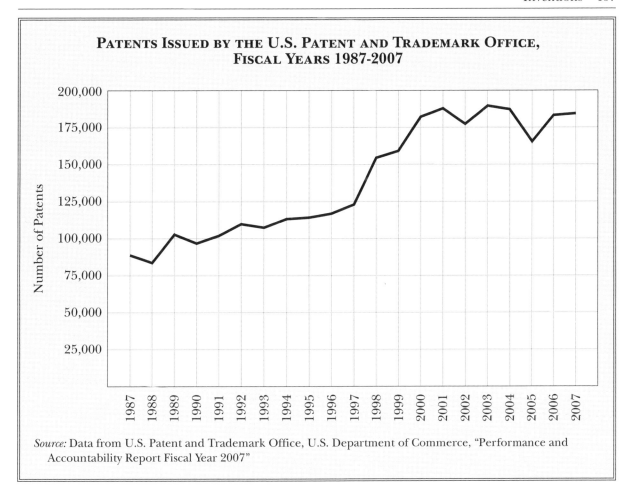

PATENTS ISSUED BY THE U.S. PATENT AND TRADEMARK OFFICE, FISCAL YEARS 1987-2007

Source: Data from U.S. Patent and Trademark Office, U.S. Department of Commerce, "Performance and Accountability Report Fiscal Year 2007"

An invention may be labor saving, capital saving, or neutral, depending on whether it tends to lower the relative share of labor, lower the relative share of capital, or leave relative shares unchanged. An example of a labor-saving invention would be automated machines that build robots that can perform a number of the manual and intellectual tasks of wage-earners. An example of a capital-saving invention would be a cheap computer that enables firms to manage their inventories more efficiently, allowing them to avoid investing capital in inventory that sits in warehouses unsold. Any invention, labor or capital saving, that lowers the cost of production can benefit the first competitor who introduces it.

Even though inventions have enabled individuals and entire societies to control their environment and to live healthier and longer lives, there are contrarians who hold that much of the technology underlying inventions, even economically useful ones, is detrimental to humanity. They mention such downsides as the low-level radiation from computers and cell phones, the negative consequences of some chemicals used as drugs, food additives, fertilizers, growth hormones. and so on. They also cite the near-meltdown of Unit 2 of the Three Mile Island nuclear power plant outside Harrisburg, Pennsylvania, in 1979. As elsewhere, the costs and benefits of inventions must be balanced to determine whether the rewards are worth the risks.

COMMERCIALIZATION

Inventors may be inspired to invent through a simple desire to create something new or better—whether out of altruistic, social, or commercial motives. An invention may also result from a combination of these motivations. The entrepreneurial and open spirit of inquiry has thrived in the United States, which embodies a profit-driven, private-ownership, capitalist system. Americans, moreover, often demonstrate a widespread belief that something new is necessarily better than something old. These factors have helped create an economic environment that stimulates inventions and innovations to such an extent that at times it lapses into gimmickry. This explains in part why the U.S. government issues some 100,000 new patents annually. Additionally, there are millions of unpatented minor technological or procedural refinements that typify economic progress.

Although many inventors may be driven by the rewards from commercialization of their products, very few will secure the funding and support often needed to develop and launch a novelty in the marketplace, and fewer still will experience lasting commercial success or the economic reward they may have expected. However, organizations such as inventor associations, clubs, business incubators, think tanks, and even some government agencies can provide the boost private inventors often lack. Entrepreneurship and sensitivity to the demands of the marketplace are typical characteristics of successful inventors, but the process may not be easy. Most great inventors go through countless prototypes, changing their designs innumerable times, as was the case when Edison sought the right noncombustible element to use as the filament of his incandescent lamp.

Inventions are an important example of a "positive externality," that is, a beneficial side-effect enjoyed by those outside a transaction or activity. Unless some of the benefits of these externalities are captured, inventors will be under-rewarded for their creations, and systematic under-rewarding will lead to under-investment in activities that lead to inventions. The latter, together with the other traditional factors of production—natural resources, human resources, physical capital, and social capital—underlie economic growth. However, different societies combine these factors with varying degrees of effectivity. The United States has been particularly effective in its this regard. For example, one important function of the U.S. patent system is to coordinate these factors and ensure that an optimum amount of resources are invested in the process of invention.

Inventions are a public good, in the sense that they can be used by many without being diminished. An addition to a specific innovative inventory does not reduce its productivity, since an individual user will still enjoy its maximum benefits regardless of the number in the market. However, low-quality imitations ("knock-offs") can undermine the original invention's value to its inventor as well as the reputation of the entire class of products in the marketplace. Such imitations may be created through reverse engineering—that is, analyzing the product's component parts to learn how to emulate them or their functions.

LIKELIHOOD OF COMMERCIALIZATION

There are specific characteristics of inventions that increase the likelihood of their successful commercialization. They relate to individual, firm, and industry characteristics, as well as the nature of the inventions themselves. First, there arc advantages to the outside sourcing of new technologies that extend a firm's technological horizon. Outside sourcing increases a firm's knowledge base, and knowledge that is broader in scope allows trial and error processes that are essential to new product development. For instance, the discovery of aspirin as a treatment for heart problems came about through experimentation. Second, a broader scope allows several successful applications to emerge from the same discovery—for instance, the graphical user interface found in all modern computers flowed from research conducted by Xerox PARC and Apple Computer.

Past research has supported the relationship between scope of knowledge and its impact on future invention activities. Thus, all other things being equal, the greater the scope of an invention, the greater the likelihood of its commercialization. Since one of the primary reasons for a firm to pursue innovation is to secure a steady stream of profits (economic rents), initial advantages are considered valuable as they can sometimes form the base for sustainable competitive benefits.

Inventions that are more pioneering enhance commercialization efforts for several reasons. First, the firm seeks to obtain learning-curve advantages by focusing on technologies that are different from those of other firms. The greater the similarity between a new invention and existing competitive technologies, the greater the chance that other firms will be able economically to reverse engineer competing products. Thus, the greatest financial advantages may accrue to firms that create the most novel components and production methods as well as the most novel products. Incremental inventions based on prior skills provide patent protection to a narrower base of intellectual property than do pioneering, original inventions. In short, all other things being equal, the more original the invention, the greater the likelihood of successful commercialization.

Sourcing inventions from outside a given firm yields advantages to both the source providing the invention and the firm that licenses it. However, the rules that allow an innovation to be protected against imitation may have an impact on the likelihood of commercialization. If the sourced invention is also available to other firms or is part of the public domain, it can lead to knowledge spillovers. Thus, all other things being equal, the greater the exclusivity of the product or process, the greater the likelihood of commercialization. Finally, there is an inverse relationship between the likelihood of commercialization and the age of the product. The bottom line is that firms should actively seek to source inventions that are broad in scope and original in nature. It may be useful to wait for these inventions to emerge from the laboratory stage, but firms cannot wait until too far along in the development process when licensing products created outside their organizations.

Peter B. Heller

Further Reading

Barnes, Patrick W., ed. *Economic Perspectives on Innovation and Invention.* New York: Nova Science, 2007. Collects essays that highlight two of the primary engines of economic progress—inventions and innovations—in the context of adoption and diffusion, funding, tariffs, labor supply, and diversity.

Beane, Thomas L., ed. *Economics of Technological Change.* New York: Nova Science, 2007. Essay collection discussing technological advances that have stimulated industrial innovation, production efficiency, economic growth, and societal development.

Brockman, John. *Greatest Improvements of the Past Two Thousand Years: Today's Leading Thinkers Choose the Creations That Shaped the World.* New York: Simon & Schuster, 2000. Some of the most creative thinkers of the time identify not only familiar inventions such as the computer but also nonmaterial innovations such as capitalism, democracy, social justice, the scientific method, and other nonphysical discoveries.

Cockburn, Iain M., et al. "Untangling the Origins of Competitive Advantage." *Strategic Management Journal* 21, nos. 10/11 (2000): 1123-1145. Explains the role of inventions and innovations in providing companies with competitive advantages in the marketplace.

Lander, Jack. *All I Need Is Money: How to Finance Your Invention.* Berkeley, Calif.: Nolo, 2005. A how-to book for those with inventive or innovative ideas; explains how to find capital from various sources in the private and public sectors to put those ideas into effect.

Schumpeter, Joseph A. *Capitalism, Socialism, and Democracy.* New York: McGraw-Hill, 1934. Explains the importance of commercial inventions and innovations for the growth of individual firms and of the economy as a whole.

Shane, Scott. "Prior Knowledge and the Discovery of Entrepreneurial Opportunities." *Organization Science* 11 (2000): 448-469. Inventions are among the entrepreneurial opportunities detailed here.

See also: Aircraft industry; Automation in factories; Bell, Alexander Graham; Computer industry; Edison, Thomas Alva; Industrial research; Patent law; Pharmaceutical industry; Railroads; Steamboats.

Iraq wars

The Events: International wars fought against Saddam Hussein's regime in Iraq in which the United States played a leading role

Dates: Gulf War, January 16-February 28, 1991; Iraq War, started in March, 2003

Place: Iraq, Afghanistan

Significance: Although the U.S. government cited a number of reasons for each of these wars, both wars were fought, at least in part, to protect the American economy and its businesses from the threatened loss of access to petroleum. As with earlier American wars, these conflicts stimulated American business and technological development in unforeseen ways.

From colonial times through the early twenty-first century, nearly all American wars have been fought at least partially over economic resources of one kind or another. Throughout the entire history of warfare, the struggle to control resources has played a part in military conflicts, whatever rationalizations may be given by political leaders and historians regarding the causes of war.

Since shortly after World War II, access to oil from the countries surrounding the Persian Gulf has been a key element in U.S. foreign policy. In the immediate post-World War II era, the United States was very successful in maintaining access to oil. However, as time went on, American hegemony in the Middle East weakened. In 1972, Iraq nationalized American and other foreign oil companies operating in the country. Although American companies were still able to buy oil from Iraq, they no longer had direct control of its production. By the end of the twentieth century, Iraq had the third-largest known conventional oil reserves in the world, after its neighbors, Saudi Arabia and Iran.

THE GULF WAR

Although Iraq had substantial oil revenues, it did not invest in developing its oil fields. Because Iraqi oil extraction was inefficient and exploration had been limited, many oil experts believed that the Iraqi oil fields were the most important potential source of oil on the globe. Rather than increasing oil exploration, Iraqi president Saddam Hussein sought to increase his control over oil by openly invading his small southern neighbor, Kuwait, in August, 1990. Kuwait then had the fourth-largest known conventional oil reserves. Combining Iraqi and Kuwaiti oil reserves would make Iraq a close second to Saudi Arabia in its ability to control the world's oil. However, Iraq was mistaken in thinking that no nation would come to the aid of occupied Kuwait.

Hussein's open aggression provoked the United States to demand that Iraq withdraw from Kuwait and to threaten an international military response if it did not. Although this was the most important reason given by the U.S.-led coalition, the United States also argued that the Iraqi army was in a position to threaten conquest of the Saudi Arabian oil fields, which would give Iraq control of more than half of the world's oil reserves.

Shortly after the invasion, the United Nations Security Council issued a resolution ordering Iraq to leave Kuwait. In January, 1991, after Iraq had refused to comply, the United Nations authorized the

United States to form a coalition to drive Iraqi forces out of Kuwait. The ensuing Persian Gulf War began with U.S.-led United Nations coalition air assaults on Iraq on January 17. The ensuing war was brief. By the end of February, Iraq agreed to withdraw from Kuwait and a cease-fire was in place. After Iraqi forces were out of Kuwait, a United Nations commission redrew the nation's border with Iraq. The United Nations then created safe zones and no-fly zones within Iraq to protect Kurds and other Iraqi minorities. The United Nations also arranged for ongoing inspections of Iraqi facilities to monitor the situation and force the destruction of any nuclear, biological, or chemical weapons. It also continued trade sanctions on Iraq.

THE 2003 IRAQ WAR

The war that began in Iraq in 2003 was an outgrowth of issues left unresolved after the 1991 war. In contrast to the earlier conflict involving a United Nations coalition, this new conflict was undertaken as a U.S. initiative. After Hussein's government was destroyed in just a few weeks in 2003, the United States shifted to maintaining its presence in Iraq against guerrilla-style warfare conducted by anti-American forces from within and without Iraq. The United States offered several different justifications for invading Iraq other than oil, but it was widely believed that access to Iraqi and Persian Gulf oil was the underlying cause of war. Analysts who claim oil to be the main cause of the 2003 Iraq War point to the 2008 contract between a major American oil company in Iraq for access to Iraqi oil fields—ending the thirty-six-year Iraqi oil nationalization policy—as a confirmation of this view. American business and economic interests in oil seem to have had a large role to play in both Iraqi wars.

NEW TECHNOLOGY

In response to the threat during wartime, typically a nation's scientists and engineers focus on improving war-related technology, and these inventions or modifications often find applications in the peacetime economy that follows. For example, the eighteenth century French and Indian War and the Revolutionary War produced the long rifle known as the Kentucky rifle. The U.S. Civil War saw the development of repeating rifles and ironclad warships. The first military airplanes, tanks, and machine guns made their appearance during World War I.

The development and use of the atomic bomb was the most dramatic of a host of new technologies to come out of World War II. Business plays a key role in the development of each new military technology and weapons system and in the production of multiple copies and replacement parts for each successfully developed system. Business also takes the wartime developments and turns them into important civilian goods in peacetime. The American wartime experience is hardly unique in this regard.

By considering the two Iraqi wars as a single conflict with about a decade of low-level military action in between active fighting, it is possible to see innovations more clearly. Some of the weapons and weapons systems were originally developed for use against the Soviet Union during the Cold War but had never been tested in combat before. These weapon systems initially seemed unnecessary once the Cold War ended, but the Iraqi wars provided a new justification for many systems.

For example, radar-evading stealth airplanes, such as the B-2 Spirit bomber and F-117 Nighthawk fighter-bomber had been developed during the Cold War but were first battle-tested in Iraq. These stealth aircraft were used in the opening days of the war to knock out radar and communication facilities so that other aircraft could fly over Iraq without fear of being shot down. Both stealth aircraft performed better than expected. Both also represented a staggering number of new technologies, many of which had civilian applications. The radar-deflecting composite coverings that they use have numerous civilian applications. They both use global positioning system (GPS) technology and fly-by-wire flight control systems with wide application in the peacetime world. Although air and land forces have the largest role to play in the Iraqi wars, missiles were launched from naval vessels stationed offshore, the first test of this technology during battle.

Bradley fighting vehicles and M-1 Abrams main battle tanks had been developed for use against the Soviet Union but had never been used in combat until the two Iraqi wars. Each weapons system involves a wide range of new technologies in communications, computerized fire-control systems, infrared night-vision technology, and powerful new engines. Both make use of innovative new metals such as the depleted uranium used in shells and tank armor. Although civilian uses of this equipment are less obvious, they are nonetheless quite

	MILITARY COST OF MIDDLE EAST WARS	
War	Years of War Spending	Military Cost ($ billions)
Persian Gulf War	1990-1991	96
Afghanistan	2001-	171
Iraq	2003-	648

Source: Data from Stephen Daggett, "CROS Report for Congress: Costs of Major U.S. Wars," Congressional Research Service, July 24, 2008

Note: Includes appropriations enacted through June 30, 2008. Cost is in constant fiscal year 2008 dollars.

real. Businesses are involved not only in creating the military equipment but also in manufacturing new civilian goods.

In the first Gulf War, Hussein's armed forces used primitive conventional missiles called Scuds, which had sufficient range to reach Israel. This was especially dangerous because if the Iraqis had damaged Israel significantly, Israel might have intervened to protect itself, and its intervention might have alienated the Arab countries in the American-led anti-Iraqi coalition. The United States provided additional defenses for Israel in the form of a newly developed but untested Patriot missile air defense system in return for a promise not to intervene. The Patriot was battle-tested by the Israelis during the conflict with generally good results. The experience during the first Iraqi war led to improvements in the system, which greatly expanded its utility in the U.S. military arsenal. Smart bombs using internal guidance systems and global positioning system technologies were tested and improved during the two wars. The Iraqi wars have seen continued improvements in ground-support airplanes, helicopters, and other vertical takeoff and landing aircraft. Still the air war in Iraq is most likely to be remembered for the development of unmanned aerial vehicles (UAVs). First used only for reconnaissance, improvements made it possible for them to actually take an active combat role by carrying and firing so-called smart bombs and missiles as part of their repertoire.

The two wars also brought about developments in a wide variety of infantry supplies and weapons. The first Iraqi war saw the first deployment of a utility vehicle called a high-mobility multipurpose wheeled vehicle (Humvee), which quickly made the transition to civilian life as the country's most expensive sport utility vehicle (SUV), the Hummer. Numerous small arms innovations occurred, but soldiers probably most appreciated the development of new ceramic plates for use in body armor, new designs in camouflage uniforms, and infrared technologies for use in night vision goggles. All these improvements made infantrymen safer and reduced casualties. When casualties occurred, new emergency medical techniques were employed, and these improvements were quickly incorporated into civilian medical practice. In the process of retreating from Kuwait, the Iraqi army set fire to many of the Kuwaiti oil wells, creating massive fires that required weeks to bring under control. This led to the creation of new environmental technologies and fire-suppression strategies for dealing with the situation.

PRIVATIZING FUNCTIONS AND PROVISIONING

Beyond these hardware and software improvements, certain innovations in operations have had far-reaching consequences. The Iraqi wars placed a tremendous burden on United States Armed Forces in terms of human resources. One way to solve this problem was to use private corporations to provide certain functions. This need for additional people coincided with an ideological preference for privatization of government on the part of the presidential administrations that managed both wars. The personal and political connections of Vice President Dick Cheney, former head of Halliburton, may have led to the granting of multibillion-dollar no-bid contracts to Halliburton and its subsidiary Kellogg Brown & Root (later KBR) to provide many functions that had previously been the task of noncombat auxiliaries of the Armed Forces. Although private businesses have always played a large role in provisioning the U.S. Armed Forces, the extensive privatization of formerly governmental functions seems dramatically new, especially when the number of civilian contractors exceeds the number of members of the Armed Forces who were in Iraq throughout the second Iraq war.

Another major example of privatization is the use of private quasi-military forces such as those employed in security operations for the State Department and other U.S. government departments in the war zone. The personnel of these private groups are not subject to the laws of war and are therefore immune from prosecution for wrongdoing in ways that U.S. military personnel are not. Some consider this immunity to be a strategic advantage, but others have roundly condemned how these private forces are used. Blackwater USA (later Blackwater Worldwide) was perhaps the most notorious of these private contractor groups because of incidents involving fatalities in 2004 and 2007.

All these changes created a large number of new opportunities for American businesses to participate in both Iraqi wars. Criticism of privatization has been growing, and it is impossible to say whether such practices will continue in the future. It is undeniable, however, that American business will continue to have a very large role in the Iraq War and in any future wars involving Americans.

Richard L. Wilson

FURTHER READING

Gordon, Michael R., and Bernard E. Trainor. *Cobra II: The Inside Story of the Invasion and Occupation of Iraq.* New York: Vintage Books, 2007. As its title indicates, this book provides a detailed account of the military operations in the overthrow of Hussein's regime in Iraq and the occupation of the country that followed.

Kelly, Orr. *King of the Killing Zone.* New York: W. W. Norton, 1989. Detailed evaluation of the Abrams main battle tank and many variations.

Munro, Alan. *Arab Storm: Politics and Diplomacy Behind the Gulf War.* London: I. B. Tauris, 2006. The importance of access to oil as a key component of both of the Iraq wars is a central theme of this examination of the diplomacy surrounding Iraq from 1990 onward.

Ricks, Thomas E. *Fiasco: The American Military Adventure in Iraq.* New York: Penguin, 2006. This book is one of the most popular journalistic accounts of the second Iraq war in the administration of President George W. Bush. As the title indicates, the account is very critical, and it deals extensively with the business-related issues of the war.

Seahill, Jeremy. *Blackwater: The Rise of the World's Most Powerful Mercenary Army.* New York: Nation Books, 2007. This book provides a critical analysis of the privatization of the military function by the most prominent private military armed force, which the author characterizes as a mercenary army.

Smith, Jean Edward. *George Bush's War.* New York: Henry Holt, 1992. Journalistic account of the 1991 Persian Gulf War.

Wright, Steven. *The United States and Persian Gulf Security: The Foundations of the War on Terror.* Reading, England: Ithaca Press, 2007. This academic book analyzes the foreign policy of both Bill Clinton and George W. Bush to provide a long-term perspective on both Iraqi wars against the backdrop of U.S. policy toward Iran, Saudi Arabia, and the other countries in the Persian Gulf region.

SEE ALSO: Asian trade with the United States; Energy crisis of 1979; "Gas wars"; Korean War; Military-industrial complex; Organization of Petroleum Exporting Countries; Petroleum industry; Private security industry; Vietnam War; War surplus; Wars.

Irrigated farming

DEFINITION: Crop farming on lands using an artificial supply of water rather than rainfall

SIGNIFICANCE: Irrigated farming led to the profitable cultivation of acres that otherwise would not have been suitable for crop growing, the establishment of numerous subsidiary enterprises, and significant shifts in population.

Although most regions of the eastern United States receive sufficient rainfall for farming, lands west of the one-hundredth meridian, which runs from the Dakotas southward to Texas, are generally arid and need irrigation to be farmed. In areas where rainfall permits growth but is not abundant, irrigation can increase crop yields dramatically.

Early steps to encourage farming in the West met with limited success. During the 1870's and 1880's, a number of private irrigation companies were formed, but generally they were unable to deliver water to distant tracts and most failed within a few years. The Desert Land Act of 1877 allowed would-be farmers to buy land at a low price, provided part of the land came under irrigation within three years, a requirement often impossible to meet. The Carey Act of 1894 offered land to the states for irrigation projects, although few took advantage of it.

Far greater success came with the formation of the Bureau of Reclamation, created by the Newlands Reclamation Act of 1902. Under the bureau's guidelines, the federal government financed and oversaw the damming of rivers, the creation of reservoirs, and the digging of canals, allowing water users to repay the costs gradually. Such projects, which initially employed large numbers of laborers, resulted in the cultivation of vast tracts of land and increased settlement in the western states. The spread of irrigated farming also encouraged the manufacture and marketing of farm equipment, fertilizers, and pesticides.

By the middle of the twentieth century, advances in technology made it possible to pump water from rivers and aquifers and deliver it to elevations beyond the reach of earlier systems. Irrigation systems featuring automated sprinkling also became widespread. Toward the end of the century, irrigated farming became increasingly common in the southeastern United States. The number of large, corporate farms increased significantly, while small, family farms and farm jobs decreased. People also began to express concern about the long-term negative consequences of irrigation: salinization of soils, damage to riverine ecology by dams, and concentration of pollutants caused by irrigation runoff. In 2003, barely a century after the creation of the Bureau of Reclamation, nearly 53 million acres of the United States were under irrigation.

Grove Koger

FURTHER READING

Pisani, Donald J. *Water and American Government: The Reclamation Bureau, National Water Policy, and the West, 1902-1935.* Berkeley: University of California Press, 2002.

Reisner, Marc. *Cadillac Desert: The American West and Its Disappearing Water.* Rev. ed. New York: Penguin, 1993.

Rowley, William D. *The Bureau of Reclamation: Origins and Growth to 1945, Volume 1: Reclamation—Managing Water in the West.* Denver, Colo.: Bureau of Reclamation, U.S. Department of the Interior, 2006.

SEE ALSO: Agribusiness; Agriculture, U.S. Department of; Colorado River water; Dams and aqueducts; Farm labor; Interior, U.S. Department of the; Land laws; Rice industry; Water resources.

J

Japanese trade with the United States

SIGNIFICANCE: The United States forcefully entered into a trade treaty with Japan in 1853 to bolster its profitable trade with China. From that time until World War II, Japan was an important U.S. trading partner, and after the war, American exports helped rebuild Japan. Beginning in 1965, Japan began to export more to the United States than it imported, raising American trade fears during the 1970's and 1980's. By 2008, Japan had become America's fourth-largest trading partner.

During the mid-nineteenth century, Japanese ports were closed to all but some Dutch and Chinese traders. However, American business interests had begun expanding across the Pacific Ocean into China, so the United States wanted to establish trade relations with Japan to gain bases for its China trade. On July 14, 1853, U.S. Navy commodore Matthew C. Perry led a squadron of ships to land at a harbor near present-day Tokyo. Perry conveyed American demands for a trade agreement to a reluctant Japanese government. He was subsequently credited for opening Japan to Western trade. Significant Japanese trade with the United States began with the Tariff Treaty of 1866, which set import and export duties, allowing only a 5 percent duty to be placed on goods imported to Japan, and permitted American merchants to deal directly with their Japanese counterparts.

EARLY TRADE

From 1866 until 1932, American businesses imported more from Japan than they exported. The first top imports from Japan were raw silk, which American factories turned into consumer products, and tea for U.S. consumption. America exported primarily cotton yarn to Japan. As natural-resource-poor Japan embarked on industrialization, American manufacturers, like their Western European counterparts, began to export machinery, iron, and steel to Japan.

Initially, Japanese trade was a welcome but small by-product of America's trade with China. In 1866, American exports to Japan were worth $1 million,

and imports from Japan $2 million. Trade with Japan accounted for only 0.4 percent of U.S. trade. By 1914, exports to Japan had reached $51 million, and imports from Japan $107 million, raising Japan's share of America's foreign trade to 3.6 percent.

Japanese trading companies soon sought to control the trade with American businesses that was supporting Japan's rapid industrialization, so they opened branches in the United States The first to arrive was Mitsui Company, which established an office in New York City in 1879 and was soon followed by others.

Trade between America and Japan led to collaboration on economic policy. In 1899, Japan supported America's Open Door Policy to keep China accessible to international trade. In 1904, American banks sold $350 million of Japanese war bonds to help finance Japan's successful 1904-1905 war with Russia. In 1911, the United States accepted Japan's tariff autonomy when that country modestly raised import duties.

TRADE FROM 1914 TO 1941

When World War I broke out in 1914, Japan joined the Allies and increased trade with the United States. The American and the Japanese economies were booming, but as of 1917, a huge difference remained in the importance of their trade for each partner. Japanese trade accounted for 4.7 percent of U.S. trade, with American exports to Japan valued at $186 million and imports from Japan worth $254 million. In contrast, the United States was Japan's largest trading partner with a share of 29 percent of all Japanese foreign trade.

As Japan's industry expanded, U.S. companies formed joint ventures there to manufacture goods under U.S. licenses. Western Electric (1899) and General Electric (1905, 1908) were pioneers, followed in 1917 by the rubber company Goodrich. Ford (1925) and General Motors (1927) set up factories in Japan. Other U.S. firms, such as Columbia (1927), United Steel and Signal (1928), RCA (1929), and Otis Elevator (1932), followed suit.

Japanese firms continued to form branches and subsidiaries in the United States to support Japan's trade with America. By the early 1930's, Yokohama Specie Bank alone financed more than 50 percent of Japan's purchases in the United States. Japanese ships transported 73 percent of its imports from and 63 percent of its imports to the United States.

After the Depression hit, global trade shrunk. Due to demand caused by its military aggression in China beginning in 1931, Japan continued to buy U.S. exports. From 1932 until 1940, for the first time, U.S. exports to Japan exceeded imports from Japan, and American businesses earned some much needed revenues. However, Japan was an ally of Germany, which entered into World War II in Europe in 1939. The U.S. government froze all Japanese assets in America and launched an oil embargo after July, 1941, to protest Japan's aggression in China and Indochina. Trade was terminated with Japan's attack on Pearl Harbor on December 7, 1941.

POSTWAR TRADE HELPS JAPAN RECOVER

After the Japanese surrender on September 2, 1945, the United States conducted all Japanese trade until August, 1947. American businesses began exporting their goods to Japan again, and Japanese imports to the United States generated strongly needed revenues for the island nation. Until 1965, Japan imported more U.S. goods than it exported to America.

American exports shored up the Japanese economic recovery. In 1949, Japan enacted the Foreign Exchange and Foreign Trade Control Law to protect its industries, and set up the Ministry of International Trade and Industry (MITI) to promote its exports. Japan welcomed the 1949 U.S. decision to fix the exchange rate at 360 yen to 1 dollar, making dollars earned abroad very valuable. To safeguard weakened Japanese companies from takeover by foreign, primarily American, companies, the Foreign Investment Law was enacted in 1950. Japanese banks and trading companies reopened their American branches after 1951.

When Japan regained sovereignty on April 28, 1952, the United States accepted Japan's export-oriented trade strategy. This was done from a position of strength and with the goal of helping a Cold War ally. The United States supported Japan's joining the General Agreement on Tariffs and Trade (GATT) and extended most-favored-nation status to Japan in 1955. In 1961, the United States accepted Japanese tariff policies that set low rates on desirable American imports, such as raw materials and essential goods, but imposed barriers on goods that were being produced by Japan's rebuilding industry. The United States championed Japan's becoming a member of the Organization of Economic Cooperation and Development (OECD) and the International Monetary Fund (IMF) in 1964. All of this was done in the spirit of free trade with Japan, even though American companies setting up branch offices in Japan, such as International Business Machines (IBM), could not transfer their earnings from Japan to the United States.

Trade with Japan was brisk and growing by 1964. American companies exported goods valued at $2 billion to Japan and imported goods worth $1.8 billion from Japan. Trade with Japan accounted for 8.3 percent of America's foreign trade.

THE TRADE BALANCE SHIFTS

Since 1965, Japan has had a trade surplus with the United States. That year Japanese exports to the United States, worth $2.4 billion, first exceeded American exports to Japan, worth $2.1 billion. In the United States, the best-selling Japanese imports were radios and television sets, liked for their high quality and low prices. By 1971, Japanese exports to the United States had almost tripled, to $7.3 billion, while U.S. exports to Japan merely doubled, to $4.1 billion. At this peak, imports from Japan accounted for 16 percent of all imports in the United States.

The steady growth of Japanese imports in the United States led to a series of U.S. countermea-

---

UNITED STATES TRADE WITH JAPAN, 1985-2005, IN MILLIONS OF DOLLARS

Year	Exports	Imports	Balance
1985	22,631	68,783	–46,152
1990	48,580	89,684	–41,104
1995	64,342	123,479	–59,137
2000	64,924	146,479	–81,555
2005	55,484	138,003	–82,519

Source: Data from U.S. Census Bureau, Foreign Trade Division, Data Dissemination Branch, Washington, D.C. 20233

Note: Trade figures are from the U.S. perspective.

sures. American businesses demanded Japanese reciprocity in free trade and objected to the many legal and administrative barriers that protected Japanese manufacturers and markets. Beginning with Sony Corporation in 1970 and continuing until 1974, U.S. courts charged some Japanese companies with dumping products, or selling them below cost, in the United States. Japan received its biggest shock when President Richard Nixon slapped a 10 percent tariff surcharge on all Japanese imports to the United States in 1971.

TRADE FRICTION

The 1973 oil crisis made fuel vastly more expensive and exacerbated U.S.-Japanese trade friction. Fuel-thrifty Japanese cars became a hit in the United States, taking market share from U.S. automakers. To earn money to pay for the rising cost of oil, all of which it must import, Japan pursued the American market with tenacity. Even as U.S. exports to Japan jumped from $5 billion in 1972 to $10.5 billion by 1977, Japanese imports to the United States doubled from $9 billion to $18.6 billion. This trade was generally conducted by Japanese companies that handled 86 percent of Japanese exports to the United States and 94 percent of U.S. exports to Japan in 1974.

Japanese businessmen and politicians were not oblivious to the changing mood in the United States. One alternative was for Japanese companies to manufacture directly in the United States. Sony was the first to open a color television plant in America in 1972. By 1979, five other Japanese companies had begun manufacturing products in the United States. Japanese foreign direct investment in the United States rose from $0.3 billion in 1973, or 1.4 percent of foreign investment in the United States, to $4.3 billion in 1980, a 6.2 percent share.

The United States confronted Japan over the barriers to its domestic market during the GATT Tokyo Rounds from 1973 to 1979. Although progress was made in eliminating Japanese legal protectionist measures and Japan opened its market to U.S. bulk film, pharmaceuticals, computers, and semiconductors, Japanese agriculture remained protected and many administrative barriers remained. In 1977, Japan agreed to voluntary limits on the export of color television sets, and later of steel and automobiles, to the United States.

The abolition of Japan's Foreign Investment Law and the liberalization of its Foreign Exchange and Foreign Trade Control Law in 1979 freed more Japanese capital to invest abroad. New Japanese-owned factories in the United States such as those of Honda (1982) and Toyota (1988) created jobs for Americans. However, American apprehension over losing vital national security technology canceled the Fujitsu purchase of U.S. manufacturer Fairchild Semiconductor in 1987.

As the Japanese trade gap with the United States widened from $10 billion in 1980 to $46 billion in 1985 and Japanese trade accounted for 15.6 percent of U.S. foreign trade, the United States sought to balance the situation through a variety of economic policy initiatives. From 1984 to 1985, the Market Oriented Sector Selective (MOSS) talks covered the contentious issue of U.S. access to Japanese markets

Toyopets arrive in San Francisco in 1958. They were the first four-door sedan passenger car exported by Japan. (AP/Wide World Photos)

in four key fields. Two currency agreements strengthened the yen versus the dollar in 1985 and 1987.

U.S.-Japanese trade frictions reached their climax during the 1988 U.S. presidential primaries, when Democrat Richard Gephardt charged that unfair Japanese barriers made Chrysler's K-car too expensive in Japan. Congress passed the Trade Act of 1988, under which Japan was charged with unfair trading in three business fields. The 1989 Structural Impediments Initiative led to a series of agreements in 1990 to remove Japanese domestic barriers for U.S. exports and ended in 1993.

A CALMER RELATIONSHIP

In 1990, American business feared that Japanese competition would challenge America's global economic position. Strong American consumer demand for Japanese goods and a still tightly guarded Japanese domestic market maintained the trade imbalance, as trade with Japan accounted for 15.6 percent of all American trade. Japan had become the second-largest foreign investor behind Great Britain in the United States, owning U.S. assets worth $83 billion. Sony's acquisition of CBS Records and Columbia Pictures in 1988 and 1989, as well as Matsushita Corporation's purchase of MCA/Universal for $6.6 billion in 1990 raised some U.S. cultural anxieties. However, just as American concern over Japanese economic strength peaked during the early 1990's, the Japanese bubble economy burst. This plunged Japan into a recession from which even its strong exports to the United States could not save it immediately.

Intense economic negotiations preceding the foundation of the World Trade Organization (WTO) on January 1, 1995, led to significant opening of Japanese markets for U.S. products. As Japanese consumers had to economize, demand for cheap American goods rose. In a highly symbolic move, after Japan ended its post-World War II ban on rice imports in 1994, Emperor Akihito dined on American rice.

As Japanese trade with the United States matured and the Japanese economy remained troubled, growth of Japanese exports to the United States slowed significantly. Exports rose only from $123 billion in 1995 to $145 billion in 2007. At the same time, weak Japanese domestic demand kept U.S. exports to Japan in the $50 billion to $60 billion range from 1995 to 2007. Even though Japan was America's fourth-largest trading partner, Japan's share of U.S. trade fell to just 6.7 percent in 2007, less than half of what it had been in 1995.

During the early twenty-first century, Japanese trade with the United States was more harmonious than in the two preceding decades. American business enjoyed greater access to Japanese markets, and Japanese companies continued to do brisk business with their American trading partners.

R. C. Lutz

FURTHER READING

Bailey, Jonathan. *Great Power Strategy in Asia: Empire, Culture and Trade, 1905-2005.* New York: Routledge, 2007. Covers Japanese trade with America; emphasis is on Japan's military politics up to 1945 and trade's importance for the postwar U.S. relationship.

Cohen, Stephen. *An Ocean Apart: Explaining Three Decades of U.S.-Japanese Trade Friction.* Westport, Conn.: 1998. Compares different American and Japanese views of Japan's trade surplus with the United States from 1965 to 1996. Balanced, informative coverage.

LaFeber, Walter. *The Clash: U.S.-Japanese Relations Throughout History.* New York: W. W. Norton, 1997. Best overview of the subject from the beginning to 1995. Japanese trade with the United States is well analyzed and put into larger perspective. Illustrated, notes, bibliography, index.

Ota, Fumio. *The US-Japan Alliance in the Twenty-first Century: A View of the History and a Rationale for Its Survival.* Honolulu: University of Hawaii Press, 2006. Puts the strengths and troubles of the relationship in their historic context; includes thoughts on the role of trade for the alliance.

Sumiya, Mikio, ed. *A History of Japanese Trade and Industry Policy.* Reprint. Oxford, England: Oxford University Press, 2004. Covers Japan's post-World War II economic recovery. Very useful for understanding Japanese views of interacting with American business and of the economy.

Wilkins, Mira. "Japanese Multinationals in the United States: Continuity and Change, 1879-1990." *Business History Review* 64 (Winter, 1990): 585-629. Best historical coverage of Japanese foreign investment in the United States.

SEE ALSO: Asian financial crisis of 1997; Asian trade with the United States; Automotive industry; Chinese trade with the United States; Deming, W. Edwards; Electronics industry; General Agreement on Tariffs and Trade; International economics and trade; Korean War; Taiwanese trade with the United States; Tariffs.

Jewelry industry

DEFINITION: Manufacturers, designers, distributors, wholesalers, and retailers of precious and semiprecious personal adornments

SIGNIFICANCE: The lucrative jewelry industry provides Americans with fashion accessories, miniature art, and other precious objects. Jewelry is valuable in itself, but it also takes on symbolic value, as it is used to identify social position, marital status, and religious and lodge affiliations.

Early American jewelry imitated European designs, chiefly those of French and English jewelers. Later, an Italian-inspired fashion in cameos led native artisans to fashion images of U.S. presidents George Washington and Andrew Jackson on pliant shells. The wedding ring remained the most prevalent item of jewelry. For many women, such rings contained the only gold or diamonds they would own. Many also came to anticipate receiving engagement rings. The American jewelry industry successfully promoted wedding rings for men as well as women, in part by falsely tracing the custom of the man's wedding band to the Middle Ages. Attempts to market male engagement rings failed, however, perhaps because of the more limited purchasing power of American women.

In the nineteenth century, a distinctive form of American jewelry developed on the Navajo, Hopi, and Zuñi reservations of the Southwest. These Native Americans fashioned coin silver and turquoise bracelets, bolos, rings, and necklaces. Their squash blossom necklaces became popular, employing crescent shapes that seemed to echo the Moorish-Islamic heritage of Spain. Though numerous Native American craftspeople developed genuine artistry, their products were labor intensive, their competition was keen, and their market was eventually diluted with fake "Indian" jewelry made in Asia for tourist consumption.

Gold and silver jewelry, adorned with precious stones, remained a privilege of the affluent, but by the nineteenth century democratizing forces were at work in the jewelry trade as elsewhere. New, cheaper materials such as vulcanite were developed, along with white- and gold-colored metals. Colored glass could mimic expensive jewels, and synthetic stones were later developed that were almost identical in properties to natural ones.

Americans excelled in the design and manufacture of costume jewelry, or jewelry made of inexpensive materials and sold for everyday wear. Such items were often designed to showcase the creative artistry of their designers, rather than to create authentic imitations of precious stones. Produced with varying degrees of skill, costume jewelry could be sold in pricey boutiques, in department stores, or even in thrift stores. When Kenneth Jay Lane produced faux pearl necklaces for First Lady Barbara Bush and former First Lady Jacqueline Kennedy Onassis, costume jewelry became widely respectable.

Until the mid-twentieth century, Providence, Rhode Island (home of the Rhode Island School of Design), was the costume jewelry capital of the United States. At its height, the industry employed over 13,500 workers, chiefly immigrants and women drawn by the flexible hours. During World War II, many factories were converted into war production facilities, and by the end of the century Providence's jewelry district had become chiefly a tourist locale rather than an active manufacturing center.

Fascination with jewelry continued into the twenty-first century, despite a decline in craftsmanship, as several companies licensed their names to producers of inferior products. By the beginning of the century, international sales of jewelry had risen to $146 billion per year, and the United States enjoyed a market share estimated at 26 percent. Furthermore, jewelry making, especially beading, became a major American hobby: Bead shops flourished in major American cities, and seventeen periodicals were devoted to the craft. Online commerce and auction Web sites, such as eBay, provided a market for amateur craftspeople to sell their jewelry.

Allene Phy-Olsen

FURTHER READING

Marshall, Suzanne. *Two Hundred Years of American Manufactured Jewelry and Accessories.* Atglen, Pa.: Schiffer, 2003.

Newman, Harold. *An Illustrated Dictionary of Jewelry.* New York: Thames and Hudson, 1981.

SEE ALSO: Home Shopping Network; Mineral resources; Native American trade.

The Jungle

IDENTIFICATION: Novel by Upton Sinclair about the early twentieth century meatpacking industry
DATE: Published on February 28, 1906
SIGNIFICANCE: By raising the consciousness of consumers to the shocking conditions in the stockyards, slaughterhouses, and meatpacking facilities of Chicago, *The Jungle* helped launch federal regulation of the food industry.

Seldom does a work of fiction have dramatic, long-term effects on the day-to-day operations of a major industry. Such, however, was the case with Upton Sinclair's 1906 novel *The Jungle*, which became the catalyst for creating new structures regulating health and safety in U.S. food production. In 1904, the socialist weekly newspaper *Appeal to Reason* sent Sinclair on an investigative visit to "Packingtown," a slum district of Chicago where many of the nation's meatpackers lived and worked. The result of this visit was to be a novel exposing American readers to the hardships of urban working-class life. Though Sinclair hoped the novel would establish his reputation, neither he nor those financing his trip could have foreseen the impact it would have.

The plot of *The Jungle* follows the fortunes of the Rudkus family, Lithuanian immigrants living in the slums of Chicago. The protagonist, Jurgis Rudkus, works in the meatpacking industry, and during the course of the novel he endures imprisonment, the deaths of his wife and young son, and a long series of injuries and humiliations at work. The book shined a harsh light on the horrors of life in desperate poverty. It revealed the filthy and dangerous working conditions in the stockyards, slaughterhouses, and meatpacking plants where profit motives gave rise to corner cutting, corruption, and shocking abuses of workers.

The Jungle was published in early 1906 and immediately made an international splash. As the editors of *Appeal to Reason* had intended, readers learned about the deprivations of America's urban slums.

Upton Sinclair. (Library of Congress)

Far more disturbing to many readers, though, were revelations of the dangerous and dirty conditions through which much of the nation's meat supply passed. Descriptions of workers injured and killed by heavy machinery were horrifying enough. Even worse was the realization that meat sold around the United States (and exported abroad) was frequently contaminated with filth and rat poison from unsanitary packing plants, and even with human blood and body parts.

Public outcry was so loud that government action soon became all but inevitable. Steps were taken to improve conditions in the industry and to counteract corruption. Legislation passed in the summer of 1906, mere months after *The Jungle's* publication, mandated more stringent inspections of both the meat itself and the plants where it was processed. The Pure Food and Drug Act led to the establishment of the agency that later became the Food and Drug Administration; it was thus a major milestone in the increasing federal oversight of industry, labor, and commerce in the United States.

Janet E. Gardner

FURTHER READING

Barrett, James R. *Work and Community in the Jungle: Chicago's Packinghouse Workers, 1894-1922.* Chicago: University of Illinois Press, 2002.

Mattson, Kevin. *Upton Sinclair and the Other American Century.* New York: John Wiley & Sons, 2006.

SEE ALSO: Beef industry; Food and Drug Administration; Food-processing industries; Literary works with business themes; Meatpacking industry; Pork industry; Poultry industry.

Junior Achievement

IDENTIFICATION: Organization providing applied economic and business education to students in grades 4-12

DATE: Founded in August, 1916

SIGNIFICANCE: Originally founded as the Boys' and Girls' Bureau in 1916, Junior Achievement has grown into the largest supplier of applied economic and business education curricula in the United States, reaching well over one million students in grades 4-12 annually.

Originally created as a program for preteens in Springfield, Massachusetts, Junior Achievement shifted its focus to teach teenagers the responsibilities of citizenship, the value of self-reliance, and respect for America's free-market economy as safeguards for American democracy. During the 1920's-1950's, teens between the ages of sixteen and twenty-one formed Junior Achievement clubs that were structured like mini-businesses. Under adult guidance, club members raised funds, made products, marketed and sold their products, and returned a portion of their profits to shareholders in the form of annual dividends. Junior Achievement clubs provided hands-on experience in all aspects of business operations. During the Great Depression of the 1930's, Junior Achievement clubs provided job training and an opportunity to earn money for teens who were neither attending school nor employed.

Shortly after its founding, Junior Achievement began to allow coed membership in its clubs, and it was one of the first organizations to provide entrepreneurial training to young women. Junior Achievement clubs were also racially integrated at a time when such a policy was not common in many parts of the United States. During the 1940's, when U.S. industry was heavily involved in producing supplies to support the military in World War II, many Junior Achievement clubs functioned as subcontractors to manufacture simple but necessary defense industry products. During the 1950's and 1960's, Junior Achievement expanded its programs to operate in all fifty states. Junior Achievement has always had a policy of refusing to compete for funds against other nonprofit agencies. Its local programs must be supported by local business communities, which provide funds for start-up costs and materials, as well as expertise in various areas of business operations.

By the late 1960's, American teenagers were opposed to both the war in Vietnam and the nation's general business culture. Participation in Junior Achievement dropped steadily. In conjunction with the National Business Alliance, Junior Achievement began to develop curricula in financial literacy, applied economics, and business operations for use in high school classrooms across the country.

Since the 1940's, Junior Achievement had fostered strong ties with high schools to provide students with practical business experience, but it had not yet participated in activities in the classroom. Junior Achievement had been run as clubs that met after school hours. Beginning during the 1970's, however, Junior Achievement began to provide schools with business educators, as well as approved classroom materials, all paid for by local business sponsors. Eventually, Junior Achievement expanded its curricula to include materials and activities for more than 2 million students in grades 4-12 annually.

In addition to providing real-world experience running small businesses, Junior Achievement clubs compete against and learn from one another in regional trade fairs. Junior Achievement members also participate in leadership development programs at national business conferences, where they network with supportive business executives.

Victoria Erhart

FURTHER READING

Box, John M. "Twenty-First Century Learning After School: The Case of Junior Achievement Worldwide." In *The Case for Twenty-First Century Learning,* edited by Eric Schwarz and Ken Kay. San Francisco, Calif.: Jossey-Bass/Wiley, 2006.

Francomano, Joe, Wayne Lavitt, and Darryl Lavitt. *Junior Achievement: A History.* Colorado Springs, Colo.: Junior Achievement, 1988.

See also: Business schools; Education.

Junk bonds

Definition: Speculative, high-yield debt instruments that are generally classified as being below investment grade because they are riskier for default than higher rated bonds

Significance: The junk bond industry arose during the 1970's in response to an increasingly desperate need for capital by American corporations, which issued high-risk bonds that attracted investors tempted by the prospect of high returns. However, the popularity of so-called junk bonds waned during the 1990's, when some of their major issuers went into default.

Effectively loan contracts with fixed maturity dates that promise to pay back the amount borrowed, along with interest at specified rates, bonds play a major role in the financial world. They are used for a number of financial purposes. Corporations may issue bonds to expand their operations, to acquire other companies, or simply to refinance their existing debt. Government institutions also issue bonds for a variety of reasons, such as financing the construction of bridges, hospitals, or harbors. They generally get authorization for bond issues through special ballot measures.

CLASSIFICATION OF BONDS

Some bonds are classified as investment grade, generally rated by Moody's as BBB- or higher, at the time of their issuance. However, with the passage of time, their credit rating slips because their financial strength deteriorates, resulting in their reclassification as speculative, or junk bonds. Bonds suffering this reclassification are often called fallen angels.

Some bonds are marketed initially as speculative simply because their credit ratings are marginal, based on the borrower's inability to demonstrate a more promising financial future. Occasionally these speculative instruments become investment grade over time as the corporations involved demonstrate improved results in their business operations. Such bonds, reflecting improved credit ratings, are often termed rising stars.

Often purchasers of bonds are limited in how far down the line they can go in terms of bond credit ratings. Pension funds, banks, and insurance companies, for example, may be prohibited by their charters from purchasing speculative bonds. Junk bonds consequently attract a different type of investor than that attracted by the bonds issued by more conservative financial institutions.

Individual investors who wish to purchase speculative bonds are generally wise to go through high-risk bond funds. Through the funds, investors can avail themselves of the advice of professionals who are aware of the risks involved in each particular issue.

BOND CREDIT RATINGS BY MOODY'S INVESTORS SERVICE AND STANDARD & POOR'S

Moody's	S&P	Definition
Aaa	AAA	Prime, lowest risk
Aa1, Aa2, Aa3	AA+, AA, AA–	High grade, low risk
A1, A2, A3	A+, A, A–	Upper medium grade
Baa1, Baa2, Baa3	BBB+, BBB, BBB–	Lower medium grade
Ba1	BB+	Noninvestment grade
Ba2, Ba3	BB, BB–	Speculative
B1, B2, B3	B+, B, B–	Highly speculative
Caa1	CCC+	Substantial risk
Caa2, Caa3	CCC, CCC–	In poor standing
Ca		Extremely speculative
C		May be in default
	D	Defaulted

Source: Data from Moody's Investors Service, Standard & Poor's, and BondsOnline

Note: Bonds receiving ratings below the double rule are considered junk bonds.

Fund professionals research the bond markets constantly and diversify their investments over a number of different types of assets. This spread of risk in a portfolio of speculative bonds can be preferable to concentrating on one or just a few issues.

CHANGING INVESTMENT INSTRUMENTS

A dramatic change in bond investment quality began developing during the 1970's. Before then, most bonds issued were of investment quality. During the late 1970's, investment houses began to issue bonds that were speculative from their inception. This change occurred for one compelling reason—the growing need for capital by private industry to meet rapidly changing economic fundamentals. Companies were facing new challenges from foreign competition and technological innovations. Existing bond markets for meeting corporate needs for more capital had failed to meet the challenge. The answer to the problem lay in turning, increasingly, to the issuance of speculative bonds by corporations pressed to acquire additional capital.

Moreover, a number of investment experts determined that the risk to bond purchasers involved in investing in these high-risk instruments was more than offset by the higher yields the bonds offered. Until the late 1980's, the issuance of high-risk bonds expanded rapidly. However, during the late 1980's and early 1990's, the tide turned. An increasing number of high-risk bonds became subject to default. This resulted in the failure of a handful of financial institutions that had invested too heavily in the high-risk category. For example, this activity led to the bankruptcy of the investment house of Drexel Burnham.

Critics of the move into junk bonds complain that these bonds have been used as devices by corporate raiders to seize control of existing companies. Raiders typically employ substantial debt instruments in the acquisition of such control. However, many experts think that these buyouts have led to the ultimate expansion of the targeted companies rather than to their demise.

Despite some negative results, junk bond activity has continued to expand as the mutual fund activity in this category has demonstrated. Figures from 1983 indicated that high-risk bond issues accounted for one-third of the bonds in force. In 2003, issuance of high-risk bonds more than doubled over 2002.

Carl Henry Marcoux

FURTHER READING

Altman, Edward I., and Scott A. Nammacher. *Investing in Junk Bonds: Inside the High Yield Debt Market.* Washington, D.C.: Beard Books, 2002. An examination of the pros and cons of junk bonds as investments.

Schilit, W. Keith. *Dream Makers and Deal Breakers: Inside the Venture Capital Industry.* Englewood Cliffs, N.J.: Prentice Hall, 1991. Discusses the use of high-risk bonds by the venture capital industry.

Shapiro, Eli, and Charles R. Wolf. *The Role of Private Placements in Corporate Finance.* Boston: Harvard University Press, 1972. Presents an alternative approach to long-term borrowing by smaller, less financially secure companies.

Yago, Glenn. *Junk Bonds: How High Yield Securities Restructured Corporate America.* New York: Oxford University Press, 1991. Yago looks at how, despite the risks involved, the junk bond industry has played a leading role in American economic expansion.

Zey, Mary. *Banking on Fraud: Drexel, Junk Bonds and Buyouts.* New York: Aldine de Gruyter, 1993. This critical look at the junk bond industry examines the 1981-1982 recession, the stock market crash in 1987, and the Drexel Burnham Lambert bankruptcy of 1990.

SEE ALSO: Bond industry; Interest rates; Mutual fund industry; Securities and Exchange Commission.

Justice, U.S. Department of

IDENTIFICATION: Cabinet-level department in the U.S. government responsible for enforcing federal laws, defending the legal interests of the national government, and ensuring and offering equal and impartial justice for all U.S. citizens

DATE: Established in 1870

SIGNIFICANCE: Various agencies within the Justice Department specialize in the investigation and prosecution of white-collar and corporate crime on the federal level.

The Judiciary Act of 1789 created the Office of the Attorney General, a part-time position for an individual who was appointed by the president. The attorney general was charged with prosecuting federal suits and advising the president on legal matters. The role and responsibilities of the office grew, and assistants were hired. The caseload expanded after the U.S. Civil War, requiring the hiring of private attorneys. Partly in response to this, Congress passed an act to establish the Department of Justice (DOJ) in 1870. The department officially began operating on July 1.

RESPONSIBILITIES

The Department of Justice is responsible for various duties assigned to the department by the executive branch of the federal government. The department is directed by the U.S. attorney general, who is a full member of the president's executive cabinet. Major duties of the department include maintaining the entire system of federal prisons, enforcing all immigration laws and processing new applications, investigating and prosecuting all federal laws, and representing the United States in all legal matters, including cases that may be tried in front of the U.S. Supreme Court. As of 2008, the department employed close to 115,000 people in the United States and abroad, and had an annual operating budget of close to $44 billion.

LAW-ENFORCEMENT AGENCIES

Most of the law-enforcement agencies responsible for the investigation of possible violations of federal statutes are housed within the Justice Department. These agencies include the United States Marshals Service; Drug Enforcement Administration (DEA); Bureau of Alcohol, Tobacco, Firearms, and Explosives (ATF); and the Federal Bureau of Investigation (FBI). Of these four agencies, the FBI conducts the most white-collar and corporate crime investigations for the Department of Justice. The FBI has a white-collar crime division that specializes in crimes committed by corporate officers and employees of for-profit and not-for-profit organizations and businesses. FBI investigators played a major role in the investigation and subsequent prosecution of many of the top officials involved in well-known corporate scandals at Enron Corporation, WorldCom, Adelphia Communications, Rite Aid, and Tyco International.

After a crime has been investigated and a case has been built, it is handed over to one of the divisions within the Office of the Attorney General for prosecution. The attorney general is supported by nu-

NUMBER OF FINANCIAL CRIME CASES UNDER INVESTIGATION BY THE FBI, FISCAL YEAR 2007	
Type of Fraud	Pending Cases
Mass marketing	127
Insurance	209
Corporate	529
Money laundering	548
Securities and commodities	1,217
Mortgage	2,007
Health care	2,493

Source: Data from Federal Bureau of Investigation, "Financial Crime Report to the Public, Fiscal Year 2007" (Washington, D.C.: Author, 2007)
Note: Fiscal year 2007 is 10/1/2006 to 9/30/2007.

merous deputy and associate attorneys general throughout the United States. Each state has one or more associate or assistant attorneys general who are responsible for all prosecutions of both civil and criminal cases involving federal legislation. The major legal divisions that prosecute violations of federal law are antitrust, civil, criminal, civil rights, environment and natural resources, justice management, tax, and national security. The Justice Department legal divisions—especially the antitrust, civil, criminal, and environmental and natural resources divisions—have started to increase the number of prosecutions of corporate white-collar offenders.

The Federal Bureau of Prisons also falls under the auspices of the Department of Justice. Once a person has been convicted of a crime and sentenced to prison by the federal court system, that person is housed in one of the more than one hundred federal prisons throughout the United States. Those who commit white-collar offenses tend to be housed in lower-security prison camps, away from inmates sentenced for more violent offenses.

Through its Office of Justice Programs, the Justice Department both conducts and sponsors research projects dealing with crime and numerous types of legal matters. Since their start during the mid-1960's, these projects have been an effective learning tool in regards to various types of crime, crime patterns, crime prevention techniques, and criminal behavior in general. The Department of Justice also offers services for victims of federal crimes through the Office for Victims of Crime.

Paul M. Klenowski

FURTHER READING

Dunn, Lynne. *The Department of Justice.* New York: Chelsea House, 1989. Covers the history of the Department of Justice and describes the structure and function of each of the operating agencies and offices within the department.

Nossen, Richard A. *The Investigation of White-Collar Crime: A Manual for Law Enforcement Agencies.* New York: Books for Business, 2002. The go-to manual for law-enforcement agencies of all levels to investigate various forms of business-related crimes.

Rosenberg, Morton. *Congressional Investigations of the Department of Justice, 1920-2007: History, Law, and Practice.* New York: Nova Science, 2008. This book chronicles the dark side of the Justice Department and the various scandals that have plagued this department since its inception.

U.S. Department of Justice. *U.S. Department of Justice Manual.* 2d ed. Gaithersburg, Md.: Aspen Law and Business, 1999. Gives a detailed description of the roles and responsibilities of the major divisions and agencies within the Justice Department.

U.S. Department of Justice and the Federal Trade Commission. *Antitrust Enforcement and Intellectual Property Rights: Promoting Innovation and Competition.* Washington, D.C.: Author, 2007. Discusses how enforcement of antitrust laws promotes capitalistic ideas.

SEE ALSO: Antitrust legislation; Business crimes; Enron bankruptcy; HealthSouth scandal; Identity theft; Organized crime; Ponzi schemes; Tyco International scandal; WorldCom bankruptcy.

K

Kaiser, Henry J.

IDENTIFICATION: Industrialist who founded more than one hundred companies
BORN: May 9, 1882; Sprout Brook, New York
DIED: August 24, 1967; Honolulu, Hawaii
SIGNIFICANCE: Kaiser achieved renown through the innovative techniques he introduced to the many operations that he developed. His interests included construction, engineering, medicine, automobile manufacturing, and community development.

Henry J. Kaiser left school at the age of thirteen and began working in a dry goods store in Utica, New York. He soon developed a particular interest in hardware and photography. In 1901, before he was twenty, he bought his own photography store and studio in Lake Placid, New York. Using that town as his base, he traveled seasonally to the state of Florida, working as a photographer. In 1907, when he was twenty-five, he married. To overcome his father-in-law's objections to his itinerant life as a photographer, he moved west to Spokane, Washington, where he took a job clerking in a hardware store. This work led him into the contracting field. In 1914, he started his own road-paving firm in Vancouver, Canada. His company, which pioneered in the use of heavy machinery, began building roads throughout the West and was the first to build concrete roads in Cuba. Revenue from his Cuba operation allowed him to expand his operations. During the late 1920's, his firm was one of the major contractors that helped build the Hoover and Grand Coulee dams. Around that time, he expanded his operations into gravel and cement production.

Kaiser's expansion into shipbuilding during World War II led to his earning a worldwide reputation for innovative engineering. Kaiser Shipyard in Richmond, California, turned out Liberty ships as the rate of one every thirty days. In 1942, his company set a record by completing an entire ship in only four days. One of his significant innovations was using welding rather than riveting to join large metal parts. He was also innovative in hiring women as welders. However, it was his general streamlining of shipbuilding assembly that was responsible for his company's high production rate.

As the war was nearing its end, Kaiser began expanding into other fields, including the manufacture of aluminum, gypsum, and household products, and the construction of homes. His biggest new operation was automobile manufacturing. That branch of his industrial empire ultimately failed, but his Jeep division lived on. Meanwhile, during his shipbuilding years, Kaiser had established an innovative health program for his workers. In 1945, the program was made available to the public. Called Kaiser Permanente, the plan would become been a model for health maintenance organizations globally.

During the mid-1950's, Kaiser turned to what would be the final phase of his busy career. He moved to Hawaii and developed the Kaiser (later Hilton) Hawaiian Village. He spent the rest of his life in Hawaii, where he supervised the construction of what he regarded as his dream city, while leaving one of his sons in charge of his other interests.

Carl Henry Marcoux

SEE ALSO: Automotive industry; Construction industry; Health care industry.

Klondike gold rush

THE EVENT: Large influx of people looking for gold in the Klondike region of Canada's Yukon Territory, to which the U.S. territory of Alaska was the principal gateway
DATE: 1896-1898
PLACE: Klondike region near Alaska
SIGNIFICANCE: News that gold had been discovered in and around the Klondike River caused a stampede northward through Alaska of those hungry for wealth.

Discovery of gold in the Klondike region of the Yukon River basin came at a time when Americans were very much in need of good economic news, as the country was suffering through a depression that had started in 1893. Wheat prices had bottomed out in 1894, causing eastern immigrants to the West to head back east with signs reading "In God we trusted, in Kansas we busted" painted on their wagons. Furthermore, the United States had yet to establish a gold standard for currency. Coinage was based on both gold and silver at a set ratio. Gold was not to become the official standard until 1900, but in the meantime, the federal government was running short of gold to back the partial standard.

THE RUSH IS ON

The hysteria started when two ships landed on the West Coast: the *Excelsior* at San Francisco on July 16, 1897, and the *Portland* at Seattle on July 17, 1897. Eighty miners were aboard these ships. They were from various walks of life and various places. Many of them had been searching for gold in the Yukon for years. What they all had in common was gold, packed in suitcases, boxes, jam jars, and an array of containers. They were all men who had gone into the Yukon with no money and were coming out millionaires.

When the local papers printed the news, people headed in droves north to the Yukon to get rich. Many of them had only vague notions of where the Yukon was. Most of them had no idea how difficult the journey would be or how challenging it would be to get the gold out of the frozen tundra. Still, be-

fore the "stampede" was over, 100,000 people had headed to Alaska from the United States and other places. By 1929, $175 million worth of gold had been taken out of the Yukon. However, as in most gold rushes in the West, most of the easy gold vanished early, and most of the profit went to a select few: those who discovered the gold, those who got there early, or those who got lucky. Some estimate that businesses that supplied the miners as they traveled to the Yukon and while they mined for gold made more money than most of the miners. Still, people came by the thousands, risking all they had and even dying along the road, all in a desperate attempt to get rich. Of the 100,000 who set out for the gold fields, only 30,000 actually got there. The "stampede" itself lasted only two years.

LEGEND AND REALITY

The gold that was discovered in the Klondike region had been washed down the mountain by the two-thousand-mile Yukon River over a period of thousands of years. Because gold has a specific gravity nineteen times that of water, it did not make it to the sea. Instead it settled in sandbars and beaches along tributaries of the Yukon River. Long before the United States bought Alaska from the Russians, there had been rumors that gold could be found there. The natives of the region had brought specimens of gold to the Russians, but the Russians could never find large quantities of it. Further, they were concerned about announcing it to the world for fear that a rush would hurt the fur trade in the region.

The big break came after the United States purchased Alaska, when the Dyea-Chilkoot Pass was opened to American prospectors through negotiations with native Alaskans. This led to the discovery of gold on August 17, 1896, on what was then called Rabbit Creek but would later be renamed Bonanza Creek. Accounts vary as to who actually discovered the gold, but all agree that the three men there at the mo-

Miners climb the Chilkoot Trail during the Klondike gold rush. (Canadian National Archives)

ment were George Washington Carmack, Tagish Charley, and Skookum Jim Mason. In one account, Carmack panned for the gold beside their camp, a mile or so from the point at which Rabbit Creek empties into the Klondike, a tributary of the Yukon River. In another he was sound asleep as Skookum Jim Mason washed a pan after cleaning a moose they had killed and discovered gold in the creek. What no one disputes is that their accounts of gold on the Klondike caused a stampede to the Dawson Creek area of the Yukon River Valley. At first, it was a local stampede, but when the *Excelsior* and the *Portland* docked in San Francisco and Seattle almost a year later, it became worldwide.

Much of the legend surrounding the Klondike gold strike grows out of the difficulty that miners faced in getting to the gold fields and in extracting the ore from the ground. The easy route was expensive: Miners traveled by sea to the mouth of the Yukon River at Saint Michael, then down the river to

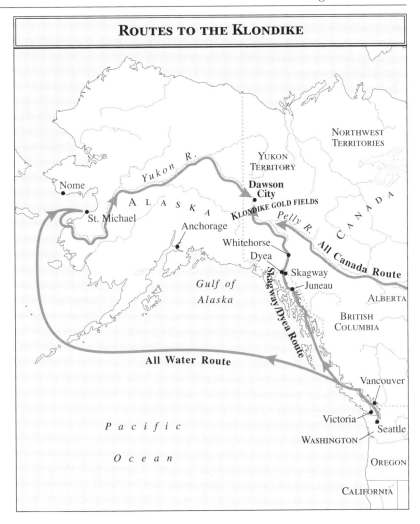

ROUTES TO THE KLONDIKE

Dawson City. The cheaper route, and the one that most took, was a treacherous overland trek through Canada and up and over either the Chilkoot or the White Pass. The trails up these passes were forbidding and steep. The Chilkoot trail was too steep for pack horses, forcing miners to carry their belongings in bits and pieces. Many left their belongings on the trail or gave up all together. The White Pass was so steep and slick that three thousand pack animals died trying to cross it, causing it to be nicknamed "dead horse trail." Those who made it over the passes still had to travel five hundred miles by boat (often making their own boats) to get to Dawson City.

When prospectors got to Dawson City, their work was only beginning. They had to extract the ore from beneath the permafrost layer of earth, building fires to thaw the ground as they went. Further-

more, by the time the bulk of miners had arrived, most of the accessible gold was gone, having been extracted by locals. The Klondike strike, like so many other strikes, enriched a handful of people, created an enormous number of legends and stories, and broke the hearts of thousands.

H. William Rice

FURTHER READING

Deans, Nora L. *Klondike Trail: North to the Yukon.* Anchorage: Alaska Natural History Association, 2007. An account of the path to Klondike gold.

Evans, Barbara A., ed. *Klondike Gold Rush Anthology, 1897-1997.* Seattle: Klondike Gold Rush Centennial Committee of Washington State, 1997. A collection of writings on the Klondike gold rush published on the hundred-year anniversary.

Haskell, William B. *Two Years in the Klondike and Alaskan Gold-Fields, 1896-1898: A Thrilling Narrative of Life in the Gold Mines and Camps.* Fairbanks: University of Alaska Press, 1998. A firsthand account of life during the peak of the gold rush by a miner.

Haugan, Jevne. "Klondike Gold: One Thousand Miles from Anywhere." *Maritime Life and Traditions* 33, no. 1 (Winter, 2006): 62-73. Though this article focuses primarily on the ships and bodies of water that were associated with the gold strike, it contains very good information about the event itself. Further, it provides details not found in other publications.

Johnson, Julie, and Nora L. Deans. *Klondike Gold Rush National History Park.* Anchorage, Alaska: Alaska Natural History Association, 2007. An account of the park, with substantial history of the gold rush and early settlers.

Morgan, Murray. *One Man's Gold Rush: A Klondike Album.* Seattle: University of Washington Press, 1967. Murray's book features the photographs of Eric A. Hegg. Journeyman photographer Hegg went north to Alaska not to find gold but to chronicle the "stampeders." His photographs provide a compelling record of what happened in the Klondike gold rush.

SEE ALSO: American Bimetallic League national convention; Black Hills gold rush; California gold rush; *Coin's Financial School*; "Cross of Gold" speech; Currency; Exploration; Gold standard; Mineral resources.

Knickerbocker Trust Panic. *See* Panic of 1907

Knights of Labor

IDENTIFICATION: National labor union

DATE: November 25, 1869-1917

SIGNIFICANCE: As one of the most powerful national labor unions in the United States during the post-Civil War industrial era, the Knights of Labor, which welcomed both women and African Americans, championed a progressive agenda designed to define the rights and protect the interests of an emerging urban workforce.

As increasing industrialization shaped the northeast United States after the U.S. Civil War, the growing gap between the rich and the poor resulted in numerous attempts to organize workers. On Thanksgiving, 1869, Uriah Smith Stephens, a Philadelphia tailor, invited eight other tailors to inaugurate what he envisioned as the Noble and Holy Order of the Knights of Labor, a fraternity of workers and artisans regardless of ethnicity, gender, or religion, designed to promote the dignity of work. Initially the order was based on Stephens's familiarity with the Freemasons. He conceived of the order as a way to organize Philadelphia's immigrant Catholic workers, who were banned from the Masons. Rosters were kept secret, and the meetings resembled religious rituals, with scripture readings and visionary sermons.

Initially growth was unremarkable: By 1879, the order maintained only twenty-three assemblies, mostly around Philadelphia. After Stephens resigned as the order's master workman in 1879 and the order came under the progressive leadership of Terence V. Powderly, it abandoned its secrecy and rituals, trimmed its name, and began to address worker issues more forthrightly. Most notably, the new leadership championed an eight-hour workday, a ban on hiring children under fourteen for factory work, an end to using convicts as cheap labor, an upgrade in factory safety standards, a graduated income tax, public ownership of utilities, government assistance for farmers, and equal pay regardless of gender or race. Because the Knights of Labor welcomed all workers (excluding only "nonproductives," such as bankers, doctors, stockholders, professional gamblers, and liquor producers) and because it welcomed both women and African Americans, by 1886, the Knights of Labor was the most powerful labor organization in the country with more than 700,000 members. In 1884, the organization achieved its most significant victory: the settlement of the Union Pacific Railroad strike.

The decline in the Knights of Labor's influence, however, has been traced to its opposition to strikes (it advocated arbitration and limited boycotts), a strategy out of step with an evolving radical labor underground that saw disruption as the workers' best hope. Ironically, it was the growing outcry against unions, particularly after the 1886 Haymarket Riot (which did not actually involve the Knights of Labor), and the resulting blackballing of union members by company owners that caused a sharp drop in membership. With the rise of craft-unions, most notably the American Federation of Labor, Knights of Labor membership dropped to 74,000 by 1893, a decline exacerbated by disputes among the organization's leadership and among its autonomous assemblies and by several failed investment schemes. The Knights of Labor, however, maintained a headquarters until it was disbanded in 1917.

Joseph Dewey

FURTHER READING

Fink, Leon. *Workingmen's Democracy: The Knights of Labor and American Politics.* Urbana: University of Illinois Press, 1985.
Leavitt, John McDowell. *Kings of Capital and the Knights of Labor: For the People.* Adamant, Vt.: Adamant Media, 2001.
Weir, Robert E. *Beyond Labor's Veil: The Culture of the Knights of Labor.* State College: Pennsylvania State University Press, 1997.

SEE ALSO: AFL-CIO; Gilded Age; Gompers, Samuel; Haymarket Riot; Industrial Workers of the World; Labor history; Labor strikes; National Labor Union; United Mine Workers of America.

Korean War

THE EVENT: Military conflict that involved the United States after North Korea invaded South Korea in 1950
DATE: June 25, 1950-July 27, 1953
PLACE: Korean peninsula
SIGNIFICANCE: The Korean War forged the link between U.S. defense spending and manufacturing, normalized government agencies controlling business, and helped develop Japan's manufacturing capabilities.

By the late nineteenth century, Korea's agrarian economy was intertwined with Japan's, trading for food, manufactured goods, clothing, silver, and gold. In 1910, Japan annexed Korea through a treaty. Korea's economy slowly changed from purely agrarian to include some manufacturing. Although the Japanese built roads and railroads and developed Korean industry, they treated Koreans as racial inferiors—particularly after militarists came to power during the 1930's. After World War II, it was decided that Korea would be divided in half. Land above the thirty-eighth parallel would be supervised by the Soviet Union and that below the parallel by the United States. The two halves were to be reunited after a government was organized, a constitution written, and Korea stabilized for self-rule. This division of Korea caused protests all through the country.

COMMUNISM VS. DEMOCRACY

Joseph Stalin, leader of the Soviet Union, sought to increase the Soviet Union's presence in Asia and ordered that a communist government be established in northern Korea. In May, 1946, Kim Il Sung—a Korea-born major in the Soviet Army—was made head of the North Korean Communist Party. In August, 1946, nationalization of northern Korean industry began, at first including only industries that did business with Japan. However, all large and nearly all medium-sized Korean businesses had done business with the Japanese. Similarly, the Americans nationalized southern Korean companies owned by Japan or by Japanese nationals.

In 1947, President Harry S. Truman handed control of southern Korea to the United Nations (U.N.), which called for unifying elections. The Soviets refused. South Korea was thereafter considered a separate country by the United Nations. That same year, North Korea printed its own currency. In the spring of 1948, Stalin secretly approved a North Korean constitution, which was immediately passed by the People's Assembly, and the Democratic People's Republic of Korea (DPRK, commonly known as North Korea) was born. North Korea proclaimed it had the single constitution for the entire peninsula and refused to recognize South Korea. South Koreans were labeled separatists working for the Americans. Kim became secretary general of North Korea. In October, Stalin sent North Korea an invitation to establish friendly relations with the Soviet Union.

North Korea began a rapid economic advance. Harsh rule limited corruption, and a great deal of money and supplies flowed into the country from other communist nations. In return, North Korea exported raw materials and what little manufactured goods it produced. The North bought gas and oil at reduced rates and had guaranteed markets for its goods in the Soviet Union. Its military received the latest Soviet equipment. The Soviets also sent industrial machinery with the assumption that a prosperous North Korea would in time pay them back.

In 1948, Syngman Rhee, with active support from the United States, was elected by a large majority as the first president of the Republic of South Korea (ROK, commonly known as South Korea). Rhee had lived abroad for many years, was a baptized Christian, and had a degree from Georgetown University and a Ph.D. from Princeton in international law. During the Japanese occupation, he was president of the Korean government in exile. Rhee was a fervent nationalist who hated communists and wanted capital development, but he was not above enriching himself from government funds. His government was corrupt, and Rhee was dictatorial and cruel to political opponents. South Korean leadership governed a country in social turmoil. There were street demonstrations in which police and demonstrators were killed, worker strikes, a communist insurrection in part of the South Korean army, a million refugees from the North entering the South's major cities, food shortages, and South Korean communists agitating for reunification under Kim. President Rhee ordered South Korean communists jailed and tortured. With the help of the United States, he gave the large farms owned by landlords to one million sharecroppers. South Korea remained dependent on millions of dollars of foreign aid received each year from the United States. A South Korean military was organized in 1948 but was given few tanks or armor.

A WIDENING SPLIT

By 1948, the Korean peninsula was home to two separate countries with vastly different economies and philosophies, both wholly reliant on sworn enemies who were commencing the Cold War. Border skirmishes between North Korean and South Korean forces began almost immediately. The ideological and economic split between the two countries widened rapidly. A North Korean army was quietly assembled in 1948, with permission from Moscow. As a soldier, Kim gave considerable attention to building a formidable, well-trained, politically indoctrinated military. However, he overestimated support for communism in the South. In 1949, the United States Army began leaving South Korea. By 1950, there were fewer than five hundred American advisers left in the country. Stalin agreed to an invasion of the South, which began on June 25, 1950.

The next day, Kim accused South Korea of attacking the North.

Seoul fell to the communists in three days, and by August, 1950, 90 percent of South Korea was occupied. In September, General Douglas MacArthur's army landed at Inchon and drove North Korean forces back into the mountains near the Korean-Chinese border. In November, the Chinese attacked across this border with 300,000 men, taking over the majority of fighting from the North Koreans. The U.N. forces retreated southward a second time. By December, Kim was back in Pyongyang in an underground bunker as the city was being bombed into ruins by U.N. planes. In the spring of 1951, U.N. forces counterattacked the exhausted Chinese, pushed them northward up the peninsula, until the thirty-eighth parallel was once again the dividing line between the two Koreas. In March, 1953, Stalin died, and the Soviets and Chinese made immediate peace overtures. A cease-fire was signed in July, 1953, although South Korea refused to sign it.

IMPACT ON U.S. BUSINESS

After World War II, President Truman greatly cut the defense budget. By 1947, the U.S. Army had shrunk to 700,000 men, with two divisions fully ready for deployment. Much of the U.S. Navy's equipment was placed in storage or cut up for scrap. Money saved was diverted to social programs. Truman ended World War II price-and-wage controls in 1946, creating a huge jump in prices and inflation that settled down within two years. Meanwhile, the United States was experiencing both an economic and a baby boom. The government eased the housing shortage by insuring mortgages for returning veterans up to 95 percent of their cost, and the building boom grew larger. By 1950, there were fewer than 2 million unemployed, and the United States was a global economy—in fact, the strongest economy in the world. By 1950, inflation was again low and consumer goods were rolling off assembly lines into the homes of an enlarging middle class. Less-developed nations, particularly in Latin America, were tapped for cheap raw materials. The military regimes that dominated these countries were tolerated by the Americans because they kept communists out and resources flowing. The 1950 census tallied 151 million Americans, with an average wage of $60.53 per week—a new high.

Good times ceased at the close of 1950. The Chi-

MILITARY COST OF KOREAN WAR, 1950-1953

- In current year dollars = $30 billion

- In constant fiscal year 2008 dollars = $320 billion

- War cost as percentage of gross domestic product in peak year, 1952 = 4.2%

- Total defense cost as percentage of gross domestic product in peak year, 1952 = 13.2%

Source: Data from Stephen Daggett, "CROS Report for Congress: Costs of Major U.S. Wars," Congressional Research Service, July 24, 2008

---

nese entered the Korean War in November, and by December, the military budget increased to $50 billion (from a postwar low of $13.5 billion), and inflation soared to 7.9 percent. Corporate taxes and income taxes were raised and credit tightened. Nonmilitary spending, including social programs, was slashed 28 percent. Citizens and companies hoarded goods. In December, 1950, Truman declared a state of emergency, which gave him wide executive powers. His Economic Stabilization Agency immediately canceled price increases by Ford, General Motors, and Chrysler, and reduced worker pay raises to put the economy on a war footing. Charles E. Wilson, head of the Office of Defense Mobilization (ODM), was given nearly free reign to channel materials into war industries, withholding a portion of them from the production of civilian goods. The ODM prohibited the expansion of factories producing domestic items but authorized the building of new defense factories in the South and the West.

By 1951, the war had affected U.S. businesses by tightly connecting industries to military spending, placing the U.S. economy on a war footing that would go on for decades, making federal regulation of businesses an accepted practice, and establishing Japan as a future business competitor.

The Cold War with the Communist bloc began before the Korean War and continued into the 1990's. The war pumped millions of dollars for equipment and supplies into U.S. companies through defense contracts. The U.S. economy was so strong it could afford such massive expenditures (14 percent of gross domestic product) and still build and maintain military bases within the country and across the globe. Federal budgets were written enabling the U.S. military to go to war at any moment. Companies such as General Electric, Boeing, Electric Boat, Northrop Grumman, Lockheed Martin, Raytheon, and BAE Systems grew huge and prosperous and employed tens of thousands. Defense plants and the money they generated were a large piece of the economy. The Korean War jump-started the link between business and the government that President Dwight D. Eisenhower called the "military-industrial complex."

At the same time, federal regulation of the national economy and private business became more common. The Truman administration used nineteen war mobilization agencies to control the economy during the Korean War. The ODM managed and penalized private business. Government intervention to ensure economic stabilization became routine; federal agencies were created; and the size of U.S. bureaucracy increased.

IMPACT ON JAPAN

The Korean War had the effect of making Japan a major manufacturer of domestic goods. Japan's industries had been destroyed during the war, and the country was struggling economically. The United States felt it was important that Japan recover quickly to fend off communist influence. It also needed supplies for its military, many of whom were based in Japan before going to the Korean War. Large contracts were written with the Japanese for supplies—ships, pharmaceuticals, oil, beer, and more—and large manufacturing companies, such as Mitsubishi, Sumitomo, and Mitsui, were saved from bankruptcy by U.S. investment. The U.S. government paid the Japanese government large sums for "special military procurement." These payments amounted to 27 percent of Japan's total export trade. Supplies from Japan totaled $149 million in 1950 and $809 million in 1953. Japan's economy grew 10 percent a year. Toyota was given a contract to build trucks for the United Nations, and Sony was given a contract to produce tape recorders for American Armed Forces

Radio. These early contracts helped Japanese manufacturers reestablish themselves. Soon, they began exporting goods to countries such as the United States. During the 1970's, Japan gained market share in quality electronics and then automobiles. The United States became Japan's biggest customer, buying 35 percent of what it made. In 2007, Japan's trade imbalance with the United States was $82.8 billion.

James Pauff

FURTHER READING

Facts About Korea. Rev. ed. Elizabeth, N.J.: Hollyum, 1998. Great resource providing sections on history, the economy, and foreign relations.

Halberstam, David. *The Coldest Winter: America and the Korean War.* New York: Hyperion, 2007. Last chapter provides consequences of the war.

Hickman, Bert G. *The Korean War and United States Economic Activity, 1950-1952.* New York: National Bureau of Economic Research, 1955. A book of statistics and graphs that presents U.S. economic trends of the period.

Martin, Bradley K. *Under the Loving Care of the Fatherly Leader.* New York: Thomas Dunne Books, 2004. The best text on North Korea and its economic ties with the Soviet Union.

Pierpaoli, Paul G. *Truman and Korea: The Political Culture of the Early Cold War.* Columbia: University of Missouri Press, 1999. In-depth information on U.S. economics and society.

_____. "Truman's Other War: The Battle for the American Homefront, 1950-1953." *Organization of American Historians Magazine of History* 14, no. 3 (Spring, 2000): 15-19. Short, excellent article on politics and business during the war.

SEE ALSO: Asian trade with the United States; Chinese trade with the United States; G.I. Bill; Government spending; Japanese trade with the United States; Military-industrial complex; Steel mill seizure of 1952; War surplus; Wars.

L

Labor, U.S. Department of

IDENTIFICATION: Federal cabinet-level department charged with promoting and protecting the rights of workers in the United States and assuring their safety on the job

DATE: Established in 1884; became a cabinet-level department in 1913

SIGNIFICANCE: The Department of Labor is directly related to business communities in the United States by its official charge to foster, promote, and develop the welfare of wage earners of the United States; improve their working conditions; and advance their opportunities for profitable employment.

As the United States became increasingly industrialized in the last half of the nineteenth century, it was evident that some governmental controls had to be imposed on industry to protect its workers. In 1884, responding to this need, Congress established the Bureau of Labor as an adjunct of the Department of the Interior. Before the turn of the century, the bureau had expanded to the point that it became an independent agency called the Department of Labor. As such, however, it did not have cabinet status, which very much impeded its activities and limited its director's access to the highest administrative levels of the federal government.

In 1903, the department was returned to the status of a bureau with the establishment of the new cabinet-level Department of Commerce and Labor. With the creation of this new department, whose secretary had direct access to the president, the Bureau of Labor actually experienced a decrease in its power and influence.

Realizing the need for a separate department designed to deal with the status and problems of wage-earners, President Woodrow Wilson pushed for the creation of a new cabinet-level Department of Labor (DOL) with its own secretary who reported to the president. On March 4, 1913, Congress voted to establish this new department, and on the following day, President Wilson appointed William Bauchop Wilson to be the first secretary of labor, a post in which he served for eight years.

SUBDIVISIONS

The responsibility for the enforcement of federal labor laws falls to the Department of Labor. By the mid-twentieth century, approximately 150 such laws were in existence. They affected such areas as minimum wages, overtime pay, workers' compensation, unemployment insurance, workers' involvement in labor unions, and discrimination in the workplace based on gender, sexual orientation, age, or race.

The department is also charged with providing opportunities for workers to enhance their employment possibilities through training programs that

The Labor Department helped soldiers returning from World War I get jobs, as this 1917 poster shows. (Library of Congress)

are sponsored by the department and are designed to improve and expand the employment opportunities of those whose previous skills are obsolescent or have been supplanted by new technologies. Closely associated with such job training programs is the establishment of protocols for job placement.

The United States Employment Service (USES), a branch of the Department of Labor, maintains more than twenty-five hundred public employment offices throughout the nation to help workers through job placement. Special mandates that apply to the USES establish specific aid for rural workers, aliens, veterans, and young people about to enter the workforce.

Related to the USES is the Office of Comprehensive Employment Development. This agency, with nearly five hundred offices scattered throughout the nation, provides workplace training for those about to join the workforce. Related to such programs are the Summer Youth Employment Program, designed to introduce new workers to the workplace while they are still quite young; the Job Corps; the Apprenticeship and Training Program, designed to provide youths with supervised on-the-job training; and the Private Sector Initiative Program, sponsored largely by private industry. Each of these vital programs is administered and overseen by the Employment and Training Administration of the Department of Labor.

ORGANIZATION

The Department of Labor, which in 2007 had 16,126 full-time employees, is organized around four major divisions. The Office of the Inspector General is responsible for auditing the programs of the department and for ensuring adherence to existing labor laws. This office works closely with the solicitor of labor, who is responsible for all of the department's legal activities and actions.

The Office of Information, Publications, and Reports is concerned with disseminating the basic research findings and statistics of the department, making them readily available to the public and to the American business community. The information provided through this office directly affects much of the long-term planning done by American businesses.

The matter of fair wages is a salient one in many situations involving labor. Matters relating to wages are handled within the Department of Labor by the Wages Appeal Board. This board investigates and passes judgment when wage disputes arise. Its members are well versed in labor laws as they pertain to wages and fair employment practices.

Finally, the Women's Bureau was established in 1920, the year in which the Nineteenth Amendment to the United States Constitution granted American women the right to vote. This bureau, which became an independent office of the Secretary of Labor in 1977, has ten regional offices that monitor labor practices involving gender discrimination in both hiring and compensation and is directly concerned with the rights of women in the workplace. The Women's Bureau gained considerable strength when Frances Perkins, appointed by Franklin D. Roosevelt, served as secretary of labor from 1933 to 1945. Perkins was the first female cabinet member in the history of the United States and enjoyed one of the longest tenures of any cabinet member. The Women's Bureau grew considerably during the last quarter of the twentieth century because of the large numbers of women entering the workforce. The bureau paved the way for this change and has overseen its implementation through the years.

MONITORING AND ENFORCING LABOR LAWS

The undersecretary of labor is responsible for assuring adherence to and enforcement of established labor laws. This oversight falls under the jurisdiction of three boards, the Employees' Compensation Board, which is authorized to render decisions under the Federal Employees' Compensation Act of 1916; the Office of Administrative Law Judges, which conducts formal hearings relating to compensation, hours, health, welfare, and safety; and the Benefits Review Board, which considers appeals from the administrative law judges in cases involving the Harbor Workers' Compensation Board and the Black Lung Benefits Act (1972).

The fair compensation of workers is of prime importance to the Department of Labor, second only to the department's concern with the health and safety of those in the American workforce. The staff of the solicitor of labor deals with cases that come before the aforementioned agencies.

LABOR UNIONS

Labor unions have been a major part of the American labor movement throughout the twentieth century. The Department of Labor and the unions often have similar aims, those of protecting workers and assuring them of fair treatment in the work place, although the department and labor unions often have quite different means of achieving these ends.

To guarantee that union bosses do not use strong-arm tactics to gain and retain their power, the Department of Labor enforces legislation assuring the fair and honest election of officials of labor unions. The department observes union elections scrupulously to make sure they are even-handed and legitimate. It also assures that workers will not be penalized for participation in union activities.

OCCUPATIONAL SAFETY AND HEALTH ADMINISTRATION

Perhaps the agency of the Department of Labor most visible to the average American is the Occupational Safety and Health Administration (OSHA). Whenever an industrial or mining accident occurs, OSHA is on the scene almost immediately to investigate it and to finds means of preventing similar accidents in the future. OSHA establishes and enforces safety standards for the workplace on its own initiative as well as through the Mine Safety and Health Administration, which oversees health and safety matters in mines within the United States.

Despite its emphasis on protecting workers, OSHA has been one of the most controversial agencies in the Department of Labor. Few people in industry would deny the need for an agency of this sort to help inform workers and managers of workplace health and safety measures. Many business leaders, however, complain that OSHA has gone too far in imposing difficult restrictions on the private sector. Considerable discontent with OSHA stemmed from its issuance in 1980 of the first comprehensive national report that recognized and sought to control the use of cancer-causing substances in the workplace. There was considerable disagreement about the linkages that OSHA appeared to assume between certain substances commonly found in the workplace and the subsequent development of cancer in some workers. A great deal was at stake financially for substantial numbers of manufacturing enterprises that often depended on the use of some of the substances the report had pinpointed. Categorical proof was difficult to establish because of the considerable time spans that separated workers' exposure to such substances and the onset of cancer.

Despite such caveats, OSHA has weathered the storms of protesters who objected to many of the agency's findings that suggested links between the development of cancer and the use of seemingly carcinogenic substances in the work place. The agency has introduced new record-keeping mandates and has demanded that documents containing medical records and exposure to toxins be made available to OSHA as well as to workers and their representatives at their request.

OSHA's concern with mining safety has resulted in safety, health, and accident investigations of coal mines at the rate of about fifty thousand annually. Such inspections have resulted in the issuance of an average of some 120,000 citations a year. Despite a rash of dramatic mining accidents during the early twenty-first century, American mines are among the safest in the world. When accidents occur, OSHA is on site immediately and works doggedly to support rescue efforts and to take positive steps to prevent the recurrence of such accidents.

Many decisions made by America's business community are directly affected by reports created and distributed by the Bureau of Labor Statistics. Its publication, *Monthly Labor Review*, is widely read by business leaders. Among its other publications, the *Consumer Price Index* provides a guide to the direction in which the American economy is headed at any given time. The *Occupational Outlook Quarterly* is an important indicator of employment trends, while *Producer Prices and Price Index* measures and reports on such important trends as consumer spending.

R. Baird Shuman

FURTHER READING

Borrelli, MaryAnne. *The President's Cabinet: Gender, Power, and Representation.* Boulder, Colo.: L. Rienner, 2002. A feminist account of the functions of the presidential cabinet and of how it helps to shape attitudes about race and gender.

Justice, Keith, comp. *Presidents, Vice Presidents, Cabinet Members, Supreme Court Justices, 1779-2003.* Jefferson, N.C.: McFarland, 2003. Comprehensive listing of those who have held public office, including the presidents' cabinet members.

Morris, Richard B., ed. *The U.S. Department of Labor: History of the American Worker.* Washington, D.C.: U.S. Government Printing Office, 1976. Despite its age, this overview is worth reading for its comprehensive overview of how the Department of

Labor has helped to direct the course of American business.

Ossian, Lisa L. "Always Working for Labor." In *The Human Tradition in America Between the Wars, 1920-1945*, edited by Donald W. Whisenhunt. Wilmington, Del.: SR Books, 2002. Appreciative account of the contributions of Secretary of Labor Frances Perkins to gender equality.

Pasachoff, Naomi E. *Frances Perkins: Champion of the New Deal.* New York: Oxford University Press, 1999. Appropriate for young adult readers, this is an account of the impact that Frances Perkins had on the status of women as the first female cabinet member in United States history.

Sarkela, Sandra J., Susan Mallon Ross, and Margaret A. Lowe, eds. *From Megaphones to Microphones.* Westport, Conn.: Praeger, 2003. Frances Perkins's speech, "Social Insurance for U.S.," delivered on February 25, 1935, is reproduced and sets forth some of the tasks for the Department of Labor under President Roosevelt's New Deal.

U.S. Department of Labor. *2001 Summer Employment Program.* Washington, D.C.: U.S. Department of Labor, 2001. One of many annual reports that reflect how the Department of Labor helps train youth for the workplace.

SEE ALSO: Affirmative action programs; Commerce, U.S. Department of; Education, U.S. Department of; Labor history; Labor strikes; Occupational Safety and Health Act; Presidency, U.S.

Labor history

DEFINITION: The history of the working people in the United States, as shaped by various labor organizations and social developments

SIGNIFICANCE: The working conditions and compensation of workers have a profound effect on American society and the economy. Working people are both laborers and consumers, affecting the bottom line of businesses in many ways.

Labor history is a broad and complex topic, especially because even the basic definitions of key terms such as "labor" and "history" shift across time and place. In relation to American business history, labor history is an integral part of international and national patterns of social and economic life, and therefore, it cannot readily be separated from these broader trends. For many historians, labor history refers specifically to the long history of labor relations emerging as the modern economy of North America developed; others view it as the social history of working people.

HISTORICAL OVERVIEW

European colonization of the Americas brought various economic and cultural practices to the New World. The established economies of the indigenous people were largely disrupted and displaced by colonial economic expansion, which sometimes involved the appropriation of Indian land and labor. Varied European models of commerce and concepts of property relations and law eventually dominated the continent, as did international markets and trade.

Workers in North America in the eighteenth and early nineteenth centuries included slaves, indentured servants, wage laborers, farmers, merchants, traders, soldiers, guild members, and business managers. Various forms of working, middle, managing, and owning classes emerged in the United States, creating class stratification that affected American business and social history. Race, religion, and gender also played a part in the development of American society and labor.

During the early nineteenth century, the southern states began developing plantation agriculture, depending largely on slaves for labor. At the same time, the economy in many other parts of the country began a significant shift from agrarianism to industrialization and urbanization. During the early national period, workers began to organize to exert more control over working conditions and compensation. Slaves organized informally and covertly, their protests taking the form of slave revolts and uprisings. At the same time, workers in the larger industries, including coal, steel, iron, textiles, and mining, began forming labor unions, guilds, and worker organizations and leagues, and farmers in the West and Midwest began forming leagues. Their protests took the form of work stoppages and strikes. The first unions were regional in nature. One of the first national unions, the Knights of Labor, was formed in 1869 and championed a progressive agenda. During the early 1870's, the National Grange of the Patrons of Husbandry (also known as the Grange), a fraternity for farmers, started to engage in political action.

UNION MEMBERSHIP IN THE UNITED STATES, 1970-2003

Year	Number of Members
1970	18,088,600
1980	17,717,400
1990	16,739,800
2000	16,258,200
2003	15,776,000

Source: Data from Jelle Visser, "Union Membership Statistics in Twenty-four Countries," *Monthly Labor Review* 129, no. 1 (January, 2006): 38-49

Partly in response to the need for labor created by industrialization, starting in the nineteenth century, immigrants began arriving in the United States, first from southern and eastern Europe, then from Asia, Mexico, and other areas. Immigrant workers brought with them a range of models and traditions of labor organizing in both agriculture and industry. Companies viewed them as a source of cheap labor, sometimes using them to replace more experienced workers. Immigrants therefore faced social prejudice from other sectors of the American workforce and were rarely welcomed by labor unions.

After the U.S. Civil War resulted in the freeing of slaves, especially those engaged in agricultural work in the South, these freed slaves briefly engaged in organizing, but the economic failures of Reconstruction forced them to abandon these efforts. Like immigrants, they were often banned from joining labor unions.

CYCLES AND POLITICS

Business cycles in the United States have dramatically affected labor. Times of expansion, recession, and depression have all sparked different strategies from labor organizers and responses from business owners. In general, during business expansion, companies employ more workers and on better terms, but in times of recession or depression, they employ fewer people and with less compensation and under poorer working conditions. Unions typically try to minimize the effects of economic down-

turns on their members and to gain benefits for them in upswings. Booms, crashes, and panics have had a profound impact on public support for labor organizing, particularly in their influence on the attitudes of members of the American middle and upper middle classes. Similarly, wars and wartime economies have affected labor organizing, as the government tends to regard strikes and work stoppages during war as detrimental to the war effort. For example, in 1952, during the Korean War, President Harry S. Truman seized steel mills that were about to go on strike, although the U.S. Supreme Court later ruled his actions were illegal.

American labor has a complex political relationship with the international and domestic Left. American labor's socialist experiments and left-wing activities have included agrarian utopian communities, cooperative commonwealth movements, workingmen's parties, communist labor organizing, and a long tradition of democratic participation in labor organizing. The Communist Party had some influence in unions such as the Congress of Industrial Organizations (CIO) and United Automobile Workers (UAW) but was never a dominating force.

American business and governmental policy has been predominantly and often emphatically pro-capitalist, and therefore, labor organizing has often involved a political and ethical critique of the social and economic practices of capitalism in the United States. Conflict with owners, the government, and law enforcement (as enforcers of business policy) has been not only ideological but also physical. At times, workers involved in strikes, marches, and other protest have been met with repressive action, including violence and mass arrest. For example, a conflict between workers and Chicago police officers in 1886 erupted into the Haymarket Riot, and an 1892 strike by workers at the Homestead Steel Works Company ended in violence when Pinkerton agents and state militia were sent in to break the strike.

Some labor organizations (including the AFL-CIO), however, have been essentially sympathetic to capitalism and have argued for more power and benefits for union workers but not for changes in the capitalist structure of business. Needless to say, the political winds of American history have had a significant impact on, and been strongly affected by, the politics and philosophies followed by labor organizations.

Many historians agree that organized labor was in its heyday from the late nineteenth century until the middle of the twentieth century. During this time, labor unions and workers' organizations made remarkable gains in membership, political influence, and economic security. After World War II, however, labor organizations began to decline in number and political power, particularly in the increasingly conservative business and political climate of the late twentieth and early twenty-first centuries. Some observers anticipate a rebound in labor organizing as American workers are increasingly affected by the globalization of capitalist markets. Others believe that the future of organized American labor remains uncertain at best and bleak at worst.

Sharon Carson

FURTHER READING

Clark, Christopher, Nancy A. Hewitt, and Roy Rosenzweig. *Who Built America? Working People and the Nation's History.* 3d ed. Boston: Bedford/St. Martin's, 2007. Remarkably detailed and thoroughly researched study of all periods of American labor history.

Drucker, Peter F. *The Essential Drucker: Selections from the Management Works of Peter F. Drucker.* New York: HarperBusiness, 2001. Collection of essays by Drucker, a prolific and insightful business philosopher. He analyzes labor history in the context of management theory and social philosophy.

Dubofsky, Melvyn. *Hard Work: The Making of Labor History.* Urbana: University of Illinois Press, 2000. Collection of essays by a founding scholar in academic labor history, exploring the changes in methods and presumptions guiding labor history as a scholarly discipline and analyzing labor in relation to social and political history.

Fraser, Steven, and Joshua B. Freeman. *Audacious Democracy: Labor, Intellectuals, and the Social Reconstruction of America.* Boston: Mariner/Houghton Mifflin Company, 1997. Stimulating collection of essays by labor activists, social historians, and political philosophers.

Jones, Jacqueline. *American Work: Four Centuries of Black and White Labor.* New York: W. W. Norton, 1998. Excellent comparative study of black and white workers within the full sweep of American labor history, using race and labor as key analytical categories to illuminate American social history.

Nicholson, Philip Yale. *Labor's Story in the United States.* Philadelphia: Temple University Press, 2004. Excellent and very readable survey of American labor history, combining historical context with rich detail regarding specific movements, people, events, and organizations.

SEE ALSO: AFL-CIO; Bracero program; Gompers, Samuel; Immigration; Industrial Workers of the World; International Brotherhood of Teamsters; International Ladies' Garment Workers' Union; Knights of Labor; Labor, U.S. Department of; Labor strikes; Lewis, John L.; National Labor Union; Supreme Court and labor law.

Labor law, Supreme Court and. *See* Supreme Court and labor law

Labor Management Relations Act of 1947. *See* Taft-Hartley Act

Labor strikes

DEFINITION: Work stoppages by laborers who organize to demand higher pay and improved working conditions

SIGNIFICANCE: American businesses regard strikes as a hindrance to productivity as well as an interference with management rights. Workers, on the other hand, see strikes as a last resort in trying to level the playing field with management. Strikes have become less common than they were in the past as a negotiating tactic.

Work stoppages have been part of the economic climate of the United States since before the nation won its independence during the late eighteenth century. The growth of organized labor during the late nineteenth century helped bring focus to many strikes. Business owners have generally opposed strikes as interfering with their rights to run a business as they see fit. They often emphasize that strikes hamper the productivity of the American economy and interfere with their property rights. Government at all levels has often sided with management, at times providing support for crushing strikes through the courts and overt intervention including use of the police and troops to attack strikers.

Workers often agree that strikes provide an economic hardship, including one to themselves through lost wages or even jobs. Nonetheless, strikes have always been one weapon in the arsenal of organized labor to try to force management to bargain in good faith or to observe work agreements. Commonplace in some industries up to the 1960's, strikes were used less thereafter as unions turned to other means to try to gain concessions.

There is some disagreement among theorists as to the fundamental nature of strikes. Some argue that strikes express only economic issues and should be treated as simply an economic issue. Others contend that strikes often express political and social issues and have wider implication for society than just economic concerns.

THE FIRST FIFTY YEARS

The period of growth for the American economy during the late nineteenth century saw numerous strikes in industries such as coal, steel, or railroads as workers tried to assert demands for higher wages and better working conditions. The growth of organized labor helped to channel strikes toward achieving identifiable goals that often included management recognition of a union as a first step toward achieving better working conditions.

Two mass strikes during the 1890's are illustrative of these developments. The first occurred at the Carnegie Steel Company plant at Homestead, Pennsylvania, in 1892. The Amalgamated Association of Iron and Steel Workers had secured a union contract in 1889 and with a short strike and collective bargaining had achieved some improvements in wages and working conditions. Henry Clay Frick, the chairman of Carnegie Steel, who had long opposed unions, decided to force a confrontation that he hoped would enable him to destroy the union when the union contract came up for renewal in 1892. Frick imposed new work rules, and the union went on strike at the Homestead Works.

Frick tried to send a flotilla of boats carrying replacement workers and Pinkerton detectives up the Monongahela. The strikers drove off the flotilla. Although the workers enjoyed a good deal of local support, Frick appealed to the governor of Pennsylvania, who ordered in the state militia to restore or-

der. With the troops in place, Frick brought in replacement workers and fired most of the strikers. Union membership dropped from twenty-four thousand to eight thousand by 1895. Even though the strike damaged Andrew Carnegie's reputation as a benevolent factory owner, Carnegie Steel's profits increased dramatically after the strike. In this case, Carnegie Steel was willing to suffer a short-term loss to achieve long-term gains realized through cutting wages and demanding higher worker productivity after the strike.

The Pullman Strike of 1894 started in the Pullman Palace Car Company outside of Chicago when workers were faced with wage cuts while the rents in their company-owned houses remained the same. The American Railway Union refused to handle Pullman cars and nearly brought the railroads in the eastern United States to a standstill. This action gave the railroad owners an opportunity to crush the union. The railroads put Pullman cars on all trains, and when the American Railway Union refused to handle the trains, the owners turned to the U.S. government, claiming that the union was interfering

Striking Polish coal miners battle with coal and iron police near Shenandoah City, Pennsylvania, in this 1888 newspaper illustration. (Library of Congress)

with the mail. Here, too, the strike brought disastrous results for the workers, as the Pullman and railroad workers were forced to accept management's terms, which destroyed the respective unions. The intervention of troops on the side of management had tipped the balance, as the strike had been relatively peaceful up to that point, and the strikers enjoyed a good deal of public support in Illinois.

Economic downturns have often led to strikes, as workers tried to preserve gains made in happier times. Such was the case in the years after World War I. Coal miners and textile workers in particular had profited (as did the mine and textile owners) from wartime production. When demand dropped after the war, owners began to lay off workers and increase production demands for the same (or lower) rates of pay. One of the most violent strikes, known as the Matewan massacre, occurred in the coal fields in Mingo and Logan Counties, West Virginia, in 1920. The mine operators almost seemed to welcome a confrontation. Shooting and dynamiting began to be part of the strikers' tactics, and the owners turned to the Baldwin-Felts detective agency, which also engaged in violence against the strikers.

Finally, a large group of miners attempted to march from Mingo County to Logan County to emphasize their demands for a living wage and for improvements in the harsh and dangerous working conditions. The local United Mine Workers of America leader, Frank Keeney, tried to dissuade the miners from the march for fear of governmental intervention, but to no avail. The miners and local militia engaged in a number of conflicts, including a major encounter that became known as the Battle of Blair Mountain, in which somewhere between ten to fifty miners died. The West Virginia governor, a former attorney for the coal companies, called on the U.S. government for aid. President Warren G. Harding ordered twenty-one hundred Army regulars to the area, supplemented by machine guns and aircraft. Unwilling to confront the troops of their country, the miners halted their march, although not until a National Guard plane had dropped dynamite bombs on them. Soon thereafter, the strike collapsed, as public opinion had turned against the miners and they had no other source of income save to go back into the mines on the owners' terms.

A Change in Effectiveness

Although labor leaders won some early confrontations by striking, they often lost. That situation began to change during the 1930's, as the U.S. government and some state governments adopted stances that were more neutral during strikes. Without being able to call on the power of government to help break strikes, some businesses found it advantageous to agree to negotiations when a strike occurred. During the 1930's, the United Auto Workers confronted the automotive industry with a series of strikes that led to union recognition and some concessions. Some violent strikes still occurred, as happened at Honea Path, South Carolina, in 1934, when seven strikers in the General Textile strike were shot as they fled from the local textile plant as strikebreakers inside the mill opened fire on them.

Immediately after World War II, many unions became assertive, striking to gain from wartime prosperity or to defend gains already made. A long-running strike in the eastern coal fields led President Harry S. Truman, who was usually friendly to organized labor, to threaten to federalize the mines temporarily to restart production. The political climate toward labor was changing, fostered in part by some of the postwar strikes, and in 1947, Congress passed the Taft-Hartley Act over President Truman's veto. This legislation placed limits on organized labor, most notably one allowing state governments to declare their states "right-to-work" states, which made union organizing more difficult. Bureau of Labor Statistics data indicate that from 1947 through 1974 the number of work stoppages involving one thousand workers or more remained high, averaging 314 per year. The number during the early 1950's had been even higher, averaging 396 strikes a year. Organized labor and big business gradually developed a more accommodating approach that was intended to prevent work stoppages and that saw over 30 percent of the private workforce as union members during the mid-1950's.

A New Labor Climate

When Ronald Reagan was elected president in 1980, business saw that it had a president who would be supportive of a more aggressive approach to unions and the use of strikes. In addition, the American workforce was changing, with a growing number of workers in service jobs or technical jobs, both of which were harder to organize.

Many Americans have been ambivalent about union power, especially strikes, but most have been opposed to strikes by unions representing public employees. The air traffic controllers union, Professional Air Traffic Controllers Organization (PATCO), called a strike in 1981, and President Reagan enjoyed wide public support when he fired the striking controllers and hired replacements. Since the Depression, there had not been such a widespread firing of striking workers, yet the PATCO members did not even have the full support of the labor movement.

The shifting climate for labor and lack of public support for strikers can be seen in the strikes at the Caterpillar, Staley, and Firestone/Bridgestone plants in the industrial heartland of Decatur, Illinois, during the 1990's. Decatur had long been a bastion of unionism, but the strikers found little public support when the management of each company took advantage of strikes to break the unions and enforce harsher working conditions with lower wages. In each case, the company claimed the necessity of competing in a global marketplace as the reason for imposing the cuts that led to the strikes.

In one sense, strikes, which have been used by workers to try to secure better conditions, have often been used by businesses as an excuse for weakening unions. Not all mass strikes have been failures, though. The strikes by automobile workers during the 1930's gained them better pay and working conditions. Some small strikes have also been quite effective for the workers. Nonetheless, while business has stated its opposition to strikes, some business leaders have been able to take advantage of governmental and public support to attack and weaken unions during strikes.

Strikes will continue to be used by workers as a means of enhancing their bargaining power, but many unions are turning to other tactics, such as political activism, public relations campaigns, and nonviolent protests, as means of affecting the work environment. In some cases, unions have organized successful boycotts of a business's products, as the farmworkers' union in California did during the 1970's and 1980's. Strikes will continue to occur when workers think they have no other choice. By the early twenty-first century, many businesses re-

turned to the hard-line antiunion approach of the past, while others tried to avoid labor trouble by offering such attractive wages and benefits that workers would be disinclined to join unions or strike.

John M. Theilmann

FURTHER READING

Brecher, Jeremy. *Strike!* Rev. ed. Cambridge, Mass.: South End Press, 1997. Good historical analysis of strikes. Written from a prolabor viewpoint.

Brown, Cliff. *Racial Conflicts and Violence in the Labor Market: Roots in the 1919 Steel Strike.* New York: Garland, 1998. An exploration of the 1919 steel strike that focuses on the divisiveness it fostered between white and black workers. Includes tables and figures, bibliography, and index.

Chaison, Gary, and Barbara Bigelow. *Unions and Legitimacy.* Ithaca, N.Y.: Cornell University Press, 2001. Broad economic analysis of labor unions and strikes.

Franklin, Stephen. *Three Strikes.* New York: Guilford Press, 2001. Examination of three strikes in Decatur, Illinois, during the 1990's that illustrated the growing weakness of the strike tactic.

Lens, Sidney. *The Labor Wars: From the Molly Maguires to the Sitdowns.* Garden City, N.Y.: Doubleday, 1973. Essential account of strikes in American society in the period from the 1870's through the 1930's that includes an excellent account of the organizing drive in the steel industry in 1919, the packinghouse strike that preceded it, and the role of William Z. Foster in both. Places events in the context of the ongoing battles that marked the rise of the American labor movement.

Lichtenstein, Nelson. *The Most Dangerous Man in Detroit.* New York: Basic Books, 1995. Insightful biography of Walther Reuther including information on strikes in the automobile industry.

_____. *State of the Union.* Princeton, N.J.: Princeton University Press, 2002. Comprehensive reinterpretation of the effectiveness of unions and strikes.

SEE ALSO: Air traffic controllers' strike; Baseball strike of 1972; Coal strike of 1902; Haymarket Riot; Homestead strike; Labor, U.S. Department of; Labor history; Private security industry; Pullman Strike; Railroad strike of 1877; Sit-down strike of 1936-1937; Supreme Court and labor law.

Land law, Supreme Court and. *See* Supreme Court and land law

Land laws

DEFINITION: Statutes, ordinances and treaties enacted by the U.S. Congress and state legislatures governing the acquisition, ownership, distribution, development, and conservation of the vast lands under U.S. sovereignty

SIGNIFICANCE: Land laws helped determine the development and distribution of perhaps the United States' greatest economic resource—its land. They were designed to encourage settlement and farming of the North American continent; raise revenue and reduce the public debt; extract resources; reward key constituencies and populations; promote education, business, and economic growth; and conserve wilderness for future generations.

Great Britain claimed sovereignty over part of the eastern seaboard of North America by right of discovery and conquest, despite the presence of Native Americans. In charter and grants, England divided this land among thirteen colonies, although the western boundaries of the colonies were not clearly defined. In the Proclamation of 1763, Parliament forbade settlement of the lands west of Appalachia, and the Quebec Act of 1774 redrew several of the boundaries of the larger colonies. By purchases, statutes, and treaties, the American colonies—and subsequently the United States—took away the rights of the Native Americans to occupy much of what had been their traditional homelands and confined or relocated them to reservations.

THE NEW NATION

The destiny of the new nation, as well as its economy and wealth, was inextricably linked with its land laws, policies, and politics. Real property has traditionally been the greatest source of wealth in human affairs. After gaining its independence, the United States inherited sovereignty over a portion of the North American lands claimed by England. The disposition of those lands, as well as the then-foreign lands stretching to the Pacific, would play a critical role in the economic development of the new nation. The states of South and North Carolina, Georgia, New York, Connecticut, Virginia, and Massachusetts ceded their lands west of Appalachia to the newly formed federal government under the Articles of Confederation. The Confederation was desperate for revenue as it lacked the power to tax and was liable for the debts of the Revolutionary War. Therefore, the goal of the first of the Confederation's land laws was simply to sell public lands to private citizens to raise revenue. The first major land ordinance in 1785 created the rectangular survey system of townships and sections that remained in the twenty-first century. The ordinance also preserved the Confederation's ownership of one-third of the precious metal mines on the lands it sold. The Northwest Ordinance of 1787 authorized the lands that had been ceded to the central government by the states to be settled in an orderly fashion, to be organized into territories, and to be admitted into the Union as new states.

With the enactment of a constitution in 1789, Congress had the means to make land laws with a more sophisticated purpose than retiring the public debt. Thomas Jefferson proposed selling public lands in compact units to create a democratic bedrock of small farmers. Secretary of the Treasury Alexander Hamilton favored selling the land wholesale to investors and manufacturers to promote rapid growth and industrialization. The Land Act of 1796, steered by Senator Albert Gallatin, further regularized the rectangular survey system in an attempt to promote land sales to individual settlers and discourage land speculators. It also created the office of surveyor general. The Frontier Land Bill of 1800 aimed at making lands on the western frontier more attractive to productive settlement.

EXPANSION

In the nineteenth century, although the federal government converted many of its public lands to private ownership, it added vast new tracts to its holdings. Over the course of the century, the United States acquired lands from Spain, France, Mexico, and Russia, extending the country's borders to the Pacific Ocean and multiplying its size more than fourfold. The largest addition came in 1803, when by treaty with France, the United States purchased the Louisiana Territory. Its 530 million acres doubled the size of the country. In 1812, Congress created the General Land Office to superintend the acquisition, maintenance, and disposition of federal lands. From its start to 1946, when it became the Bureau of Land Management, this office sold more than 1 billion acres of public land for settlement, development, and other purposes.

Florida was purchased from Spain in 1819. Texas was annexed in 1845. By the 1848 Treaty of Guadalupe-Hidalgo (which ended the war with Mexico), California, Nevada, Utah, New Mexico, and other territories were added to the United States. The Oregon territories were acquired in 1846, and Alaska was purchased in 1867. Federal laws arranged for these lands to pass into private hands in myriad ways, accomplishing numerous objectives. The overriding objective was to foster ownership by small farmers, who would productively cultivate the lots. In the Land Act of 1820, the price of federal land was reduced to $1.25 an acre, but purchases on credit were eliminated, which had been a device used by land speculators. The Preemption Act of 1841 gave preferential rights to settlers on public lands, despite public ambivalence toward "squatters." With land sales having greatly reduced the public debt, Congress could undertake more ambitious land policies. Military veterans were given bounties of land, amounting to some 61 million acres. Territories were given federal lands on admission to statehood. In the first half of the nineteenth century, Congress gave hundreds of millions of acres to states, entrepreneurs, and commercial interests to promote the construction of roads, canals, railroads, and other infrastructure.

In 1862, Congress enacted perhaps the two most significant land laws in U.S. history. The Homestead Act allowed any family to gain ownership of 160 acres of land if the family would settle on and cultivate it for at least five years. This historic act opened up the western United States to a wave of settlement and farming. The Morrill Land-Grant Act (also known as the Agricultural College Act) gave every state hundreds of thousands of acres to endow colleges of agricultural and mechanical arts. This act helped spur the creation of state universities devoted to the improvement and promotion of state economies.

Similar legislation followed these two historic laws. The Timber Culture Act of 1873 granted 160 acres of land to settlers who planted and grew trees on 40 acres of the land for ten years. The Desert Land Act of 1877 made available lots of 640 acres to settlers who constructed irrigation systems in the desert. The Timber and Stone Act of 1878 allowed people to purchase 160-acre blocks of land deemed fit for logging and mining, not farming, for $2.50 per acre. The Dawes General Allotment Act of 1887 brought the theory of private division and disposition of public land to the Native American reservations. Land that had been held by tribes in common was allotted to Native American families in 160-acre tracts, with the title to vest after five years of occupancy. Under the Alaska Statehood Act of 1958, the Bureau of Land Management was directed to begin the process of transferring 104.5 million acres of land to Alaska. The Alaska Native Claims Settlement Act of 1971 transferred the title of lands in Alaska to thirteen Alaska Native regional corporations and more than two hundred local village corporations.

RESOURCES AND CONSERVATION

Whereas the nineteenth century was characterized by disbursement of public land and associated resources to private hands, the twentieth century saw a welter of laws designed to conserve the public endowment. The initial policy of the United States toward resources, as with land, was to see them developed by private interests. The 1785 reservation of mining rights had been allowed to expire. The General Mining Law of 1872 allowed miners to stake claims to hardrock minerals on federal lands. The Taylor Grazing Act of 1934 legalized putting cattle and sheep to pasture on federal land.

By the end of the nineteenth century, with the fixing of America's borders and the closing of the frontiers, there was increasing concern about loss of public lands and the riches they contained. Presidents Benjamin Harrison and Grover Cleveland reserved 33 million acres for national timber. However, it was during the administration of Theodore Roosevelt, spurred by conservationists and naturalists such as Gifford Pinchot and John Muir, that federal conservation began in earnest. President Roosevelt signed the Newlands Reclamation Act of 1902 to support the creation of dams and irrigation works. The Act for the Preservation of American Antiquities of 1906 (known as the Antiquities Act) allowed Roosevelt to reserve 132 million acres of forest land and create national wildlife refuges and monuments. The Weeks Act of 1911 permitted the buying of land to enlarge the National Forest

System, and the Clarke-McNary Act of 1924 expanded this act. The Bankhead-Jones Farm Tenant Act of 1937 allowed the government to purchase land to rehabilitate it. Numerous laws governing development of water resources have been enacted since 1974 to promote the effective use of water, river, and lake resources. The Alaska National Interest Lands Conservation Act of 1980 set aside 79.54 million acres in Alaska as wilderness areas and national parks.

STATE LAND LAWS

As the United States expanded, federal law determined the acquisition, organization, use, and disposition of the new territories. However, state laws have always been most important in determining the uses of local real estate, usually by common, or judgemade, law. State common law determines the process of buying, selling, donating, and transferring real property and the attached structures. It also determines contracts of sale, the obligations and rights of landlords and tenants, and the doctrines of caveat emptor and caveat lessee, which ascertains the quality of the land and buildings that are purchased or leased. State law determines whether a state follows a community or common law property system. Likewise the law of fixtures—structures attached to the land—has traditionally been part of state common law. The technical aspects of land law are usually governed by state statute. For example, most states have statutes governing the maintenance of public records that reflect ownership of land ("recording systems"), requirements for a valid deed, and the warranties, registration, and marketability of titles. Likewise, the law of mortgages has been a matter of state law, although modern economic forces have seen the federalization of the mortgage system, with the creation of the federal home loan corporations Fannie Mae (Federal National Mortgage Association) and Freddie Mac (Federal Home Loan Mortgage Corporation).

Large-scale regulation of land use by the states is by and large a phenomenon of the twentieth century. In the nineteenth century, states implemented some laws controlling nuisances on land and regulating such private land controls as easements, covenants, and servitudes. However, comprehensive regulation of land use by state government has resulted from four modern areas of land law: zoning, landlord-tenant law, antidiscrimination statutes, and the law of eminent domain.

States, cities, and towns have used their regulatory power to zone land by industrial use, also known as Euclidean zoning, since 1916, when New York City divided the city into different use zones. Probably no system of land laws has had as pervasive an effect on the shape of modern economic life and its relation to the living patterns of workers as zoning laws. With zoning well established by the 1920's, states began regulating private landowners' use of their properties for health concerns, aesthetic and historic preservation considerations, noise control, and demographic mix.

DISPOSITION OF LANDS IN THE PUBLIC DOMAIN, 1781-2005

Type of Disposition	Acres (millions)
Land Laws	
Homestead Acts, grant or sale	287.5
Timber Culture Act, grant or sale	10.9
Desert Land Act, sale	10.7
Timber and Stone Act, sale	13.9
State of Alaska, grant	91.4
Alaska Native Claims Settlement Act, grant	37.4
State Grants	
Support of common schools	77.6
Swampland reclamation	64.9
Railroad construction	37.1
Canals and rivers	6.1
Construction of wagon roads	3.4
Support of miscellaneous institutions	21.7
Unclassified purposes	117.6
Other Grants and Claims	
Railroad corporations, grant	94.4
Veterans as military bounties, grant	61.0
Confirmed as private land claims	34.0

Source: Data from U.S. Department of the Interior, Bureau of Land Management, "Public Land Statistics," 2005

The 1960's and 1970's saw a revolution in landlord-tenant law as the old rules gave way to a consumer-oriented movement that aimed to guarantee tenants habitable and enjoyable premises. The wholesale revisions in landlord law were again largely the work of the state judiciary. However, for political reasons, it was the federal government that took the lead in antidiscrimination land law. The historic Fair Housing Act of 1968, as subsequently amended, prohibits discrimination in the sale, purchasing, or leasing of land on the basis of race, national origin, religion, sex, disability, or familial status. Many states have extended antidiscrimination prohibitions in their own laws.

The power of eminent domain—to take the property of private landowners—has always been an inherent power of state government, although circumscribed by the U.S. Constitution. The Fifth Amendment limits the exercise of eminent domain to circumstances of public use and for just compensation. In recent years, in response to the controversial Supreme Court case of *Kelo v. City of New London* (2005), numerous states have enacted legislation to further limit the ability of local governments to exercise their powers of eminent domain.

Howard Bromberg

FURTHER READING

Berry, Wendell. *Home Economics.* New York: North Point Press, 1987. Fourteen essays in which novelist and nature writer Berry pleads for protection of land and the lifestyles associated with it.
Dombeck, Michael, Christopher Wood, and Jack Williams. *From Conquest to Conservation: Our Public Lands Legacy.* Washington, D.C.: Island Press, 2003. Argues for increased conservation based on the legacy of public land laws and policies.
Friedman, Lawrence. *A History of American Law.* 3d ed. New York: Touchstone Books, 2005. An outstanding survey of American legal history, with diverse sections on land law in the eighteenth, early and late nineteenth, and twentieth centuries.
Gates, Paul. *History of Public Land Law Development.* Washington, D.C.: Government Printing Office, 1968. The official history of federal lands, authorized by the Public Land Review Commission. Scholarly, immense, and definitive.
Hall, Kermit. *The Magic Mirror: Law in American History.* New York: Oxford University Press, 1989. A history of American legal culture that argues that the variety of American land laws acted both to encourage and to arrest economic development.
Lehman, Scott. *Privatizing Public Lands.* New York: Oxford University Press, 1995. Study of public lands and the effects of selling them into private hands.
Turner, Frederick Jackson. *The Frontier in American History.* Tucson: University of Arizona Press, 1994. Reprinting of Turner's famous 1893 essay on the closing of the American Frontier as well as his other essays relating to American land history, policy, and law.
Wolf, Michael, ed. *Powell on Real Property.* Albany, N.Y.: Matthew Bender, 2000. Thorough and respected summary of property law.

SEE ALSO: Agriculture; Environmental movement; Homestead Act of 1862; Housing and Urban Development, U.S. Department of; Indian removal; Mexican War; Northwest Ordinances; Real estate industry, commercial; Real estate industry, residential; Supreme Court and land law; Zoning, commercial.

Latin American trade with the United States

SIGNIFICANCE: Historically linked by their geographical proximity and their shared histories of being created by European colonialism, the United States and the many nations of Latin America have long been important trading partners. The late twentieth century rise in globalization has pushed these nations' economic development closer together and prompted the creation of new treaty relationships that are moving the entire Western Hemisphere toward a single free trade zone.

As former colonies of European nations that won their independence during the same era, around the turn of the nineteenth century, the United States and the nations of Latin America in Central and South America and the Caribbean share similar histories. Efforts of Great Britain's North American colonies to conduct trade with the Latin American colonies were resisted by imperial Spain and Portugal. However, after most of the Western Hemisphere's nations were independent, U.S. trade with Latin America began to grow. Differences among the countries in climate, topography, and raw materials ensured that they would produce many products that their trading partners could not produce for themselves, and their physical proximity to one another encouraged their trade.

The decades surrounding the turn of the twenty-first century have seen a new impetus in regional trade that produced new treaty arrangements fostering free trade. The success of the majority of these agreements indicates that their emphasis has been on the reduction or elimination of tariff rates and duties, serving to stimulate trade among the signatories. Other issues that the agreements address are the climate for private investment by foreigners and their potential effect on the standard of living of the poorer segments of the nations involved.

NORTH AMERICAN FREE TRADE AGREEMENT

A major stimulus to U.S.-Latin American trade has been the North American Free Trade Agreement (NAFTA), which the United States, Mexico, and Canada signed in 1994. That agreement transformed the three North American nations into something like a free trade zone, greatly increasing trade among those nations. By 2006, Mexico accounted for 11.5 percent of U.S. trade, as measured by value, and accounted for 60 percent of all of U.S. trade with Latin America. The United States exported goods valued at $134 billion to Mexico in 2006. In turn, the Mexicans shipped $198 billion worth of goods to the United States during the same period.

The NAFTA treaty did not discontinue all tariffs and duties immediately but began phasing them out over a fourteen-year period. This staggered approach was adopted so as to soften the effect that cheaper prices of imported goods would have on existing domestic markets. Even so, many Mexican peasant farmers found themselves unable to compete with some imported American agricultural products. The main challenge the farmers faced was the difficulty of shipping their own products over poor roads and through inadequate railroad service. NAFTA officials have sought to aid the farmers by investing in a series of improvements designed to support their marketing capabilities. Nevertheless, many Mexican farmers have continued to oppose the treaty. Despite this problem and several minor

disputes, NAFTA is generally regarded as an outstanding success as a trade stimulus. It has been one of the world's most successful trade agreements in terms of the combined gross domestic product produced for all three parties. The positive results achieved have given rise to the development of other agreements of a similar nature.

CENTRAL AMERICAN FREE TRADE AGREEMENT

In 2004, the success of NAFTA led to the formulation of the similar Central American Free Trade Agreement (CAFTA), involving the United States and the Central American nations of Costa Rica, El Salvador, Guatemala, Honduras, and Nicaragua. Shortly afterward, the Caribbean island nation of the Dominican Republic joined the agreement, which became known as DR-CAFTA.

The goal of DR-CAFTA has been to create a free trade area similar to that of the NAFTA agreement. It has been designed to remove upward of 80 percent of the tariffs imposed on U.S. imports entering the Central American nations and the Dominican Republic. When the agreement was signed, most exports from those nations to the United States were already duty-free because of the U.S. government's existing Caribbean Basin Initiative. The new agreement created an export market for the United States second only in size to that of NAFTA.

By 2008, two-way trade within the DR-CAFTA nations amounted to $32 billion annually. The plan was designed to help modernize the economies of the six smaller countries, improve their labor laws, raise their environmental standards, and encourage private investment in all the nations. One concern expressed by some economists in the small Latin American countries was the possible harm from the U.S. mass producers of competing goods to the fledgling industries within their own borders.

DR-CAFTA and other agreements similar to it are considered by many free trade advocates as steps in the direction toward the ultimate goal of many—a Free Trade Area of the Americas (FTAA) that will encompass North, Central, and South America and the island nations of the Caribbean. Most economists regard free trade as largely positive because it reduces the need for domestic subsidies, encourages formation of capital investment, and helps promote full employment for the parties involved as well. An obvious advantage in the adoption of a hemisphere-wide FTAA would be in the reduction in rules governing each separate agreement. The adoption of such a plan would make trade activity easier to manage by all the parties concerned.

OTHER FREE TRADE AGREEMENTS

In 2004, a free trade agreement between the United States and Chile went into effect. This bilateral treaty soon resulted in a 154 percent increase in the value of trade between the two countries. By 2008, the United States was Chile's primary trading partner for both imports and exports. The United States sends Chile electronic goods, motor vehicles, road-building equipment, fertilizers, tractors, and petroleum oil. Chile ships the United States copper, wine, cheeses, and a wide variety of fruits and vegetables and wood products. As a Southern Hemisphere exporter of agricultural products, Chile is a particularly valuable trading partner of the United States because it grows summer crops during the Northern Hemisphere's winter.

The United States entered similar trade agreements with Peru in 2005 and Colombia in 2006 and has negotiated a trade agreement with the Central American nation of Panama. In these new agreements, both the U.S. and Latin American representatives have addressed an additional challenge—the problems arising from gross disparities in income distribution in the Latin American nations. The business sector believes that increased trade will increase job opportunities for the poorest sectors of their respective economies. Representatives of the International Labor Organization have argued that the agreements should spell out the labor sector's rights, such as provisions against the exploitation of child labor.

MERCOSUR

The United States does not have an exclusive prerogative to form trade agreements throughout the Western Hemisphere. Other countries in the region have also recognized the necessity to inaugurate free trade programs to help them meet the challenges of economic globalization. As early as 1991, four countries in South America's so-called Southern Cone—Brazil, Argentina, Uruguay, and Paraguay—initiated a treaty designed to increase economic cooperation and to expedite trade within the

UNITED STATES TRADE WITH SELECTED LATIN AMERICAN COUNTRIES, 2007, IN MILLIONS OF DOLLARS

Country	Imports	Exports	Balance
Chile	8,314	8,999	−685
Costa Rica	4,581	3,942	639
Columbia	8,558	9,434	−876
Dominican Republic	6,084	4,216	1,868
El Salvador	2,313	2,044	269
Guatemala	4,065	3,026	1,039
Honduras	4,461	3,912	549
Nicaragua	890	1,604	−714
Panama	3,740	365	3,375
Peru	4,120	5,272	−1,152

Source: Data from U.S. Census Bureau, Foreign Trade Division, Data Dissemination Branch, Washington, D.C. 20233

Note: Trade figures are from the U.S. perspective.

group, which is known as Mercosur (Mercado Común del Sur) or Mercosul (Mercado Comun do Sul). In 2006, Venezuela became the fifth member of the group, which has steadily reduced tariffs on imports and exports traded among the members of the group. The original assessment of the group's trading potential has proven to be correct, as the volume of trade among the five nations has increased markedly since the inauguration of the treaty. Although competition within the group in some products has continued, the overall trade balances among them produces a positive flow of commerce.

Since Mercosur's founding, Bolivia, Chile, Colombia, Ecuador, and Peru have become associate members. By 2008, Mercosur had announced its goal to make all South and Central American nations members. However, Mercosur's quest to expand its membership may present long-range problems to an overall trade program for the Western Hemisphere. For example, Brazil, a Mercosur leader, and the United States have shown little willingness to move closer to each other on a number of trade issues. Both Brazil and Argentina have continued to maintain strong restrictions on their trade with the United States. Venezuelan president Hugo

Chávez has openly expressed his opposition to any expansion of U.S. influence in Latin American affairs. However, Chávez is more concerned with American political influence than he is with economic relationships with the United States. Meanwhile, the United States has continued to buy large quantities of Venezuelan petroleum, and Venezuelan imports of American products have continued to increase. Meanwhile, increasing government control of industry in Bolivia and Ecuador has tended to inhibit the growth of commerce between these two South American nations and the United States.

Trade continues to be a major consideration in U.S.-Latin American relations. It is one of the areas in economic policy that is subject to a great deal of wrangling and debate among traders on all sides. Mexico has remained the leading Latin American trading partner of the United States. Mexico's imports from the United States increased by 11.5 percent in 2006 alone, but trade between the United States and many other Latin American countries has also generally increased. U.S. trade has even increased with Venezuela, despite growing political friction between the two nations.

Carl Henry Marcoux

FURTHER READING

Bognanno, Mario, and Kathryn J. Ready, eds. *The North American Free Trade Agreement: Labor, Industry, and Government Perspectives.* Westport, Conn.: Quorum Books, 1993. Report on a 1991 conference in Minneapolis at which representatives of labor, industry and government from all three countries participating in the North American Free Trade Agreement discussed a wide range of issues dividing them.

Irwin, Douglas A. *Free Trade Under Fire.* Princeton, N.J.: Princeton University Press, 2005. Douglas discusses two major threats to the global expansion of free trade—programs of protectionism adopted by individual countries to defend their domestic economies and the actions of so-called public interest groups that seek to block free trade progress.

Machinea, Jose Luis, and Guillermo Rozenwurcel. *Macroeconomic Coordination in Latin America: Does It Have a Future?* Santiago, Chile: United Nations Publications, 2005. Obstacles and opportunities in global financial markets.

Roett, Riordan, ed. *Mercosur Regional Integration, World Markets.* Boulder, Colo.: Lynne Rienner Publishers, 1999. A discussion of Mercosur connections with other trade associations and countries.

Von Bertrab, Hermann. *Negotiating NAFTA. A Mexican Envoy's Account.* Westport, Conn.: Praeger, 1997. A banker, Von Bertrab joined the Mexican government to help plan the NAFTA agreement in Washington, D.C., from 1990 to 1994. He headed up the Mexican office there, coordinating all government and public relations activities.

Weintraub, Sidney. *Development and Democracy in the Southern Cone: Imperatives for U.S. Policy in South America.* Washington, D.C.: Center for Strategic and International Studies, 2000. Discussion of future possibilities in the trade relationships between the United States and Argentina, Brazil, Chile, and Paraguay.

SEE ALSO: Asian trade with the United States; Canadian trade with the United States; Chinese trade with the United States; Drug trafficking; European trade with the United States; General Agreement on Tariffs and Trade; Immigration; International economics and trade; Japanese trade with the United States; Mexican trade with the United States; North American Free Trade Agreement.

Legal services

DEFINITION: Advice, representation, and other services provided by lawyers and other legal professionals, including drafting official legal documents and filing them with courts of law

SIGNIFICANCE: The United States is a nation of laws, and from its inception, the legal profession has been at the heart of its government, culture, and economy. Lawyers have been essential to the orderly operation of American business. With the proliferation of lawyers, opportunities for lawsuits, and large damage awards, the provision of legal services has become a huge industry.

In colonial America, the legal profession was small, fluid, and somewhat mistrusted. Lawyers were few, because in the wide-open spaces of the American frontier, farmers, soldiers, and merchants were needed, not legal technicians. The norms of the profession were flexible: Almost anyone with a command of legal terminology could begin a legal practice. Lawyers were often mistrusted, because they were associated with the established order deriving from the English crown, increasingly at odds with the colonies. However, the approach of independence saw major changes in the legal profession. Recourse to the law became a protection against English tyranny.

With the development of an economic infrastructure in the colonies, lawyers were necessary to draft contracts for merchants, probate wills and estates, register land titles, and construct accurate pleadings. A system of apprenticeship and the printing of legal treatises, especially *Commentaries on the Laws of England* (1765-1769) by Sir William Blackstone, enhanced the prestige of the legal profession. Commercial lawyers such as Alexander Hamilton rose to prominence. Property law—the centerpiece of civil law in an agricultural society—shifted from a static view of rigid inheritances and fixed estates to the free alienability and exchange of land. The conception of the corporation—favored under the law as a "legal person"—shifted from that of a public body to a private, commercial enterprise.

In the beginning of the nineteenth century, the federal and state governments created legal franchises and monopolies to promote banks, canals, ferries, mills, and railroads. Alexis de Tocqueville described lawyers as the American aristocracy, indicating their role in shaping the new economic order. Although the bulk of legal services throughout American history would be provided by unheralded solo practitioners, famous lawyers such as Lemuel Shaw and Daniel Webster earned tens of thousands of dollars in legal fees representing American businesses and corporations.

THE GILDED AGE

During the middle of the nineteenth century, the political and legal crisis over slavery and southern secession overwhelmed both the nation and the legal profession, and questions of business receded in importance. In the decades after the U.S. Civil War—a period often called the Gilded Age—the United States underwent a period of enormous economic growth and industrialization. Lawyers who represented the great American commercial and manufacturing enterprises garnered prestige and wealth. The legal profession itself was transformed, as were the other learned professions such as medicine, teaching, and engineering. Admission to the practice of law was made more rigorous, professional standards and canons were adopted, and jurists searched for scientific principles to undergird legal doctrine.

During the 1870's the first true law schools—as opposed to legal departments of undergraduate colleges—were established. With the implementation of the case method at Harvard Law School by Dean Christopher Langdell, law students were given a common mode of training, useful for dealing with complex commercial issues. Bar associations were organized in most states to raise professional standards and to create business opportunities for lawyers. The American Bar Association (ABA) was established in 1878 and would soon become one of the more powerful professional organizations in the country. The composition of the legal profession was transformed as well. It was increasingly seen as a path of upward mobility for children of the middle classes. Although barriers of all sorts remained, there was greater ethnic, even racial diversity, in the legal profession, reflecting the waves of immigration of late nineteenth century America. Women, mostly barred from voting and politics, found occasional opportunities in law.

For a century, leading lawyers had been assisting the growth and influence of business corporations. In the beginning of the twentieth century, elite lawyers organized themselves into their own corporations, acquiring the size, diversity, and legal advantages necessary to dominate the profession and take a leading role in the financial world. The symbol and innovator of this trend was the New York City law firm of Cravath. With the arrival of Paul Cravath to a New York law partnership in 1899, the characteristics of the modern Wall Street law firm were swiftly established: steady growth in the number of law partners; specialization of the firm into departments so as to serve the increasingly complex legal needs of businesses and wealthy clients; billing of hefty retainers and hourly fees; and the recruitment, training, and forming of the best graduates of top law schools. A lawyer such as Elihu Root, distinguished in public life and respected for his legal expertise, was able to earn $100,000 in 1900 practicing law on Wall Street.

NEW DEALS FOR LAWYERS

The decades from the 1920's to the 1950's were characterized by economic boom and bust, marked by depression, war, and a growing pulse of prosperity. The leaders of the legal profession took on the mission of bringing order to turbulent economic times. In public life, lawyers were instrumental in devising, enacting, and administering New Deal legislation and regulations. In private law, the most notable achievement was the Uniform Commercial Code (UCC) completed in 1950. The UCC was a complete revision and codification of the laws concerning commercial transaction and payments that underlie the American economy: buying and selling goods, securing credit, negotiating instruments, and regulating consumer transactions.

During the 1960's, the practice of law would become ever more diverse, if not stratified. The corporate law firms found their services in great demand, in part due to the revolution in tort (injury) law, with new causes of action for product liability, professional malpractice, mass torts, and environmental wrongs. To attract top-performing graduates, Cravath and other firms began paying first-year associates as much as $15,000 per year, a princely sum at the time. For the middle class, traditionally served by smaller or individual practice lawyers, companies such as Pre-Paid Legal Services and Hyatt Legal Services began offering lower-cost legal representation.

The Civil Rights movement, the social upheavals of the 1960's, and the Great Society legislation spurred new legal services for the poor, elderly, minorities, and disadvantaged. Legal aid societies had existed for centuries; during the 1960's, they were transformed into active agents of social change. Staffed with more lawyers, with a renewed sense of mission, and better funded, legal aid societies were busy defending the indigent and the criminally accused, accorded more procedural and constitutional rights under the U.S. Supreme Court presided over by Chief Justice Earl Warren. As a reflection of their prominence, various legal aid societies were consolidated into the congressionally funded Legal Services Corporation in 1974. A new kind of law firm came into prominence as well—the public interest law firm, often paid from the enhanced fees created by Congress to encourage civil rights lawsuits.

By the end of the twentieth century, the legal profession, which always took a major role in assisting business, had become a big business itself. There were now more than a million lawyers in the United States. One major corporate law firm had grown to an astronomical 3,117 lawyers. Already in 1977, the U.S. Supreme Court, in a majority opinion written by Associate Justice Harry Blackmun in *Bates v. State Bar of Arizona*, had struck down the traditional ban on lawyer advertising as unconstitutional. New lawsuits proliferated at dizzying speed.

A paradigm shift had taken place in the law. At the nation's origin, questions of property dominated legal practice and jurisprudence. Contract law rose to prominence in the nineteenth and early twentieth centuries, reflecting the free-market, commercial transformation of the American economy. At the end of the twentieth century, however, the tort action would become the paradigmatic lawsuit, dominating the courts and the headlines. By 2002, the direct cost of the U.S. tort system was approaching 2 percent of the gross domestic product (GDP). Advocates of this new phenomenon argued that it meant greater access to justice for all Americans and a fairer and safer America; critics argued that it meant the enrichment of lawyers at the expense of society.

Lawyers had reached the status of celebrities and entrepreneurs, with opportunities for money making that rivaled the richest capitalists. Elite lawyers had always received handsome hourly wages for their representation, but two new methods of compensation opened unlimited chances at wealth for personal injury lawyers. The contingency fee allowed for plaintiffs' attorneys to collect at least one-third of their clients' awards. As juries awarded record damages, lawyers walked away with million-dollar prizes. Even more lucrative was the class-action lawsuit. Originally created during the 1970's as a tool to favor consumers, the class-action lawsuit allowed lawyers to assemble thousands of plaintiffs for even the smallest alleged wrong, arrange an out-of-court settlement with the defendant's lawyers, and walk away with a fortune, while individual plaintiffs were often left with a pittance.

In securities class-action litigation, shareholders could feel doubly punished—first, by the decline in the share price of a given security and second, by the class-action suit brought in their name against their own company. The firm of Milberg Weiss brought 149 shareholder class actions in the year 2000 alone. Lawyer Richard Scruggs made an estimated $400 million to $1 billion from the tobacco settlement of 1998, part of the estimated $15 billion that private lawyers collected from this litigation; an article in the March, 2007, issue of the *ABA Journal* described the big winners of the settlement as the tobacco companies, state treasuries, and lawyers. In an April, 2002, report, the White House Council of Economic Advisors estimated that the United States was paying an excessive "litigation tax" of over $136 billion. The political controversy over tort reform revolved around the question of whether all of this represented justice for hitherto unrepresented victims or a threat to American prosperity.

In the years between the world wars, revenues from the federal income tax grew steadily, from $35 million in 1913 to $4 billion in 1920 to $20 billion by 1941. Nevertheless, the income tax was insignificant in the lives of most citizens. As late as 1939, only 6 percent of Americans were liable for any income tax at all. Thus, tax-preparation services consisted mostly of accountants, lawyers, and other agents advising the extremely wealthy on how to reduce their tax burden. This would change with World War II and the postwar years, as the personal income tax came to loom large in the lives of average Americans.

TAX PREPARATION

In 1939, there were only 3.9 million payers of the federal income tax. By war end in 1945, the number of taxpayers had risen to 42.6 million and tax collection to $35.1 billion. Over 74 percent of Americans were now liable for federal income tax. For most middle-income payers, tax planning was not necessarily the first priority. Rather, people clamored for help in preparing the complex array of Internal Revenue Service tax forms. Henry Bloch, a student at Harvard Business School, realized the opportunity this represented. In 1946, Bloch and his two brothers Leon and Richard opened a bookkeeping service in Kansas City, Missouri, with an emphasis on

---

TAX-PREPARATION SERVICES

Tax preparers assist businesses and individuals in planning, preparing, and paying taxes owed to the government. This industry is dominated by a single law—the federal tax code. Already in 1884, Congress had authorized the secretary of the Treasury to regulate the commercial provision of tax representation. In 1887, the American Institute of Certified Public Accountants was created; accountants would always play the central role in tax preparation for businesses.

The ratification of the Sixteenth Amendment to the U.S. Constitution in 1913 authorized an individual federal income tax. From that point on, tax preparation services would grow, as tax revenues increased and tax forms became more complex. For example, the accounting firm of Arthur Andersen reported an increase in its fees to $188,000 in 1919 and $322,000 in 1920 as a result of growth in the demand for tax-preparation services.

---

tax management for small businesses. In 1955, they incorporated the company under the name H&R Block, offering services exclusively in income tax preparation. Business boomed as has all tax preparation in the postwar years.

By 1979, 55.8 percent of individual tax returns would be prepared by professional tax preparers. Corporations were subjected to ever more extensive and expensive federal taxes as well. These were handled mostly by certified public accountants, with the "big eight" accounting firms dominating tax preparation for the largest companies. With the Internal Revenue Code reaching ever greater complexity with each congressional session, tax preparation services remain a growth industry in the United States.

Howard Bromberg

FURTHER READING

Aaron, Henry J., and Joel Slemrod, eds. *The Crisis in Tax Administration.* Washington, D.C.: Brookings Institution Press, 2004. Collection of essays on questions of tax policy and implementation, including a chapter on tax preparers.

Bloomfield, Maxwell. *American Lawyers in a Changing Society, 1776-1876.* Cambridge: Harvard University Press, 1999. Demonstrates the dramatic changes in nineteenth century legal services through profiles of major figures in the law.

Brownlee, W. Elliot. *Federal Taxation in America.* 2d ed. Cambridge: Cambridge University Press, 2004. A concise, much-cited history of federal taxation.

Friedman, Lawrence. *A History of American Law.* 3d ed. New York: Simon & Schuster, 2005. Seminal, brilliantly written history of American law and the legal profession, from a social perspective.

Goulden, Joseph. *The Money Lawyers: The No-Holds-Barred World of Today's Richest and Most Powerful Lawyers.* New York: St. Martin's Press, 2006. Journalistic account "super-lawyers," those garnering billions of dollars in damage awards.

Horowitz, Morton. *The Transformation of American Law, 1780-1860.* Cambridge, Mass.: Harvard University Press, 2006. An influential book emphasizing the legal contributions to the growth of nineteenth century capitalism, although perhaps overestimating the transformation of law in service to the wealthy classes.

Speiser, Stuart. *Lawyers and the American Dream.* New York: M. Evans, 2005. A favorable, autobiographical account of modern tort law.

SEE ALSO: Bankruptcy law; Business crimes; Contract law; Copyright law; Justice, U.S. Department of; Merger and corporate reorganization industry; Patent law; Service industries.

Lend-Lease Act

THE LAW: Federal law allowing the president of the United States to give material aid to the Allies before and after the United States entered World War II

DATE: March 11, 1941-August 21, 1945

SIGNIFICANCE: The Lend-Lease Act, which provided war material to Allied nations, created massive production for American industry and employment for labor.

When World War II began in Europe during the late 1930's, President Franklin D. Roosevelt said that although the United States could remain neutral in deed, it could not remain neutral in spirit. His government was firmly committed to the side of the Allies and hoped to aid them by making the United States the arsenal of democracy and sending war materiel and other goods to the Allied nation while embargoing the same for the Axis. In June, 1940, Roosevelt announced his intentions. However, U.S. law demanded that only goods that were paid for in cash (the cash-and-carry policy) could be delivered, and Great Britain could not pay in advance.

In July, Roosevelt sent fifty destroyers to Britain in exchange for ninety-nine-year leases on bases for American ships and troops in the Caribbean and Newfoundland. In the 1940 presidential campaign, while running for an unprecedented third term, Roosevelt pledged to keep the United States out of the war. However, after the election, Roosevelt proposed on December 8, 1940, the Lend-Lease Bill, which provided that the United States could send material for the defense of any nation whose survival was vital to American interests. Payment could be made directly or indirectly in any manner that the president determined. Roosevelt used the analogy that if a neighbor's house was burning, no one would refuse to lend that person a garden hose.

A great debate followed over whether the bill would bring about American involvement in the war. The administration, led by Secretary of War Henry L. Stimson, argued that providing Great Britain with the material would help the United States stay out of the conflict and, at the very least, give the United States time to build up its military strength.

Congress passed the bill in March, 1941. Although initially the act was intended to apply only to the United Kingdom, it soon was extended to other nations fighting the Axis. In April, it was extended to China and, in September, to the Soviet Union. Furthermore, the controversial action was in fact a violation of U.S.-declared neutrality, and during the period between the passage of the bill and December, when the United States entered the war, German submarines attacked U.S. ships delivering war material. On October 31, 1941, a U-boat sank the famous destroyer the USS *Reuben James* as it escorted a convoy carrying lend-lease material.

Over forty nations had received aid by the end of the war. Great Britain (63 percent) and the Soviet Union (22 percent) received the most. The total amount was $49.1 billion in value. Much of it was not repaid and counted as gifts. However, the Allied countries gave $8 billion in aid to American troops stationed in their countries, the so-called reverse lend-lease.

Frederick B. Chary

FURTHER READING

Dobson, Alan P. *U.S. Wartime Aid to Britain, 1940-1946.* Dover, N.H.: Croom Helm, 1986.

Kimball, Warren F. *The Most Unsordid Act: Lend-Lease, 1939-1941.* Baltimore: Johns Hopkins University Press, 1969.

Weeks, Albert Loren. *Russia Life-Saver: Lend-Lease Aid to the U.S.S.R. in World War II.* Lanham, Md.: Lexington Books, 2004.

SEE ALSO: Military-industrial complex; War surplus; World War II.

Lewis, John L.

IDENTIFICATION: American labor leader
BORN: February 12, 1880; Lucas, Iowa
DIED: June 11, 1969; Alexandria, Virginia
SIGNIFICANCE: Through his persistent work and vision as a labor union leader, Lewis helped shape the modern American labor union and boost the financial standing of the average American worker.

John L. Lewis. (Library of Congress)

During his younger years, John L. Lewis worked as a coal miner, farmer, construction worker, and small-business entrepreneur. He became involved in the labor movement in 1906 and helped organize the American Federation of Labor (AFL) in 1911. In 1920, he was elected president of the United Mine Workers of America (UMWA), the largest trade union in the United States.

As unemployment grew in the United States during the 1930's, membership in the UMWA dropped from 500,000 to less than 100,000. Lewis helped form the Committee for Industrial Organization (CIO; later Congress of Industrial Organizations) in 1935. When he was elected president of the CIO in 1937, it had more members than the AFL. During the 1940's, Lewis led a series of strikes that produced increased wages for mine workers. Membership in the UMWA grew to over 500,000. Lewis served as president of the UMWA until 1960.

Lewis stood up against business tycoons and was insistent that every worker in the United States, including those in menial factory jobs, should have a middle-class existence. He fought vigorously and ag-

gressively against the antilabor Taft-Hartley Act of 1947. He regularly advised the president of the United States and challenged America's corporate leaders. Through his influence, unfair labor practices diminished, wages continued to increase, health benefits and retirement plans were established and enhanced, and work safety regulations were passed. The standard of living of millions of American workers was raised because of his persistent work on their behalf.

Alvin K. Benson

FURTHER READING

Dubofsky, Melwyn, and Warren Van Tine. *John L. Lewis: A Biography.* Champaign: University of Illinois Press, 1986.

Kurland, Gerald. *John L. Lewis: Labor's Strong-Willed Organizer.* Charlotteville, N.Y.: SamHar Press, 1973.

SEE ALSO: AFL-CIO; Labor history; Labor strikes; Taft-Hartley Act; United Mine Workers of America; World War II.

Lewis and Clark expedition

THE EVENT: Expedition that traversed the Great Plains and the American Northwest in search of trade routes to the Pacific Ocean

DATE: May 14, 1804-September 23, 1806

PLACE: The Great Plains and northwestern America

SIGNIFICANCE: Acting as official representatives of the United States government, Lewis and Clark explored and charted territories newly acquired through the Louisiana Purchase. Their expedition helped spur westward movement by U.S. citizens who would eventually establish homesteads, cities, and businesses, taking advantage of the country's abundant natural resources and connecting the far-flung parts of the nation through a series of roads and railways.

In 1803, when President Thomas Jefferson issued detailed instructions to Meriwether Lewis for the conduct of an expedition up the Missouri River to the Pacific Ocean, he stated explicitly that the mission was "for the purposes of commerce." Under this broad umbrella, Jefferson justified sending two army officers with a party of nearly thirty men called the Corps of Discovery on a two-year journey. The expedition would encounter dozens of Native American tribes already engaged in a brisk and complex trading system not only among themselves but also with traders representing the interests of the French and British governments.

For some time, Jefferson had been worried about efforts by the British and French to establish claims to lands west and northwest of the Mississippi River, thereby threatening the security of the fledgling United States. In Jefferson's view, security along the western border of the country would be better secured through trade than through warfare. He realized that to bring about commercial exchanges, the U.S. government would need sound knowledge of the landscape and its inhabitants. Hence, although the Louisiana Purchase was not completed until December, 1803, Jefferson began laying out to Congress the rationale for cross-continental exploration nearly a year earlier.

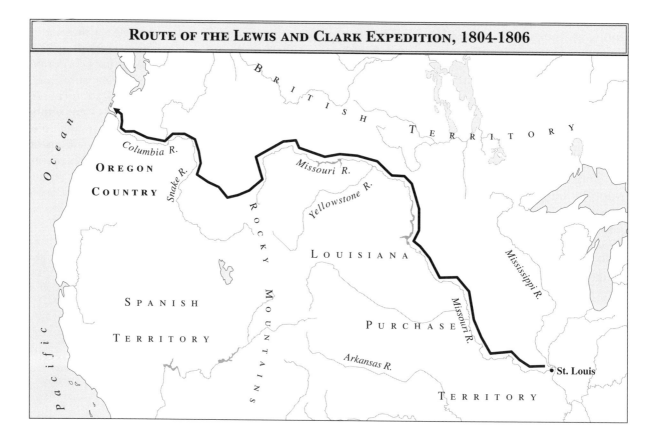

ROUTE OF THE LEWIS AND CLARK EXPEDITION, 1804-1806

Lewis and his co-commander William Clark were charged with documenting routes, specifically river passages, that might provide an unimpeded pathway from the Mississippi to the Pacific Ocean. Jefferson believed the population of his country would inevitably expand. The nation of farmers he envisioned would require additional land to thrive. He realized, however, that trade was key to the success of sophisticated agrarian communities, which would need to get goods to market and to obtain items they could not manufacture or grow locally.

Therefore, when Lewis began preparing for the expedition that eventually was launched in 1804, in addition to purchasing large quantities of weapons, ammunition, foodstuffs, medical supplies, and scientific equipment needed by his men, he spent about 30 percent of the funds allocated to him on sewing items, knives, and jewelry for the Native Americans the party would meet along the way. These goods were not specifically for trade, however; they were intended to show good faith toward the local tribes and to introduce them to materials Americans could provide in the future. Lewis and Clark also took along commemorative medals inscribed with a bust of Jefferson on one side and symbols of peace on the other to signal their intention of establishing friendly relationships with local tribes. The medals were also meant to make it clear that Lewis and Clark represented a government claiming sovereignty over the territory and wishing to engage in commerce with its new "citizens."

During the two years in which Lewis and Clark traversed the continent westward to the Pacific Ocean and back again, they made it a point to meet peaceably with Native American tribes, exchanging gifts and trading for foodstuffs and information that would help them locate the best routes to the west. Many tribes found their claim to be interested in trade rather curious, since these white men had little interest in fur pelts. Lewis and Clark knew, however, that, if they were successful, government officials would follow them later to establish trading posts all along the route they were mapping. When the explorers returned to the East in 1806, they provided information about potentially lucrative commercial opportunities and about the customs of tribes that might make good trading partners. Even before their journals were published in 1814, Americans had learned enough about their exploits to realize that there was great promise for trade and settlement west of the Mississippi.

The immediate result of the Corps of Discovery's trek was an increase in activity by private traders operating out of St. Louis, which quickly became the hub for America's dealings with Native American tribes west of the Mississippi. Only after the United States had obtained additional territory as a result of its war with Mexico in 1848 and gold was discovered in California was there wide-scale migration into the regions Lewis and Clark had traversed. Although their expedition had set the tenor for peaceful coexistence with Native Americans based on trade, subsequent actions by U.S. citizens and their government would instead be driven by a desire to remove indigenous peoples from locations that would be most beneficial to the white population for agriculture, mining, or manufacturing.

Laurence W. Mazzeno

FURTHER READING

Ambrose, Stephen E. *Undaunted Courage.* New York: Simon & Schuster, 1996. Detailed account of the Lewis and Clark expedition, focusing on the hardships faced by the participants and their determination to carry out the mission assigned to them by President Jefferson.

Fritz, Harry William. *The Lewis and Clark Expedition.* Westport, Conn.: Greenwood Press, 2004. Useful handbook outlining the course of the expedition; provides brief biographies of principal participants and information on scientific and ethnographic contributions made by the party.

Hoxie, Frederick, and Jay Nelson, eds. *Lewis and Clark and the Indian Country: The Native American Perspective.* Urbana: University of Illinois Press, 2007. Collection of essays examining the impact of the expedition on Native Americans living in areas explored by Lewis and Clark; includes commentaries on matters of trade and commerce and a section discussing changes that occurred as a result of future incursions into the area by U.S. citizens.

Ronda, James. *Jefferson's West: A Journey with Lewis and Clark.* Charlottesville, Va.: Thomas Jefferson Foundation, 2000. Brief account of Jefferson's vision for the territories he sent Lewis and Clark to explore and of the realities the two leaders and their men discovered as they journeyed westward.

Seefeldt, Douglas, et al., eds. *Across the Continent: Jefferson, Lewis and Clark, and the Making of America.* Charlottesville: University Press of Virginia, 2005. Essays speculating on the impact of Lewis and Clark's initial overtures to Native American tribes and commenting on the political and economic ramifications of the expedition for the development of the United States.

SEE ALSO: Exploration; Fur trapping and trading; Indian removal; Louisiana Purchase; Native American trade; Pike's western explorations.

Literary works with business themes

SIGNIFICANCE: The mainstream American novel has evolved as a fundamentally individual-centered form of representation. As a result, most realistic antibusiness American novels tend to represent corporations and other collective capitalist entities as detrimental to individual happiness and well-being. By the same token, the few probusiness novels tend to focus on successful individuals and their personal experiences of prosperity, rather than on corporations as a whole.

The earliest American writers were busy surviving and had a Puritan suspicion of worldly enterprises, but the first literary portraits of American business were for the most part positive and promotional. Samuel Sewall's *Diary*, for example, written from 1673 to 1729, reflects the business values that accompanied the early growth of the colonies by a man who was an important Boston merchant and public servant. Sewall describes balancing his business interest with his religious and romantic interests. Sewall also wrote one of the first antislavery tracts in America, *The Selling of Joseph* (1700). Clearly, there were conflicts between commerce and human development even in early American history.

The first important American writer to identify peculiar American business values was Benjamin Franklin, whose *Poor Richard Improved* (1757; also known as *The Way to Wealth*)—probably the most reprinted work in all of American literature—outlined in pithy and humorous form the values and attitudes that would underpin American business for the next centuries. His aphorisms include

"Necessity never made a good bargain"; "Early to bed and early to rise, makes a man, healthy, wealthy, and wise"; "Lost time is never found again"; and "The used key is always bright." Franklin later reiterated these values in his *Autobiography* (1791), emphasizing—even when he did not practice them—frugality, industry, moderation, and other virtues.

The first generation of American leaders—George Washington, Thomas Jefferson, and the other Founders—bore out Franklin's positive picture, which emerged as what came to be known as the Protestant work ethic, the belief that hard work results in success and salvation. The first phase of the literary treatment of American business can be said to have ended with J. Hector St. John Crèvecœur's *Letters from an American Farmer* (1782), which described in eloquent language a vision of the New World in which—in contrast to England—"industry" and "good living" prevailed over class and fashion, and farmers and merchants carved out their places on the American frontier by dint of these values.

THE INDUSTRIAL REVOLUTION

By the middle of the nineteenth century, the positive view of American business was coming under increasing attack. In Henry Wadsworth Longfellow, one of the most popular poets of the nineteenth century, the Protestant work ethic was already beginning to sound a bit hollow. "Let us, then, be up and doing," Longfellow urged in his most famous poem ("The Psalm of Life," 1838), "Learn to labor and to wait."

Although work was a purposeful enterprise in the time of Franklin and Crèvecœur, by Longfellow's time it had become an end in itself. Slavery was now a reality few Americans could ignore—a war would be fought over it within the quarter century—and wage slavery, which accompanied the Industrial Revolution to the United States, soon became a second target of writers. Although the American values of hard work and frugality were still present (witness the portraits of working Americans in Washington Irving's sketches), the truth was moving closer to Herman Melville's stories "Bartleby, the Scrivener: A Story of Wall Street" (1853) and "The Paradise of Bachelors and the Tartarus of Maids" (1855), which represent the destructive effects of routine and meaningless work. Already, Transcendentalists such as Ralph Waldo Emerson and Henry David Thoreau in the second third of the nineteenth century were warning readers of their spiritual impoverishment as a consequence of the American Industrial Revolution.

Rebecca Harding Davis's *Life in the Iron Mills* (1861) only confirmed what earlier writers had touched on: The Industrial Revolution had arrived, and it stifled human life and growth. In one of the first works of American realism, a form that would dominate American literature for the next half century, Davis depicted graphically what industrial growth was doing to human potential. The Gilded Age, the first boom time after the U.S. Civil War, was named in a novel of that title by Mark Twain and Charles Dudley Warner (1874) that depicted the worst excesses of the period's speculation and government collusion with business. Novel after novel described the excesses of the period, including, among other wrongs, how immigrant labor was being exploited.

Frank Norris represented the monopolistic railroads at the turn of the century in *The Octopus* (1901), while Abraham Cahan depicted the needle trades and early unions, in *The Rise of David Levinsky* (1917), the story of a man who achieved business success by exploiting his fellow immigrants. The most famous of these works was Upton Sinclair's study of the Chicago meatpacking industry, *The Jungle* (1906). It was not only fiction that portrayed this period, however; at the turn of the century, journalists labeled "muckrakers" by President Theodore Roosevelt were investigating various industries in this era of unchecked economic growth. Lincoln Steffens (*The Shame of the Cities*, 1904), Ida Tarbell (*The History of the Standard Oil Company*, 1904), and others wrote exposés for the leading magazines of the period that were often collected into books. It was this literature that helped bring on the antitrust legislation at the beginning of the twentieth century, as Sinclair's novel helped produce the Pure Food and Drug Act of 1906.

There was a popular antidote to this critical literature at the end of the nineteenth century in dime novels such as the Horatio Alger series, which glorified individual industry and honesty, and in the many works such as Andrew Carnegie's autobiography *How I Served My Apprenticeship* (1896) that reinforced Alger's rags-to-riches narratives. The American Dream may have remained just a dream in the lives of increasing numbers of immigrant mill and factory workers, but it was everywhere in the popular literature of the end of the nineteenth century. Perhaps the best example of this phenomenon was not a book but a lecture, Russell H. Conwell's "Acres of Diamonds," which he delivered over six thousand times after 1870. In his lecture, Conwell told the story of a man who left home in a search for diamonds—which were discovered after he died on the very land that he had abandoned. The lesson in this and other popular literature was clear, that the American Dream was possible by staying with the job, no matter how boring and meaningless. Popular literature functioned, like education, to help provide the workforce for a growing industrial economy. As *McGuffey's Fifth Eclectic Reader* phrased it to students in 1879, in a poem by Eliza Cook,

> Work, work, my boy, be not afraid;
> Look labor boldly in the face;
> Take up the hammer or the spade,
> And blush not for your humble place.

Ida Tarbell, muckraking journalist. (Library of Congress)

THE AMERICAN RENAISSANCE

Forty years later, readers were more likely to come upon Sarah N. Cleghorn's poem "The Golf Links" (1917), which read

> The golf links lie so near the mill
> That almost every day
> The laboring children can look out
> And see the men at play.

The American Renaissance, as the literary period from 1910 to 1940 is known, saw the sensational debut of American literature on the world stage, and it was a period noted for its experimentation, criticism, and disillusionment, particularly with American business. Sinclair Lewis's *Babbitt* (1922) portrayed the American businessman as a shallow and spiritually empty booster; Theodore Dreiser's Frank Cowperwood trilogy (*The Financier*, 1912, *The Titan*, 1914, and *The Stoic*, 1947) made a similar attack on an unscrupulous magnate of big business. Eugene O'Neill's *The Hairy Ape* (1922) and Elmer Rice's *The Adding Machine* (1923) were plays depicting the dehumanizing effects of technological progress.

During the 1930's, this criticism of American business became even more strident. Proletarian literature (such as Mike Gold's novel, *Jews Without Money*, 1930, or Clifford Odets's play, *Waiting for Lefty*, 1936) blamed American capitalism for the crisis and glorified the worker. John Dos Passos's *U.S.A.* trilogy—*The 42nd Parallel* (1930), *1919* (1932), and *The Big Money* (1936)—chronicled the decline of its characters in the first decades of the century through commercialism and exploitation. Probably the best novel of the decade, John Steinbeck's *The Grapes of Wrath* (1939), followed uprooted Dust Bowl refugees facing exploitation in California at the hands of agribusiness. These and other works of the Great Depression faulted American business and called for an overhaul of the American economic system.

POSTWAR AMERICA

Nonfiction after World War II sought to confirm the growing number of negative fictional portraits of American business. Sociological studies such as David Reisman's *The Lonely Crowd* (1950) and William Allan Whyte's *The Organization Man* (1956) detailed the dehumanizing and conformist nature of work in the American corporation. Fiction such as

Sloan Wilson's *The Man in the Gray Flannel Suit* (1955) or the stories of John Cheever only intensified this picture. The Beat Generation of the late 1940's and early 1950's (Jack Kerouac, Allen Ginsberg, and their cohorts) rejected American business entirely in the search for adventure and spiritual fulfillment.

Novels written after the war painted a generally bleak picture of American business. In Saul Bellow's *Seize the Day* (1956), the hero loses everything gambling on commodities. In Ken Kesey's *One Flew Over the Cuckoo's Nest* (1962), an insane asylum becomes a metaphor for all American institutions. In E. L. Doctorow's *Ragtime* (1975), the leaders of American business—J. P. Morgan and Henry Ford—are pictured as slightly insane, and only the revolutionaries have life. Tom Wolfe's *Bonfire of the Vanities* (1987) portrays the world of New York investment bankers with satiric savagery, and Don DeLillo's *Cosmopolis* (2003) portrays greed and power as empty and aimless.

It was in drama, more than in any other genre, that American business took the most direct criticism. Arthur Miller's *All My Sons* (1947) told the story of a corrupt manufacturer of aircraft parts, while his *Death of a Salesman* (1949) recounted the powerful story of a man used up and tossed aside by American business. The pictures of business and businessmen, from Edward Abbey's *The Zoo Story* (1959) through David Mamet's *Glengarry Glen Ross* (1984), continued this portrait of a selfish, rapacious American business culture. Some positive treatments of business continued into the twentieth century—notably Ayn Rand's *The Fountainhead* (1943) and *Atlas Shrugged* (1957), which celebrate individualism and self-interest—but they were a minority voice.

American literary history demonstrates that American literature and business are not perfectly compatible. It is often noted that some of the greatest poets of the twentieth century were businessmen. Wallace Stevens was vice president of an insurance company, T. S. Eliot worked for a leading London publisher, and William Carlos Williams was a medical doctor. Rarely, however, did their work find its way into their poetry. There has always been an American suspicion of accumulated wealth and power stretching all the way back to the Puritans and their early equation of money and evil. Also working against the subject was the very nature of American literature. Some of the greatest American novels—from Mark Twain's *Adventures of Huckleberry Finn* (1884) through Ernest Hemingway's *The Sun Also Rises* (1926) to John Updike's *Rabbit, Run* (1960)—are about running away from family, work, and responsibility. It is a strain that exists from the nineteenth century on. In the twentieth century, modernism elevated aesthetic concerns above those of subject and further erased American business from the literary picture.

David Peck

FURTHER READING

French, Bryant Morey. *Mark Twain and "The Gilded Age": The Book That Named an Era.* Dallas: Southern Methodist University Press, 1965. Detailed study of Mark Twain and Charles Dudley Warner's novel about corruption in business and government during the decade following the Civil War.

Mukherjee, Arun. *The Gospel of Wealth in the American Novel.* London: Croom Helm, 1987. More than half this study is devoted to the novels of Dreiser, but Mukherjee also analyzes William Dean Howells (*The Rise of Silas Lapham*, 1885), Norris (*The Pit*, 1903), and other late nineteenth century writers.

Polland, Arthur, Geoffrey Carnall, et al., eds. *The Representation of Business in English Literature.* London: Institute of Economic Affairs, 2000. Serves as a useful counterpoint to studies of business themes in American literature, demonstrating the similarities and differences in representations of commerce on either side of the Atlantic.

Spindler, Michael. *American Literature and Social Change.* Bloomington: Indiana University Press, 1983. A Marxist analysis of American literature from the "production" economy (Howells, Norris, Sinclair) of the late nineteenth century to a "consumption" model (Dreiser, F. Scott Fitzgerald, Lewis, Miller) in the twentieth.

Taylor, Walter F. *The Economic Novel in America.* Chapel Hill: University of North Carolina Press, 1942. The classic study of the treatment of Gilded Age capitalistic industrialism in the novels of Twain, Howells, Norris, and other writers.

Watts, Emily Stipes. *The Businessman in American Literature.* Athens: University of Georgia Press, 1982. Probably the best survey of literary attitudes toward business, from the Puritans' condemnation of the accumulation of wealth, through Franklin, to postwar American writers. Watts provides plentiful evidence of the American literary treatment of businessmen as greedy and unethical.

Westbrook, Wayne W. *Wall Street in the American Novel.* New York: New York University Press, 1980. Uncovers an association of money and evil going back to the Puritans, and evident also in Melville and Nathaniel Hawthorne. Perceptive analyses of Louis Auchincloss, Edith Wharton (*The House of Mirth*, 1905), William Faulkner (*The Sound and the Fury*, 1929), and other American novelists.

SEE ALSO: Book publishing; Copyright law; Films with business themes; Gilded Age; *The Jungle*; Magazine industry; Television programming with business themes.

Lotteries, state-run

DEFINITION: Type of state-sanctioned gambling in which winners are selected by the drawing of lots from people who have paid to participate

SIGNIFICANCE: In early American history, lotteries were responsible for funding some of the major institutions of higher learning, public buildings, roads, canals, and bridges. Modern state-run lotteries produce revenue that results in lower levies being imposed on businesses and individual taxpayers.

Common in colonial America, lotteries were abolished throughout the United States by the end of the nineteenth century, primarily because of scandals. In 1963, voters in New Hampshire revived the practice by approving a state-run lottery in a referendum. The lottery began operation the following year, and other states soon followed suit. In the United States, as of 2008, forty-two states and the District of Columbia had state-run lotteries.

Lotteries have had to overcome strong religious opposition to their operation. Biblical mention of lotteries clearly designates them as suitable only for the resolution of profoundly important matters, because in theological terms, they are seen as a blasphemous intrusion into God's decision-making domain. Ultimately, financial necessity overcame religious reservations, and a colonial lottery was authorized in 1612 for the Virginia Company of London, the first of numerous programs heralded with great fanfare. Franchises were sometimes granted to private promoters who paid a licensing fee, and proceeds typically were earmarked for benevolent purposes. Lotteries began to disappear from the American scene after notorious scandals regarding their operation came to light, and the excessive profits appropriated by the promoting businesses fueled public indignation and legislative bans.

In 1830, a total of 420 state lotteries were in operation, producing earnings five times the total of the federal budget. However, following the U.S. Civil War, only Louisiana continued to permit lotteries and soon ended the practice. In 1890, Congress prohibited the use of the mail service for lottery sales.

NUMBERS

Between the late nineteenth century and 1964, when the New Hampshire lottery began operation, lotteries were replaced by the numbers business, an illegal form of gambling that became particularly prominent in the slums of large cities. Playing the numbers, also called "policy," "bolita," "the figures," and "the digits," involved as many as half a million daily bettors in New York City during the 1970's and provided employment for more than 100,000 workers in the city's five boroughs. The employees fell into a strict hierarchy of positions, from those responsible for laying off bets at the top, down to pickup men, and below them runners who took bets directly from customers.

The odds normally were 600 to 1 against a person selecting a winning three-digit number, although the eventual earnings were on the order of 540 to 1 because the winner was expected to pay the runner 10 percent of the take. In Chicago, the numbers business was believed essential to the economic well-being of the minority and low-income communities because of the jobs that it created in these areas. Publications, so-called "dream books," were sold openly, each claiming to offer clues to winning numbers.

Competition in the numbers business was eliminated either by mergers or by police action against potential entrants into the field. Police were paid off on a sliding scale, with patrolmen receiving the least money, plainclothesmen a middle amount, and headquarters' officers the most. Honest police officers often found themselves transferred to out-of-the-way beats, such as the cemetery area.

LOTTERIES REAPPEAR

Gradually, the religious opposition to lotteries began to fade. Moral objections to lotteries were undercut by the Roman Catholic Church's widespread sponsorship of bingo contests, a form of gambling. Most important, chronically starved state and municipal governments turned to lotteries to increase state revenues. Lotteries offered governments the opportunity to obtain money without raising taxes, a move that was likely to offend voters and lessen the popularity of the officials behind the tax increase.

Lotteries have become the most popular form of gambling. About 66 percent of the U.S. population plays at least once during the year, and 13 percent participate weekly, even though the odds of winning a Mega Millions jackpot have been calculated at 1 in 175.7 million. Lottery tickets typically are sold at businesses such as convenience stores, gas stations, and supermarkets. The wait between the purchase of a lottery ticket and the announcement of the results of the drawing are believed to avoid creating the intense emotional state that characterizes compulsive gambling. Research indicates that a lottery outperforms voluntary giving as a means to finance public projects and that lotteries that offer the highest payoffs are particularly successful in raising funds for beneficial purposes.

New York, which was the next state after New Hampshire to legalize lotteries, at first restricted lottery ticket sales to banks (though this was later declared to be unconstitutional), hotels, motels, and local government offices. Lottery participants had to provide their name and address, and drawings took place once a month. These conservative measures were largely abandoned when earnings fell far short of estimates. New Jersey, the next state to legalize a lottery, learned a lesson from its neighbor. It held weekly drawings and decorated each of the tickets, which were sold in strips, with a four-leaf clover. New York followed suit and its lottery program has become one of the best run in the country.

Like most of the states in which lotteries are held, New Jersey employs high-powered advertising agencies to create marketing strategies to draw lottery customers. In Tennessee, for example, the chief promoter of the lottery was filmed on television during halftime at a University of Tennessee football game waving a huge symbolic check made out for a billion dollars, the amount at stake in the state's lottery. The Tennessee impresario, in the words of

LOTTERY SALES AND PROFITS BY STATE, FISCAL YEAR 2006

State or Jurisdiction	Sales ($ millions)	Profits ($ millions)	Profit as Percentage of Sales	State or Jurisdiction	Sales ($ millions)	Profits ($ millions)	Profit as Percentage of Sales
Arizona	468.7	141.1	30.1	New Hampshire	262.7	80.3	30.6
California	3,585.0	1,240.6	34.6	New Jersey	2,406.6	849.3	35.3
Colorado	468.8	125.6	26.8	New Mexico	154.7	36.9	23.9
Connecticut	970.3	284.9	29.4	New York[a]	6,803.0	2,203.0	32.4
Delaware[a]	728.0	248.8	34.2	North Carolina[b]	229.5	64.6	28.1
District of Columbia	266.2	73.4	27.6	North Dakota	22.3	6.9	30.9
Florida	4,030.0	1,230.0	30.5	Ohio	2,221.0	646.3	29.1
Georgia	3,177.6	822.4	25.9	Oklahoma	204.8	69.0	33.7
Idaho	131.1	33.0	25.2	Oregon[a]	1,104.0	483.0	43.8
Illinois	1,964.8	637.7	32.5	Pennsylvania	3,070.0	975.9	31.8
Indiana	816.4	218.0	26.7	Puerto Rico	334.5	115.9	34.6
Iowa	339.5	80.9	23.8	Rhode Island[c]	1,731.5	323.9	18.7
Kansas	236.1	67.1	28.4	South Carolina	1,144.6	319.4	27.9
Kentucky	742.3	204.3	27.5	South Dakota[c]	686.2	119.0	17.3
Louisiana	332.1	118.8	35.8	Tennessee	996.3	277.7	27.9
Maine	229.7	51.7	22.5	Texas	3,774.7	1,036.1	27.4
Maryland	1,560.9	501.0	32.1	Vermont	104.9	22.9	21.8
Massachusetts	4,534.1	951.2	21.0	Virginia	1,365.0	454.9	33.3
Michigan	2,212.4	688.0	31.1	Washington	477.9	117.0	24.5
Minnesota	450.0	121.3	27.0	West Virginia[a]	1,522.0	610.0	40.1
Missouri	913.5	260.7	28.5	Wisconsin	508.9	150.6	29.6
Montana	39.9	9.1	22.8				
Nebraska	113.1	30.3	26.8	Total	57,435.6	17,102.5	29.8

Source: Data from the North American Association of State and Provincial Lotteries

Note: Fiscal year ends March 31 for New York, August 31 for Texas, and September 30 for District of Columbia and Michigan; all others end December 31.

[a] Includes net video lottery terminal sales.

[b] Instant sales began March 30, 2006; online sales began October, 2006.

[c] Includes gross video lottery terminal sales.

a *New York Times* feature story, "reshaped state-sponsored gambling into highly sophisticated commercial enterprises peddling products that are as ubiquitous as Cokes or Snickers." The promoter had introduced twenty-nine instant-ticket and two online games and paid out $227.5 million in prizes. In just four months, state education programs in Tennessee were allocated an additional $123 million, and an additional $2 million went to after-school programs.

Some states permitted lotteries because they were viewed as less likely to foster problem gambling than casinos, but by the early years of the twenty-first century, lottery-only states were losing revenue as their citizens crossed their borders to indulge in blackjack, roulette, and other gambling opportunities at well-appointed casinos. In addition, apparent boredom with picking numbers and anticipating results was significantly reducing the amount of money states were generating from lotteries. Even so, lotteries continue to earn about $60 billion annually.

MULTISTATE LOTTERIES AND VLTs

In 1985, three New England states joined together to create an interstate lottery. Three years later, Oregon, Iowa, Kansas, Rhode Island, West Virginia, Missouri, and the District of Columbia formed the Multi-State Lottery Association and offered the Powerball, a lottery featuring a large payout. In 1996, another group of states joined together to offer the Big Game (later Mega Millions) lottery.

To pump up their lottery business, some states began introducing video lottery terminals (VLT), basically slot machines. VLTs account for about 70 percent of the income from legal gambling in the United States. Their primary appeal is that there is no waiting for the result of a bet. Ten states have approved these terminals in conjunction with their lotteries.

In Rhode Island, the VLTs that were installed at the Lincoln Park greyhound racetrack in 1992 reversed the decline in the track's income. VLTs also have been installed at an old jai alai arena in Newport, Rhode Island, and have boosted the state's gambling take to more than $1,500 per citizen, the highest ratio in the nation. Rhode Island's VLTs account for 80 percent of the state's lottery income, an income that makes up slightly more than 10 percent of the state's operating budget.

THE PRIVATIZATION MOVEMENT

During the first decade of the twenty-first century, privatization became the next development in the world of lotteries. During 2006 and 2007, three state legislatures—Illinois, Indiana, and Texas—rejected bids from private investors for their lottery programs. In September, 2007, the brokerage firm of Lehman Brothers offered the state of California $37 billion to purchase its lottery program, money that the governor wanted to use to finance health care innovations. The bid failed, but the issue remained very much in play.

Privatization could take the form of investors buying a lottery franchise outright and operating it as a monopoly, or negotiating a lease arrangement under which the state would continue to receive a share of the profits. Private investors believe that with more aggressive marketing tactics and innovative technology, they could significantly increase profits. For example, some states do not sell lottery tickets near welfare offices or adult bookstores, re-

strictions that private companies might abandon. If lotteries were to go private, this would represent the largest privatization of a government enterprise in American history, but a national survey by Independent Lottery Research found that more than half of the respondents opposed privatization, primarily because they believed that fewer funds would be available to finance public needs.

State-run lotteries and video lottery terminals have come under criticism for several reasons. One concern is that these gambling venues, particularly VLTs, may result in compulsive gambling. Some lottery operations seek to compensate for the risk of addiction that they may induce by making contributions to facilities that rehabilitate compulsive gamblers. Operators of gambling facilities argue that compulsive gambling may reflect basic personality problems that could result in more serious, disabling behavior if lotteries and slots were not available. Another objection to state-sponsored gambling, especially lotteries, is that they rely primarily on low-income people who cannot readily afford the wagers. Therefore, the lottery acts like a regressive tax. Lottery operators, for their part, emphasize that lotteries offer hope, however statistically unreasonable, to those who often are living a drab and dreary existence.

Gilbert Geis

FURTHER READING

Bobbitt, William R. *Lottery Wars: Case Studies in Bible Belt Politics, 1985-2005.* Lanham, Md.: Lexington Books, 2007. Basing his conclusions on a review of thousands of media reports, government documents, and interviews with religious and political leaders, Bobbitt outlines the debates and communication strategies relied on in determining if and how lotteries will be permitted.

Clotfelter, Charles T., and Philip J. Cook. *Selling Hope: State Lotteries in America.* Cambridge, Mass.: Harvard University Press, 1989. A sophisticated and even-handed consideration of all aspects of the lottery that can provide ammunition both for those who favor lotteries and those who oppose them.

Kearney, Melissa. *State Lotteries and Consumer Behavior.* Cambridge, Mass.: National Bureau of Economic Research, 2002. The author notes that spending on lotteries does not detract from other forms of gambling and that it accounts for

$38 per month per family, or about 2 percent of household consumption. She concludes that lottery participants are making fully informed economic decisions.

Nibert, David A. *Hitting the Lottery Jackpot: Government and the Taxing of Dreams.* New York: Monthly Review Press, 2000. Emphasizes the economic and social costs involved in the generating of state revenue by means of lotteries and maintains that lotteries represent a pernicious tax on the poor and primarily benefit advertising agencies, television stations, and ticket vendors.

Pierce, Patrick A., and Donald E. Miller. *Gambling Politics: State Government and the Business of Betting.* Boulder, Colo.: Lynne Rienner, 2004. The authors focus on the political maneuvering associated with gambling endeavors and explore the relationship between state-run gambling and its possible consequences, including crime, job creation, and economic development. They note that participation in lotteries is correlated with involvement in illegal gambling.

SEE ALSO: Gambling industry; Organized crime; Privatization; Taxation.

Louisiana Purchase

THE EVENT: Sale by France to the United States of much of what would become the central and western portions of the United States

DATE: Finalized in December, 1803

PLACE: Louisiana Territory, between the Mississippi River and the Rocky Mountains

SIGNIFICANCE: The largest single acquisition of territory by the United States, the Louisiana Purchase more than doubled the size of the nation, creating a vast new territory to be explored and incalculable commercial opportunities to be exploited. The purchased territory accounts for 23 percent of the territory of the modern United States.

Before the era of the railroads, water transportation was by far the most efficient way to move large, bulky cargoes. American commerce tended to move in a counterclockwise direction because of the Ohio and Mississippi Rivers and their tributaries. Farm commodities, lumber, and other bulk goods from the trans-Appalachian west moved down the river systems, eventually reaching the Mississippi and the port of New Orleans. From New Orleans, these goods would be taken by sea to the eastern coast or exported to Europe. Because of the importance of this river traffic, it was imperative that the United States maintain access to the port of New Orleans.

While New Orleans and what was considered the "Louisiana Territory" was under Spanish control, the United States negotiated the Pinckney Treaty with Spain in 1795. Under this agreement, American shippers were granted the "right of deposit" in New Orleans—the right to ship goods in and out of New Orleans and to store goods there while awaiting shipment.

When Napoleon I of France came to control Spain as part of his European empire, he forced the Spanish government to give control of Louisiana back to the French in 1800; this cession was formalized in the Treaty of Madrid in March, 1801. Even though France technically controlled the Louisiana territory after that date, Spanish colonial officials remained in place in America until the region was turned over to U.S. control. In October, 1802, the Spanish colonial administrators in Louisiana revoked the right of deposit for American shippers.

THE OFFER

When President Thomas Jefferson learned of the revocation of the right of deposit, he sent James Monroe to Paris to assist Robert Livingston, the U.S. ambassador to France, in making an offer to the French for the purchase of New Orleans. They were authorized to offer $2 million for New Orleans, or up to $10 million for New Orleans and what was then called "West Florida"—the coastal region of present-day Alabama and Mississippi.

Monroe arrived in Paris in April, 1803, and was astonished to learn that Napoleon's prime minister, Charles Talleyrand, had already offered to sell the United States all of the Louisiana region for $15 million. Livingston and Monroe had no authorization to proceed with such negotiations, but they immediately wrote to Jefferson and Secretary of State James Madison for instructions, indicating that they were proceeding on the assumption that the forthcoming instructions would be to make the purchase. Monroe and Livingston signed a draft treaty on April 30, 1803, and the U.S. Senate

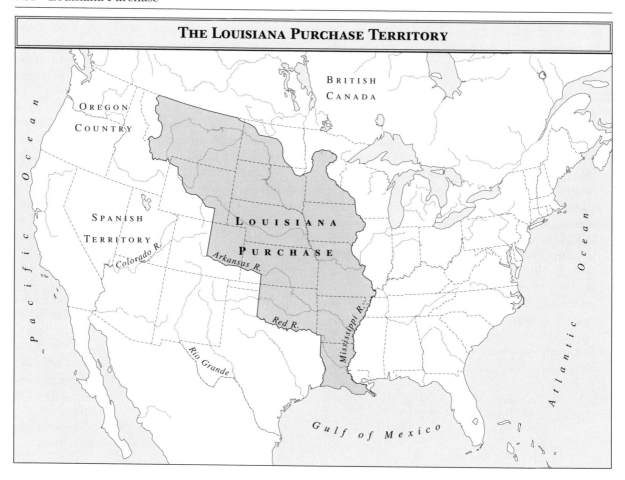

THE LOUISIANA PURCHASE TERRITORY

ratified the purchase treaty on October 20, 1803. On December 20 of that year, the U.S. took formal possession of the region in a ceremony at New Orleans.

THE PURCHASE

The purchase price of $15 million was agreed on, but the United States did not pay that much directly to France. Citizens of the United States had claims for damages against France amounting to $3.75 million, and the United States agreed to pay those claims, and remitted to France the balance of $11.25 million. To make the purchase, the U.S. borrowed money from the London firm of Baring Bank and from Hope and Company of Amsterdam.

In the short run, the major significance of the Louisiana Purchase was that the right of American commerce to navigate the Mississippi was permanently secured. Even before much settlement advanced into the lands the United States had acquired, the economic development of the area between the Appalachian Mountains and the Mississippi caused the traffic flowing through New Orleans to boom. In the long run, the settlement and economic development of the vast territory gained in this acquisition had an even more pervasive impact on American economic history. The purchase increased the size of the United States by approximately 140 percent. Eventually, all or part of more than a dozen states would be created out of this territory.

Mark S. Joy

FURTHER READING

DeConde, A. *This Affair of Louisiana.* New York: Charles Scribner's Sons, 1976. Long considered the standard work on the Louisiana Purchase.

Joy, Mark S. *American Expansionism, 1783-1860: A Manifest Destiny?* London: Pearson Education,

2003. Brief introduction to the subject of America's expansion; includes many learning aids, such as a time line, glossary, who's who, and bibliography.

Kuka, Jon. *A Wilderness So Immense: The Louisiana Purchase and the Destiny of America.* New York: Alfred A. Knopf, 2003. Major work on the Louisiana Purchase; detailed and well-written.

Owsley, Frank L., and Gene A. Smith. *Filibusterers and Expansionists: Jeffersonian Manifest Destiny, 1800-1821.* Tuscaloosa: University of Alabama Press, 1997. Valuable work that puts the purchase of Louisiana into the overall context of the foreign policy of Presidents Jefferson, Madison, and Monroe.

Perkins, B. *The Creation of a Republican Empire, 1776-1865.* Vol. 1 in *The Cambridge History of American Foreign Relations.* New York: Cambridge University Press, 1993. A standard history of American diplomacy that covers the Louisiana Purchase in detail.

Weeks, William Earl. *Building the Continental Empire: American Expansionism from the Revolution to the Civil War.* Chicago: Ivan R. Dee, 1996. Brief, accessible treatment of American continental expansion, with suggestions for further reading.

SEE ALSO: Exploration; Hurricane Katrina; Indian removal; Lewis and Clark expedition; Native American trade; Pike's western explorations.

M

McDonald's restaurants

IDENTIFICATION: Fast-food corporation

DATE: Founded on April 15, 1955

SIGNIFICANCE: By the mid-1950's, automobiles and drive-in restaurants were part of the American lifestyle. McDonald's successfully met the need for fast service, low-cost meals, convenience, and a child-friendly atmosphere. It became the world's largest fast-food restaurant chain and a symbol of American culture. The term "McDonalization" was coined to describe the homogenization accompanying the globalization of American culture.

The original business concept behind McDonald's restaurants emerged in 1948 with the first such restaurant, in San Bernardino, California. At this hamburger, french fries, and milkshake stand, brothers Maurice and Richard McDonald implemented their revolutionary "Speedee Service System," the basic format of the modern fast-food restaurant. This self-service, assembly-line system eliminated the need for waiters, carhops, dishwashers, and bus boys. Paper plates and plastic utensils replaced dishware, glassware, and silverware.

In 1954, Ray Kroc, the exclusive distributor of the Multimixer milkshake mixer, was intrigued that the McDonald's restaurant was running eight Multimixers at once. After observing the restaurant's busy daily operations, he was impressed with how efficiently and cheaply it was able to produce and sell large quantities of food.

Kroc proposed a franchise program. On April 15, 1955, he opened the first franchised McDonald's restaurant in Des Plaines, Illinois; he incorpo-

The first McDonald's restaurant in Des Plaines, Illinois, pictured in 1982. (AP/Wide World Photos)

rated later that year. Kroc sold franchises, requiring owners to become restaurant managers and to follow the McDonald's automation and standardization models. In 1961, Kroc purchased the McDonald brothers' equity in the business for $2.7 million. By then, sales had reached $37 million and there were 228 restaurants. Over one billion hamburgers had been sold by the end of 1963. McDonald's issued stock, becoming a publicly traded company in 1965. When Kroc died in 1984, there were more than 7,500 McDonald's restaurants worldwide.

McDonald's created famous symbols and products to define its brand. The rooftop "golden arches" were replaced by the trademark double-arch "M" logo in 1962. In 1963, the iconic Ronald McDonald clown appeared, and in 1974, the first Ronald McDonald House opened in Philadelphia to house families of critically ill children away from home.

McDonald's introduced the Big Mac sandwich in 1968, the Egg McMuffin in 1973, Happy Meals for children in 1979, Chicken McNuggets in 1983, salads in 1985, and a premium salad line in 2004. In 2006, McDonald's premium coffee made its debut to compete with Starbucks and Dunkin' Donuts coffee. In response to health concerns, McDonald's began including nutritional information on packaging.

By early 2008, the McDonald's Corporation had 30,000 local restaurants in more than one hundred countries. With 75 percent of the restaurants owned and operated by franchisees and affiliates, McDonald's was serving more than 54 million customers daily.

Alice Myers

FURTHER READING

Kroc, Ray, and Robert Anderson. *Grinding It Out: The Making of McDonald's.* New York: St. Martin's Paperbacks, 1987.

Love, John F. *McDonald's: Behind the Arches.* Rev. ed. New York: Bantam Books, 1995.

Spurlock, Morgan. *Don't Eat This Book: Fast Food and the Supersizing of America.* New York: G. P. Putnam's Sons, 2005.

SEE ALSO: Beef industry; Drive-through businesses; Fast-food restaurants; Food-processing industries; Restaurant industry; Retail trade industry.

Magazine industry

DEFINITION: Enterprises publishing magazines for the general public

SIGNIFICANCE: The magazine industry was one of the major disseminators of information, cultural material, and entertainment before the advent of broadcast media. During the late twentieth and early twenty-first centuries, it has had to readjust its methods to compete and integrate with television and the Internet. Through specialization and fast technological printing processes, magazines have continued to lure paying customers, both readers and advertisers.

The publication of American magazines began in 1741 in Philadelphia, when Andrew Bradford's *American Magazine* and, days later, Benjamin Franklin's *General Magazine* were published. By the end of the eighteenth century, about one hundred magazines were providing information and entertainment to the populace in and around Philadelphia, New York, and Boston.

These earlier periodicals catered to a rather elite readership inasmuch as literacy was largely the province of the educated, financially better off segment of society. The early nineteenth century produced scholarly journals such as Boston's *The North American Review,* which was modeled after the British publications *Quarterly* and *Edinburgh Review.* By 1831, *Godey's Lady's Book* carried articles relating to women's fashions and issues of morality and taste. Its circulation reached an impressive 150,000. *Harper's Magazine* (founded in 1850) published serialized novels by the English writers Charles Dickens, William Thackeray, and George Eliot, often paying them more handsomely than did its English counterparts.

COMPETING FOR READERS

By the time of the U.S. Civil War, magazine publication had expanded. Low postal rates allowed for wide distribution of periodicals throughout the ever-expanding nation. With growing competition, some publishers reduced the price of their magazines in a bid to capture a wider audience. The more expensive magazines such as *Harper's Magazine* and *Scribner's Magazine* sold for 25 to 35 cents a copy, which was a considerable sum at the time. *Harper's Magazine,* for instance, had an annual subscription price in 1870 of $4. An advertisement in the magazine cost $1.50 per line per insertion on an inside page and $2.00 per line on the outside cover. *McClure's Magazine*, published in 1893 by Samuel S. McClure, went on sale for only 15 cents a copy. The success of *McClure's Magazine* prompted other magazine publishers to lower their prices: *Cosmopolitan* dropped its price to 12½ cents, and *Munsey's Magazine* dropped its price to 10 cents. The magazines' lower prices increased their readership between 1893 and 1899, and circulation grew from 250,00 to 750,000 readers.

Improvements in production methods and wider use of photoengraving processes to produce illustrations made mass production cheaper; advertising revenues increased with the periodicals' wider distribution. Increased advertising revenues made it possible to sell magazines for less than they cost to publish. The advent of easier-to-produce color illustrations made magazines more attractive, leading to even greater circulation. During the 1890's, the newly developed multicolor rotary press made color printing easier and cheaper. In addition, advertising agencies had grown in size and capabilities; their inventive copywriters, artists, and page designers presented their business clients' products in visually appealing and stimulating formats. Photography and the use of the halftone block created timely images of news events and other contemporaneous visuals that captured the interest of the reading public.

Even after automated processes were available, women's magazines continued to print hand-tinted fashion illustrations. As many as 150 women had to be hired to do the tinting, an expensive proposition, but there was a strong audience for such visual embellishment throughout the nineteenth century. Women's magazines with illustrations debuted and thrived; among these successful publications were *Ladies' Home Journal* (1883), *Ladies' Home Companion* (1886), *Vogue* (1892), and *McCall's Magazine* (1807). Although *Good Housekeeping* (1885) was not quite in the same category as these fashion magazines because it was geared toward homemakers, it still had a strong appeal to women readers.

The Impact of Advertising

Many early American magazine publishers resisted advertising, patterning their periodicals after the more literary or scholarly British periodicals. The appearance of consumerism was thought to be crass and contradicted the image they wanted to convey. By the twentieth century, however, businesses of all types were acutely aware of the need to stand out from the competition, and one of the best ways to do so was to advertise their products to the widest possible audience. Thus, the demand for advertising venues increased dramatically, and the expanding circulation of magazines, especially to bases of committed subscribers, further motivated businesses to offer top dollar to advertise in these periodicals. Some magazines gave in quickly to the enticement of increased revenue from the sale of advertising space. They used the money to produce more copies with as much or more content as before and to generate greater profits.

Others, however, such as *Reader's Digest* (founded in 1922), held off until mid-century before succumbing to the lure of advertising. For years, *Reader's Digest* boasted that it contained no ads; it could afford to resist as long as it did because of its huge, devoted readership. By 1922, *The Saturday Evening Post* had built its circulation to more than 2 million readers, and its advertising revenues had reached more than $28 million. It initially charged relatively low advertising rates, but as its circulation and popularity increased, so did its rates.

Verification of Circulation

It soon became apparent that a magazine's circulation was important in determining both the kinds of advertising the magazine could publish and the rates it could charge. As a result, advertisers needed a way to verify magazines' circulation figures. An impartial resource was needed to research which magazines people were reading, how many people were reading each particular magazine, and what specific topics and formats held their interest. The first organizations to track this kind of information were a market research organization established by the Curtis Publishing Company in 1911 and the Audit Bureau of Circulation, which was founded in 1914.

Most magazines published in 1900 devoted about 50 percent of their content to advertising, much of which was clustered in the back pages so as not to interrupt the magazines' unpaid content. By 1947, 65 percent of the average magazine's content was advertising. Colorful, sometimes intriguing or humorous ads were scattered throughout magazines, interrupting the flow of essays and fiction.

DRAWBACKS OF ADVERTISING

The content of most magazines is written either by freelance writers, whose main allegiance is to their own research, intent, and style, or by salaried staff writers, who are bound to adhere to the standards, philosophy, and purposes of the magazine's publisher and owner. On occasion, an article or story gets published that creates a backlash among readers or causes advertisers to feel their products were denigrated in some way. When that happens, the business department of the magazine often hastens to rectify the situation, reassuring the readership that no insult was intended and the advertisers that no harm was done. Especially when an offended advertiser provides a large portion of the periodical's budget, the magazine must strive to avoid losing that business as a client.

Many magazines have had to yield to financial pressure from advertisers who disagree with editorial decisions of the magazines and print retractions, expunge their stable of writers, or do whatever will best appease their advertisers. Others, however, have such wide popularity and financial strength that they can afford to hold firm to their policies and insist that advertisers either accept those policies or cancel their advertisements. Still, the tendency has been for magazines, no matter their financial or philosophical stance, to try to give minimum offense to both advertisers and readers and to avoid radical departures from the middle ground of their chosen readership.

SPECIALIZATION

The success of women's magazines proved that "niche" publications could be profitable. The women's magazines themselves splintered into even more specialized publications dealing with fashion, health, sexual concerns, weddings and marriage, family and home, and, during the 1970's, feminism. Innovative distribution of these publications in supermarkets opened yet another outlet for such magazines and increased readership and circulation.

Early men's magazines and or those catering mostly to men's interests, such as *Burton's Gentlemen's Magazine* (founded in 1840) and *Popular Science Monthly* (founded in 1872), always had an audience, as most of the individuals with the financial means to purchase magazines and the education to read them were men. During the twentieth century, specialization increased. Magazines geared to boys,

girls, or young people of both genders were successful as the populace became more literate. Ads for clothes and accessories produced greater sales and lucrative profits for both the advertisers and the magazines.

By the mid- to late twentieth century, there was considerable diversity in specialized magazines. Indeed, general magazines were losing favor with readers, who preferred more narrowly focused publications. Although men's and women's magazines might still provide general information about health, fitness, fashion, and leisure activities, some magazines adopted much narrower approaches. Some men's magazines dealt with such masculine interests as automobiles, fishing and hunting, sports, guns and knives, and outdoor activities. Women's magazines focused more narrowly on becoming a bride, weddings and marriage, relationships, true confessions about crises in women's lives, family life, home decoration, romance, pregnancy, and baby care. Magazines for youngsters proliferated during the mid- to late twentieth century. News magazines such as *Time* and *Newsweek* continued to be popular even after the advent of online versions of news dispatchers, in part because they developed their own competing online presence. They continued to be profitable as well, with increased advertising revenues.

ECONOMIC CONCERNS

New production technology developed during the 1980's allowed magazine publishing to proceed ever faster and more profitably. As the twentieth century wound down, however, recessionary trends set in, causing advertisers to reduce their budgets to maintain reasonable profits. Publishers responded in part by introducing niche periodicals geared so precisely to a specific readership that advertisers were assured of a closely matched audience for their advertisements. The spectrum of niche publications expanded to include more kinds of comic, lifestyle, travel, music, and family magazines. Markets that had previously been overlooked or ignored, such as certain ethnic groups or esoteric activities and issues (snowboarding or electronic innovations, for example), were soon targeted by niche publications.

The leading advertisers by the beginning of the twenty-first century were automobile makers (including General Motors, Toyota, Ford, and Daimler-Chrysler), consumer goods companies (including Johnson and Johnson, Procter and Gamble, and

L'Oreal USA), tobacco companies such as Philip Morris, and entertainment groups such as AOL Time Warner. The top fifty magazine advertisers spent $6.4 billion in 2002, making the business of magazine publishing an attractive, profitable enterprise. Hundreds of magazine publishers and entrepreneurs, wishing to cash in on such a lucrative business, launched magazines each year only to struggle and disappear amid the fierce competition for both readers and advertisers. As many as 50 percent of these new launches failed within one to two years.

The outlook for magazine publishing in the twenty-first century is problematic. With the growing popularity and lower cost of electronic magazines (ezines) and with the rising costs of paper, wages, distribution, and other traditional costs of magazine publishing, the magazine industry faces several concerns. It has already responded, though, by aggressively marketing itself online, and—almost without exception—every major print periodical maintains a significant Web site, which both encourages traditional print subscriptions and distributes unique content, enhancing the print publication's revenue with online advertisements. The direction taken by the industry in the future will depend on the continuing desire of Americans for the tactile satisfaction of holding a printed periodical in their hands as opposed to the gratification some feel to have almost instantaneous electronic access to information and entertainment.

Jane L. Ball

FURTHER READING

Angeletti, Norberto, and Alberto Oliva. *Magazines That Make History: Their Origins, Development, and Influence.* Gainesville: University Press of Florida, 2004. Explores the strategies of the founders of eight American and European magazines to show their beginnings, evolution, and impact on business decisions and practices. Of particular interest is its treatment of *Time, Life,* and *Reader's Digest.*

Daly, Charles P., Patrick Henry, and Ellen Ryder. *The Magazine Publishing Industry.* Boston: Allyn and Bacon, 1997. Discusses in detail advertising, marketing, circulation, production, and editorial techniques. Examines the state of the industry during the last years of the twentieth century in terms of social, economic, and technological concerns.

Johnson, Sammye, and Patricia Prijate. *The Magazine from Cover to Cover.* 2d ed. New York: Oxford University Press, 2007. Overview of magazine publishing, analyzing industry trends, how magazines reflect and influence the world around them, and the role of advertising. Covers American magazine publishing history, case histories of selected magazines, and historical trends.

Renard, David, et al. *Last Magazine: Magazines in Transition.* New York: Universe, 2006. Discusses issues and pressures that will cause a decline in publication of print magazines and lead to two types of future magazines: those in electronic form and "style press" magazines. Chapters are devoted to each type.

Sumner, David E., and Shirrel Rhoades. *Magazines: A Complete Guide to the Industry.* New York: Peter Lang, 2006. Details magazine production processes from article conception through printing and distribution. Comprehensive look at industry trends, history, issues, and business basics. Contains lists, charts, glossaries.

SEE ALSO: Advertising industry; *Barron's*; Book publishing; *The Economist*; *Forbes*; *Fortune*; Muckraking journalism; Newspaper industry; *Reader's Digest.*

Mail, U.S. *See* Postal Service, U.S.

Mail-order shopping. *See* Catalog shopping

Major League strike of 1972. *See* Baseball strike of 1972

Management theory

DEFINITION: Body of thought that seeks to explain and improve the administrative control of businesses and their employees

SIGNIFICANCE: Since the early twentieth century, a wide variety of management theories have been offered to solve the principal-agent problem so that important objectives of business managers can be achieved. Such theories are important to a wide variety of complex business enterprises.

Management is hierarchical by definition. Managerial and worker interests may diverge, and critical managerial instructions will not always be followed. Getting workers to act on the behalf of management and the company's investors is known as the principal-agent problem. Management theory attempts to find ways that essential compliance can ensured. During the nineteenth century, most American businesses were small enterprises managed directly by owners who supervised their employees directly. By the end of the nineteenth century, much larger enterprises had arisen, and it was becoming increasingly difficult for business owners to manage enterprises on an industrial scale. Owners then began trying to seek out alternative management structures that gave them assurance that the objectives of the firm would prevail over any divergent objectives by the workers.

SCIENTIFIC MANAGEMENT

One of the earliest management theories was developed by Frederick Winslow Taylor, who called his management theory scientific management. Taylor's theory stressed the importance of strict time-and-motion studies of the industrial process. With the development of the assembly line, such time-and-motion studies seemed appropriate for breaking large industrial processes down into their smallest components and then training workers to perform only one small part of the manufacturing process. Based on time-and-motion studies, Taylor recommended the use of written instructions, as in a handbook, and strict training of employees to ensure they followed the manual.

Taylor was an engineer, and his theories tended to treat workers as if they were machines. Taylor's scientific management seemed to have some success, and it was very popular in the first three decades of the twentieth century. Still, its effectiveness declined over time, as workers and some researchers found processes based on Taylor's theory dehumanizing.

LATER THEORIES

A variety of researchers conducted studies that indicated that eventually the time-and-motion studies led to worker demoralization and increased inefficiency rather than efficiency in industrial processes. Mary Parker Follett challenged Taylor by suggesting that industrial situations were too com-

plex to be measured solely by a manual covering an entire enterprise. Instead, she asserted, they required giving supervisors close to the work the authority to make changes based on the logic of the situation. Follett did rely on material incentives as the principal motivating force, just as Taylor did. While scientific management never died out entirely, other theories of management arose to challenge its supremacy.

By the middle of the twentieth century, Abraham Maslow and Douglas McGregor were challenging the use of material incentives as the primary motivating factor for workers. Using a variety of experiments in different industrial settings, they showed that incentives based on nurturing a worker's self-worth were more likely to increase efficiency and productivity than were instructions based on machine-like time-and-motion studies.

The management theories of W. Edwards Deming, shown in 1987, were followed by the Japanese. (AP/Wide World Photos)

Although the work of McGregor and Maslow improved efficiency by improving the workplace conditions and attitudes of the workers, it became clear that a greater level of compliance with managerial directives was required. One of the management theorists who sought to advance beyond the work of McGregor and Maslow was Peter F. Drucker, whose dozens of books on management theory have become classics in the twentieth century. Drucker recognized the importance of uniform objectives governing workplace processes but stressed the importance of involving workers in the establishment of those uniform objectives. The concept of management by objectives is the phrase most widely recognized from Drucker's work.

Another management theorist, W. Edwards Deming, took worker involvement in the setting of objectives one step further by urging management to create small groups of employees to discuss how efficiency could be improved within their work unit. Calling such groups quality circles, Deming believed that worker involvement in brainstorming in small groups (or quality circles) was the best way to improve efficiency. Deming also argued that management must promote quality in the goods and services their institution produces or else face insurmountable competition from businesses in foreign countries who have adopted similar management techniques. Improvements are constantly being developed in management theory and these are critically important to all business enterprises.

Richard L. Wilson

FURTHER READING

Baker, George P., and George David Smith. *The New Financial Capitalists.* New York: Cambridge University Press, 1998. Management theory is applied to leveraged buyouts and other financial manipulations.

Deming, W. Edwards. *The New Economics: For Industry, Government, and Education.* 2d ed. Cambridge, Mass.: MIT Press, 2000. Issued after Deming's death, this book represents the culmination of his management theory.

Drucker, Peter F. *The New Realities.* New Brunswick, N.J.: Transaction, 2003. This is the last book in a long list of books of managerial theory published by Drucker.

Follett, Mary Parker. "The Giving of Orders." In *Scientific Foundations of Business Administration,* edited by H. Metcalf. Baltimore: Williams and Wilkins, 1926. This article was one of the first challenges to Taylor's scientific management.

McKenna, Christopher. *The World's Newest Profession: Management Consulting in the Twentieth Century.* New York: Cambridge University Press, 2006. This book examines the role played by management consultants in developing new management theory.

Miner, John B. *Organizational Behavior: Foundations, Theories, and Analyses.* New York: Oxford University Press, 2002. Addresses topics of motivation, leadership, and decision making in organizations and offers introductory material on the origins and history of management theory.

Taylor, Frederick W. *Scientific Management.* New York: Harper & Row, 1947. This book is a later version of the time-and-motion study principles that Taylor developed early in the twentieth century.

SEE ALSO: Business schools; Education; How-to-succeed books; Labor history; Labor strikes.

Marketing. *See* Christmas marketing; Online marketing

Marshall Plan

IDENTIFICATION: Large economic assistance program provided by the United States to Western European nations to help them recover from World War II

DATE: July 12, 1947-1951

SIGNIFICANCE: The Marshall Plan helped reopen the wealthy foreign markets of Europe to American products. Fear existed that, if Western Europe was not rebuilt, the U.S. economy could slide back into depression. The success of the Marshall Plan contributed to an extended period of U.S. economic dominance.

When World War II ended in 1945, the United States had recovered from the Great Depression. The American economy was responsible for producing as much as one-half of the world's output at the time. Europe and Asia, however, had been devastated by the war. Their economies were still experiencing a depression. Recognizing the importance of foreign markets, the United States feared that its economy could also fall back into depression if previously wealthy foreign consumers did not reacquire the resources they needed to buy American goods.

COLD WAR CONCERNS

The United States had another great fear as well. Though aligned with the Soviet Union during the war, the United States had already begun to perceive this former ally as a threat. The Soviets maintained a troop presence in the nations of Eastern Europe after the war and imposed one-party dictatorships on those countries. In addition, they required them to adopt government-owned, centrally planned economies, thus mostly preventing private businesses from operating. The United States believed that the Soviet Union sought to spread communism globally.

To address both of these fears, the United States adopted the Marshall Plan, also known as the European Recovery Program. Named after Secretary of State George C. Marshall, who initially proposed it, the program provided $13 billion in financial assistance and preferential treatment in trade to participating nations. Furthermore, it required countries receiving assistance to coordinate their efforts to rebuild their economies. This required cooperation led to the creation of the Organization for European Economic Cooperation (OEEC), the precursor to the Organization for Economic Cooperation and Development, which further facilitated trade among the wealthiest countries in the world.

The goal of the program was twofold: to prevent communists from acquiring power in Western Europe and to reopen markets in the region to American products. These national security and economic goals appeared to be linked. If the Soviet Union expanded its influence, it would not only enhance its ability to attack the United States and its allies but also reduce the number of markets available to American business. Thus, by keeping communists out of power, the United States believed it would be protecting its national security as well as its economic interests.

HISTORICAL BASIS

The Marshall Plan was part of a broad approach to U.S. foreign economic policy after 1945. The

One of the posters created by the Economic Cooperation Administration to promote the Marshall Plan in Europe. (Economic Cooperation Administration)

United States realized that its response to the onset of the Great Depression in 1929 failed. At the time, American leaders pursued protectionist policies in an attempt to recover from the severe economic downturn. In 1930, the United States passed the Smoot-Hawley Tariff Act, which significantly increased tariffs on imported products. In response, other powerful countries also raised their tariffs, leading to a reduction in global trade and exacerbating the world economic crisis.

As World War II was coming to an end, the United States embraced more open trade. It took the leading role in creating a new global financial system by establishing the Bretton Woods institutions—the International Monetary Fund (IMF) and the International Bank for Reconstruction and Development (the World Bank)—as well as the General Agreement on Tariffs and Trade (GATT). Together, these institutions encouraged free trade by aiding countries that developed balance-of-payments problems and reducing tariff rates. As long as many countries remained crippled by the damage caused by the war, however, it would be extremely difficult for these new global institutions to create a more open exchange of goods and services across international borders. Thus, a large economic aid package to those states severely damaged could easily be justified, and the United States had the economic clout to provide this kind of assistance.

SUCCESSES

The Marshall Plan is widely considered to have been a successful U.S. foreign policy initiative. In regard to national security, recipient countries became major allies of the United States, as most joined the North Atlantic Treaty Organization (NATO), a military alliance initially formed to contain possible Soviet expansion into Western Europe. Though the communist parties were relatively strong in France and Italy, they never came to power in those countries.

The Marshall Plan also produced favorable results for the U.S. economy. Though the program represented approximately 3 percent of the American gross national product (GNP), it helped recipient countries recover from the devastation caused by World War II. In doing so, trade between the United States and Western Europe increased dramatically after 1945. Foreign investment expanded substantially as well. The United States did not fall back into depression, as many had feared might happen. European cooperation partially fostered by the program has continued. Furthermore, the United States remains the richest country in the world, long after World War II and the Great Depression. Finally, global trade is much more open now than it was in 1945, serving as evidence of progress toward the U.S. economic goal established at the time.

Kevin L. Brennan

FURTHER READING

Behrman, Greg. *The Most Noble Adventure: The Marshall Plan and the Time When America Helped Save Europe.* New York: Free Press, 2007. Examines the history of the Marshall Plan and provides a detailed account of the roles of various individuals who contributed to its creation and deployment.

Djelic, Marie-Laure A. *Exporting the American Model: The Post-War Transformation of European Business.* New York: Oxford University Press, 2001. Analyzes the strengths and weaknesses of the U.S. business model as applied in France, Italy, and West Germany.

Gaddis, John Lewis. *We Now Know: Rethinking Cold War History.* New York: Oxford University Press, 1997. Utilizes information declassified soon after the Cold War ended to revisit several events of that era. Suggests the prolonged heightened tensions between the United States and Soviet Union were unavoidable.

Mills, Nicolaus. *Winning the Peace: The Marshall Plan and America's Coming of Age as a Superpower.* Hoboken, N.J.: John Wiley & Sons, 2008. Makes a strong case that the Marshall Plan serves as an example of successful nation-building. Provides a rich history of the program as well.

Schain, Martin A., ed. *The Marshall Plan: Fifty Years After.* New York: Palgrave, 2001. Collection of articles that address the impact of the Marshall Plan on the evolution of political and economic integration in Western Europe as well as the region's postwar recovery.

SEE ALSO: Agency for International Development, U.S.; Bretton Woods Agreement; European trade with the United States; Export-Import Bank of the United States; Food for Peace; International economics and trade; World War II.

Meatpacking industry

DEFINITION: Enterprises that process and package meat for wholesale or retail sale

SIGNIFICANCE: From its earliest beginnings during colonial times to the second half of the nineteenth century, the meatpacking industry in the United States underwent steady development, always moving westward along with shifting human settlement. During the 1860's, it underwent rapid expansion into a highly centralized, highly industrialized system that offers a prime example of late nineteenth century economic growth.

The processing and packing of meat for commercial purposes in the United States began in colonial times. Animals, primarily hogs and cattle, were either driven alive to urban centers or killed and pro-

Workers knocking cattle before slaughter at Swift & Co.'s packing house in Chicago around 1906. (Library of Congress)

second quarter of the nineteenth century, railroads also began to be used as a means of shipment.

By the second half of the nineteenth century, as the nation's rail system grew, cities further west began to replace the earlier processing centers. Following the U.S. Civil War, Chicago became a major rail and meat-processing hub. This development coincided with a rapid growth in beef production, in an era sometimes called the Cattle Kingdom. Cattle raised on the open plains of the West were driven along cattle trails to shipping points on the newly constructed western railroads. They were then loaded into railroad cars and carried to Chicago, where the slaughtering and processing took place. The Chicago Union Stock Yards, which opened in 1865, eventually became the largest livestock-receiving center in the world, and around it a new, more industrialized system of meat processing developed.

cessed at the place where they were raised. Local processing was done chiefly during the winter months, and the meat was transported in the spring, since no method of refrigerated storage existed. Meat intended for export or intercolonial shipment was placed in barrels filled with brine for preservation.

As settlement spread westward into the Ohio River Valley during the early years of the nineteenth century and agricultural production expanded, the meatpacking industry also grew in significance. Hogs raised on corn became a major commodity, and Cincinnati, often referred to by the nickname "Porkopolis," became an early meat-processing center. Animals continued to be driven overland to processing centers, where they were then slaughtered, and the salted meat was shipped by river or canal to the East. During the

THE INDUSTRIAL AGE

Among the pioneers of the new system were Philip Armour and Gustavus Swift, both of whom opened meatpacking plants in Chicago after the Civil War. Both introduced new industrial techniques, especially the use of the assembly line, into meat processing. In this method, the meat was moved by a conveyor system from the point of initial killing to the product's final stage, while workers remained at fixed positions along the line, performing the same task over and over again. Nearly all parts of the animal were utilized, creating smaller, subsidiary industries that produced such items as leather, fertilizer, soap, and glue. Refrigerated railroad cars, introduced during the 1870's, further revolutionized the industry, allowing fresh meat to be transported over greater distances.

Armour's, Swift's, and several of the other large

TOP EIGHT MEATPACKING COMPANIES, BY SALES, 2008

1. Tyson Foods: cattle, hogs, poultry
2. ConAgra: cattle, hogs, poultry
3. Smithfield Foods: cattle, hogs, poultry
4. Cargill Meat Solutions: cattle, hogs, poultry
5. Swift/JBS SA: cattle, hogs, poultry
6. Pilgrims Pride/Gold Kist: poultry
7. Geo. Hormel: cattle, hogs, poultry
8. Perdue: poultry

Source: Hoovers, SEC

Chicago-based packing plants of the period eventually opened other regional processing centers at places such as Kansas City, Missouri; Sioux City, Iowa; and South St. Paul, Minnesota. By the late 1880's and early 1890's, the scale of the industry had grown to nearly monopolistic proportions, with several large companies—known variously as the Big Five or the "beef trust"—meeting secretly to fix prices and divide up territory and business. Although the government made periodic efforts to break up these large concentrations, its efforts were never completely successful. The major packers also led in the development of modern management structures. Swift, for example, developed a vertical organization of his company, creating a series of divisions based on primary functions—a stockyards division, a meatpacking division, a sales division, and so forth—each of which was overseen by a manager who reported directly to corporate headquarters.

REGULATION AND UNIONS

Regulation in the area of consumer protection proved more successful than antitrust action against the big companies. A scandal following the Spanish-American War, in which several packers were accused of selling tainted meat to the government, along with the publication in 1906 of *The Jungle*, Upton Sinclair's fictionalized (but thoroughly researched) exposé of the industry, eventually led to the passage of the Federal Meat Inspection Act of 1906. This legislation, which required the Department of Agriculture to inspect all meat processed for interstate shipping, stands as one of the earliest examples of consumer-protection legislation undertaken at the national level.

Although Sinclair's novel had also documented the desperate state of packinghouse workers—low pay, long hours, and dangerous working conditions—the attempt to improve the lot of these individuals involved a long, difficult struggle. With the growth of the United Packinghouse Workers of America (UPWA) during the 1930's and early 1940's, major gains were eventually made in wages, hours, benefits, and workplace safety. By this time also, large numbers of African American workers had replaced the European immigrant workers of the earlier period.

During the 1950's and 1960's, a major change occurred in the meatpacking industry. Cost considerations and the rise of interstate trucking led to growing decentralization, with smaller processing plants being located closer to the centers of beef production. During the 1950's, both Swift and Armour closed their Chicago plants, and in the years that followed, most of the large regional processing centers were also shut down. During this time, the composition of the workforce shifted once again, with growing numbers of Latino workers finding employment in the smaller rural processing plants. With these changes, an epic period of the industry had come to an end.

Scott Wright

FURTHER READING

Halpern, Rick. *Down on the Killing Floor: Black and White Workers in Chicago's Packinghouses, 1904-1954.* Chicago: University of Illinois Press, 1997. Focuses on the issue of race and its impact on efforts to organize packinghouse workers during the first half of the twentieth century.

Magoc, Chris J. *Environmental Issues in American History: A Reference Guide with Primary Documents.* Westport, Conn.: Greenwood Press, 2006. Chapter 9, "Progressive Women and 'Municipal Housekeeping': Caroline Bartlett Crane's Fight for Improved Meat Inspection," offers an excellent case study in the role of women in this important area of Progressive reform.

Skaggs, Jimmy. *Prime Cut: Livestock Raising and Meatpacking in the United States, 1607-1983.* College Station: Texas A&M University Press, 1986. Historical overview of meatpacking in America from colonial to modern times.

Wade, Louise Carroll. *The Stockyard, Packingtown,*

and Environs in the Nineteenth Century. Urbana: University of Illinois Press, 1987. A history of the meatpacking industry in Chicago in its early years with special emphasis on the community life of packinghouse workers.

Walsh, Margaret. *The Rise of the Midwestern Meat Packing Industry.* Lexington: University Press of Kentucky, 1982. Examines the growth of pork packing in the Midwest prior to the rise of the meatpacking giants of the late nineteenth century.

SEE ALSO: Agriculture, U.S. Department of; Beef industry; Dairy industry; Food and Drug Administration; Food-processing industries; *The Jungle;* Pork industry; Poultry industry; United Food and Commercial Workers.

Medicare and Medicaid

IDENTIFICATION: Federal programs that provide health care assistance for the elderly (Medicare) and the poor (Medicaid)

DATE: Signed into law on July 30, 1965

SIGNIFICANCE: Medicare and Medicaid have had positive impacts on the health care, insurance, pharmaceutical, and related industries, as well as on states' economies.

Legislative proposals for federal programs for elderly and indigent health care assistance before 1965 were denounced as "socialized medicine" by medical-industry, insurance, and pharmaceutical lobbies, which helped prevent their enactment. Medicare and Medicaid (Titles XVIII and XIX, respectively, of the Social Security Act of 1965) were successful political compromises, however. Medicare covered hospital expenses, while participation for coverage of doctors' fees was optional for patients and physicians. Medicaid was administered by states.

Starting in 1975, a series of cost-containment measures reduced physicians' compensation rates. However, the private sector benefited from the increase in health care facilities related to Medicare coverages, the creation of private "Medigap" insurance to pay for excluded services, and additional Medicare options, such as Part C, which provides benefits through private insurance plans. Starting in 2003, Medicare Part D prescription drug cover-age generated profits for the insurance and pharmaceutical industries by using private-sector insurance and prohibiting the government from negotiating for discounted drug prices or reimporting less expensive drugs from foreign countries.

Public officials have expressed concerns regarding Medicaid costs. However, numerous studies have shown that Medicaid payments to health care providers and institutions are a major stimulus to state economies. Medicaid spending is the second-largest state budget expenditure, and the federal government matches states' spending at a rate of 50 percent or more, generating the greatest amount of federal grant money in every state. The program is directly beneficial to nursing homes, hospitals, pharmacies, community and home health care agencies, and insurance companies, and it creates jobs in other related industries. It also increases the amount of money in circulation, which has benefited businesses in general.

Jack Carter

SEE ALSO: Food and Drug Administration; Government spending; Health care industry; Pharmaceutical industry; Social Security system; Wages.

Merger and corporate reorganization industry

DEFINITION: Late twentieth century industry that arose to facilitate corporate mergers, leveraged buyouts, liquidations, and other forms of business reorganizations

SIGNIFICANCE: As the variety of business mergers became more complicated, a new industry arose from businesses designed to provide specialized accounting and legal and financial expertise that would facilitate all manner of reorganizations. In principle, these firms were supposed to act as neutral parties to aid all parties involved in mergers to gain fair and equitable evaluations of the assets of the parties, but genuine neutrality has not always existed.

Early in American history, colonial charters were sometimes based on joint-stock companies, but most early American businesses were either sole proprietorships or partnerships with very simple legal structures. No assistance beyond perhaps that of an attorney was needed to combine or dissolve most business structures. Over the next two centuries, the legal structures became more complex, and the various kinds of mergers required more legal and accounting assistance.

During the late nineteenth century, many businesses merged into what became known as trusts or holding companies. Some of these clearly aimed at monopoly control of certain sectors of the economy. By the first half of the twentieth century, concern that mergers were producing monopolies with too much economic power had led to these monopolies either being broken up or subjected to increased regulation. From that moment, mergers required sophisticated accounting, financial, and legal services to achieve their objectives. The antitrust and regulatory environment limited the number of successful mergers. During the 1980's, the administration of President Ronald Reagan successfully pushed for substantial deregulation of the financial industry, and various forms of mergers again became popular. Because mergers were once again attractive, an entire industry grew up from the specialized services needed for complex mergers.

MERGERS

Mergers may be combinations of two willing partners of roughly the same size or they may be acquisitions of smaller companies by larger companies. Sometimes mergers are of successful companies acquiring distressed or insolvent companies; these are popularly known as liquidations. Mergers may be vertical or horizontal integrations or conglomerations. Conglomerations involve the joining of unrelated businesses. Their main business advantage is that they may allow for more efficient allocation of capital. A horizontal integration is the merger of two or more businesses in the same sector with similar modes of production. The aim is to reduce competition, and therefore, the approval of the antitrust division of the U.S. Department of Justice has often been required. Vertical integration is the merger of one or more businesses representing different stages of the production of a final product. Although vertical integration may raise monopoly concerns and require Justice Department clearance, this type of integration can usually be justified because of reduced transaction costs and therefore is easier to achieve.

The AOL Time Warner building in New York. The 2000 merger of AOL and Time Warner ended in a goodwill write-off of AOL in 2002, after the value of the Internet company fell. (AP/Wide World Photos)

LEVERAGED BUYOUTS

Leveraged buyouts are a type of merger that may represent either vertical or horizontal integration. The key issue in the leveraged buyout is that the purchaser does not have sufficient cash to directly buy the target or a controlling share of its stock. The purchaser can overcome this problem by borrowing money and using the assets of the business being purchased as collateral for the loan. After completing a leveraged buyout, the buyer often sells off units of the purchased company to pay back the loan.

Targets of leveraged buyouts frequently resist being taken over because they oppose having their assets broken up and sold in this way. In such cases, leveraged buyouts are known as hostile takeovers.

Leveraged buyouts of businesses of all sizes were popular during the 1980's, when about two thousand companies with assets totaling about $250 million were bought out. During that same decade, some controversial hostile takeovers occurred that helped give the profitable merger industry a poor reputation.

During the 1990's and the early twenty-first century, leveraged buyouts and hostile takeovers, along with a variety of other mergers, remained popular. However, some of these leveraged buyouts were based on inflated evaluations of the assets of the companies being acquired. When enough such buyouts took place at the same time, they created various economic bubbles that ultimately burst, creating instability in the larger financial markets. The first of these was the dot-com bubble that began during the late 1990's and continued into the next decade. Only a few years later, a comparable bubble involving subprime mortgages led to first a burst bubble and then a crash, creating a very difficult situation for investment banks, the mortgage industry, and the real estate market. Nonetheless, the merger industry has continued to play a significant role in the financial sector.

Richard L. Wilson

FURTHER READING

Baiman, Ron, Heather Boushey, and Dawn Saunders. *Political Economy and Contemporary Capitalism: Radical Perspectives on Economic Theory and Policy.* Armonk, N.Y.: M. E. Sharpe, 2000. Collection of essays that examines mergers and leveraged buyouts from a perspective sympathetic to socialism.

Burrough, Bryan. *Barbarians at the Gate.* New York: Harper & Row, 1990. Study of the leveraged buyout of a large tobacco company that became such a well-known example of a hostile takeover that it was made into a Hollywood film with the same title as the book.

Johnston, Moira. *Takeover: The New Wall Street Warriors—The Men, the Money, the Impact.* New York: Arbor House, 1986. Still one of the best studies of the merger mania of the mid-1980's; however, it was written before some of the biggest and most important deals were concluded.

Levinson, Marc. *The Box: How the Shipping Container Made the World Smaller and the World Economy Bigger.* Princeton, N.J.: Princeton University Press, 2006.

A detailed analysis of a famous merger with some positive consequences.

Smith, Roy C. *The Money Wars: The Rise and Fall of the Great Buyout Boom of the 1980's.* New York: Dutton, 1990. Clear and well-informed discussion of the takeover movement of the 1980's.

Stewart, J. B. *Den of Thieves.* New York: Simon & Schuster, 1991. Critical examination of the merger, acquisitions, and leveraged buyout industry.

Wasserstein, Bruce. *Big Deal: Mergers and Acquisitions in the Digital Age.* Rev. ed. New York: Warner Books, 2001. History and tactics of media corporate mergers, with emphasis on businesses and personalities behind the scenes.

SEE ALSO: Bankruptcy law; Federal Trade Commission; Incorporation laws; Petroleum industry.

Metric system

DEFINITION: System of physical measurements used in most countries outside the United States

SIGNIFICANCE: Because the metric system is in common use in all major countries except the United States, American businesses are at a serious disadvantage in marketing a wide variety of products abroad.

There are two important components of the international metric system of weights and measures. The first is the fact that all measures are interrelated. Thus, any unit can be converted to others by simple operations involving powers of ten. The second is the establishment of standard values for the base units of each type of measurement. Thus, the unit of length is established as the distance light travels in a certain given amount of time. For mass, the base unit is established as the mass of a carefully guarded platinum-iridium cylinder located in Sevres, France.

In common usage, certain of the possible powers-of-ten values for the base units have become more common than others. For distance and size, for example, the meter, the centimeter (one-hundredth of a meter), the micrometer (one-millionth of a meter), and the kilometer (one thousand meters) are commonly used. For weight, the gram, the milligram (one-thousandth of a gram), and the kilogram (one thousand grams) are common. In some businesses, the metric ton is used. This represents is a megagram (one million grams).

Metric units of volume are based on the meter. Thus, a liter is a volume of one cubic decimeter and a kiloliter is a cubic meter. Areas are usually expressed in terms of square meters or square centimeters, but in some applications, as in agriculture, areas are given in terms of the unit "hectare," which is a square 100 meters on a side, or 10,000 square meters.

METRICS IN THE UNITED STATES

The U.S. government recognized the importance of adopting metric units as early as the mid-nineteenth century. To promote the metric system, Congress issued each state a set of standard metric units of weights and measures in 1866. In 1875, together with most other major countries of the world, the United States signed the Treaty of the Meter, an international agreement to use metric units in international matters, especially business. However, for more than one hundred years, American business has failed to realize fully the advantages of using the same units as adopted in other countries.

The U.S. government has made many attempts to promote a countrywide conversion from common ("English") units to metric units, but with little success. A U.S. Metric Study was authorized in 1968, resulting in a recommendation from the National Bureau of Standards that the country be predominantly metric by 1981. Congress passed the Education Amendments Act of 1974, which asked schools to prepare their students for the metric system. In the next year, the Metric Conversion Act of 1975 was passed and the U.S. Metric Board was created to coordinate a voluntary conversion. One of the first conversions occurred when the Bureau of Alcohol, Tobacco, and Firearms required wine and distilled spirits producers and importers to use metric bottles for wine and hard liquor. Metric speed limit signs began to appear, and distances on maps and road and trail markers were given in metric units. However, in 1982, President Ronald Reagan disbanded the U.S. Metric Board, and conversion activity ended. Metric speed limit signs were taken down. In 1991, President George H. W. Bush signed an executive order directing all federal agencies and executive departments to convert to the metric system.

BUSINESS AND THE METRIC SYSTEM

The problem for American business is that a complete conversion to metric units would be expensive. To satisfy the world market, it would not be enough to re-label a manufactured item; it must be redesigned to have metric dimensions. Currently, most manufactured items in America include a metric measurement on their labels, but it is given in parentheses and is usually not a round number—for instance, "net weight 20 oz. (566 g)." The world market would prefer to have the metric unit be the primary one on a label and to have the measure be a simple one to permit comparison pricing. For small-scale goods, this would require re-scaling the machinery that produces and packages the items.

Some American food and household products are sold in metric sizes. For example, soft drinks are offered in two- and three-liter bottles, and wine is almost universally sold in standard 750 milliliter bottles. However, other food items, such as meat and dairy products, have not been successfully converted.

In some commercial fields, there has been a curious hybrid conversion to metric units. For example, the tread of automobile tires is measured in millimeters, while the tires' diameters are measured in inches. Otherwise, car manufacturers throughout the world use metric units for all parts, except for the lug bolts for wheels.

Although the American automobile manufacturing companies are using mostly metric units, manufacturers of other products have been reluctant to convert. Perhaps the most notable current case of a large, global business that has resisted metrification is the Boeing Company, which is still basing its design of airplanes on traditional units. For a small manufacturer, the advantage of a world market may not obviously warrant an expensive retooling of the plant. For computers, there has been a gradual conversion to metric-sized products. Digital versatile discs (DVDs) are 120 millimeters in diameter, but some computer components are still manufactured in traditional units, most conspicuously computer monitors.

FINANCIAL MEASURES

In finance, there is still a double standard for certain measurements. International production figures are usually given in metric units, such as metric tons; however, American statistics are often quoted in old units, such as bushels for wheat, barrels for oil, and pounds for certain other commodities. Unlike the case of Britain and various other traditionalist countries, U.S. currency has been decimal-based since the country began. However, only in 2001 did Wall Street cease to use the archaic fractional system of eighths in trading in stocks.

The gradual metrification of American business has proceeded very slowly, to the detriment of its potential global customers. However, with the ascent of European unity and prosperity, American business is realizing the importance of accelerating the conversion process.

Paul W. Hodge

FURTHER READING

Fenna, Donald. *A Dictionary of Weights, Measures, and Units.* Oxford, England: Oxford University Press, 2002. For a comprehensive account of the International Metric System and related systems of measurements, this fairly technical book is an excellent resource. Both the history of the system and its scientific foundations are covered.

Halsey, Frederick. *The Metric Fallacy: An Investigation of the Claims Made for the Metric System and Especially of the Claim That Its Adoption Is Necessary in the Interest of Export Trade.* 1919. Reprint. Whitefish, Mont.: Kessinger, 2008. Influential book that went to great lengths to demonstrate that the United States could get along without the metric system by showing how it had failed in other countries. The book's twenty-five chapters examine the metric system in individual countries and regions, in different scientific fields, and in different economic systems. A fascinating historical document.

Law, Merry. *Guide to International Measurement Systems: Practical Details About Metric, U.S. and Imperial Measures, with Paper, Clothing, Cooking, and Computer Measurements.* Highland Park, N.J.: WorldVu, 2005. An examination of the metric system, with conversion guides.

U.S. National Archives and Records Administration. *The United States and the Metric System: A Capsule History.* Washington, D.C.: National Institute of Standards and Technology, 1992. Brief federal government report surveying the history of American efforts to adopt the metric system.

Whitelaw, Ian. *A Measure of All Things: The Story of Man and Measurement.* New York: St. Martin's, 2007. Covers the history of measurement, including the metric system.

SEE ALSO: International economics and trade; Time zones.

Mexican Contract Labor Program. *See* Bracero program

Mexican trade with the United States

SIGNIFICANCE: A key to modern Mexican-U.S. trade relations lies in the 1994 North American Free Trade Agreement, more commonly known as NAFTA, which was signed by the United States, Mexico, and Canada. NAFTA's purpose is to eliminate restrictions such as tariffs and quotas on trade and investment among the three participants. After the agreement went into effect, trade among the three countries increased significantly.

As neighbors sharing a nearly two-thousand-mile border through two centuries, the United States and Mexico have long been important trade partners. The United States has long been Mexico's biggest trading partner, and after the adoption of the North American Free Trade Agreement (NAFTA) in January, 1994, the economic and trade ties between the two countries grew even stronger. The change has been particularly important for Mexico, whose trade with the United States tripled in value after NAFTA. By 2008, nearly 90 percent of Mexican exports were going to the United States, and about 56 percent of Mexico's imports came from the United States. Moreover, NAFTA provisions liberalizing foreign investment restrictions have also resulted in a marked increase in American investments within Mexico.

MEXICAN MANUFACTURING

In 1965, the Mexican government established a program to encourage the building of factories to assemble and build products primarily for the countries from which they import the products' materials.

Known as the *maquiladora* program, after the Spanish word for factory, this program became the centerpiece in Mexico's manufacturing industry. By 2008, approximately three thousand such plants were providing jobs for more than 500,000 Mexican workers—mostly near Mexico's northern border with the United States.

Maquiladoras import most of their materials and equipment (generally from the United States), assemble and manufacture products, and then export the finished goods, often to the countries from which they imported the materials. Mexico imposes no duties or taxes on the incoming materials. After NAFTA was signed, manufacturers no longer even had to pay duty on the value-added portions of their finished goods.

Maquiladoras produce electric equipment, clothing, plastics, furniture, appliances, and automobiles and auto parts. The *maquiladora* industry is second only to oil in producing income from exports to foreign countries. In addition to the United States, other countries, including Japan and Germany, have established factories in Mexico to take advantage of NAFTA and Mexican government inducements under the *maquiladora* plan. The program's chief attraction has been the low cost of Mexican labor. However, new competition from low-cost Chinese labor has caused a substantial number of Mexican factories to close.

PETROLEUM

During the early twentieth century, oil was Mexico's most important export to the United States. American and British oil companies furnished the technical skill and capital necessary to develop the Mexican oil industry after commercially exploitable reserves were discovered by a British railroad building firm around the turn of the twentieth century. The British formed the Mexican Eagle Oil Company, which played a major role in the industry during this period. The British were joined by other oil companies from the United States and Europe. In 1938, however, the Mexican government, under president Lázaro Cárdenas, expropriated the foreign oil companies and nationalized the industry. The United States, Great Britain, and the Netherlands promptly instituted a boycott on Mexican oil, but increased demand for oil brought on by the outbreak of World War II saved Mexico's oil industry.

U.S. TRADE WITH MEXICO, 1985-2005, IN MILLIONS OF DOLLARS

Year	Exports	Imports	Balance
1985	13,635	19,132	−5,497
1990	28,279	30,157	−1,878
1995	46,292	62,100	−15,808
2000	111,349	135,926	−24,577
2005	120,365	170,109	−49,744

Source: Data from U.S. Census Bureau, Foreign Trade Division, Data Dissemination Branch, Washington, D.C.

Note: Trade figures are from the U.S. perspective.

Eager to block the sale of Mexican oil to Nazi Germany, the Allies lifted their boycott on Mexican oil.

The Mexican oil industry is managed by a government bureaucracy, Petróleos Mexicanos—better known by its acronym, PEMEX. The tenth-largest oil company in the world, as measured by revenue, PEMEX provides one of its country's major sources of tax revenue. Along with Canada and Saudi Arabia, PEMEX is one of the three major suppliers of oil to the United States, but it has been slow to drill new wells and is plagued by corruption from within as well as by interference from the politically powerful Petroleum Workers Union.

AGRICULTURE

Immediately before NAFTA was signed in 1994, the two-way trade in agricultural products between the United States and Mexico amounted to about $6 billion per year. By 2008, that figure had quadrupled, to about $24 billion annually. In January, 2008, all restrictions on agricultural products traded between the two countries were lifted, so the value of the trade was expected to continue to increase. The exchange of agricultural products between Mexico and the United States has been mutually beneficial. Mexican exports to the United States have been mostly fresh fruits, vegetables, and beer. American exports to Mexico have been mostly corn (maize), soybeans, meat, poultry, and tobacco.

Some Mexican peasants have complained about the competition they have encountered from American agricultural products because of the cost benefits of mass-production methods in the American agricultural industry. Farmers in Mexico's interior states have been at a further disadvantage in shipping their products because of the comparatively poor railroad and highway facilities. However, American NAFTA officials have contributed millions of dollars to help improve marketing facilities for local Mexican farmers.

TOURISM

Mexico's third-largest generator of foreign exchange is tourism, which has grown rapidly during the early twenty-first century. With long coastlines on both the Atlantic and Pacific Oceans, extensive and spectacular archaeological sites, and many vibrant cities, Mexico has a great deal to offer to tourists. By 2008, as many as two million foreigners—mostly Americans—visited the country each year. The Mexican government established a long-term plan for tourist development, under a department called Fonatur, to ensure development without causing damage to the environment. The government has made a point of establishing resort areas throughout the entire country to spread the economic benefits from the tourism industry as widely as possible.

A serious downside of the tourist boom has been an increase in attacks by criminal gangs on foreigners, many of whom use their visits to Mexico to seek out recreational drugs. This problem is aggravated by the efforts of Mexican gangs to use tourists to carry illicit drugs into the United States. The problem has become so acute that the government of Mexico has employed its army to combat criminal activity.

IMMIGRATION INTO THE UNITED STATES

The immigration of Mexicans into the United States has long complicated U.S.-Mexican trade relationships. Thousands of undocumented aliens, the overwhelming majority from Mexico itself, have crossed the U.S. border illegally in search of jobs in agriculture, factories, restaurants, hotels, construction, and American homes. Many American employers have come to rely on undocumented workers, especially in agriculture. Since September 11, 2001, American concern about illegal immigration has been heightened by the fear of terrorists infiltrating the United States from Mexico. To help slow the influx of illegal immigration, the U.S. government began building a chain of fences along the Mexican border.

Of great importance to the economy of Mexico is the substantial amount of money that immigrant workers in the United States remit to their families in their homeland. The approximately ten million Mexican laborers in the United States remit at least $20 billion a year to Mexico. These remittances constitute one of the most important sources of foreign exchange in Mexico. An estimated 6 percent of all Mexican households benefit from this influx of U.S. money. Families in four states in particular—Michoacán, Durango, Guanajuato, and Zacatecas—account for more than one-third of the total amount. Any substantial reduction of remittances resulting from tighter border controls could have a drastic impact on many Mexican families.

Virtually all studies of Mexican immigration into the United States agree that a continual supply of Mexican workers to the United States is critical to the economies and trade development of both countries. Mexico on its own cannot provide the necessary jobs for its rapidly growing population, and the United States cannot fill all the unskilled and semiskilled jobs required for its own economic expansion.

Carl Henry Marcoux

FURTHER READING

Bognanno, Mario F., and Kathryn Ready, eds. *The North American Free Trade Agreement: Labor, Industry and Government Perspectives.* Westport, Conn.: Quorum Books, 1993. Report on a 1991 conference in Minneapolis at which representatives of labor, industry, and government from the United States, Mexico, and Canada discussed a wide range of issues relating to NAFTA.

Irwin, Douglas A. *Free Trade Under Fire.* Princeton, N.J.: Princeton University Press, 2005. Discusses two major threats to the global expansion of American free trade—protectionism adopted by individual countries to defend their own industries and the actions of so-called public interest groups that seek to block free trade progress.

O'Driscoll, Gerald P., ed. *Free Trade Within North America: Expanding Trade for Prosperity.* Boston: Kluwer Academic, 1993. Twenty-one experts on foreign trade met in Texas in 1991, sponsored by the Federal Reserve bank of Dallas, to measure the potential for expanded global trade and the problems that this expansion presents.

Von Bertrab, Hermann. *Negotiating NAFTA: A Mexi-*

can Envoy's Account. Westport, Conn.: Praeger, 1997. Detailed account of the work of the Mexican negotiating team, headed by the author, an experienced Mexican financier, charged with addressing the concerns of internal Mexican groups as well as the multiplicity of American interests, with a tentative agreement for a proposed trade treaty.

Weintraub, Sidney. *NAFTA: What Comes Next?* Westport, Conn.: Praeger, 1994. The author, an experienced economist with a deep understanding of Latin American political and economic affairs, discusses the future for international trade and the role that NAFTA is playing in its global expansion.

SEE ALSO: Asian trade with the United States; Bracero program; Canadian trade with the United States; Chinese trade with the United States; European trade with the United States; Gadsden Purchase; Immigration; International economics and trade; Japanese trade with the United States; Latin American trade with the United States; Mexican War; North American Free Trade Agreement; Texas annexation.

Mexican War

THE EVENT: Military confrontation between Mexico and the United States over the annexation of Texas to the United States in 1845

DATE: 1846-1848

PLACE: Mexico, Texas (Lone Star Republic), California (Bear Flag Republic), and New Mexico

SIGNIFICANCE: The Mexican War resulted in Mexico ceding an area from Texas to California to the United States, extending the country to the Pacific Coast and immensely increasing its territorial assets and economic potential. The acquisition benefited the gold, silver, iron, copper, cattle, farming, banking, real estate, railroad, and telegraph industries, decisively advancing U.S. industrialization and financial strength.

The Mexican War ended with the signing of the Treaty of Guadalupe Hidalgo on February 2, 1848. Mexico ceded California, Nevada, Utah, and parts of Arizona, Colorado, New Mexico, and Wyoming

to the United States. With this transfer, Mexico lost half a million square miles, almost half its territory. For the United States, the Mexican cession would prove an economic bonanza of extraordinary proportions and the catalyst for the United States becoming a world economic power.

In August, 1848, gold was discovered in California. Tens of thousands of people flocked to the region in the following decade. San Francisco changed from a village into a maritime metropolis of intense commercial and financial activity equivalent to billions of dollars in modern currency. California immediately became so wealthy and populated that the U.S. Congress granted it statehood in 1850. Subsequent to the discovery of gold in California, some of the largest stores of silver in the world were uncovered in Nevada and Colorado. The capital accumulated from gold and silver reserves gave the United States a unique advantage as a developing country by allowing it to finance its own growth. Innovations in mining industry techniques benefited not only precious metal enterprises but also those dealing in iron, copper, and semiprecious stones.

Mining brought many other businesses to San Francisco. In 1853 Levi Strauss, a young German immigrant, arrived in the city, intending to help clothe the miners. Within a generation, he had developed an industry around blue jeans with distinctive rivets and stitching that would become a symbol of American style.

The San Francisco-based Bank of California opened in 1864 and immediately became one of the richest banks in the country, financing extensive commercial, manufacturing, and real estate enterprises.

MULTIPLIER EFFECTS

Along the East Coast, the need to transport goods to the gold fields stimulated business development. The long route by sea, around the southern tip of South America, required fast ships. Shipbuilding industries accelerated their production of clippers, the fastest vessels on the sea. In 1840, the Cunard Line introduced transoceanic steamship travel, which eventually replaced clipper transport.

Companies providing rapid overland transportation also emerged. Wells Fargo (founded in 1852) developed rapid pony and stagecoach delivery of passengers, goods, and communications. During the 1860's, the Union Pacific and the Central Pacific railroads extended their lines from California and Nebraska, respectively, to meet in Utah, linking the country from coast to coast. A multiplier industry, railroads stimulated a host of businesses, including iron, steel, coal, and oil enterprises. The Western Union Telegraph company (founded in 1851) had established a transcontinental communication line by 1861.

MILITARY COST OF MEXICAN WAR, 1846-1849

- In current year dollars = $71 million
- In constant fiscal year 2008 dollars = $1,081 million
- War cost as percentage of gross domestic product in peak year, 1847 = 1.4%
- Total defense cost as percentage of gross domestic product in peak year, 1847 = 1.9%

Source: Data from Stephen Daggett, "CROS Report for Congress: Costs of Major U.S. Wars," Congressional Research Service, July 24, 2008
Note: Data for war costs extends past war's end.

FURTHER ADVANCES

Wherever transportation and communication improved in the West, settlement and land values of adjacent areas increased. The Great Plains became an agricultural breadbasket, exporting foodstuffs to the industrializing East and Europe. The states formed from the Mexican cession became cattle country, a further source of foodstuffs. One of the largest cattle enterprises was the King Ranch (founded in 1853) in Texas, which eventually reached more than a thousand square miles and supplied countless herds to the railroad shipping pens in Kansas. Along with the cattle industry, various leather goods enterprises developed, producing saddles, saddle bags, boots, shoes, and other accouterments. Range wars raged between cattlemen and farmers, but the introduction of barbed wire in Texas during the mid-1870's and the state's mass commercialization over the next two decades rapidly reduced the amount of open range. The occupation of the West was sometimes violent and subject to attack by native fauna and indigenous populations. Facilitating and accelerating this violence were advances in gunsmithing, with companies such as Browning, Winchester, and Smith and Wesson manufacturing ever more powerful guns and rifles.

Further wealth came from California. The vast central valley of California became a major producer of fruits and vegetables. Watered by the Sacramento and San Joaquin Rivers, the land became doubly productive as engineering enterprises devised more effective water distribution and irrigation systems. Accumulated western transportation and communication projects would produce one of the largest construction companies in the world, the San Francisco-based Bechtel Corporation. The horticulturalist Luther Burbank settled in California in 1875, laying the foundation for its innovative agricultural businesses by developing seeds for hybrid, more productive types of fruits, vegetables, grains, flowers, and grasses. His work would be complemented by the horticultural and retailing advances of the Burpee seed company, with operations on both the East and West coasts.

The Mexican War fundamentally changed the nature of how business was conducted in the West. Under Mexico, enterprise in the region had been corporate and regulated. After the U.S. acquisition of the land, businesses became entrepreneurial and shaped by market competition. Moreover, a culture that was mostly Hispanic and Catholic became predominantly Anglo-Saxon and Protestant.

Edward A. Riedinger

FURTHER READING

Crawford, Mark, David S. Heidler, and Jeanne T. Heidler, eds. *Encyclopedia of the Mexican-American War.* Santa Barbara, Calif.: ABC-Clio, 1999. Concise compilation of information on the issues, regions, and individuals engaged in the events leading up to and through the conclusion of the war.

Frazier, Donald S., ed. *The United States and Mexico at War: Nineteenth-Century Expansionism and Conflict.* New York: Macmillan Reference USA, 1998. Examines both the war and the desire of the United States to expand to the West Coast.

Hine, Robert V., and John Mack Faragher. *The American West: A New Interpretive History.* New Haven,

Conn.: Yale University Press, 2000. The middle chapters of this work concentrate on the development of the mining, cattle, and transportation industries in the decades immediately after the Mexican War. Includes maps and extensive bibliography.

Rayner, Richard. *The Associates: Four Capitalists Who Created California.* New York: Atlas, 2008. Traces the lives of Collis Huntington, Leland Stanford, Mark Hopkins, and Charles Crocker, four nineteenth century U.S. railroad and banking investors who laid the foundations of the entrepreneurial wealth of California.

Torr, James D., ed. *The American Frontier.* San Diego, Calif.: Greenwood Press, 2002. An examination of the history of the American West that looks at how the area was settled and developed. Contains essays covering mining and cattle operations.

SEE ALSO: Alaska purchase; California gold rush; Railroads; Robber barons; Texas annexation; Transcontinental railroad; Wars.

Military-industrial complex

DEFINITION: Cautionary description of a symbiotic relationship between a national military establishment and a nation's armaments industry

SIGNIFICANCE: President Eisenhower dedicated his farewell address to a warning about the dangers represented by the "military-industrial complex." Since then, the term has been used to suggest the opportunities for collusion between defense contractors and government agencies that could cause corporate interests in amassing profit to overwhelm governmental interests in the welfare of the nation and its citizens.

On January 17, 1961, delivering his farewell address to the nation, U.S. president Dwight D. Eisenhower acknowledged the dangers that accompanied the new need for standing defense. He expressed his worries, in particular, about the simultaneous growth in power of both the private arms industry and the national military bureaucracy:

This conjunction of an immense military establishment and a large arms industry is new in the American experience. The total influence—economic,

political, even spiritual—is felt in every city, every state house, every office of the Federal government. . . . we must guard against the acquisition of unwarranted influence . . . by the military-industrial complex. . . . We must never let the weight of this combination endanger our liberties or democratic processes.

An earlier draft of the speech spoke still more explicitly of a "military-industrial-scientific complex." Even in the final text, Eisenhower warned against both the "domination of the nation's scholars by Federal employment, project allocations, and the power of money" and the "danger that public policy could itself become the captive of a scientific-technological elite." The president had little remedy to recommend, except "statesmanship" and "balance," but his naming of the problem was itself a lasting contribution.

MILITARISM AND ITS DANGERS

In the United States, Republican leader Thomas Dewey asserted, "politics is the shadow cast on society by big business." Eisenhower's speech continues to shape the debate over the proper relationship between business and government in general and that relationship within the defense industry in particular. The concept of the military-industrial complex serves as a reference point for critics who warn of the dangers of American militarism. It is also implicated in discussions of responsible oversight of the assignment and fulfillment of government contracts to private companies.

The immense military market tempts suppliers to secure government contracts by any means necessary. A "revolving door" system results in former bureaucrats gaining employment as executives in the very industries they were recently responsible for regulating, creating conflicts of interest, or the appearance of them. The scale of defense spending ensures fierce competition among countless individual communities—and their elected representatives—for contracts to build and service military bases and to develop and maintain weapons systems. In the resulting atmosphere of constant competition for governmental contracts, it becomes difficult to differentiate legitimate defense needs from pork-barrel spending.

On one hand, leftist critics such as Noam Chomsky and Henry Giroux argue that the vast power of corporations in pursuit of defense dollars can distort educational practice, democratic citizenship, and basic research. The tendency to privatize war as a business may further warp national priorities, at home and abroad. On the other hand, many believe that continuing development of a robust array of technologies to defend U.S. national security interests depends on the kind of innovativeness "free market" competition is thought to encourage. Eisenhower's warning about the military-industrial complex serves to highlight the ability of established market players to influence, in their drive for corporate profits, what counts as a national security interest.

American business and government have both grown enormously since Eisenhower issued his warning. In a globalized world, national boundaries and even national interests begin to seem less significant to multinational corporations trying to maximize their influence and profits. Moreover, as scholar James Adams points out, the balance between government and industry in terms of technological leadership has shifted significantly since the Cold War to favor civilian industries. Interconnections among business, government, and culture have expanded the military-industrial complex into an all-encompassing military-industrial-technological-entertainment-scientific-media-corporate matrix.

SCIENCE AND ITS PROFITS

Analysts have discerned the idea of the military-industrial complex in the work of sociologist C. Wright Mills and in still earlier cultural trends, but for Eisenhower it was largely a consequence of World War II. That war, during which atomic weapons (among other science-based innovations) were first developed, irreversibly shifted military attitudes toward scientific research. Under the leadership of such individuals as Vannevar Bush, President Franklin D. Roosevelt's science adviser, the organization of academic scientists plainly contributed materially to military victory. Even before the end of the war, planning for the role of scientific research in postwar life was under way.

Those plans addressed the relationship between research and the military and business worlds. U.S. senator Harley Kilgore of West Virginia, an active proponent of the postwar establishment of the National Science Foundation, argued that patents on inventions developed with public funds should fall into the public domain. Bush, on the other hand, argued that the ability to profit from intellectual property rights would drive innovation by private corporations, which should therefore retain patents even on publicly funded projects. Critics have viewed Bush's laissez-faire approach as sustaining a system of "corporate welfare," in which the risks and costs of innovation and investment are borne by the public (through subsidies, tax relief, bailouts, and so on), while the profits of successful ventures primarily benefit private companies. Supporters, however, believe that profit is the only motive powerful enough to drive the level of innovation necessary to keep Americans safe.

Edward Johnson

FURTHER READING

Adams, James. *The Next World War: Computers Are the Weapons and the Front Line Is Everywhere.* New York: Simon & Schuster, 1998. Places the military-industrial complex in the context of the information revolution.

Borden, Penn. *Civilian Indoctrination of the Military: World War I and Future Implications for the Military-Industrial Complex.* Westport, Conn.: Greenwood Press, 1989. Locates the origins of the complex during the early twentieth century Progressive era.

Giroux, Henry A. *The University in Chains: Confronting the Military-Industrial-Academic Complex.* Boulder, Colo.: Paradigm, 2007. Leftist critique of militarism's influence on higher education.

Singer, P. W. *Corporate Warriors: The Rise of the Privatized Military Industry.* Updated ed. Ithaca, N.Y.: Cornell University Press, 2007. General survey of the emergence of the business of twenty-first century war.

Turse, Nick. *The Complex: How the Military Invades Our Everyday Lives.* New York: Henry Holt, 2008. Extension of the concept of the military-industrial complex to include military influence on all aspects of contemporary American culture.

Walker, Gregg B., ed. *The Military-Industrial Complex: Eisenhower's Warning Three Decades Later.* New York: Peter Lang, 1992. Anthology examining the implications of the concept of the military-industrial complex.

Weber, Rachel Nicole. *Swords into Dow Shares: Governing the Decline of the Military-Industrial Complex.* Boulder, Colo.: Westview Press, 2001. Argues that the dependence of defense-industry businesses on public resources implies that corporate control should extend beyond shareholders.

Zachary, G. Pascal. *Endless Frontier: Vannevar Bush, Engineer of the American Century.* Cambridge, Mass.: MIT Press, 1999. Biography of one of the chief architects of the military-industrial-academic complex.

SEE ALSO: Arms industry; Government spending; Industrial research; Industrial Revolution, American; Wars; World War II.

Military surplus. *See* War surplus

Mineral resources

DEFINITION: Natural resources that include metals, coal, and stones

SIGNIFICANCE: The abundance of mineral resources available in the United States has allowed the rapid growth of American businesses to meet domestic needs and enabled the country to become a global force. Mineral resources have provided the raw materials and energy needed by businesses to produce goods, construct infrastructure, and provide mass transportation.

Mineral resources are an important primary input of production for businesses. As economic development grew and became more sophisticated, increasingly larger amounts and more diverse mineral resources were needed for business activities. The availability of mineral resources depends on the geological abundance of the minerals and their distribution.

Some mineral resources such as stone, coal, and iron are widely distributed and are commonly found in useful concentrations in many parts of the world. Other mineral resources such as copper and platinum are scarcer and require a much higher level of concentration to be useful. This makes their worldwide distribution uneven and their availability more restricted. A geographically larger country is likely to have more favorable areas of geology than a smaller country. Important mineral producers include Australia, Brazil, Canada, China, the Democratic Republic of the Congo, Russia, South Africa, and the United States. Smaller countries such as Chile, Ghana, and Indonesia can also have important mineral resources based on their favorable geology, but such countries have less diversity in their products. The types and amounts of mineral endowment in a country will affect the way business develops in that country. This was particularly true for early American business, as the physical and political isolation of the new country made it difficult to transport bulky raw materials from other regions.

During the colonial period and the early years of the new American republic, business activities were based on primary production, especially agriculture. Energy for business activities came mainly from animals and people, with some supplementation from wood and water. American businesses were small scale and primarily focused on directly using or exporting natural resources. The northern colonies had been a disappointment to their colonizers in terms of mineral resources because there were no easily exploited outcroppings of gold or silver as in other explored regions of the Americas. However, there were numerous small sites of poorer grade iron ore that could be used for small metalworking business operations (as in Valley Forge) and other small deposits of useful minerals. Exploration of Pennsylvania found that the state was well endowed with large deposits of anthracite coal that would become a vital material for the development of steel and transportation industries as the country moved from wood to coal for heating purposes during the early business years.

INDUSTRIALIZATION BEGINS

The business direction of the United States began to change significantly early in the nineteenth century. The troubled relationship between the United States and its major trading partner, Great Britain, as exemplified by the Embargo Act of 1807 and the War of 1812, made it apparent that the United States needed to become less dependent on Great Britain and Europe. Greater economic independence would require that the United States had the ability to produce its own manufactured goods and the necessary transportation infrastructure to move resource inputs and products around a rapidly growing country.

As the United States grew in size with the Louisiana Purchase, the addition of Texas, the territory gained from the Mexican War, and later additions such as Alaska, Americans moved steadily westward to look for new business and economic opportunities. Mineral resources discovered and produced in the newly available lands were an important source of economic opportunity for many Americans and new immigrants, and the raw materials served as inputs for new manufacturing industries. The 1840's and 1850's were a time of development of important mineral resources: the California gold rush, the discovery of large copper deposits in the Upper Peninsula of Michigan, and the lead-zinc mines of Wisconsin. The development of these mineral resources corresponded with the beginning of the second phase of the American Industrial Revolution (around 1850) that radically changed the nature of business in the United States. This phase of the American Industrial Revolution was initially based on the introduction of the steam engine both in industry and in transportation (first steamboats and then railroads). Steam engines and the new railroads needed large amounts of coal and steel, and steelmaking requires iron ore, coal, and limestone. All of these minerals were abundant and conveniently located in the United States.

American businesses went through a rapid period of growth and industrialization during the late nineteenth and early twentieth centuries as the United States became a manufacturing power. During this era, the country became the world's largest economy and leading producer of manufactured goods. To fuel this growth in manufacturing and create a transportation infrastructure, the country depended on the efficient exploitation of its abundant mineral resources, particularly iron, coal, and copper, and other minerals in smaller amounts. For example, iron ore production went from 1 million metric tons in 1860 to 76 million metric tons in 1916. The United States was the world's leading mineral producer of this era—both in quantity and in variety. Users of these minerals often sought to own and control these vital materials; for example, the United States Steel Corporation owned iron ore sites and the railroads owned coal mines.

Another resource abundant in the United States, petroleum, became very important in this era. The ready availability of oil—the fuel powering automobiles and trucks—allowed the mass production of cars for personal use and completely changed the nature of life and business in the country. As oil production grew, a whole new industry was created to discover, extract, and refine the crude petroleum. This activity led to the creation of one of the great trusts of the era, Standard Oil. Under the Sherman Antitrust Act of 1890, Standard Oil was broken up into a number of different oil companies. Meanwhile, coal usage shifted from powering steam engines to generating electrical power, which

Mules pull a coal car from a mine in Starkville, Colorado, in the early 1900's. Coal remains an important mineral for the United States. (Library of Congress)

GEMSTONES

Natural gemstones were some of the earliest mineral resources used in the United States. Native Americans used gemstones such as chalcedony, freshwater pearls, tourmaline, and turquoise for tools and decorative purposes. In the twenty-first century, gemstones are used mainly for decorative purposes, with some limited industrial use (as with diamonds, feldspar, and garnet). Natural gemstones are found in all parts of the United States, and more than sixty different types have been mined and used at some time. Examples of commercially used gemstones include chalcedony, diamond, feldspar, garnet, opal, freshwater pearls, peridot, quartz, sapphire, tourmaline, and turquoise. Tourmaline was first commercially mined in 1822 in Maine, and the commercial mining of other gemstones followed during the 1800's.

The gemstone industry tends to consist of small firms and individuals widely spread throughout the country, but it can be locally important, as in the cases of turquoise in the Southwest and freshwater pearls in Tennessee. The states of Tennessee, Oregon, Arizona, California, Arkansas, Alabama, Idaho, Montana, and Nevada account for most of the commercial value of natural gemstones produced in the United States. American resources are supplemented with imports and laboratory-created materials.

in turn dramatically changed the nature of life and business in the United States.

MODERN BUSINESS

As the U.S. economy continued to grow during the twentieth century, mineral needs were also growing. Much of this demand continued to be met through the use of domestic sources. Petroleum and coal (largely bituminous coal resources at this time) were used to produce gasoline and electricity to supply energy needs. Iron ore and base metals such as copper, lead, and zinc were produced in large amounts to provide the raw materials necessary for manufacturing and mass production. Industrial minerals such as potash and phosphate rock were mined to provide fertilizers needed for intensive agriculture. Other industrial minerals were used by the chemical industry. Rock and gravel were consumed in huge amounts to produce new roads, bridges, and other construction.

The diversification of American business led to products and industries that required minerals not available domestically. This shift was evident by the 1940's and the 1950's. Tin and aluminum products needed imported raw materials. The creation of new specialty steel products such as stainless steel required the importation of metals such as chromium, cobalt, manganese, and nickel. Platinum and titanium had to be imported. Even for the minerals that American businesses could buy domestically, the 1950's was a turning point. The rapidly growing economy and the depletion of the best domestic mineral resources had made it increasingly difficult for businesses to depend fully on domestic sources. Mineral output was not keeping up with demand, and new foreign sources cost less. American businesses were moving into a new era in which they could not depend solely on domestic sources of minerals for their needs.

Although American businesses have had to look to foreign sources of mineral resources to supplement their mineral needs, this does not mean that the United States can no longer view its domestic mineral resources as an important asset. The country is still one of the largest mineral producers in the world, but the ability to produce all the minerals its businesses need is gone. This is particularly true in energy production, where the country's demand for petroleum products has grown much faster than the country's ability to find and produce these products. The United States has gone from being self-sufficient to needing to import nearly half of its petroleum needs.

The nature of American business and its use of minerals has also changed since the peak of domestic mineral consumption during the mid-twentieth century. Large traditional, industrial users of minerals such as iron ore (steel) and base metals have slowed in growth or declined because of growing foreign competition, and new industries have arisen based on new technologies and services. These types of business do not depend as much on the availability of mineral resources. Service industries are usually less mineral-intensive in their business activities. High-tech industries require smaller amounts of specialized minerals that are easily transported and may or may not be available from U.S. sources. This means that the United States is now finding itself in the position of increasingly sourcing its iron ore and some base metals from other countries such as China.

The availability of some mineral resources is still a must for the success of American business. Coal is still the main fuel for electrical power generation, despite concerns about global warming. The United States (along with China) is one of the leading producers of coal in the twenty-first century and has the world's largest reserves. There is no immediate substitute to meet the tremendous demand for electricity. U.S. businesses also depend on the availability of industrial and construction minerals. These types of minerals must be produced locally because of their low-value, high-bulk-per-unit nature. These minerals are absolutely necessary for road work, construction, cement, and industrial purposes. Most of the physical output of minerals and more than half the dollar value (excluding energy minerals) of U.S. mineral production are of these basic materials.

The mineral resources of the United States have played a very important role in the history of American business and continue to do so. It was the abundance of key minerals such as iron ore, coal, copper, and petroleum that allowed the country to undergo rapid industrialization, to become a world economic power, and to achieve high levels of wealth for its citizens. Despite the nation's large consumption of minerals in the past, mineral resources are still adequate to meet many of the needs of business as business activity continues to evolve and grow.

Gary A. Campbell

Further Reading

Auty, R. M., ed. *Resource Abundance and Economic Development.* Rev. ed. New York: Oxford University Press, 2004. A scholarly book about the link between resources and a country's economic development. The chapter "Natural Resources and Economic Development: The 1870-1914 Experience" is of particular interest.

Coyne, Mark S., and Craig W. Allin, eds. *Natural Resources.* Pasadena, Calif.: Salem Press, 1998. This three-volume reference set has numerous entries about natural resources and their use. A particularly useful entry is "United States, resources and resource use in."

Peach, W. N., and James A. Constantin, eds. *Zimmermann's World Resources and Industries.* 3d ed. New York: Harper & Row, 1972. This older reference book is an excellent source of information about the historical use of resources in society and business. Part 3 deals with minerals.

United States Geological Survey. *Minerals Yearbook.* Washington, D.C.: U.S. Government Printing Office, 2005. This three-volume reference periodical is published annually by the U.S. Geological Survey. It discusses the production and consumption of all commercial minerals in the United States and the rest of the world by mineral and location for the year and historically. It is an excellent introduction to the business use of particular minerals in the United States.

Vogely, William A. *Economics of the Mineral Industries.* 3d ed. New York: American Institute of Mining, Metallurgical, and Petroleum Engineers, 1976. This Seeley W. Mudd Series handbook is a good source of information about the historical use of minerals in society.

See also: Black Hills gold rush; California gold rush; Coal industry; Commodity markets; Exploration; Interior, U.S. Department of the; Jewelry industry; Klondike gold rush; Petroleum industry; Steel industry.

Minimum wage laws

Definition: Statutes establishing minimum hourly wages that employers must provide to workers

Significance: One of the first significant government restrictions placed on American industry, the minimum wage permanently altered the dynamic between employer and employee by guaranteeing a basic level of compensation for most workers. After surviving a number of legal challenges, the minimum wage became a permanent and often controversial fixture of the U.S. economy.

The origin of minimum wage laws in the United States can be traced to the Progressive movement of the late nineteenth and early twentieth centuries.

Concern for women and youths working in garment factories and other "sweatshop" environments, where low wages and long hours were common, prompted progressive organizations such as the National Consumers' League to call for legislation requiring employers to pay workers at a minimum hourly rate. These proposals met with vehement opposition from politicians and industrialists, who argued that the free market alone should set wages and who embraced a contemporary political philosophy supporting a strictly limited role for government in regulating economic activity. Despite this opposition, the movement for minimum wage laws in the United States slowly gained momentum, bolstered by the enactment of the first minimum wage laws in Australia in 1896.

In 1912, Massachusetts passed the first minimum wage law in the United States. The law applied only to women and children and provided few sanctions for violators. Fourteen other states followed suit during the 1910's and early 1920's, and in 1918, the U.S. government established a minimum wage for female workers in the District of Columbia. The U.S. Supreme Court ruled these laws unconstitutional in *Atkins v. Children's Hospital* (1923), holding that they violated the due process clause of the Fifth Amendment by interfering with the implied contract that exists between employer and employee.

FEDERAL MINIMUM WAGE LEGISLATION

Despite continued opposition from business and the courts, public interest in minimum wage laws was revived during the Great Depression. President Franklin D. Roosevelt attempted to establish a national minimum wage of 25 cents per hour in 1933 as part of his New Deal program to combat the effects of the Depression, but the Supreme Court, citing *Atkins* as precedent, again declared minimum wage laws unconstitutional in 1935. Several states nevertheless passed minimum wage laws during the early 1930's, with Oklahoma passing the first such statute to cover men as well as women and children. The Supreme Court reversed its opposition to minimum wage laws in 1937, ruling that states can use their police powers to restrict contracts in the interest of public health and safety. Emboldened by the ruling, Roosevelt revived the national minimum wage as part of the Fair Labor Standards Act, which the U.S. Congress passed in June, 1938.

The national minimum wage of 25 cents per hour

established in 1938 was increased periodically by amendments to the Fair Labor Standards Act. The minimum wage reached $1.00 per hour in 1956, and by 1963 it had reached $1.25 per hour. Although these increases were implemented in response to economic growth and inflation, the purchasing power of low-income workers increased as a result. This purchasing power reached its peak in 1968, when the minimum wage was increased to $1.60, an amount equivalent to approximately $9.50 in 2008 dollars.

SLOW GROWTH

The federal minimum wage began to increase more slowly during the 1980's, prompting critics to decry its failure to keep pace with inflation and changes in the American economy that had increased the number of lower-paying service jobs. Increased to $3.85 in 1981, the minimum wage was not raised again until 1990, when Congress approved a gradual increase to $4.25 by mid-1991. Two additional raises during the 1990's set the wage at $5.15 by 1997, where it would remain for the next ten years. In 2006, Congress voted to increase the wage incrementally to $7.25 by 2009, returning the purchasing power of minimum-wage earners to its highest level since the early 1980's.

The slow growth of the federal minimum wage during the late twentieth and early twenty-first centuries prompted many states and localities to pass laws establishing minimum wages that exceeded federal standards. In 2008, the states with the highest minimum wages were Massachusetts and California, at $8.00 per hour, and Washington at $8.07 per hour. The city of San Francisco, California, raised its minimum wage to $9.36 in 2008.

IMPACT

By mandating a basic level of compensation for low-income workers, the enactment of minimum wage laws eliminated one of the most common means of worker exploitation in U.S. industry during the late nineteenth and early twentieth centuries. Minimum wage laws also influenced the wages of all hourly workers by establishing a benchmark for fair compensation in many jobs. The true impact of minimum wage laws on the American economy has been the source of much debate, however. Some economists and political theorists have argued that these laws decreased job opportunities for low-income workers by discouraging employers from hiring low-income employees, as well as placing undue pressure on small businesses and fueling inflation by placing upward pressure on wages and prices. Recent studies have indicated that while the presence of a minimum wage has not significantly reduced the number of jobs available to low-income workers, its effectiveness in reducing the overall poverty rate has been modest. Others have suggested that the slow growth of the federal minimum wage during the late twentieth century effectively rendered it obsolete by the early twenty-first century.

Michael H. Burchett

FURTHER READING

Burkhauser, Richard V., and Joseph J. Sabia. "The Effectiveness of Minimum Wage Increases in Reducing Poverty: Past, Present, and Future." *Contemporary Economic Policy* 25, no. 2 (April, 2007): 262-282. This examination of the effectiveness of minimum wage laws in combating poverty concludes that their effects, while significant, have been limited, primarily as a result of historically low federal minimum wage levels.

Neumark, David, and William Wascher. *Minimum Wages and Employment.* New York: Now, 2007. Analysis of the effects of minimum wage laws upon employment in various economic sectors. Includes comparative analyses of the effects of minimum wage laws in other countries.

Pollin, Robert, et al. *A Measure of Fairness: The Economics of Living Wages and Minimum Wages in the United States.* Ithaca, N.Y.: ILR Press, 2008. Comparative analysis of the impact of federal minimum wage laws and state laws establishing minimum wages higher than the federal minimum wage.

Waltman, Gerold. *The Politics of the Minimum Wage.* Champaign: University of Illinois Press, 2000. This comprehensive history of the minimum wage in the United States focuses upon the legal battles and political maneuvering behind changes in federal and state minimum wage laws.

Whittaker, William G. *The Fair Labor Standards Act.* New York: Novinka Books, 2003. This overview of the Fair Labor Standards Act includes detailed discussion of federal minimum wage law and the ongoing debate over its implementation.

SEE ALSO: Bracero program; Child labor; Congress, U.S.; Labor history; Labor strikes; New Deal programs; Supreme Court and labor law; Wages; Women in business.

Mint, U.S.

IDENTIFICATION: U.S. Treasury branch that produces national coinage

DATE: Established on April 2, 1792

SIGNIFICANCE: Before the establishment of the national mint, the United States had to depend on foreign or individual states' coins. After the U.S. Mint was created, it provided the standardized coinage necessary for the nation to conduct business, including banking and domestic trade. Through the years, the U.S. Mint has also fostered a numismatic industry that has served coin collectors.

In 1777, the U.S. Congress under the Articles of Confederation first recognized the need for a national mint to produce and distribute coinage for circula-

A worker punches out coin blanks at the U.S. Mint in New Orleans in the late 1890's. (Library of Congress)

tion throughout the country. In 1785, the Continental Congress adopted a decimal coinage system, and in 1787, the U.S. Constitution gave Congress the power to coin money and regulate its value. When the Department of the Treasury was created in 1789, Alexander Hamilton became the first secretary of the Treasury. Hamilton submitted his report on a national mint in 1791, and on April 2, 1792, Congress passed the Coinage Act, establishing the first mint, which was to be located in Philadelphia, the nation's capital. The Mint became the first federal building constructed under the Constitution. President George Washington appointed scientist David Rittenhouse as the first director of the Mint. Since the Mint was then within the Department of State, its director reported directly to President Washington and Secretary of State Thomas Jefferson.

The Coinage Act authorized the Mint to produce gold, silver, and copper coins. The first coins struck were silver "half-dimes," but the first circulating coins were 11,178 copper cents delivered in March, 1793. In 1799, the U.S. Mint became an independent agency. Under the Coinage Act of 1873, it became a branch of the Department of the Treasury.

MINT FACILITIES

The Mint's function is to provide enough circulating coinage for the U.S. economy to function. This function is critical to American trade and commerce. During the first years of the twenty-first century, the Mint produced between 11 billion and 20 billion circulating coins annually. Mint facilities in Philadelphia, Denver, San Francisco, and West Point produced the country's domestic, bullion, and foreign coins, disbursed gold and silver for authorized purposes, and distributed coins to the Federal Reserve Banks. Fort Knox, in Kentucky, has stored the country's metal bullion reserves. Relocated from Philadelphia to Washington, D.C., in

1873, the Mint headquarters has managed marketing operations, customer services, policy formulation, and research and development.

Former mint facilities included three that President Andrew Jackson authorized in 1835: New Orleans, Louisiana; Charlotte, North Carolina; and Dahlonega, Georgia. The discovery of gold in the South in the nineteenth century had necessitated additional branches. The Confederate government closed these mints in 1861. However, the New Orleans mint resumed coining operations in 1879, and it functioned as an assay office from 1909 until 1942. The oldest surviving Mint structure, this building was designated a National Historic Landmark in 1975.

The discovery of gold in California and the resulting westward movement led to the opening of mint branches in San Francisco in 1854 and Denver in 1863. Mint or assay facilities opened after the U.S. Civil War but ultimately closed in St. Louis, Missouri; Seattle, Washington; Boise, Idaho; Helena, Montana; Deadwood, South Dakota; Salt Lake City, Utah; and New York. The famous Carson City, Ne-

---

MAJOR U.S. COMMEMORATIVE COINS, 1982-2009

George Washington 250th anniversary half dollar, 1982
1984 Los Angeles Olympics series, 1983-1984
Statue of Liberty series, 1986
Constitution bicentennial series, 1987
Congressional bicentennial series, 1989
Eisenhower centennial dollar, 1990
Mount Rushmore golden anniversary series, 1991
Christopher Columbus quincentennial series, 1992
Bill of Rights bicentennial series, 1993
Civil War battlefield series, 1995
Centennial Olympics series, 1995-1996
Jackie Robinson series, 1997
Franklin D. Roosevelt gold five-dollar coin, 1997
Black Revolutionary War patriots' dollar, 1998
Leif Ericson millennium series, 2000
First flight centennial series, 2003
Lewis and Clark silver dollar, 2004
Chief Justice John Marshall silver dollar, 2005
Little Rock Central High School desegregation silver dollar, 2007
Jamestown 400th anniversary series, 2007
Bald Eagle series, 2008
Abraham Lincoln silver dollars, 2009

vada, mint, which opened in 1870 after the discovery of the Comstock Lode, the country's largest silver strike, discontinued coining production in 1893, was an assay office until 1933, and reopened as a museum in 1941.

COMMERCIAL PRODUCTS AND SPECIAL ISSUES

In 1874, the U.S. Mint was first authorized to produce coins for foreign governments. The first foreign coins it produced were two million 2½ centavo and 10 million 1 centavo denominations, coined between 1875 and 1876 for the government of Venezuela. By the early 1980's, the Mint had struck coins for more than forty foreign governments.

The U.S. Mint has also been authorized to create proof, uncirculated, and commemorative coins and medals for sale to the general public. Annual sets of proof and uncirculated coins have been a staple of the numismatic industry. Proof sets, composed of noncirculating coins with the highest quality strike and sharp details, have been highly prized by coin collectors. In 1999, the Fifty State Quarters program began. Commemorative, noncirculating coins have been authorized by Congress to raise money for organizations and causes helping the community. The first commemorative coin was the 1892 Columbian Exposition half dollar. From 1892 to 1954, the Mint produced 157 silver and gold commemorative coins. For instance, to commemorate peace between the United States, Germany, and Austria, the Peace Dollar was issued from 1921 to 1928 and from 1934 to 1935.

Congress has also authorized commemorative medals to honor people, events, and places. Bronze replicas of congressional gold medals have been made available for sale to the public. Commemorative medals have included those honoring the Dalai Lama, the Tuskegee Airmen, Jesse Owens, Robert F. Kennedy, Simon Wiesenthal, and the American Red Cross.

Alice Myers

FURTHER READING

Evans, George Greenlief. *Illustrated History of the United States Mint with a Complete Description of American Coinage, from the Earliest Period to the Present Time.* 1885. Rev. ed. Rockville Centre, N.Y.: Sanford J. Durst, 2002. Includes biographical essays about mint officers and descriptions of silver and gold coin production. Illustrated. Tables and glossary.

Goe, Rusty. *The Mint on Carson Street.* Reno, Nev.: Southgate Coins and Collectibles, 2004. Chronicle of the famous Nevada mint; includes stories about the Comstock miners, mint personnel, 111 coin issues between 1870 and 1893, special collections, and scandals. Illustrated. Appendixes, bibliography, and index.

Kelly, Richard, and Nancy Oliver. *Mighty Fortress: The Stories Behind the Second San Francisco Mint.* Hayward, Calif.: OK Association, 2004. This complete history covers subjects such as the rare 1870-*S* half-dime, the theft of $30,000 in gold coins in 1901, and the 1906 San Francisco earthquake. Illustrated. Bibliography and index.

Lange, David W., and Mary Jo Mead. *History of the United States Mint and Its Coinage.* Atlanta: Whitman, 2006. A well-researched, comprehensive history; covers the precolonial era to the Fifty State Quarters program. Beautifully illustrated on every page. Bibliography.

Taxay, Don. *The United States Mint and Coinage: An Illustrated History from 1776 to the Present.* Rockville Centre, N.Y.: Sanford J. Durst, 1996. Originally published in 1966, this popular classic is a standard reference. Bibliography.

Turner, Lisa, and Kimberly Field. *Denver Mint: One Hundred Years of Gangsters, Gold, and Ghosts.* Denver, Colo.: Mapletree, 2007. Well-researched, entertaining, and often humorous history that includes interviews and insiders' stories. Illustrated. Bibliography and index.

SEE ALSO: American Bimetallic League national convention; Bank of the United States, First; Bank of the United States, Second; Confederate currency; Counterfeiting; Currency; Fort Knox; Gold standard; Hamilton, Alexander.

Mississippi and Missouri Rivers

IDENTIFICATION: Principal rivers in the largest drainage basin in the United States

SIGNIFICANCE: In addition to draining nearly one-half the continental United States, the Mississippi-Missouri River system was historically the principal transportation artery of the Midwest. It consequently played a major role in facilitating domestic trade and the development of the interior of the United States.

Two steamboats and a raft navigate the Mississippi River in the 1860's. (Library of Congress)

The Mississippi and Missouri Rivers and their many tributaries drain an area of about 1.23 million square miles in the center of the United States. Extending 2,341 miles, the Missouri River is the longest river in the United States. The Mississippi and the Missouri, its principal tributary, together form the fourth-longest river in the world—a system measuring 3,900 miles.

Early in the nineteenth century, the U.S. Army Corps of Engineers began surveying the Mississippi River and its major tributaries, notably the Missouri, Ohio, and Tennessee Rivers. Though the rivers' potential as a major transportation system was great, the many rapids, sandbars, and other hazards— such as naturally occurring log jams—had to be reduced to make the rivers safely navigable.

COMMERCIAL POTENTIAL

The potential value of the Mississippi River system as a transportation route for passengers and cargo was recognized by early European explorers. Until the third decade of the nineteenth century,

however, that potential was severely limited by the difficulty of moving boats upriver. By the early nineteenth century, large amounts of timber and other heavy cargoes were being floated down the river on rafts, which were dismantled and sold at New Orleans, and on keelboats, which relied on humans using poles to work their slow, tortuous way back upriver. The full potential of the rivers for transportation was realized only after the development of practical steam engines made possible steam-powered boats that could carry cargo and passengers upstream. As expanding steamboat traffic carried goods and settlers up the Mississippi and Missouri Rivers and into their many navigable tributaries, economic development followed. A large portion of the first cities built in the Mississippi River basin naturally arose as riverports.

The first steamboat reached Minneapolis and St. Paul in 1823. During the following decades, the development of the increasingly large and powerful high-pressure Mississippi River steamboats made it necessary to deepen the shallowest stretches of the channel from four to six feet by 1910. Later in the twentieth century, the further evolution of tow boat and barge technology required further deepening to nine feet. As the use of the rivers for logging decreased under the pressures of a growing agricultural economy, and with the railroads offering an economically viable, and more flexible, alternative for shipping bulk products, the Army Corps of Engineers found it necessary to consider the cost-benefit ratio of continuing to improve and deepen the channel. Added to the fundamental issues of profitability were the new concerns about the impact of the system of dams and locks necessary to maintain a deeper channel on the marshes, floodplain area, and meanders that keep a river ecosystem healthy.

Traditionally, the Missouri River delivers high discharge from the early spring to the early summer when the snow melts first in the Midwest and then in the Rocky Mountains. With the intense evaporation of the summer, the low-discharge period extends until December, making traveling on these rivers more treacherous. Although Congress had approved the plans to deepen the Mississippi-Missouri Rivers during the 1920's, President Herbert Hoover blocked the funding necessary for construction. It was only in 1933, in the midst of the Great Depression, that work began under President Franklin D. Roosevelt. Seven years later, in 1940, the last of the twenty-nine locks and dams was completed and heavier commercial barges began moving upstream, carrying oil, coal, chemicals, fertilizers, and raw materials for the industrial centers of the Midwest, and returning laden with enormous quantities of corn, wheat, and soybeans produced by midwestern farmers. As a further benefit of the project, the lakes formed behind these locks offered new opportunities for recreational fishing and boating.

FLOOD CONTROL

The Mississippi River system has been plagued with major floods—most notably in 1912, 1913, 1927, 1973, 1993, and 2005. The flood of 1927 was especially severe; more than 200 people lost their lives, and more than 600,000 others had to be evacuated. Moreover, crops were destroyed, and virtually all economic activity was paralyzed for weeks until floodwater receded. As a result of the calamity, Congress passed the Flood Control Act of 1928, which funded a new round of ambitious projects aimed at managing floodwaters through improvement and

stabilization of the channel, and the construction of new levees and floodways. The most immediately apparent of these projects were the levees, which raised the banks of the rivers above expected flood levels. More than 2,200 miles of levees and floodwalls were built along the Mississippi and tributaries. For almost fifty years, these monumental efforts appeared to control the river.

Despite all these flood-control efforts, the Mississippi River reached its highest level in more than 150 years in the spring of 1973. The stage for the 1973 flood was set during the late fall and winter of 1972, when heavy rainfall all along the river and its tributaries was followed by equally heavy snowfall in the north and west. The month of February, 1973, was unusually warm, and the consequent snowmelt collected in a drainage basin that was already saturated. On March 13, following a warm spell that rapidly melted the snow in the northern part of the drainage basin, flooding conditions were reported on the Missouri River. The flooding was worsened by heavy precipitation, in which some areas of the drainage basin received more than fourteen inches of rainfall in forty-eight hours.

Because the Mississippi River floods annually, the Army Corps of Engineers had previously built a series of structures that would allow the diversion of excess water to the Atchafalaya River, a shorter route to the Gulf of Mexico. Unfortunately, the flood control system was overwhelmed by the magnitude of the event, which was the worst flood in the region since 1927. In the lower Mississippi River valley, 17 million acres were inundated, as well as 600,000 acres in the delta. The flood, which did not completely recede until June, caused more than $180 million in property damage and took a terrible toll on the wildlife living in the delta. More than thirty people died, and thirty-five thousand people were left homeless.

The combination of unusual events that led to the 1973 flood was repeated in 1993. Intense late spring precipitation, twelve inches above normal, fell in the eastern Dakotas, southern Minnesota, Kansas, Wisconsin, Iowa, southern Nebraska, and Missouri. The resulting flood on the Mississippi River and 150 major rivers and tributaries that flow into it caused forty-five casualties and almost $15 billion in property damage. In this event, the water control system was more than overwhelmed; hundreds of levees broke along the Missouri and Mississippi Rivers, severely disrupting both land transportation, by the flooding of highways and destruction of bridges, and barge traffic, for which hazardous waterways made movement impossible for more than seven weeks.

On August 29, 2005, levees and flood walls suddenly failed in New Orleans under the pressure of the storm surge of Hurricane Katrina. This was the worst engineering disaster in United States history. It caused the death of 1,464 people and the collapse of the region's economic activities.

No river system has had a greater role in the expansion and development of the United States than the Mississippi-Missouri system. With its tributaries, it forms a network of navigable waterways 12,350 miles in length that was the primary route by which the regional economy developed in the nineteenth century. Even in the twenty-first century, this river system remains immensely important, as vessels carry more than 300 million tons of goods on its waters every year.

Denyse Lemaire and David Kasserman

FURTHER READING

Ambrose, Stephen E., Sam Abel, and Douglas Brinkley. *The Mississippi and the Making of a Nation: From the Louisiana Purchase to Today.* Washington, D.C.: National Geographic, 2002. The book gives a detailed history of the development of the Mississippi River basin.

Barry, John M. *The Great Mississippi Flood of 1927 and How It Changed America.* New York: Simon & Schuster, 1998. This book traces one of the country's worst natural disasters.

Brinkley, Douglas. *The Great Deluge: Hurricane Katrina, New Orleans, and the Mississippi Gulf Coast.* New York: HarperCollins, 2007. Thorough study of the economic impact of Hurricane Katrina on New Orleans and the lower Mississippi region.

O'Neill, Karen M. *Rivers by Design: State Power and the Origins of U.S. Flood Control.* Durham, N.C.: Duke University Press, 2006. An examination of river development that looks at both the Mississippi and the Sacramento Rivers. Focuses on the early development of the Mississippi as a waterway.

Twain, Mark. *Life on the Mississippi.* 1883. Facsimile reprint. New York: Oxford University Press, 1996. Classic work on the golden age of steamboating in which Twain recounts his years as a steamboat pilot on the Lower Mississippi during the late 1850's and describes the immense changes that

had taken place when he returned to the river in 1882. Includes chapters on the earlier history of the river and devotes considerable space to the river's economic impact on the United States.

SEE ALSO: Canals; Colorado River water; Dams and aqueducts; Erie Canal; Exploration; Hurricane Katrina; Lewis and Clark expedition; Louisiana Purchase; Pike's western explorations; Steamboats; Transportation, U.S. Department of; Water resources.

Monetary policy, federal

DEFINITION: Regulation of interest rates and the money supply by the Federal Reserve Bank to influence the economy

SIGNIFICANCE: Federal monetary policy exerts a powerful influence on aggregate demand for goods and services and thus on output, prices, interest rates, and foreign-exchange rates.

Before 1914, federal monetary policy involved the monetary standard, banks, and paper currency. The Coinage Acts of 1792 and 1834 provided for gold, silver, and copper coins. Congress chartered the First Bank of the United States (1791-1811) and Second Bank of the United States (1816-1841), which provided high-quality banknotes and performed some rudimentary central banking functions, but antagonism from President Andrew Jackson put an end to these experiments.

In 1862, during the U.S. Civil War, Congress authorized issue of legal-tender United States notes called greenbacks. They were paid out to employees and suppliers. Their value was not fixed in terms of precious metals, and they depreciated substantially as prices escalated. Efforts to withdraw them after the war were blocked in an effort to keep prices from falling—but they fell anyway. The National Banking Acts of 1863 and 1864 created a safe and uniform national banknote currency.

Both types of currency became convertible at par into precious metals, beginning in 1879. Deflation generated strong political pressure for monetary expansion through "free coinage of silver," advocated by Democratic presidential candidate William Jennings Bryan in 1896. After his defeat, the Gold Standard Act of 1900 linked the dollar to gold alone.

THE FEDERAL RESERVE SYSTEM

The Federal Reserve Act of 1913 was intended to eliminate bank panics, which had plagued the economy for a century. It authorized the Federal Reserve banks to issue Federal Reserve notes, expected to provide an "elastic currency." In a panic, the Federal Reserve (the Fed) could lend newly created Federal Reserve notes to distressed banks. The notes were convertible into gold at the par value of $20.67 an ounce. The Federal Reserve was also authorized to buy and sell U.S. government securities through "open-market operations." Only gradually did people discover that the Federal Reserve had the power to create bank reserves when it made loans or purchased securities.

When the United States entered World War I in 1917, the Department of the Treasury had to issue bonds to finance the big rise in expenditures. The Federal Reserve helped by buying Treasury securities and by lending newly created reserves to the banks so that they could buy more Treasury securities. Between 1914 and 1920, both the money supply and the price level approximately doubled. When new bond issues ceased in November, 1919, the Federal Reserve tightened policy to put an end to the inflation, raising its interest charge on loans to banks. Beginning in May, 1920, a sharp recession set in. The Federal Reserve began lowering its interest rate in May, 1921, and recovery was achieved by 1922.

During the rest of the decade, Federal Reserve authorities undertook to counter business cycle fluctuations. They maintained some degree of credit restraint during the stock market boom of the late 1920's but felt obligated to meet the expanding demand for credit by banks.

THE GREAT DEPRESSION

Beginning in 1929, expenditures for national output declined precipitously, falling by about half by 1933, when the downswing ended. During the Great Depression (1929-1939), the money supply declined from $27 billion in 1929 to $20 billion in 1933. The Federal Reserve did not cause this, but it could have prevented it. The economy was swept by an epidemic of bank failures beginning in 1930. Had the Federal Reserve been willing to buy securities more aggressively, it could have alleviated this deflationary process. However, it was constrained by fear that international gold withdrawals would endanger the par convertibility of the dollar.

When Franklin D. Roosevelt was inaugurated president in March, 1933, he suspended the convertibility of the dollar into gold. A national "bank holiday" restored confidence in the surviving banks. When the price of gold was raised in 1934 to $35 an ounce, gold began to flow into the United States from other countries, leading to a rapid increase in bank reserves and the money supply and gradual economic recovery.

When the United States entered World War II in December, 1941, unemployment stood at 10 percent. The expansion of government expenditures stimulated increased production without serious inflationary pressure. To maintain the extremely low interest rates from the Depression era, the Federal Reserve pegged the prices of Treasury securities by standing ready to buy them if their prices fell. Fed-

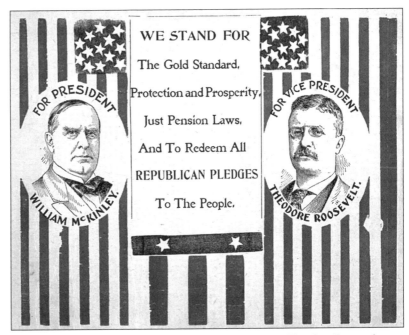

This 1900 campaign poster for William McKinley and Theodore Roosevelt mentions their support for the gold standard. (Library of Congress)

eral Reserve security holdings increased from $2 billion in 1940 to $24 billion in 1945; these purchases greatly expanded bank reserves, bank lending, and the money supply. Price controls helped limit wartime inflation to about 30 percent, but when controls were lifted in 1946, prices leaped further. Most important, however, was that there was no postwar deflationary disaster.

A new bout of inflation accompanied the outbreak of the Korean War in the summer of 1950. Tax increases and restoration of price controls helped end the price run-up in mid-1951. The Federal Reserve then reached an accord with the Treasury, which gave it greater leeway to permit interest rates to increase, as it did.

After 1966, increasing U.S. involvement in the Vietnam War brought a renewed acceleration of monetary growth and inflation. Conditions worsened when international petroleum prices escalated in 1973. Federal Reserve authorities felt obligated to expand money and credit to try to alleviate the resulting unemployment. However, this aggravated inflation, which reached double digits in 1974 and again in 1979-1981. Fed officials misinterpreted high interest rates to indicate a restrictive policy, when the high rates actually reflected expectations of high inflation. The episode convinced many economists that the money supply was the underlying source of inflation, with Fed open-market operations the key instrument of control.

The appointment of Paul Volcker to the Federal Reserve chair in 1979 and Ronald Reagan's victory in the presidential election of 1980 brought a reversal of Federal Reserve policy. The monetary growth rate was slowed, causing a painful but brief recession beginning in January, 1980. Both inflation and interest rates soon declined. In 1987, Alan Greenspan became chair of the Federal Reserve. Skillful open-market operations targeting the federal-funds interest rate enabled the economy to avoid either serious inflation or serious depression for the next twenty years.

THE 2008 FINANCIAL CRISIS

The financial crisis of 2008 led the Federal Reserve outside its customary role. Normally the Federal Reserve would try to combat a business recession by lowering its target interest rates and aggressively buying securities in the open market. In 2008, it tried to address the breakdown of tightly integrated financial markets. These markets were accustomed to short-term lending arrangements that could be concluded in a matter of minutes with minimal transactions costs.

Because the Federal Reserve has the power to create money, it could provide emergency funding in large amounts on short notice. In March, 2008, it played a major role in the merger of Bear Stearns into JPMorgan Chase. This was a preemptive move to prevent default on Bear's large outstanding short-term debt. In September, 2008, the government allowed Lehman Brothers, another huge investment bank, to fall into bankruptcy. This demonstrated the kind of chain reaction the authorities wanted to avoid. Lehman's huge amount of short-term debt went into default, spreading the crisis to other firms that held those debts, notably money-market mutual funds.

The experience clearly led top officials to avoid a repetition. A few days later the Federal Reserve Bank of New York loaned $85 billion to AIG (American International Group) to keep it operating.

As private short-term lending froze up in fear of borrower defaults, the Federal Reserve developed a number of innovative lending options. Traditionally, its direct lending had been confined to commercial banks. However, in March, 2008, the Federal Reserve created a primary dealer credit facility, to accommodate investment banking firms. By mid-October, this facility had over $100 billion in loans outstanding. Its lending to banks also reached very high levels, so that its total direct lending exceeded $400 billion in October. To offset inflationary effects, the Federal Reserve reduced its holdings of U.S. government securities (which traditionally made up more than 90 percent of its assets). The Federal Reserve also created a commercial paper funding facility to make loans for this very extensive form of short-term credit. At the same time, it entered into agreements with other major central banks to provide them with dollar exchange.

By mid-November, 2008, Federal Reserve assets were more than double their level of the previous September. Over the same period, commercial-bank reserves ballooned from $47 billion in September to an unheard-of $653 billion in mid-November. In late November, 2008, the Federal Reserve committed itself to buying up to $600 billion of debt issued by or backed by Fannie Mae, Freddie Mac, and other mortgage agencies. They also committed to lending up to $200 billion to investors holding securities based on student loans, car loans, credit card debt, and small-business loans.

In October, 2008, the Fed began to pay interest on bank reserve deposits held by Federal Reserve banks. This created a new instrument for monetary policy. By lowering this interest rate, the Fed effectively encouraged banks to hold smaller reserves and expand their lending.

Paul B. Trescott

FURTHER READING

Hester, Donald D. *The Evolution of Monetary Policy and Banking in the U.S.* Berlin: Springer, 2008. Traces the history of U.S. monetary policy as it affected banking.

Hetzel, Robert L. *The Monetary Policy of the Federal Reserve: A History.* New York: Cambridge University Press, 2008. Examines the agency's monetary policy from its inception through Greenspan's chairmanship.

Meltzer, Allan H. *A History of the Federal Reserve.* Chicago: University of Chicago Press, 2003. A leading monetary economist presents the definitive account of the history of monetary policy.

Mishkin, Frederic S. *The Economics of Money, Banking, and Financial Markets.* 7th ed. New York: Pearson/Addison-Wesley, 2004. Chapters 14-18 deal at length with monetary policy of the 1970's and later.

Trescott, Paul B. *Money, Banking, and Economic Welfare.* New York: McGraw-Hill, 1960. Chapters 14-17 give a thorough exposition of the evolution of U.S. monetary policy to 1958.

SEE ALSO: Bank of the United States, First; Bank of the United States, Second; Banking; Currency; Federal Reserve; Financial crisis of 2008; Gold standard; Great Depression; Greenspan, Alan; Inflation; Interest rates.

Montgomery Ward

IDENTIFICATION: Retail department store
DATE: Founded in 1872
SIGNIFICANCE: Montgomery Ward pioneered mail-order retailing during the 1870's and established a company that later became one of the largest department store chains in the United States.

As a young dry-goods salesman in the Midwest, Montgomery Ward experienced firsthand the economic difficulties of rural and small-town Americans, who often endured high prices and limited choices when purchasing consumer goods. Ward conceived a business model in which goods would be purchased from manufacturers in large quantities to reduce per-unit costs and sold by mail, taking advantage of proliferating railroad lines to deliver orders to rural areas. With the assistance of partner George R. Thorne, Ward established Montgomery Ward and Company in Chicago in 1872, publishing a single-page price list of hardware items that served as the first catalog.

The business grew rapidly during its first few years of operation, as its volume of orders grew exponentially, aided by the relatively low prices Ward charged for his merchandise and his money-back guarantee to customers dissatisfied with their purchases. Rural residents no longer had to rely on local merchants and traveling jobbers for goods; instead, they enjoyed access to a wider variety of items as the company's catalog grew from year to year, reaching 150 pages by 1876. Despite the emergence of competitors such as Sears, Roebuck and Company by the 1880's, Montgomery Ward continued to grow into the twentieth century, attaining gross annual sales of $1 million by 1891 and $40 million by 1913.

Throughout the early twentieth century, Montgomery Ward continued to challenge its chief competitor, Sears, Roebuck, for dominance of the mail-order market. Its catalog, which became known as the "wish book" (a name later adopted by Sears) weighed over four pounds by the early 1990's and was mailed to millions of customers across the United States. Known simply as "Wards," the company and its catalog exerted a significant influence on American culture during the early twentieth century. In 1939, Wards employee Robert L. May created the popular song "Rudolph, the Red-Nosed Reindeer" as part of a Christmas promotional campaign.

Montgomery Ward joined Sears and other competitors in entering department store retailing during the early twentieth century, opening its first department store in Plymouth, Indiana, in 1926. The company lagged behind its competitors, however, in moving its stores from downtown to suburban locations during the post-World War II era, and by the

1960's it had lost a significant share of both the department-store and mail-order markets. Company profits continued to decline during the late twentieth century, as discount and Internet-based retailers began to replace traditional department stores in the retail sector. The company filed for bankruptcy in 1997 and by 2001 was defunct, reemerging in 2004 as an online retailer.

Michael H. Burchett

FURTHER READING

Holland, Thomas W. *More Boy's Toys of the Fifties and Sixties: Toy Pages from the Great Montgomery Ward Christmas Catalogs, 1950-1969.* Waterloo, Ont.: Windmill Press, 1998.

Kaufman, Leslie. "Montgomery Ward Closes Its Doors." *The New York Times,* Dec. 29, 2000, p. C1.

Sobel, Robert. *When Giants Stumble.* Paramus, N.J.: Prentice Hall, 1999.

SEE ALSO: Advertising industry; Catalog shopping; Christmas marketing; International Brotherhood of Teamsters; Retail trade industry; Sears, Roebuck and Company; Warehouse and discount stores.

Morgan, J. P.

IDENTIFICATION: American financier and banker
BORN: April 17, 1837; Hartford, Connecticut
DIED: March 31, 1913; Rome, Italy
SIGNIFICANCE: Morgan exercised tremendous economic power through J. P. Morgan and Company, the nation's most prosperous private banking house; a railroad empire built by reorganizing bankrupt lines and gaining a controlling interest in many of the nation's major lines; and the United States Steel Corporation, then the world's largest business. His consolidation and domination of industries aroused vehement criticism.

J. P. (John Pierpont) Morgan played a crucial role in the financial development of the United States. The son of prominent international banker Junius Spencer Morgan, he studied at English High School in Boston and the University of Gottingen in Germany and joined Duncan, Sherman and Company as an accountant in 1857. Three years later, Morgan joined his father's London-based financial firm, George Peabody and Company, as American agent

and attorney. In 1871, he established a private banking company with Anthony Drexel and emerged as the leading dealer in federal securities. On Drexler's death in 1895, the firm became J. P. Morgan and Company, the nation's most prosperous private banking firm and one of the world's most powerful banking institutions.

Morgan acquired, consolidated, and restructured many of the nation's major railroad lines, applying his own regulations and standards in an unregulated industry. Inefficient management, inflated security structures, and unrestrained competition financially jeopardized many railroad corporations. Morgan demonstrated exceptional organizational skills, eliminating inefficiency, costly competition, and instability. Morgan controlled the Albany and Susquehanna, New York Central, New Haven and Hartford, Lehigh Valley, Pennsylvania, Reading, Southern, Erie, Chesapeake and Ohio, and Northern Pacific Railroads. On 1901, Morgan, James Jerome Hill, and Edward H. Harriman created the Northern Securities Company, a holding company that controlled major railroads in the Midwest and Northwest.

Morgan created business monopolies by reorganizing and consolidating numerous industrial corporations. Because his railroads required large quantities of steel, he founded and acquired large steelmaking operations. In 1901, Morgan formed the United States Steel Corporation (U.S. Steel) by merging Carnegie Steel Works with his other steel companies. U.S. Steel became the world's largest and first billion-dollar corporation. Morgan controlled virtually all the basic American industries, including shipping, communication, insurance, and coal, and he sat on many boards. Between 1892 and 1904, he helped form General Electric, American Telephone and Telegraph, Western Union Telegraph Company, and International Harvester.

Morgan also provided financial backing for the U.S. government. In 1877, he, August Belmont, and the Rothschilds floated $260 million in U.S. government bonds. When the government experienced a gold shortage in 1895, Morgan's firm replenished the Federal Reserve with $62 million. Detractors criticized him for the harsh terms of the loan. Morgan's company helped the U.S. Treasury thwart a stock market panic in 1907. New York financiers were forced to obey his directives for stabilizing the stock market.

J. P. Morgan. (Library of Congress)

Morgan, acting as the main force behind his trusts, came to symbolize concentrated economic power. His wealth, power, and influence attracted much federal government scrutiny. In 1911, the government filed suit against the U.S. Steel Company. The Pujo Committee of the U.S. House of Representatives investigated his monopoly finances. Morgan adamantly denied charges of undue influence in his control of the nation's industries and financial institutions, but the Pujo Committee found that eleven House of Morgan partners held seventy-two directorships in forty-seven major corporations. Although reformers criticized his corporate domination, Morgan remained largely unscathed and America's foremost financier. He amassed $80 million, but his power rested in the billions he controlled.

Morgan donated extensively to schools, hospitals, libraries, churches, and museums. The Metro-politan Museum of Art in New York City houses his vast art collection, and the Morgan Library in New York City contains his massive accumulation of rare books.

David L. Porter

FURTHER READING

Carosso, Vincent P. *The Morgans: Private International Bankers, 1854-1913.* Cambridge, Mass.: Harvard University Press, 1987.

Chernow, Ron. *The House of Morgan: An American Banking Dynasty and the Rise of Modern Finance.* New York: Grove/Atlantic, 2001.

Strouse, Jean. *Morgan: American Financier.* New York: Random House, 1999.

SEE ALSO: Banking; Carnegie, Andrew; Gilded Age; Northern Securities Company; Panic of 1893; Panic of 1907; Railroads; Robber barons; Steel industry; United States Steel Corporation.

Morris Plan banks

IDENTIFICATION: Banking business founded on the principle of providing small loans to consumers possessing little or no credit

DATE: Founded on March 23, 1910

SIGNIFICANCE: Morris Plan banks allowed Americans of limited economic means to build credit. The demand for more consumer credit resulted in more than one hundred Morris Plan banks opening during the 1910's and 1920's, providing enormous economic opportunities to an untapped consumer group. The Morris Plan banks encouraged financial responsibility for their borrowers and introduced a new approach to lending that proved successful through the Great Depression.

In 1910, Arthur J. Morris, a Virginia lawyer, founded the first Morris Plan bank, the Fidelity Savings and Trust Company, in Norfolk. Morris understood the need to expand credit to Americans unable to secure banks loans because of their limited economic means. He believed that a combination of character and earning power should determine a person's credit. Morris declared that through small loans that could be repaid over lengthy periods, borrowers could establish credit, practice thrift, make useful investments, and eventually achieve financial independence. At the time, many borrowers unable to secure loans from banks relied on loan sharks and other unscrupulous sources of credit. Morris demonstrated the Progressive Era desire to improve the lives of the less fortunate, while opening up a huge market for his business plan.

Morris developed his model on cooperative industrial banks in Europe and his knowledge of various banking laws in the United States. Potential borrowers could qualify for small loans (customers in 1936 averaged a loan of $250) by securing two cosigners willing to guarantee the payment or by offering acceptable collateral. To avoid state usury laws, the qualified borrower purchased an installment investment certificate from the bank instead of making an actual loan. For a certificate worth $100, the plan carried an approximate interest rate of 8 percent (about double the standard rate of the time). Parties agreed on the length and amount of installment payments, depending on the financial status of the borrower.

By the end of the 1920's, Morris Plan banks were operating in more than thirty states, with the most locations in Massachusetts. This expansion reflected the great economic success of the banks. During the Depression, the number of Morris Plan banks stabilized at just over one hundred locations in 120 cities across thirty-two states. By the end of the Great Depression, new installment credit programs, credit cards, and competition from other financial institutions banks challenged the Morris Plan banks to remain relevant. During the postwar years, Morris Plan banks focused on consumer loans and abandoned the economic model established by Morris.

Aaron D. Purcell

FURTHER READING

Allen, Larry. *The Global Financial System, 1750-2000*. London: Reaktion Books, 2001.

Chapman, Charles C. *The Development of American Business and Banking Thought, 1913-1936*. New York: Longmans, Green, 1936.

Herzog, Peter W. *The Morris Plan of Industrial Banking*. Chicago: A. W. Shaw Company, 1928.

SEE ALSO: Bank failures; Banking; Postal savings banks; Supreme Court and banking law.

Mortgage industry

DEFINITION: Enterprises that negotiate, broker, issue, underwrite, bundle, and exchange loans secured with real estate

SIGNIFICANCE: Mortgage loans have long been a major form of credit for households and business firms, and they provide major assets for banks and other financial firms.

From colonial times, the pursuit of income and profit led many people to borrow extensively to buy and develop land. Several colonial governments created land banks, lending on mortgage security by issuing paper currency.

During the nineteenth century, the majority of Americans lived on farms. Farmers relied on mortgages to finance the acquisition and improvement of land, construction of buildings (including the family home), and other expenses. Mortgage credit was also important for business firms. As railroad building expanded after the 1830's, many of the railroad bond issues involved mortgage claims on the land involved in the right-of-way.

As commercial banking developed, there were misgivings about mortgage lending by banks. Mortgage loans were not very liquid and were quite risky. When the national banking system was created in 1863, the national banks were forbidden to make mortgage loans. By that time, however, there were other financial institutions for which mortgage lending was appropriate, notably savings banks and insurance companies. Bankers in rapidly developing areas would initiate mortgage loans, sell them to Eastern investors, and continue to service the loans for a commission. Nonnational banks had much more freedom to initiate mortgages, and by 1909, one-fourth of their assets were mortgage loans. However, as late as 1910, three-fourths of farm mortgages were held by individual investors.

In 1900, total mortgage debt was around $6.7 billion, of which one-fourth was farm debt. Despite urbanization, farm mortgages increased to $11 billion in 1922, 40 percent of the total mortgage debt, reflecting boom times for farmers. The Federal Farm Loan Act of 1916 authorized the creation of federal land banks, which became large farm-mortgage lenders. By 1927, they held $1 billion of farm mortgages. In that year, over $2 billion was held by life insurance companies and over $1 billion by commercial and savings banks. Joint-stock land banks, also created by the 1916 legislation, held $600 million.

Urbanization brought rapid growth in nonfarm residential mortgages. By 1900, these totaled about $2.9 billion, of which half was held by financial institutions. Mutual savings banks were the largest lenders ($632 million), followed by savings and loan associations (which had developed primarily to provide home-mortgage loans—$371 million).

The proportion of nonfarm residents who were homeowners rose steadily in the prosperous early twentieth century, from one-third around 1900 to nearly half by 1930. By then nonfarm residential mortgages exceeded $30 billion, two-thirds held by financial institutions. Savings and loan associations were the largest lenders, accounting for over $6 billion.

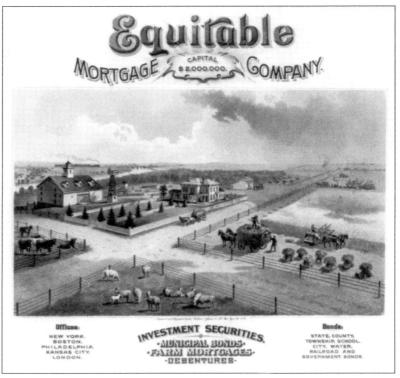

An 1888 advertisement for the Equitable Mortgage Company. (Library of Congress)

THE GREAT DEPRESSION

Plummeting incomes and prices following 1929 increased the burden of debts of all kinds. During the Great Depression, in some cities, half of all residential mortgages were in default, dragging down banks and other lenders. New loans for home building virtually ceased.

The federal government created a multitude of new agencies and programs designed to ease debt burdens and promote new home building. The Reconstruction Finance Corporation (created in 1932) lent $100 million to savings and loan institutions and lesser sums to federal land banks, joint-stock land banks, and mortgage loan companies. A system of Federal Home Loan banks was created in 1932; by mid-1933, they had lent $22 million to mortgage-finance institutions.

Under President Franklin D. Roosevelt, mortgage programs multiplied. The Federal Farm Mortgage Corporation (created in 1933) issued bonds and made loans to the federal land banks. The Home Owners Loan Corporation (HOLC, created in 1933) bought many defaulted mortgages from lenders and restructured most of them. By the time it closed in 1936, the HOLC had made about one million loans totaling $3 billion and refinanced about one-fifth of all mortgaged dwellings. By the end of 1935, the federal government had plowed nearly $6 billion into mortgage markets, about equally divided between farm and nonfarm. The Federal Housing Administration (FHA), created in 1934, was authorized to insure long-term amortized home mortgages. This insurance primarily protected mortgage lenders against loss from borrower default. By 1941, FHA insurance covered about $3 billion of the $18 billion of nonfarm home-mortgage debt. Nonfarm home mortgages had reached $30 billion in 1930; they declined to $23 billion during the mid-1930's and returned to $30 billion only in 1946. By then, a new mortgage guarantee program had been created for military veterans.

Expansion of home ownership and mortgage lending were important parts of the economic growth and prosperity that followed World War II.

High income-tax rates provided a subsidy for home ownership, as interest paid on mortgage debt was a deductible expense. The proportion of homes that were occupied by their owners rose from 53 percent in 1945 to 63 percent in 1970. Over the same period, nonfarm residential mortgage debt rose from $25 billion to $338 billion. Of this total, $280 billion covered one-family to four-family structures, of which $60 billion was FHA-insured and $37 billion was insured by the Veterans Administration. Almost 90 percent of nonfarm residential mortgages were held by financial institutions, of which savings and loans were the largest, with $139 billion.

A relatively new institutional player was Fannie Mae (Federal National Mortgage Association, FNMA), which had been created in 1938 to provide a secondary market for home mortgages but did not purchase on a large scale until the 1960's. It became a shareholder-owned corporation in 1968. At that time, Ginnie Mae (Government National Mortgage Association, GNMA) was spun off from Fannie Mae to provide a secondary market for government-guaranteed mortgages. In 1970, the Home Loan Bank Board created Freddie Mac (Federal Home Loan Mortgage Corporation, FHLMC). All three of these sold their own bonds and used the proceeds to buy mortgages.

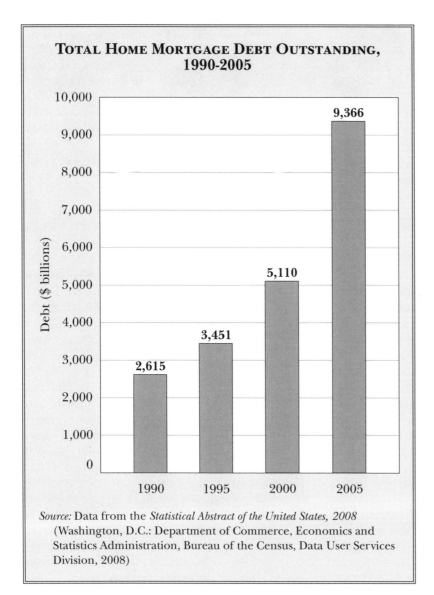

TOTAL HOME MORTGAGE DEBT OUTSTANDING, 1990-2005

Source: Data from the *Statistical Abstract of the United States, 2008* (Washington, D.C.: Department of Commerce, Economics and Statistics Administration, Bureau of the Census, Data User Services Division, 2008)

TURBULENT TIMES

Rising interest rates following 1965 brought on deregulation of deposit institutions and the savings and loan crisis. Longstanding institutional differentiation of mortgage lenders largely disappeared. A new crisis emerged in the twenty-first century, focused even more sharply on home mortgages. A rapid rise in house prices encouraged both home buyers and mortgage lenders into speculative activities. Subprime loans (loans made at above-prime rates to borrowers who do not qualify for prime-rate loans) were made without much attention to the buyer's ability to repay, on the assumption that increases in the value of the house would enable the buyer to refinance at a lower interest rate. A huge number of mortgages were used as the basis for collateralized debt obligations (CDOs), issued in large amounts by Fannie Mae, Freddie Mac, Lehman Brothers, and other private firms. These were layers of bonds differing in priority and risk. The highest priority bonds were regarded as risk-free and were eagerly purchased by conservative investors at home and abroad, at very low interest rates. Often these came with guarantees against default from the issuing agency or from firms specializing in creating credit-default swaps. A second layer of bonds received payment only after the first layer was paid in full. These had higher risks and required high interest rates. A final layer represented an equity interest with lowest priority and highest risk. These appealed to speculative buyers such as buyers of hedge funds.

As mortgage default rates began to rise in 2007, financial firms with substantial mortgage operations rapidly showed signs of trouble. They were holding long-term assets (mortgages or CDOs) financed by short-term loans whose lenders were reluctant to renew. Fannie Mae, Freddie Mac, and other mortgage operators had very small capital accounts; thus, the value of their assets barely exceeded their liabilities. When mortgage defaults began to reduce asset values, these operators soon showed indications of insolvency. This was accentuated by marking-to-market accounting rules requiring that reported assets be reported at their (supposed) current market value.

Mortgage involvements brought about bank failures involving IndyMac, Washington Mutual, and Wachovia. Lehman Brothers, a large issuer of CDOs, went bankrupt. Its closing precipitated its creditors falling into financial distress. Fannie Mae and Freddie Mac were taken over by the government. Under the supervision of the Federal Housing Finance Agency, they became the chief source of continued credit to the home-mortgage sector.

The mortgage crisis was especially acute in California. Although U.S. home prices declined about 10 percent over the year ending October, 2008, prices in California fell by one-third. About one-third of all the mortgages in an average mortgage-backed security were written on California properties. California mortgages were a major reason for the failures of Countrywide, IndyMac, and Washington Mutual. Housing and housing finance were in a severe slump by late 2008. In the second quarter of 2008, more than 9 percent of home mortgages were in default, compared with 6.5 percent a year previous. Sales of foreclosed properties made up 45 percent of existing-home sales in October.

Paul B. Trescott

FURTHER READING

Bogue, Allan G. *Money at Interest: The Farm Mortgage on the Middle Border.* Ithaca, N.Y.: Cornell University Press, 1955. Case studies humanize the interactions among lending institutions, agents, and farm borrowers in the nineteenth century.

Chandler, Lester V. *America's Greatest Depression, 1929-1941.* New York: Harper & Row, 1970. Devotes much attention to the debt crisis and the extensive federal programs that attempted to deal with it.

"Credit and Housing Markets." *Economic Report of the President, 2008.* Washington, D.C.: Government Printing Office, 2008. Simple but comprehensive review of the subprime mortgage mess and its macroeconomic effects.

Markham, Jerry W. *A Financial History of the United States.* Vol. 3. Armonk, N.Y.: M. E. Sharpe, 2002. Chapter 2 reviews the savings and loan crisis; Chapter 5 gives an excellent overview of the complexities arising for mortgage markets from the 1970's on.

Quigley, John M. "Federal Credit and Insurance Programs: Housing." *Review,* July/August, 2006, pp. 281-321. Recommends limiting the activity of the FHA and government-sponsored enterprises to first-time home buyers.

SEE ALSO: Banking; Construction industry; Deregulation of financial institutions; Farm Credit Administration; Housing and Urban Development, U.S. Department of; Interest rates; Real estate industry, commercial; Real estate industry, residential; Savings and loan associations.

Motel industry. *See* Hotel and motel industry

Motion-picture industry

DEFINITION: Enterprises that plan, finance, produce, distribute, and exhibit motion pictures

SIGNIFICANCE: The motion-picture industry, part of the greater entertainment industry, employs vast numbers of people in the creation and distribution of its products. The industry has spawned many other businesses and services, some related to the production of films and others related to their marketing and sales.

Nickelodeons (storefront movie theaters) were a popular entertainment for the working classes beginning in 1906. With increased urbanization due to the increase in factories in the cities, attendance grew steadily to the point where large movie theaters were built in place of the nickelodeons. Early studios, such as the New York Motion Picture Company, Mack Sennett's Keystone Studios, and American Mutoscope and Biograph, eventually made way for the five major studios of the first half of the century, Metro-Goldwyn-Mayer (MGM; begun as Loew's in 1910), Paramount (1916), Warner Bros. (1923), FOX (1915), and RKO (1928).

The American film industry was able to become the leader in releasing and distributing films during the early 1920's thanks in part to World War I and the fact that the United States did not suffer the extensive physical damage and disruption that Europe did. Soon, the major studios were building their own large theaters in which to show their films.

THE STUDIO ERA

By the 1920's, there were eight significant studios in the American motion-picture industry. In addition to the five major studios, three smaller studios (Universal, Columbia, and United Artists) were also producing and distributing films. Because of various scandals and fears of increased government regulation, a regulatory group was formed, the Motion Picture Producers and Distributors of America (MPPDA). The group, which later evolved into the Motion Picture Association of America (MPAA), hired former postmaster Will Hays to create a code of conduct for films. The Hays Code was released in 1930 but not really put into effect until 1934. The code remained in effect until 1966 and was replaced by the MPAA ratings system in 1968.

The theaters that the studios owned beginning during the 1920's played a major role in their success. In addition to each studio running only its own films in its own theaters, the studios had a practice of "block booking" with independently owned theaters; this practice required theaters to book all of a studio's current film titles on offer in order to exhibit any of them. So, if a theater wanted the latest hit film from Paramount, it had to also book the studio's three B-pictures as well. Block booking ensured that even the smaller pictures would make money for their studios. The practice had an added benefit: If a theater was fully booked with the films

of one studio, it was impossible for it to book films from other studios.

In 1928, when Warner Bros. introduced modern sound films with the release of the *Jazz Singer,* the other studios realized they too would need to convert to sound. However, equipping both their film equipment and movie theaters to accommodate sound films was a major expense, and the film studios took on a lot of debt. Going to the movies had become an important part of most Americans' lives, and in 1929, over 100 million people bought tickets to see films, making it the industry's best year to that point.

The Great Depression did not hit the film industry hard during its first couple of years. However, by 1934, ticket sales were down by about 40 million annual sales, and the studios were feeling the pinch from the conversion to sound. Approximately one-third of the movie theaters in the United States closed during the Depression. The ones that remained open lured viewers by slashing ticket prices, having giveaways, and—most popularly—through "bank nights," when a ticket holder would win money through a drawing. Despite the Depression, the 1930's were seen as the golden era of the studio system, with major successes such as *Gone with the Wind* (1939) making use of new technologies such as Technicolor. It was also seen as the era when the studio system was at its most efficient, with stars and technicians under long contracts and many films being produced cheaply.

In 1938, the three smaller studios sued the five major studios for violating the Sherman Antitrust Act of 1890 through their use of block booking and ownership of theaters. This lawsuit took ten years to make it through the court system, but its final ruling had a major impact on the industry. In the meantime, World War II helped bring movie ticket sales out of their slump, as people were beginning to do better financially.

POST WORLD WAR II TO THE LATE 1970'S

The end of World War II brought about a series of changes for the film industry, particularly for the major studios. The small studios won their antitrust suit. Studio-owned theaters and block booking were declared illegal. No longer able to count on the revenue from these practices, the studios began cutting costs by releasing actors and technical staff from their contracts. The anticommunist "red scare" and blacklist led to a further loss of talent in Hollywood, as well as smearing the industry's public image when it could least afford it. The industry was faced with trying to win people back into downtown theaters, despite the growing popularity of television, with its increasingly suburban audience.

During the 1950's, drive-in theaters' ticket sales increased, but all other movie ticket sales went down. Studios tried to bring moviegoers back with big, all-star film spectacles such as *Ben-Hur* (1959), but for the most part it did not work. In 1957, RKO, one of the original major studios, went out of business. During this same period, other studios such as Warner Bros., MGM, and Universal diversifed into television and music recording. During the 1970's, major corporations began taking over film companies, such as Paramount, Warner Bros., and MGM, and studios sold off the big lots where they had previously shot their films.

THE BLOCKBUSTER ERA

With the release and major successes of *Jaws* in 1975 and of *Star Wars* and its toy merchandising in 1977, film studios began to realize the potential of blockbuster films with sequels, increased marketing, and related merchandising. Merchandising, such as toys for fast-food children's meals, tie-in books, action figures, and even clothing became a requisite part of every blockbuster film release. Film studios had produced blockbusters and event pictures before, but instead of emphasizing the star power of the cast, studios began to pour money into marketing budgets and tie-ins. As film historian Joel Finler notes, "What big companies are now selling are not so much blockbuster movies as brands or franchises." The marketing and advertising budgets for films have only increased over time, with more money being spent on advertising than ever before. During the late twentieth century, advertising budgets increased more than film production budgets.

During the 1980's, Disney began to become a bigger player in the motion-picture industry, just as MGM and United Artists were declining. Foreign invest-ment in film studios was also becoming a trend, with Rupert Murdoch buying Twentieth Century-Fox and Japanese companies Sony and Matsushita buying Columbia and Tri-Star, and MCA and Universal, respectively. During the late 1980's and early 1990's, many film companies either changed hands or merged with larger companies (Warner Bros. merged with Time, for example). At the same time, many smaller film companies that had made a dent in the film industry, such as Orion, were going out of business. During the period from 1985 to 1995, Disney was the only major studio to avoid a takeover or merger.

NEW REVENUE STREAMS AND OUTSOURCING

Merchandising and ticket sales came to account for only a portion of film companies' revenues. During the 1980's, the advent of the videocassette recorder (VCR), cable television, IMAX theaters, and pay-per-view channels gave film companies new ways to extend the revenue life of their films. With the arrival of the digital versatile disc (DVD) during the 1990's, with its ability to contain extra features and commentary, the studios were able to realize new profits from their extensive film libraries by rereleasing classic films on DVD. The importance of film libraries can be highlighted by Ted Turner's purchase of MGM's movie library in 1986 for over $1 billion. Sales of films to foreign markets also became a major revenue stream. The viewing of films over the Internet is a potential new source of revenue (as well as of piracy).

TOP TEN HIGHEST GROSSING FILMS WITHIN THE UNITED STATES

1.	*Titanic* (1997)	$600.8 million
2.	*The Dark Knight* (2008)	$526.7 million
3.	*Star Wars* (1977)	$460.9 million
4.	*Shrek 2* (2004)	$436.5 million
5.	*E.T. the Extra-Terrestrial* (1982)	$434.9 million
6.	*Star Wars: Episode 1—The Phantom Menace* (1999)	$431.1 million
7.	*Pirates of the Caribbean: Dead Man's Chest* (2006)	$423.0 million
8.	*Spider-Man* (2002)	$403.7 million
9.	*Star Wars: Episode III—Revenge of the Sith* (2005)	$380.2 million
10.	*The Lord of the Rings: The Return of the King* (2003)	$377.0 million

Source: Internet Movie Database, October, 2008

In 1994, the latest major studio arrived with the creation of DreamWorks SKG. However, during the 1990's fewer films were made by major studios than in previous decades. Many films, while financed in part by major studios, are produced primarily by subsidiaries, such as Miramax, a subsidiary of Disney. This sharing of the work in making a film has become a new way for the major studios to hedge their bets when creating a film. By partnering with a smaller company (which usually handles the film production while the major studio handles the marketing and distribution), the studio is able to share any risks as well as profit with its partner.

In a move reminiscent of block booking, in the past couple of decades, film companies—with the cooperation of the cinema multiplexes that began cropping up during the 1970's—have begun saturation booking, in which a film opens on three thousand screens or more. These saturation bookings tend to occur during times of peak movie ticket sales, such as summer or the Thanksgiving holiday. By filling multiple screens at each location, blockbusters reinforce their status as a destination or event film, while preventing smaller films from sharing the same theater.

Julie Elliott

FURTHER READING

Acheson, Keith, and Christopher J. Maule. "Understanding Hollywood's Organization and Continuing Success." In *An Economic History of Film*, edited by John Sedgwick and Michael Pokorny. London: Routledge, 2005. Compares the Hollywood studio system to those of England and Europe, accounting for its initial and continued successes.

Bergman, Andrew. *We're in the Money: Depression America and Its Films*. New York: Harper, 1971. Focuses on films and the film industry during the Great Depression. Good coverage of "bank nights" and other attempts to get people into movie theaters.

Casper, Drew. *Postwar Hollywood, 1946-1962*. Malden, Mass.: Blackwell, 2007. Section 2 of the book, "Business," provides a good overview of the fallout from the Paramount antitrust lawsuit.

Dickenson, Ben. *Hollywood's New Radicalism*. New York: I. B. Tauris, 2006. Looks at Hollywood during the transition from the twentieth to twenty-first centuries, mainly from a liberal perspective.

Finler, Joel W. *The Hollywood Story*. 3d ed. New York: Wallflower Press, 2003. Includes an opening chapter on Hollywood finance; each section on a major studio includes financial details as well. This is the book to read for a concise historical overview of motion-picture industry finances.

Mintz, Steven, and Randy Roberts. *Hollywood's America: United States History Through Its Films*. St. James, N.Y.: Brandywine Press, 1999. Provides analysis of early studio practices, as well as good primary source material related to film finances, such as the Supreme Court's 1948 opinion on the antitrust case and a 1907 review of nickelodeons from *Harpers*.

SEE ALSO: American Society of Composers, Authors, and Publishers; Copyright law; Disney, Walt; Films with business themes; Hughes, Howard; Music industry; Photographic equipment industry; Radio broadcasting industry; Sherman Antitrust Act; Television broadcasting industry; Video rental industry.

Muckraking journalism

DEFINITION: An activist, investigative form of reporting that seeks to unearth and document socioeconomic and political abuses

SIGNIFICANCE: With federal controls on greedy, corrupt, and unlawful business practices ineffectual at best and nonexistent at worst, a wave of muckraking journalism arose during the late nineteenth century. Spearheaded by a new brand of "slick" magazines, it sought to correct the laissez-faire practices of robber barons, corporations, and the often complicit government bureaucracies.

The turn of the twentieth century brought about the rise of the so-called quality, or "slick," magazines: *Collier's Weekly, Cosmopolitan, McCall's Magazine, McClure's Magazine, Munsey's Magazine, Saturday Evening Post*, and others. Combining popular appeal with serious purpose, these magazines printed news and commentary side by side with fiction. More often than not, these features were the product of investigative journalism. The new generation of magazines sold for a dime a copy—less than the cost of printing—making their profits from advertising.

McClure's Magazine, in a typical example, began with a circulation of eight thousand in 1892; two years later, it boasted more than one-quarter million subscribers. By 1906, in the heyday of the muckraking era, the combined sales of the top ten muckraking magazines ran in the millions.

The term "muckraking" was coined disparagingly by President Theodore Roosevelt in a 1906 *New York Tribune* article, "The Man with the Muck-Rake." It became a phenomenon of the early twentieth century, driving the unheard-of sales of the new magazines. The articles evinced a hard edge and topical realism, reflecting the fact that crime in America was no longer seen in terms of isolated pockets of brutality perpetrated by society's dregs. Rather, it had come to seem endemic to a corrupt sociopolitical system requiring urgent and active response.

With the approval of magazine and newspaper owners and editors, muckraking journalists carried the reformist banner by attacking social injustice, exposing business abuses, and drawing the general public's attention to political complicity in both. Even President Roosevelt embraced the muckraker's progressivist agenda, until *Cosmopolitan* ran a series of articles entitled *Treason in the Senate* that involved a censure of some of Roosevelt's political allies. Incensed, he gave the speech that was later printed in the *New York Tribune*, implicitly tarring the crusading journalists by comparing them to the muckraker in John Bunyan's allegory *The Pilgrim's Progress* (1678-1684), establishing the name but ultimately turning the tide of public support against the pen-wielding crusaders.

In the 1932 study *The Era of the Muckrakers*, C. C. Regier documented the staggering number of social, political, and business reforms that flowed from muckraking exposés in the first decade and a half of the twentieth century. Among numerous other accomplishments, the muckrakers helped bring about the dismantling of the convict and peonage systems in some states; substantial prison reforms; the passage of a federal pure food act and a federal employers' liability act; the setting aside of forest reserves and the passing of the Newlands Reclamation Act (1902), which made possible reclamation of millions of acres of land; and the preservation of Niagara Falls and even Alaska from the greed of corporate interests. Even more important, the muckrakers were responsible for adoption of partial child

labor laws in some states, passage of eight-hour workday laws for women and mothers' pension acts in some states, passage of worker's compensation laws by roughly half of the states, adoption of the income tax amendment to the Constitution; dissolution of monopolies such as Standard Oil and the tobacco companies, and passage of better insurance laws and packing-house laws. Far from being a mere historical curiosity, in modern-day America—where business and political interests are often hard to distinguish—muckraking journalism and the muckraking spirit are enjoying a renaissance.

Peter Swirski

FURTHER READING

Center for Public Integrity. *Citizen Muckraking: Stories and Tools for Defeating the Goliaths of Our Day.* Monroe, Maine: Common Courage Press, 2000. This collection of accounts of average Americans who fought corruption also serves as a user-friendly instruction manual from a nonpartisan, nonprofit nongovernmental organization (NGO). It is aimed at arming reformist-minded citizens with practical strategies to combat corporate and bureaucratic abuse.

Hofstadter, Richard. *The Age of Reform.* New York: Vintage, 1960. Classic account of the populist and progressivist reform movements between 1890 and 1940 that attempts to synthesize their historical roots.

Miraldi, Robert. *Muckraking and Objectivity: Journalism's Colliding Traditions.* Westport, Conn.: Greenwood Press, 1990. Scholarly investigation of the classic and the modern eras of muckraking journalism that aims to redefine the role and purpose of journalism in American democracy in terms of reformist activism, ideologically driven partisanship, and professional neutrality.

_____, ed. *Muckrakers: Evangelical Crusaders.* Westport, Conn.: Praeger, 2000. Collection of essays aiming at a comprehensive picture of the muckraking period; takes a fresh look at the ideology behind America's first generation of investigative reporters with a view to reaffirming journalism as a moralistic and crusading enterprise.

Serrin, William, and Judith Serrin, eds. *Muckraking! The Journalism That Changed America.* New York: New Press, 2002. Organized chronologically and topically, this inclusive and varied collection reprints more than one hundred seminal muckraking articles selected from daily newspapers, magazines, books, and even broadcasts from the past 250 years.

Tichi, Cecelia. *Exposés and Excess: Muckraking in America, 1900-2000*. Philadelphia: University of Pennsylvania Press, 2005. Focusing on the laissez-faire practices of the gilded ages at both ends of the twentieth century, this lively book examines the classic muckraking publications, the rise of the contemporary generation of muckraking journalists, and the relationship between journalism and literature.

Weinberg, Arthur, and Lila Weinberg, eds. *The Muckrakers*. Urbana: University of Illinois Press, 2001. Anthology of twenty-nine muckraking articles from the first decade of the twentieth century by such luminaries of the genre as Ida Tarbell, Lincoln Steffens, Upton Sinclair, Ray Stannard Baker, Samuel Hopkins Adams, Thomas W. Lawson, Charles Edward Russell, and Mark Sullivan, accompanied by concise commentaries from the editors on the sociohistorical background and political reverberations of each piece.

SEE ALSO: Antitrust legislation; Child labor; Food and Drug Administration; Health care industry; *The Jungle*; Labor history; Literary works with business themes; Magazine industry; Newspaper industry; Rockefeller, John D.; Standard Oil Company.

Multinational corporations

DEFINITION: Companies that have capital assets in—and conduct business within—one or more foreign countries

SIGNIFICANCE: American-based multinationals have contributed to the growth of the U.S. economy by acquiring greater access to foreign markets and increasing international sales. Foreign-based multinationals have provided additional employment opportunities to the American workforce, as well as greater product choices for consumers. These multinational corporations have also increased competition among business firms in the United States and contributed to the maintenance of a free market economy.

Multinational corporations may be organized according to three different structures: horizontal, vertical, and diversified. If a multinational corporation is structured horizontally, it manages production facilities in different countries that all produce the same product. Each facility performs the same operations, from beginning of production to completion of the finished product. Vertically structured multinationals manage facilities in different countries that perform usually only one part of the production process. The facility produces a part or good that will be used in another facility to continue the manufacture of the product or receives a part or good from another facility that it will use to continue the manufacturing process. Multinationals that have a diversified structure produce a variety of products. The various facilities in the different countries are not integrated either horizontally or vertically.

Multinational corporations play an important role in the global economy with their direct foreign investment. Corporations make direct foreign investment by either establishing production and marketing facilities or purchasing existing facilities to create a subsidiary in a foreign country, or by acquiring an ownership interest in a foreign business. Most countries welcome direct foreign investment. The installation of a multinational in a country provides additional tax revenue and increased employment opportunities, and it acts as a stimulus to economic activity. Thus, multinationals are usually offered incentives to set up facilities in other countries. These incentives may include tax breaks, assurance of government assistance, and even at times a relaxation of environmental or other standards.

THE UNITED STATES AND MULTINATIONALS

One of the first American multinational corporations was the sewing machine manufacturer I. M. Singer and Company, later called the Singer Manufacturing Company. Isaac Merrit Singer established his first European manufacturing and marketing facilities in 1890. By the end of the century, Westinghouse, General Electric, Western Electric, and Eastman Kodak had opened manufacturing facilities in Europe, and Standard Oil had established refineries on the continent as well. During the early years of the twentieth century, American-based firms began to set up factories and offices in Canada and Mexico. During the century, an increasing number of American-based companies—including Ford, Gen-

The Singer Building, headquarters of the Singer Manufacturing Company in New York. At the time of its completion, 1908, it was the tallest building in the world. (Library of Congress)

MULTINATIONALS AS EMPLOYERS

Approximately 70 percent of the workers in foreign countries employed by American multinationals are in developed countries with high wage scales. The greatest number of these employees are found in Western Europe. The greatest number of overseas employees of American multinationals are working in the manufacturing sector. The transportation sector plays a significant role in this employment, as many of the workers are employed in the foreign assembly plants of American automakers.

European-based foreign multinationals make up the largest percentage of foreign-based firms employing American workers in the United States. However, in regard to the actual number of workers employed, United Kingdom-based multinationals and Japanese-based multinationals are the largest foreign employers of American workers in the United States. Canadian-based firms are the next largest employer.

Shawncey Webb

FURTHER READING

Almond, Phil, and Anthony Ferner. *American Multinationals in Europe: Managing Employment Relations Across National Borders.* New York: Oxford University Press, 2006. Examines American multinationals operating in foreign countries such as the United Kingdom, Germany, Spain, and Ireland from a cultural viewpoint. The analysis of what is American and how it contrasts with local customs and practices is especially useful.

Chandler, Alfred, and Bruce Mazlish, eds. *Leviathans: Multinational Corporations and the New Global History.* New York: Cambridge University Press, 2005. A good overview of reasons for development of multinationals, how they operate, and their significant impact worldwide, both culturally and socially.

Geppert, Mike, Dirk Matten, and Karen Williams, eds. *Challenges for European Management in a Global Context: Experiences from Britain and Germany.* New York: Palgrave Macmillan, 2002. Discusses the problems faced by American multinationals operating in foreign countries in their employment of local workers. It stresses that the expectations of these employees are different from those of American employees.

Jones, Geoffrey, and Lina Gávez-Muñoz, eds. *Foreign Multinationals in the U.S.: Management and Perfor-*

eral Motors, Coca-Cola, International Business Machines (IBM), and McDonald's—established facilities and factories in foreign countries.

European multinationals including Nestlé and Japanese companies such as Toyota and Sony joined the American business community. In 1984, Nestlé acquired Carnation, and in 2002, it bought animal food manufacturer Ralston Purina, Dreyer's (sold as Dreyer's Ice Cream and Edy's Ice Cream), and Chef America, the manufacturer of Hot Pockets. In 1982, through a joint venture with General Motors, Toyota established its first manufacturing facility in the United States. Sony Corporation, headquartered in Tokyo, set up its subsidiary Sony Corporation of America. These developments increased the role of multinationals in the American economy.

mance. New York: Routledge, 2001. Offers a good overview of the experiences, successes, and failures of foreign multinationals with offices and production facilities in the United States. There are sections on Japanese, French, Dutch, and British multinationals.

Osterhammel, Jurgen, and Niels P. Petersson. *Globalization: A Short History*. Translated by Dona Geyer. Princeton, N.J.: Princeton University Press, 2005. Appropriate for both the general reader and the student of economic history, this work traces the evolution of globalization from early trading among European countries, through the expanding trade that developed with exploration and colonization, to modern-day international trade. The focus is on economic developments; cultural and political events play a secondary role. There is a large section on the Bretton Woods Agreement negotiations.

SEE ALSO: Agribusiness; General Electric; Income tax, corporate; Incorporation laws; International economics and trade; Military-industrial complex; Petroleum industry; Price fixing.

Music industry

DEFINITION: Companies that record, produce, distribute, promote, and market recorded music

SIGNIFICANCE: The music industry has brought listeners numerous types of music in various, changing formats. These changes in format as well as changes in music tastes challenged companies to adapt while protecting copyrights and finding ways to profit using the new technology.

Copyright and fair compensation for work have always been the major concerns for not only music publishers and producers but also composers and artists. While testifying to the Senate and House Patent Committee's copyright hearings in 1906, composer John Philip Sousa said his writing ability rose with his compensation. In 1909, Sousa was one of the composers who successfully lobbied for a copyright law that would force record companies to compensate composers for using their music. The law gave artists copyright of their work for twenty-eight years, with one renewal for the same time period. The law also stipulated that record companies compensate composers for recording and selling their music (then 2 cents per pressing of a music cylinder of printed sheet music). Since Sousa's time, the laws for copyright have continued to change. Although copyright laws have protected the music industry in the United States to some degree, international piracy is still a major problem.

EARLY HISTORY

Printed sheet music was an early product of the music industry. Although the early publishers of printed music were independents, during the 1880's, a number of sheet music firms began establishing themselves in a section of Manhattan near Twenty-eighth Street and Broadway that became known as Tin Pan Alley. This group of publishers began to streamline the composing and producing of sheet music, paying a given rate per song. The Tin Pan Alley group also began marketing their songs through vaudeville performers, something earlier music publishers did with minstrel performers. Tin Pan Alley also targeted its marketing toward white upper-middle-class Americans, who preferred waltzes, marching music, and vaudeville songs. Anything that had an ethnic or African American sound was avoided.

In 1877, Thomas Alva Edison created the phonograph. He did not intend his invention to be used for distribution of popular music; rather, his main intent was for the device to function as a secretarial aid for dictation. During the late 1890's, when some vendors of the phonograph began selling it to saloons and train stations for use as "coin-in-the-slot" music machines, Edison was displeased. By the 1890's, the phonograph had become a popular way to hear music throughout the country, and other phonograph companies were trying to cash in on the music arcade movement. In response, in 1896, Edison gave Columbia Phonograph Company permission to use his phonograph technology to create the first machines that could play cylindrical records at home. A competing company, Victor Talking Machine, was also working on the home phonograph market and eventually bested Edison and Columbia, thanks to its savvy use of both a better way of cranking the machine (a modified knitting machine motor) and of celebrity—creating several recordings of songs sung by popular singers. Both Columbia and Victor survived, however, because although each company used certain items patented by the other, neither decided to sue.

In 1919, the radio was first introduced to the American home. The Radio Corporation of America (RCA) began marketing affordable radios to families, and by the early 1920's, most households had one. At first, the phonograph companies were worried that radios would hurt their market and reacted to the new technology by trying to fight it. The industry soon realized, however, that radio was a useful tool for marketing their singers and merchandise.

One outcome of the advent of the radio was the success of smaller record companies through the promotion of African American and hillbilly music, two markets ignored by the major phonograph companies and Tin Pan Alley. Smaller companies, such as Okeh Records, began to make money by selling records by African Americans and rural country artists. Because the songs by the major labels and composers were the songs that were being featured on the radio, there was not as strong a need to purchase those records. However, records by African Americans and rural southerners were not being played on radio, so those who wished to hear those songs had to buy them from the smaller independent labels.

In 1921, record sales hit a peak of $106 million, a figure that would not be topped until 1945. Record sales hit their lowest point during the Great Depression, with only $6 million dollars in sales in 1933. The Depression hit the music industry hard, forcing early phonograph innovators such as Thomas A. Edison, Inc., to close. Other larger companies that were successful during the early phonograph era folded because of their reluctance to cooperate with radio.

RECORDS AND ROCK

After World War II, the music industry experienced a mini-boom between 1945 and 1947. The brittle shellac 78-revolutions-per-minute (rpm) phonograph records gave way to long-play (LP) $33\frac{1}{3}$- and 45-rpm records made of vinyl, which were less fragile and had better sound quality. The LP record could play more music per side than a phonograph (twenty minutes per side as compared with four). The 45s allowed for a single song to be purchased and listened to, and reminiscent of the nickel arcades of the 1890's, the jukebox became popular. During the 1950's, a number of smaller record companies, such as Sun Records and Chess Records, began marketing rhythm and blues and eventually rock and roll.

The major music labels were not receptive to rock and roll when it appeared during the 1950's, and despite the fast-rising popularity of the genre, they were slow to sign rock acts. Filling in the void were numerous small record labels, such as Chess Records, Sun Records, and Atlantic Records, which made fortunes selling records in the new musical style. The peak of independent record companies came in 1962, when they accounted for 75 percent of music sales. By that time, the major labels had begun to realize that to survive, they needed to sign more rock-and-roll acts.

As rock music became more popular during the 1950's, the demand for personal appearances and tours by artists began to increase. Disc jockey Alan Freed held several popular concerts in Cleveland that featured a variety of artists. He twice broke the record for money made from a concert. Soon Dick Clark, Murray "the K" Kaufman, and other celebrity disc jockeys began holding concert promotions across the United States.

VIDEO, CASSETTES, AND NEW GENRES

During the 1970's, many of the independent labels that made their fortunes through the signing of rock-and-rolls acts were bought out by major labels.

The major labels had learned from their mistake in rejecting new music and greatly profited from promoting first disco, then punk, new-wave, and heavy-metal acts. An ally in their promotion efforts came in the form of music videos.

In 1981, a cable television channel called MTV (Music Television) ushered in the era of music videos. Initially, the music industry resisted producing music videos, thinking that the cost would exceed the returns from record sales, but in the first half of the decade, at least, that proved not to be the case. As it had with radio earlier, the industry soon embraced music videos, and a number of bands and artists—notably Duran Duran, the Eurythmics, Michael Jackson, and Madonna—successfully marketed themselves through elaborate music videos. Also during this decade, a new genre, hip-hop music, emerged. Hip-hop featured a rhythmic style of speaking called rap, over percussive sounds. The major labels were slow to sign hip-hop artists, to their financial detriment. A number of indepen-

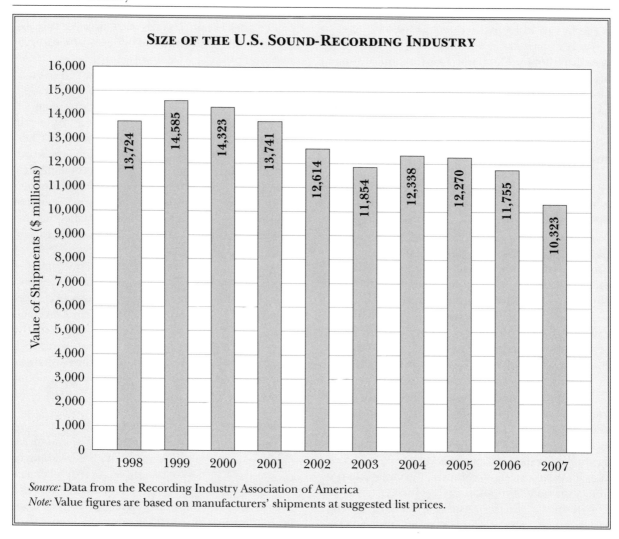

SIZE OF THE U.S. SOUND-RECORDING INDUSTRY

Source: Data from the Recording Industry Association of America
Note: Value figures are based on manufacturers' shipments at suggested list prices.

dent labels, such as Def Jam Recordings and Tommy Boy Records, began producing and distributing hip-hop music at a profit.

By the mid-1980's, music sales again began to plummet. Part of this could be attributed to the availability of cassette tape recorders, which allowed people to copy music at no cost, a kind of low-tech piracy. The advent of compact discs (CDs), first introduced in 1983 and more widespread toward the end of the decade, helped bring industry sales back somewhat.

As the 1980's came to a close, a number of major record companies merged. Many of the independents who had specialized in hip-hop music were bought out (Def Jam by Polygram, Tommy Boy by Warner Bros.), and major labels were purchased by international conglomerates (RCA by the Bertelsmann Music Group, or BMG; CBS-Columbia by Sony). The mergers continued, and by the beginning of the new millennium, 80 percent of the music being distributed was owned by four major companies, the highest concentration in the industry since the Tin Pan Alley days.

DOWNLOADABLE MUSIC

During the 1990's the Moving Picture Experts Group Phase 1 (MPEG-1)Audio Layer 3, or MP3, was created. MP3 allows computers to compress quality audio files into an easily downloadable format. Soon Web sites became available for downloading songs, with many sites offering song downloads for free, without compensation to the recording artists or companies, causing them to pursue legislation to protect their interests. In 1998, President Bill Clinton signed into law the Digital Millennium Copyright Act, which was designed to help protect both the music and film industries from piracy.

In 1998, the first MP3 players were marketed, and as with radio and music videos, the music industry's first response was to fight the new technology vigorously, as it was feared that downloadable music would reduce sales of CDs. However, with the opening of Apple's iTunes online store in 2003, which sold downloads for use on computers and iPods, record companies began to realize that, like radio and music videos, the MP3 format could be a tool to help market their offerings. Record companies have further protected their content through digital rights management, in which the music that consumers download is encrypted and cannot be shared. However, some consumers have complained that digital rights management prevents them from listening to their downloaded music on all their various electronic music players.

Despite the growing popularity of downloads, the revenue generated has not made up for the drop in the sales of CDs, which in 2007 accounted for 77 percent of revenue (down from 91 percent in 2005). According to the Recording Industry Association of America, from 2006 to 2007, downloaded singles saw a rise of 38 percent, and downloaded albums rose 54 percent, while the number of CDs shipped fell 17.5 percent. Overall, the industry experienced an increase of 11.6 percent in total digital and physical units sold but an 11.8 percent decline in the total value of units.

Julie Elliott

FURTHER READING

Chapple, Steve, and Reebee Garafolo. *Rock 'n' Roll Is Here to Pay.* Chicago: Nelson-Hall, 1977. Written in a chatty style but does provide good information on rock music from the 1950's to the mid-1970's. The section on concert promotion is particularly informative.

Espejo, Roman, ed. *What Is the Future of the Music Industry?* Detroit, Mich.: Greenhaven, 2008. A collection of articles discussing the music industry's future. Topics include illegal file sharing, CDs, and digital rights.

Krasilovsky, M. William, et al. *This Business of Music:* *The Definitive Guide to the Music Industry.* 10th ed. New York: Billboard Books, 2007. Considered the bible of the music industry, the book, written by law experts, provides an overview of the music industry in the twentieth century and discusses how new copyright laws and piracy legislation affect musicians and their distributors.

Stamm, K. Brad. *Music Industry Economics: A Global Demand Model for Pre-recorded Music.* Lewiston, N.Y.: Edwin Mellen, 2000. While very academic in tone, Stamm's work provides an excellent overview of American copyright laws as well as the issue of international piracy.

Tschmuck, Peter. *Creativity and Innovation in the Music Industry.* New York: Springer, 2006. Provides an excellent economic overview of the U.S. and international music industry from the emergence of the phonograph to MP3s. Uses tables to show how independents made money from rock and roll and other genres.

SEE ALSO: American Society of Composers, Authors, and Publishers; Apple; Computer industry; Copyright law; Digital recording technology; Motion-picture industry; Radio broadcasting industry; Television broadcasting industry.

Mutual fund industry

DEFINITION: Branch of the financial investment industry comprising institutions that use investors' money to collectively invest in stocks, bonds, or money market instruments

SIGNIFICANCE: Since the creation of the first mutual fund in 1929, the mutual fund industry has enjoyed the fastest growth rate of the financial investment industry. In 1949, all mutual fund companies combined controlled $2 billion; fund assets soared to $6.5 trillion at the outset of 2003, and more than $12 trillion in 2007, making the funds America's largest financial investment vehicles.

The mutual fund industry consists of investment companies that sell shares in one or more portfolios of financial assets. Fund managers determine the composition of the portfolio, which may include stocks, bonds, government securities, shares in precious metals, and other financial assets. As open-end funds, they are sold publicly, and their shares must be redeemed by the investment company on request of the shareholder.

Mutual funds are categorized by their general investment objectives. Equity funds consist of common stocks and are organized to achieve capital growth. Bond funds are composed of corporate, U.S. government, or municipal bonds and emphasize regular income. Income funds have the same objective as bond funds but include Government National Mortgage Association securities, government securities, and common and preferred stocks as well as bonds. Money market mutual funds consist of short-term instruments, such as U.S. government securities, bank certificates of deposit (CDs), and commercial paper. Short-term municipal bond funds are composed predominantly of tax-exempt, short-term municipal securities.

The mutual fund industry is regulated by the Securities and Exchange Commission (SEC) and by state regulations and securities laws. The first mutual fund was developed on March 21, 1924, when three Boston securities executives pooled their money to establish the Massachusetts Investors Trust. In just one year, the mutual fund grew from $50,000 to $392,000 in assets. Investors welcomed the innovation and invested in this new vehicle heavily; however, the stock market crash of 1929 slowed its growth. To instill investors with confidence, the U.S. Congress passed the Securities Act of 1933, the Securities Exchange Act of 1934, and the Investment Company Act of 1940, which set standards with which mutual funds must comply.

By the end of the 1960's, there were approximately 270 funds with $48 billion in assets. One of the largest contributors to the mutual funds' growth was the provision added to the Internal Revenue Code in 1975 that allowed individuals already in a corporate pension fund to contribute up to $2,000 per year to an individual retirement account (IRA). Mutual funds became popular in employer-sponsored 401(k) retirement plans, IRAs, and Roth IRAs.

In 1976, John Bogle founded the first retail index fund (a passively managed fund that tries to mirror the performance of a specific index, such as the S&P 500), named First Index Investment Trust. Later renamed Vanguard 500 Index Fund, it revolutionized investing, becoming one of the world's largest mutual funds, with more than $115 billion in assets. Mutual fund assets first reached the trillion-dollar mark in January, 1990. By the end of 1990, the industry had also posted new records, both in the number of funds (3,108) and in the number of individual accounts (62.6 million). By 1996, total mutual fund assets reached $3 trillion. The industry blossomed in the dawn of the new millennium, and in 2007, there were 8,015 mutual funds, with a combined worth of $12.4 trillion.

Rikard Bandebo

FURTHER READING

Jacobs, Bruce. *All About Mutual Funds.* Columbus, Ohio: McGraw-Hill Companies, 2001.

Mobius, Mark. *Mutual Funds: An Introduction to the Core Concepts.* Hoboken, N.J.: John Wiley & Sons, 2007.

SEE ALSO: Bond industry; 401(k) retirement plans; Internal Revenue Code; Junk bonds; New York Stock Exchange; Stock markets; Supreme Court and banking law.

N

NAFTA. *See* **North American Free Trade Agreement**

NASDAQ

IDENTIFICATION: Second largest of the United States' three major stock exchanges

DATE: Began operations on February 8, 1971

SIGNIFICANCE: As the first computerized stock exchange, the NASDAQ revolutionized the stock market trading system by allowing the easy trade of small stocks by permitting ordinary people to use electronic trading to buy and sell stocks without the need for a broker. During the 1990's, the NASDAQ became the favored exchange for new Internet companies, though the crash at the start of the twenty-first century diminished the exchange's relevance.

As the oldest stock exchanges in the country, the New York Stock Exchange (NYSE) and the American Stock Exchange (AMEX) included mostly large companies that could afford the high fees charged for listing those companies. Smaller companies with lower priced stocks and a low volume of trading were sold on the more rudimentary over-the-counter (OTC) market. The OTC market was not a single room where brokers and traders bought and sold as if at an auction. Instead, OTC trading occurred over the phone between brokers and one of scores of traders who held stock. Lacking a central place for trading in small stocks, traders found it nearly impossible to know the exact price of any stock sold over the counter. The OTC market would become the favorite of the new technology companies that would bring the United States into the computer age.

The OTC market went unnoticed by regulators and by most market traders until 1962, when a sudden dive in the market created chaos in OTC trading. Brokers could not keep up with the sudden and massive price declines as they sold stock over the phone. It became apparent that the OTC market had outgrown its origins, and only a change in technology would allow smaller stocks to continue to be traded. On February 8, 1971, stock trading moved into the computer age, as the National Association of Securities Dealers Automated Quotations (NASDAQ) began operations.

THE BEGINNING

Formation of the NASDAQ system raised concerns in the NYSE that the new computerized trading would compete with the stock exchange's floor trading and eventually replace the NYSE. For that reason, the NASDAQ was limited to selling smaller companies not listed on the New York exchange.

During the 1980's, the NASDAQ was transformed from a niche exchange, familiar to only a few professional traders, to a market that traded the stocks the public wanted to own. Companies such as Microsoft, Apple Computer, and Oracle—all on the forefront of new technology—traded on the NASDAQ, eventually earning the exchange a reputation as a technology-heavy market.

The exchange also earned the highest form of compliment, as the NYSE imitated some of the electronic trading systems used by its competitor, but, even with these changes, by the late 1980's the trading volume on the NASDAQ was beginning to approach the levels of the NYSE. By 1987, though, speculation had seized the markets, with stocks becoming overvalued and computerized trading systems setting up investors for a sudden and large fall. October 19, 1987, would expose the weaknesses of technology stocks, as a sudden drop in their value triggered a cascade of computerized sell orders. Because machines rather than people were making trading decisions, when stocks reached a certain price, they were automatically sold, deepening the market's decline. Unlike other market declines, during which human traders used price declines to scoop up stocks that were oversold and undervalued, the computers ruthlessly sold stocks without regard to such details or to companies' outlooks. Much of the 1987 crash could be attributed to the computerized sell orders.

THE INTERNET

The NASDAQ would become the star of the stock-buying binge of the 1990's, as Internet companies dominated the exchange and drew in trillions of dollars in investments. Because the exchange catered to start-up businesses lacking proven track records, new companies such as Google, Amazon.com, eBay, and Yahoo sold their shares on the NASDAQ. Public excitement about the Internet age drew in many small investors, and these companies soon became worth more than established stocks in the NYSE. The rampant speculation drove the NASDAQ to extraordinary highs, as its index value increased nearly 700 percent in less than six years. Speculators' investments in initial public offerings of NASDAQ technology stocks were responsible for the development of many Internet start-up companies, but the crash of 2000 laid low many of these new companies, leading to bankruptcies and worthless stock. The resulting disaster took some of the shine off the NASDAQ, as the more established stocks on the NYSE suffered fewer losses and became more popular among investors over the next decade.

Douglas Clouatre

Men watch stock prices fall at the NASDAQ MarketSite in Times Square on October 24, 2008. (AP/Wide World Photos)

FURTHER READING

Dalton, John. *How the Stock Market Works.* New York: Prentice-Hall, 2001. Amateur stock market investors and those curious about how stocks are bought and sold are the main audience for this book, which explains the differences between the three market exchanges.

Frewles, Richard, and Edward Bradley. *The Stock Market.* New York: John Wiley & Sons, 1998. Looks at all of the American stock markets and how they trade in stock; includes a detailed analysis of the NASDAQ market.

Ingerbretsen, Mark. *NASDAQ.* Roseville, Calif.: Forum, 2002. Historical look at the development of the OTC market and the formation and growth of the NASDAQ stock exchange through the latter years of the twentieth century.

Little, Jeffrey B., and Lucien Rhodes. *Understanding Wall Street.* New York: McGraw-Hill, 2004. Relates the methods of stock trading, including the OTC market and the NASDAQ.

Sobel, Robert. *The Big Board.* Frederick, Md.: Beard Books, 2000. Written by an economic historian, this work details the history of stock market trading and includes sections on the role of the NASDAQ in developing the modern stock market system.

SEE ALSO: American Stock Exchange; Black Monday; Dot-com bubble; Google; New York Stock Exchange; Stock markets; Wall Street.

National Association of Securities Dealers Automated Quotations. *See* NASDAQ

National Broadcasting Company

IDENTIFICATION: Radio and television network
DATE: Launched on November 15, 1926
SIGNIFICANCE: The founding of NBC established the structure within which U.S. radio, and later television, stations would operate: a system of local independent affiliates to a nationwide network.

When the Radio Corporation of America (RCA) acquired several radio stations from American Telephone and Telegraph (AT&T) in 1926, broadcasting was still in its infancy. AT&T had just pioneered commercial advertising on the air. The company referred to such advertising as "toll radio," after toll calls, but it actually employed a model more akin to newspaper advertising. It used its long-distance telephone lines to relay programming to the more distant stations, so all stations on its network could carry the same programs.

RCA decided to expand this system and create a nationwide network under the name of the National Broadcasting Company (NBC). To signal local affiliates to broadcast their station identification calls, NBC developed the distinctive three-note NBC chimes, a sequence of the musical notes G-E-C. NBC quickly split into two networks, NBC Red and NBC Blue, according to the colors of the grease pencils used to lay out the systems on a map. Each of the two networks developed its own personality: The Red Network concentrated on programming that already had a guaranteed listener base to ensure sponsorship, while the Blue Network aired less-tested programs that sought to cultivate both a listener base and sponsors.

The two distinctive styles of operation were not enough to satisfy the Federal Trade Commission's concerns about monopolistic practices, and in 1943, RCA spun off the Blue Network to avoid an antitrust suit. It was later bought by an outside concern and renamed the American Broadcasting Company, or ABC.

Because RCA was one of the primary developers of American television technology, NBC expanded into commercial television as soon as broadcast licenses became available. Although early NBC logos were based on the RCA logos of the time, after RCA's compatible color system was approved by the Federal Communications Commission (FCC), NBC began to use a multicolored peacock logo to designate its color broadcasts. A more stylized version of the peacock subsequently became NBC's general corporate logo.

After the retirement of NBC founder David Sarnoff from RCA in 1970, the company went into decline. It was ultimately sold to General Electric (GE), and NBC become part of the NBC Universal media branch of GE. After the success of the Cable News Network (CNN), NBC developed two cable news channels, the business-oriented CNBC and the general-interest MSNBC (the latter being a joint venture with Microsoft). Both cable channels and the regular network remained branded with the NBC peacock logo.

Leigh Husband Kimmel

FURTHER READING
Edgerton, Gary R. *The Columbia History of American Television.* New York: Columbia University Press, 2007.
Lewis, Tom. *Empire of the Air: The Men Who Made Radio.* New York: Edward Burlingame, 1991.
Sobel, Robert. *RCA.* New York: Stein and Day, 1986.
Tinker, Grant, and Bud Rukeyser. *Tinker in Television: From General Sarnoff to General Electric.* New York: Simon & Schuster, 1994.

SEE ALSO: CNBC; Federal Communications Commission; Gates, Bill; General Electric; Radio broadcasting industry; Television broadcasting industry.

National Labor Relations Board

IDENTIFICATION: Federal government agency charged with arbitrating between business and labor interests

DATE: Established on July 5, 1935

SIGNIFICANCE: The National Labor Relations Board organized and monitored union-recognition elections and protected workers and unions against employers' unfair practices. Later it also restricted abusive union practices.

Before 1935, organized labor in the United States was quite limited in scope. About 10 percent of the nonfarm labor force was unionized. Most unions were affiliated with the American Federation of Labor (AFL), and most were identified by the craft or occupation of the individual worker—carpenters, electricians, and so forth. A few unions, notably the United Mine Workers of America (UMWA), were industrial unions, ready to organize all workers in a given industry, whatever their particular job. Unions were strong in some sectors, such as the building trades and the railroads. Union power was severely limited by the likelihood that a strike (union-instigated work stoppage) would be met by a court injunction to forbid it and perhaps assess financial damages on the union. Both the Clayton Act of 1914 and the Norris-LaGuardia Act of 1932 attempted to limit the scope of injunctions in labor disputes, but with only limited success.

As the Great Depression set in after 1929, working conditions worsened. The unemployment rate rose steadily, until by 1933, one-fourth of the labor force was unemployed. Employers insisted on cutting wage rates. One of the first "recovery" measures of Franklin D. Roosevelt's New Deal program was the National Industrial Recovery Act (NRA) of 1933. Section 7a of the act asserted that workers had a right to organize and bargain collectively without interference or reprisal by employers. Aggressive actions to extend union membership provoked much labor disturbance in 1933 and 1934. In June, 1934, Congress authorized the president to appoint a board to handle disputes relating to Section 7a of the NRA. This led to the creation of the first National Labor Relations Board (NLRB) in July, 1934.

THE RIGHT TO ORGANIZE

The NRA was held to be unconstitutional in May, 1935. The labor provisions were quickly reenacted in the National Labor Relations Act of 1935, also known as the Wagner Act. The law provided for a new National Labor Relations Board of three persons with no direct connections with either unions or management. The NLRB was empowered to restrain employers from specific unfair labor practices, including coercing or otherwise interfering with workers' organizing and bargaining activities; dominating or financing a labor organization; discriminating against union members and organizers or against persons filing grievances; or refusing to bargain collectively in good faith with an accredited labor organization.

The NLRB was also authorized to conduct elections to determine whether a group of workers wanted to bargain through a particular union. J. Warren Madden, dean of the law school of the University of Pittsburgh, was appointed chair. Many business leaders were passionately opposed to unionization and to the principles of the National Labor Relations Act, so the early days of NLRB were very turbulent. Some leaders of organized labor, notably John L. Lewis and Sidney Hillman, saw the opportunity to use the protection of the new law to extend unionization to the unorganized—particularly in mass-production industries. Conservative craft

union leaders in the AFL did not share this commitment. As a result, a group of industrial unions calling themselves the Committee for Industrial Organization (CIO; later the Congress of Industrial Organizations) formed within the AFL and ultimately (1938) broke away.

The CIO was able to add millions of workers to union rolls, particularly in the steel, automobile, and textile industries. The process was often not peaceable—most noteworthy was a sit-down strike against General Motors from the end of 1936 into 1937. Workers occupied company facilities for a six-week period. In February, 1937, GM agreed to accept the United Automobile Workers as the sole bargaining agent for its members. Ford Motor Company maintained an antiunion stance until 1941—company thugs seriously injured several organizers in a violent encounter at the River Rouge plant in May, 1937. In April, 1941, worker protests against discharge of union members culminated in an NLRB election supporting the union, and Henry Ford agreed to terms in June, 1941.

Once the constitutionality of the National Labor Relations Act was upheld in April, 1937, the NLRB became very busy. In its first five years, the board acted in nearly thirty thousand cases involving 6.4 million workers. It administered elections for 1.2 million workers, representing 3,379 bargaining units. About 80 percent of the votes favored unionization. Where employer violations were found, the NLRB often ordered workers to be reinstated with back pay or to receive pay adjustments.

A challenge for the NLRB in conducting elections was to determine the appropriate bargaining unit— whether the entire firm, or merely those workers practicing a traditional craft specialty covered by the AFL. For the most part, board members favored broader measures, thus giving an edge to the CIO. In many cases, the ballot offered the workers a choice between a CIO union, an AFL union, and no union.

Although the labor violence of the late 1930's probably impeded economic recovery, the economy did expand. Unemployment declined, and wages increased. After the European war began in 1939, the American economy shifted increasingly to a war footing. Prosperity reduced business resistance to unionization and union demands. Between 1935 and 1939, union membership increased from 3.7 million to 9 million, representing 29 percent of nonfarm workers. The spread of industrial unions transformed the labor movement. Unions now welcomed unskilled workers, women, and racial minorities. Unions became a political force, aligned overwhelmingly with the Democratic Party.

WORLD WAR II

The war strengthened union positions further. Business firms were often under pressure from government to avoid work interruptions. Defense contracts could be sweetened to cover generous labor settlements. Attention shifted away from the NLRB; representation questions and unfair labor practices were less frequent. The government had created in early 1942 the National War Labor Board, dealing with the major issues of pay and working conditions until its termination in 1945. By war's end there were 15 million union members, representing 36 percent of nonfarm workers. When the war ended, they flexed their muscles, greeting the end of wage-price controls with large wage demands. A wave of strikes in the winter of 1945-1946 involved coal, steel, automobile, and rail workers, but there was no return to the labor violence of the mid-1930's.

The NLRB required employers to bargain in good faith with unions. This involved deciding what topics were appropriate for collective bargaining. A landmark NLRB decision in 1948 rendered private pension benefits a bargainable issue. This contributed to a great increase in the extent of company-managed pension programs.

Public dislike for unions rose, as people blamed them for inflation and for work stoppages, helping bring passage in 1947 of the Taft-Hartley Act. The law altered the NLRB mandate, prohibiting unfair practices by unions. These included the closed shop, under which an employer could hire only people who were already union members; indeed, state governments were authorized to go further if they chose, outlawing making union membership a condition of employment. This provision produced so-called right-to-work laws, which had been adopted in nineteen states by 1963. Unions were forbidden to coerce or restrain workers or employers in relation to union organization and bargaining. They were forbidden to pressure an employer to discriminate against a worker or to charge excessive union initiation fees. "Featherbedding"—pressuring an employer to pay for work not performed—was outlawed, as were secondary boycotts: These involved union pressure on one firm to cease doing business with another firm that is the union's actual target. Unions seeking help from the NLRB were required to submit financial statements, and their leadership was obliged to sign noncommunist affidavits. This provision was repealed in 1959.

THE LANDRUM-GRIFFIN ACT OF 1959

A series of congressional investigations during the 1950's highlighted corruption and criminality in labor unions. The Landrum-Griffin Act of 1959 tightened restrictions on picketing and outlawed "hot-cargo" actions, whereby unions (notably the International Brotherhood of Teamsters) would refuse to handle goods of a firm that unions were targeting. Internal affairs of unions were regulated: Financial reports were required, restrictions were imposed on the use of dues, and union office-

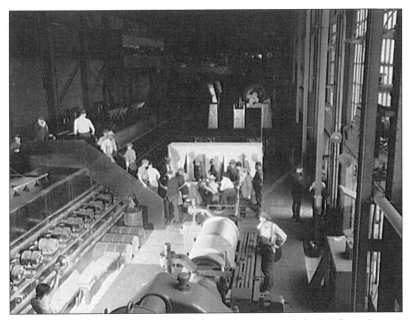

Workers cast ballots at the National Labor Relations Board election for union representation at the River Rouge Ford plant in Dearborn, Michigan. (Library of Congress)

holding was restricted for felons and communists.

Union membership reached its peak in 1979, when there were 21 million members. However, as a percentage of the labor force, union membership had been gradually declining from a maximum of around one-third in 1954. After the 1960's, there was a great expansion of union membership in government employment—but most of these workers were not under NLRB jurisdiction. By 2006, there were about 15 million union members, but only 7.4 million of these were in private employment, where they represented only 8 percent of workers.

As the tide of union organizing receded, the activities of the NLRB became less exciting. Representation elections, which numbered above eight thousand per year during the 1980's, had fallen below four thousand per year by 1994. From the mid-1970's, unions lost more elections than they won. The number of complaints to the NLRB against employers leveled off around three thousand per year.

Paul B. Trescott

FURTHER READING

Bernstein, Irving. *Turbulent Years: A History of the American Worker, 1933-1941.* Boston: Houghton Mifflin, 1970. Colorful, if somewhat biased, overview of the period that produced Section 7a, the Wagner Act, and the CIO.

Freeman, Richard B. "Spurts in Union Growth: Defining Moments and Social Processes." In *The Defining Moment: The Great Depression and the American Economy in the Twentieth Century,* edited by Michael Bordo, Claudia Golden, and Eugene White. Chicago: University of Chicago Press, 1998. Very critical of the Wagner Act as a defining framework for modern labor relations; views the parallel system for state government employees as generally superior.

Higgins, John E., Jr., et al., eds. *The Developing Labor Law: The Board, the Courts, and the National Labor Relations Act.* 5th ed. 2 vols. Washington, D.C.: Bureau of National Affairs, 2006. Comprehensive, scholarly coverage of the legal rights and duties of employees, employers, and unions.

McCulloch, Frank W., and Tim Bornstein. *The National Labor Relations Board.* New York: Praeger, 1974. The first five chapters give an excellent historical overview; the remainder describes structure and operations. McCulloch was NLRB chair for nearly a decade.

Taft, Philip. *Organized Labor in American History.* New York: Harper & Row, 1964. Encyclopedic history, with separate chapters on the NRA, the Wagner Act, and the Taft-Hartley Act, all in context.

SEE ALSO: Commerce, U.S. Department of; Labor, U.S. Department of; Labor history; Labor strikes; New Deal programs; Supreme Court and labor law.

National Labor Union

IDENTIFICATION: Short-lived labor organization that worked to reform labor laws and practices in favor of workers by campaigning to elect government officials sympathetic to laborers' rights
DATE: 1866-1872
SIGNIFICANCE: The goal of the National Labor Union was to improve working conditions by campaigning for and helping elect political candidates who promised to push for labor-reform legislation, including passage of laws mandating an eight-hour workday. In some state and national elections, the National Labor Union put forward its own candidates to run for public office.

The National Labor Union was the precursor to the Knights of Labor and the American Federation of Labor. Though in existence for only a short period, from 1866 to 1872, the National Labor Union did manage in 1868 to gain congressional passage of the eight-hour workday, its foremost issue. Employers retaliated, however, by cutting workers' hourly wages. President Ulysses S. Grant issued an order that employers were forbidden to continue the practice of cutting wages, but his order was largely ignored by private industry and even by some government agencies.

Begun by William Sylvian, leader of the Iron Molder's International Union, the National Labor Union was open to all white male workers in skilled trades. Eventually, its membership expanded to include white male farmers and unskilled workers. Chinese and African American workers were excluded, as were women. African American workers formed the Colored National Labor Union, but it remained ineffective as a result of widespread racism in American politics. Rather than acting through strikes and collective bargaining, the National Labor Union attempted to improve working conditions through legislative reforms and third-party arbitrations, as well as by trying to form a third political party, the National Labor Party. This would permit the National Labor Union to run political candidates independently of both the Democratic and the Republican political parties.

Despite its significant victory in winning passage of the legislation mandating the eight-hour work-day, the National Labor Union was not effective in the long run. Farmers and unskilled and skilled craftspeople did not share a united political agenda except on narrowly focused labor issues. The National Labor Union did help form several industry-specific national unions. Sylvian, however, died unexpectedly in 1869, just as the National Labor Union was increasing its political clout and gaining members.

At its zenith, the National Labor Union counted approximately 700,000 workers among its members. The union selected its own candidate, David Davis of Illinois, to run in the 1872 presidential election, but when the candidate dropped out of the race, the union members found that they had little in common with one another. The National Labor Union collapsed shortly thereafter. The Depression of 1873 caused many unions to back away from labor reforms in an attempt to preserve jobs. The National Labor Union's ideas of progressive social policies and labor reforms were taken up by later labor organizations, especially the Knights of Labor. None of those organizations, however, agreed with the National Labor Union's idea of labor reform via legislation or arbitration.

Victoria Erhart

FURTHER READING

Leavitt, John McDowell. *Kings of Capital and the Knights of Labor: For the People.* Adamant, Vt.: Adamant Media, 2001.

Voss, Kim. *The Making of American Exceptionalism: The Knights of Labor and Class Formation in the Nineteenth Century.* Ithaca, N.Y.: Cornell University Press, 1993.

Weir, Robert E. *Beyond Labor's Veil: The Culture of the Knights of Labor.* State College: Pennsylvania State University Press, 1997.

SEE ALSO: AFL-CIO; Debs, Eugene V.; Knights of Labor; Labor history.

National Road. *See* Cumberland Road

National Science Foundation

IDENTIFICATION: Scientific research funding organization

DATE: Founded in 1950

SIGNIFICANCE: The National Science Foundation provides funding for basic research and development to promote and advance science and engineering in the United States.

The National Science Foundation (NSF) was created by the National Science Foundation Act of 1950. The act was an outgrowth of the important contributions science and engineering made to advancing technology during World War II. The foundation's mission is unique among all United States government scientific research agencies. The NSF supports the development of all scientific and engineering disciplines, awarding annual funding for research and educational advancement to over two thousand universities, colleges, primary and secondary schools, businesses, and public and private research institutions within the United States. Many other government agencies support research, but they usually focus on specific areas such as space exploration, medicine, or defense.

The NSF promotes interdisciplinary research and supports the overall development of science and engineering, seeking to expand the number of trained scientists, engineers, and science educators within the United States. The NSF annually provides almost half of all federal support for nonmedical basic research conducted at academic institutions. Nearly all NSF funds are grants and cooperative agreements resulting from competitive, peer-reviewed proposals submitted to the foundation. The proposal review and decision process involves nearly 60,000 scientists and engineers each year. The NSF annually receives about 40,000 proposals for research, fellowships, and projects. It makes about 16,000 awards, supporting the work of over 200,000 scientists, teachers, students, and engineers.

The foundation is administered by a director, who is appointed by the president of the United States and confirmed by the U.S. Senate. It is overseen by the National Science Board (NSB), whose membership consists of twenty-four eminent scientists appointed by the president and confirmed by the Senate to six-year terms. The role of the NSB is to establish policies for the foundation, to oversee its programs and activities, and to approve strategic directions and budgets.

Board decisions and directions for the NSF are often based on political agendas and the perceived strategic or economic needs of the nation, and budgets are set accordingly. The NSF's annual budget for research and development is approximately $6 billion, accounting for approximately 5 percent of all U.S. government-funded research. The role the NSF plays in promoting and maintaining basic research is vital to American scientific and engineering advancement.

Economic estimates suggest that much of American industrial, financial, and intellectual growth after World War II has been the result of federally funded scientific and engineering research and development. Estimates also suggest the annual monetary return on investment for government-funded research and development is between 25 and 30 percent, a significant economic dividend. The transfer of basic scientific discoveries and engineering developments to the private sector results in new products, growing industrial and financial markets, higher standards of living, improved quality of life, further intellectual advancement, and increased national prestige.

Randall L. Milstein

FURTHER READING

Belanger, D. O. *Enabling American Innovation: Engineering and the National Science Foundation.* West Lafayette, Ind.: Purdue University Press, 1998.

England, J. M. *A Patron for Pure Science: The National Science Foundation's Formative Years, 1945-1957.* Washington, D.C.: National Science Foundation, 1983.

Federal Research and Development Budget and the National Science Foundation: Hearing Before the Subcommittee on Science, Technology, and Space of the United States House of Representatives. Washington, D.C.: U.S. Government Printing Office, 2004.

Kleinman, D. L. *Politics on the Endless Frontier: Postwar Research Policy in the United States.* Durham, N.C.: Duke University Press, 1995.

SEE ALSO: Government spending; Internet; Inventions; Military-industrial complex.

Native American trade

SIGNIFICANCE: Trade between Native Americans and white settlers enabled the newcomers to develop ways to survive and to profit from the rich resources of North America. However, the settlers depleted many of these resources, and contact with whites ultimately destroyed the traditional lifestyles of many Native American tribes.

Trade was occurring among Native American tribes long before Europeans set foot on the North American continent. The need and desire for food, shelter, and tools drove tribes to travel long distances and establish trade with neighbors. Trade provided tribes not only with new resources but also with opportunities to observe new patterns of behavior, new tools, and new techniques and later to incorporate them into their lives. The transformation brought by intertribal trade, however, was insignificant when compared with that brought by trade with whites.

FIRST EUROPEAN CONTACTS

When the Pilgrims landed at Plymouth (later in Massachusetts) in November of 1620, they were ill equipped to establish a life there. Winter loomed ahead, and they feared that their supplies would not last. When they discovered several bushels of maize buried in a rush basket, they took it, intending later to provide recompense to the owner. When they subsequently "paid" the Native Americans for the maize, they began the process of trade that would enable them to survive and prosper and would transform the Pokanokets, the Narragansetts, and other tribes in the region. Although the Pilgrims had brought wheat, barley, and peas to plant in the New World, they soon made maize, a vegetable introduced to them by Native Americans, a staple part of their diet. It grew much better in the New World than the seed that they had brought with them.

The Pilgrims arrived in the New World indebted to those who had financed their voyage. Therefore, trade with the indigenous people in the region was indispensable not only for their survival but also for meeting their financial obligations. By the early 1630's, the Puritans had established trading posts up and down the eastern shores of New England, extending from the Connecticut River to what is now Castine, Maine. From the Dutch, the Pilgrims learned to use wampum, white and purple beads made from shells, as a medium of exchange. In his book *Mayflower: A Story of Courage, Community, and War* (2006), Nathaniel Philbrick estimates that the Pilgrims exported several million dollars worth of pelts (mostly beaver) to England between 1631 and 1636. This was a part of the product of trade with Native Americans. The Pilgrims also used wampum and English goods (such as clothing and firearms) to trade for land. There was a clear intent among the early settlers to be sure that the indigenous people were fairly compensated in trade, whether it was for land or beaver pelts.

Despite this early example of goodwill on the part of white traders, the outbreak of Metacom's War (1675-1676) a generation later demonstrates the ultimate outcome of trade between the English colonists and the Native Americans. The overhunting of beaver had brought about its near extinction in New England and eliminated one of the prime sources of pelts to be traded. Furthermore, the English had acquired more and more Native American land, so that the tribes in the region were beginning to feel crowded. Finally, Native Americans had come to rely so much on European goods, including firearms, that they needed desperately to maintain trade with the colonists. The war was in part an attempt by some Native Americans in New England to rid themselves of the English. However, by the end of Metacom's War, all the tribes in the region had been transformed. Native American culture in the region had been decimated. In his book, Philbrick estimates that the indigenous people in the area lost 60 to 80 percent of their population as a direct or indirect result of the war. This pattern of contact, trade, and transformation continued across the country as the United States developed.

The Nez Perce, whom the Lewis and Clark expedition encountered in 1805 near the Columbia River in the northwest portion of what is now the United States, helped the expedition, as did the Nez Perce's eastern neighbors, the Shoshone. Sacagawea, a Shoshone, guided the group and was a vital resource for them. When Meriwether Lewis and William Clark encountered these tribes, both of these tribes had developed a lifestyle based in part on trade. The Nez Perce had the largest horse herd on the continent. They were able to establish such a herd partly because of their homeland, which had a wide expanse of grasslands and meadows along the Grande Ronde and Wallowa streams. However, the horse was not indigenous to this area or even to North America. The horse herds owned by the Nez Perce were the product of trade.

HORSES

Horses initially came to the Nez Perce through trade with the Cayuse, a neighboring tribe. The Cayuse had acquired these horses from their neighbors,

Navajo at a trading post in Cañon Diablo, on the reservation in Arizona in 1903. (Library of Congress)

the Shoshone, who had sent a trade expedition southward to trade for horses. There would have been no stock for them to acquire had the Spanish not left horses and cattle in what is now Mexico during the sixteenth century. The descendants of those horses spread northward and beyond, becoming a dominant feature and resource for many Native American tribes in the West and enabling tribes such as the Sioux and the Kiowa to establish large patterns of trade with whites and other tribes. It also enabled these tribes to establish a largely nomadic existence that depended almost entirely on hunting buffalo on the Great Plains.

Lewis and Clark's famous expedition opened the way for trade in the West. The first whites who came to the Great Plains after Lewis and Clark were in search of furs, in particular beaver pelts, which were in great demand in the East and in Europe. They trapped beavers and other animals, and they often lived among, traded with, and eventually intermarried with Native Americans. These trappers quickly discovered other resources—in particular the buffalo—in the course of their contact and trade with Native Americans. The demand for buffalo hides and tongues (a delicacy in the East) became so great that within a mere fifty to sixty years, the herds on which the Plains Indians had depended were gone, and their whole way of life was transformed. This happened not because whites traded with Native Americans for buffalo hides but because whites saw in the vast herds of buffalo something the indigenous tribes did not: an opportunity for a quick profit.

BUFFALO

To the Native Americans, the buffalo herds were a resource they lived among, one that provided them with food, shelter, and even spiritual support. Many tribes on the plains incorporated the buffalo into their religious traditions. The reaction of the white frontiersmen to this vast resource can be characterized in a phrase that became a virtual mantra of those who settled the West: Get in, get rich, get out. With gold, with the buffalo, and even with land speculation, "getting out" occurred after the resource was depleted. Because the buffalo was the center of Native American life, the depletion of this resource transformed tribal life in previously unimaginable ways. Native Americans were placed on reservations and forced to adapt to a life sustained by farming and inadequate government rations.

The promises made to Native Americans as they were forced onto reservations exemplify the unfair trading that sometimes occurred between whites and indigenous tribes. In exchange for their land, the tribes were promised reservation life and government rations. However, most of them were given no option other than to take the trade. This pattern was repeated across the country, with the end result that Native Americans lost access to resources that had previously sustained their lives and their cultures. The Nez Perce, who had helped Lewis and Clark, suffered the same fate as the other Native Americans in the West, ultimately losing their homeland.

NEGATIVE INFLUENCES

Trade brought other threats to Native American life. Trading posts became a fixture in frontier existence, and all too often, alcoholic beverages were among the items traded. Native Americans were introduced to alcohol by whites. Their reaction to it was pronounced, leading some scientists to subsequently conclude that Native Americans are genetically more susceptible to alcoholism than whites. What this meant to traders was that alcoholic beverages became not only something to trade but also an inducement for Native Americans to rely on trade. Paul H. Carlson, in *The Plains Indians* (1998), states that trading was a time of celebration on the plains. Carlson quotes a British trader:

> At a few yards distance from the gate (to the Trading Post), they salute us with several discharges of their guns. On entering the house, they are disarmed, treated with a few drams and a bit of tobacco. Indian leaders related the yearly news, relaxing in proportion to the quantity of rum they have swallowed, till at length their voices are drowned in a general clamor.

Although alcohol was banned in some regions and at some trading posts, no one could keep alcohol from playing a significant role in the relationship between Native Americans and whites. All too often, the trading post was the place where this impact was most pronounced. As trade with whites became a common feature of Native American life, it created divisions within tribes. Tradition-following tribe members stood in contrast to what was called the commissary Indian, a tribe member who frequented trading posts for easy access to alcohol and other goods that the whites offered. In the mid-1800's, Native American leaders, including Crazy Horse of the Lakota Sioux and Sitting Bull of the Hunkpapa Sioux, attempted to persuade their tribes to maintain independence from the whites and the goods that they provided, and to live in traditional ways. These leaders and their followers defined themselves in opposition to those Indians who had succumbed to white influences. Ultimately, they were unsuccessful. Nonetheless, in twenty-first century Native American culture, this division still exists. Those Indians who resist the influence of white culture are called traditionals, while those who succumb to the temptations of mainstream culture are known as "apples," red on the outside but white on the inside. The American Indian Movement (AIM), well known for its protests and demonstrations during the 1970's and 1980's, is the modern-day embodiment of the movement for a separate, traditional way of life.

In his book, Carlson argues that trade between whites and Native Americans was embarked on with different expectations, creating a disadvantage for Native Americans. Tribal cultures in general emphasized sharing wealth, even to the point that citizens acquired status in the culture according to the amount they gave away. The philosophy that undergirds such an understanding of material wealth is circular: What a person gives away comes back to that person. Black Elk stated to John G. Neihardt in *Black Elk Speaks* (1932) that everything that Native Americans do is circular; even the houses they build are circular. In some respects this reflects the circularity of the cycles of nature. A culture that reflects the cycles of nature would clearly take a different view of material wealth than a culture that reflects the "mastery" of nature through industrialization.

The whites who traded with Native Americans sought material gain in whatever way possible. The Industrial Revolution in Europe bequeathed to the British culture a sense of respect for those who accumulated goods, not those who gave them away. Thus, the whites who traded with Native Americans by and large sought profit, not merely an equal exchange. Ironically, one theory of the origin of the pejorative expression "Indian giver" underscores the difference between the Native American and the white European understanding of trade. Indians gave and took back because they considered wealth something that passed from one person to another and then back again: What a person gives away will come back to the giver and then back to the recipient in a continuous cycle. However, to whites, trade did not work this way. Their view was that what is gained in trade is kept, never to be returned.

Native Americans were also disadvantaged in trade because of their failure to view land ownership in the same way that whites did. Native Americans inhabited land; whites owned it and profited from it. Philbrick describes the process by which, in 1642, Massasoit, sachem of the Pokanokets, sold to the Pilgrims the land that would become the township of Rehoboth. The deed reports that he "chose out ten fathoms of bead . . . and put them in a basket, and affirmed that he was full satisfied for his land . . . , but he stood upon it that he would have a coat more." What Massasoit could not know was what the Pilgrims would ultimately do with the land. They would raise not only food on it but also cattle. Furthermore, they would clear the land, driving away game that the Pokanokets relied on for food. Finally, more and more settlers would come, driving the price of the land up and crowding the Indians out of the very land they had occupied for generations. Ironically, what the Indians had sold for beads was finally worth much more than that because the whites did with the land what Indians would never have thought to do: turn a profit.

H. William Rice

FURTHER READING

Black Elk. *Black Elk Speaks.* New York: W. Morrow, 1932. A holy man of the Oglala Sioux describes his life to poet and writer John G. Neihardt.

Carlson, Paul H. *The Plains Indians.* College Station: Texas A&M Press, 1998. Presents a very detailed overview of the Plains Indians, including an excellent chapter on trade.

Josephy, Alvin. *The Nez Perce Indians and the Opening of the Northwest.* New York: Houghton Mifflin, 1997. Josephy's account of the opening of the Northwest is rich in detail about the culture of the Nez Perce, their contact with whites (particularly Lewis and Clark), and Chief Joseph's brave struggle to maintain their way of life.

Lewis, Meriwether, and William Clark. *The Journals of Lewis and Clark.* Abridged by Anthony Brandt. Washington, D.C.: National Geographic Adventure Classics, 2002. Lewis and Clark's journey west not only involved trade with the Indians but also was instrumental in opening the West to the hordes of traders that would come after them.

Philbrick, Nathaniel. *Mayflower: A Story of Courage, Community, and War.* New York: Viking, 2006. Philbrick's study of the first century of life among the Pilgrims and their descendants and their Native American neighbors is carefully researched and consequently is a storehouse of information about how trade with Native Americans started in the United States.

SEE ALSO: Alcoholic beverage industry; French and Indian War; Fur trapping and trading; Horses; Indian removal; Interior, U.S. Department of the; Lewis and Clark expedition.

Navigation Acts

THE LAWS: English parliamentary acts restricting the use of non-English ships to conduct trade with England and its colonies

DATES: Passed on October 9, 1651, and September 13, 1660

SIGNIFICANCE: The Navigation Acts tied the American colonies into the British imperial market, restricting the colonies' trade with other powers and encouraging smuggling. Because colonial ships were considered to be English, the acts contributed to the growth of American shipbuilding. After the American Revolution, American ships were no longer colonial vessels, so the acts restricted the ability of the United States to trade with Great Britain.

The Navigation Act of 1651 prohibited non-English vessels from importing goods into England or Ireland. The Navigation Act of 1660 expanded this prohibition to include imports into England's colonies. The second act required that all imports and exports of the colonies be carried in either English or colonial vessels. Goods produced in foreign countries and imported in vessels of their country of origin were exempt. Although colonists were free to trade to foreign countries in their own ships, the act of 1660 also mandated that certain commodities, including many important colonial crops such as sugar, tobacco, and cotton, could be exported only

to England or another English colony. Over time, more commodities were added to this list of restricted goods.

Subsequent amendments and modifications to the Navigation Acts tightened the restrictions on foreign trade to the colonies and imposed duties on trade between colonies. Scottish traders were originally excluded from colonial trade by the acts, but that changed after Scotland united with England to form Great Britain in 1707. Enforcement of the acts was never complete, but they nevertheless aroused much resentment in the colonies, contributing to the outbreak of the American Revolution. After the revolution, American ships were defined as "foreign," and the United States' ability to trade with Britain was restricted. The acts were finally repealed in 1849, as part of the British free trade movement.

William E. Burns

SEE ALSO: Colonial economic systems; European trade with the United States; Gadsden Purchase; International economics and trade; Royal Charters of North American colonies; Stamp Act of 1765; Townshend Act.

NBC. *See* National Broadcasting Company

Neutrality Act of 1794

THE LAW: Federal legislation that prohibited American nationals from being commissioned in a foreign army, hiring people to serve a foreign government, or outfitting ships for the military of a foreign government

DATE: Passed by Congress on June 4, 1794

SIGNIFICANCE: Although the Neutrality Act technically reduced business opportunities by making it illegal to build warships for sale to foreign governments, the main effect of the law was to increase Americans' opportunities for trade with foreign countries that were at war by defining key aspects of American neutrality.

At the beginning of President George Washington's second administration, tensions between Great Britain and France erupted into open warfare. Within the U.S. government, one faction remembered France's support of the Americans during the Revolutionary War and took note of the fact that France had become a republic. Another faction recognized that U.S. trade was conducted almost exclusively with Great Britain. In 1793, the newly appointed French minister to the United States started commissioning Americans as privateers to attack British ships. He also established pseudo-French courts within the United States to confiscate captured cargoes from the British. Thus, for adventurous ship owners who could afford to turn their ships into military vessels, the war presented a golden opportunity.

These privateering actions within its borders were unacceptable to the United States, however. President Washington proclaimed that the United States would remain neutral in the conflict, and he sought to expel the French minister. France's actions and its willing American accomplices motivated the passage of the Neutrality Act of 1794. The law banned such activities by American citizens on behalf of warring nations in conflicts in which the United States was not a participant. An indirect result of the law was that American ships, as vessels of a formally neutral country, would have free passage into the ports of trade of all nations. American shipping made huge gains. However, there were hindrances as well. For example, when the French sought to open their ports in the West Indies to American ships, the British blocked them. Overall, the law has been useful in restricting economic activities that could be harmful to American foreign policy.

Donald A. Watt

SEE ALSO: Constitution, U.S.; Gadsden Purchase; International economics and trade; Revolutionary War; Wars.

New Deal programs

IDENTIFICATION: President Franklin D. Roosevelt's liberal public programs to provide relief for the needy, promote economic recovery, and increase governmental regulation of private businesses

DATE: Launched on March 4, 1933

SIGNIFICANCE: The New Deal programs empowered the federal government to exercise greater control over the national economy, to assist poor and unemployed persons, to recognize and en-

force the right of collective bargaining, and to administer the complex system of Social Security.

The term "New Deal" was first used by Franklin D. Roosevelt in his 1932 speech accepting the Democratic Party's nomination to run for president of the United States. Although vague about specific programs, he promised to govern with "liberal thought," "planned action," and "bold, persistent experimentation." He also advocated a balanced budget and the elimination of "unnecessary functions of government." During this time, the country was in the depths of the Great Depression, with an unemployment rate of 25 percent. In the presidential election, Roosevelt won in a historic landslide (57 percent of the popular vote), and his coattails helped Democrats gain firm control of Congress. The victorious Democrats possessed a popular mandate to pursue policies different from those of the defeated Republicans.

FIRST PHASE, 1933-1934

When Roosevelt took office on March 4, 1933, more than five thousand banks had been forced to close, and the entire banking system appeared to be on the brink of collapse. In his inaugural address, Roosevelt asserted his belief that "the only thing we have to fear is fear itself," and he pledged to "wage war against the emergency" with "direct, vigorous action." In the next few months, called the Hundred Days, the Roosevelt administration cooperated with Congress to enact an unprecedented amount of legislation.

On March 5, Roosevelt unexpectedly declared a four-day "bank holiday." He and his advisers hoped to stop the run on the banks and restore public confidence in the banking system. Officials quickly drafted the Emergency Banking Act, proposing that Department of Treasury inspectors examine the banks and then announce which ones were financially sound. Congress approved the legislation on March 9, and within three days almost one thousand banks were operating without fear of panic. To secure lasting confidence in the system, Congress passed the Glass-Steagall Act, which created the Federal Deposit Insurance Corporation (FDIC), giving the government's guarantee that depositors might safely keep their money in banking accounts.

Additional laws of the Hundred Days further enlarged governmental intervention into the nation's

A 1934 political cartoon satirizes the proliferation of New Deal legislation. (Library of Congress)

economy. The Civilian Conservation Corps (CCC) was a popular program employing two million young men to work in environmental projects. The Federal Emergency Relief Act created the Federal Emergency Relief Administration (FERA), which provided relief funds for the destitute. The first Agricultural Adjustment Act taxed distributors and processors of food to provide funds to farmers in exchange for limiting production of livestock and specific crops, with the goal of increasing the prices of agricultural products.

The Tennessee Valley Authority (TVA) was a massive construction project consisting of thirty dams to control flooding and thirteen power plants to provide cheap electricity for one of the nation's depressed regions. The controversial National Industrial Recovery Act (NRA), with its symbol of the Blue Eagle, provided for the organization of business and governmental officials into industry boards empowered to set minimum wages, price guidelines, and working conditions in particular industries.

In 1934, the first phase of the New Deal came to an end with a flurry of legislation that established new regulatory structures. The Securities Exchange Act prohibited abuses such as insider trading and es-

tablished the Securities and Exchange Commission (SEC), which was authorized to make rules and regulate the trade in stocks. The Corporate Bankruptcy Act permitted the reorganization of corporations if two-thirds of their creditors consented. The Federal Communications Act imposed new rules on radio broadcasting and established the Federal Communications Commission (FCC), which was authorized to regulate interstate and foreign communications by telegraph, cable, and radio. The National Housing Act founded the Federal Housing Administration (FHA) for the purpose of insuring loans made by banks, building and loan associations, and other private lending institutions.

SECOND PHASE, 1935-1938

While continuing relief and recovery programs, the second phase of the New Deal put a new emphasis on social and economic reforms designed to help working people, the unemployed, and the elderly. Roosevelt announced this change of direction in his annual address to Congress on January 4, 1935. In large part, Roosevelt was reacting to the left-wing critics of the New Deal, particularly Huey Long, who advocated a massive redistribution of wealth, and Francis Townsend, who proposed an expensive program of benefits for older citizens.

The two most significant legislative reforms of the New Deal's second phase were the National Labor Relations Act (NLRA) of 1935 and the Social Security Act (SSA) of 1935. The NLRA, or the Wagner Act, guaranteed that workers could organize unions for collective bargaining, outlawed a large number of unfair employer practices, and established the National Labor Relations Board (NLRB) to enforce the right of workers to choose their union representatives. The Social Security Act enrolled working Americans in a pension program that guaranteed retirement income, and it also provided states with funds for disability and unemployment insurance, as well as for single mothers with dependent children. This ambitious entitlement program was financed by a tax on employer payrolls, a policy that many progressives denounced as regressive in its impact.

Other important programs were also started in 1935. The Works Progress Administration (WPA) dwarfed previous relief programs by giving employment to almost one-third of the country's jobless. The Revenue Act of 1935 made the personal and corporate income taxes more progressive, increasing the surtax rate on incomes over $50,000 and taxing incomes in excess of $5 million at the rate of 75 percent. The Public Utility Holding Company Act broke up the oligopoly that some thirteen holding companies exercised over gas and electric operating companies, and it restricted such companies to operations within a single area.

A number of programs were designed to improve conditions in rural areas. The Soil Conservation and Domestic Allotment Act of 1935 established the Soil Conservation Service as a permanent unit to control and prevent soil erosion. The Rural Electrification Administration (REA), established by executive order as authorized by Congress, made extremely low-interest loans to farmers' cooperatives and utility companies to extend electrical power to 90 percent of the population that lacked such power. The Resettlement Administration, which was absorbed by the Farm Security Administration in 1937, resettled low-income families from areas of limited potential and loaned them money to purchase farmlands and equipment.

The Supreme Court's decision in *Schechter Poultry Corp. v. United States* (1935), which struck down the National Industrial Recovery Act as unconstitutional, marked the beginning of a bitter conflict between the Roosevelt administration and the Court. Even though Roosevelt had become dissatisfied with the controversial NRA, he feared that the Court might strike down his more successful programs. In 1936, these fears were reinforced by *United States v. Butler,* which invalidated the way that the Agricultural Adjustment Administration was financed. Democratic landslide victories in the elections of that year provided evidence of public support for the New Deal. Convinced of his popular mandate, Roosevelt in early 1937 proposed a "court-packing" bill that would have added an additional justice for each justice over the age of seventy. Although Congress refused to pass the bill, one moderately conservative justice began to vote with the four liberal justices, a change often called the "judicial revolution of 1937." Soon thereafter, Roosevelt was able to appoint justices with liberal perspectives on constitutional jurisprudence, thereby ending the conflict.

In 1937, Roosevelt signed into law the National Housing Act, which appropriated $500 billion for a program of slum clearance and public housing, establishing a foundation for the expanded programs of the postwar years. By this time, Roosevelt, concerned about large deficits and believing that the economy was rebounding, decided to cut back on relief programs. Unfortunately, the stock market reacted negatively, and the unemployment rate grew to an alarming extent. In 1938, Congress enacted the second Agricultural Adjustment Act, which satisfied the Supreme Court's objection to the way that the first act had been financed. Later that year, Congress enacted the last major piece of New Deal legislation, the Fair Labor Standards Act, which outlawed child labor and set a minimum wage of 40 cents per hour and a maximum workweek of forty hours. In addition to helping exploited workers, the act was motivated by the desire of northern manufacturers to minimize the competitive advantage that the low wages paid in the South gave to southern firms.

LEGACY OF NEW DEAL PROGRAMS

By 1938, New Deal liberals, increasingly under attack, were forced into a defensive position. A powerful coalition of Republicans and conservative southern Democrats was able to slash appropriations and reduce corporate taxes. Conservatives on the House Committee on Un-American Activities launched a well-publicized investigation of communist influences within New Deal agencies. In the mid-term Democratic primaries, voters reacted negatively to Roosevelt's attempts to "purge" anti-New Deal Democratic senators, and in the November elections, Republicans made major gains in both the Senate and the House, as well as in state contests. In his state of the union address of January, 1939, Roosevelt expressed the need to "preserve our reforms," while he proposed no new domestic policies.

With the outbreak of World War II, the growing demand for labor eliminated the need for relief programs such as the Civil Conservation Corps and the Works Progress Administration. In a press conference of 1943, Roosevelt observed that New Deal programs had been enacted during a period in which the United States was "an awfully sick patient," and he declared that it was now time for "Dr. New Deal" to be replaced by "Dr. Win-the-War." Although conservatives continued to denounce the New Deal, they made almost no attempts to abrogate its core programs: Social Security, subsidies for farmers, minimum-wage legislation, the banning of child labor, defense of collective bargaining, and banking and securities regulations. These programs had become firmly entrenched as foundations within the new economic and social order produced by the New Deal.

In subsequent years, moreover, many of these programs would be expanded on a piecemeal basis. When the United States entered World War II in December, 1941, Roosevelt would be able further to institutionalize the New Deal's most important legacy, governmental regulation of the economy. Following the war, the number of New Deal-inspired programs would continue to proliferate in Harry S. Truman's Fair Deal and even more in Lyndon B. Johnson's Great Society.

Thomas Tandy Lewis

FURTHER READING

Alter, Jonathan. *The Defining Moment: FDR's Hundred Days and the Triumph of Hope.* New York: Simon & Schuster, 2007. Compelling narrative account of how President Roosevelt and his advisers dealt with the banking crisis and cooperated with Congress to enact the many significant laws of early 1933.

Kennedy, David M. *Freedom from Fear: The American People in Depression and War, 1929-1945.* New York: Oxford University Press, 1999. The first half of this Pulitzer Prize-winning book presents an informed account of the New Deal within its historical context.

Leuchtenburg, William. *Franklin D. Roosevelt and the New Deal, 1932-1940.* New York: Harper & Row, 1963. Written by a Roosevelt admirer who lived during the period, this popular book has long been recognized as one of the best syntheses ever written about the New Deal.

Rosen, Elliott A. *Roosevelt, the Great Depression, and the Economics of Recovery.* Charlottesville: University Press of Virginia, 2007. Discussing corporate regulations, social welfare, and monetary and fiscal policies, Rosen takes a critical view of the government's efforts to regulate the economy.

Sitkiff, Harvard. *New Deal for Blacks: The Emergence of Civil Rights as a National Issue.* New York: Oxford University Press, 1981. Discusses the extent to which the New Deal benefited African Americans, emphasizing the roles of persons like Mary McLeod Bethune and Robert Weaver.

Smith, Jason Scott. *Building New Deal Liberalism: The Political Economy of Public Works, 1933-1956.* New York: Cambridge University Press, 2005. In this historical account of public works programs, Smith argues that the New Deal produced a revolution in economic development and laid the foundations for postwar development.

Smith, Jean Edward. *FDR.* New York: Random House, 2007. Probably the most interesting and well-written biography ever written about Roosevelt, with a good balance between his personal life and public policies.

SEE ALSO: Banking; Farm Credit Administration; Federal Deposit Insurance Corporation; Federal Trade Commission; Food Stamp Plan; Great Depression; National Labor Relations Board; Presidency, U.S.; Social Security system; Tennessee Valley Authority; World War II.

New York Stock Exchange

IDENTIFICATION: Facility in New York at which traders and brokers buy and sell stock and securities
DATE: Opened on May 17, 1792
SIGNIFICANCE: The New York Stock Exchange (NYSE), nicknamed the Big Board, is the oldest and largest stock exchange in the United States, and the largest stock exchange in the world by dollar volume.

The New York Stock Exchange (NYSE) is a platform for buyers and sellers to trade shares of stock in publicly registered companies. Trading on this exchange is conducted in bonds and stocks as well as financial futures and options. Generally, to be listed on the NYSE, a company must submit a title; descriptions of its properties; a statement of its status under the Federal Securities Act; a list of any companies with which it is affiliated; details of its management, dividend records, capitalization, and conversion rights; information about labor relations and any pending legal matters; and its financial statements, including its debt and policies of account keeping.

The NYSE is divided into "seats." Originally, the number of seats increased or decreased as members joined or resigned. In 1868, the number of seats was fixed at 533, but in 1953, this number was extended to 1,366 seats. Owning a seat enables a person to trade on the floor of the exchange, either for that individual's personal account (floor trader) or as an agent for someone else (floor broker).

HISTORY

The New York Stock Exchange originated on May 17, 1792, when twenty-four New York city stockbrokers and merchants signed the Buttonwood Agreement outside 68 Wall Street under a buttonwood tree. By this two-sentence agreement, they promised to trade only with each other and abide by a 0.25 percent commission. Thus, three government bonds and two bank stocks began to be traded.

On March 8, 1817, the Buttonwood Agreement was drafted into a constitution, by which the organization was renamed the New York Stock and Exchange Board. With Anthony Stockholm as its first president, the exchange raised the trading level to thirty stocks. That same year, the exchange moved to bigger premises at 40 Wall Street. In 1863, the name of the organization was shortened to its current form, the New York Stock Exchange.

From the establishment of the NYSE until 1871, trading on the exchange was done in a "call market" fashion, a system by which only one company's stock trades across the whole exchange at any one time. The members would sit in their seats and participate in the buying and selling of desired stocks as if they were at an auction. After 1871, the trading of stocks became simultaneous, and floor trading became the norm. Prices for seats on the exchange are determined by supply and demand, and they have ranged from $500,000 during the mid-1930's to $4 million during the early 1990's.

The first half of the twentieth century was marked by not only innovations but also struggles. The NYSE was not immune to the ravages of warfare. It closed at the beginning of World War I (July, 1914); however, it reopened on November 28 of that same year, in an effort to boost the economy by trading bonds. On September 16, 1920, a bomb ex-ploded outside the NYSE, killing thirty-three people and injuring more than four hundred. The bombers were never found. In 1929, the Great Depression was precipitated, if not caused, by the crash of the NYSE on October 24, 1929, known as Black Thursday, and the subsequent sell-off panic on October 29, known as Black Tuesday.

On October 1, 1934, the NYSE was registered as a national securities exchange with the U.S. Securities and Exchange Commission. The organization consisted of a president and thirty-three board members. To help the economy and bolster investor confidence in the markets, the NYSE created an investor protection program on October 31, 1938.

In 1966, the exchange created the NYSE Composite Index, a market-value-weighted price index that includes all common stocks listed on the NYSE, including American Depositary Receipts (ADRs), Real Estate Investment Trusts (REITs), and tracking stocks. The index measures all common stocks listed on the exchange and four subgroup indexes: industrial, transportation, utility, and finance. It encompasses 61 percent of the total market capitalization of all publicly traded companies around the world. The base was set at 50 points when the index was established, but it was recalculated to reflect a base value of 5,000 as of December 31, 2002. Because the index tracks change in the market value of

---

NYSE TRADING VOLUME FIRSTS

Volume	Year First Reached
1 million	1886
5 million	1928
10 million	1929
50 million	1978
100 million	1982
500 million	1987
1 billion	1997
2 billion	2001
3 billion	2005
4 billion	2007
5 billion	2007

Source: Data from the New York Stock Exchange
Note: Volume is number of stocks traded in a single day.

common stocks, it is a fairly good indicator of the strength of the market.

On February 18, 1971, the NYSE was first incorporated as a not-for-profit corporation, and the number of board members was reduced to twenty-five.

THE BUILDING

The NYSE was first located outside 68 Wall Street, by a buttonwood tree, and when the weather was inclement, at the Tontine Coffee House. In 1812, the exchange moved to its first permanent home, a rented room at 40 Wall Street.

In 1903, the NYSE moved to 18 Broad Street. The exchange commissioned the construction of the building to architect George B. Post. The neoclassic building was ornamented with a pediment designed by John Quincy Adams Ward, a prolific American sculptor. The figures in the pediment represent American commerce. The central figure symbolizes integrity, flanked by figures personifying sources of wealth: agriculture and mining to the left, and science and industry and invention to the right. The building is considered one of Post's masterpieces, and it is a New York and national landmark.

BUSINESS

The last two decades of the twentieth century and first of the twenty-first were full of distress and controversy. On Black Monday, October 19, 1987, the world stock markets crashed, and the Dow Jones Industrial Average dropped 508 points. By the end of October, the NYSE had fallen more than 22 percent. A lesser crash took place on October 27, 1997. Then, for the second time in its history, the NYSE closed its doors, ceasing business after the September 11, 2001, attacks on the World Trade Center, to reopen on September 17, 2001.

In September, 2003, the news of its chair, Richard Grasso, receiving $140 million in a deferred compensation package shocked NYSE shareholders. Grasso was subsequently replaced by John S. Reed, former chair of Citigroup.

In 2005, the NYSE launched an initiative to reorganize itself to become a publicly traded company. On December 6, it acquired Archipelago Holdings, which operates an open all-electronic stock market in the United States. The newly publicly traded company was renamed the NYSE Group on March 8, 2006.

In August of 2006, NYSE chief executive officer John Thain made public his plan to create a blended electronic and floor-based auction market. Chief Technology Officer Roger Burkhardt was commissioned to create this hybrid market. The NYSE had been keeping up with technological innovations; traders already had such tools as wireless handhelds, but under the new system, stocks could be traded as an immediate response to a customer's electronic order. The NYSE hybrid market was launched on January 24, 2007.

On April 4, 2007, the NYSE merged with Euronext, the pan-European stock exchange, creating a truly global financial marketplace group and the world's largest and most liquid exchange group. Jan-Michiel Hessels became chair, with Marshall N. Carter as the deputy chair. The NYSE Euronext is the first trans-Atlantic stock market, with exchanges in New York, Paris, Brussels, Amsterdam, and Lisbon, in addition to automated trading desks and six derivatives and futures markets, including Liffe, which trades more than two trillion euros worth of derivatives a day. In 2007, the NYSE listed more than 4,800 companies, including most of the largest U.S. and international corporations, whose combined capitalization was $25 trillion.

The NYSE has declared that its mission is to add value to the capital-raising and asset-management processes by providing a self-regulated marketplace for the trading of financial instruments, and to serve as a forum for discussion of relevant national and international policy issues.

Rikard Bandebo

FURTHER READING

Buck, James E. *The New York Stock Exchange: Another Century.* Old Saybrook, Conn.: Greenwich, 1999. Limited revised edition containing the history of the NYSE up to 1999, illustrated with more than 250 photographs of the trading floor.

Gasparino, Charles. *King of the Club: Richard Grasso and the Survival of the New York Stock Exchange.* New York: Collins, 2007. Well-documented reconstruction of the events that led to the rise and fall of New York Stock Exchange chair Richard Grasso. The author uses the scandal to offer the reader a look inside the boardroom and at the technological changes initiated at the NYSE during the 1990's.

McPherson, Aaron. *NYSE and Euronext: The Crow*

Tastes Pretty Good Here! Framingham, Mass.: IDC Research, 2007. In-depth review of all the causes, financial terms, and consequences of the merger of the NYSE and Euronext.

Noble, Henry George Stebbins. *The New York Stock Exchange in the Crisis of 1914.* Detroit: University of Michigan Library, 2005. Detailed examination of the first time that the NYSE was forced to close its doors; essential to understand the effects of World War I in the United States and the role of the NYSE.

Sobel, Robert. *The Big Board: A History of the New York Stock Market.* Knoxville, Tenn.: Beard Books, 2000. An insightful short account of Wall Street and of American economic growth from the eighteenth century to 1965.

Weiner, Eric J. *What Goes Up: The Uncensored History of Modern Wall Street as Told by the Bankers, Brokers, CEOs, and Scoundrels Who Made It Happen.* Newport Beach, Calif.: Back Bay Books, 2007. Weiner, a former Wall Street journalist, offers the reader an insightful perspective based on primary sources, mostly interviews.

SEE ALSO: American Stock Exchange; Black Monday; Bond industry; Commodity markets; Dow Jones Industrial Average; Financial crisis of 2008; NASDAQ; Securities and Exchange Commission; Standard & Poor's; Stock market crash of 1929; Wall Street.

Newspaper industry

DEFINITION: Enterprises that market, print, and distribute, as well as produce or secure content and advertisements for, daily or weekly news publications

SIGNIFICANCE: Early newspapers fostered the growth of democracy and promoted citizen participation in national, state, and local governments. Over time, they continued to create interest in society's concerns, and their use of advertising not only furthered their own financial profits but also affected the profits of other businesses.

Newspapers are daily and weekly publications sold to the public that convey information about current events. Their avowed reason for being is to impart news. However, they have also become important sources of information about products and services, thanks to the relatively large amount of advertising they contain.

NEWSPAPERS IN THE AMERICAN COLONIES

A Boston printer named Benjamin Harris of Boston published the first American newspaper in 1690. A single-page newssheet called *Publick Occurrences, Both Forreign and Domestick,* it reported on Indian raids, fever and flu outbreaks, and a scandal about France's Louis XIV. Harris's first issue, however, was also his last, as two ministers, Increase Mather and Cotton Mather, suppressed the paper's publication because Harris had failed to obtain a publishing license.

Three other American newspapers were publishing by 1730: *The Boston Newsletter,* begun in 1704, and for fifteen years the only paper in the colonies; *The Boston Gazette,* started in 1719; and *The New England Courant,* started in 1721 by Benjamin Franklin's half brother. These papers carried mostly news about arrival and departure times for ships traveling the Atlantic, three-month-old news from England, and simple advertisements for lost, found, or for-sale items. Each copy, bought mainly through subscription by the more prosperous colonists, was read by as many as twenty people, passed from person to person eager to receive European and colonial news or read aloud in a coffee shop or on someone's porch. Printing these newspapers involved a slow, laborious process, as each issue was produced with a manually operated hand press, using hand-inked, hand-set type on flat sheets of paper.

When the colonies' rebellion started, the newspapers carried opinions about revolution and letters to the editors with reactions to those views. By the 1730's, some newspapers had been openly or covertly subsidized by political officials desiring a way to present their "official" versions of public affairs. The papers, often atrociously printed with old-fashioned type, contained hearsay items; short obituaries of upper-class colonists or foreign royalty; notices of rewards for runaway apprentices, servants, and slaves; and even excerpts from books or European periodicals as space fillers. The actual reporting of news along the model of modern journalism was unheard of. The printer of the newspaper was the editor, publisher, and writer.

When the colonies became the United States, the

First Amendment to the Constitution established freedom of the press in 1791, guaranteeing the press the right to print information and opinions without prior government restraint. A trial in 1735 against John Peter Zenger, publisher of the *New York Weekly Journal*, confirmed that critical comments published in a newspaper are not libelous if they are true.

NINETEENTH CENTURY PROGRESS

Newspaper circulation increased to a few thousand readers during the nineteenth century as a result of faster printing presses and mechanical typesetting. The Hoe cylinder press, patented in 1847, revolutionized the printing process. Where earlier printing involved manually pressing hand-inked, hand-set type on flat single sheets, the Hoe press used a revolving cylinder to hold the type, which could roll rapidly over the paper and produce eight thousand one-sided copies per hour. A later, improved model, called the Hoe web perfecting press, could print on both sides of the sheet and produce eighteen thousand sheets per hour.

The telegraph and the telephone made it possible to compile far-ranging news in a more timely manner; more and fresher news increased circulation. Costs for publishing newspapers fell as circulation increased. Circulation increased as the newspaper publishers printed more news of interest to "lower stratum" readers, who bought papers to read courtroom news, stories advocating social reform, or crime or human interest stories. This growing interest in news led to the use of newsboys and newsgirls hawking one-cent-a-copy papers on city streets for readers on their way to work or shopping.

Whereas early newspapers were available mostly by subscription, newspapers such as *The New York Tribune*, founded by Horace Greeley in 1841; *The New York Sun*, Benjamin Davis's paper founded in 1833; and *The New York Morning Herald*, later *The Herald*, founded by George Gordon Bennett in 1835, were among the 715 American newspapers being sold to a wider readership, on the streets as well as by subscription. The West Coast was able to receive East Coast and European news much faster. Before the telegraph was invented, it took three months for news to travel by ship around Cape Horn to the West Coast; the new technology brought it in a matter of days.

NEW TECHNOLOGIES AND METHODS

As the U.S. Civil War approached, the new technologies and the increased desire of readers to follow current events caused the newspaper business to develop new ways to engage its readerships. Illustrations were more widely used in papers such as New York's *Frank Leslie's Illustrated Newspaper* and *Harper's Weekly*. These newspapers printed the news of the day, exposés, sports news, and even fiction—illustrated by accomplished artists such as Thomas Nast, best known for his political cartoons, and Winslow Homer. Matthew Brady was taking extraordinary photographs of the war at the time, but news presses could not yet reproduce photographs.

The cost of the new technologies could not be recovered by subscriptions and street sales alone. The newer presses, paper, and workers' wages required a constant outlay of money that cut into profits. Consequently, advertisements were sought from any feasible source, with little regard to the quality of the product or service being advertised. Soon, anyone who could afford it was buying space in newspapers, whose circulation numbers almost guaranteed wide exposure for advertisers. Because greedy newspapers allowed practically anyone to advertise, for a time brothels, individual prostitutes, vendors of quack medicines and treatments, and other questionable sellers bought ads. This period was not an admirable one, but the revenues generated from such ads helped the industry progress.

Another innovation during this era was the use of correspondents who did on-the-spot reporting. As far back as 1849, newspapers had relied on a news-gathering agency, the Associated Press, to supply reports of what was happening around the nation and the world. When the Civil War began, many newspapers realized they could send their own reporters to battle sites for firsthand stories. The Confederate States' newspapers, however, did not have sufficient individual reporters, so they started the Press Association of the Confederate States of America, an agency that gathered war news for dissemination among the Confederate newspapers. The Confederate States' papers also had another problem: Nearly all American paper mills were located in the North, so there was a severe shortage of newsprint. The shortage became so severe that many of the southern newspapers had to cease publication altogether, while those remaining in operation used any paper they could find, including wrapping paper and even wallpaper.

By the end of the nineteenth century, innovative machines brought newspaper publishing to a new zenith. Aside from the machine that mechanically folded the papers, there was the Linotype machine, developed by Ottmar Mergenthaler. Its typewriter-type keyboard decreased typesetting time to one-third the time it took by hand, producing whole lines of type on metal slugs. It had more than ten thousand moving parts, and its operators needed more than four years of training and experience to learn to operate the machine correctly. The web-perfecting press, meanwhile, could print on both sides of a sheet of paper, which by this time was mounted on huge rolls instead of flat sheets. A half-tone engraving technique gave a three-dimensional shading effect to illustrations for greater realism. Cheaper paper was available, made of wood pulp instead of the previously used, more expensive rag paper. Typographical errors were reduced with the use of the newly invented, more efficient typewriter.

ERA OF GREAT AMERICAN NEWSPAPERS

In 1870, there were 5,091 newspapers operating in the United States. *The Washington Post* was started in 1877, with a circulation of ten thousand and a cost of 3 cents per copy. Other great American newspapers were established before the end of the century. Joseph Pulitzer started the *St. Louis Post-Dispatch* and then New York City's *The World*, which was said by some to be the "greatest of all newspapers." William Randolph Hearst started the *New York Journal* and helped start the trend of "yellow journalism" (named for the rival *World*'s comic strip character the Yellow Kid, after the *Journal* and the *World* began a feud). Hearst also published a tabloid, *The Daily Mirror*, that reported on tragedies, murders, disasters, and scandals of the rich and famous. His papers and Pulitzer's are believed to have helped instigate American participation in the Spanish-American War of 1898.

The New York Times, started by Adolph Ochs in 1895, set a different standard from its raucous contemporaries, saying its aim was to publish "all the news that's fit to print," referring to its goal of limiting itself to serious news coverage. *The Kansas City Evening Star* and *The Chicago Tribune* also began publishing between 1880 and 1900. Edward W. Scripps, publisher of the Cleveland *Press*, set up the Scripps-McRae League in 1895, the first newspaper chain in the United States. With the publications of Scripps, Pulitzer, and Hearst, the great American newspaper empires of the twentieth century had begun.

MODERN CONTROVERSIES

After World War II, even faster machines and potentially damaging labor concerns stirred up the newspaper business as never before. Photocomposition machines again changed the printing process, setting type six times faster than earlier machines and using 25 percent less ink than before. The highly trained, unionized Linotype operators believed, rightfully, that the new technology would eliminate their jobs, because the new machines could be operated by anyone with decent motor skills. To resolve their concerns and forestall damaging labor strikes, newspaper publishers, seeking ways to reduce costs and increase profits, and the workers, seeking mainly to hold on to their jobs, negotiated until a satisfactory agreement was reached and progress continued. The newspapers improved: More color pictures and photographs were used, and more copies were printed faster—the new presses could print eighty-five thousand copies of a sixty-four-page paper in about an hour.

Many Americans headed for the suburbs during the 1940's and 1950's, and readership of daily papers dropped. However, more Sunday papers were read, and during the 1980's, an innovative national daily, *USA Today*, featuring a mix of national news and other items of interest, soon became the

---

PRIMARY NEWS SOURCES FOR INTERNET USERS, 2005

Television, 60%
National televison, 49%
Radio, 49%
Local newspaper, 38%
Internet, 35%
National newspaper, 14%

Source: Data from the *Statistical Abstract of the United States, 2008* (Washington, D.C.: Department of Commerce, Economics and Statistics Administration, Bureau of the Census, Data User Services Division, 2008)

second-most-read daily in the country, after *The New York Times*. Radio and television began cutting into newspaper advertising revenues, however. Serious decreases began in the twenty-first century, although certain factors in 1990 already predicted a slide in revenue. These included a weakening national economy, changes in the industry, and slumps in the markets that purchased advertising. Some newspapers, such as *The San Francisco Chronicle*, suffered serious financial losses of as much as $1 million per week. Advertising revenue records showed a 10 percent drop between 2006 and 2007. Circulation revenue, newspapers' second-largest source of revenue after advertising, grew some 5.5 times between 1975 and 2005. During this time, circulation revenue reached 31 cents to every dollar of advertising revenue. By 2005, it had dropped to 24 cents.

In spite of the industry's problems, about 51 million people continued to buy newspapers during the early twenty-first century; at least 124 million read them. The industry, acutely aware of a decrease in interest in its print versions, sought new ways to keep its customers and attract new ones. They began to experiment with different revenue models based on online journalism, an extremely popular source of information for millions of Americans, but one that users expected to be free.

Jane L. Ball

Further Reading

Blau, Judith R., and Cheryl Elman. "The Institutionalization of U.S. Political Parties: Patronage Newspapers." *Sociological Inquiry* 72, no. 4 (Fall, 2002): 576-599. Examines the implications of the emergence of federal political parties and the establishment of newspapers in Washington, D.C.

Douglas, George H. *The Golden Age of the Newspaper.* Westport, Conn.: Greenwood Press, 1999. Discusses newspaper history from early penny papers through tabloids.

Fink, Stanley. *Sentinel Under Siege: The Triumphs and Trouble of America's Free Press.* Boulder, Colo.: Westview Press, 1997. An examination of freedom of the press and media criticism's endeavors to create a greater sense of responsibility among the press.

Horn, Maurice. *One Hundred Years of American Newspaper Comics.* New York: Gramercy, 1996. An illustrated history of significant American comic

strips. Useful in spite of some factual inaccuracies.

Madigan, Charles M., ed. *The Collapse of the Great American Newspaper.* Chicago: Ivan R. Dee, 2007. A series of essays and articles theorizing about the decline of the newspaper industry.

Meyer, Philip. *The Vanishing Newspaper: Saving Journalism in the Information Age.* Columbia: University of Missouri Press, 2004. Discusses ways to reverse the growing failure of the newspaper business by addressing the factors affecting it and incorporating the changing technologies that could help save it.

See also: Advertising industry; Book publishing; Cable News Network; Magazine industry; Muckraking journalism; Papermaking industry; Printing industry; *USA Today*; *The Wall Street Journal*.

9/11. *See* September 11 terrorist attacks

Nixon's China visit

The Event: A visit by the U.S. president to the People's Republic of China that signaled an end to China's isolation and opened a new era of Sino-American relations

Date: February 21-27, 1972

Place: People's Republic of China

Significance: Nixon's visit was one of the defining moments of the Cold War, signifying a tremendous shift in relations between the United States and China as part of a grand strategy of Nixon and his national security adviser to use China as a counterweight to the Soviet Union. Although undertaken for diplomatic and geopolitical purposes, Nixon's trip opened China to greater contact with the United States and provided greater opportunities for Americans to engage in business with China, especially exporting products, technology, and services to China's vast population.

Shortly after taking office in January, 1969, President Richard M. Nixon indicated to National Security Adviser Henry Kissinger that he sought to improve relations with the People's Republic of China. At roughly the same time, China was seeking to move closer to the United States because of its tensions with its huge neighbor, the Soviet Union. Nixon feared opposition from the U.S. State Department and kept the role of Secretary of State William Rogers to a minimum. The first significant contact between the two nations was made via the U.S. ambassador to Poland, Walter Stoessel, who expressed to Chinese diplomats Nixon's desire for talks with China. Back-channel negotiations were also conducted through Romania and Pakistan, with the Pakistani contacts yielding an indication from Chinese prime minister Zhou Enlai (Chou En-lai) that China would accept a visit from a high-level American official.

President Richard Nixon shakes hands with Mao Zedong during his 1972 visit to China. (AP/Wide World Photos)

Kissinger made a secret trip to China from July 9 to 11, 1971, met with Zhou, and arranged for a formal invitation to be extended to the president. In a televised statement on July 15, 1971, Nixon announced that he would visit China in 1972. U.S. policy shifted to support admission of China to the United Nations and its Security Council. Subsequent visits by Kissinger and other American officials finalized the details for Nixon's visit to China, which took place in February of 1972.

Seeking maximum publicity for his historic journey, Nixon insisted on prominent television coverage. He met several times with Zhou and once with the ailing chair of the Chinese Communist Party, Mao Zedong. Kissinger had numerous discussions with Zhou and other Chinese officials. The visit also included sightseeing and several state banquets. Although Kissinger played down trade issues, the official communiqué presented on February 27, 1972, did note that both countries sought to "facilitate" trade. However, the main points of the communiqué focused on "normalization" of relations between China and the United States. It stipulated that there was one China and Taiwan was part of it, and that the United States would withdraw troops from Taiwan.

Although Taiwan was furious and felt betrayed, Nixon's efforts were hailed elsewhere as a tremendous breakthrough. In April, 1972, the Chinese table-tennis team visited the United States, and the nations exchanged animals: The United States received pandas, and China received musk oxen. Further progress between China and the United States was hindered by the Watergate crisis and Mao's deteriorating health. Real advances came subsequent to President Jimmy Carter's decision to accord diplomatic recognition to China in 1979 and to leadership changes in China.

Mark C. Herman

FURTHER READING

Dallek, Robert. *Nixon and Kissinger.* New York: HarperCollins, 2007.

MacMillan, Margaret. *Nixon and Mao.* New York: Random House, 2007.

SEE ALSO: Asian financial crisis of 1997; Asian trade with the United States; Chinese trade with the United States; International economics and trade; Japanese trade with the United States; Taiwanese trade with the United States.

NLRB. *See* National Labor Relations Board

Nooyi, Indra K.

IDENTIFICATION: Chair and chief executive officer of a global beverage and food corporation

BORN: October 28, 1955; Madras (now Chennai), Tamil Nadu, India

SIGNIFICANCE: As the head of PepsiCo, the world's fourth-largest beverage and food producer, Nooyi was ranked the most powerful businesswoman in the world by *Fortune* magazine in 2006 and 2007.

Indra K. Nooyi graduated from Holy Angels School in Madras in India before attending Madras Christian College. After graduating with a bachelor's degree in chemistry in 1974, she received a graduate degree from the Indian Institute of Management in Calcutta in 1976. She then transferred to Yale School of Management, where she received a master's degree in 1980. After graduation, she began working for the Boston Consulting Group but quickly moved on to strategy positions at Motorola and Asea Brown Bovari.

Her employment with PepsiCo began in 1994 as a senior vice president for strategic management. She recommended that the company spin off its fast-food holdings—Taco Bell, KFC, and Pizza Hut—into Tricon Global Restaurants (which later became Yum! Brands) and acquire Tropicana and Quaker Oats. In 2001, she was named the president and chief financial officer (CFO) of PepsiCo. After she became the CFO, PepsiCo's revenues rose 72 percent on an annual basis, and its net profits more than doubled, reaching $5.6 billion in 2006. She was named the chief executive officer of PepsiCo on October 1, 2006, and became chair of the board in May, 2007.

Nooyi has also served on the boards of Motorola Corporation, the Federal Reserve Bank of New York, the International Rescue Committee, and the Lincoln Center for Performing Arts. She has been the Successor Fellow at Yale and was ranked third on *Forbes* magazine's 2008 list of the World's One Hundred Most Powerful Women.

Richard L. Wilson

SEE ALSO: Coca-Cola Company; Cola industry; Fast-food restaurants; Restaurant industry; Women in business.

North American Free Trade Agreement

IDENTIFICATION: Trilateral trade and common tariff agreement among the United States, Mexico, and Canada

SIGNFICANCE: The North American Free Trade Agreement significantly altered the economic relationship among businesses in the United States, Canada, and Mexico by approximating the conditions of a common market. The agreement created the largest free trade area in the world and sparked considerable controversy over exactly who benefits most from its terms.

The North American Free Trade Agreement (NAFTA) was negotiated between 1991 and 1992, with additional agreements incorporated in 1993 to shore up U.S. ratification and allow the accord to go into effect on January 1, 1994. The two supplemental agreements were the North American Agreement on Environmental Cooperation (NAAEC) and the North American Agreement on Labor Cooperation (NAALC). NAFTA's main objectives included the promotion of a more harmonious development and a greater expansion of trade among its member nations. All of its objectives were consistent with the interests of broad sectors of the American, Canadian, and Mexican business communities. For this reason, the passage of NAFTA largely symbolized the triumph of probusiness lobbies in the three member countries.

NAFTA also increased the pressure on labor unions, particularly in the United States and Canada, and enlarged the possibilities that environmental regulations in these countries could be bypassed by "environmental dumping," that is, relocation of contaminating industries to Mexico, where environmental protection and enforcement is generally weaker. For Mexico, closer ties with American business through NAFTA meant driving a wedge between it and the rest of Latin America. It also required reforms of certain aspects of its development model, including an earlier liberalization of the restrictive rules of collective land tenure that dated back to the Mexican Revolution of 1910. In Canada, NAFTA seemed to reinforce the image of Ottawa's subservience to Washington, D.C., creating new hurdles for longstanding grievances between the two countries, particularly with respect to environmental issues. In sum, NAFTA provided a lightning rod of protest for organized labor and various social movements in all three member countries.

A POLITICAL TRIUMPH FOR BUSINESS

NAFTA represented the culmination of years of business lobbying efforts aimed at opening up new markets and investment opportunities. The notion of a trade agreement was generally embraced by the U.S. Republican Party and was thrown into high gear during the administration of President George H. W. Bush. Although the terms of agreement were reached in October, 1992, substantial opposition in the U.S. Congress, spearheaded by labor and environmental interests, prevented the Bush administration from achieving quick ratification. Before this tripartite agreement, a U.S.-Canada Free Trade Agreement had been finalized in 1989. The Conservative Party administration of Brian Mulroney in Canada worked closely with the Bush administration to bring NAFTA to fruition. However, stiff opposition on both sides of the border made passage in the U.S. Congress impossible until the Democratic Party regained the White House. It was ultimately the administration of President Bill Clinton that rallied sufficient bipartisan support for congressional ratification, only after two separate sidebar agreements addressing labor and environmental concerns were added to the agreement. Once ratified in Washington, NAFTA went into effect on January 1, 1994.

NAFTA was designed to create a free trade area across the three member countries by eliminating tariff and nontariff barriers on agricultural and manufacturing goods as well as services. In addition, it was meant to significantly reduce restrictions on foreign investment among the three countries and offered specific protections of intellectual property rights. Nearly half of all trade was to be stripped of tariff protections at the start of the agreement, and subsequent tariff reductions were to take place in phases over a fourteen-year period. At the time the agreement took effect, the combined free trade area represented $6 trillion and included more than 365 million inhabitants.

In effect, NAFTA ratified a trend toward economic liberalization in the Mexican economy that was already well under way. A shift in political orientation on the part of the ruling Institutional Revolutionary Party had prepared the way for the agreement by systematically dismantling statist protections and opening the country to foreign investment in previously restricted spheres of the economy. Especially notable was the *maquiladora* sector along the Mexican side of the U.S. border, which consisted of a duty-free, tariff-free platform for assembly-line factories for manufactured goods destined for U.S. consumers. The *maquiladora* factories grew rapidly during the 1980's, providing cheap labor for American businesses investing across the border, thus helping pave the way for NAFTA.

The American small-business sector was especially attracted to NAFTA because it promised the possibility of an international market for products that had been limited to local and national markets. Ultimately, however, larger businesses such as agribusiness proved to be better positioned to take advantage of the opportunities posed by the expanded markets offered by this agreement. In the final analysis, NAFTA encouraged an already well-established trend, the increasing concentration of transnational capital into the hands of fewer and larger firms.

A PERSISTENT CONTROVERSY

When NAFTA was still being negotiated in 1992, independent third-party presidential candidate H. Ross Perot became famous for his slogan "you will hear the giant sucking sound" if NAFTA is eventually ratified. He was referring to the anticipated loss of American industrial jobs heading across the border. As in all free trade agreements, there were indeed winners and losers after NAFTA went into effect. In Mexico, small peasant farmers were most adversely affected, being unable to compete with the massive agricultural food imports from the United States.

Perhaps corn production best illustrates the downside of NAFTA for Mexico's peasantry because the crop is grown on more than half of that country's cultivable land and its production involves nearly half of the agrarian labor force. American producers are heavily subsidized by their government, as are large Mexican producers (albeit on a smaller scale), but the majority of Mexico's small

UNITED STATES TRADE WITH NAFTA COUNTRIES, 2005-2007, IN BILLIONS OF DOLLARS

Year	Country	Exports	Imports	Trade Balance
2005	Canada	183.2	287.5	−104.3
	Mexico	101.7	169.2	−67.5
2006	Canada	198.2	303.0	−104.8
	Mexico	114.6	197.1	−82.5
2007	Canada	213.1	312.5	−99.4
	Mexico	119.4	210.2	−90.8

Source: Data from United States International Trade Commission, *The Year in Trade 2007* (Washington, D.C.: Author, 2008)
Note: Trade figures are from the U.S. perspective.

farmers have no governmental support. They rely on subsistence farming techniques and plow the least fertile lands with the lowest yields. Predictably, these small farmers were ill-equipped to compete with the influx of American-grown corn that occurred after NAFTA came into effect. In a country in which around 25 percent of the population works in the agricultural sector, NAFTA became a hated symbol of liberalization by peasants and the poor. The very day that NAFTA went into effect, a peasant uprising took place in the largely indigenous region of Chiapas, led by the Zapatista Front for National Liberation (EZLN), which declared war on Mexico's federal government. Since then, frequent and often large protests have taken place in Mexico, demanding the repeal of the most sensitive sections of NAFTA regarding agricultural liberalization policies.

IMPLICATIONS FOR BUSINESS

NAFTA was originally touted as a move toward regional integration of the Americas. The Bush administration argued that NAFTA was the first major step toward an eventual Free Trade Area of the Americas (FTAA) agreement that would integrate the hemisphere from Canada to the tip of South America. It is important to understand, however, that NAFTA is a trade and investment agreement. It contains none of the political institutions associated with the kind of comprehensive integration created by the European Union. The primary goal of NAFTA was to open up trade and investment markets. Many observers also point to the strategic geopolitical significance that such economic pacts hold for Washington. Clearly, however, these free trade and investment agreements never envisioned a move toward a common currency or even free mobility of labor between their member countries. Indeed, the only move toward expanding NAFTA involved various proposals over the years to increase its geographical reach by including other nation members. Eventually, separate U.S. free trade agreements were signed on a bilateral basis with Chile, Peru, and others, including a subregional trade and investment agreement signed with Central American countries and the Dominican Republic. This has left the original terms of NAFTA intact and increasingly under political fire due to persistent opposition on the part of farmers, trade unions, and environmental groups.

The proposed FTAA eventually stalled because of considerable social protests all across the hemisphere. This opposition led important regional actors such as Brazil to pull back, preventing any final agreement under the original timetable of negotiations. In the United States, the possibility of renegotiating NAFTA has steadily gained currency among major political figures, mostly in the Democratic Party. In Mexico, a broad coalition of peasant organizations and social movements as well as leftist political parties have continued to demand renegotiations on portions of NAFTA that are key for that country. Because opposition to the agreement, particularly over environmental concerns, also remains considerable in Canada, the long-term future of the agreement remains uncertain.

Richard A. Dello Buono

FURTHER READING

Belous, Richard S., and Jonathan Lemco, eds. *NAFTA as a Model of Development.* Washington, D.C.: National Planning Association, 1993. Collection of twenty-one conference papers presents a variety of viewpoints, including several from the perspective of Canada and Mexico.

Cameron, Maxwell A., and Brian W. Tomlin. *The*

Making of NAFTA: How the Deal Was Done. Ithaca, N.Y.: Cornell University Press, 2000. Provides some background on the diplomatic process and presents a full account of the negotiations that resulted in the agreement.

Gerson, Timi, et al. *Another America Is Possible: The Impact of NAFTA on the U.S. Latino Community and Lessons for Future Trade Agreements.* Washington, D.C.: Labor Council for Latin American Advancement and Public Citizen's Global Trade Watch, 2004. An examination of the adverse impact that NAFTA has had on U.S. Latino communities, particularly in the areas of job security, health, and environment. The report shows how NAFTA weakens federal, state, and local public interest laws through unrestricted empowerment of business interests.

Harr, Katie. "NAFTA, CAFTA-DR, and the Role of the Environment." *COHA Opinion* 6, no. 2 (2006). The incorporation of the environmental protection sidebar agreement (NAEEC) into NAFTA had great symbolic importance. This essay written for the Council on Hemispheric Affairs journal suggests, however, that loose mandates for strengthening enforcement of existing environmental laws and encouraging greater public participation in conservation and pollution control fell short of offering real environmental protections.

Scott, Robert E., Carlos Salas, and Bruce Campbell. *Revisiting NAFTA: Still Not Working for North America's Workers.* Washington, D.C.: Economic Policy Institute, 2006. This report details the ways in which NAFTA serves business interests in all three member countries while at the same time weakening the existing social contract and exacerbating existing social inequalities.

Shefner, Jon. "Rethinking Civil Society in the Age of NAFTA: The Case of Mexico." *Annals of the American Academy of Political and Social Science* 610 (2007): 182-200. This article establishes the connection of NAFTA to the broader issue of the neoliberal development model. It is particularly useful for understanding the persistence of social movement opposition to free trade agreements such as NAFTA.

Solomon, Joel. *Trading Away Rights: The Unfulfilled Promise of NAFTA's Labor Side Agreement.* New York: Human Rights Watch, 2001. A comprehensive and detailed analysis of the weaknesses of the sidebar agreement on labor (NAALC) that was ratified as part of NAFTA. The report shows how the NAALC avoided embracing international labor rights norms or the establishment of multinational judicial processes in favor of calling on each signatory country to enforce its existing laws.

SEE ALSO: Canadian trade with the United States; Congress, U.S.; Environmental movement; General Agreement on Tariffs and Trade; International economics and trade; Labor history; Latin American trade with the United States; Mexican trade with the United States; Tariffs; World Trade Organization.

Northern Securities Company

IDENTIFICATION: Holding company that consolidated several railroads in the Northwest and Midwest

DATE: Founded in 1901

SIGNIFICANCE: The U.S. government successfully brought suit against the trust formed by the Northern Securities Company for violations of the Sherman Antitrust Act. This victory demonstrated the government's power to break up industrial monopolies.

The late nineteenth century saw the rapid industrial development of the United States, including the growth of corporations and trusts. Although capitalism supposedly guaranteed competition, business consolidation had instead resulted in monopoly conditions. The Sherman Antitrust Act of 1890 was an attempt, based on the interstate commerce clause of the U.S. Constitution, to restore competition to the marketplace. However, in *United States v. E. C. Knight* (1895), involving a sugar trust, the Supreme Court ruled that manufacture was not commerce and that the Sherman Antitrust Act did not apply.

In 1901, James Jerome Hill, president of the Great Northern Railroad, and Edward H. Harriman, who controlled the Union Pacific, tried to buy the Burlington (Chicago, Burlington, and Quincy) for its access to the hub of Chicago. Although Hill succeeded in buying the Burlington, Harriman made a bid for control by buying stock in the Northern Pacific, which controlled nearly half of the

Burlington's stock. His actions drove the Northern Pacific's stock price to $1,000 per share. However, Hill and financier and railroad consolidator J. P. Morgan, working together, were able to purchase enough shares to gain majority control of the Northern Pacific. This battle over stock disrupted the stock market and the U.S. economy. For primarily financial reasons, Hill, Morgan, and Harriman joined forces to create the Northern Securities Company, a holding company that controlled the major railroads of the Midwest and Northwest. This basically created a monopoly over rail transportation in the region.

The creation of the Northern Securities Company was significant but not unique among business dealings at the time. What made it different was the response of President Theodore Roosevelt. On February 19, 1902, under Roosevelt's direction, Attorney General Philander Knox filed suit against the Northern Securities Company for violations of the Sherman Antitrust Act. Roosevelt's motives were several. As a New York patrician and as a progressive, Roosevelt was distrustful of the growing power of industrial capitalism. Politically, with his eye on his reelection in 1904, an attack on one of the more notorious trusts (it is estimated that 30 percent of the stock of the Northern Securities Company was "watered" or inflated) would be popular with U.S. producers and consumers. Also, Roosevelt had little faith that the conservative Republican majority in Congress would establish meaningful laws to regulate corporate power.

This lithograph from the 1930's depicts the empire builders, some of whom were involved in the Northern Securities Company: (from left) James Jerome Hill, Andrew Carnegie, Cornelius Vanderbilt, John D. Rockefeller, J. P. Morgan, Jay Cooke or Edward H. Harriman, and Jay Gould. (Library of Congress)

The suit against the Northern Securities Company produced shock on Wall Street. In 1904, the Supreme Court ruled, in a five-to-four decision, that the Northern Securities Company had violated the Sherman Antitrust Act by its restraint of trade. The holding company was dissolved. It was the first meaningful demonstration of the government's power to attack industrial monopolies. Roosevelt was reelected in 1904 and gained the nickname of "the Trust Buster." Ironically, he actually favored federal regulation rather than the breaking up of business trusts.

Eugene Larson

FURTHER READING

Dalton, Kathleen. *Theodore Roosevelt.* New York: Knopf, 2002.

Meyer, Balthasar Henry. *A History of the Northern Securities Case.* New York: Da Capo Press, 1972.

Morris, Edmund. *Theodore Rex.* New York: Random House, 2001.

SEE ALSO: Antitrust legislation; Morgan, J. P.; Presidency, U.S.; Railroads; Sherman Antitrust Act.

Northwest Ordinances

THE LAWS: Legislation to govern political and economic growth in the Northwest Territory

DATES: 1784, 1785, and 1787

SIGNIFICANCE: The three Northwest Ordinances defined the Northwest Territory and provided that territory with a blueprint for governance and economic development. The sales of this land provided the new government with significant revenue.

Shortly after the Revolutionary War, American settlers and land speculators began to press westward into the Ohio Country across the Appalachian Mountains, territory officially closed to settlement by the Proclamation of 1763. The new government recognized the need to frame a process for expansion and a method to extend its jurisdiction over the new territory with its significant economic potential (several states claimed parts of the territory).

The first Northwest Ordinance, drafted by Thomas Jefferson in 1784, recommended that the states abandon individual claims to the territory and that the land be eventually divided into new states, each self-governing but part of the Union (Jefferson outlined seventeen such states, roughly identical rectangles). Although Congress did not pass Jefferson's recommendation, it did move quickly to survey the new territory—the Northwest Ordinance of 1785 set up thirty-six-square-mile townships and provided a mechanism for selling the rest of the land at a minimum of a dollar per acre (the land sales were the fledgling government's most lucrative income).

The landmark 1787 Northwest Ordinance proposed dividing the territory into at least three and no more than five territories and that when each territory reached 60,000 settlers, it would write its own constitution and apply for admission to the Union. Thus, no new rival nations could be carved out of the territory. Initially, each territory would be governed by congressional appointees until the population reached 5,000—then free white men would vote for an assembly and send a nonvoting representative to Congress. Moreover, the ordinance proposed fair treatment for indigenous people and recognized their right to property, although this would not be sustained as policy. The ordinance also guaranteed civil rights to settlers, including religious freedom, freedom of speech, and trial by jury (guarantees that predate the Bill of Rights by five years). Far more important, the ordinance prohibited slavery in the territory, thus setting the stage for a half-century of incendiary legislation governing slavery in new territories as the continent expanded.

In this far-reaching ordinance, the new government defined expansion and established a method in which any new territory and its residents would maintain allegiance to a central government and contribute to its economy. The ordinance boldly created the blueprint for ensuring that a single nation would emerge from the settlement of a continent, the actual reach of which had yet to even be mapped.

Joseph Dewey

FURTHER READING

Gunderson, Jessica. *The Second Continental Congress.* Mankato, Minn.: Compass Point Books, 2008.

Hindraker, Eric. *Elusive Empire: Constructing Colonialism in the Ohio Valley, 1673-1800.* New York: Cambridge University Press, 1999.

Winik, Jay. *The Great Upheaval: America and the Birth of the Modern World, 1788-1800.* New York: Harper, 2007.

SEE ALSO: Articles of Confederation; Constitution, U.S.; Land laws; Slave era.

NSF. *See* National Science Foundation

Nuclear power industry

DEFINITION: Public and private utilities using nuclear reactors to generate electrical power

SIGNIFICANCE: Nuclear power provides an alternative to fossil fuels for delivering electric power. Plagued by some accidents, public fears of nuclear energy, and massive construction cost overruns, the industry has grown little since the 1980's, although by the early twenty-first century there were some indications of a revival of the industry, as the United States sought a "clean" alternative to fossil fuels such as coal and oil.

The nuclear power industry originated during the 1950's, as the United States began to investigate peaceful uses for nuclear energy to complement the military nuclear weapons program. In 1955, a research reactor provided some electric power for the town of Arco, Idaho, and in 1957, the first commercial nuclear power plant began operation in Shippingport, Pennsylvania. During the 1950's and early 1960's the Atomic Energy Commission (AEC; the agency that had charge of civilian nuclear energy) investigated several types of reactors, such as the breeder reactor, sodium-graphite reactor, and pressurized water reactor. Ultimately, the AEC settled on the pressurized water reactor, which had been developed by the U.S. Navy for submarine use. The Shippingport and subsequent commercial reactors were all pressurized water reactors. Elsewhere, research continued, and nuclear power industries in some foreign countries, such as France, adopted different types of reactor design.

To induce private industry to participate in the development of nuclear power, Congress passed the Price-Anderson Indemnity Act in 1957 to protect reactor builders and operators from liability suits if accidents occurred. By the early 1960's, several electric utilities had contracted for the construction of nuclear reactors, reasoning that these plants would decrease their costs and enable them to expand their power generation capabilities. Nuclear power was often cited as the energy source of the future during the late 1950's.

SAFETY AND FEARS OF ACCIDENTS

Aware of the potential for major accidents at nuclear power plants, the nuclear industry adopted a policy of engineering safety mechanisms designed to prevent and contain any accident. All commercial nuclear reactors would be surrounded by massive containment buildings intended to contain any radioactive material emitted in an accident. Plants were designed with large margins of error to try to prevent any sort of operating accident from occurring. At every stage of operation, redundancies were built into safety mechanisms so that should one fail there would be others in place to prevent runaway chain reactions that could lead to the emission of radioactive material.

Companies that used nuclear reactors for power generation conducted extensive training of their personnel to further a process of safe operations. Many early nuclear power plants even provided tours for the public as a means of emphasizing the safety of their operations. The early strategies of the AEC had emphasized the containment of any radioactive material in the case of an accident. During the 1960's and early 1970's, the industry was plagued by construction cost overruns, and the AEC began to shift its strategy to prevention as a means of cutting construction costs yet maintaining safe operation. Spurred by ever-increasing demands for electric power, the electric power industry ordered larger and larger reactors, so by the early 1970's, several reactors with 1,000-megawatt or higher capacities were being constructed in different parts of the country.

The initial support for nuclear power was, however, beginning to decline during the early 1970's, as some Americans became quite concerned by the possibility of accidents and radiation leaks. From 1966 to 1976, the time required to obtain a permit to build a reactor increased from slightly over a year to nearly three and one-half years. Construction delays also increased. Some electric companies began

A cooling tower of the Three Mile Island nuclear power plant looms behind an abandoned playground in March, 1979. (AP/Wide World Photos)

to reconsider the feasibility of nuclear power and canceled orders for new reactors. The electric power industry ordered no new reactors after 1978, and some plants under construction were not completed.

Already-declining support for nuclear power received a further shock in March, 1979, when an accident occurred at the Three Mile Island reactor outside Harrisburg, Pennsylvania. The Three Mile Island accident confirmed that the defense-in-depth strategy worked, as almost no radiation (15 curies) was released to the atmosphere. Nonetheless, the errors that occurred in dealing with the initial accident, such as shutting down the emergency cooling loop, led to severe criticism of the industry. The problems at Three Mile Island were primarily human failures rather than design problems, but the widespread negative publicity, coupled with the impact of the nuclear-safety-themed movie *The China Syndrome* (1979), led many Americans to doubt the safety of nuclear power.

The nuclear power industry received another black eye in April, 1986, with the major accident at the Soviet power reactor at Chernobyl. The Chernobyl accident occurred because of several design flaws in Soviet reactors, as well as numerous human errors. The Chernobyl accident released 100 million curies of radioactivity into the atmosphere, and several people died trying to cope with the accident. The Chernobyl reactor was a graphite reactor that suffered a runaway reaction—something that was not possible in American light-water reactors. In addition, the Soviet reactors did not have a full containment shield, unlike those in all Western countries. This flaw led to much of the radioactivity release. The Soviet operators deliberately ignored several warnings during a test that disabled the cooling mechanism for the reactor and kept the test running in spite of several warnings of danger.

Ironically, the Chernobyl accident helped confirm the strengths of U.S. reactor design and training. U.S. power reactors did not follow the Soviet design, and all had extensive containment mechanisms. American operators are unable to override the safety mechanisms as the Soviet operators had done. Nonetheless, the Chernobyl accident and its continuing environmental and health impacts confirmed the opinions of many Americans that nuclear power was an unsafe technology. Although American power companies did not shut down any of their reactors, the negative public opinion coupled to the enormous cost of completing the reactors they had under construction made it impossible to engage in any expansion of nuclear power capability.

By the late 1980's, questions were also being raised about nuclear waste. Reactor operation produces several types of nuclear waste, from slightly radioactive shop towels to spent fuel rods that remain radioactive for several thousand years. France followed a policy of reprocessing its fuel rods to extend their usable life. This process, however, also produces weapons-grade plutonium, adding a different hazard. Throughout the decade of the 1990's, Congress debated what to do with nuclear waste, and a decision was reached late in the decade to bury most of the waste in geologically stable formations in the western United States. The facility for storage of spent control rods is not yet complete, so utilities store the material in special facilities on site. The questions concerning nuclear waste added support to the opponents of nuclear power.

The nuclear power industry remained moribund throughout the 1990's and into the twenty-first century. Public fears and high construction costs ensured that no reactors were constructed. In some cases, additional safety and operating issues were raised by nuclear power opponents concerning existing reactors. Power reactors were initially permitted for twenty years, and these permits were extended for some reactors, raising potential safety concerns. Even so, the potential costs and hazards of dismantling an out-of-service reactor remain a troubling issue.

ENERGY COSTS AND GLOBAL WARMING

During the 1990's, energy prices began to rise at a steep rate in the United States, as oil and natural gas prices increased. Coal prices remained relatively low, but burning coal contributes significantly to global warming and other environmental problems such as acid rain. Reactor construction costs had made nuclear plants an uneconomical source of energy, but the increase in the prices for other sources of energy began to make nuclear power appear to be a somewhat better alternative. The increasing awareness of the atmospheric problems caused by burning coal and oil began to raise some tough environmental questions for these industries. Coal power remained quite cheap during the early twenty-first century, but its environmental costs became increasingly evident, making it a less desirable fuel. Initially, the fears of nuclear power accidents and questions concerning nuclear wastes were dominant, precluding any consideration of expanding nuclear power capacity. In some cases, fears of terrorism directed against reactors added to the force of these questions.

Gradually, critics of global warming theories and advocates of American energy independence have begun to refocus their attention on nuclear energy. There is a good deal of uranium available in Canada and the Western United States, so obtaining fuel is less of a political concern than is obtaining oil from unstable countries in the Middle East and Asia. Several geologists have pointed out that supplies of oil and natural gas are limited and cannot be relied on far into the future.

Coal power remains the cheapest form of electric power. Coal is readily available, U.S. energy companies have numerous coal plants already paid for, and construction of a new coal-fired plant is cheaper than constructing other types of power plants. The indirect costs of burning coal are steadily mounting. These include carbon emissions that constitute a major source of global warming, as well as various forms of acid rain. Although burning natural gas produces fewer environmental problems, burning oil produces many of the same environmental problems as burning coal. Some environmentalists as well as energy analysts have come to advocate nuclear power as a potential means of increasing energy supply in the United States. Nuclear power produces no greenhouse gases or compounds that lead to acid rain. The available supply of uranium is large enough to supply American energy needs well into the future. The problems of high costs associated with construction and dealing with nuclear wastes will have to be addressed, however, before nuclear energy can compete with other forms of energy.

By late 2007, sixteen utilities had announced plans for potential reactor construction. Three had filed applications for early site permits to begin construction, and four had obtained a combined license to build and conditionally operate one or more commercial reactors (one of these had also obtained an early site permit). If all these reactors were constructed, approximately nineteen gigawatts of nuclear electric power capacity would be added to the power grid. None of these utilities has started construction, and some of these potential reactors may not be built. Nonetheless, the nuclear power industry appears to be making a resurgence, driven largely by environmental issues and a desire for energy independence.

John M. Theilmann

FURTHER READING

Herbst, Alan M., and George W. Hopley. *Nuclear Energy Now.* Hoboken, N.J.: John Wiley & Sons, 2007. Primarily an economic analysis that concludes that nuclear power is a better source of energy for the future of the United States.

Hore-Lacy, Ian. *Nuclear Energy in the Twenty-first Century.* Burlington, Mass.: Academic Press, 2006. Easily understood examination of the technical aspects of nuclear reactor operation worldwide. A good starting point for further reading.

Macfarlane, Allison M., and Rodney C. Ewing, eds. *Uncertainty Underground.* Cambridge, Mass.: MIT Press, 2006. Essays from several different perspectives concerning the development of the repository for high-level nuclear waste at Yucca Mountain, Nevada.

Morone, Joseph G., and Edward J. Woodhouse. *The Demise of Nuclear Energy?* New Haven: Yale University Press, 1989. Good analysis of the early history of nuclear energy and its safety and economic problems.

Morris, Robert C. *The Environmental Case for Nuclear Power.* St. Paul: Paragon House, 2000. Analysis of environmental issues that argues that nuclear power is environmentally superior to other forms of energy.

Ramsay, Charles B., and Mohammad Modarres. *Commercial Nuclear Power.* New York: BookSurge, 1998. Extensive analysis of nuclear reactor operation and safety.

SEE ALSO: Coal industry; Energy, U.S. Department of; Environmental movement; Petroleum industry; Public utilities; Tennessee Valley Authority; Three Mile Island accident.

NYSE. *See* New York Stock Exchange

O

Occupational Safety and Health Act

THE LAW: Federal legislation designed to ensure the safety and health of American workers

DATE: Passed on December 29, 1970

SIGNIFICANCE: The Occupational Safety and Health Act created the Occupational Safety and Health Administration, an agency of the U.S. Department of Labor. The administration has two principal functions: setting standards and conducting workplace inspections to ensure that employers are complying with those standards and providing a safe and healthful workplace for their employees.

The Occupational Safety and Health Act of 1970 extends to all employers and their employees in the fifty states, the District of Columbia, Puerto Rico, and all other territories under the jurisdiction of the federal government. The act does not cover self-employed persons; farms that employ only immediate family members of the farmer; working conditions regulated by other federal agencies, such as mining, nuclear energy, nuclear weapons manufacture, and many segments of the transportation industry; or employees of state and local governments.

FEDERAL OSHA STANDARDS

The mission of the Occupational Safety and Health Administration (OSHA) is to prevent work-related injuries, illnesses, and deaths. It seeks to accomplish this mission by enforcing rules (called "standards"). OSHA standards may require employers to adopt certain practices to protect workers on the job. It is employers' responsibility to become familiar with standards applicable to their industries, to eliminate hazardous conditions to the extent possible, and to comply with the standards. Compliance may include ensuring that employees use protective equipment when required for safety or health. Employees must also comply with the rules and regulations applicable to their own actions and conduct.

States with OSHA-approved job safety and health programs must set standards that are at least as effective as the equivalent federal standard. Most of the state-plan states have adopted standards identical to the federal ones. New York, New Jersey, Connecticut, and the Virgin Islands have plans covering only public employees. In 2000, the United States Postal Act made the U.S. Postal Service the only quasi-governmental entity under the purview of OSHA.

Standards fall into four major categories, each of which imposes requirements that are unique to particular industries. The categories are general industry, construction, maritime (including shipyards, marine terminals, and longshoring), and agriculture. Areas that impose similar requirements on all industry sectors are those dealing with access to medical and exposure records, personal protective equipment, and communication. Employers must grant employees access to any of their medical records maintained by the employer and to any records maintained by the employer dealing with the employee's exposure to toxic substances.

HAZARDOUS MATERIALS

For each industry segment except agriculture, employers are required to provide employees, at no cost to the employees, with personal protective equipment designed to protect them against certain hazards. This equipment might include protective helmets for construction and cargo handling work, eye protection, hearing protection, hard-toed shoes, special goggles for welders, or gauntlets for ironworkers. The hazardous-communication provision of the law requires that manufacturers conduct an evaluation of the hazardous materials they manufacture or import. If a product is found to be hazardous under the terms of the standard, containers of the material must be appropriately labeled and the first shipment of the material to a new customer must be accompanied by a material safety data sheet. Employers must then train their employees to recognize and avoid the hazards presented. Any hazard not covered by an industry-specific standard may be covered by a general industry standard. Generally, employers must keep their workplace free of hazards that may cause death or serious bodily injury to employees.

OTHER STANDARDS

OSHA also imposes regulations covering activities such as record keeping, reporting, and posting. Records of job-related injuries and illnesses must be maintained by all employers except those in low-hazard industries such as retail, real estate, finance, and insurance. Employees are granted several important rights, including the right to complain in confidence to OSHA about the safety and health conditions in their workplace, to contest the time allowed by OSHA to correct the violations, and to participate in OSHA work inspections. To enforce OSHA'S standards, the agency's compliance and safety officers, chosen for their knowledge and experience of occupational hazards, are authorized to conduct workplace inspections of establishments covered by the act. States with their own occupational safety and health programs conduct inspections using qualified state inspectors. Fines and sanctions may be assessed for violations of the act, depending on the severity of the violation. Citations and penalties can be reviewed and may be appealed by employers and employees.

Much debate about OSHA's regulations and enforcement policies revolves around the cost of regulations and enforcement rather than the actual benefit in reduced rates of worker injury, illness, and death. OSHA has come under criticism for the ineffectiveness of its penalties, particularly criminal penalties (available only when a willful violation of a standard results in the death of a worker). The maximum penalty is a misdemeanor conviction carrying a maximum jail term of six months.

INDUSTRIAL SAFETY REGULATIONS

Some of the changes in industrial safety regulation that are attributed to OSHA include guards on all parts of machinery where contact is possible, defining maximum concentrations of chemicals and dusts in the workplace, broader use of protective personal equipment, requirements for locking energy sources in the "off" position when performing

OSHA officials are called in to investigate accidents such as this crane collapse at a construction site in Grand Junction, Colorado, in March, 2007. (AP/Wide World Photos)

repairs or maintenance, and requirements for air sampling and use of a "buddy system" when working inside tanks, manholes, pits, bins, and other enclosed areas. In addition, employers must communicate with employees regarding the hazardous chemical products used in the workplace and must engage in process safety management to reduce large-scale industrial accidents, especially in the petrochemical industry. OSHA has issued a standard designed to prevent health care workers from exposure to blood-borne pathogens such as hepatitis B and the human immunodeficiency virus (HIV) and requires safeguards for workers in trenches and excavations at a depth of more than five feet.

Marcia J. Weiss

FURTHER READING

Collins, Larry R., and Thomas D. Schneid. *Physical Hazards of the Workplace.* Boca Raton, Fla.: Lewis, 2001. Comprehensive list of potential workplace hazards and how to avoid them.

Hofmann, David A., and Lois E. Tetrick, eds. *Health and Safety in Organizations: A Multilevel Perspective.* San Francisco: Jossey-Bass, 2003. Examination of different portions of management and the labor force and the role of each in protecting workers from harm.

McGarity, Thomas O., and Sidney A. Shapiro. *Workers at Risk: The Failed Promise of the Occupational Safety and Health Administration*. Westport, Conn.: Praeger, 1993. Two administrative law scholars criticize OSHA as far from meeting its mandate to protect American workers; they suggest ways the agency can get back on track. Good for historical context.

Mendeloff, John. *Regulating Safety: An Economic and Political Analysis of Occupational Safety and Health Policy*. Cambridge, Mass.: MIT Press, 1979. Detailed examination of OSHA with emphasis on economic and social policy.

Reese, Charles D. *Occupational Health and Safety Management: A Practical Approach*. Boca Raton, Fla.: CRC Press, 2003. Offers an approach management can take to occupational health and safety issues.

SEE ALSO: Health care industry; Labor, U.S. Department of; Labor history; Triangle Shirtwaist Company fire.

Oil. *See* Petroleum industry

Oil boycott. *See* Arab oil embargo of 1973

Online marketing

DEFINITION: Promotion of goods and services over the Internet though coordination of various online strategies, including World Wide Web advertising, search optimization, e-mail, blogs, and other online technologies

SIGNFICANCE: Since its advent during the mid-1990's, online marketing has become a vital part of the overall marketing strategies of most major American companies. The growth of online marketing has overtaken that of traditional marketing. Tens of billions of dollars are spent annually on online marketing.

Advertising on the Internet started simply with companies developing Web sites and posting advertising (webvertising) in the form of banner advertisements on other Web sites. This leveraged two of the most important advantages of online marketing: the inexpensive nature of placing advertisements on the Internet compared with the cost of traditional media advertisements and the ability to reach a global market instantly.

Online marketing differs from online advertising in that it also includes design, development, and sales as well as incorporating the electronic management of customer data and customer relationships. It grew naturally of a combination of traditional marketing and businesses started to take n-ternet includi all parcel of text er). Strategies usi ned and used to tar-get markets

BENEFITS

The benefits of online marketing itional marketing are varied and numerous. One of the largest benefits is the ability to provide a one-on-one approach to marketing because advertisements can be targeted to specific behaviors or interests rather than reaching out to a broad demographic, as traditional marketing does. Online marketing can do this more easily because it is much simpler to keep track of user activity through the use of cookies and through the ease of accessing statistics from Web servers. On the average, thousands of pieces of data are collected monthly about each user as the person visits Web sites. Most Web servers have built-in software that can analyze the stored data so that nearly all aspects of a marketing campaign can be measured quickly. The effectiveness of a campaign can be checked constantly, and the campaign can be altered on the fly to take advantage of indicated trends. Traditional marketing results take months to collect and analyze.

Online marketing has become ubiquitous as technology continues to spread, a phenomenon that further increases its effectiveness. It can include other wireless media such as cell phones and smart phones. Most companies now include their Web site on the products that they sell, and retailers commonly place their Web site information on receipts and in-store literature.

TRENDS

Web 2.0 technologies have brought an even more personal approach to online marketing. Companies can be found on social networking sites and added as a "friend." Customers can be constantly provided information on products in which they are interested by reading a company's blog or subscribing to an RSS (Really Simple Syndication) feed that supplies them with information about a company or new product as soon as it is released.

Search engine marketing (SEM) has allowed companies to reach their target audience much more quickly than before. Billions of dollars are spent annually on SEM, and it is growing faster than traditional marketing and other online strategies. Once the target audience is identified, experts use a variety of techniques to get their company listed toward the top of Web searches so that consumers looking for a specific product are directed to their company. Advertisements on Web sites can also be targeted to a specific user who is browsing the site by accessing the user's browsing history.

Online marketing is also much more fluid than traditional marketing. The costs associated with traditional advertising on radio and television and in print do not allow for an easy change in the marketing campaign, so it is usually run until the cost for the campaign is recouped. Online marketing allows companies to test market much more effectively, and changes to the campaign can be made at little or no cost. Unlike print advertisements, online media have no permanence and allow for fast changes in corporate image and sweeping strategy changes because the Web site code is very easy to alter.

There are some drawbacks that companies must be aware of when implementing an online marketing strategy. E-mail campaigns can be seen as spam, so most companies offer consumers the chance to opt out, or to no longer receive the company's e-mails. There are also concerns about privacy. Many consumers have an aversion to their browsing habits being tracked and analyzed online. The issues associated with online marketing are regulated in part, and many watchdog groups make sure

ONLINE RETAIL SPENDING, 2001 AND 2006, IN BILLIONS OF DOLLARS		
Category	2001	2006
Computer hardware and software	11.0	20.0
Apparel, accessories, footwear, and jewelry	4.7	16.8
Books, music, and videos	3.8	9.3
Grocery and pet food	0.8	5.4
Tickets	1.8	5.3
Flowers and specialty gifts	1.2	3.6
Toys and video games	1.0	3.6
Consumer health	0.4	3.2
Sporting goods	0.7	2.3

Source: Data from the *Statistical Abstract of the United States, 2008* (Washington, D.C.: Department of Commerce, Economics and Statistics Administration, Bureau of the Census, Data User Services Division, 2008)

abuses do not go unnoticed. Those with little access to technology are left out of many campaigns unless there is an intensive effort to coordinate an online campaign with an offline marketing effort.

Tens of billions of dollars are spent every year by businesses of all sizes on online marketing. This medium is growing much faster than marketing in other media by a large percentage and has transformed some industries by taking them almost wholly online, from marketing to product distribution. Online marketing may become necessary for a company to remain competitive.

James J. Heiney

FURTHER READING

Chaffey, Dave. *Internet Marketing: Strategy, Implementation, and Practice.* 3d ed. New York: Pearson Education, 2006. A comprehensive guide to how organizations can use the Internet to support their marketing activities.

Hanson, Ward A., and Kirthi Kalyanam. *Internet Marketing and E-Commerce.* Mason, Ohio: Thomson/South-Western, 2007. Covers marketing strategies, technologies, and practices as well as application of individual online behaviors.

Meyerson, Mitch, and Mary Eule Scarborough. *Mastering Online Marketing.* Irvine, Calif.: Entrepreneur Press, 2008. A practical guide to online marketing covering the best practices and the pitfalls to be avoided.

Roberts, Mary Lou. *Internet Marketing: Integrating Online and Offline Strategies.* Boston, Mass.: McGraw-Hill/Irwin, 2003. Uses extant marketing theory and applies it to the field of online marketing so that marketers can successfully use the Internet for marketing.

Scott, David Meerman. *The New Rules of Marketing and PR: How to Use News Releases, Blogs, Podcasting, Viral Marketing, and Online Media to Reach Buyers Directly.* Hoboken, N.J.: John Wiley & Sons, 2007. Stresses the use of some of the more advanced technologies that can be used in the field of online marketing with real-world examples.

See also: Advertising industry; Apple; Catalog shopping; Computer industry; Dot-com bubble; eBay; E-mail; Google; Internet; Outsourcing, overseas; Video rental industry.

OPEC. *See* Organization of Petroleum Exporting Countries

Organization of Petroleum Exporting Countries

Identification: International cartel of oil-exporting countries dedicated to controlling the price of oil in the international market

Date: Founded September 10-14, 1960

Significance: OPEC's founding challenged the power of the "Seven Sisters," the seven giant international petroleum companies—five of which were incorporated in the United States—that at the time dominated the production, shipping, and refining of oil outside the United States and Russia. Thirteen years later, control over the international price of oil slipped into OPEC's hands.

The early growth of the international petroleum industry was significantly driven by two developments: the turn-of-the-century switch to oil as the fuel of preference of navies in a world where security was widely measured in sea power and the 1911 court-ordered breakup of John D. Rockefeller's Standard Oil monopoly, which forced many of its parts to look overseas for the oil on which their refining and marketing operations depended. Demand for oil rose with the development of a private automobile industry—made affordable via Henry Ford's assembly-line production techniques—and a recognition of oil's competitive advantages over coal as an energy source. The industry grew in size and evolved in structure to meet this increased demand.

The Seven Sisters

By the time that the governments of the major petroleum-exporting states began to discuss a cooperative effort to capitalize on the growing demand for oil after World War II to gain greater revenue, the industry had gone through several stages. From its origins in a concession system in which individual oil companies acquired the right to a country's petroleum reserves for a one-time fee, it had evolved into a 50-50 profit-sharing system, under which the producing companies paid the governments of oil-producing states 50 percent of the price of oil on the global market.

The Seven Sisters' economic model was geared toward deriving profits from selling oil cheaply in extremely high volumes. The companies were thus reluctant to increase the price of oil precipitously, lest demand and the volume of their trade decrease. Meanwhile, the oil-producing states were growing dissatisfied with their revenue under the 50-50 profit-sharing system. In September, 1960, representatives of Iran, Iraq, Saudi Arabia, Kuwait, and Venezuela met in Baghdad to found the Organization of Petroleum Exporting Countries (OPEC) with the expressed short-term goal of lobbying the Seven Sisters to increase the price of oil, and the long-term goal of regaining control over their petroleum reserves from Western oil companies.

Oil and the U.S. Economy

Much of OPEC's subsequent history can be written in terms of its successful and unsuccessful responses to events that it only occasionally set in motion. The major developments occurred during the 1970's and early 1980's, when three political events—the Arab-Israeli Yom Kippur War in October, 1973, the fall of the shah of Iran in early 1979, and the Iraq-Iran war later that year—transformed the international oil market and challenged the ability of Western economies to absorb the cost of imported oil, whose price increased twelvefold between 1973 and 1979. The Yom Kippur War resulted in the members of the Organization of Arab Oil Exporting Countries (OAPEC) declaring an embargo on oil shipments to any country aiding Israel during that war. The threat of that embargo produced such panic in the oil-importing world that OPEC's members were able to regain control over the ownership of their petroleum assets by buying out the Western oil companies and then hiring them to continue to produce their oil for sale on the world market.

Six years later, the fall of the shah and the advent of the Iraq-Iran War produced more panic buying by oil-importing countries. Imported petroleum's price quickly soared from $16 per barrel to over $36 per barrel, and record profits accrued to both the oil industry and OPEC's member states. Over the long term, however, the higher price of oil proved to be too costly to all concerned. A prolonged "stagflationary" period ensued during the 1980's, as inflation caused by the price increase and unemployment resulting from the counter-inflationary policies adopted to curtail that inflation produced a deep, long global recession. OPEC's member states resorted to underselling one another when the demand for their oil plummeted with the global economy. The price of oil eventually fell below $7 per barrel before Saudi Arabia's efforts to reestablish discipline inside OPEC succeeded and the price of oil restabilized around $24 to $26 per barrel on the eve of Iraq's 1990 invasion of Kuwait.

The Iraqi invasion produced a new jump in the price of oil before the U.S.-led war against Iraq culminated in Iraq's defeat, the restoration of Kuwait's oil industry, and the restabilization of oil prices around $20 per barrel throughout most of the 1990's—a price structure that allowed the American economy and other Western economies to grow again.

The first decade of the twenty-first century once more found OPEC benefiting from outside events, and the soaring cost of oil again threatened to disrupt the economy of oil-importing states, including that of OPEC's largest consumer, the United States. By the early years of the new millennium, the growing demand for oil in the Western world, along with

Drivers form a long line at a gas station in Miami in 1973 during the oil embargo. (AP/Wide World Photos)

India and China's increasing demand for oil, was producing a tight oil market even before the March, 2003, U.S. occupation of Iraq and the subsequent fighting there that crippled Iraq's oil industry. On the fifth anniversary of that invasion, OPEC oil was selling for over $100 per barrel—a fourfold increase over the cost when that war began—with negative effects on Western economies.

Joseph R. Rudolph, Jr.

FURTHER READING

Amuzegar, Jahangir. *Managing the Oil Wealth: OPEC's Windfalls and Pitfalls.* Rev. ed. New York: I. P. Tauris, 2001. Excellent study of OPEC's ability to exploit political events for its member states' financial benefit.

Kalicki, Jan H., and David L. Goldwyn, eds. *Energy and Security: Toward a New Foreign Policy Strategy.* Baltimore: Johns Hopkins University Press, 2005. Regionally organized study of energy dependency throughout the world that attests well to how important OPEC's decisions are to security—and life—in the contemporary world.

Sampson, Anthony. *The Seven Sisters: The Great Oil Companies and the World They Created.* Rev. ed. London: Coronet, 1998. Masterful portrait of the rise and fall of the private petroleum cartel that controlled the international oil industry for half a century.

Yergin, Daniel. *The Prize: The Epic Quest for Oil, Money, and Power.* New York: Simon & Schuster, 1991. Epic history of the world of oil, from the industry's origins through its growth into a global industry based on oil production in Latin America, Africa, and the Middle East.

SEE ALSO: Arab oil embargo of 1973; Asian trade with the United States; Commodity markets; Energy crisis of 1979; "Gas wars"; Inflation; Petroleum industry.

Organized crime

DEFINITION: Organizations set up to operate illegal businesses, frequently through the use of criminal tactics, with profits being reinvested into legitimate operations

SIGNIFICANCE: The diverse enterprises in which various organized crime elements have engaged

since the late nineteenth century have created a black market for goods and services in the United States, siphoning off profits from legitimate firms, reducing tax revenues to states and the federal government, and requiring law-enforcement agencies to invest significant resources in attempting to stem illegal activities.

For most Americans the term "organized crime" conjures up images of armed gangsters running bootlegging or gambling operations and taking out rivals by violent means, all at the behest of a revered "boss" who heads their "family." Although these characteristics may be accurate, they do not provide a comprehensive picture of organized crime or its impact on American business since the first formal groups were established during the late nineteenth century.

NATURE AND STRUCTURE

Terms such "mafia," "mob," and "Cosa Nostra" have been used to designate criminal organizations, especially those whose membership is largely Italian American. Actually, however, "organized crime" is an umbrella term describing a number of criminal groups of various ethnicities. These entities have common characteristics that distinguish them from bands of ordinary criminal gangs. In the latter there are few attempts to establish formal hierarchies; most operate like bands of brigands or pirates, sometimes with a titular leader but with few other levels of authority. By contrast, many organized crime groups have created structures similar to those found in legitimate corporations or military units. A chief executive, often called the boss, assisted by principal deputies often known as "capos," supervises a group or "family" of between fifty and several hundred individuals who carry out most of the illegal activities, such as pressuring small-business owners to provide a portion of their profits to the mob, collecting illegal payoffs, running gambling and prostitution operations, and using physical force against individuals who refuse to comply with the organization's directives.

Additionally, unlike gang activity, part of the efforts of organized crime have been aimed at generating a steady stream of revenues by illegal means that can be used not only to support members of the crime group directly, but also to reinvest in legitimate businesses that can supplement, often handsomely, funds derived directly from illicit activities. Everyone within the illegal group shares in the spoils—at differing levels, as the top bosses frequently take a major share of these illegal earnings for their personal use and investment. Some have become millionaires and set themselves up as community leaders and philanthropists, distancing themselves from the illegal activities on which their fortunes had been built. Finally, most organized crime "families" establish some form of succession planning, in which those higher up in the organization designate a successor to take over operations upon the arrest, retirement, or death of the group's leader. In this way, organized crime elements have been able to sustain operations even when an individual is removed from the group.

History in the United States

The earliest organized crime groups were founded in immigrant communities, where law enforcement was often lax or even hostile to new arrivals. Certain criminal leaders saw ways to extract money from immigrants for "protection," guaranteeing their homes and businesses would be safe if the leaders were paid. These same men also set up operations supporting gambling, counterfeiting, and prostitution, from which they profited without having to pay any taxes. Frequently organized crime groups were abetted by corrupt local law enforcement and local politicians, who were bribed to provide protection from law enforcement or secure contracts for mob-affiliated businesses. By the 1920's, organized crime elements were operating in virtually every major American city along the eastern seaboard and in the Midwest, with major centers in New York and Chicago. Other groups operated in large metropolitan areas such as Philadelphia, Miami, Boston, Cleveland, New Orleans, St. Louis, and Kansas City, and in small communities such as Little Rock, Arkansas, and Reading, Pennsylvania.

The era of Prohibition proved a boon for organized crime, as various discrete crime organizations entered into commerce with other groups to form networks for production, distribution, and sales of illegal alcohol. At the same time "families" expanded their operations into a number of other areas. By the 1940's, organized crime elements had branched out from gambling, prostitution, loan sharking, and protection services into activities such as hijacking, smuggling, mail and wire fraud, and trafficking in counterfeit goods. Their favorite targets among legitimate businesses were those operating principally on a cash basis, since it was easier to skim funds from these operations. Consulting regularly, the various leaders entered into informal syndicates whereby they agreed to parcel out certain activities or territories to reduce competition and thereby maximize profits for everyone.

Organized crime elements also infiltrated a number of legitimate businesses, where they bought in as partners (often silent) or became major investors. Over time, they became deeply enmeshed in a number of unions, where they controlled elections and often siphoned off money from pension funds. Organized crime became a major influence in unions serving the garment industry, trucking and transportation, shipping, entertainment and food service, waste disposal, and construction. An especially nefarious alliance was struck with the International Brotherhood of Teamsters, whose pension fund provided a lucrative source for loans or outright theft.

After World War II, leaders of organized crime made a concerted effort to expand westward, beefing up activities in the motion-picture industry and in the emerging legalized gambling industry in Las Vegas. As they had done on the East Coast, mafia operatives made inroads into the principal businesses as part owners of film studios and casinos, and also infiltrated a number of service industries, including the one for stagehands, through their union connections. The mob's connections with various political leaders who controlled government budgets and the various licensing agencies for businesses often meant they could obtain both government and private contracts for companies at inflated prices, pad payrolls with friends or associates in their organizations, and receive kickbacks on work being done at various legitimate enterprises. If bribery was not sufficient motivation for politicians, union leaders and members, and business owners, local mafia would resort to tactics such as property damage or bodily injury to get their way.

Law-Enforcement Efforts

Until the 1920's, efforts to control organized crime were left to local and state law-enforcement agencies. When Prohibition was enacted, federal agencies began seeking to curtail the activities of organized crime. The most famous efforts were made by the Department of the Treasury, which went after a number of high-profile mobsters (including Al Capone in Chicago) for tax evasion. Because Federal Bureau of Investigation Director J. Edgar Hoover was reluctant even to admit the existence of organized crime, the Federal Bureau of Investigation (FBI) did little in this area until after Hoover's death in 1972. Congress became involved as early as 1950, however, as a committee chaired by Tennessee Senator Estes Kefauver and ably run by its counsel Robert F. Kennedy exposed the activities of organized crime to the American public. Kennedy launched his own crusade against organized crime when he became United States Attorney General in 1961. Subsequently, mob leaders were often arrested and charged with various crimes, and some went to prison. Their operations continued, however, as structures had been put in place for carrying on the business when a leader was removed from his office.

Additionally, despite having their activities revealed, many mob bosses avoided prosecution because the actual crimes were being committed by underlings, most of whom abided by a "code of silence" that members of organized crime units imposed on all members. Few leaders were ever identified as having participated in or directed illegal activities.

Continuing pressure from various government and law-enforcement agencies finally led to the passage of the Racketeer Influenced and Corrupt Organizations (RICO) Act in 1970. Under terms of this law, the government could prosecute individuals who were involved in activities considered illegal even if the accused had not committed a criminal act personally. As a result, a number of high-ranking officials in organized crime outfits were tried and sentenced, and a dent was made in the influence organized crime had on legitimate businesses. The impact of the RICO law became evident when Atlantic City, New Jersey, authorized gambling during the 1970's. Although organized crime elements were able to exert influence and take profits from the service industries, they could not buy into the casinos themselves, as government regulations made it virtually impossible for criminal figures to become investors. Additionally, during that same decade mafia figures were forced to divest themselves of holdings in Las Vegas casinos.

To counter this loss and others brought on by increased government scrutiny, innovative leaders of crime families began infiltrating the financial services industry, and by the 1990's they had gained notable influence in that enterprise. The remaining crime families also entered an area where they had not been a major factor in the past. Although initially reticent to become engaged in selling illegal drugs, by the 1980's many organized crime groups became heavily involved in this lucrative business. Eventually "families" in the United States became part of various international enterprises, including drug smuggling and sales, transnational sales of illegal arms and equipment, and human trafficking activities involving the sale of women and children for illicit purposes.

Reputed Gambino family crime boss John Gotti during his trial in 1990. (AP/ Wide World Photos)

IMPACT ON BUSINESS AND SOCIETY

The impact of organized crime on American business and society has been significant and insidious. Because operations have always been secretive, it is not possible to get an accurate gauge on the profits organized crime elements have generated from their operations. What is known is that, for more than a century, legitimate operations in a number of industries have been forced to use a portion of their income to make payoffs, insure for property damages that might be caused by elements of organized crime, or purchase goods and services from mob-controlled suppliers. These costs are passed on to consumers in the form of inflated prices. At the same time, those receiving income from illegal activities have managed to shield much of it from government agencies assessing taxes. A single example illustrates the significance of this tactic: In 1985, law-enforcement officials in New York estimated the gross income of the city's five major crime families at $48 billion, half of which was profit. In the same year Exxon, the largest legitimate business in the United States, grossed $51 billion—with a net profit of only 5 percent.

Although law enforcement managed to make significant progress in curtailing operations of organized crime during the 1980's and 1990's, its efforts were not without significant cost. The government spent an estimated $75 million to put away New York crime boss John Gotti in 1992. By 1995, the Federal Bureau of Investigation had spent more than $4 billion on efforts to eliminate organized crime. Nearly a decade later, however, a 2004 study suggested the profits from organized crime still ranged as high as 2 percent of America's gross national product—a sum in excess of $250 billion. The total may well be higher; in 2005 the Federal Bureau of Investigation estimated that worldwide organized crime was a $1 trillion business.

Laurence W. Mazzeno

FURTHER READING

Jacobs, James B. *Mobsters, Unions, and Feds: The Mafia and the American Labor Movement*. New York: New York University Press, 2006. Documents the long-standing relationship between organized crime and labor unions in America. Explains how both the unions and federal agencies have worked to sever those ties.

Reppetto, Thomas A. *American Mafia: A History of Its Rise to Power*. New York: Henry Holt, 2004. Sketches the history of organized crime from its emergence in poverty-stricken neighborhoods in America to the heyday of its operations during the three decades following World War I. Explains how various local and regional organizations were structured and controlled. Also explains relationships between organized crime and various politicians.

_____. *Bringing Down the Mob: The War Against the American Mafia*. New York: Henry Holt, 2006. Outlines efforts of various federal, state, and local agencies to break up organized crime activities. Provides insights into the changing nature of organized crime as its leaders adapted to increased pressure from law enforcement.

Ryan, Patrick J. *Organized Crime: A Reference Handbook*. Santa Barbara, Calif.: ABC-Clio, 1995. Describes various activities of organized crime, outlines the structure of groups in cities throughout America and abroad, provides brief biographies of key leaders, and details efforts by law enforcement to control illegal activities.

Woodiwiss, Michael. *Organized Crime and American Power: A History*. Toronto: University of Toronto Press, 2001. Concentrates on the relationships between organized crime and various local, state, and federal politicians and law-enforcement agencies in the United States. Explains how organized crime leaders have managed to use their sway over these individuals and organizations to maintain their operations and even influence the way legitimate business is regulated.

SEE ALSO: Business crimes; Gambling industry; Hoffa, Jimmy; Identity theft; Justice, U.S. Department of; Muckraking journalism; Ponzi schemes; Private security industry; Prohibition; Racketeer Influenced and Corrupt Organizations Act; Secret Service, U.S.; Treasury, U.S. Department of the.

Outsourcing, overseas

DEFINITION: The transfer of day-to-day business functions to an external third-party service provider located overseas

SIGNFICANCE: Advances in technology have allowed U.S. companies to transfer some functions previously done within the country to overseas contractors or vendors. This has reduced costs for these companies but also eliminated many jobs in the United States.

Overseas outsourcing has seen a huge growth, beginning during the 1990's. The lowering of trade and political barriers and major technical advances have made it possible to do business almost anywhere, and at any time, instantly around the globe. Although many companies outsource business functions such as information technology, human resources, and accounting, they can also outsource customer support, Web site design, telemarketing, marketing, and content writing. Consequently, companies can often experience unheard-of savings, as much as 30 to 40 percent, in labor costs during the first year—thus vastly improving their annual cash flow.

THE UPSIDE AND DOWNSIDE

Experts argue that overseas outsourcing helps globalization by raising the standard of living in countries to which jobs are outsourced and that this improves the American economy by providing low-cost products and services to American consumers. In the long run, they argue, this will lead to higher paying service jobs within the United States. American companies benefit not only from lower labor costs but also from offshore tax benefits. Small companies that outsource jobs can position themselves to be far more competitive against larger corporations. However, although overseas outsourcing is viewed by many companies as an extremely profitable business venture, for workers with well-paying jobs in the United States who lose their jobs to professionals in such countries as India and China, it is an economic and psychological nightmare. Simply put, big layoffs follow when companies outsource service jobs to developing countries.

Outsourcing is a business practice used by many of the *Fortune* 500 companies, such as Microsoft, IBM, Hewlett-Packard, and American Telephone and Telegraph Company (AT&T), but it has become a point of contention because Americans continue to lose jobs when companies contract with overseas vendors that provide low-paying labor in such countries as India, China, Brazil, the Philippines, and Mexico. The jobs that are lost are not lower-paying manufacturing jobs: Highly educated professionals find themselves having to compete against people with comparable college degrees willing to work harder for a fraction of the pay in developing countries. A poll during the 2004 elections revealed that 71 percent of voters believed that outsourcing hurts the American economy and wanted government intervention through increased taxes on companies that outsource. For small towns, overseas outsourcing can be particularly destructive because the workers in a small town may not be able to find comparable work unless they leave the area.

Outsourcing can be highly risky for American businesses because service providers may be disreputable or simply may not be able to perform vital work to American standards. In addition, huge layoffs by companies can lead to heavy financial losses as a result of poor planning on the part of the company and the lowered motivation levels of the remaining workers. After companies outsource services, they often find it more difficult to retain well-trained, experienced staff in the United States and, as a result, can lose key personnel to their competitors. Similarly, the contractor providing the outsourced function can experience high turnover, causing it to replace its staff with less-qualified workers, and may purchase inferior technology. Often contractors fail to live up to the promises they initially make to the client company, leading to poorer quality service. In particular, customer satisfaction questionnaires reveal that call centers that are expected to provide professional customer service are problematic when inferior language skills prevent smooth communications between the service provider and the customer.

Some critics insist that outsourcing exploits lower-paid overseas workers, but supporters of the practice note that it benefits these workers by giving them relatively well-paid employment and enriching their quality of life. However, although they enjoy a higher standard of living, workers at the outsource company remain insecure because they realize their jobs are only temporary and that their jobs could be easily moved to another developing country, where wages are even lower. Critics also note that highly skilled workers such as accountants and computer programmers are being exploited because they are being paid far lower wages than their American counterparts.

Businesses that choose not to outsource overseas run the risk of failing because their competition can offer similar services at far lower prices. In this regard, customers who frequent businesses that practice overseas outsourcing are often blamed as the ultimate cause of the problems caused by outsourcing.

PAST, PRESENT, AND FUTURE

Economists see outsourcing as an evolutionary process that happened first in the manufacturing industry, when companies relocated factories to such areas as Canada, Mexico, and South America to cut costs. During the 1990's, outsourcing heavy-industrial low-skilled work to developing nations allowed Americans to specialize in higher-paying technical jobs. Later, it was these higher-paying information technology (IT) jobs that became affected by overseas outsourcing. In the past, outsourcing took place at a slower pace, with factories often taking years to fully relocate. In addition, the movement of large amounts of equipment and raw materials to the new factory created new jobs. However, in the age of the digital revolution, white-collar jobs can be moved overseas very quickly, with no additional job creation involved.

Jobs in the United States involving information technology, marketing, human resources, customer services, and accounting have been lost to outsourcing. Vendors in other countries such as India, China, the Philippines, and Romania, which have become known as outsourcing centers, employ large numbers of qualified people to handle a variety of service jobs required by client businesses in the United States. These jobs involve such personnel as software engineers, computer staff, editorial workers, and credit-card bill collectors. Recruiting and training personnel for a telemarketing operation in the United States is cost prohibitive, while contracting for telemarketing services from a company with the latest equipment and lower-paid but qualified staff already in place is much more cost-effective.

Health care companies often outsource medical billing to India to cut costs. India's advanced and stable governmental network and strong economy make the nation a particularly appealing outsource destination. In addition, India, which can boast of a computer-literate and English-speaking labor force, has become the preferred site for mainframe operations that involve computer systems, monitoring and systems recovery, and business operations necessitating high-level salaried employees.

Many American companies have engaged outsourcing companies to perform accounting functions and business processes for far less than these services would cost in the United States. In particular, many companies are outsourcing accounts-payable management functions. Another fast-growing sector in the outsource business is human resources, where outsource companies handle functions such as payroll, benefits, and the hiring and training of personnel. High-end research and design jobs have been outsourced as well.

Much has been said and written about the financial and psychological mayhem created in the United States as a result of overseas outsourcing. Some people view outsourcing as the reason for the demise of traditionally good-paying American jobs. However, economists maintain that transformational outsourcing, in which corporations use outsourcing not just to save money but also to promote corporate growth, will have a positive effect on the U.S. economy. American corporations can become much more efficient, increase their pace of innovation, and raise productivity. Therefore, they will be able to hire more Americans and make far better use of their skilled staff in the United States by freeing them from routine office tasks. Indeed, some economists view outsourcing as a catalyst for a larger plan to reinvent outdated American office operations and as an effective means of creating radical business models to overtake competition.

M. Casey Diana

FURTHER READING

Bendor-Samuel, Peter. *Turning Lead into Gold: The Demystification of Outsourcing.* Provo, Utah: Executive Excellence Publishing, 2000. Written for companies interested in contracting with outsource companies to save money and companies interesting in providing outsource services to make money. Uses statistics and case studies.

Carmel, Erin, and Paul Tjia. *Offshoring Information Technology: Sourcing and Outsourcing to a Global Workforce.* New York: Cambridge University Press, 2006. Written by an expert in global information technology for college students and business executives, this work provides insights into outsourcing information technology. Covers such subjects as managing contractors and legal issues in addition to cultural and language problems.

Dobbs, Lou. *Exporting America: Why Corporate Greed Is Shipping American Jobs Overseas.* New York: Business Plus, 2004. The host of the television show *Lou Dobbs Tonight* on Cable News Network (CNN) argues that free trade through outsourcing jobs overseas has led to runaway trade deficits and the loss of hundreds of thousands of jobs in the United States. Dobbs negates twelve "myths" associated with outsourcing jobs.

Friedman, Thomas L. *The World Is Flat: A Brief History of the Twenty-first Century.* New York: Farrar, Straus and Giroux, 2005. The author, who won a Pulitzer Prize as a *New York Times* foreign correspondent, discusses how the partial dismantling of trade and political barriers along with advances in digital technology have so changed the planet that it is possible to do business instantly across the planet.

Kern, Thomas, and Leslie P. Willcocks. *The Relationship Advantage; Information Technologies, Sourcing, and Management.* New York: Oxford University Press, 2002. Academic work focusing on five longitudinal case studies that address factors involved in outsourcing to improve relationships between clients and outsource companies.

SEE ALSO: Federal Emergency Management Agency; Internet; Printing industry; Privatization; Service industries.

P

Panama Canal

IDENTIFICATION: Artificial waterway that permits oceangoing vessels to travel between the Caribbean Sea and the Pacific Ocean by passing through Panama

DATE: Opened to shipping in 1914

SIGNIFICANCE: The canal allowed the United States to transport goods in ships from the East Coast to Asia easily and efficiently, opening up new markets and creating profit for manufacturers, shippers, and the canal operators.

The late nineteenth century was a bleak time for the United States, which experienced a great economic slump as it began the transition from an agricultural to an industrial economy. The Panic of 1873, which mostly affected the countryside, was followed by the Panic of 1893, the first true crisis of the newly industrialized economy of the United States. Railroads collapsed, as did banks and their investors. Credit markets became shaky, and defaults on bond payments led to an even greater crisis. Countless workers—perhaps numbering in the millions—lost their jobs. The economy was in a shambles. However, the American victory in the Spanish-American War (1898) created a wave of optimism. The war had produced enormous political and economic benefits, including an expansion of overseas markets, at very little cost to the national treasury.

In the midst of this optimism, legislators and the American public were soon faced with plans for the construction of a Central American isthmian canal with an estimated price tag of some $400 million. This plan was part of the Republican platform of 1896, on which William McKinley had been elected president. The platform proposed the following course of action: the building of a "steel, blue-water" navy; the construction of an isthmian canal somewhere in the Western Hemisphere, so as to defend American commercial interests; and the expansion of U.S. markets abroad, especially in Asia.

During his involvement in the Spanish-American War, President Theodore Roosevelt had become convinced of the absolute necessity of such a canal, and by 1902, Congress had passed the Spooner Bill, which authorized the building of a canal through Panama. Congress appropriated $40 million for the president to purchase the property and supplies of the New Panama Canal Company in Paris. Then, it authorized the president to opt for one of two plans: If the canal was to be routed through Panama, Congress earmarked $135 million to begin the project, whereas if the canal was to pass through Nicaragua, $180 million could be spent.

In 1903, the United States and Panama signed the Hay-Herrán Treaty, in which Colombia, the power that controlled Panama, consented to the project. Opposition to the project arose in Colombia, but the government soon had to deal with other matters, when a revolutionary junta, under the command of José Agustín Arango, mounted a rebellion. On November 6, 1903, President Roosevelt recognized the revolutionary junta as the official government of Panama. On November 11, the Panamanian representative, Philippe-Jean Bunau-Varilla, concluded a Panama Canal convention with Secretary of State John Hay. The Hay-Bunau-Varilla Treaty was ratified on December 2, and the U.S. Senate approved it on February 23, 1904.

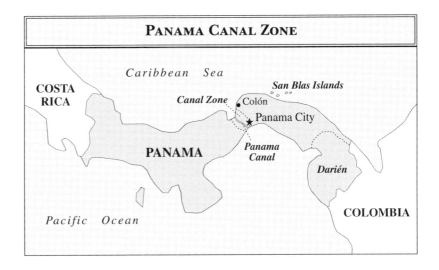

PANAMA CANAL ZONE

Caribbean Sea

COSTA RICA

Canal Zone   Colón

San Blas Islands

★ Panama City

PANAMA

Panama Canal

Darién

Pacific Ocean

COLOMBIA

By 1908, the year William Howard Taft was elected, expenditure on the canal had reached $33.2 million, only to be surpassed by the expenditures of the following year, which brought the total to $170 million, $35 million more than had been appropriated by Congress in 1902. Another appropriation of $397 million, to be raised with 3 percent bonds, was added to the $135 million to see the project through to completion. The United States built the canal in ten years, and it was officially opened on August 15, 1914. Through the Torrijos-Carter Treaties (1977), the canal was ceded back to Panama by the United States in 2000.

Since its opening, the Panama Canal has been enormously important to business in the Western Hemisphere, as well as lucrative. In the eighty-five years that it belonged to the United States, the canal took in approximately $1.9 billion, while, in contrast, revenues from 2000 to 2006 were $2.8 billion. On the average, 12,000 ships pass through the canal every year, accounting for almost 5 percent of total world shipping. On October 22, 2006, the citizens of Panama overwhelmingly approved a national referendum to construct new locks, widen and deepen the canal, and excavate new access channels. These improvements are designed to allow for passage of larger and heavier ships, and thereby bring an increased volume of passage and profits to the Panama Canal Authority. In the twenty-first century, the Panama Canal remains of extreme importance to world trade and to U.S. security interests in the Western Hemisphere.

Mark DeStephano

FURTHER READING

Cosmas, Graham A. *An Army for Empire: The United States Army in the Spanish-American War.* Columbia: University of Missouri Press, 1971. A detailed and carefully documented history and analysis of the role of the army in every aspect of the Spanish-American War, with a fine recounting of discussions regarding the need for an isthmian canal and the plans to execute its construction.

McCullough, David. *The Path Between the Seas: The Creation of the Panama Canal.* New York: Simon & Schuster, 1977. This is the single most authoritative work on the history of the Panama Canal. Written in a clear and accessible style, McCullough's book is filled with essential information about the entire canal project—from its inception to its completion.

Maurer, Noel. *What Roosevelt Took: The Economic Impact of the Panama Canal, 1903.* Boston: Division of Research, Harvard Business School, 2006. An outstanding study of the economic benefits garnered by the United States from the construction and operation of the canal—benefits that were not shared fully by the Panamanian people.

Meditz, Sandra W., and Dennis M. Hanratty, eds. *Panama: A Country Study.* 4th ed. Washington, D.C.: U.S. Government Printing Office, 1989. This outstanding fact book was prepared under the auspices of the Department of the Army. It is the single most complete source of data on Panama and, despite its age, still offers a superb introduction to the history and workings of the nation.

Parker, Matthew. *Panama Fever: The Epic Story of One of the Greatest Human Achievements of All Time—The Building of the Panama Canal.* New York: Doubleday, 2007. An excellent historical study of the planning and construction of the canal, with new insights into the design process.

Speller, Jon L. *The Panama Canal: Heart of America's Security.* New York: Robert Speller & Sons, 1972. This brief study answers criticisms of U.S. policy that have been raised over the decades since the building of the canal. It is especially helpful as a resource for analysis of the original treaty documents.

SEE ALSO: Canals; Erie Canal; Latin American trade with the United States; Shipping industry; Spanish-American War; Transatlantic steamer service.

Panic of 1819

THE EVENT: American credit collapse resulting from upheavals accompanying the transition to a market-based economy

DATE: 1819-1820

PLACE: United States, primarily the South and Midwest

SIGNIFICANCE: The Panic of 1819 revealed the consequences of the lack of a national currency system controlled effectively by a federal bank.

The Panic of 1819 had multiple causes, among the most important of which were the opening up for settlement of the public lands in Alabama and Mississippi following the removal of Native Americans from those lands, the emergence of short-staple cotton as a major worldwide commodity, and the resumption of specie payments that had been suspended during the War of 1812. These developments were all manifestations of the conversion of the U.S. economy from one based in subsistence agriculture to one based in marketing commodities.

President Jackson's battle against the Second Bank of the United States is reflected in this political cartoon, which shows Jackson, with Martin Van Buren hanging on to his discarded coat, fleeing from Nicholas Biddle. (Library of Congress)

CAUSES AND CRISES

The United States experienced rapid population growth during the years after 1789, limited in the original colonies to a fixed land base east of the Appalachian Mountains. This situation also affected the panic: The victories of European American settlers over American Indian tribes freed land beyond the Appalachians for settlement. The creation of a public land system, surveyed as rapidly as possible following the end of military activities, induced huge numbers of people to leave their old homes along the eastern seaboard and seek new homesteads, in both the Northwest (Ohio, Indiana, and Illinois) and the Southwest (Tennessee, Alabama, and Mississippi).

To serve the needs of this wave of immigrants, the various newly created western states authorized numerous state banks. These, in turn, supplied immigrants with credit in the form of state banknotes. In addition, a number of branches were established in the new states by the inept management of the Second Bank of the United States, which likewise issued banknotes freely. These notes circulated widely among the immigrants to the newly opened public lands, resulting in significant inflation.

Existing rules allowed squatters to take up residence on the new public lands even before the land was offered for sale at the various government land offices that were being established in the new areas. Although there was extensive demand for surveyors, it took time for crews to be recruited and for the plots to be established according to the preferred system of rectangular townships with six miles on each side. Purchasers buying directly from the government were required to buy at least 640 acres. Many plots were sold to those with capital, who paid one-fourth down and promised to pay the remainder over the next five years. Land speculators, who bought land they intended merely to resell, abounded.

The land rush into Tennessee, Alabama, and Mississippi was motivated by a soaring demand for cotton. The price of cotton rose from a few cents per pound to 33 cents per pound in 1818. As cotton-growing areas, Alabama and Mississippi drew settlers expecting to sell cotton at this exorbitant price. In the spring of 1819, world commodity prices collapsed, and cotton prices fell by more than 50 percent. Settlers who had borrowed money on the assumption that in two to three years they would be selling huge quantities of cotton at high prices became unable to pay back the money they had borrowed, so foreclosures rose dramatically.

Additionally, the Second Bank of the United States began calling in its loans to individuals, as well as the funds it had lent to numerous state banks, and demanding that the loans be repaid with specie (gold and silver), not with the deflated state banknotes that circulated widely. As a result, many state banks also were unable to repay the money they had borrowed, and many collapsed. The leaders of the various state and territorial governments did what they could to rescue the state banks, because their operators were often local political leaders, but many failed.

Sales of public lands also collapsed. Many plots that had already been purchased reverted back to the government when their purchasers were unable to make payments on the remainder of their commitment. The huge optimism that had fueled the land boom gave way to a deep pessimism that may have played into the religious revival that occurred in the succeeding years. Where it looked as if the government debt would shortly be extinguished by the sale of public land, that solution was now put off for at least a decade.

RECOVERY

The economy slowly recovered during the 1820's, but the lessons of the Panic of 1819 remained. Conservative leadership of the Second Bank of the United States under Nicholas Biddle kept a rein on easy financing until Andrew Jackson, the seventh president of the United States, refused to countenance its re-authorization. The conversion of the United States to a market-based economy defined by capitalism remained permanent, along with the occasional panics that seemed to be a natural feature of the business cycle.

Nancy M. Gordon

FURTHER READING

Kindleberger, Charles, and Robert Aliber. *Manias, Panics, and Crashes: A History of Financial Crises.* 5th ed. Hoboken, N.J.: John Wiley & Sons, 2005. The classic treatment by longstanding specialists in the field; more analytical than chronological.

North, Douglass C. *The Economic Growth of the United States, 1790-1860.* New York: Norton, 1966. A classic survey by a Nobel Prize-winning economist.

Rockoff, Hugh. "Banking and Finance, 1789-1914." In *The Cambridge Economic History of the United States,* edited by Stanley Engerman and Robert E. Gallman. Vol. 2. New York: Cambridge University Press, 2000. This comprehensive survey of the history of the American economy treats each of the various sectors in turn.

Rohrbaugh, Malcolm. *The Land Office Business.* London: Oxford University Press, 1968. The most comprehensive treatment of the Land Office.

Rothbard, Murray N. *The Panic of 1819: Reactions and Policies.* New York: Columbia University Press, 1962. Focuses on the development of the panic and the sequence of events; a good starting point.

Rothman, Adam. *Slave Country: American Expansion and the Origins of the Deep South.* Cambridge, Mass.: Harvard University Press, 2005. Provides many details about the emergence of the cotton economy in the American South.

Sellers, Charles. *The Market Revolution: Jacksonian America, 1815-1846.* New York: Oxford University Press, 1991. Masterly account of the conversion of the subsistence economy to one based on markets.

SEE ALSO: Bank failures; Bank of the United States, Second; Business cycles; Currency; Depression of 1808-1809; Monetary policy, federal; Panic of 1837; Panic of 1857; Panic of 1873; Panic of 1893; Panic of 1907.

Panic of 1837

THE EVENT: National depression precipitated by loss of faith in the banking system

DATE: 1837-1843

PLACE: United States

SIGNIFICANCE: The Panic of 1837 undermined the state banking system established during President Andrew Jackson's administration. The failure of large eastern and small rural banks to handle the panic began a movement toward hard money and a distrust of speculation. The resulting depression also wiped out much of the slowly growing labor movement.

Several factors contributed to the Panic of 1837 and the depression that followed. The Andrew Jackson administration's banking policy may have started the depression, as Jackson ordered the withdrawal of federal deposits from the Second Bank of the United States and the placement of federal money in state banks. This shift eliminated the stabilizing effect of a national bank able, with sufficient central power, to inject liquidity into the financial system. The federal government paid off the national debt in 1835, leaving it with excess revenues that it distributed to the states, exacerbating the growing inflationary pressures. As the amount of paper money in the economy exploded, Jackson issued an order requiring all public land sales to occur in gold or silver, rather than banknotes. Jackson hoped to end speculation by limiting the currency available to purchase land. The result was a squeezing of the money supply and a financial panic.

FAILURES AND CONSEQUENCES

The first firms to fail were cotton exporters, whose buyers in London lost their credit as the Bank of England refused to lend money for purchases in the United States. The financial panic hit New Orleans first, as cotton prices collapsed. Cotton speculators and producers suffered, and their financial losses moved to the New York banking industry. As depositors tried to remove their assets from threatened banks, those same banks were forced to halt payments in gold starting in May, 1837. Without a national bank to provide liquidity, credit tightened, and a depression followed.

Cotton mills in Lowell, Massachusetts, and all over New England shut down, as demand for clothing declined and mass unemployment swept through factory towns. The British economy also slipped into depression, deepening the American downturn, as exporters saw their overseas markets dry up just as their domestic markets also weakened. American business received one benefit, as the growing union movement was crushed under the weight of unemployed workers. The 1837 depression was the first major economic downturn of the industrial era. Thousands of workers lost their jobs and were without the benefit of a government safety net.

The real estate industry suffered, because land speculation had been a major cause of the depression. As the value of land declined, speculators abandoned their property to their creditors, further depressing prices. Without people buying land, the need for internal improvements such as roads and canals also eased. This led to rising unemployment, further undermining the economy.

The decline in cotton prices spread the depression into the agricultural South; landowners abandoned their property and headed west in search of cheaper land. Many in the South headed toward the Republic of Texas, an independent country, hoping to escape the poor economic conditions in the United States. For those plantation owners who had not speculated, their slave-based economy escaped

This caricature of President Van Buren issued during the Panic of 1837 portrays him as a monarch in a princely cloak, treading on the Constitution. (Library of Congress)

some of the worst aspects of the depression, convincing some that the southern slave system was superior to the wage-based economy of the North.

The consequences of the depression for the American economy were profound. For only the second time in the country's history, Congress passed a federal bankruptcy law, attempting to protect creditors and debtors alike. The number of bankruptcies skyrocketed from 1841 through 1843, when the law was repealed.

BANKING CRISIS

The banking system was also bruised by the depression. Jackson's attempt to restructure the country's financial system had left the country without the mechanisms for handling a panic or banking crisis. The replacement of the second national bank with state banks led to more speculation, deepening the depression and forcing Jackson's successor, Martin Van Buren, to retreat from Jackson's policies. Most of Van Buren's term in office was consumed by a political debate over creating an independent treasury that could provide liquidity to state banks. The law eventually passed near the end of Van Buren's term, and state banks tried to reopen and pay their depositors in gold, but another banking collapse in 1839 extended hard times through 1843.

The Panic of 1837 highlighted the weakness of a new form of business, the corporation, and its impersonal nature. Spread across a single state or several states, corporations had limited loyalty to their workers, responding to economic depressions with layoffs and plant closures. The buying and selling of stock and the issuing of bonds by corporations provided economic opportunities and risk for ordinary citizens, as they could make or lose a fortune quickly and easily. Many American workers also experienced the negative aspects of wage labor, losing their jobs and unable to find replacements. Unlike farmers, who could produce their own food and owned their land, manufacturing workers were left without an income. As unemployment increased, wages were depressed, as more workers sought fewer and fewer jobs.

The political consequences of the panic were felt in 1840, as President Van Buren, mocked as "Martin Van Ruin," lost a close presidential race to William Henry Harrison.

Douglas Clouatre

FURTHER READING

Feller, Daniel. *The Jacksonian Promise*. Baltimore: Johns Hopkins University Press, 1995. Wide-ranging discussion of the political era and of economic changes that promised prosperity for the middle and working classes of the period.

Remini, Robert. *The Jacksonian Era*. Wheeling, Ill.: Harlan Davidson, 1997. Written by a preeminent Andrew Jackson scholar, this book is a brief description of the political, social, and economic changes that occurred during the 1820's and 1830's.

Rousseau, Peter. "Jacksonian Monetary Policy, Specie Flows, and the Panic of 1837." *Journal of Economic History* 62, no. 457 (2002). Economic analysis of how Andrew Jackson's banking policy and his specie circular contributed to the Panic of 1837.

Sellers, Charles. *The Market Revolution*. London: Oxford University Press, 1991. Expansive book that describes the rise of the market economy in the United States from 1815 to 1846. Includes a description of the 1837 depression and the economic conditions that led to it and followed it.

Widmar, Ted. *Martin Van Buren*. New York: Times Books, 2005. Van Buren's careers as a political operative, secretary of state, and president are the book's primary focus. Widmar also describes how the 1837 depression dominated the Van Buren presidency and his inability to revive the economy.

SEE ALSO: Bank failures; Bank of the United States, Second; Business cycles; Currency; Panic of 1819; Panic of 1857; Panic of 1873; Panic of 1893; Panic of 1907.

Panic of 1857

THE EVENT: Economic downturn that ended a period of prosperity following the end of the Mexican War and the discovery of gold in California

DATE: Began on August 24, 1857

PLACE: New York, New York

SIGNIFICANCE: The Panic of 1857 was linked to the absence of a central banking system in the United States. Many banks independently suspended payments, despite having enough specie to meet demand, perhaps frightening others into following their examples: A core of principles and safeguards could thus have prevented or mitigated the panic. Its effects set the stage for bank reform and the eventual passage of the National Banking Act in 1863.

The Panic of 1857 began in August of that year, but the complex events that gave rise to the crisis originated much earlier. Alarms were sounded following the close of the Crimean War in 1856, when Russia's dependence on American crops ended with the return of Russian soldiers to their farms. In the agricultural regions of the United States, the boom period of the 1850's, based on the discovery of gold in California and in Australia in 1851, had fueled enormous land speculation and railroad commitments. The decrease in Russian demand for grain exports was damaging to agricultural land speculators. Moreover, certain instabilities in the financial structure of Great Britain, America's strongest economic ally, were ominous. By 1856, the credit structure of the United States was seriously overextended and in need of credit reduction.

THE PANIC BEGINS

On the morning of August 24, 1857, the New York branch of the Ohio Life Insurance and Trust Company announced that the bank had failed and closed its doors. News spread quickly that the entirety of the bank's assets had been embezzled by its cashier, and Wall Street immediately suffered a decline in stocks. Within hours of Ohio Life's failure, other New York banks closed, sending public distrust and loss of confidence soaring.

In September, 1857, the steamer *Central America*, loaded with $2 million in Californian gold and headed for New York to renew the dwindling specie (gold coin) reserves of the eastern U.S. banks, sank during a hurricane off the coast of North Carolina. The shipment had been needed to maintain the ratio between deposits and specie in the banks. The toll of human lives and the catastrophic loss of largely uninsured gold further undermined public confidence in the banking system, and many Americans feared the government's paper currency was worthless.

On September 20, 1857, news came from Philadelphia of a run on the banks, and two days later

Newspaper illustration showing the failed Ohio Life Insurance and Trust Company bank with other banks about to topple around it. (Library of Congress)

banks there suspended specie payments to customers. In New York, despite the stability of the state's own currency, banks found themselves faced with unreliable banknotes, but they desperately reassured customers that they would not suspend payments. However, early in October, panic-stricken depositors in New York withdrew $4 million. Bank stocks fell sharply, and by the following week, after a run of depositors for gold, all New York banks suspended specie payment on October 14.

RECOVERY

The panic itself was relatively brief, and by December 14, two months after total suspension, the New York banks resumed specie payments, aided by a massive influx of gold from California and abroad. By the end of the year, banks in Boston, New England, and New Orleans, and very soon those in Philadelphia and Baltimore, also resumed paying specie in full.

The economic recession had lasting effects on merchants and property owners. Hundreds of thousands of men in New York, Chicago, and other large cities were unemployed throughout the winter. Protests were made in the cities hardest hit, most of which adopted relief measures. Within a year, more than five thousand businesses had failed.

Many sections of the country were ravaged by the Panic of 1857: Only California was unscathed. The severity of the panic in the Midwest precipitated a prolonged period of misery with few signs of recuperation. While the East and the larger cities in the West were recovering, midwestern farmers struggled with crop failure and severe drought that resulted in shortages of grain for humans and animals. Thousands of farmers whose farms had been mortgaged to the railroads, now bankrupt, saw no immediate relief for their dismal plight. The South, too, despite its economic reliance on cotton, suffered a paralysis of trade.

The inequities in conditions across the United States exacerbated sectional differences and political tensions. Issues surrounding states' rights, particularly the question of state banknotes and a need for a sound banking system, remained bitterly divisive through the beginning of the U.S. Civil War.

Mary Hurd

FURTHER READING

Huston, James L. *The Panic of 1857 and the Coming of the Civil War.* Baton Rouge: Louisiana State University Press, 1987. Explores the impact of the Panic of 1857 on political attitudes and partisan behavior.

Kindleberger, Charles P., and Robert Aliber. *Manias, Panics, and Crashes: A History of Financial Crises.* Hoboken, N.J.: John Wiley & Sons, 2005. Witty look at the role that mismanagement of money and credit plays in financial crises.

Sobel, Robert. *Panic on Wall Street: A History of America's Financial Disasters.* Washington, D.C.: Beard Books, 1999. Analysis of the complexity and causes—political, military, and economic—of various financial panics.

Stampp, Kenneth. *America in 1857: A Nation on the Brink.* New York: Oxford University Press, 1992. Discusses the Panic of 1857 as a factor in the escalation of North-South tensions that led to the Civil War.

Van Vleck, George W. *The Panic of 1857: An Analytical Study.* New York: AMS Press, 1967. Contains lengthy discussion of the effect of the world economy on the Panic of 1857, particularly the roles of England and France.

SEE ALSO: Bank failures; Banking; Business cycles; Civil War, U.S.; Currency; Mexican War; Panic of 1819; Panic of 1837; Panic of 1873; Panic of 1893; Panic of 1907.

Panic of 1873

THE EVENT: Six-year depression caused by economic instability in the wake of growing railroad speculation

DATE: Began on September 18, 1873

PLACE: Eastern, southern, and midwestern regions of the United States

SIGNIFICANCE: The Panic of 1873 represented the first great crisis of industrial capitalism in the United States, and it altered the nature of economic enterprise, political ideology, and labor rights. The resulting depression caused widespread tension between laborers and capitalists, dividing the country along class lines.

After the end of the U.S. Civil War, the United States experienced a period of economic expansion that arose from a northern railroad boom and the passage of protective tariffs. Between 1866 and 1873,

Jay Cooke and Company's office during the Panic of 1873. (Library of Congress)

thirty-five thousand miles of track were laid throughout the country, bringing the railroads a great infusion of cash from speculation. The Philadelphia banking firm of Jay Cooke and Company handled most of the government's loans during the Civil War. It began to invest heavily in the railroads but needed more funds to complete its investment plans. Cooke and other entrepreneurs planned to build a second transcontinental railroad, the Northern Pacific Railway, but by September, 1873, the firm had overextended itself and declared bankruptcy. Cooke was engaged in the dangerous practice of advancing short-term funds for long-term use. This unregulated, speculative credit created a vast overexpansion of the nation's railroad network. Paper money soon depreciated, and the impact fell on the domestic economy.

FROM BAD TO WORSE

The situation worsened when New York banks loaned money to railroads that expected to raise funds for repayment by selling bonds before the notes came due. There was no central national bank to shield the economy from the brunt of the railroads' collapse, so a chain reaction of bank failures resulted. The stock market plummeted, and the New York Stock Exchange was closed for ten days. Between 1873 and 1878, eighteen thousand businesses failed and the unemployment rate reached 14 percent.

One-quarter of New York City's labor force was unable to find work in 1874. The panic caused companies to hoard cash receipts rather than depositing them in banks, so payrolls could not be met. In previous decades, workers had concentrated on such issues as greenbacks, cooperatives, and the eight-hour workday. Now, they simply sought to maintain their predepression wages or find unemployment relief. Some moved toward socialism.

Worker unrest led to social class tensions and labor demonstrations, especially in northern urban centers. The Work or Bread movement in New York turned violent on January 13, 1874, when police dispersed a crowd of seven thousand demonstrators at Tompkins Square. In 1875, a long strike in Pennsylvania's anthracite coal fields ended with the defeat of the Workingmen's Benevolent Association and resulted in the infamous trials of leaders in the Molly Maguires.

President Rutherford B. Hayes had to send in federal troops to quell a railroad strike that left more than one hundred dead in 1877. One year later, fifteen thousand textile workers went on strike for two months in an unsuccessful attempt to halt wage reductions. Farmers encountered falling agricultural prices and land values, and they fell into debt as a result. Small farmers in midwestern states began to join the National Grange of the Patrons of Husbandry, better known as the Granger movement, in larger numbers from 1870 until 1890 to prevent the high freight prices for agricultural products imposed on their group by the railroad industry. The Grange advocated strong railroad regulation, government controls to prevent currency inflation, a return to the gold standard, and putting a stop to high freight rates.

IMPACT

The emergence of the corporation in the United States coincided with the rise of the railroad industry and of organized labor movements to counter the influence of monopolistic practices. Political leaders were reluctant to involve the federal government too heavily in the private sector, but this mentality shifted during the late nineteenth century, when unions began asking the government to intercede on their behalf. Congress finally enacted the Interstate Commerce Act of 1887 to regulate railroads and the Sherman Antitrust Act of 1890 to prevent monopolistic companies from gaining total control in an industry. By the turn of the twentieth century, politicians and Progressive reformers created many of the United States' modern regulatory agencies; these departments included the Interstate Commerce Commission, the Food and Drug Administration, and the Federal Trade Commission.

The Panic of 1873 represented a shift in political power. Voters reacted to the depression by turning against the party in power and reversing the Republican stranglehold on Congress by the mid-1870's. It would not be until 1896 that Republicans would gain control of both houses. Northerners began to turn away from Reconstruction policies, and African Americans' hopes for social reform began to fade, as educational opportunities and social and industrial progress stagnated in the South. The effects of the panic were devastating because of the emerging factory system in the region. Poor whites and African Americans were forced to depend on cotton as the primary cash crop once again, and they became dependent on sharecropping and tenant systems until the mid-twentieth century.

Gayla Koerting

FURTHER READING

Fels, Rendigs. "American Business Cycles, 1865-1879." *American Economic Review* 41, no. 3 (June, 1951): 325-349. Analyzes the causes and effects of the Panic of 1873, contending that businesses undergo cyclical cycles of peak and decline.

_____. "The Long-Wave Depression, 1873-1897." *The Review of Economics and Statistics* 31, no. 1 (February, 1949): 69-73. Argues that scholars Alvin Hansen and Joseph Schumpeter are too dependent on comparing the causes of the Great Depression with that of the Panic of 1873. Contends that specific causal factors for the Panic of 1873 must be taken into account and studied within the context of that time period.

Foner, Eric. *Reconstruction: America's Unfinished Revolution, 1863-1877.* New York: Harper & Row, 1988. Provides an overview of the Panic of 1873 in the context of the political, social, and economic factors of the Reconstruction era.

Juglar, Clement. *A Brief History of Panics and Their Periodical Occurrence in the United States.* Reprint. New York: Augustus M. Kelley, 1966. Day-to-day account of the events that took place immediately following September, 1873.

Wicker, Elmus. *Banking Panics of the Gilded Age.* New York: Cambridge University Press, 2000. Major study of post-Civil War banking panics; argues that the suspension of cash payments had the greatest impact on the working class during depressions during the late nineteenth century.

SEE ALSO: Business cycles; Granger movement; New York Stock Exchange; Panic of 1819; Panic of 1837; Panic of 1857; Panic of 1893; Panic of 1907; Railroads; Sherman Antitrust Act.

Panic of 1893

THE EVENT: Stock market collapse following the failures of the Reading Railroad and the National Cordage Company

DATE: February-May, 1893

SIGNIFICANCE: The Panic of 1893 marked a major shift in investment techniques, as investors began to place more money in stocks than in bonds.

The economic climate surrounding the Panic of 1893 was unique. Most of the United States' financial panics were precipitated by inflation caused by investors speculating in one or more industries. Markets collapsed and panics ensued when this speculation caused securities to become dramatically overvalued. Credit proved difficult or impossible to obtain, and repricing the assets that underlay the overvalued securities took more time than investors expected. Some investors were left holding securities that proved to be essentially worthless, because the companies holding title to the assets had filed for bankruptcy; only investors with extraordinarily deep pockets could work their way through these price adjustments.

THE CAUSE

By contrast, between the end of the U.S. Civil War in 1865 and the early 1890's, the United States experienced a long period of monetary deflation, so securities were not overvalued in 1893. The immediate cause of the Panic of 1893, rather, was the necessity of refinancing America's railroads. The vast expansion of America's railroads after the Civil War had required sums that could not be generated from the profits of the railroad companies themselves. The railroads amassed the huge sums required to build more tracks and buy more engines and other equipment by issuing bonds, whose interest rates were fixed.

The United States was operating on the gold standard during the 1890's. Thus, while the demand for money was growing rapidly, the money supply was fixed by the amount of gold in the reserve. As a result, prices declined. Increasingly, the railroad companies found themselves with overexpanded lines that did not generate enough returns to pay the interest on their bonds. The companies began to default on their bonds. Between 1893 and 1897, companies owning about one-third of the railroad mileage in the United States passed through bankruptcy. This enabled them to free themselves from the obligation to pay interest on their bonds, and those that were viable recapitalized, mostly by selling stock (which carried no commitment to make fixed regular payments).

A significant number of those who had purchased railroad bonds were foreign investors. When the companies defaulted on their obligations, America's reputation as a good place to invest suffered significantly. Those who had strong financial backing—financiers such as J. P. Morgan and Edward H. Harriman—were able to take over the companies and to reorganize them. Many foreign investors withdrew funds from the United States, however, and they insisted on being paid in gold, placing a heavy strain on the U.S. gold supply. Many banks, especially smaller banks in the South and West, lacked enough gold in reserve to repay these investors, and they went bankrupt as a result. These bank failures wiped out the savings of many small businessmen and particularly farmers, who still constituted a substantial portion of the U.S. population. Those banks that survived stopped making loans, which also harmed farmers, because they lacked the cash to finance their operations until the fall harvest. Thus, many farms also went bankrupt.

Many Americans believed that the central cause of these problems was the lack of sufficient gold.

Since the Civil War, there had been no major additions to the nation's gold supply, but the nation's economy had nevertheless continued to grow. Many people believed that the solution to the problem was to convert from a gold standard to a bimetallic system in which currency was supported by silver as well as gold. The requirement that loans be repaid in gold had been halted during the Civil War, when the government had issued the famous "greenbacks" as legal tender. In 1875, Congress decided that "species redemption," the ability of banks to require that loans be repaid in gold, would be resumed in 1879.

Meanwhile, the issuance of paper money was very restrained, so there was very little inflation. In 1879, a $1 paper note was worth about $1 in gold. In 1878, Congress had ordered the Treasury to buy a specified amount of silver and create silver coins

Newspaper illustration depicting the panic in the New York Stock Exchange on May 5, 1893. (Library of Congress)

with it. Congress tried to increase the amount of silver the Treasury was required to buy in 1890, but in 1893, President Grover Cleveland persuaded Congress to repeal the requirement, causing the gold holdings of the Treasury to drop to a new low.

IMPACT

The bankruptcy of railroads and numerous other firms continued. Many people had depended on the interest payments on railroad bonds. The crisis harmed them both directly and indirectly, as it dampened financial institutions' willingness to lend. Under these circumstances, company financing shifted from bonds to stocks, which were traded much more heavily on the New York Stock Exchange than had hitherto been the case for bonds. Many trusts (essentially banking holding companies) were created, further consolidating control of the American manufacturing sector.

Nancy M. Gordon

FURTHER READING

Cochran, Thomas C., and William Miller. *The Age of Enterprise: A Social History of Industrial America.* New York: Macmillan, 1960. Highly useful synthesis of the economic developments in the United States.

Engerman, Stanley, and Kenneth Sokoloff. "Technology and Industrialization, 1790-1914." In *The Cambridge Economic History of the United States*, edited by Stanley Engerman and Robert Gallman. Vol. 2. New York: Cambridge University Press, 2000. Overview of the influence of modern technology and industrial culture on U.S. economic history.

Kindleberger, Charles, and Robert Aliber. *Manias, Panics, and Crashes: A History of Financial Crises.* 5th ed. Hoboken, N.J.: John Wiley & Sons, 2005. The classic treatment by longstanding specialists in the field; more analytical than chronological.

Martin, Albro. *Railroads Triumphant: The Growth, Rejection, and Rebirth of a Vital American Force.* Oxford, England: Oxford University Press, 1992. Popular account that is loaded with many details.

Neal, Larry, and Lance E. Davis. "Finance Capitalism and the Second Industrial Revolution." In *Financing Innovation in the United States, 1870 to the Present*, edited by Naomi Lamoreux and Kenneth Sokoloff. Cambridge, Mass.: MIT Press, 2007. Significant study of the process of financing America's industrial sector.

Rockoff, Hugh. "Banking and Finance, 1789-1914." In *The Cambridge Economic History of the United States*, edited by Stanley Engerman and Robert Gallman. Vol. 2. New York: Cambridge University Press, 2000. Good, comprehensive history of the economic development of the United States.

SEE ALSO: Bond industry; Business cycles; Currency; Panic of 1819; Panic of 1837; Panic of 1857; Panic of 1873; Panic of 1907; Railroads; Stock markets.

Panic of 1907

THE EVENT: Stock market crash that accompanied the failure of many New York banks but was mitigated by massive investments made by J. P. Morgan

DATE: October, 1907

PLACE: New York, New York

SIGNIFICANCE: The Panic of 1907 led to the creation of the Federal Reserve system.

Beginning in 1896, the U.S. economy entered a sustained period of prosperous activity, especially on the stock market. The market was the means whereby a major consolidation of U.S. businesses was carried out, largely through the efforts of men of great wealth, such as John D. Rockefeller, Edward H. Harriman, Andrew Carnegie, and, above all, J. P. Morgan. These business consolidations were driven by a widespread conviction that the gyrations of the business world should be suppressed through monopoly control of important parts of the economy. Rockefeller's effective control of the oil market was the model for the consolidations.

One consequence of this period of consolidation was the establishment of numerous "trusts," that is, investment houses that traded in the securities of many businesses. In 1906, there were some one thousand of these trusts. Although they resembled banks, trusts were not required to hold a certain percentage of the money they managed as "reserves," that is, as cash or its ready equivalent. In 1906, New York State introduced a requirement that trusts keep 15 percent of their total assets in reserves, though only one-third of this amount (5 percent of total assets) had to be in cash. This requirement was still being implemented in 1907, so many trusts were still almost entirely dependent on the marketability of their assets when the panic broke.

Another major factor in the Panic of 1907 was an event that could not have been foreseen: the earthquake and subsequent fire that struck San Francisco in April of 1906. The almost total destruction of large parts of the city put many insurance companies at risk, and in 1906-1907, Wall Street experienced a substantial sell-off of insurance company stocks. The value of insurance-sector stocks dropped by 15 to 30 percent, and railroad stocks dropped by more than 15 percent. As a result of these market pullbacks, there was insufficient capital available to finance the 1907 crop year.

THE TRIGGER

The immediate trigger of the Panic of 1907 was the attempt of a couple of speculators to corner the market in copper. As they proceeded to buy up shares of companies with copper holdings in Montana, they discovered that the market was dealing in more shares than they had calculated, meaning that the shares had been used as collateral for other purchases. The two leading speculators had used funds they had borrowed from the Knickerbocker Trust Company to pay for the copper company shares they were amassing. As soon as it became known that the Knickerbocker company

The market problems of 1907 are depicted in this political cartoon showing "common honesty" erupting from the volcano and people fleeing with "secret rate schedules," "rebates," "stocks," and "frenzied accounts." (Library of Congress)

had provided the funding for their speculation, the company became the object of a bank run.

The financial unrest associated with the Panic of 1907 began in earnest on October 21 and extended through the next two weeks. The Knickerbocker Trust Company lacked the cash to pay all the depositors who lined up to withdraw their funds. On October 22, the trust suspended payments to depositors. On the same day, the National Bank of Commerce let it be known that it would no longer accept checks from the Knickerbocker Trust; lines then formed around other banks, as depositors tried to withdraw their deposits. The National Bank of Commerce was sometimes known as J. P. Morgan's bank, and Morgan became the leader of a group of financiers trying to prevent the bank runs from spreading. At the same time, banks outside New York City that had deposits in New York City banks joined individual depositors and began trying to withdraw their deposits.

Morgan and a coterie of other financiers of the leading New York banks began a series of meetings, to which the secretary of the Treasury was invited. By Thursday, not only Morgan but also the U.S. Treasury had begun to make loans to all the major New York banks to ensure that their cash supplies would be sufficient to meet all demands. When these demands increased, threatening to exceed supply, Morgan pressured the other leading financiers to advance additional funds to cover the banks' needs. By the weekend, Morgan had learned that a shipment of gold was on its way to New York from London. The New York clearing-house banks agreed, on being pressured by Morgan, to issue clearinghouse certificates that could temporarily supplement their cash supplies.

On Monday, October 27, Morgan learned that the City of New York would be unable to meet its payroll obligations. He agreed to buy revenue bonds from the city that would replenish its cash supply, enabling it to pay its employees. By this time, the panic was spreading to Wall Street, and a number of well-known firms such as Westinghouse Electric announced that they would be forced to declare bankruptcy.

RECOVERY AND RESULT

By the beginning of November, the turmoil began to subside. In the end, only six banks failed, along with a number of companies listed on the New York Stock Exchange. As those directly involved began to reflect on the panic, however, it became clear to them that the country needed a central bank or its equivalent. Congress, under the leadership of President Theodore Roosevelt, began to investigate the panic and its causes. By 1912, government leaders had come to the conclusion that a central reserve was needed. On December 23, 1913, they passed the Federal Reserve Act.

Nancy M. Gordon

FURTHER READING

Allen, Frederick Lewis. *The Great Pierpont Morgan.* New York: Harper & Row, 1965. Popular biography that provides many of the details of how Morgan engineered the rescue of the New York banks in 1907.

Bruner, Robert F., and Sean D. Carr. *The Panic of 1907: Lessons Learned from the Market's Perfect Storm.* Hoboken, N.J.: John Wiley & Sons, 2007. Well-researched account of the events of the Panic of 1907.

Cochran, Thomas C. *The Age of Enterprise: A Social History of Industrial America.* New York: Macmillan, 1960. Essential background for the events of 1907 by a leading business historian.

Kindleberger, Charles, and Robert Aliber. *Manias, Panics, and Crashes: A History of Financial Crises.* 5th ed. Hoboken, N.J.: John Wiley & Sons, 2005. Economic analysis of the factors that brought about the panics of the nineteenth and early twentieth centuries.

Rockoff, Hugh. "Banking and Finance, 1789-1914." In *The Cambridge Economic History of the United States*, edited by Stanley Engerman and Robert Gallman. Vol. 2. New York: Cambridge University Press, 2000. Excellent survey of U.S. economic history during the nineteenth century.

SEE ALSO: Bank failures; Banking; Business cycles; Federal Reserve; Morgan, J. P.; Panic of 1819; Panic of 1837; Panic of 1857; Panic of 1873; Panic of 1893.

Papermaking industry

DEFINITION: Companies manufacturing and distributing paper and paper products

SIGNIFICANCE: Paper is a necessary component for a wide range of industries, including the publishing, card, stationery, printing, postal, shipping, disposable cup and dishware, packaging, office supply, and school supply industries.

The first facility to create paper in America was a paper "plant" in Germantown, Pennsylvania, established about 1690. Paper had been invented in China during the early centuries of the common era; it had made its way to Europe by 1100. By 1500, rag-based paper had spread widely throughout Europe, just in time for the invention of movable type

The Old Washington Paper Mill in Germantown, Pennsylvania, in 1900. (Library of Congress)

by Johann Gutenberg. Papermaking was a craft industry at this time, conducted in small shops with a few workers. The major problems were acquiring a sufficient number of rags and breaking them down into their constituent fibers.

During the eighteenth century, papermaking spread throughout colonial America, but it was not until the early nineteenth century that new technology enabled papermaking to become a real industry, with the introduction first of the Hollander, a device for beating rags into fibers, and then of the more sophisticated Fourdrinier machine, which further sped the reduction of rags to their constituent fibers.

INDUSTRIALIZATION

The modern industry got its start after the U.S. Civil War, when it was discovered that wood fiber derived from softwood trees lent itself to conversion to fiber and that fiber could be converted in turn into pulp—a watery slurry of tree fibers that could be formed into sheets or rolls by laying it out on a flat or curved surface. Various processes were used to produce pulp, either grinding the wood (groundwood) or dissolving the substances holding the fibers together, or exposing them to chemicals.

The last part of the nineteenth century saw the creation of a full-fledged papermaking industry, starting with large installations that turned wood fiber into pulp. These facilities were all located along rivers or lakes, because turning wood into pulp requires large quantities of water. Also needed were large forests of softwoods, especially spruce and fir. At the same time, demand for paper to print books and especially newspapers grew at a very rapid rate, particularly in the United States. As a result, an industry producing newsprint in very large quantities emerged, especially in Canada and the northern tier of the United States, where large forests of softwood grew.

The machines that turned fiber into pulp and pulp into paper were large and very expensive; thus the paper industry was very capital-intensive. New capital investment mostly took the form of upgrading machinery, though operating that machinery required specialized skills that led to a stable, largely unionized workforce. Demand for paper generally tracks the business cycle, so the paper market is cyclical. The high capital costs of the industry, however, compel the machines to be operated at nearly full capacity to remain profitable. Thus, the paper industry is always balanced on a "hinge," the 90 percent of capacity operation that is essential to keep the invested capital employed.

Paper is a product of the developed world, where demand is located. The United States, because of its large geographic extent, has the largest paper industry in the world, followed by Canada, which delivers most of the paper it produces to the United States. Europe is another area of high demand for paper, a significant portion of which comes from the United States and Canada. It also has its own paper industry, located largely in Scandinavia, which markets its pulp and paper in the European Union. Japan also has a substantial paper industry, and though it has forested land in its north, it imports pulp to make enough paper to supply its needs.

Besides paper for newspapers and for writing and printing, paper developed during the early twentieth century into a major raw material for packaging. Paper for this purpose required greater strength than newsprint or even writing paper, and some companies specialized in packaging paper and in paper used to make cartons and boxes. This part of the market grew with the expansion of markets for consumer products, particularly as self-service stores multiplied.

AFTER 1950

In the last half of the twentieth century, papermaking became a global industry. It got a major boost when it was discovered, before World War II, that fiber for paper need not come from softwood trees. Hardwood trees, the most prevalent variety in the temperate and tropical zones, could also be used for making paper. These areas had longer growing seasons that made it possible to grow trees specifically for pulpwood in twenty years, or sometimes less. As a result, much of the paper industry in the United States moved south: International Paper Company, an American paper company and the largest in the world, steadily reduced its holdings in the northern United States and Canada, replacing them with lands and facilities in the southern United States.

During the late twentieth century, methods began to be developed for making pulp for paper from other fiber sources, such as sugarcane residues in Brazil. Pulp has long been a commodity that can be acquired anywhere suitable fibrous sources are located, and recycled paper has become a major "raw material." Papermaking remains water and energy intensive, as well as capital-intensive, continuing to require constant operation to remain profitable. The reduction in printing in favor of electronic communication in the twenty-first century may provide a further challenge to the industry.

Nancy M. Gordon

FURTHER READING

Arpan, Jeffrey S., et al. *The United States Pulp and Paper Industry: Global Challenges and Strategies.* Columbia: University of South Carolina Press, 1986. Comprehensive account of the industry by a group of business school researchers.

Hunter, Dard. *Papermaking: The History and Technique of an Ancient Craft.* New York: Alfred A. Knopf, 1943. Many historical details but most useful for an exhaustive chronology.

Roach, Thomas R. *Newsprint: Canadian Supply and American Demand.* Durham, N.C.: Forest History Society, 1994. Part of a series published by the society; tells the story of the newsprint portion of the papermaking industry.

U.S. Department of Energy. *Setting the Industry Technology Agenda: The 2001 Forest, Wood and Paper Industry Technology Summit.* Atlanta: Tappi, 2002. A technology summit meeting that examined technological aspects of the papermaking industry.

SEE ALSO: Book publishing; Currency; Forestry industry; Magazine industry; Newspaper industry; Printing industry; Retail trade industry; Shipping industry.

Parliamentary Charter of 1763

THE LAW: British royal charter granting the Crown a monopoly on many types of trade, including the fur trade, in Britain's American colonies

DATE: Passed on October 7, 1763

SIGNIFICANCE: The Parliamentary Charter of 1763 was issued at the conclusion of the Seven Years' War between France and Britain. Despite its victory, Britain needed fresh sources of revenue to pay its large war debt. The charter forbade colonists from settling west of the Appalachians and prohibited anyone other than a representative of the Crown from negotiating the purchase of Native American lands.

The Parliamentary Charter of 1763 drove up the purchase price of Native American land by giving the British crown monopolistic control over land purchases. By forbidding settlement west of the Appalachians, the charter shut out colonists from the lucrative fur trade while also denying them access to productive agricultural lands, despite the fact that colonists had already purchased land and started settlements west of the Appalachians. The colonists had fought for Great Britain in the just-concluded French and Indian War (the American portion of the Seven Years' War), and they felt that they had sacrificed enough for the home country. They therefore resented Parliament's decision to force them to help pay for the costs of the war in Europe as well.

In an attempt to placate Native Americans and French colonists now under British jurisdiction in the New World, the Parliamentary Charter of 1763 granted these subjects more political rights than loyal British colonists enjoyed. The charter was the first in a series of acts—including the Stamp Act of 1765, Sugar Act of 1764, and Tea Act of 1773—that required British colonists to pay higher taxes on an increasing number of imported goods. These acts together represented a growing trend toward taxation of the British colonies without granting them representation, which became one of the causes of the American Revolution.

Victoria Erhart

SEE ALSO: Boston Tea Party; European trade with the United States; French and Indian War; Native American trade; Navigation Acts; Revolutionary War; Stamp Act of 1765.

Patent law

DEFINTION: Body of statutes and common law that governs the intellectual property rights adhering to inventors and inventions

SIGNIFICANCE: Patents encourage and reward invention. In addition, patents promote the disclosure of inventions to the public, which in turn stimulates further innovation and economic development.

Businesses in industries ranging widely from manufacturing, biotechnology, and financial services to information technology, chemicals, and pharmaceuticals consider patents to be valuable assets that can enhance market share and provide an overall competitive advantage. Furthermore, the licensing of patents can generate significant royalties that can serve as an additional revenue stream for a business. A patent is a public privilege, granted by the U.S. government, that confers on an inventor the exclusive rights to use and control his or her invention. The government grants an inventor these rights in exchange for fully disclosing the invention to the public in a patent application. After the inventor files the application, it is subject to an examination process. If the invention meets the statutory requirements for patentability, the inventor is granted a patent. A U.S. patent confers on an inventor the right to exclude all others from making, using, selling or offering for sale, and importing into the United States the invention for twenty years, as measured from the date the patent application was filed.

Magazine illustration from 1869 showing patent officers at work. (Library of Congress)

HISTORICAL DEVELOPMENT

By the sixteenth century, patent laws existed in Italy, France, Germany, the Netherlands, and England. In 1624, the English parliament enacted the Statute of Monopolies, which forbade monopoly privileges granted by the Crown, with the exception of patents. This law was the foundation of the English patent system, which served as the basis for patents issued by several of the American colonies. After the American Revolution, the states continued to issue patents, but this inevitably led to conflicts and confusion when multiple inventors were issued patents on the same invention by different states. During the drafting of the United States Constitution, the power to issue patents was delegated to Congress, by Article I, section 8, clause 8, of the Constitution.

Over the years, the U.S. Congress has enacted a series of patent statutes to define the requirements for patent protection and the exclusive rights of the patentee. The first patent statute was enacted in 1790, and it was quickly replaced in 1793. The Patent Act of 1790 had established a system whereby an application for a patent on an invention was to be examined by federal government officials, including the secretary of state, to determine if it met the legal requirements. The 1793 statute abandoned this approach and created a registration system under which patent applications were not examined for compliance with the requirements for patentability. Instead, inventors simply registered their inventions and received a patent, leaving the federal courts to determine the validity of the patent if the inventor ever brought suit to enforce the patent.

By 1836, however, Congress had become concerned that the registration system had resulted in too many patents on inventions that were in fact not patentable. The Patent Act of 1836 reinstituted an examination system and created the Patent Office to oversee this system. Congress superseded this statute with the Patent Act of 1870, which retained the

The Beginnings of Patent Law

The term "patent" is actually an abbreviated version of "letters patent," derived from the Latin term *literae patentes*, which means "open letters." Letters patent were issued by the sovereign and recited a grant of a special privilege to favored merchants and manufacturers. Although there are a few scattered references to monopolies or franchises granted by sovereigns to artisans and guilds from other countries in an attempt to gain access to their skills and knowledge, the first true patent system did not emerge until the European Renaissance.

The Venetian Republic is believed to have enacted the first known patent statute on March 19, 1474, which provided that

> every person who shall build any new and ingenious device in this City, not previously made in our Commonwealth, shall give notice of it to the office of our General Welfare Board when it has been reduced to perfection so that it can be used and operated. It being further forbidden to every other person in any of our territories and towns to make any further device conforming with and similar to said one, without the consent and license of the author, for the term of 10 years.

All of the requirements for obtaining patent protection can be found in this early statute.

examination system and added the requirement that the applicant for a patent define the invention by way of written claims that specifically describe the invention in detail. Judicial treatment of patents changed dramatically during the Great Depression. The economic downturn and strong antimonopoly attitude of that era led to hostility to patent enforcement in the courts that finally ended with the onset of World War II and the need to develop new military technologies. In 1952, a new Patent Act was enacted, marking a significant overhaul of the U.S. patent system.

The 1952 Act

The Patent Act of 1952 spells out the procedure and legal requirements for obtaining a patent. Once the invention has been built, the inventor may file an application with the U.S. Patent Office to obtain a utility patent protection for the invention. A patent application is a document that discloses the details and operation of the invention to the Patent Office. The central part of a patent application is the claims, which describe and delineate the scope of the invention sought to be patented. The language used in the claims to detail the invention becomes important in reviewing the prior art (everything publicly known before the invention) during the examination process and in proving infringement of the patent if it is subsequently granted.

Once a complete application is filed, it is assigned to a patent examiner knowledgeable in the field of technology for examination to determine whether the invention meets the standards for patentability. To qualify for utility patent protection, the invention must meet four distinct legal requirements, all of which were first included in the Venetian patent statute enacted in 1474. The invention must be of the type of subject matter that may be patented, and it must be useful, novel, and nonobvious.

The Patent Act defines the subject matter that may be patented to include any process, machine, manufacture, composition of matter, or improvement on any of these. The U.S. Supreme Court has explained that patentable subject matter consists of any product or process created by humans. Although the range of patent-eligible subject matter is quite broad, excluded from patent protection are laws of nature, natural phenomena, mathematical formulas, and abstract ideas. As such, a newly discovered mineral or chemical element, the law of gravity, natural phenomena such as tides or volcanic eruptions, scientific principles such as the law of thermodynamics, and abstract mathematical formulas are not patentable.

The invention must also be useful, not merely theoretical. An invention is useful if it is operable and has a practical purpose. As long as the invention is capable of performing its proposed function, it need not be the best or the only way of doing so. Accordingly, an invention lacks utility only if the invention is totally incapable of achieving some useful result or if it requires further research to identify or confirm a practical use or application.

In addition, the invention must be new; that is, it must be something that no one else, including the inventor, has publicly made or used before in the United States, or patented or described in a printed publication anywhere else in the world. The novelty requirement furthers the policy that a patent should not be granted for something previously invented or already freely available in the public domain. When the same device was previously known, used, or described in a printed publication before the date that the inventor claims to created the invention, the invention is said to be anticipated by the prior art.

Another aspect of novelty relates to how the inventor has used the invention and whether that use may lead to a loss of the ability to patent the invention. Even if an inventor was the first person to invent the subject matter claimed in the patent application, he or she will be barred from being granted a patent if the invention was patented or described in a printed publication in the United States or a foreign country, or in public use or on sale in the United States, more than one year before the filing date of the patent application.

Further, the invention must not be "obvious" to a person with ordinary skill in the art and who understands the technical field of the invention. Instead, it must represent a significant inventive "next step," "leap forward," or meaningful advancement in the current state of the technology. Under the Patent Act, the question is whether the invention would have been obvious to a person with ordinary expertise and knowledge in the pertinent field. If so, then the invention is not patentable. Thus, the nonobviousness requirement prevents new but merely routine or marginal variations on existing technology from receiving patent protection.

Finally, the patent application must adequately disclose and describe the invention and its preferred embodiment. The application must disclose a precise written description of the invention. The disclosure must be enabling in the sense of explaining how to make and use the invention. Finally, the disclosure must identify the best mode—inventor's preferred way of making and using the invention. This requirement is based on the premise that full disclosure of technical information will spur further invention and innovation. Even if the invention meets all of the other requirements of patentability, if the patent application does not fulfill the disclosure requirement, the applicant will not be granted a patent. In a sense, therefore, the disclosure requirement represents part of a "bargain" between the government and inventors: full disclosure of the invention to the public in exchange for exclusive rights for a period of twenty years.

TRENDS

The late twentieth century witnessed a number of major developments in patent law and the patent system. One the most significant developments occurred in 1982, when Congress passed legislation creating a new federal court of appeals to hear all appeals from district courts involving patents. The purpose of this new appellate court was to bring more consistency to patent law and enhance the status of patents in an industrial economy. Another important development resulted from the membership of the United States in the World Trade Organization, which in 1994 concluded an international agreement among its members to bring greater international harmonization to patent law in the age of an increasingly global economy.

American patent law has also had to respond to new innovations in biotechnology and information technology, including the emergence of the Internet as a marketplace. During the 1970's, the courts struggled with the issue of whether computer-related inventions were patentable. Some argued that computer programs were merely unpatentable abstract mathematical algorithms, but in 1981, the Supreme Court ruled that software that applies mathematical algorithms to achieve a practical result was patentable. The decision proved to be critical to computer industry.

A second important Supreme Court decision in 1980 established that genetically altered living organisms were patentable, spurring rapid developments in the biotechnology industry. Likewise, responding to trends in agriculture and industrial designs for useful products, Congress enacted amendments to the Patent Act providing for plant patents and design patents. A plant patent confers the exclusive right to reproduce a new and distinctive variety of asexually reproducing plants. A design patent protects new, original, and nonobvious ornamental designs for articles of manufacture.

By the mid-1990's, electronic commerce became a reality, as businesses recognized the potential of the Internet as a new market. The development of new methods of doing business online soon raised the issue of whether such business methods were patentable. Although traditionally the courts had been reluctant to extend patent protection to business models and systems, in a landmark holding the federal court of appeals responsible for reviewing patent cases ruled that such business methods were in fact patentable. As the scope of patentable inventions has expanded, the U.S. Patent Office has seen the number of patent applications dramatically increase and has continued to adjust its examination procedures accordingly.

Kurt M. Saunders

FURTHER READING

Adelman, Martin J. *Patent Law Perspectives.* 2d ed. 8 vols. New York: Matthew Bender, 2002. Provides a detailed analysis of ongoing developments in patent law and an evaluation of the implications of these developments on patenting and patent law practice.

Durham, Alan L. *Patent Law Essentials: A Concise Guide.* 2d ed. Westport, Conn.: Praeger, 2004. A useful and concise guide to patent law basics and the patenting process intended for nonlawyers.

Merges, Robert P., and John F. Duffy. *Patent Law and Policy: Cases and Materials.* 3d ed. Newark, N.J.: LexisNexis, 2002. Contains the leading court cases on patent law and intersperses these with useful notes, illustrations, and references.

Mueller, Janet M. *An Introduction to Patent Law.* 2d ed. New York: Aspen, 2006. Provides a comprehensive summary of the law of patents and the patenting process, in addition to examples and practical illustrations.

Pressman, David. *Patent It Yourself.* 12th ed. Berkeley, Calif.: Nolo, 2006. A step-by-step guide through the patent application and examination process for nonlawyers.

Schechter, Roger E., and John R. Thomas. *Principles of Patent Law.* St. Paul, Minn.: Thomson West, 2004. Provides an understandable overview of the key concept and rules of patent law, along with an explanation of their underlying rationale and numerous hypothetical examples.

SEE ALSO: Constitution, U.S.; Copyright law; Edison, Thomas Alva; Industrial Revolution, American; Inventions; Pharmaceutical industry.

Penn, William

IDENTIFICATION: English Quaker who founded the colony of Pennsylvania
BORN: October 14, 1644; London, England
DIED: July 30, 1718; Ruscombe, England
SIGNIFICANCE: Penn was the founder and owner of the colony of Pennsylvania. As one of America's earliest proprietors, his business practices were unique in that he maintained an amicable business relationship with local Native Americans instead of seeking to conquer them.

On March 4, 1681, King Charles II of England granted William Penn a charter for the land located in America that was west of the Delaware River and between New York and Maryland. The king made this grant in settlement of a debt owed to Penn's deceased father, Admiral Sir William Penn. Penn viewed the colonization of Pennsylvania as both a business opportunity and a chance to create a community providing religious freedom to anyone who believed in God. By selling parcels of land relatively cheaply and marketing the colony in Europe, Penn succeeded in selling more than 620,000 acres to approximately five hundred buyers by August, 1682. Thousands of persecuted people moved to Pennsylvania in search of religious freedom.

In October, 1682, Penn arrived in Pennsylvania for the first time. That same year, he made a treaty of friendship with the local Native American tribe, the Lenni Lenape (also known as Delaware), and paid them for the land that King Charles had already given him. Penn lived in the colony until 1684 and continued to maintain a business relationship with the indigenous people. In 1683, Penn founded the town of Philadelphia and named it Pennsylvania's capital. Unfortunately, by the time Penn returned to England in 1684, he viewed the colony as a business failure, because it had not yet yielded him a profit. He and his family retained ownership of the colony until the American Revolution.

Bernadette Zbicki Heiney

SEE ALSO: Colonial economic systems; Native American trade; Revolutionary War.

Pension and retirement plans

DEFINITION: Savings plans administered by an employer, employee, or third party meant to provide a steady source of income in retirement

SIGNIFICANCE: Pension and retirement plans became expected job benefits during the twentieth century, increasing the overhead of employment for many firms but also providing workers with significant income on retirement. Late in the century, many pension funds failed, as it was revealed that major employers had borrowed money from their employees' pensions that they were unable to pay back.

Government pensions in the United States began with pensions to veterans of the Revolutionary War and to their dependents. Each subsequent war brought its own pension program. By 1917, the federal government had paid out over $5 billion in pensions, 90 percent of which were paid to veterans of the U.S. Civil War. The number of military pensioners rose steadily from 126,000 in 1866 to nearly one million in 1893-1906. Annual payments surpassed $100 million in 1890, and World War I took them over $200 million. Veterans' pensions were enlarged as a form of relief during the Great Depression, rising above $300 million in 1934. World War II sent the programs into new magnitudes, passing $1 billion in 1946 and $2 billion in 1948.

Retirement pensions for federal civil service workers were created in May, 1920, initially covering 330,000 workers and providing annual annuities of $180 to $720. Numbers of pensioners and expenditures rose very slowly. Not until 1947 did the number of pensioners exceed 100,000 and the payments exceed $100 million. Many state and local governments also created employee pension programs after 1920. By 1930, ten states had adopted general old-age pension programs, beginning in 1923 with Nevada, Montana, and Pennsylvania.

All of these were dwarfed by the creation of Social Security and Railroad Retirement programs. Under the initial 1935 statute, Social Security retirement pensions began only gradually; monthly benefits did not begin until 1940, when only $40 million was paid, while railroad benefits (originating in 1934) were then $117 millions. Modifications to Social Security accelerated pension payout, and benefits passed the $10 billion mark by 1960, by then being ten times railroad benefits. Public employee retirement benefits were then about $2.6 billion.

PRIVATE PENSIONS

As early as the 1740's, some churches provided pensions for clerical widows and orphans. Railroads, the nation's first really big business, began pensions during the 1870's. American Express, then a railway freight forwarder, initiated a program in 1875. The program offered old-age assistance up to $500 a year to persons injured or "worn out" in service to the firm. The Baltimore and Ohio Railroad offered a more systematic plan in 1880, responding to violent labor unrest throughout the country in 1877. Pensions were free but not large—the maximum was one-third of former wage.

The Pennsylvania Railroad adopted an informal pension program in 1886, then formalized it in 1900 to encourage workers to retire. By 1900, five other major business firms were offering pensions, including such well-known names as John Wanamaker,

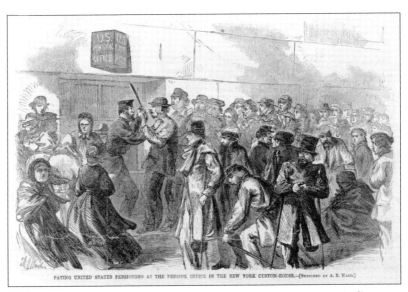

PAYING UNITED STATES PENSIONERS AT THE PENSION OFFICE IN THE NEW YORK CUSTOM-HOUSE.—[SKETCHED BY A. R. WARD.]

This magazine illustration shows veterans, some disabled, waiting in line to receive pensions in 1866. (Library of Congress)

Sherwin-Williams, and Procter and Gamble. By 1919, thirty-eight railroads had pension programs, and these covered 75 percent of the industry workforce. Most followed the Pennsylvania model. Programs did not involve employee contributions, and they provided defined benefits based on level of previous pay and length of service. Retirement was compulsory at the age of seventy.

TEACHER PENSIONS

Universities also initiated pensions during the 1890's, when Columbia, Harvard, and Yale led the way. In 1905, generous donations from Andrew Carnegie extended pensions to many professors: too many, in fact—the financial base had to be reorganized. This involved the creation in 1918 by the Carnegie Foundation of the Teachers Insurance and Annuity Association (TIAA). TIAA was incorporated as an insurance company, and its inception became a model for the modern private pension system, of which it has remained an important part. Contributions could be made by both teacher and employer, and would be invested in the manner of life insurance reserves, chiefly in bonds and mortgages. Benefits, paid monthly on retirement, were based on the actuarial analysis of the accumulated reserve. Except for a death benefit, the program reserves could not be withdrawn and were not subject to employer control. Programs were vested—that is, the qualifying teacher had a contractual right to the benefits. The programs were transferable from one university employer to another.

Company pension plans were typically treated as current expenses, without accumulated reserves. In 1923, the Morris Packing Company, a meat processor, went bankrupt and ceased payments to its four hundred retirees. Current employees had contributed to the pension plan; they now lost those contributions. Corporate bankruptcies have remained a problem area ever since. The Metropolitan Life Insurance Company entered the business of managing pension plans in 1920, recognizing its close parallels with life insurance. Their pension business expanded rapidly. Most pension programs were, by 1929, not supported by segregated, dedicated assets.

THE GREAT DEPRESSION

As the unemployment rate increased after 1929, many firms used forced retirement as a way of reducing their workforce. The number of pensioners doubled from 1927 to 1932. Plans that depended on current corporate revenues were in trouble. Surprisingly, a number of new plans came into force between 1927 and 1932, almost all managed by insurance companies. The extensive system of railroad pensions came under severe stress. In response, railroad workers pressed successfully for the government to take over providing railroad pensions.

The original Social Security Act of 1935 conformed very closely to the conservative actuarial guidelines of insured private pensions. Contributions were to be accumulated and benefits paid only after such accumulation. The result was a program that was initially more of a revenue system than a pension system. Amendments in 1939 accelerated payouts, but potential benefits were not generous, especially for higher-paid workers. Paradoxically, then, private pension plans expanded in numbers and dollar amounts. Between 1930 and 1940, the number of persons receiving private pensions rose from 100,000 in 1930 to 160,000 in 1940, and annual payout increased from about $90 million in 1930 to $140 million in 1940.

Tax rates on corporate profits and personal incomes increased greatly during the 1930's. Contributions to pension funds offered either tax avoidance (for corporations) or tax deferral (for individuals). Therefore, pension plans were developed aimed chiefly at higher-paid employees. Tax law was changed in 1942 to provide that pension-fund contributions could be deducted as business expenses (thus reducing measured profits and tax liability) only for plans that covered the vast majority of a firm's employees.

By 1939, twelve national labor unions provided pensions for members, with payouts of about $2 million. World War II brought a vast increase in union membership and power. The Welfare and Retirement Fund of the United Mine Workers of America (UMWA) was established as the outgrowth of a major strike in 1946. Revenue came from royalties paid by employers on every ton of coal. By 1955, pension payout was about $70 million. The fund had only a small reserve; benefits were mostly paid out of current revenues. In 1949, the Supreme Court held that pensions were a subject on which employers were obligated to bargain with unions. Major corporate programs were then negotiated in such Congress of Industrial Organizations (CIO) strongholds as steel and automobiles. They brought pension benefits to rank-and-file workers, achieved high funding levels (though uninsured), and provided defined-benefit pensions. Largely as a result of union pressure, private pension coverage expanded from 19 percent of the workforce in 1945 to 40 percent in 1960 (about 42 million workers). Over the same period, the number of pensioners increased from 310,000 to 1.8 million, and payout increased from $220 million to $1.7 billion. Government retirement benefits were much larger: In 1960, Social Security retirement payments were $8.2 billion, and government employee retirement benefits totaled about $2 billion.

About two-thirds of private pension plans were uninsured. Most had trustees, often major banks and trust companies. Employers valued the flexibility of such plans, which often took advantage of the small percentage of retirees relative to total employment. In many cases, an employee who left the firm before retirement would retain no benefits from that employer. Because so many programs did not accumulate large reserve funds, pensions depended on the survival of the sponsoring corporation. When Studebaker closed its automobile manufacturing operations in 1964, it left some seven thousand workers with little or no pension benefit.

Pension funds were vulnerable to abuse. An example was the Central and Southern States Pension Fund (CSPF) created by Jimmy Hoffa's International Brotherhood of Teamsters in 1955, which loaned generously to union officials, paid bribes to government officials, and subordinated pensioner welfare.

In 1974, Congress adopted the first comprehensive federal program to regulate private pension funds: the Employee Retirement Income Security Act (ERISA). Major provisions included the creation of the Pension Benefit Guaranty Corporation (PBGC—"Penny Benny"), which insures defined-benefit pension programs (defined-contribution programs are adequately secured by accumulated assets). Coverage per person in 2004 was around $40,000. Covered employers pay a premium into the insurance fund. Covered pensions were to be vested, assuring benefits to workers who remained with the firm for ten years. Many companies permitted vesting after five years.

The Department of Labor was given authority to monitor pension-fund financing. Firms were required to achieve full funding for vested pension claims—though this goal was not achieved. Individual Retirement Accounts (IRAs) were authorized. Individuals were permitted to invest tax-deferred funds into approved programs, subject to withdrawal limits. By 1981, the nation's IRA accounts totaled $400 billion.

The Twenty-First Century

In 2000, the Pension Benefit Guaranty Corporation had accumulated assets exceeding liabilities by $10 billion. Then rough times set in. The shaky condition of stock prices impaired pension fund assets. A series of major corporate closings began with Bethlehem Steel (October, 2001), which imposed $3.7 billion of unfunded liabilities on the insurance agency. Nearly twice as much arose from United Airlines in 2005. By 2006, PBGC liabilities exceeded assets by $19 billion. The liabilities were the present value of expected future

---

Money Spent on Pensions in 2005

Census data covering 207 million persons with income in 2005 indicated that 41 million were receiving Social Security or railroad retirement pension benefits. Some 11 million were receiving company or union pension benefits, and 7 million were receiving government retirement pensions.

Pension Type	Amount ($ billions)
Social Security	512
Private pensions	333
State and local government retirement	155
Federal civil service	55
Veterans	32
Railroad retirement	9

Source: Data from the *Statistical Abstract of the United States, 2008* (Washington, D.C.: Department of Commerce, Economics and Statistics Administration, Bureau of the Census, Data User Services Division, 2008)

Note: Private pension amount is for 2004.

payouts. Current cash flows met current cash needs (as was true for Social Security as well). The asset shortfall was a forecast of problems to come, as pension obligations would increase over time. Underfunding of insured pensions was estimated to total $350 billion in 2006. By 2006, PBGC covered about 44 million workers involved in thirty thousand defined-benefit pension plans.

Whatever their difficulties, pension funds had become, in the new millennium, a major financial force. With total assets of $4.7 trillion in 2004, they held about one-fourth of all corporate stock. Stock investment had expanded rapidly following the pioneering establishment in 1952 of the College Retirement Equity Fund by TIAA.

In 2006, about half the civilian labor force was covered by private pension plans, including 80 percent of union workers and 60 percent of full-time workers, but only 24 percent of service workers. Employers had taken a strong move toward defined-contribution plans, which held little risk for employers compared with defined-benefit plans. Employers also strongly promoted 401(k) plans, first authorized in 1982. These were voluntary for employees, who would contribute to their choice of approved investment programs, often with matching funds from the employer.

Paul B. Trescott

FURTHER READING

Brown, Jeffrey R. "Guaranteed Trouble: The Economic Effects of the Pension Benefit Guaranty Corporation." *Journal of Economic Perspectives* 22, no. 1 (Winter, 2008): 177-198. Good update on the evolution and problems of Penny Benny.

Costa, Dora L. *The Evolution of Retirement*. Chicago: University of Chicago Press, 1998. Provides a comprehensive context for pensions, which are the focus of chapter 8.

McGill, Dan. *The Fundamentals of Private Pensions*. 2d ed. Homewood, Ill.: Richard D. Irwin, 1964. McGill was longtime head of the Pension Research Council. Successive editions of this classic work provide a good updating.

Myers, Robert J. *Social Security*. 4th ed. Philadelphia: Pension Research Council, 1993. Myers was a longtime high administrator in the Social Security system and wrote authoritatively as an insider.

Sass, Steven A. *The Promise of Private Pensions*. Cambridge, Mass.: Harvard University Press, 1997.

The evolution of private pensions is superbly developed in the context of business management.

SEE ALSO: Banking; Bush tax cuts of 2001; 401(k) retirement plans; Savings and loan associations; Social Security system; Taxation; Wages.

Petroleum industry

DEFINITION: Enterprises locating, extracting, refining, processing, distributing, marketing, and selling petroleum

SIGNIFICANCE: The United States petroleum industry became a major factor in the country's emergence as the world's dominant economy and a global superpower during the twentieth century, even as its major corporations were becoming the anchor of the international cartel of petroleum corporations (the Seven Sisters) that dominated the production, refining, and marketing of oil outside the United States and Soviet Union through the half century leading up to 1973.

Civilizations are deeply rooted in their energy sources. When physical labor was the most versatile form of energy, those who controlled large slave populations were able to erect monuments to themselves that still punctuate the landscape in Egypt, Mexico, and Peru. The Industrial Revolution flourished on "King Coal," and those countries that possessed indigenous coal reserves were able to flourish during the nineteenth century, whereas those without (like the Austrian-Hungarian and Ottoman empires) declined. In the twentieth century, oil's higher energy value and versatility made it the fossil fuel of choice, and by the century's end two countries with large domestic petroleum holdings, Russia and the United States, had established themselves as the world's dominant powers. Along the way, the availability of large amounts of cheap oil and gas reshaped American society and economy into the world's most affluent.

THE U.S. INDUSTRY AT HOME

Although the first United States oil well was drilled before the U.S. Civil War, in 1859, it was not until John D. Rockefeller began to assemble the Standard Oil Company in 1870 that the U.S. petroleum industry—then focusing on the production of kerosene for home lighting—began to develop. Over the next four decades, Rockefeller's empire not only spread into the mass production of transportation fuels and acquired such industry dominance that it drew antitrust action, but also it established the model for the industry giants that were to follow it: vertical integration. Thus, although Rockefeller founded his empire by acquiring a monopolistic dominance over petroleum refining operations, by the time that the Supreme Court in 1911 ordered the dismemberment of Standard Oil into its state components, Rockefeller had internally integrated its operation from the production of oil in fields it owned, through refining operations and transportation, and into local sales marketing, as well as research and development activity in the petroleum field.

The breakup of the Standard Oil Company, as intended, created more competition and opportunities for competition in all phases of the industry; however, so dominant had it become that its dismemberment scarcely produced an even playing field. The largest petroleum company in the world at the time of the antitrust action, it was broken up into state units which, in terms of wealth, continued to constitute most of the world's major oil companies, including Standard Oil of New York (later Mobil), Standard Oil of New Jersey (Jersey Oil, later Exxon), and Standard Oil of California (later Chevron). In fact, the most lasting impact of the action was its effect on the international oil market. State units like Standard Oil of New York and Jersey Oil, which were rooted in refining or marketing operations, were forced to look abroad for their oil supply. There, they quickly developed as among the world's first multinational corporations and shortly thereafter established themselves as among its dominant multinational corporations.

In the meantime, the entry of the United States into the mechanized arena of World War I underscored the national security importance of a strong petroleum industry, and five years after the forced breakup of Standard Oil, the United States government was encouraging a level of internal cooperation inside the domestic petroleum industry that has never been extended to other U.S. industries. That same importance of oil to national security, and to the affluent way of life of twentieth century Americans, later led Washington to extend a wide range of tax benefits to U.S. corporations seeking oil

at home and abroad as the widespread demand for oil continued to grow.

Within the United States, the product of this action was essentially a three-tiered domestic petroleum industry, measured in terms of the level of vertical integration of the units composing it, surrounded by a variety of petroleum-related industries (pipeline companies, natural gas companies, fertilizer plants, and so on) in the country's economy. At the bottom were the numerous small firms involved in the production of oil. At the next tier were the "independents," the term generally assigned to the large domestic corporations like Getty Oil and Ashland Oil, which were small only in comparison to the giant United States-based multinationals and most of which were also involved in refining or regional marketing operations. Finally, there were the industry's "majors," the giant, often multinational corporations—most notably Mobil, Exxon, Gulf, Texaco, and Standard Oil of California. This industry structure was in place when the 1973 Arab oil embargo made energy policy a priority in oil-consuming countries throughout the world. By then, however, domestic production had not been meeting the growing oil appetite of Americans for more than fifteen years, and the United States economy had become increasingly dependent on imported oil for more than 30 percent of its petroleum and nearly a sixth of its total energy needs.

THE AMERICAN INDUSTRY ABROAD

The five giant United States petroleum corporations—Mobil, Exxon, Gulf, Texaco, and Standard Oil of California—combined with Royal Dutch-Shell and British Petroleum constituted the Seven Sisters, the international oil cartel that by the 1930's was maintaining stability in the global oil market and that as late as 1960 continued to account for approximately 90 percent of all petroleum production and 80 percent of all refining activity outside North America and the Soviet Union. Just as the power of each of these corporations rested on its scale of operations and high internal degree of vertical integration, their power as a cartel rested on their collective cooperation. Producer states either sold to them at the price they offered, or the producer states rarely sold their oil, and the production needs of any Sister unable to gain agreement from its producer government were met by other members of

Oil well derricks on the beach along the California coast in 1944. (Library of Congress)

the cartel increasing the production in their fields until the wayward state fell into line.

Ironically, it was the arrival of other United States oil firms that ultimately led to the downfall of the Seven Sisters cartel. Most of these "independents"—like Occidental in Libya—were dependent on a single country for their overseas supply of oil and were thus often forced to offer their host a higher price for oil than the Sisters were offering their producing countries. Those deals, in turn, usually had to be met by the Seven Sisters and then, to cover the cost, offset by the cartel revising upwardly its earlier established price for oil on the world market. Thus, even before the 1973 oil crisis enabled the Organization of Petroleum Exporting Countries (OPEC) to replace the Seven Sisters as the international cartel controlling oil prices and production, the Sisters' ability to establish and maintain the international price of oil had already been slipping away.

Subsequently, U.S. and other western oil compa-nies have often become the contracting partners of the oil-producing states, charged with producing their oil in return for a percentage of the value of their production operations. Thus, they have continued to profit, sometimes handsomely, from upward spirals in the cost of OPEC oil. Moreover, although the producing states now frequently engage in their own refining operations and have acquired their own tanker fleets, the United States oil industry and its associated industries have continued to be at the vanguard of the international petroleum business, whether measured in the ability to produce oil in difficult locales, to extinguish fires in the oil fields of Kuwait or on off-shore platforms in the North Sea, or to build a pipeline across the Arctic without damaging the permafrost.

THE NEW MILLENNIUM

Throughout their nearly half century of controlling the international price of oil, the Seven Sisters practiced price restraint. Vertically integrated, they made their profits from their refining, transportation, and marketing operations as well as the production of oil, and in each area, their focus was on small unit profits from a very large volume of transactions. They therefore focused on maintaining price stability and avoiding any sudden surge in cost, which would reduce demand. By contrast, the members of the OPEC cartel were initially involved in only the production of oil. Additionally, many were committed to costly development schemes whose financing depended on high earnings from their oil exports. Consequently, when political events like the outbreak of the Iraq-Iranian war in 1979 reduced the exportable supply of petroleum, OPEC states have often pushed the price of their exports ever higher—for example, from $3 per barrel to nearly $12 per barrel in October, 1973, and to over $36 per barrel by the end of the decade. During the 1980's, that action ignited a global recession that reduced significantly the demand for oil throughout the western world.

The impact of that recession was not confined to OPEC's exports. Oil exporting states inside the United States also found the demand for their product and its price plummeting, and like other U.S. industries caught in a prolonged recession, America's petroleum corporations began to retrench their operations and sought better means of functioning efficiently. One result of that search was a significant increase in mergers during the 1980's, which included such major corporations as Chevron (which acquired Gulf Oil) and Texaco (which purchased Getty Oil).

The recession ended during the 1990's, but for most of that decade, oil prices remained flat at around $25 per barrel, and the merger boom did not end with the revival of the postrecession demand for oil. In fact, it is estimated that between 1990 and 2004, more than twenty-five hundred mergers occurred that involved either oil companies or industries related to them. Most important, those concentrated during the 1998-1999 period included some of the biggest petroleum corporations in the world, capped by the merger of the two giants from Rockefeller's old Standard Oil monopoly: Mobil and Exxon.

As a result of these mergers, the United States petroleum industry not only continues to represent three of the ten largest corporations in the United States—Exxon Mobil (number one), Chevron-Texaco (number seven) and Conoco-Phillips (number eight)—but these same corporations also account, respectively, for the second-, seventh-, and ninth-largest corporations in the world, as well as the most profitable (Exxon Mobil). They are also only the tip of the petroleum industry in the American economy, where, nearly a century after the breakup of the Standard Oil monopoly, that industry remains as important a component of the United States economy as ever, just as its product remains deeply intertwined with the country's way of life.

Joseph R. Rudolph, Jr.

Further Reading

Blair, John M. *The Control of Oil.* New York: Random House Vintage Books, 1976. A scholarly study focusing on the public's interest in the political economy of oil, the monopolistic tendencies in the American and international oil industries, and the transformation of those industries following the first oil crisis.

Engler, Robert. *The Brotherhood of Oil: Energy Policy and the Public Interest.* Chicago: University of Chicago Press, 1977. Written after the first energy crisis, Engler's work examines the fraternal network characterizing the American petroleum industry, the political economy of oil in the last quarter of the twentieth century, and the political and economic power of that industry in a country whose way of life had become dependent on oil's availability and affordability.

Falola, Toyin. *The Politics of the Global Oil Industry: An Introduction.* Westport, Conn.: Praeger, 2005. Well-titled, Falola's book provides an update to the work of Blair and Engler, in detailing the global oil industry during the early years of the twenty-first century, with due attention to the violent conflicts still being waged in many countries in order to control it, and the wealth and power it represents.

Para, Francisco. *Oil Politics: A Modern History of Petroleum.* New York: I. B. Tauris, 2004. Examination of the international petroleum industry written by a former secretary general of OPEC, this book is highly recommended for its slightly different perspective as companion reading to the other books in this list.

Rutledge, Ian. *Addicted to Oil: America's Relentless Drive for Energy Security.* New York: I. P. Tauris, 2006. Insofar as OPEC's power is heavily rooted in the oil-importing world's demand for oil and the absence of any short-term energy alternatives, the thirst for oil of its biggest customer explains much of OPEC's ability to push prices ever higher in the twenty-first century's first decade.

Sampson, Anthony. *The Seven Sisters: The Great Oil Companies and the World They Created.* Rev. ed. London: Coronet, 1998. Less detailed than Yergin but nonetheless an award-winning portrait of the rise and fall of the cartel that long controlled the international oil industry.

Yergin, Daniel. *The Prize: The Epic Quest for Oil, Money, and Power.* New York: Simon & Schuster, 1991. Epic history of the world of oil, from its birth in the fields of the eastern United States through its growth into a global industry. Particularly interesting are those chapters on Rockefeller's Standard Oil monopoly, its dismemberment under antitrust action, and the growth of its constituent parts into national and global supercorporations.

See also: Alaska Pipeline; Arab oil embargo of 1973; Automotive industry; Coal industry; Energy crisis of 1979; "Gas wars"; Getty, J. Paul; Mineral resources; Organization of Petroleum Exporting Countries; Standard Oil Company; Teapot Dome scandal.

Pharmaceutical industry

DEFINITION: Enterprises researching, developing, producing, marketing, and distributing prescription drugs and medications

SIGNIFICANCE: The United States leads the world in pharmaceutical research, spending more money than any other industry; in 2007, $58.5 billion was committed to the search for new medicines and vaccines. The U.S. pharmaceutical industry is also one of the nation's most profitable industries and earns almost half of the entire world's industry revenues.

The U.S. pharmaceutical industry was thrust into world prominence in 1941, when Great Britain—devastated by World War II—sought help from the United States in the production of penicillin, which had been discovered by Alexander Fleming several years earlier. The manufacturing and distribution processes had to be developed and deployed quickly if they were to benefit the many soldiers in Europe with infected wounds. Fermentation was completed at a U.S. agricultural station by 1943, and the Merck, Pfizer, and Squibb pharmaceutical companies collaborated to produce huge amounts of the "miracle drug." Meanwhile, Abbott, Lily, Merck, and Frederick Stearns were producing large amounts of Atabrine to treat malaria. Merck was also leading the way in the production of streptomycin, a curative for tuberculosis, and of the new remedy for pernicious anemia, vitamin B_{12}.

During the 1950's, new technology and instruments were developed, and the pharmaceutical industry continued to develop antibiotics. Many new medicines were developed, including cortisone, more potent tuberculosis medication, anesthetics, tranquilizers, and Thorazine (chorpromazine), an antipsychotic drug. Government funding for scientific research was prominent, especially following the launch of the Soviet satellite *Sputnik* in 1957. The discovery of polio vaccine by Jonas Salk, and its modification by Albert Sabin, resulted in the marketing of both injected and oral vaccines. The discovery of the structure of deoxyribonucleic acid (DNA) and of the structure of proteins and their functions thrust the industry toward biotechnological medicine. Those discoveries and continuing study of cells, proteins, and DNA provided more possibilities for drug development.

The 1960's brought forth a proliferation of new drugs to a society that was forever changed by them. The first contraceptive pill was marketed in 1960, and it was followed by the first in-vitro fertilization. Besides experimenting with women's reproductive systems, scientists had developed tranquilizers aimed at reducing tension. Following the success of Librium (chordizepoxide, an anxiety drug), Valium (diazepam), marketed in 1963 by Roche, soon became the most popular and the most prescribed of the sedatives, tranquilizers, and stimulants available during the 1960's. The production of high-blood pressure medication escalated, and studies of blood proteins resulted in a huge spike in the sale of plasma products.

Also during the 1960's, a European morning sickness pill for pregnant women, thalidomide, caused severe birth defects. Though the drug was not

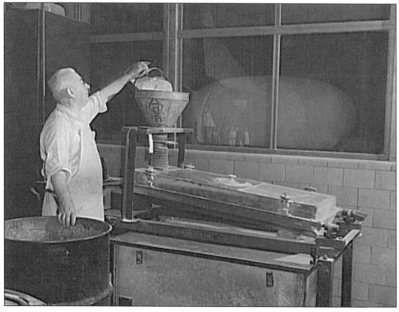

A worker mixes powders for pharmaceutical products at Parke, Davis, and Company in Detroit, Michigan, in 1943. (Library of Congress)

marketed in the United States, the uproar over the drug caused concern about the safety of drugs in general and prompted renewed U.S. regulation of pharmaceutical companies. In 1962, Congress amended the 1938 Food, Drug, and Cosmetic Act, which banned dangerous drugs and required drug testing for safety, including a stipulation that drugs must be subjected to defined clinical trials before being marketed.

EXPANSION

During the 1970's, the pharmaceutical industry expanded, renewing efforts to find a cure for cancer. The 1980's posed new complications and problems for the industry. The emphasis placed on treating acquired immunodeficiency syndrome (AIDS) and heart disease resulted in rising costs and some reshuffling within the industry. Some larger companies "partnered" with smaller ones that were in danger of going under, with benefits to both.

Pharmaceutical research and development requires enormous investments to guide any potential new drug on its journeys from a discovered compound through all phases of its development and testing to become a new medication. As the total cost of developing a successful drug includes that of abortive and failed attempts along the way, it has been estimated to exceed $1 billion for the period of development. Patents secured by the developing company to protect its investment give it the sole right to market the medication for a specified purpose for up to twenty years. After that, other companies can produce cheaper, generic versions of the brand-name medication.

Efforts to offset enormous pharmaceutical costs during the 1980's involved the rise of Health Maintenance Organizations (HMOs), which emphasized disease prevention. Armed with the potential risk factors of individuals for certain diseases, health organizations focused on the lifestyle choices made by individuals that placed them at risk. The risk of having heart disease, lung and colon cancers, and AIDS all could be influenced by lifestyle choices. The idea of individual responsibility for one's health was highly controversial.

In 1983, Congress passed the Orphan Drug Act, which required drug companies to develop drugs for illnesses afflicting fewer than 200,000 individuals. In return, pharmaceutical companies reaped advantages of guaranteed sole rights in the market-ing of those medications for a period of seven years, along with huge tax credits to mitigate the costs of development. One of the drugs to emerge from this measure was Azidothymidine (AZT), a medication to slow the growth of AIDS. Initially intended for cancer, AZT had proven ineffective against that disease.

Support for speeding up the approval process for AZT gained ground, but the Food and Drug Administration (FDA), remembering the 1960 thalidomide scandal and fearing the dangers of AZT, insisted on a full period of testing. Eventually, public outcry, protests, and a quick testing period led to the production of AZT by the end of the decade. In 1984, Congress passed the Drug Price Competition and Patent Term Restoration Act, which lengthened the duration of some medical patents and exempted drugs that were the equivalent of those already approved from the clinical trial process, thereby facilitating the proliferation of generic drugs.

CONSOLIDATION

During the 1990's, consolidation within the pharmaceutical industry brought about mergers between many biotechnical companies that experimented with living cells and genetics. Also, the restructuring of the FDA, under pressure from consumer demand and protests, resulted in a loosening of its grip on pharmaceutical regulations. In 2003, Congress enacted the Medicare Prescription Drug, Improvement, and Modernization Act (MMA) to provide medication for the disabled and the elderly—a plan that should increase the revenues of drug companies by billions of dollars.

Mary Hurd

FURTHER READING

Angell, Marcia. *The Truth About the Drug Companies: How They Deceive Us and What to Do About It.* New York: Random House, 2004. Blistering attack on drug companies as corrupt organizations that lie about exorbitant costs for research and development to justify high prescription prices. Angell claims their costs really come from marketing, much of which is in the form of bribes for doctors.

Carroll, Jamuna, ed. *The Pharmaceutical Industry.* Detroit, Mich.: Greenhaven, 2009. An examination of the industry that focuses on drug research and development.

Ng, Rick. *Drugs: From Discovery to Approval.* Wilmington, Del.: Wiley-Liss, 2004. Detailed account of the lengthy process of drug development.

Shorter, Edward. *The Health Century.* New York: Doubleday, 1987. This companion volume to a Public Broadcasting Service documentary details the history of vertical health interventions in the twentieth century. Provides insights into the business and the inside politics of the pharmaceutical industry.

Vogel, Ronald J. *Pharmaceutical Economics and Public Policy.* New York: Pharmaceutical Products, 2007. This book, published by an industry publisher, analyzes the cost of developing, manufacturing, and marketing products, and how that is affected by public policy regarding safety, insurance, and patents.

SEE ALSO: Chemical industries; Counterfeiting; Drug trafficking; Federal Trade Commission; Food and Drug Administration; Genentech; Health care industry; Medicare and Medicaid.

Photographic equipment industry

DEFINITION: Industry that produces cameras and related accessories, such as plates, film, lights, memory cards, and other accouterments

SIGNIFICANCE: Over the decades since the photographic equipment industry's beginnings during the nineteenth century, it has evolved from serving a small, exclusive group of professionals to supplying cameras to a vast population of amateur photographers and hobbyists.

The earliest photographic images and processes—the daguerreotype and the calotype—were developed in Europe during the early nineteenth century. These photographic images were captured on sensitized metal plates in a rather arduous procedure. To begin with, cameras were large and cumbersome, weighing as much as forty pounds. They were made of wood and had bellows for adjusting the lens made of leather or fabric. The plates used to record images were made of glass and consequently heavy and subject to breakage if not handled carefully.

Chemicals used to develop photographs included collodion and silver nitrate, used to coat the glass plates, and the fixative required to render images permanent. The wet collodion process required that the glass plate, coated with the solution, be exposed to the image while still wet, because its light sensitivity was lost once the plate dried. Consequently, the plates had to be coated with the solution just moments before the picture was to be taken, and the development process had to take place immediately after exposure. This process required photographers to travel not only with their cameras but also with all the equipment and chemicals needed to prepare and process the plates, the equivalent of complete portable studios and darkrooms.

Late nineteenth century cameras came equipped with a single view lens, and they cost about $38 in 1896. For an extra $14 or $15, one could add an extra three-speed shutter to the apparatus, making it a fairly expensive device.

EARLY U.S. COMPANIES

The Scovill Manufacturing Company and the American Optical Company made cameras during the 1880's. Between 1893 and 1900, Rochester, New York, was considered America's optical center. Many camera manufacturing companies were established there, including Rochester Optical, Rochester Camera, Ray Camera, Monroe Camera, Century, and Seneca. By 1900, the Western Camera Manufacturing Company was operating in Chicago. Several older companies went out of business or merged by 1900. By 1887, George Eastman, a young businessman in New York, developed a camera that used paper film instead of the wet collodion process. He introduced his first Kodak camera in 1888. Eastman switched to a more durable celluloid film in 1889, and by 1896, he had sold one hundred cameras. By the beginning of the twentieth century, his company was making several models of low-priced box and folding cameras that amateurs could use and enjoy.

Eastman's first camera, the Kodak, was a box-style camera with a fixed-focus lens and a single shutter speed. It sold for $15. It came preloaded with enough film to take one hundred pictures. Once all one hundred exposures were taken, the camera had to be sent back to the factory, along with a $10 processing fee. There, the film was developed, prints were made, the camera was reloaded, and the prints and camera were returned to the customer. (This process was revived in modified form with the advent of single-use or disposable cameras that enjoyed popularity during the 1990's and the early twenty-first century.)

EARLY TWENTIETH CENTURY INNOVATIONS

In 1901, Eastman introduced the Kodak Brownie, which sold for between 25 cents and $1.00, making it affordable for practically everyone. The Brownie was a square camera made at first of wood, metal, or leather; after 1930, Brownies were of plastic construction. They were extremely simple to use, allowing amateur photographers merely to point and shoot. Unlike the earlier Kodak camera, however, the Brownie required customers to purchase film separately and load it into the camera themselves. After the film had been exposed, customers would unload it and send it to the Kodak factory, where it was processed and the prints were mailed back.

Eastman's slogan for the popular Brownie was "You press the button, we do the rest." From a business point of view, the Brownie increased the amount of money Eastman's customers could spend by making it possible for them to purchase and expose multiple rolls of film at once. Owners of the earlier Kodak camera temporarily lost the use of the camera whenever they sent it to the processing plant.

Thirty-five millimeter (mm) film for use in still cameras became popular during the mid-1920's after a German, Oskar Barnack, designed the Leica, a camera that used 35mm film. American companies soon came up with their own versions of the 35mm camera, including the Simplex and the Tourist. The small size of 35mm cameras and their ability to take up to thirty-six exposures in fairly rapid succession made them extremely popular among serious photographers. Thirty-five millimeter cameras were more expensive than other cameras on the market, however. Even Kodak's Retina I, introduced in 1938, was too expensive for the average consumer. In 1939, the more affordable Argus cameras came on the market, and the popularity of the 35mm camera remained very high into the 1960's. Argus sold thirty thousand of its low-cost (around $12.50) cameras in their first week on the market. The Argus Model C3 was the best-selling 35mm camera in the world for thirty years.

It became easier to take pictures in a broader array of settings in 1930, when flashbulbs were developed. Previously, a dangerous flash powder was used

A photographer holds a large-format camera in 1914. (Library of Congress)

when there was insufficient natural light. Flash powder was made from the waxy spores of club moss, a substance called lycopodium powder. Quite flammable, it was also used in fireworks. Even professional photographers had to handle flash powder with extreme caution. Flashbulbs by contrast were small glass globes containing an illuminant, a magnesium-coated wire, that, when set off, created a bright flash sufficient to light photographic subjects. The advent of the flashbulb was thus a boon to all photographers, professional and amateur. General Electric produced a popular version of the flashbulb, which it named the Sashalite. Flash photography increased the popularity of the hobby by making it possible to take snapshots almost anywhere.

Kodak started marketing color film in 1935, and a new era of photography began. Kodacolor film increased the realism of snapshots. Color film relieved professional portrait photographers of the need to hand-tint their pictures; the film produced more natural skin tones and other colors than could be achieved with tinting.

American scientist Edwin Land developed a process of instant photography during the 1940's. He made a camera, the Polaroid, that could develop black-and-white pictures within minutes of their exposure. The film packs used in the camera contained the chemicals needed to develop the pictures; the camera started the development process and ejected pictures on which images then gradually emerged. The instamatic camera was an immediate success. Not only was it easy to use, but it also provided instant gratification. The drawback of the instamatic process was that it lacked a negative, so only one copy of a photograph could be made. When color snapshots began to dominate the field, Polaroid developed instant color pictures in 1963.

INDUSTRY-CHANGING INNOVATIONS

Easy-to-use cameras were a boon to the photographic equipment industry. Cameras were inexpensive, disposable, instamatic, and capable of taking high-speed action shots or close-up shots of distant subjects. Cameras became popular gifts for recipients of all ages, and the wide spectrum of quality and features resulted in cameras coming at many different price points. With the surge in camera users, there was a concomitant growth in the photo finishing industry, which processed the thousands of rolls of film being exposed. The laboratories that processed film restructured their facilities to adopt assembly-line methods of processing. It became possible to move two hundred to five hundred feet of roll film on racks through huge tanks full of developing chemicals, producing two thousand to three thousand finished prints per hour.

Eventually, however, cameras stopped using film, as the industry transitioned from analog to digital photography. The electronic camera had preceded the digital camera in 1972, signaling the eventual loss of favor of film cameras, but it was nearly twenty-five years before a consumer-friendly, relatively inexpensive camera incorporating digital technology came on the market. When it did, the need for film was greatly reduced.

Photographic companies adjusted. Kodak eventually joined with the computer company Microsoft in an arrangement that allowed its digital cameras to transfer their images to compatible computers for printing and e-mailing. In addition to being stand-alone devices, cameras began to be incorporated into other digital devices, especially cell phones, and these devices' manufacturers also made compatibility arrangements to ensure that users could print or share photographs taken with such cameras.

Digital cameras, unlike conventional analog cameras, translate visual information into a digital language and store the resulting images electronically. To accomplish this, they incorporate computer technology. Conventional cameras, by contrast, require chemical and mechanical processes to operate. Some people consider their picture quality to be superior to that of digital cameras, but the ease and convenience of the latter have made digital cameras more popular than analog cameras. Prices of both conventional and digital cameras have dropped sufficiently for photography to remain a widely enjoyed pastime. Argus, for example, manufactures some of the market's lowest-priced models with color liquid crystal display (LCD) screens and sells digital cameras for less than $50.

The instant camera business has suffered from the advent of digital technology. In 2008, the Polaroid Company, which was devoted primarily to self-developing film cameras, closed down factories in Massachusetts, Mexico, and the Netherlands and eliminated more than four hundred jobs, as its instamatic cameras lost popularity to digital cameras. The company ceased production of film cameras altogether, and after years of successful marketing—with its sales peaking in 1991 at nearly $3 billion—it shifted its focus to digital photography. Polaroid developed an eight-ounce photograph printer that can almost fit into the palm of one's hand and can print pictures from digital cameras.

Digital cameras' capacity to take and store a large number of pictures has increased the growth of online services that can create and share online photo albums. These services store photographs online, where a photographer can access them from any Internet-enabled computer, share them with friends and family, or publish them publicly for anyone to see. Such services often allow viewers to see and download digital images for free, but they charge to print and ship physical copies of photographs, either as individual prints, as books, or incorporated into novelty gift items such as mugs. The services will also ship compact discs-read only memory (CD-ROMs) or digital versatile discs (DVDs) full of photographs to consumers. The American consumer's involvement with photography seems only to grow, and businesses continue to find new ways to profit from it.

Jane L. Ball

FURTHER READING

ASMP Professional Business Practices in Photography. 6th ed. New York: Allworth Press, 2001. More than twenty industry experts discuss pricing, using electronic technology, standard practices in stock and assignment photography, and financial tips. Clarifies accepted business standards.

Jenkins, Reese V. *Images and Enterprises: Technology and the American Photographic Industry, 1839-1925.* Baltimore: Johns Hopkins University Press, 1987. Explores business, technical, and social factors influencing the photography industry from 1839 to 1925. Eastman's impact on amateur photography is discussed.

Marien, Mary Warner. *Photography: A Cultural History.* 2d ed. Columbus, Ohio: Prentice Hall, 2006. Discusses the historical, social, and economic development of photography from its origins before the nineteenth century.

Moran, Barbara. "The Preacher Who Beat Eastman Kodak." *American Heritage of Invention and Technology Magazine,* Fall, 2001, 44-51. Recounts a patent battle between George Eastman and a minister over flexible film technology.

Wensberg, Peter C. *Land's Polaroid: A Company and the Man Who Invented It.* Boston; Houghton Mifflin, 1987. Biography of Edwin Land presents behind-the-scenes activities as the company is formed and managed. The Eastman Kodak attempt to usurp the instant photo effort is given attention.

Zimberoff, Tom. *Photography: Focus on Profit.* New York: Allworth Press, 2002. Discusses the requirements for successfully operating a profitable photography business, including required equipment, business management, and accounting practices.

SEE ALSO: Digital recording technology; Edison, Thomas Alva; Inventions; Motion-picture industry.

Pike's western explorations

THE EVENTS: Two military expeditions commissioned to explore and locate the sources of the Mississippi and the Arkansas Rivers, evaluate the natural resources of the newly acquired Louisiana Territory for the United States, and report on the current state of settlement and the fur trade

DATES: August 9, 1805-April 30, 1806; July 15, 1806-July 1, 1807

PLACE: Upper Mississippi River, southern Great Plains, eastern Rocky Mountains

SIGNIFICANCE: Pike's journals provided detailed and colorful descriptions of the resources of the upper Mississippi Valley and the southern Great Plains, with data on their distribution and possibilities for future commercial exploitation. His reports on numerous major river systems were used in the planning of the network of antebellum steamboat lines that were in operation well into the nineteenth century.

On June 24, 1805, General James Wilkinson, one of the two commissioners appointed by President Thomas Jefferson to govern the Louisiana Territory and commander in chief of the western army, wrote to Lieutenant Zebulon Montgomery Pike, who was then commanding the military post at Kaskaskia. Pike was ordered to come to St. Louis and prepare an expedition that would follow the Mississippi to its northernmost source. At this time, much of the Louisiana Territory remained unknown and unexplored by Americans; most of those who had traveled the area were British or French fur traders. The goals of the survey were to gather information on all Native American groups along the river, with an eye toward the military threat they might present; to report on the influence of British or French fur traders in the area; and to collect astronomical and scientific data that would allow the U.S. government to establish the northernmost boundaries of the territory and to assess the soils and natural resources of the region, the usability of its rivers, and the best places to create new forts and trading posts.

The successful completion of the first expedition prompted Wilkinson to commission a second one on June 24, 1806, with the dual objectives of establishing diplomatic relations with several Native American nations and mapping the courses of the Arkansas and Red Rivers. Pike's company was the first American group to traverse the middle plains, and his notes on the diet of Native Americans revealed what crops were already adapted to the region and reported on the immense herds of buffalo later used as a staple meat source on the transcontinental journey. The ascent of the Arkansas began on October 28, 1806, and on November 15, the expedition first sighted the mountain that bears Pike's name as well as the front range of the Rocky Mountains, which the group regarded as a natural frontier between the Louisiana Territory and Mexico. The expedition was taken into custody by Mexican authorities and brought to Santa Fe, from where the group made their return to U.S. territory.

The information gathered by the Pike expeditions represented the first eyewitness account of the physical nature of much of the newly acquired territory. This information was essential for the expansion of existing trading networks and ultimately the flow of business enterprises into these untapped regions. Pike's treaty purchase, for $200, of 100,000 acres of land near the Falls of St. Anthony from the Sioux nation laid the foundation for the eventual founding and settlement of Minneapolis and St. Paul and the development of Minnesota.

Robert B. Ridinger

FURTHER READING

Hart, Stephen Harding, and Archer Butler Hulbert, eds. *The Southwestern Journals of Zebulon Pike, 1806-1807.* Albuquerque: University of New Mexico Press, 2006.

Hollon, W. Eugene. *The Lost Pathfinder: Zebulon Montgomery Pike.* 1949. Reprint. Westport, Conn.: Greenwood Press, 1981.

Hutchins, John M. *Lieutenant Zebulon Pike Climbs His First Peak: The U.S. Army Expedition to the Sources of the Mississippi, 1805-1806.* Lakewood, Colo.: Avrooman-Apfelwald Press, 2006.

SEE ALSO: Cumberland Road; Fur trapping and trading; Lewis and Clark expedition; Louisiana Purchase; Mississippi and Missouri Rivers; Pony Express; Wilderness Road.

Piracy, maritime

DEFINITION: Robbery perpetrated at sea by the crew of one ship against another ship

SIGNIFICANCE: Ships and goods of uncountable value have been lost to piracy from the colonial days to modern times.

Piracy affected American business almost as soon as it existed. Pirates were criminals who stole goods and ships that they captured at sea. Privateers, by contrast, were commissioned by sovereign nations in times of war to attack and steal goods from the vessels of enemy nations. Privateers carried letters of marque authorizing their actions, and they often gave a portion of their bounty to the countries issuing those letters.

EARLY PIRACY

Pirates stole goods from any ships they encountered and sold them at ports. Ships in American waters carried valuable trading resources such as medicine and commodities, as well as the profits of their trade (money and goods). Many were laden with gold, silver, and jewels taken from the continents. They also carried the spoils of the Aztec and Incan civilizations. As a result, American shipping lanes were particularly ripe for piracy.

Shares of the loot were divided among the crew members of a ship. Pirates also ransomed individuals for profit. In one instance, the pirate Blackbeard (Edward Teach) kidnapped prominent South Carolinians and blockaded the wealthy port city of Charleston, South Carolina. He threatened to bombard the city if he was not delivered a valuable chest of medicine. The city complied, but Blackbeard was hunted down soon afterward. Slaves were also run for huge profits by some, but not all, pirates. Jean Laffitte ran a piracy ring based in New Orleans, Louisiana, and at one point provided roughly one-tenth of the employment in the city through his various illegal activities. He was outlawed for trading slaves but was pardoned when he defended New Orleans from attack in 1812.

Pirates brought a lot of money into a port when they landed. The goods that they traded were valuable to the port city, but even more lucrative for the port was the money that pirates spent on recreation and gambling. Skilled shipbuilders became wealthy for the quality of the ships they could provide and kept the pirates coming back to specific ports. Pirates and privateers helped make port cities the largest and wealthiest cities of the times with a combination of trading, carousing, shipbuilding, and ship support services.

Privateers both were militarily useful and saved the American government vast amounts of money fighting against the British in the Revolutionary War. During the war, the Continental Navy numbered well under seventy ships, so letters of marque were issued to merchants, and their ships were outfitted for battle. These letters caused the naval fighting force to grow to well over twenty times its original size. Philadelphia was the largest port at the time, and it supplied the privateers. British trading was cut off, and valuable supplies intended to reach British troops were instead delivered to American troops who were sorely lacking in such supplies. Gold was plundered as well, and individual ships came to port with prizes worth millions of dollars. The same tactic was used in the War of 1812. The American navy had a mere 23 ships at the time, but it mustered 150 privateers to its cause. Privateers captured British supplies and prizes worth over $40 million and caused around the same amount in damage to the British navy.

The castle of Edward Teach, known as Blackbeard, on the Island of St. Thomas in the Virgin Islands. (Library of Congress)

MODERN PIRACY

Modern pirates have traded the cannon of their early brethren for automatic weapons. They generally fall into three types: small pirates who break onto ships—usually in port—solely to rob the crew and passengers; pirates who board a ship, rob the crew, and steal the cargo; and pirates who capture the ship itself and either sell it or reflag it. Reflagging ships allows them to take on cargo, and the pirates can then steal any that gets consigned to them. Modern ship crews are much smaller than they were during the age of sail, and they rarely carry firearms, so pirates remain mostly unchallenged when they attack. The most prevalent form of piracy in the United States is small pirates. The U.S. Coast Guard pursues pirates and keeps them in check in American waters, at a cost to taxpayers.

Most attacks against American ships happen as they travel through foreign shipping lanes. It is difficult to assess how widespread this problem is, since ships that have their cargo stolen often choose not to report it. It is estimated that between 40 and 60 percent of attacks are unreported. In many cases, the cost of higher insurance premiums resulting from reported cases is simply greater than the cost of writing off the lost cargo. The average loss comes out to pennies on every $10,000 worth of goods that are shipped. The more important aspect of combating piracy is preventing injury to the crew. Although piracy and its effects have diminished in modern times, they still have an impact on many industries, including insurance and trading.

James J. Heiney

FURTHER READING

Bradford, Alfred S. *Flying the Black Flag: A Brief History of Piracy.* Westport, Conn.: Praeger, 2007. History of piracy from its beginning to modern times.

Burnett, John S. *Dangerous Waters: Modern Piracy and Terror on the High Seas.* New York: Dutton, 2002. Journalist's look at modern piracy, including firsthand accounts.

Exquemelin, A. O. *The Buccaneers of America.* Mineola, N.Y.: Dover, 2000. Eyewitness account of piracy on the Spanish Main.

Lehr, Peter. *Violence at Sea: Piracy in the Age of Global Terrorism.* New York: Routledge, 2007. Studies links between piracy, terrorism, and organized crime; details efforts to combat piracy, as well as new trends and developments.

Roland, Alex, W. Jeffrey Bolster, and Alexander Keyssar. *The Way of the Ship: America's Maritime History Reenvisioned, 1600-2000.* Hoboken, N.J.: John Wiley & Sons, 2008. History of shipping in America focusing on American merchant marines.

SEE ALSO: Colonial economic systems; Insurance industry; Revolutionary War; Shipping industry; Slave era; War of 1812.

Plantation agriculture

DEFINITION: Large-scale, labor-intensive agricultural operations that developed primarily in the American South and produced huge quantities of staple crops for both the domestic and international markets

SIGNIFICANCE: A combination of favorable geographic conditions, climate, and world demand for the staple crops of the South led to the growth of these large-scale agricultural operations beginning during the early seventeenth century. Before the U.S. Civil War, the agricultural products of southern plantations, especially cotton, played a major role in American exports and the balance-of-trade equation.

During the early seventeenth century, English colonists in the southern part of the East Coast found a land with a warm climate and adequate soils. Much of this land was near rivers or coastal waters that provided economical transportation. Few places north of Maryland had this combination of conditions, which the colonists recognized as suitable for large-scale agriculture.

EARLY PLANTATIONS

The word "plantation" originally meant simply a piece of cleared, farmable land. Over time, southern plantations came to specialize in the production of a few staple crops: tobacco, cotton, sugar, and rice. In the co-

lonial period, indigo, a plant grown to make a rich deep-blue dye, was also significant, but its production ended around the time of the American Revolution. Hemp, which was grown for its fiber for making rope and burlap, later became an important staple in the upper areas of the South.

Early colonial plantations favored indentured servants and slaves because, in a region where land could be obtained easily, hired laborers tended to migrate to their own farmsteads. The majority of the laborers during the early colonial period were white indentured servants. An indentured servant sold the right to his or her labor for a period of time (usually five to seven years) in return for transportation to America and sometimes the payment of other debts. Until the early eighteenth century, indentured servitude was much more common on southern plantations than black slavery. By 1725, this had changed, and black slaves predominated, primarily because plantation owners had become wealthy enough to afford the extra cost of slaves.

THE ANTEBELLUM SOUTH

In the nineteenth century South, the term "plantation" came to refer to a farm with twenty or more slaves. The status of a plantation depended on the

A cotton plantation in Richmond, Mississippi, in 1890. (Library of Congress)

number of slaves owned, not the number of acres farmed. Although many variables make it difficult to generalize about plantations, a "typical" plantation was probably around one thousand acres and had sixty to one hundred slaves.

Large plantations could take advantage of economies of scale to cut production costs. With the gang system, in which many slaves worked under the direction of an overseer, the rhythm of work could be controlled and a large number of workers kept focused on a particular task. Plantation owners were generally convinced that slave labor was not highly efficient; therefore, to produce crops profitably, they believed the slaves had to be worked long hours per day and many days per year.

Many people associate plantation agriculture with the production of cotton. However, the cotton boom was a relatively late occurrence. Before the invention of the cotton gin, the difficulty of removing the seed from short-fiber cotton meant it was not very profitable to grow—but this was the only type of cotton that would grow in much of the South. Eli Whitney's invention of the cotton gin in 1793 was a timely innovation, for it allowed a vast expansion in the production of short-fiber cotton precisely when English factories were creating unprecedented demands. In 1793, the United States produced 5 million pounds of cotton. By 1800, this had increased to 40 million pounds. During the early nineteenth century, cotton production doubled every decade, and by 1860, the South produced 2 billion pounds of cotton, more than two-thirds the total world supply. Cotton achieved a dominant position in the U.S. export market. In 1860, earnings from cotton exports totaled $190 billion. The export of cotton was one of the principal ways that Americans earned foreign currency to purchase foreign goods.

Besides the major staple crops, most plantations also produced food crops: livestock, vegetable crops, and corn, wheat, and other grains. Much of this production was consumed by the people on the plantation, and some of the grains were fed to livestock. Some planters, however, followed the model of the English West Indies plantations by putting all of their land into one cash crop and buying the food and livestock fodder they needed from other producers.

Historians have debated the economic viability of slavery. Many early scholars argued that by 1860 slavery was unprofitable and likely to be discontinued in the near future. However, later scholars have rejected this view, arguing that slavery, for all its moral evils, was economically viable, and therefore it was unlikely that southern planters would have abandoned this labor system voluntarily.

After the U.S. Civil War, plantation owners often subdivided their lands into thirty- to forty-acre units that were farmed by sharecroppers. Because each sharecropping family operated somewhat independently, there was less sense of the plantation as a single, large entity. In the twentieth century, all forms of commercial farming became larger and more mechanized, and this also contributed to the disappearance of the distinctive character of the old-style plantation.

Mark S. Joy

FURTHER READING

Fogel, Robert W., and Stanley Engerman. *Time on the Cross: The Economics of American Negro Slavery.* 2 vols. Boston: Little, Brown, 1974. This work prompted major debates over many issues involving slavery, especially concerning the extent to which slaves were exploited.

Genovese, Eugene G. *Roll, Jordan, Roll: The World the Slaves Made.* New York: Pantheon Books, 1974. A major study of the daily lives of slaves in the antebellum South.

Hughes, Jonathan, and Louis P. Cain. *American Economic History.* 6th ed. Boston: Addison-Wesley, 2003. Especially valuable for putting slavery and the plantation system into the overall context of the American economy.

Otto, John Solomon. *The Southern Frontiers, 1607-1860: The Agricultural Evolution of the Colonial and Antebellum South.* Westport, Conn.: Greenwood Press, 1989. Provides many details about farming practices, something surprisingly absent in many works about the antebellum South.

Phillips, Ulrich Bonnell. *American Negro Slavery: A Survey of the Supply, Employment, and Control of Negro Labor as Determined by the Plantation Regime.* 1918. Reprint. Baton Rouge: Louisiana State University Press, 1966. Phillips created a whole school of historical interpretation, which later was criticized for having an overly benign view of slavery and the plantation system.

Stampp, Kenneth. *The Peculiar Institution: Slavery in the Ante-Bellum South.* New York: Vintage Books,

1956. One of the first major revisionist works to challenge the Phillips school of interpretation.

SEE ALSO: Agriculture; Colonial economic systems; Cotton gin; Cotton industry; Farm labor; Indentured labor; Sharecropping; Slave era; Slave trading; Washington, George.

Pony Express

IDENTIFICATION: Horse-and-rider postal delivery service that connected St. Joseph, Missouri, and Sacramento, California

DATE: April 3, 1860-October 26, 1861

SIGNIFICANCE: The ten-day delivery period provided by the Pony Express greatly shortened communication times between the East and West Coast of the United States and helped foster the development of the West. However, the Pony Express became obsolete only eighteen months after it began when the transcontinental telegraph service suddenly made possible virtually instantaneous cross-country communication.

In 1860, a tiny advertisement appeared in many American newspapers calling for "Young Skinny Wiry Fellows not over eighteen" who were "willing to risk death daily: for twenty-five dollars per week." Now famous because it launched the creation of the Pony Express, that advertisement attracted eighty riders, forty of whom were assigned to begin carrying mail from the east and forty from the west. The young riders dressed in their distinctive costumes of gaudy red shirts and blue pants.

Pony Express service began on April 3, 1860, when the first rider left St. Joseph, Missouri. On the following day, another pony headed east from Sacramento, California. The enterprise was sponsored by Russell, Majors, and Waddell, a well-known freighting firm that recently had entered the overland mail business by consolidating the various lines along the central route into a company known as the Central Overland, California and Pikes Peak Express Company. Intense rivalry developed with the Butterfield Overland Mail Company, which had received a government contract to deliver the mails on a longer southern route from Missouri to San Francisco, running stages in a great semicircle by way of Fort Smith, El Paso, Tucson, Yuma, and Los Angeles.

ORIGINS OF THE PONY EXPRESS

Some historians claim that the Pony Express had actually begun in 1839, when a Swiss adventurer named John Augustus Sutter arrived in Monterey in Upper California. Nine years later, the discovery of gold at Sutter's Sacramento fort caused a land rush across the United States in 1849 that inspired a new name for a class of people: forty-niners. By 1860, the American population on the West Coast had grown to one-half million people, three hundred thousand of whom were in California. Transplanted from the East, they craved information, letters, newspapers, books, and magazines from "the States." They wanted news that was less than a month or two old.

William M. Gwin, a senator from California who supported all plans to improve mail service to the Pacific coast, was eager to publicize the fact that the central route, favored by emigrants, was practicable and shorter for mail delivery than the southern "oxbow" route. He suggested to William Hepburn Russell of Russell, Majors, and Waddell that Russell's firm establish a fast express and mail system with men on horseback over the central route. Gwin promised to seek congressional reimbursement for the cost of the experiment and pointed out to Russell that publicity associated with the enterprise would advertise the advantages of the stage route and might result in lucrative mail contracts.

Financial assistance was not forthcoming from the government, but Russell decided to go ahead; he notified his partners that he proposed to organize the Pony Express, with relays of horsemen that would carry the mails between Missouri and California in ten days. Alexander Majors and William B. Waddell, Russell's partners, rejected the idea at first but later agreed, although with reluctance. The public announcement of the creation of the Pony Express caused great excitement, because Russell agreed to deliver letters between St. Joseph, Missouri, and Placerville, California, for $5 per ounce within ten days—half the time required on the Butterfield route. Russell undertook the responsibility of establishing 190 way stations between ten and fifteen miles apart along the route, and he selected the fleetest horses to be ridden by men noted for their light weight, physical stamina, and steady nerves. Success depended on their ability and endurance.

A Pony Express rider passes men stringing wires for the transcontinental telegraph, which would render the Pony Express obsolete. (Library of Congress)

How the System Operated

Mail packages, wrapped in oiled silk to protect them from the weather, were placed in leather *mochilas* that fit over the riders' saddles. No more than twenty pounds of mail were carried by a single pony. The number of letters in a given package depended on their total weight. Among the most famous deliveries west were a copy of Abraham Lincoln's inaugural address and news of the outbreak of the U.S. Civil War.

The Pony Express was organized as a giant relay, with each rider driving a pony at a gallop from one station to the next, where another animal would be saddled and waiting. Only two minutes were allowed to change horses and transfer the *mochila* before the rider was off to the next station. Each man had a run of between seventy-five and one hundred miles, over which he was expected to average nine miles per hour. If his replacement was not waiting at the end of his run, he was to ride on, because the mail had to be kept moving night and day. Eighty riders were in their saddles at all times. The life was hard and dangerous because of inclement weather and the possibility of Indian attacks. In emergencies, riders such as "Buffalo Bill" Cody and "Pony Bob" Haslam made rides of several hundred miles that brought them great fame.

The pay for Pony Express riders was $125 a month, a good income for the time. The real test came in the winter of 1860-1861. Instead of covering the entire distance from Missouri to California, most trips were confined to the distance between Fort Kearney, Nebraska, and Fort Churchill, Nevada, the termini of the telegraph system then under construction. A schedule of thirteen days was maintained between the ends of the telegraph lines, with a total of seventeen or eighteen days for the entire distance between St. Joseph and San Francisco.

From the standpoint of drama, romance, and publicity, the Pony Express was an outstanding success.

FINANCIAL PROBLEMS

Although rates were high—it cost approximately $38 to deliver each letter—the numbers of letters carried increased from 49 to 350 per trip within a year. Nevertheless, Russell, Majors, and Waddell encountered financial difficulties. They lost about $1,000 per day on the operation and did not receive payment from the U.S. government for delivering freight. Losses incurred by the Pony Express alone were estimated at $500,000.

In desperation, Russell, with the cooperation of a clerk in the Department of the Interior, appropriated $870,000 in Indian Trust Fund bonds to be used as security for maintaining the firm's credit and borrowing power. Meanwhile, the Overland Mail Company had been forced to abandon its southern route through Texas after that state had joined the Confederacy at the outbreak of the Civil War, and its equipment was moved to the central route. This company was heavily indebted to Wells, Fargo, and Company for funds advanced to outfit and maintain the line. Wells, Fargo directors on the board of the Overland Mail Company forced the retirement of John Butterfield as president and elected William Dinsmore to take his place.

On March 2, 1861, the reorganized company obtained a government contract that provided for a daily overland mail and a semiweekly Pony Express on the central route with an annual compensation of $1 million. Thus, the Pony Express received financial support from the federal government after July 1, 1861, and the responsibility for its operation was transferred to the Overland Mail Company controlled by Wells, Fargo. Russell, Majors, and Waddell were forced into bankruptcy, and the Pony Express was officially discontinued on October 26, 1861, two days after the overland telegraph line was completed.

W. Turrentine Jackson and Russell Hively

FURTHER READING

Champlin, Tim. *Swift Thunder.* New York: Leisure Books, 2000. One of the few adult novels about the Pony Express, this well-written story of a Pony Express rider offers a vivid and largely authentic depiction of what life was like on the trail.

Corbett, Christopher. *Orphans Preferred: The Twisted Truth and Lasting Legend of the Pony Express.* New York: Broadway Books, 2003. Corbett sifts through the legend that is the Pony Express, examining both its truths and its fictions.

Hafen, LeRoy R. *The Overland Mail, 1848-1869: Promoter of Settlement, Precursor of Railroads.* 1926. Reprint. Norman: University of Oklahoma Press, 2004. This classic work on the subject provides the essential background for understanding the Pony Express in a single chapter.

Limerick, Patricia Nelson. *Legacy of Conquest: The Unbroken Past of the American West.* New York: W. W. Norton, 1987. Contrasts the historical myths and the reality of the American West.

Moeller, Bill, and Jan Moeller. *The Pony Express: A Photographic History.* Missoula, Mont.: Mountain Press, 2002. A pictorial history of the Pony Express, with notes to the reader, photographs of stations along the route, and the appendix "Legends of the Pony Express: Facts and Fictions."

Paul, Rodman W. *The Far West and the Great Plains in Transition, 1859-1900.* New York: Harper & Row, 1988. A history of the settlement and development of the American West in the latter half of the nineteenth century.

Settle, Raymond W., and Mary L. Settle. *Saddles and Spurs: The Pony Express Saga.* Harrisburg, Pa.: Stackpole Books, 1955. Written by authors who have spent a lifetime studying the history of the Russell, Majors, and Waddell Company, for which their ancestors worked.

SEE ALSO: Horses; Postal Service, U.S.; Railroads; Shipping industry; Telecommunications industry; Transcontinental railroad.

Ponzi schemes

DEFINITION: Fraudulent investment plans that offer a fast, high return on a seemingly low-risk investment but typically benefit only the promoter and some early investors

SIGNIFICANCE: Since Charles Ponzi perpetrated his scheme on a large scale in Boston in 1920, many others have defrauded investors through what have become known as Ponzi schemes. The story of the scheme shows how easily individuals can be attracted by promises of large profits and serves as a cautionary tale for naïve investors.

Charles Ponzi's scheme was based on a simple and seemingly credible way of making money with little risk. The idea that he sold to investors involved international reply coupons, created in 1906 as a way of sending return postage to someone in another country. The coupon could be bought in one country and redeemed for postage stamps in another. Due to changes in exchange rates following World War I, Ponzi discovered that he could exchange a dollar overseas to buy international reply coupons, which could be sent to the United States and redeemed for stamps worth more than one dollar. However, he did not have a way to convert the stamps back into dollars.

Undaunted, Ponzi set out to find investors willing to finance his idea. With an offer of 50 percent interest in ninety days, which he later changed to forty-five days, he was able to attract a few people willing to gamble modest sums on his scheme. As word spread that initial investors received the promised 50 percent, more investors, some willing to invest large sums, began to appear. Ponzi noticed that relatively few of the investors actually took their money at the end of the forty-five-day period, preferring instead to reinvest the initial sum and the interest earned. With increasingly more money being invested each month, very little of it being paid out, and none of it being used to buy International Reply Coupons, money began to accumulate, and Ponzi became a millionaire. Ponzi had started with nothing in December, 1919, and had, by the end of July, 1920, been entrusted by investors with nearly $10 million.

THE DOWNFALL

For Ponzi's scheme to continue to work, money from new investors had to cover the withdrawals of previous investors. Until July, 1920, that had not been a problem, as new people continued to invest, and relatively few withdrew their investments. Questions arose early in July, 1920, when a furniture dealer from whom Ponzi had rented furniture sued Ponzi for $1 million, claiming that he was entitled to some of Ponzi's profits for having loaned Ponzi money in December, 1919, at the outset of Ponzi's enterprise. Although the lawsuit was without merit, it aroused suspicions at the *Boston Post*, which began investigating how the Italian immigrant had come to enjoy such a meteoric rise.

In the midst of the *Post*'s allegations that his busi-

ness was a fraud and the attendant scrutiny he came under from a number of government agencies, Ponzi offered to close his business to additional investors until he had been fully investigated. His plan was to claim assets of the Hanover Trust, a bank he had come to control, as his own to prove that he was solvent, buying him time to devise a plan that would allow him to pay off all the investors. He was thwarted when the Massachusetts Bank Commissioner, Joseph Allen, took control of the Hanover Trust, and an audit of Ponzi's business, the Securities Exchange Company, revealed that his obligations to investors exceeded his assets by about $3 million. By the middle of August, 1920, Ponzi's house of cards had collapsed.

PONZI'S END

For his crime, Ponzi spent almost four years in a federal prison and seven years in a Massachusetts state prison before being deported to Italy. The man who had made getting rich quick look so easy died in the charity ward of a Rio de Janeiro, Brazil, hospital in 1949. Investors in his scheme who had not got-

Charles Ponzi. (Library of Congress)

ten their money out of his business before it was closed ended up with about 37 cents for each dollar they had invested. Ponzi was not the first to perpetrate this type of fraud, but his name continues to be linked to it.

Randall Hannum

FURTHER READING

Dunn, Donald H. *Ponzi: The Boston Swindler.* New York: McGraw-Hill, 1975. An overview of Ponzi's life is presented in a novelistic way, along with the details of the rise and subsequent fall of the Securities Exchange Company.

_____. *Ponzi: The Incredible True Story of the King of Financial Cons.* New York: Broadway Books, 2004. A reissue of the author's earlier book, in which the author reveals that he had the opportunity to interview Ponzi's wife before her death.

Ponzi, Charles. *The Rise of Mr. Ponzi.* Naples, Fla.: Inkwell, 2001. Originally self-published during his lifetime, Ponzi's autobiography displays his arrogance and optimism as he discusses the events that led to his rise and eventual fall.

Sifakis, Carl. *Frauds, Deceptions and Swindles.* New York: Checkmark Books, 2001. Contains a short, concise essay on Ponzi and his scheme among approximately 150 essays on other famous swindles.

Zuckoff, Mitchell. *Ponzi's Scheme: The True Story of a Financial Legend.* New York: Random House, 2005. Provides an interesting and extensively researched account of Ponzi's life, his scheme, and the events that eventually caused the collapse of his business.

SEE ALSO: Business crimes; Muckraking journalism; Organized crime.

Poor People's Campaign of 1968

THE EVENT: Nationally coordinated multiracial protest against poverty and economic injustice

DATE: December, 1967-June, 1968

PLACE: Washington, D.C.

SIGNIFICANCE: A grassroots movement that linked economic justice, poverty, unemployment, and homelessness to the broader Civil Rights movement during the 1960's. While the campaign may have made a statement, it failed to produce any legislation.

Collaboratively organized by Martin Luther King, Jr., and other activists in the Southern Christian Leadership Conference (SCLC), the Poor People's Campaign is best understood within the context of American business history as an attempt to illuminate the moral and political links between economic justice and participatory citizenship in American democracy. King and other organizers extended their earlier campaigns against racial segregation and white supremacy to confront what they viewed as problems of economic segregation and class supremacy.

Organizing for the Poor People's Campaign began in late 1967, with plans for building Resurrection City as a model tent-city, self-governed by poor and homeless residents. Other strategies included a mass march on Washington, D.C., pushing to improve low-income housing and antipoverty programs, and working to guarantee full employment and a livable level of income. The campaign was delayed after King's assassination on April 4, 1968, but in May of 1968, Resurrection City was raised on the Washington Mall.

The Poor People's Campaign emphasized persisting structural inequities in the economy. These problems affected all of America's working poor, unemployed, and homeless, and the campaign drew people from all regions of the country. Organizers expanded the scope of civil rights work to include multiracial coalition building along class lines. Resurrection City included poor white, Native American, and Latino residents. Solidarity Day, a mass demonstration held on June 19, 1968, at the Lincoln Memorial, drew thousands of activists from around the country and aimed to replicate the visual spectacle and national impact of the 1963 civil rights march on Washington. However, Solidarity Day failed to spark a national campaign of support, and soon afterward, the residents of Resurrection City were evicted and the Poor People's Campaign was shut down.

Historians differ in their interpretations of the successes and failures of the Poor People's Campaign. Researchers, including Robert T. Chase, have argued that by extending the scope of the Civil Rights movement to issues of poverty, unemployment, and economic justice, the campaign alienated white liberals in the movement, including those in the business community, who may have supported racial desegregation but were less sympathetic to basic structural changes in the economy. Others point to tensions among organizers and participants or to American denials of "class politics."

Although the Poor People's Campaign did not directly produce any legislation, some experts believe that it sparked some governmental reforms: food distribution to poor communities, congressional action to support low-income housing, and increased funding for economic opportunity. However, the question posed by the campaign—whether Americans have the collective will to eliminate persistent poverty, unemployment, homelessness, and economic segregation—remains unanswered.

Sharon Carson

FURTHER READING

Chase, Robert T. "Class Resurrection: The Poor People's Campaign of 1968 and Resurrection City." *Essays in History* 40 (1998). Notes how the expansion of the scope of the Civil Rights movement may have alineated white liberals.

Garrow, David. *Bearing the Cross: Martin Luther King, Jr., and the Southern Christian Leadership Conference.* New York: Harper Perennial Modern Classics, 2004.

Jackson, Thomas F. *From Civil Rights to Human Rights: Martin Luther King, Jr., and the Struggle for Economic Justice.* Philadelphia: University of Pennsylvania Press, 2006.

SEE ALSO: Affirmative action programs; Boycotts, consumer; Civil Rights movement; Coxey's Army; Labor history.

Pork industry

DEFINITION: Enterprises that breed, raise, and slaughter pigs, process them into food products, and market and distribute those products

SIGNIFICANCE: Pork, ham, bacon, and other pork products have been consistent parts of the American diet through most of the nation's history, particularly among lower-income groups, for which they represent affordable sources of protein.

The first domestic pigs were brought to the Americas by Christopher Columbus on his second voyage of exploration (1493-1499). Subsequent Spanish explorers brought more swine, some of which escaped their keepers and reverted to a feral form not dissimilar to wild boars. These feral hogs became the ancestors of the razorbacks of the Ozarks.

Early English settlers in Virginia and Massachusetts also brought domestic hogs during the seventeenth century. Typically, these hogs were allowed to roam in the woods around a settlement, eating acorns and other wild foods and turning them into edible flesh. Alternatively, they could be kept in pens within farmsteads, in which case they were generally fed table scraps (slops). In areas where no good roads existed to take wagonloads of grain to market, corn was often fed to hogs, which were subsequently walked to market themselves. Because hogs ate such a wide variety of feed and their flesh could easily be preserved by salting, pork was generally the cheapest type of meat available in America. As a result, the diet of lower-income Americans was often heavy in salt pork.

By the second half of the nineteenth century, there was an increasing interest in improving hog breeds. This period marked the development of all the modern hog breed books, which keep records of purebred stock. The modern meatpacking industry also developed at this time, centered in such cities as Cincinnati and Chicago. Indeed, Chicago turned so many hogs into canned and frozen cuts of meat that poet Carl Sandburg would call the city "hog butcher to the world." In Chicago's huge slaughterhouses and packing plants, the process of reducing a hog carcass to processed meat was systematized so that one carcass after another passed men with knives, each of whom removed a particular part. This "disassembly line" was so efficient that it may have inspired the assembly lines with which Henry Ford made the Model T affordable to ordinary workers.

The packing plants were also a driving force of social change. They employed enormous numbers of immigrants, often in appalling conditions. Upton Sinclair's 1906 novel *The Jungle*, which exposed the conditions in which these people lived and worked, led to the passage of the Pure Food and Drug Act of 1906 and the beginnings of modern regulation of food safety.

In the twentieth century, hog farming became an increasingly specialized business. Hogs were raised in confinement buildings, often in vast numbers. Some hog farms were so large that the management of the resulting waste was a serious environmental issue, and neighbors began to fight the construction of these "pork factories." Confinement also attracted criticism from animal-rights advocates, who regarded it as cruel and argued that it induced deleterious changes in the behavior of hogs.

Leigh Husband Kimmel

PORK SUPPLY AND USE, 1990-2006, IN MILLIONS OF POUNDS

Year	Production	Imports	Supply	Exports	Consumption
1990	15,354	898	16,565	238	16,031
2000	18,952	965	20,406	1,287	18,642
2003	19,966	1,185	21,684	1,717	19,436
2004	20,529	1,099	22,160	2,181	19,437
2005	20,706	1,025	22,274	2,665	19,115
2006	21,017	1,005	22,516	2,991	19,012

Source: Data from the *Statistical Abstract of the United States, 2008* (Washington, D.C.: Department of Commerce, Economics and Statistics Administration, Bureau of the Census, Data User Services Division, 2008)

Note: Weight is the weight of the animal minus entrails, head, hide, and internal organs but with fat and bone. Total supply equals production plus imports plus remaining stocks of previous year.

FURTHER READING

Pont, Wilson G., and Katherine A. Houpt. *The Biology of the Pig.* Ithaca, N.Y.: Comstock, 1978.

Rath, Sara. *The Complete Pig: An Entertaining History of Pigs.* Stillwater, Minn.: Voyageur Press, 2000.

Watson, Lyall. *The Whole Hog: Exploring the Extraordinary Potential of Pigs.* Washington, D.C.: Smithsonian Books, 2004.

SEE ALSO: Agribusiness; Agriculture; Beef industry; Commodity markets; Fishing industry; Food and Drug Administration; Food-processing industries; *The Jungle*; Meatpacking industry; Poultry industry.

Postal savings banks

DEFINITION: Banks run by the U.S. Post Office to meet the limited banking needs of rural communities and impoverished citizens

DATE: Operated from January, 1911-April, 1966

SIGNIFICANCE: The U.S. postal savings bank program provided limited banking service to an underserved population, kept money in general circulation, and provided the federal government with a cheap source of funds to help finance the public debt.

In 1867, shortly after the end of the U.S. Civil War, Postmaster John Creswell recommended that the federal government allow the post office to set up a program to serve the limited banking and savings needs of rural citizens; the poor, recent immigrants who might already be accustomed to such an arrangement in their home country; children; and hoarders who kept whatever money they possessed out of circulation. The postal savings bank would be modeled on the postal savings banking system of Great Britain, which had initiated such a system in 1861. Postmaster Creswell argued that monies collected via postal savings bank accounts should be used to finance the construction of a postal telegraph network.

THE START

Forty years later, on June 25, 1910, President William Howard Taft signed legislation establishing a postal savings bank. This type of bank opened to depositors on January 3, 1911, with one office in each state and U.S. territory. Eventually, the number of post offices authorized to serve as banks increased, though the program did begin slowly. Under the administrative oversight of the postmaster general, the secretary of the treasury, and the U.S. attorney general, the postal savings bank program was designed to avoid competing with state savings banks, while still serving its own clientele.

Some 5 percent of all postal savings deposits were

put on reserve in the U.S. Treasury. Some 30 percent of all deposits were invested in government bonds and securities, while 65 percent were to be redeposited in financially stable local and regional banks. Annual deposits were capped at $500. Postal savings bank accounts paid 2 percent annual interest. A depositor had to be at least ten years old to open an account. Deposits from 1 to 99 cents were exchanged for postal savings stamps that were pasted into a booklet. Deposits from $1 to $50 were exchanged for postal savings certificates. Larger deposits or certificates could be exchanged for postal savings bonds paying 2.5 percent annually.

During World War I, the maximum annual deposit increased to $1,000 in interest-earning funds and $1,000 in non-interest-earning funds. In 1918, the annual amount increased to $2,500 total. On June 30, 1919, the postal savings bank had more than 500,000 account holders. The average account held just under $300, for $167 million total on deposit. More than five thousand banks held postal savings funds on redeposit. The postal savings program continued throughout the Great Depression. By 1933, the program held over $1 billion in deposits.

As a result of many bank foreclosures and the shaky condition of many other financial institutions, the postal administration invested in government securities well in excess of the maximum legal allotment. The government not only allowed such a violation of the postal savings bank program's charter but even quietly encouraged such a practice as a cheap means to help finance the growing public debt. Some otherwise-stable banks refused postal savings redeposits because the banks did not have funds to cover the interest payments. To foster longer-term savings, the postal savings administration mandated a sixty-day minimum notification period if an investor wished to withdraw funds. Later, depositors were charged a fee to redeem savings certificates issued within the previous thirty days. The economy began to improve during the late 1930's, and after the United States entered World War II in 1941, the postal bank program thrived. By the end of World War II, the program held more than 4 million active accounts.

Throughout its lifespan, the postal savings bank program was highly decentralized. Local postmasters kept track of local accounts. The program was designed to be self-sustaining, but inadequate accounting methods over such a decentralized program proved unable to wither support or deny the claim to self-sufficiency.

THE END

After World War II, widespread banking reforms and a booming economy meant that the previously underserved banking population had many more banking options besides banking at the post office. The number of deposits and the amount of funds on deposit fell steadily throughout the 1950's and into the early 1960's. The postal savings bank program ceased to accept new deposits beginning April 25, 1966. On July 1, 1967, $60 million in unclaimed deposits and interest for 600,000 lost or inactive accounts was transferred to the U.S. Treasury. Account holders and their successors were allowed twenty years to come forward with claims from the program. Final disbursements were made on July 13, 1985. All monies remaining from the program reverted to the U.S. Treasury.

People line up to be the first depositors at this postal bank in New York in 1911. (Library of Congress)

Although the United States ended its postal savings program, many countries still continue to follow the practice initially modeled on the British postal bank system. The British postal savings bank program was so successful, eventually serving 25 percent of the population of Great Britain, that it was spun off into a self-standing financial institution, Girobank. Modern countries such as Japan, Germany, Brazil, and Austria still run thriving postal savings bank programs. Developing countries such as China and various countries in Africa continue to run decentralized postal savings programs to serve the rural population and those who control only small amounts of money at any one time.

Victoria Erhart

FURTHER READING

Cargill, Thomas F., and Naoyuki Yoshino. *Postal Savings and Fiscal Investment in Japan: The PSS and the FILP.* New York: Oxford University Press, 2003. An examination of the postal savings system in Japan, which remains in operation in the twenty-first century.

Kemmerer, Edwin Walter. *Postal Savings: An Historical and Critical Study of the Postal Savings Bank System of the United States.* Princeton, N.J.: Princeton University Press, 1917. The author examines the postal savings system as it operated in the United States, pointing out its benefits and flaws.

Scher, Mark J., and Naoyuki Yoshino, eds. *Small Savings Mobilization and Asian Economic Development: The Role of Postal Financial Services.* Armonk, N.Y.: M. E. Sharpe, 2004. A collection of essays looking at how postal savings banks, with their many small depositors, have played a role in the economic development of Asia.

Taft, William Howard. *Political Issues and Outlooks: Speeches Delivered Between August, 1908, and February, 1909.* Edited with commentary by David H. Burton. Athens: Ohio University Press, 2001. A collection of speeches containing a speech that touches on the postal banking system.

United States Senate Committee on Post Office and Civil Service. *Discontinuance of the Postal Savings System.* Washington, D.C.: Government Publishing Office, 1966. A government document describing the end of the postal savings system and how the remaining moneys were to be handled.

SEE ALSO: Bank of the United States, First; Bank of the United States, Second; Banking; Credit unions; Morris Plan banks; Postal Service, U.S.; Savings and loan associations; Supreme Court and banking law.

Postal Service, U.S.

IDENTIFICATION: U.S. governmental system to process and distribute various forms of correspondence, printed material, and packages
DATE: Established in 1781
SIGNIFICANCE: The postal service has been an essential tool of American business since the country was founded. It has provided quick, reliable delivery of messages and business documents to and from customers at a reasonable cost.

Great Britain's North American colonies at first did not have a common postal service but relied on informal ways of having messages and documents delivered to correspondents. The first formal postal office was a Boston tavern run by Richard Fairbanks. It was established as a mail center by the government of Massachusetts in 1639. Similar postal services appeared in other colonies during the seventeenth century, and some postal routes were established to send and receive mail between the larger cities. For example, the Boston Post Road, which has become a major highway but originally was a horse path, was established for monthly postal delivery between Boston and New York.

Postal service throughout the colonies came at the end of the seventeenth century, when the British government established a North American postal system, governed from England but run by a deputy in the colonies. The first deputy postmaster general was Governor Andrew Hamilton of New Jersey, appointed in 1692. Gradually local postmasters were appointed, most notably Benjamin Franklin, who became postmaster of Philadelphia in 1737. Franklin later became joint postmaster of all the colonies, a post he held until just before the Revolutionary War.

A NATIONAL POSTAL SERVICE

Just before and during the struggle for independence, a system for the conveyance of messages between the colonies was a vital concern of the Continental Congress, which appointed Franklin to the position of postmaster general. Franklin developed an efficient and widespread postal system to keep the colonies in communication during the war and after independence was declared in 1776. He was the first postmaster general of the new United States.

Officially created by the Articles of Confederation in 1781, the United States Post Office joined the states together with improved postal routes and a system of common rates for mail delivery. The mail service to Europe was reestablished, and new service to the western frontiers (the western parts of New York and Pennsylvania) was opened. Stagecoaches were contracted to carry the mail in addition to their passengers, and postal riders were enlisted for the various national routes.

The U.S. Constitution, finally ratified by all the states in 1789, authorized the continuation of the post office. The postmaster general was to be appointed by the president and to serve at his discretion. President George Washington appointed Samuel Osgood as his first postmaster general in 1789. The U.S. Post Office operated out of Philadelphia at first and moved to Washington, D.C., in 1800, when the national capital was established there.

As early as 1785, the U.S. Post Office was directed to give business assistance in more ways than the delivery of mail. In that year, the Continental Congress directed the postal service to use stagecoach companies for mail transportation, thus helping to provide the stagecoach lines with additional business. While he was president, Washington was concerned that the post office promote and abet businesses that would build the new country's economic health.

The acquisition of vast new lands, especially the Louisiana Territory and the Far West explored by Meriwether Lewis and William Clark, expanded the responsibilities of the post office to new levels and became a symbol of the progress and growth of the young country. Under President Andrew Jackson, the importance of the post office was strengthened by the appointment of the postmaster general to his cabinet. Not until 1872 did the post office officially become a department; before it was simply the U.S. Post Office.

Throughout the nineteenth century, there was concern among the country's leaders about the extent to which the post office should be self-supporting. Although the rates were usually reasonable, they were at first pegged to the distance as well as to the weight or size of the letter. This meant that correspondents in cities, where distances were small and numbers of letters were large, could pay less than people on farms or remote villages. Also, the routes to such places were more expensive to establish and maintain, and thus residents of these areas had to be satisfied with slower, less frequent postal service. These two issues occupied the government and post office officials for much of the mid-nineteenth century. Eventually, the decision was made to lean in the direction of public service.

The post office grew rapidly in the nineteenth century, following the country's fast-paced growth. There were only 75 post offices in the country in 1790, but by 1860, the number had increased to 28,498. Post roads increased in numbers, reaching as far west as Illinois in 1818.

In 1863, the rates paid for postal service were standardized so that instead of paying according to both the weight and the distance the mail must travel, rates would depend only on the weight of the letter. Thus the entire country paid a uniform rate, regardless of the distance that mail was carried.

TRANSPORTATION

The first mail carriers were boats and pedestrians. Postal carriers delivered mail in the cities and between villages; however, most travel was on boats, along the coast or on rivers or lakes. The post office claims to have used about every kind of boat service, including rafts, rowboats, canoes, and horse-drawn canal boats. By 1811, steamboats became available, and the post office contracted with the steamboat companies to carry the mail. This fast, safe, and reliable method of transportation greatly increased the efficiency and coverage of the mail system. The coastal waters, rivers, canals, and lakes were soon busy with steamboats carrying passengers, freight, and the mail to almost all parts of the country.

Even the Far West's mail was served by steamships. Although freight from the East Coast to the West Coast generally went around the southern tip of South America, the mail was shipped by steamer to Panama, where it was then carried overland by mule to the Pacific Ocean, where a steamship was waiting to carry it to California and the Oregon Territory. In 1855, a railroad was built across Panama, speeding up the travel time, but it still took at least three weeks to get a letter from New York to San Francisco.

A CLOSER LOOK AT THE UNITED STATES POSTAL SERVICE

- Delivers more than 210 billion pieces of mail per year, or 8,000 pieces per second
- Delivers mail to more than 300 million people at 148 million homes, businesses, and post office boxes
- Adds 1.8 million new addresses to its delivery network each year
- Has an annual operating budget of $75 billion
- Is the second-largest employer in the United States
- Employs 685,000 career employees
- Operates the largest civilian vehicle fleet in the world, with more than 219,000 vehicles
- Uses about 121 million gallons of fuel to drive 1.2 billion miles per year
- Moves mail using planes, trains, trucks, cars, boats, ferries, helicopters, bicycles, hovercrafts, subways, and mules
- Printed 42.7 billion stamps in 2007

Source: U.S. Postal Service

The Pony Express was a spectacular business venture that has remained a legend of the West. In 1860, William Hepburn Russell, who had tried unsuccessfully to interest the post office in the idea, decided to privately institute an express mail service overland to the West Coast. With two partners, he created the Central Overland California and Pike's Peak Express Company, nicknamed the Pony Express. He hired the best horsemen he could find and located a large number of strong and healthy horses. He established new relay stations along his chosen route, which went from St. Joseph, Missouri (which was reached from the East by train), to California by way of the area that would become Kansas, Nebraska, Colorado, Wyoming, Utah, and Nevada. Riders carried the mail in side pouches, covering seventy-five to one hundred miles at a time. Horses were quickly switched at each way station. In this way, mail was carried across the country at unheard-of speeds. The record was a mail packet carrying Abraham Lincoln's inaugural address, which reached California in only seven days, seventeen hours. Spectacular though it was, the Pony Express lasted only a little more than a year. It was supplanted by the intercontinental telegraph line, which was completed in 1861, and by the trains that shortly afterward made their way west to the coast.

In the East, the railroads had been used for carrying mail since 1832. Their value in serving a growing clientele was recognized by Congress, which designated all railroads as mail routes, guaranteeing both their availability to the post office and a steady revenue for the railroads. In subsequent years, many long-run trains carried mail cars, and by 1864, the first officially designated railway post offices had been designated. Rural areas were often served on the fly by devices called mail cranes, which allowed the postal workers on board the trains to grab an outgoing mail bag from a hook without stopping the train and to drop the incoming mail bags for each destination. Sorting of the mail was done by the postal workers en route.

Railroad postal delivery remained a major component of the postal service well into the twentieth century. In 1930, more than ten thousand trains carried mail. However, after passenger trains began to be unprofitable, the government released them from obligatory operation, and mail transportation moved from the railroads to the increasingly dominant highways. The last railroad post office closed in 1977. Some mail, especially parcel post, continued to be carried by train. During the 1990's, Amtrak experimented with hybrid vehicles that could travel partway by train and partway by road. Amtrak stopped carrying mail in 2004, and only a small fraction of the mail, mostly second- and third-class and parcel post, was carried by trains in the following years.

Highways dominated the mail delivery for much of the twentieth century. During the early part of the century, the nation's highway system grew rapidly as the number of automobiles grew. Federally supported highways, from U.S. Route 1 on the East Coast to Route 99 on the West Coast, created rapid and reliable routes for mail trucks. During the middle of the century, the building of interstate highways increased the speed of the mail service. By 2006, there were more than 16,000 designated highway contract routes across the country.

Airmail started experimentally in 1911 and was sufficiently promising so that it was authorized by Congress in 1916. The first regularly scheduled airmail service was a route from New York to Washington, D.C., in 1918. The post office's use of airmail gave an important boost to the aircraft and airline industries. Much of the rapid development of air travel was instigated by the post office's promotion of airports, weather stations, radio beacons, and other features essential to reliable air service. By the start of the twenty-first century, most mail in the United States was carried by air.

After 1913, when parcel post was started, this new service stimulated a whole new kind of retail business. Giant mail-order houses, such as Sears, Roebuck and Company and Montgomery Ward, sprang up, bringing the world of commerce to the previously unserved rural areas of the country. The post office's low rates for parcel post stimulated business everywhere and made it possible for many more Americans to participate in the rising standard of living. By 2000, the government estimated that the value of the American mail-order industry had reached nearly $900 billion.

UNITED STATES POSTAL SERVICE

In 1971, Congress changed the administrative nature of the post office. It became the United States Postal Service (USPS), and the postmaster general was no longer a cabinet position. The postal service no longer had a near monopoly, and private operators began to provide competition, encouraging it to increase efficiency and to use more new technology. The USPS contracted with several private carriers, such as Federal Express and United Parcel Service, for the distribution of many parcels, to the benefit of customers. It still remains an immense operation and a vital one for the business community and the convenience of the American people.

Paul W. Hodge

FURTHER READING

Bruns, James H. *Great American Post Offices.* New York: John Wiley & Sons, 1998. Written by the director of the National Postal Museum of the Smithsonian Institution, this fascinating book describes the architectural and social history of 250 famous post offices throughout the United States.

Henkin, David M. *The Postal Age: Emergence of Modern Communications in Nineteenth Century America.* Chicago: University of Chicago Press, 2006. This brief book is an authoritative account of the development of the post office during its first one hundred years and of its influence on the country's growth.

Kielbowicz, Richard. *News in the Mail: The Press, Post Office, and Public Information, 1700-1860's.* Westport, Conn.: Greenwood, 1989. The importance of the post office in communicating the news is well described in this historical account of the relationship of the news industry and its primary carrier, the post office. Until 1860, when the telegraph became available to the media, the post office was a vital element for dissemination of the news.

Luca, Eileen. *Our Postal System.* Brookfield, Conn.: Millbrook, 1999. A short history of the post office, this clear and interesting book is intended for students but can be read with profit by anyone.

Shaw, Christopher. *Preserving the People's Post Office.* Washington, D.C.: Essential Books, 2006. This book presents a convincing argument that the post office, as a major service that serves all the country's people equally, is an essential national operation that could not be replaced by private industry.

SEE ALSO: Catalog shopping; E-mail; FedEx; Franklin, Benjamin; Internet; Magazine industry; Pony Express; Postal savings banks; Shipping industry; Telecommunications industry.

Poultry industry

DEFINITION: Enterprises involving the raising, processing, and marketing of the meat and eggs of chickens, turkeys, ducks, geese, and other fowl

SIGNIFICANCE: As technological improvements in the ability to process poultry have increased and as health concerns about the consumption of beef have come to the fore, the poultry industry has increased its share of the market for meat and meat products, especially in the latter half of the twentieth century and the beginning of the twenty-first century.

Chickens were first domesticated in India thousands of years ago. Since then, they have become a mainstay of human consumption. Chickens are by far the most common domesticated fowl in the world. Early in the twenty-first century, there were more than 24 billion chickens in the world—more than any other domesticated or wild bird species.

POULTRY IN THE UNITED STATES

Early American colonists brought chickens with them from Europe to their settlements in the New World. Chickens are an important food source for several reasons. As a source of high-quality protein, chickens—pound for pound—provide a high value compared with their cost of production. Although modern industrial production relies on scientifically determined nutritious feed, chickens can subsist in a variety of conditions and on low-value foods such as scraps. Chickens very quickly grow to an age at which they can be consumed, with the average life span of a commercially grown chicken being only six weeks. Finally, chickens provide an important source of food in the form of eggs. However, early colonial settlers ate far more beef than chicken. In early United States history, chickens and eggs were produced on family farms and were marketed in small towns.

Early colonial settlers domesticated the turkey from the wild fowl they found while colonizing North America. In the United States, turkeys became a valuable food source but were far less popular than chicken until modern food production made it possible to use turkey meat as a substitute

The scene in this 1869 Currier & Ives print of a poultry yard bears little resemblance to modern chicken and egg production methods. (Library of Congress)

for beef, pork, or lamb in a wide variety of processed meats.

On a worldwide basis, waterfowl, including both ducks and geese, have been popular in those countries that engage in wet-rice or paddy rice cultivation. The ponds and reservoirs used for rice irrigation double as a habitat for domesticated ducks and geese. Waterfowl do not currently occupy a prominent place in the American poultry industry, although that may change as the number of Asian immigrants increases. Domesticated pheasants, partridges, quails, grouse, guinea fowl, button quails, and sand grouse constitute an even smaller share of the overall poultry industry, although specialized markets for each of these birds exist in the United States.

POULTRY SUPPLY AND USE, 1990-2006, IN MILLIONS OF POUNDS

Year	Production	Imports	Supply	Exports	Consumption
1990	23,468	—	23,931	1,222	22,153
2000	36,073	9	37,140	5,584	30,508
2003	38,477	17	39,595	5,498	33,131
2004	39,585	33	40,584	5,440	34,139
2005	40,935	42	41,981	5,902	34,947
2006	41,461	60	42,653	5,966	35,705

Source: Data from the *Statistical Abstract of the United States, 2008* (Washington, D.C.: Department of Commerce, Economics and Statistics Administration, Bureau of the Census, Data User Services Division, 2008)

Note: Weight is the weight of the animal minus entrails, head, feathers, and internal organs but with fat and bone. Total supply equals production plus imports plus remaining stocks of previous year.

CHANGES IN THE INDUSTRY

During the middle of the nineteenth century, scientific research began into how to make chicken feed more nutritious, produce better chickens and eggs, and improve processing for storage. Urban areas were largely dependent on farms close to the city for eggs and chicken meat. Eggs tended to break if transported great distances, and unrefrigerated chicken meat spoils easily and can cause illness, if not death. The demand for fresh produce, which was shipped similarly to chicken, also limited the amount of chicken that was transported long distances. Although processing and refrigeration of beef, pork, and lamb had progressed substantially, chickens were so small in comparison to these other animals that the same processes were not cost-effective.

During the 1920's, the first large-scale factories and chicken processing plants were established, but the Great Depression during the 1930's and World War II during the 1940's slowed their development. Factory farms confined chickens in cages to produce eggs and raised chickens for their meat in climate-controlled conditions indoors. After World War II, the industry expanded. Modern refrigeration was now available and cost-efficient enough to be used for chicken and other fowl. New synthetic materials could be used for egg cartons to minimize breakage. A mechanical deboning process increased labor productivity substantially.

During the late twentieth century, health concerns about the consumption of large quantities of beef led to an increased interest in poultry, particularly chicken and turkey. Advanced meat-processing techniques made possible the manufacture of a wide variety of processed meats, including hot dogs and sandwich meats, from chicken and turkey meat. Modern packaging and refrigeration enabled the poultry industry to grow dramatically. Advertising also helped the development of the poultry industry.

In the latter part of the twentieth century, consumers began to question the way chickens were raised and processed. Factory farms were criticized as inhumane and unsanitary, and some chicken producers began offering eggs and meat from free-range chickens, birds raised in a more traditional manner. Also, the finding of salmonella and other bacteria on chicken and several exposés about conditions in the processing plants created some questions about the way chickens are processed. However, government regulation of the poultry industry has increased public perception that chickens and chicken products are safe to eat.

Richard L. Wilson

FURTHER READING

Bell, Donald D., and William D. Weaver, Jr., eds. *Commercial Chicken Meat and Egg Production.* 5th ed. Norwell, Mass.: Kluwer Academic Publishers, 2002. A discussion of the commercial business of managing poultry designed for those in or entering the poultry industry.

Damerow, Gail. *Storey's Guide to Raising Chickens: Care, Feeding, Facilities.* Pownal, Vt.: Storey Books, 1995. This practical guide to raising chickens contains significant information about the commercial aspects of the industry.

Perrins, Christopher, ed. *Firefly Encyclopedia of Birds.* Buffalo, N.Y.: Firefly Books, 2003. This general reference book on birds contains valuable sections on the fowl included in the poultry industry.

Sherman, David M. *Tending Animals in the Global Village.* London: Blackwell, 2002. This book argues in part against the mistreatment of chickens in the poultry industry.

Smith, Page, and Charles Daniel. *The Chicken Book.* Athens: University of Georgia Press, 2000. This is a comprehensive examination of the most numerous birds in the world.

SEE ALSO: Agribusiness; Agriculture; Agriculture, U.S. Department of; Beef industry; Fishing industry; Meatpacking industry; Pork industry; United Food and Commercial Workers.

Presidency, U.S.

DEFINITION: Office of the chief executive of the United States government

SIGNIFICANCE: The president of the United States guides the federal government, oversees the implementation of laws enacted by Congress, and recommends legislation to Congress. Since 1921, the president has been required to submit an annual budget to Congress suggesting the proper federal expenditures and revenue streams for the fiscal year. The presidency has also come over time to be seen as linked to the national economy, and presidents are often given credit for good economic performance and blamed for poor economic performance.

The U.S. presidency was partly created for the economic purposes of protecting property rights and economic liberty, promoting economic growth, ensuring the payment of Revolutionary War debts, and improving the financial status of the United States government and American business with European governments and banks. As American history progressed and the American economy became more complex and interdependent, Americans developed higher expectations of the U.S. presidency regarding such issues as the development of the West and a national infrastructure for transportation, inflation, bank failures, stock market crashes, unemployment, international trade, unfair business practices, social welfare benefits, consumer protection, monopolies, and agricultural prices. By the late twentieth century, there was often a direct correlation between a president's public approval rating and the nation's economic condition.

A literal interpretation of the U.S. Constitution suggests that Congress, not the president, holds most of the federal government's powers to influence the American economy. In *The Federalist* (1787-1788), Alexander Hamilton—the first secretary of the treasury and the primary author and advocate of the office of president among the Founders—noted that, while the president wields "the power of the sword," Congress has "the power of the purse." Furthermore, a literal interpretation of the president's constitutional powers in general and those pertaining to the economy in particular suggests that they are mostly inferior and reactive to those of Congress. This pro-Congress, antipresidency interpretation of the Constitution regarding the economy is bolstered by the assumption that most Americans during the late eighteenth century preferred a laissez-faire, free market economic approach with minimal intervention, regulation, or leadership by the federal government.

A major purpose for writing, ratifying, and implementing the U.S. Constitution, however, was to provide greater order, uniformity, and direction to the American economy from a new national government, including the presidency. Among the Founders, Hamilton was the most skeptical of laissez-faire capitalism and the most favorable toward British-style mercantilism, in which executive-led, government policies would promote, protect, and subsidize a more self-sufficient, interdependent, and stable economy. In explaining and advocating the creation of the presidency in 1787 and 1788, Hamilton argued that the advantages of a powerful chief executive included the president's ability to provide "singular accountability," "energy," and "unity" in leading the nation toward long-term policy goals and vetoing legislation that threatened property rights and individual liberties.

FROM WASHINGTON TO JACKSON

As President George Washington's secretary of the Treasury, Hamilton developed, promoted, and helped Washington secure congressional passage of an economic policy agenda that included a national bank, "hard" currency, the payment of war debts, protective tariffs to raise revenue and nurture American manufacturing, excise taxes, and federal spending on interstate roads and other "internal improvements" to facilitate interstate commerce. Some of Washington's Hamiltonian economic policies proved to be bitterly divisive and controversial, especially the national bank and the Army-enforced collection of excise taxes on whiskey.

Differences about the federal government's proper role in the economy quickly became a major source of ideological, coalitional, and policy differences among presidential and congressional candidates and within the emerging two-party system. The Anti-Federalist Party, later known as the Democratic-Republican Party and then the Democratic Party, was established by future presidents Thomas Jefferson and James Madison. In contrast to the Federalist Party of Alexander Hamilton and John Adams, the Anti-Federalist Party and its successor parties opposed a national bank and high protective tariffs. It favored a more laissez-faire strategy for American capitalism until the early twentieth century.

Jefferson's presidency also saw the first major use of economic policy as a foreign policy weapon. To assert U.S. neutrality in the wars between Britain and France and to protest the British practice of "impressing" American sailors into service, Jefferson secured enactment of and vigorously enforced the Embargo Acts of 1807 and 1809, which President James Madison continued. The resulting embargo devastated the local economies of major port cities, especially in New England, and motivated some New England Federalists to consider secession.

More so than Jefferson and Madison, Democratic president Andrew Jackson regarded himself as the champion of the "common man," especially frontier settlers, laborers, and small farmers, in both politics and economics. Jackson perceived the national bank as biased in favor of the mostly Whig northern bankers and merchants. Consequently, Jackson vetoed a bill to recharter the national bank. He also withdrew federal funds from the national bank and distributed them among state banks. The U.S. economy would not have the equivalent of a central bank until the creation of the Federal Reserve system in 1913.

THE TURN OF THE TWENTIETH CENTURY

During the remainder of the nineteenth century, U.S. presidents often assumed leading roles in promoting the population growth and economic development of the West. Government subsidies of free land encouraged railroad and telegraph construction, mining, farming, and homesteading in the West. The Democratic and Republican Parties and their presidential candidates continued to differ on tariffs, the gold standard, and the extent of federal regulations on the economy. The first regulatory commission, the Interstate Commerce Commission (ICC), was established in 1887, initially and primarily for the purpose of regulating railroad rates. Despite the ICC, various economic protest movements developed among struggling farmers and rural businessmen, especially in the upper Midwest, the West, and hill country areas of the South. Furthermore, miners and railroad and factory workers increasingly believed that the president should redress their economic grievances, such as low pay, long hours, unsafe working conditions, and anti-union business practices.

Responding to these economic grievances, especially those of farmers, the Democratic and Populist Parties nominated William Jennings Bryan for president in 1896. Bryan advocated the free coinage of silver, lower tariffs, and government ownership of the railroads. Portraying Bryan as a dangerous economic radical, the Republican Party nominated William McKinley on a platform of high tariffs and maintaining the gold standard and easily won the presidential and congressional elections of 1896. Republican economic policies mostly prevailed until the New Deal of the 1930's.

McKinley was assassinated in 1901, and Theodore Roosevelt became president. Roosevelt engaged in a more vigorous, personalized type of presidential intervention in the economy. He threatened to seize control of coal mines with Army troops to end a coal strike in 1902. He directed the Justice Department aggressively to prosecute violators of the Sherman Antitrust Act of 1890, especially the Northern Securities Company and the "beef trust." Roosevelt also used the status and rhetorical position of the presidency as a "bully pulpit" to pressure Congress to pass the Elkins Act of 1903, which criminalized the giving or receiving of rebates on railroad rates, and the Hepburn Act of 1906, which gave the ICC the power to fix railroad rates. Nicknamed the Trust Buster, Roosevelt also pioneered the roles of the president as an environmentalist and a consumer advocate.

During the United States' participation in World War I, Democratic president Woodrow Wilson greatly expanded the president's powers to lead and manage the American wartime economy for foreign and defense policy purposes. He created several new executive agencies and boards to convert agricultural, mineral, and industrial production and labor relations from civilian to defense purposes and issued nearly two thousand executive orders. President Franklin D. Roosevelt relied on the precedent of Wilson's actions during World War II. During the Korean War, the Supreme Court asserted constitutional and congressional limits on a president's wartime economic powers in its 1952 decision against President Harry S. Truman in *Youngstown Sheet and Tube Co. v. Sawyer.*

FROM ROOSEVELT TO CARTER

The Great Depression and the implementation of the New Deal during the 1930's greatly increased the influence of the president's fiscal and budgetary policy on the U.S. economy. New Deal public works and relief programs reduced unemployment and poverty and stimulated consumer spending, while the Social Security Act of 1935 provided old-age and unemployment benefits. In an effort to reduce growing budget deficits, President Franklin D. Roosevelt made later budget cuts that contributed to the 1937-1938 recession. The New Deal also expanded the federal government's regulatory powers and responsibilities to include oversight of the stock market, bank deposits, agricultural production and prices, labor relations, and rural electrification.

The end of the Great Depression and World War II did not initiate a reduction of presidential powers and responsibilities in the U.S. economy.

President Harry S. Truman and Congress created the Council of Economic Advisors (CEA) in 1946 to provide the president with economic research and advice for benefiting the nation's "employment, production, and purchasing power." The CEA also helps the president prepare his annual economic report to Congress and provides economic advice to business. The CEA was instrumental in persuading Presidents John F. Kennedy and Lyndon B. Johnson to support the enactment of a major income tax cut in 1964 to stimulate greater economic growth.

The effects of high defense spending during the Vietnam War, the 1964 tax cut, and higher domestic spending through new social welfare programs such as Medicaid and Medicare contributed to high inflation, a weaker American dollar, and slower economic growth by the 1970's. Consequently, President Richard M. Nixon briefly imposed wage and price controls and removed the American dollar from the gold standard. A sharp increase in oil prices further aggravated the so-called stagflation of the 1970's, as the American economy suffered from high rates of both inflation and unemployment. In 1979, President Jimmy Carter appointed Paul Volcker as chair of the Federal Reserve Board. Volcker's policies of high interest rates and a tighter money supply aggravated the 1981-1983 recession but also contributed in the long term to low inflation, greater economic growth, and lower unemployment for the remainder of the 1980's.

FROM REAGAN TO GEORGE W. BUSH

Elected president in 1980, Ronald Reagan was the first president since the 1920's who wanted to significantly and permanently reduce the role of the federal government in the U.S. economy. Strongly influenced by monetarism and supply-side economics, Reagan's economic policy agenda included major tax cuts, less domestic spending, and deregulation of industries. While Reagan achieved tax cuts and deregulation of major industries, Congress rejected Reagan's proposals for major domestic spending cuts, Social Security reform, and welfare reform. Appointed chair of the Federal Reserve Board by Reagan in 1987, Alan Greenspan was determined to continue long-term economic growth with low inflation and low interest rates. He served as chair of the Federal Reserve until his retirement in 2006.

The Reagan administration presided over sharp increases in federal deficits and the national debt.

Elected president in 1992 partly because of the effects of the 1990-1991 recession, Bill Clinton, a Democrat, restrained congressional proposals for higher domestic spending as an economic stimulus and achieved congressional passage of tax increases to reduce the deficit and reassure the bond market. Clinton reappointed Greenspan and helped achieve the first federal budget surplus in thirty years. President George W. Bush sought to increase economic growth during his first term through tax cuts and to reduce inflation and high budget deficits during his second term with domestic spending cuts. Toward the end of his presidency, Bush's economic policies were hampered by opposition from a Democratic Congress, rising oil prices, a mortgage crisis, and the expense of the Iraq War (started in 2003).

Sean J. Savage

FURTHER READING

Campagna, Anthony S. *U.S. National Economic Policy, 1917-1985.* New York: Praeger, 1987. Useful survey of economic policies from Wilson to Reagan.

Light, Paul C. *The President's Agenda: Domestic Policy Choice from Kennedy to Clinton.* Baltimore: Johns Hopkins University Press, 1999. Detailed analysis of presidential tactics and strategies in achieving their domestic policy goals, including tax cuts, budget bills, and deficit reduction.

McDonald, Forrest. *The American Presidency: An Intellectual History.* Lawrence: University Press of Kansas, 1994. Excellent study of the origins of the U.S. presidency and Alexander Hamilton's influence on this office.

Rosenberg, Samuel. *American Economic Development Since 1945: Growth, Decline, and Rejuvenation.* New York: Palgrave, 2003. Broad study of changes in the American economy since 1945; includes an examination of presidential influence.

Stein, Herbert. *Presidential Economics: The Making of Economic Policy from Roosevelt to Clinton.* Washington, D.C.: American Enterprise Institute, 1994. Examines the similarities and differences among presidents from 1933 to 1993 in developing and promoting their economic policies.

SEE ALSO: Bank of the United States, First; Bank of the United States, Second; Congress, U.S.; Constitution, U.S.; Great Depression; New Deal programs; Sherman Antitrust Act; Taxation; Wars.

Price fixing

DEFINITION: Agreement between companies to sell products or services for certain prices to control their markets or otherwise to restrict price competition

SIGNIFICANCE: Price fixing eliminates competition and forces buyers to pay higher prices than the market would normally bear. The practice undermines the concepts that support the free enterprise economy of the United States.

The practice of price fixing is illegal in the United States, Canada, Australia, and the European Union. In other countries of the world, by contrast, it is a common practice and is often supported by the government. Price fixing is, in a general sense, artificial manipulation of the market price of a good or service to increase seller profits. The most common form of price fixing is an agreement by a group of competitors as to the price they will charge for a product or a service—that is, to fix the price. The agreement does not bind every seller in the particular market; however, agreement among major competitors significantly affects the price the majority of consumers will pay. Other forms of price fixing include agreements to eliminate discounts, maintain prices at a given point, fix credit terms, use a standard formula for figuring prices, and create price discounts. Price fixing can also be perpetrated by buyers who all agree to pay a set or fixed price for a good or service.

Several market developments may be indications of price fixing. When a large number of providers of a good or service charge the exact same price, there is a likelihood of price fixing. If sellers of the same good or service who have a history of charging different prices all begin charging the same price, they may be involved in price fixing. If a higher price is charged to local costumers than to consumers in other areas, there may be local price fixing. The elimination of discounts in a market that always used discounts and an increase in price when there is no apparent increase in cost may also be the result of price fixing by sellers.

LEGISLATION

In 1890, the Sherman Antitrust Act was passed by Congress in an effort to check the growth of monopolies. The act stated that any business grouping that attempted to restrict trade or commerce was illegal. The language of the legislation, however, proved to be too vague to curb monopolies. Then, in 1914, the Clayton Antitrust Act was passed to strengthen the Sherman Antitrust Act. It contained more precise language and declared that it was illegal for companies to enter into agreements to fix or control prices such that competition was reduced or eliminated. Price fixing was made a felony.

The Antitrust Division of the United States Department of Justice prosecutes both criminal and civil cases of price fixing. The U.S. Federal Trade Commission also prosecutes civil cases. In addition, many states' attorneys general also prosecute cases at the state level. Individual citizens and organizations also have the right to bring suit against business entities for price fixing. Cases of international price fixing by private companies or cartels that either are based or sell in the United States are also prosecuted under the United States antitrust laws.

In 1991, the Coalition Against Price Fixing attempted to get Congress to pass the Consumer Protection Against Price Fixing Act. The bill passed the Senate but failed to become law. The bill resulted from the efforts of a group of retailers from various market sectors to prohibit a manufacturer from setting a minimum price at which its product could be sold and refusing to supply retailers who sold at lower prices.

From a legal standpoint, price fixing is a complex issue. For price fixing to occur, there must be intent to restrict competition on the part of the business entities involved. The price fixing must be the result of agreement or communication among the firms, individuals, sellers, or buyers involved in the scheme. Firms may charge the same price for an item as does a major seller or market leader so long as no agreement is made. This often happens in the breakfast cereal and cigarette markets.

MAJOR CONSPIRACIES

Price fixing conspiracies have occurred on regional, national, and international scales in a wide variety of business activities, including construction, agriculture, retail trade, and manufacturing, as well as in various service industries. In 1961, the multinational General Electric, Westinghouse, and several other manufacturers of heavy electrical equipment were convicted of price fixing in regard to sales of such equipment. This was the largest price fixing case that had been prosecuted under the Sherman Antitrust Act up to that time. It was also the first time that individuals involved in price fixing were sentenced to prison.

In 1993, Archer Daniels Midland Company, an agricultural products conglomerate, was investigated and prosecuted for its role in price fixing of lysine by an international cartel. In 1997, the company was fined $100 million, which was the largest antitrust fine up to that time. Three of the company's senior officials received prison sentences in 1999. In 2005, Samsung was fined $300 million for its involvement in a an international cartel conspiracy that fixed the price of dynamic random access memory.

Shawncey Webb

FURTHER READING

Connor, John W. *Global Price Fixing*. Berlin-Heidelberg: Springer-Verlag, 2008. This study looks at the participation of American firms in global price fixing schemes and elucidates the advantages to firms and the costs to consumers. Also discusses the use of antitrust law by the United States and Europe to control and eliminate price fixing.

Greenhut, Melvin L., and Bruce Benson. *American Antitrust Laws in Theory and in Practice*. Brookfield, Vt.: Avebury, 1989. A scholarly analysis of antitrust laws and price fixing in the United States.

Rockefeller, Edwin S. *Antitrust Religion*. Washington, D.C.: Cato Institute, 2007. An examination of trusts, monopolies, mergers, "tying," and price fixing.

Schlegelmilch, Bodo. *Marketing Ethics: An International Perspective*. London: Thomson Learning, 1998. As part of an investigation of global business ethics, this study examines the ethical issues involved with price fixing. Points out that price fixing is not illegal worldwide and asks what the responsibilities of businesses are in the international marketplace.

Sullivan, Thomas E., ed. *The Political Economy of the Sherman Act: The First One Hundred Years*. New York: Oxford University Press, 1991. This compilation of essays provides an excellent overview of antitrust laws and the debate about them. It traces the history and evolution of antitrust laws from 1890 to 1990. It discusses the role of government in market regulation and presents a good analysis of how antitrust laws, which prohibit price fixing, affect American business both domestically and internationally.

SEE ALSO: Antitrust legislation; Clayton Antitrust Act; Federal Trade Commission; Justice, U.S. Department of; Sherman Antitrust Act.

Printing industry

DEFINITION: Business segment that reproduces images or written materials, such as advertisements, books, newspapers, periodicals, and stationery

SIGNIFICANCE: Because print has been necessary for businesses throughout American history, the printing industry has been an integral part of American corporate life. Changes in the printing process, including computerization, have revolutionized related industries such as publishing and presented both advantages and challenges to the printing industry.

A large number of innovations have changed the operations of the printing industry. Whereas printing was originally handwork, controlled by the printer, the introduction of the printing press made it an industrial process. Handwork started to be used less commonly after the introduction of letterpress printing, sometime in the fifteenth century. In the letterpress method, moveable type is locked together, pressed against an ink source, and then pressed or rolled onto paper. Benjamin Franklin used a letterpress printer, called the Ramage press, in England in 1725. The Ramage press was made mainly of wood but had some iron parts. This contrasted with a press made by Earl Stanhope in the beginning of the nineteenth century, which was constructed completely of iron. Philadelphia, Pennsylvania, was home to the 1817 Columbian press. In 1822, Daniel Treadwell invented the first American power press to go into production. Improvements in the inking process came in 1829, with Samuel Rust's invention of the Washington press. One year later, the Adams press, a press with a stationary platen, was created.

REVOLVING PRESS

Some of the most influential changes in printing were the result of the invention of the revolving cylinder press, which allowed for the form containing the type to curve around a cylinder that rotated as it printed. Historical accounts disagree as to who invented this type of press. Friedrich König, a German inventor, is credited with one of the first versions in 1810 or 1814. Another version was reportedly produced by D. Napier and Son in 1819. Regardless of its origin, it is generally agreed that the speed of this press greatly surpassed that of the flat press.

After Robert March Hoe designed an improved version of the revolving press in 1843, the rotary press invigorated the newspaper industry. The *Philadelphia Public Ledger* purchased a four-cylinder press in 1845. *The Sun* (New York) got an eight-cylinder press five years later, and the *New York Herald* began using a ten-cylinder press in 1857. The ten-cylinder press could print 20,000 one-sided sheets per hour. This was ten times more sheets than the smaller cylinder presses could produce. Stereotype copies of the printed pages were introduced to the newspaper industry in 1861. By 1891, printing presses could print and fold 90,000 four-page papers in an hour. One year later, the printing industry was further transformed when a four-color rotary press was invented.

LINOTYPE AND BEYOND

The Mergenthaler Linotype machine, invented by Ottmar Mergenthaler in 1886, transformed the typesetting process in a way that was roughly equal to the invention of moveable type four centuries earlier. It combined several processes into one keyboard (similar to a typewriter or computer keyboard), allowing one person to machine, typeset, justify, typefound, and type distribute.

Later changes in equipment and processes included the development of photochemical engraving, halftone cuts, color reproduction, clean feeders, folders and trimmers, mechanized bookbinding, and stereotyping for the newspaper industry, which included the standard autoplate. Photoengraving involves the process of etching the image on metal through the use of photographic techniques. It is used to make embossing and stamping dies, printed circuit boards, printing plates, and other print-integrated metal products. Halftone cuts are also related to photography, relying on dot formation to create images. Clean feeders, folders and trimmers, and mechanized bookbinding all sped up the processes involved in printing, while cutting down on the amount of handwork that printers had to do. Phototypesetting became more common in 1947. A few years later, computerized processes began to transform the industry. Digital equipment and communication technologies have further transformed the industry, forcing workers to obtain higher skill levels and creating a need for constant training updates.

PRODUCTS AND SERVICES

The products and services that the printing industry supplies are varied and often depend on each other for a final product. Advertising regularly monopolizes the largest portion of the industry (over a quarter), with packaging, catalogs, varied periodicals, and newspapers following as the largest users. In 2007, books, directories, and stationery each took up an additional 6 percent of the industry's workload. Because the industry has expanded beyond traditional print sources to include Web design, marketing communication, and other computer-related issues, it is often difficult to define exactly what processes fall under the umbrella of the print-ing industry. Secondary production, the printing jobs that are completed by companies outside of the printing industry, is not included in printing industry figures.

As of 2006, the worth of the products and services provided per year was estimated to be around $165 billion dollars. Approximately one million laborers were employed by almost 40,000 organizations. In 2004, the number of printing enterprises was about three thousand higher; however, downsizing and closings have negatively affected many segments of the industry.

CHALLENGES

The printing industry has been facing a number of challenges. Smaller companies have been consolidated into larger conglomerates covering broader geographical areas. Also, the number of employees in the industry has been falling. Aging employees have left the workplace, and fewer new students have been entering traditional printing programs in educational institutions, instead preferring to enroll in computer and graphic design programs. In-

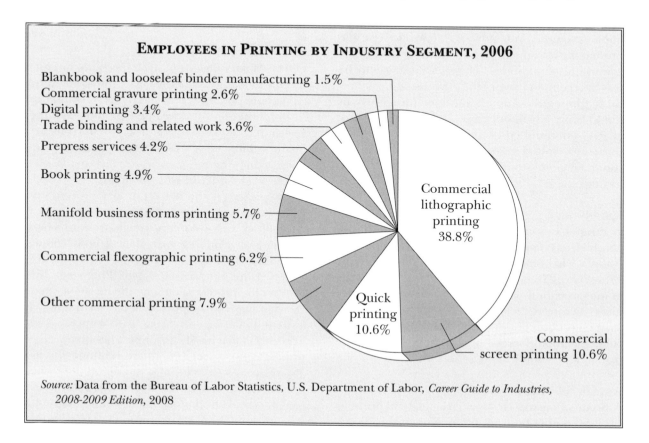

EMPLOYEES IN PRINTING BY INDUSTRY SEGMENT, 2006

Blankbook and looseleaf binder manufacturing 1.5%
Commercial gravure printing 2.6%
Digital printing 3.4%
Trade binding and related work 3.6%
Prepress services 4.2%
Book printing 4.9%
Manifold business forms printing 5.7%
Commercial flexographic printing 6.2%
Other commercial printing 7.9%
Commercial lithographic printing 38.8%
Quick printing 10.6%
Commercial screen printing 10.6%

Source: Data from the Bureau of Labor Statistics, U.S. Department of Labor, *Career Guide to Industries, 2008-2009 Edition,* 2008

creased mechanization of production equipment has meant fewer jobs are available. Cost cutting has resulted in downsizing, often through plant closures or outsourcing (using outside printing facilities, often overseas).

Increased buyer power (partially resulting from the ease of ordering and comparing prices through the Internet) has forced American printers to be competitive against other American and international companies. Printing companies must purchase new equipment and retrain workers to keep up with the technological advancements necessary to meet customers' expectations. The amount of printed material needed has also dropped, as customers increasingly make use of other media options. Electronic files have replaced many items that were traditionally printed. For printing companies to compete with electronic options, they must increase the perceived value of print items, possibly through wider product choices.

In the latter part of the twentieth century, the widespread ownership of powerful personal computers and the advent of desktop publishing allowed individuals to self-produce products that were previously the work of printers. Computerization has lowered the number of printed pages that are produced in many industries. For example, many people are printing their own cards and invitations from home rather than hiring a printing company to do the work. Also, whereas once companies would have asked printers to create a mock-up or draft of a finished product (such as reports, advertisements, and posters), they increasingly use computer-generated drafts and rely on printers only for the final product.

UNIONS

Printing unions formed after large industries began taking over printing businesses from master printers. In 1852, the National Typographical Union (which became the International Typographical Union, or ITU, in 1869), was formed. Early members included bookbinders, photoengravers, pressmen, stereotypers, and electrotypers. Separate unions formed as these groups broke away from the ITU. Pressmen created the International Printing Pressman's Union (IPPU) in 1889, which became the International Printing Pressmen and Assistants Union in 1896. In 1892, the International Brotherhood of Bookbinders (IBB) left the ITU as

machinery began to do the work that had formerly been done by hand. In 1901, the stereotypers and electrotypers formed the International Stereotypers and Electrotypers Union, and in 1904, the photoengravers formed the International Photoengravers Union.

The Amalgamated Lithographers Union attributes its origins to a group of New Jersey workers who joined together in 1882. A number of small groups from the East and Midwest united into the National Association of Lithographers of the United States and Canada four years later, modifying their name three times: the Lithographers' International Protective and Insurance Association of the United States and Canada, the Lithographers' International Protective and Beneficial Association, and finally the Amalgamated Lithographers of America in 1915.

As technological advances revolutionized the industry, further changes were made in the unions. The smaller unions began reuniting in the period between 1964 and 1983. In 2005, these smaller groups reunited to form the Graphic Communications Conference of the International Brotherhood of Teamsters (GCC/IBT).

Theresa L. Stowell

FURTHER READING

Baines, Phil, and Andrew Haslam. *Type and Typography*. New York: Watson-Guptill Publications, 2002. Fully illustrated synopsis of the definition, function, form, manufacture, design, structure, and conventions of typography in the printing industry.

Blackwell, Lewis. *Twentieth Century Type*. New Haven, Conn.: Yale University Press, 2004. Focuses on the concerns of typography through history. Outlines and illustrates the changes and challenges in typography for each decade of the twentieth century.

Fawcett-Tang, Roger. *New Typographic Design*. New Haven, Conn.: Yale University Press, 2007. Looks at type in terms of form, image, and experiment, as well as in motion. Colorful illustrations offer strong examples of each aspect discussed.

Kirschenbaum, Valerie. *Goodbye Gutenberg: Hello to a New Generation of Readers and Writers*. New York: Global Renaissance Society, 2005. Approaches the issue of declining readership by sharing a combination of artwork pieces that illustrate both old-style handprinting from around the world and newer graphic designs. Artistically beautiful volume that visually captivates while narrating the story of the written word.

Michelson, Bruce. *Printer's Devil: Mark Twain and the American Publishing Revolution.* Berkeley: University of California Press, 2006. Provides an original but historical overview of the printing industry through a focused biography of Mark Twain's own experiences in the printing industry—as both a typesetter and a book publisher. Gives details of the equipment and processes Twain used when he was a printing apprentice as well as the investments in printing machinery of his adult years.

Strauss, Victor. *The Printing Industry: An Introduction to Its Many Branches, Processes, and Products.* Washington, D.C.: Printing Industries of America, 1967. Details the multiple purposes of the printing industry. Starts with printing processes and methods, moves through a discussion of printing image carriers, printing presses, binding, and finishing, and continues through art and copy preparation, among varied additional topics.

SEE ALSO: Advertising industry; Book publishing; Franklin, Benjamin; Greeting card industry; Internet; Labor history; Magazine industry; Newspaper industry.

Private security industry

DEFINITION: Enterprises providing policing and protection services to businesses, individuals, and government entities, including the armed forces

SIGNIFICANCE: Private security agencies began in the United States during the mid-nineteenth century alongside the public police force, and the industry has grown to be worth around $150 billion.

Private security providers include security guards at banks and retail stores, armed couriers, in-house security, private investigators, and even private military organizations. Although diverse, these providers have certain general features in common. The personnel (full-time or part-time employees or self-employed) have primarily a security role. They are private, that is, nongovernmental, and act primarily as agents representing the economic interests of their employers, who may be individuals, corporations, and even nation-states. For example, a shopping mall may hire security guards to provide security for its merchants and customers.

ACCOUNTABILITY

Private security personnel are not to be confused with the public police or national armed forces, since they are typically accountable only to their employers and not to the public. Their actions are not necessarily open to public scrutiny and justice. From a public policy viewpoint, this is often problematic. For example, security personnel from Blackwater Worldwide were implicated in the killing of seventeen civilians in Iraq in 2007. The resulting U.S. military investigation described this as a criminal event. Some lawsuits were pending against the corporation as of September, 2008, but it was unclear whether the suspects should be prosecuted under civilian or military law.

The central purpose of private security agents typically is to protect the assets of their employers or to advance the employers' economic interests. This may include safeguarding merchandise, equipment, employees, intellectual property, and proprietary information.

Commenting on major growth in the industry, experts have continually cited a public perception of increased crime and police ineffectiveness. Public policing efforts are mostly reactive, and such efforts are directed mainly at crimes perceived to be threatening to the civil order, such as kidnapping, drug trafficking, and murder. Often, the public police respond only after a crime has been committed, and the commission of the crime may already have resulted in economic loss. Consequently, it is economically prudent that private, proactive security and policing measures be taken that are directed at preventing such losses before they occur. By means of electronic surveillance, drug testing, and physical deterrence, companies hope to protect themselves more effectively than the police can protect them.

HISTORY

It is quite likely that a public security industry is as old as human society. Military organizations and hired bodyguards have existed since ancient times.

A colorful example of private security in the United States is the famous Pinkerton National Detective Agency, created by Allan Pinkerton during the mid-nineteenth century. It and other agencies of its kind were formed to fill the vacuum created by incipient public police forces in major cities. These were often tiny and corrupt. Pinkerton agents were employed as spies in the U.S. Civil War in the service of the Union, and they protected President Abraham Lincoln. After the war, they served industrialists in the numerous conflicts between corporate and labor interests during the emergence of the labor movement. Trade unions often were perceived as a threat to business interests. Agents spied on labor leaders and acted as strike breakers, protecting "scabs" (replacements for striking workers). Pinkerton agents were implicated in fatal shootings during the notorious Homestead Strike of 1892.

Henry Ford of the Ford Motor Company used an in-house police force to keep track of his employees' activities, including their financial and social affairs. The "Ford Patrol," made up of former convicts, former football players, and retired police officers, patrolled local public houses and bars, using strong arms to keep employees under control. Such thuggery is much less common in the wake of improved labor relations, the establishment of legal protections for workers, the creation of sanctions against wildcat strikes, and a general reconceptualization of the labor relationship from one of physical control to one of personnel management.

NUMBERS AND PROSPECTS

Private security is a fast-growing industry. The Department of Labor predicts a healthy double digit growth rate through 2016. Statistics on the number of individuals involved in this market are difficult to ascertain because of an extremely high turnover rate and because the term "security worker" admits of different interpretations. However, there are some credible approximations.

The U.S. Department of Labor estimated the number of private security workers in 2007 at slightly over one million—about twice the number of police officers in the United States. Private security agencies themselves are often quite large. The largest security firm operating in the United States is Securitas, whose employees number more than 125,000 worldwide and whose revenues exceeded

$7 billion in 2002. Human Rights First estimates that there are almost 180,000 security workers in Iraq alone.

The median wage for security workers in the United States is a relatively low $10.85 per hour ($22,570 per annum)—this might account in part for the high turnover rate. Hospital security workers as a group earn the most, at over $26,000 per year, and the highest-paid 10 percent of workers earns an average of $37,850. Salary seems to be proportional to risk. Blackwater security employees are alleged to have earned close to $1,000 per day to guard U.S. ambassador to Iraq Paul Bremer.

It is likely that the private security industry will continue to grow. Among the many explanations offered by experts is the enduring perception of escalating domestic crime and the perceived need of private security to combat industrial terrorism by supplementing public policing efforts. Additionally, changes in U.S. demographics and property rela-

William A. Pinkerton (center), Allan Pinkerton's son, with railroad special agents Pat Connell (left) and Sam Finley in 1880. (Library of Congress)

tionships point to growth in the industry. Sociologists have documented a tendency toward privatization in contemporary U.S. society. For example, there has been a decline of public shopping venues in favor of private shopping malls. These require their own security forces, and an increase in private residential communities has similarly created an increased need for private security patrols. Finally, simple economic growth may entail a higher incidence of theft and fraud, necessitating increased surveillance measures and security personnel.

Edward W. Maine

FURTHER READING

Andress, Carter. *Contractor Combatants: Tales of an Imbedded Capitalist*. Nashville, Tenn.: Thomas Nelson, 2007. Insider story of the operations of the private American-Iraqi Solutions Group responsible for supplying coalition forces in Iraq by its exuberant cofounder, Carter Andress.

Cunningham, William C., and Todd H. Taylor. *The Hallcrest Report: Private Security and Police in America*. Portland, Oreg.: Chancellor Press, 1985. Frequently cited overview of the U.S. private security industry.

Morn, Frank. *"The Eye That Never Sleeps": A History of the Pinkerton National Detective Agency*. Bloomington: Indiana University Press, 1982. Pioneering work in the field of private policing; traces the history of the Pinkerton Agency from its inception to the twentieth century.

Nalla, Mahesh, and Graeme Newman. *A Primer in Private Security*. New York: Harrow and Heaton, 1990. Admirably clear and concise review of the private security industry, including discussion of its social history and methodologies. Contains a fine annotated bibliography that includes movies and videos.

Singer, P. W. *Corporate Warriors: The Rise of the Privatized Military Industry*. Ithaca, N.Y.: Cornell University Press, 2003. Scholarly and comprehensive study of the rise of the modern "for profit" private military industry. Contains a detailed discussion of the political and moral implications of the industry.

SEE ALSO: Homestead strike; Identity theft; Iraq wars; Labor history; Labor strikes; Organized crime.

Privatization

DEFINITION: Method by which governments outsource formerly publicly provided services

SIGNIFICANCE: Privatization exists on a continuum ranging from the complete takeover of what was once public to the mere charging of a user fee for what was previously funded by a collective account. Public managers use privatization as an administrative tool through which they can control the cost of governance.

Privatization is an important concept for all levels of government and American businesses. The process determines both the extent of state power and the scope of the free market. Opinions regarding privatization are both varied and intense. Some, including libertarians, would have government shed all noncore functions and exist in only its most minimal form. Others, including socialists, would argue for more public provision of goods and services.

Like any political controversy, most of the action, both theoretically and practically, takes place somewhere in the middle. Complicating the arguments for and against privatization is the fact that the same people who want privatization in one area might not want it in another. For instance, a citizen in favor of cost cutting who backs a jail privatization could be a strong advocate for quality public schools. As a result, debate about privatization has both an ideological and an ad hoc nature to it.

ARGUMENTS PRO AND CON

Arguments for robust privatization efforts most often center on potential cost savings to taxpayers. Indeed, politicians and public managers alike frequently mention economic necessity as the justification for scaling back government. Governments at the federal, state, and local level are experiencing increased fiscal pressure as the result of both macroeconomic conditions and a reduction in supportive cash flow from the federal government.

This financial pressure can be relieved by either raising revenue intake or cutting costs. Many politicians, if they seek to continue their careers in the public service, would rather cut costs than take the politically unpopular step of raising taxes. Consequently, in recessionary times, as experienced during the early 1980's, governments have turned to potentially saving costs through privatization rather than to increasing revenue through taxation.

Advocates of privatization believe that the introduction of market forces to a service area will drive down cost. For example, traditionally, refuse disposal was a public monopoly performed by public employees using public equipment carting trash to public land for indefinite storage. The expense of this operation is easily measured, and when compared with private firms performing a sanitation function, it has been proven that money is saved when competition is thrown into the mix.

Privatization cost savings are most heavily realized through either labor savings or increased supply-chain efficiency. Compared with governments, private firms are not as constrained in hiring choices, and they can offer cheaper benefit packages. Firms can take advantages of economies of scale when buying supplies, and they need not purchase material through an open-bidding process. Instead, a company can use expert knowledge to negotiate a better price behind closed doors.

Those who are generally against privatization argue that short-term cost savings are exaggerated and that such a goal is myopic. Instead, they reason, the country should be focused on society-wide, long-term improvement. Opponents argue that there is frequent confusion during privatization about what is best for the general public and what is best for the firms assuming the work. Citizens who need government services are not consumers in the usual sense. There have been privatization missteps in the past, and this track record is highlighted by opponents when a new discussion on the issue emerges.

HOW THE UNITED STATES USED CONTRACTORS DURING THE IRAQ WAR, 2003-2007

- $85 billion in contracts for work in the Iraq theater (Iraq, Bahrain, Jordan, Kuwait, Oman, Qatar, Saudi Arabia, Turkey, and the United Arab Emirates) was awarded by American agencies. This represents about 20 percent of funding for Iraq operations. More than 70 percent of this money went to contracts carried out in Iraq.

- $76 billion in contracts was awarded by the Department of Defense. The Army was obligated for 75 percent of this, while the U.S. Agency for International Development and the Department of States were obligated for $5 billion and $4 billion, respectively.

- At least 190,000 contractor personnel were working for the United States in the Iraq theater as of early 2008, according to estimates by the Congressional Budget Office.

- The majority of contracts were for logistics support, construction, petroleum products, or food. The contract for the Army's Logistics Civil Augmentation Program totals $22 billion.

- Between $6 billion and $10 billion was spent on private security contracts from 2003 to 2007 by the U.S. government and other parties (including the Iraqi government and other customers). About 25,000 to 30,000 private security company employees were operating in Iraq as of early 2008.

Source: Data from Congress of United States, Congressional Budget Office, "Contractors' Support of U.S. Operations in Iraq," August, 2008

ISSUES

Examples of privatized services that have not worked out well include military subcontracting, health insurance, prisons, and education. Some would include pharmaceuticals and other industries in that mix as well. Many services, such as ambulance care, water treatment, and information technology, have been commonly privatized for quite some time, and others, such as fire prevention and extinguishing, urban policing, and military combat, have been traditionally under public purview. When these commonly held traditions are challenged, controversy will arise. For example, Blackwater Corporation has made headlines by providing security functions for United States government personnel in Iraq. When Blackwater employees made a series of deadly gaffes, the media coverage of the event centered on the legitimacy of Blackwater's contracting work in the conflict.

Still, most discussion about privatization flies below the public radar, and the debate about the issue mostly takes place between interested parties with opposing points of view. When a municipality debates turning over a zoo or a museum to a private foundation, it is usually the groups' donors and administrators who hash it out among themselves.

Not all privatization issues are of international significance or on the level of administrative detail. Issues that have excited public interest include the proposed sale of a state lottery system to an investor. This would provide a state with hundreds of millions of dollars in cash in the short term but would eliminate a long-term source of revenue for the state government. Likewise, some state or local governments have researched selling toll roads to private firms.

Such large amounts of money are appealing to elected officials who are feeling pressure to provide benefits for their constituency, but the long-term cost-benefits are not clear.

The central difficulty in discussing privatization is its diversity in both topic and form. It touches on many areas of society, from education to health care, from pulse-pounding overseas military expeditions to the mundane routine of trash collection. Within these sectors it takes on many forms, from a complete sale of all assets to a small lease of public land. This complexity is what gives American business the opportunity to pick and choose where it wants to insert itself into the fray.

R. Matthew Beverlin

FURTHER READING

Avant, Deborah D. *The Market of Force*. New York: Cambridge University Press, 2005. Compares military privatization efforts of the United States to those of some smaller nations. It is a good read on a fascinating group of private contractors sometimes referred to as mercenaries.

Donahue, John D. *The Privatization Decision*. New York: Basic Books, 1989. Though written after the push for privatization by Ronald Reagan during the 1980's, this well-argued overview of the topic remains the only fair-minded critical volume tackling the subject of privatization. Its principal arguments still hold true.

Osborne, David, and Ted Gaebler. *Reinventing Government*. New York: Penguin Books, 1992. Privatization does not occur in a vacuum but is a direct response to the call for better government. This book sparked the most recent wave of reform by both Republicans and "new" Democrats.

Savas, E. S. *Privatization and Public-Private Partnerships*. New York: Seven Bridges Press, 2000. An overview of the topic written from the point of view of a privatization advocate.

_____. *Privatization in the City*. Washington D.C.: CQ Press, 2005. A noted expert and advocate of municipal privatization looks at how American cities approach the topic.

SEE ALSO: Education; Insurance industry; Iraq wars; Lotteries, state-run; Postal Service, U.S.; Private security industry; Public utilities.

Prohibition

THE ERA: Era during which an amendment to the U.S. Constitution banned the manufacture, sale, and transportation of intoxicating beverages

DATE: January 17, 1920-December 5, 1933

PLACE: United States and its territories

SIGNIFICANCE: Industrialists and businessmen who contributed heavily to the temperance movement later became Prohibition's most important opponents, primarily because of a rise in crime and hostility toward authorities and threats of increased taxation.

By 1920, more than half of the residents of American cities with populations of 100,000 or more were foreign-born, Catholic or Jewish, or children of foreign-born parents. These immigrants were feared by people living in rural Protestant areas, where public hysteria was heightened by the anti-German prejudices of World War I. For immigrants and other workers, saloons, however shabby, offered companionship but, it was feared, might also generate interest in labor unions, socialism, and communism. The Russian Revolution against the czar further increased fear, especially when revolutionary leader Vladimir Ilich Lenin predicted worldwide communism by 1920, at a time when the United States was rocked by labor unrest.

The Anti-Saloon League (ASL) was funded in

part by business leaders, including merchants John Wanamaker and Samuel Kresge and industrialists Andrew Carnegie, Pierre Du Pont, Henry Ford, and John D. Rockefeller, junior and senior. They believed abolishing saloons would eliminate the threat of revolution; working men would buy consumer goods with money previously spent on alcohol. Many naively believed that all would obey the law with little need for enforcement. ASL leader Wayne Bidwell Wheeler was the principal architect of both the Eighteenth Amendment to the U.S. Constitution, which simply abolished intoxicating beverages, and the 1919 Volstead Act, which defined these liquors as anything with an alcohol content greater than 0.5 percent, thus banning the beer and wine that were habitually drunk in the lands of origin of many of the immigrants. Enforcement was placed under the Internal Revenue Bureau (later Internal Revenue Service); 1,512 agents were initially appointed to guard 18,700 miles of national boundaries, to police production of industrial alcohol and alcohol produced for medical or religious purposes, and to destroy stills.

CONSEQUENCES

The Volstead Act allowed Americans to buy, store, and serve liquor to friends in their home or homes; the well-to-do could afford expensive, smuggled premium liquor. America's tax loss benefited Canada, Mexico, Cuba, the French Miquelon Islands near Newfoundland, and the Bahamas, as storing and smuggling became major industries; the lines formed by boats off U.S. coastal waters, waiting for liquor to be picked up, were called Rum Row. In the Bahamas alone, liquor imports rose from 27,427 gallons in 1918 to 567,940 gallons in 1921, raising government liquor revenue from $44,462 to $984,732. British liquor exports to Canada increased from 124,546 in the first quarter of 1926, to 560,444 in the first quarter of 1928. Canada's liquor exports to the United States rose from 8,335 gallons in 1921 to 1,169,002 in 1928;

Canada took in millions of dollars in export taxes. Well-to-do Americans, writers, and artists fled abroad; one Prohibitionist urged the government to revoke passports of any Americans seen drinking outside the country. Smuggled liquor supplied speakeasies, which numbered more than 30,000 in New York alone by 1927. Individual smugglers flourished at first, but by mid-decade, the liquor trade was generally gang controlled, as were nightclubs, such as Harlem's famed Cotton Club. Chicago's Al Capone considered himself to be a businessman supplying a demonstrated need and providing job opportunities. He claimed to pay $30 billion annually, however, for police and political protection.

Workers, especially immigrants, deeply resented Prohibition, especially because it accompanied other repressive actions directed against the poor, such as U.S. attorney general A. Mitchell Palmer's 1919 attempted arrest and deportation of thousands of immigrants without due process. Workers lacked money for liquor and homes to store it in. They could not afford overseas travel, imported liquor, or the better speakeasies. They drank moonshine or illegal wine and beer, produced under unsanitary conditions with questionable ingredients that sometimes caused blindness, nerve damage, and death. In Chicago, the Genna brothers (Angelo, Sam, Pete, Tony, Mike, and Jim) obtained a license to deal in industrial alcohol, redistilled it to make it drinkable, and found such demand for their

Prohibition officers raid a lunch room on Pennsylvania Avenue in Washington, D.C., in 1923. (Library of Congress)

product that they installed stills throughout Little Italy, paying workers $15 a day, then a high wage. Such decentralization of moonshine, beer, and wine production made Prohibition enforcement and quality control virtually impossible.

REPEAL

Opposing Prohibition were organizations such as the American Bar Association, the American Federation of Labor, and the American Legion. Most important was the Association Against the Prohibition Amendment (AAPA). Supporters of the AAPA included industrialists William E. Boeing and Pierre Du Pont, Du Pont's associate John Jakob Raskob, banker Charles H. Sabin, and merchant Marshall Field. Sabin's wife, Pauline, formed the influential Women's Organization for National Prohibition Reform (WONPR), opposing the claim of the Women's Christian Temperance Union (WCTU) that it spoke for all American women. Lifelong teetotaler John D. Rockefeller, Jr., now advocated repeal.

The AAPA methodically compiled its own statistics. Official Prohibition expenditures were $3.5 million in 1920; these were to rise to $44.0 million by 1930. In the AAPA's widely reported 1929 *Cost of Prohibition and Your Income Tax*, the association estimated that, without Prohibition, federal liquor taxes would have exceeded $850 million, with cities, states, and counties receiving another $50 million. The AAPA combined lost revenue with growing enforcement costs, and estimated Prohibition to have cost $936 million in 1928 alone. Moreover, the National Commission on Law Observance and Enforcement, appointed by President Herbert Hoover, issued the 1931 Wickersham Report, showing that the working classes had not become compliant consumers and employees but were bitterly resentful.

The Great Depression, which began with the financial crash of October, 1929, created millions of newly unemployed workers while tax revenue fell. On taking office in 1933, President Franklin D. Roosevelt urged modification of the Volstead Act to allow the immediate sale of beer and wine, thus defusing some working-class tension while providing some jobs and tax revenue and, above all, hope for the future. Repeal followed, backed by businessmen who otherwise foresaw catastrophically increased personal and business taxes.

Betty Richardson

FURTHER READING

Behr, Edward. *Prohibition: Thirteen Years That Changed America.* 1996. Reprint. New York: Arcade, 2006. Readable, comprehensive history. Bibliography.

Kobler, John. *Ardent Spirits: The Rise and Fall of Prohibition.* 1973. Reprint. New York: Da Capo Press, 1993. General history. Separate bibliographies cover books and pamphlets, periodical literature, and some fiction, plays, and poetry.

Kyvic, David E. *Repealing National Prohibition.* 2d ed. Kent, Ohio: Kent State University Press, 2000. Detailed study of repeal movement. Bibliography.

Nishi, Dennis, ed. *Prohibition.* San Diego, Calif.: Greenhaven Press, 2004. Excerpts from documents, including Wickersham Report and 1991 essay by anti-Prohibition economist Mark Thornton.

Sinclair, Andrew. *Era of Excess: A Social History of the Prohibition Movement.* New York: Harper & Row, 1962. Detailed history emphasizing excesses of both Prohibitionists and anti-Prohibitionists.

SEE ALSO: Alcoholic beverage industry; Business crimes; Drug trafficking; Great Depression; Income tax, corporate; Organized crime; Racketeer Influenced and Corrupt Organizations Act; Taxation; Treasury, U.S. Department of the; Whiskey Trust.

Promotional holidays

DEFINITION: Annual celebrations, such as Valentine's Day and Mother's Day, that are invented or exploited to stimulate retail trade

SIGNIFICANCE: The selling of American holidays, the extension of age-old fairs and markets, has become a multibillion-dollar industry. The rites that surround holidays have been adopted, or even invented, by the pervasive marketing that surrounds them to such an extent that the celebration of holidays and the business of holidays have become inseparable.

In February, 1900, one of the nation's leading trade papers, the *Dry Goods Chronicle*, set out the modern vision of the commercial possibilities of holidays.

Easter has already been recognized as a basis of trade attraction, and, while it commemorates an event which is sacred to many, yet there is no legitimate reason why it should not also be made an occasion for legitimate merchandising.

Two months later, the *Dry Goods Chronicle* further generalized the commercial interest in such festivals. The modern businessperson realized the economic potential in holidays, exploited them through sales and advertising, and took the lead in promoting them. Whether the occasion was Easter, the Fourth of July, Thanksgiving, or Memorial Day, "wide-awake" retailers were to conjure up "the spirit of hearty celebration" for the purposes of merchandising and consumption.

In Puritan New England, civic and religious solemnities gradually emerged in election days, militia musters, public executions, and the Harvard commencement, but the dominant rhythm of Puritan daily life was the weekly cycle of the Sabbath. The festivities of Christmas, Easter, and Whitsuntide were all rejected, as were other popular occasions such as midsummer bonfires on the eve of the feast of Saint John the Baptist.

A report from Virginia in 1719 noted that the unsettled conditions made holiday observance burdensome and impractical. Hard-pressed to subsist, colonists reportedly kept "no Holydays, except those of Christmas day and good Friday, being unwilling to loose their dayly labour." When merchants began to promote holidays, modern work discipline still remained paramount. In the United States, efforts at holiday reform were apparent in pressures to make the Fourth of July safe, sane, and sober and in attempts to make Halloween a home-centered party rather than a night of pranks and property damage.

HOLIDAY SALES

Certain products are targeted for specific holidays and have become associated with them, such as fireworks on the Fourth of July, pumpkins at Halloween, turkeys at Thanksgiving, and Santa Claus-themed decorations at Christmas. Flowers and candy are considered an essential part of Valentine's Day and Mother's Day. According to Jupiter Research, in 2001, online retailers' sales during November and December accounted for 36 percent of their annual revenues. In fact, the holiday rush at the end of the year is when merchants expect their biggest rise in sales.

The day after Thanksgiving is known as Black Fri-

day, because it is the day on which retail businesses expect to cease being "in the red" and instead go "into the black." That is, it is the day on which retail businesses begin making a profit for the year. To ensure this transition, businesses attempt to maximize sales on that day with significant discounts and promotions, and the day has become strongly associated with the beginning of the Christmas shopping season. However, the promotion of Black Friday has been too successful for some businesses: the heavy crowds that flock to shopping malls on that day have convinced many other shoppers to stay at home and shop online rather than patronize crowded brick-and-mortar stores.

In December, 2006, according to the U.S. Bureau of the Census, electronic shopping and mail-order houses accounted for $21 billion in holiday retail sales. The year before, there were 15,924 electronic shopping and mail-order houses in business in the United States, employing 253,677 workers. These stores were a popular source of holiday gifts, selling $162 billion worth of merchandise, of which 40.5 percent was attributable to online commerce. California led the nation in the number of these establishments and their employees, with 2,383 and 30,800, respectively.

HOLIDAY PRODUCTS

In 2005, there were 3,412 confectionery and nut stores in the United States. These stores thrive on holiday business, especially that associated with Valentine's Day, Mother's Day, Thanksgiving, and Christmas. Another such business is the floral industry. The combined wholesale value of domestically produced cut flowers in 2006 for all flower-producing operations with $100,000 or more in sales was $411 million. Some 21,135 florist establishments prepared, sold, and delivered Mother's Day floral arrangements in 2005. Mother's Day also accounts for a significant percentage of sales in the perfume industry.

Corned beef and cabbage is a traditional St. Patrick's Day dish. In 2006, the United States produced 42.1 billion pounds of beef and 2.6 billion pounds of cabbage. St. Patrick's Day is also strongly associated with beer sales, both in retail outlets and in bars. Many bars make as much money on St. Patrick's Day as they normally would in a month.

Independence Day celebrations drive sales of hot dogs, sausages, and beef nationwide, as millions of

Americans have barbeques on that day. In addition, July 4 is the single most important day of the year for the fireworks industry, which accounted for $206.3 million in imported Chinese fireworks in 2006. Imports from China are also the source of the majority of American flags. Of the total $5.3 million worth of U.S. flags sold in 2006, $5 million worth were imported from China.

Halloween accounts for the majority of American pumpkin sales. The major pumpkin-producing states grew 1 billion pounds of pumpkins in 2006. The value of all these pumpkins was $101 million. The holiday is also crucial for costume and formal wear rental establishments and retailers throughout the country.

On Thanksgiving Day, millions of turkeys are eaten. The six major turkey-producing states (Minnesota, North Carolina, Arkansas, Virginia, Missouri, and California) raised about 175.3 million

An 1883 advertisement for Prang's Valentine's Day cards. (Library of Congress)

turkeys in 2007. This output accounts for about two-thirds of U.S. turkeys produced in 2007. The average American eats 13.1 pounds of turkey meat each year.

December is the central holiday season in the United States, in which Christmas, Hanukkah, Kwanzaa, and pagan solstice rituals take place. The U.S. Postal Service expected to deliver 20 billion pieces of mail between Thanksgiving and Christmas in 2008. The busiest mailing day of the year is December 17, as more than three times the average daily volume of cards and letters is mailed on that day. Businesses depending on Black Friday and the rest of the holiday shopping season include department stores, bookstores, clothing stores, jewelry stores, electronics stores, and sporting goods stores. The major Christmas tree growers reported combined sales of $249 million in 2006.

The value of U.S. toy imports including stuffed toys (excluding dolls), puzzles, and electric trains from China between January and June, 2007, was $3.3 billion. China was the leading country of origin for stuffed toys coming into the United States, as well as for a number of other popular holiday gifts. These include roller skates ($79 million), sports footwear ($193 million), golf equipment ($36 million), and basketballs ($23 million).

MEDIA

One of the most important sources of holiday promotion has been the media. Along with the advertisements for holiday sales in the newspapers, films and television have done their part. Films with holiday themes are especially popular at Christmas. Usually a new crop of Christmas-themed films comes out around Thanksgiving each year. One, *Holiday Inn* (1942), included several holiday songs, including "White Christmas," which has since become a holiday standard. Another song from that film, "Easter Parade," also became so strongly associated in the popular culture with the holiday to which it pays tribute that it has become part of the holiday itself.

Holiday specials have been part of television since 1947. The major programming revolves around Christmas, Easter, New Year's, and Thanksgiving. The first special, *The Story of Easter*, aired on the National Broadcasting Company (NBC) in 1945 as an Easter Sunday evening program that told the religious story of the celebration through narration over religious paintings, scripture readings, and songs. Annual traditions include the Charlie Brown specials; the first one, *A Charlie Brown Christmas*, appeared on the Columbia Broadcasting Service (CBS) in 1965. There were also holiday specials about Charlie Brown and his friends for Thanksgiving, Easter, Halloween, and Valentine's Day. Some made-for-television films focus on special themes of forgiveness and family. Many cooking and home shows, most notably by Martha Stewart, help viewers prepare for the holidays. Many of these shows are available on digital versatile disc (DVD).

GREETING CARDS

The thread that binds all holidays together is the greeting card. The earliest known cards appeared around 1450 in Germany. Cards from woodcuts were the most prevalent and often involved the Christ Child bearing good wishes for an auspicious New Year. By 1770, greeting cards had evolved from woodcuts to finely printed messages, and engravers and printers supplied continental Europe with vast quantities of New Year's cards. In modern times, the New Year has become an integral part of the holiday season, and New Year's cards are a popular expression of hope for the future, used by businesses and individuals alike.

The first valentines in the United States were exchanged during Revolutionary days and were mostly handmade with sentimental verses written in flowing script. In 1840, Esther Howland, an imaginative artist and entrepreneur, became the first regular publisher of valentines in the United States, eventually heading her own publishing firm that specialized in Valentine's Day cards.

The rabbit and the egg are the most popular illustrations for Easter cards. The Easter bunny originates from pre-Christian legends, in which rabbits were used to symbolize new life. The custom of decorating Easter eggs dates back to the Middle Ages.

In 1863, cartoonist Thomas Nast used Clement C. Moore's description of Santa Claus in his 1823 poem "A Visit from Saint Nicholas" (also known as "The Night Before Christmas") as a model. He drew this version of Santa Claus for *Harper's Weekly* magazine. It went on to become the model for most depictions of the spirit of the Christmas holiday. The first Christmas card was produced by London artist John C. Horsley in 1843, the same year that *A Christ-mas Carol* was written by Charles Dickens. The card, created for London businessman Henry C. Cole, added "Happy New Year" to its message of "Merry Christmas."

Martin J. Manning

FURTHER READING

Bird, William L. *Holidays on Display.* New York: Princeton Architectural Press, 2006. Comprehensive overview of the art and industry of the holiday display that traces its evolution as holiday decorations moved from shop windows to building exteriors and out into the street in the form of parade floats.

Dennis, Matthew. *Red, White, and Blue Letter Days: An American Calendar.* Ithaca, N.Y.: Cornell University Press, 2002. Explores the vast political and cultural terrain of holidays, charting how Americans have defined their identities through celebration, especially through the merchants and advertisers who sell their products by linking them, often tenuously, with holiday occasions.

Lavin, Maud, ed. *The Business of Holidays.* New York: Monacelli Press, 2004. Interprets holiday commerce and design, corporate culture, and tradition (both invented and inherited).

Marling, Karal A. *Merry Christmas! Celebrating America's Greatest Holiday.* Cambridge, Mass.: Harvard University Press, 2000. Describes the prominent role commercialism plays in Christmas as America's central holiday.

Pleck, Elizabeth H. *Celebrating the Family: Ethnicity, Consumer Culture, and Family Rituals.* Cambridge, Mass.: Harvard University Press, 2000. Examines family traditions over two centuries and finds a complicated process of change in the way Americans have celebrated holidays such as Christmas, Easter, Thanksgiving, Chinese New Year, and Passover, as well as the life cycle rituals.

Schmidt, Leigh E. *Consumer Rites: The Buying and Selling of American Holidays.* Princeton, N.J.: Princeton University Press, 1995. Schmidt's book is considered the first cultural studies and historical analysis of American holidays, their origins and evolution, and the rituals of America's holiday bazaar that emerged in the nineteenth century.

Shank, Barry. *A Token of My Affection: Greeting Cards and American Business Culture.* New York: Columbia University Press, 2004. Examines the "structures of feeling" by looking at valentines, Christmas cards, and other missives that express personal feelings and sentiment on the holidays.

SEE ALSO: Advertising industry; Christmas marketing; Greeting card industry; Retail trade industry.

Public transportation, local

DEFINITION: Forms of transport, including trolleys, buses, subways, and light-rail, that convey passengers over fixed routes within metropolitan areas and among suburbs and city centers

SIGNIFICANCE: Mass public transportation was crucial to the growth of metropolitan areas and of industries employing large numbers of workers. In its heyday (1880-1930), it was also a profitable industry in its own right. Eclipsed by the private automobile since World War II, urban mass transit is slowly making a comeback, as rising energy costs make long auto commutes prohibitively expensive.

Looking from the vantage point of the interconnected early twenty-first century, it is difficult for most Americans to comprehend how limited personal mobility was before the development of railroads. An individual on foot traveled at a maximum sustained rate of four miles per hour. Although people in rural areas generally owned horses, the cost of upkeep in a city made them a luxury for most people. The need to live within close proximity to work made for dense housing and few open spaces. Families of workers in heavy industry suffered from pollution as well as overcrowding. To escape congestion and unhealthful conditions, middle-class men moved their families to more rural areas, rented rooms in town, and reserved the long, costly commute for weekends.

EARLY FORMS

The earliest form of public transportation was the omnibus, a horse-drawn vehicle with cramped seating for twelve to twenty passengers, traveling along a fixed route. A few of these operated in New York as early as 1827. They were quickly supplanted by similar but somewhat larger horse-drawn vehicles on rails. These soon became regular fixtures of large cities. Establishing a rail line required considerable

start-up capital, as well as cooperation with city government. In Boston and New York, tension erupted between private vehicle owners, who were accustomed to putting their carriages on sleigh runners when winter set in, and horse car companies, which needed tracks cleared. The car companies won the battle at the expense of undertaking street cleaning as part of their contract. Fares were too high to make this a practicable commuting method for laborers.

Steam-powered ferryboats allowed expansion of urban boundaries along rivers and estuaries. Ferries connected pre-Civil War developments at Llewellyn Park, New Jersey, and Staten Island, New York, to the city. Often, the company providing ferry or rail transport also financed a development, using the availability of inexpensive reliable transportation as a selling point for lots. In the case of Staten Island, a ninety-nine-year lease fixed passenger ferry fares at 5 cents until 1955.

URBAN RAILWAYS

The growing size of metropolitan areas and the success of steam-powered railroads in inter-city transport of goods and people prompted several avenues of development. Inter-city lines such as the Long Island Rail Road, begun in 1834 as part of a rail-ferry link between New York and Boston, carried some local traffic, which increased as spur lines were built to communities off the trunk line. Civic authorities in Brooklyn and lower Manhattan, who at first welcomed regular railroads downtown, soon discovered that the space requirements, danger to pedestrians, and pollution outweighed any advantages in built-up areas.

The earliest systematic attempts to mechanize urban transit involved cable cars, with a centralized coal-fired powerhouse operating a massive continuous cable running beneath city streets (or, in the case of New York's first elevated railway, above them). Installing a cable car system involved enormous capital outlay, running costs were high, and the maximum length of a line was only four miles. After the advent of electric trolleys drawing power from an overhead line, cable cars remained in operation only in Seattle and San Francisco, cities with numerous steep hills. On hills, the car uses the cable as a brake on the downhill slope, returning energy to the system.

To avoid congestion at street level, entrepreneurs in New York and Chicago constructed extensive networks of elevated railways, providing rapid transit between areas of the city and extending suburban commuter lines downtown. At first powered by steam locomotives, these were electrified during the 1890's. Although the "Els" speeded transport and relieved congestion, streets below them were dark and dirty. In 1893, elevated railways in New York City collected one million fares a day (transporting roughly half that number of people). They could also be dangerous. In November, 1918, an inexperienced motorman, filling in during a transit strike, ran an elevated train off the tracks at Marlboro Street Station, killing ninety-three passengers. This disaster underscored the need for greater regulation of an industry that had become absolutely essential to urban life.

Trolley cars near Boston Commons in Boston in the late 1890's. (Library of Congress)

London opened the world's first underground trains, powered by steam locomotives, in 1867. Until trains were electrified, subways were grim places from the passengers' point of view. America's first subway, a below-ground extension of surface electric trolley lines into the central business district, opened in Boston in 1897. New York's subway system, which began operation in 1904, was predominantly underground from the outset. Two private corporations underwrote the cost of installing street lines in return for a ninety-nine-year exclusive lease on operations. The city provided funds to build and maintain a tunnel under the Hudson River. The only pre-1914 single construction project that exceeded the New York City Subway system in cost was the Panama Canal. These very large start-up costs discouraged other urban areas from following suit.

DECLINE AND RESURGENCE

From 1890 to 1930, the mainstay of urban transportation in the United States was the electric trolley, typically operating on public thoroughfares increasingly shared with automobiles. Operating in small cities and between suburbs as well as within large metropolises, trolleys (and subways, in Boston and New York) were essential to the movement of armies of clerical and factory workers from residential neighborhoods to business and industrial districts. They also helped shape urban retailing. The city department store, with its wide variety of manufactured goods, only became a going concern when middle- and working-class people with modest amounts of disposable income could travel readily to a central location to do their shopping.

Although public transportation remained in private hands in the Northeast until public subsidies for the automobile industry made it unprofitable, municipalities in the more populist West took steps to make public transportation a public charge much earlier. San Francisco instituted a supplemental public trolley system in 1909, and the City of Detroit took over operating all trolleys in 1922, pursuant to a popular vote. After 1930, the rationale for public operation of public transportation changed. Before private automobiles became common, advocates of truly public transport argued that a service on which the average person depended should not be subject to the vagaries of corporate policy driven by profit. Later, when dependence on public transport was concentrated in the ranks of the poor, cities felt constrained to step in to preserve an essential service that—by nature of its clientele—could no longer pay for itself.

Public transit systems transported roughly the same numbers of people in 1920, 1930, and 1950, but the proportion of people using public transportation declined, except during gasoline rationing in World War II. Gas-powered buses replaced electric trolleys. In the long run, the total costs of running an electrical light-rail system are lower, per passenger mile, than those of a bus, but a trolley company paid to build and maintain tracks and overhead wires, whereas the city paid for streets out of its general fund. Planning in large sections of cities such as Los Angeles that expanded exponentially after 1920 assumed that residents owned automobiles. Those residents demanded, and got, a publicly funded road system to support their cars.

Between 1950 and 1970, absolute ridership on public transportation in the United States declined by half. In smaller cities, the only remaining bus service was often the school bus system. To preserve a workable level of service for the urban poor, cities were forced to take over the assets of failed private transportation companies. Poorly maintained facilities and a high level of crime discouraged middle-class commuters from using public transportation.

After 1970, civic authorities in a number of large cities realized that unrestrained urban sprawl facilitated by exponential freeway development was a swift ticket to environmental and social degradation, and that rapid mass transit offered a solution. In 1962, an act of Congress established the Federal Transit Administration as part of the Department of Transportation. The federal government provided money to cities to build and upgrade mass transit systems, including subways and light-rail systems.

Metropolitan areas with successful programs developing and expanding mass transit based on subways and above-ground light-rail included Washington, D.C.; Atlanta; Philadelphia; and the San Francisco Bay area. However, as of 2005, New York City remained the only American metropolis where a majority (55 percent) of residents commuted by public transportation. In Washington, D.C., the figure was 40 percent, and in Boston, Philadelphia, and San Francisco, 25 percent. At the other end of the spectrum, less than 5 percent of commuters in

Phoenix, San Diego, and Houston used public transportation, even though federal money also helped upgrade systems in these cities.

The history of the Atlanta system illustrates one of the success stories. Established by the Georgia State Legislature in 1965, Metropolitan Atlanta Rapid Transit Authority (MARTA) purchased the privately owned Atlanta bus system in 1972 and immediately reduced fares. During the 1970's, $800 million in federal grants underwrote construction of a regional electric light-rail system, which operates as a subway in the city core. Between 1972 and 2000, MARTA logged 3.5 billion fares. Nationwide, overall ridership on public transportation rose by 31 percent between 1995 and 2006.

ACCESS AND DISCRIMINATION ISSUES

After World War II, reliance on public transportation became increasingly concentrated in the ranks of the poor, including racial minorities, the elderly, and people with physical and mental disabilities. Simple economics, reinforced by prejudice, meant privately run transit companies offered these people inferior service. The Montgomery, Alabama, bus boycott (1955-1956), sparked when Rosa Parks, an African American woman, refused to sit in the rear seats of a segregated city bus, established that official segregation in public transportation is unconstitutional. De facto segregation remains a problem. When municipal transport systems focus their energies on light-rail systems to outlying suburbs, it is often at the expense of core areas, where obsolete equipment and overcrowding are still prevalent. Flat fares charge inner-city dwellers more for miles traveled.

The Americans with Disabilities Act of 1990 introduced opportunities and challenges for public transportation systems. Some federal money is available for infrastructure modifications to provide better access for people in wheelchairs, but the increased costs of operation are usually borne by the municipality. This in turn can force cities to curtail services to other sectors, such as poorly paid service workers, who can ill afford to subsidize the transportation needs of the handicapped. Although the growth of public funding in public transportation has produced many benefits, it has also diverted energies away from the central purpose of moving the urban masses at low cost to the pocketbook and the environment.

TRANSIT SYSTEMS OF THE FUTURE

Of the major technological advances in contemporary mass transit, automated guideway transit (AGT) trains, which require no driver or conductor and operate mainly as airport shuttles, and magnetic levitator (Maglev) trains deserve mention. There are no Maglev systems in operation in the United States. Monorails, once hailed as the wave of the future, have proved of limited use. For the foreseeable future, electric light-rail systems represent the most practical solution for most commuters.

In the short term, large employers who relocated to outer suburbs may find it cost-effective to run, or contract with, private bus companies to transport workers from residential neighborhoods, rather than demanding extensions of existing municipal public transportation systems. Several Silicon Valley companies, such as Google, have already begun such operations. The demand for public transportation is certain to grow, in which case, some services will again become profitable for private industry—but only if the laws regulating transport companies permit them to avoid less profitable routes or provide subsidies for those routes to compensate for the expense of maintaining them.

Martha Sherwood

FURTHER READING

Cheape, Charles W. *Moving the Masses: Urban Public Transit in New York, Boston, and Philadelphia, 1880-1912.* Cambridge, Mass.: Harvard University Press, 1980. Scholarly work emphasizing the impact of public policies.

Cudahy, Brian. *Cash, Tokens, and Transfers: A History of Urban Mass Transit in North America.* New York: Fordham University Press, 1990. Thorough and comprehensive in scope; devotes considerable space to financial aspects of transit development.

Demoro, Harre, and John Harder. *Light Rail Transit on the West Coast.* New York: Quadrant Press, 1989. The opening chapter provides a succinct factual background on the political, economic, and social factors that brought about the revival of trolleys. Essays on six West Coast light-rail systems are included.

Hayden, Dolores. *Building Suburbia: Green Fields and Urban Growth, 1820-2000.* New York: Pantheon Books, 2003. Though the focus is on real estate, the importance of mass transit in early suburban development receives thorough coverage.

Wolinsky, Julian. *Light Rail Transit: Planning, Design, and Implementation.* Washington, D.C.: National Academy of Sciences, 1982. A collection of papers from the Third National Conference on Light Rail Transit, which was held in San Diego in March, 1982. Provides a background in light-rail transit development and technology. The Transportation Research Board, the part of the National Academy of Sciences that produced this report, held a number of conferences and issued a number of other special reports on light-rail transit issues.

SEE ALSO: Air transportation industry; Amtrak; Automotive industry; Canals; Hotel and motel industry; Railroads; Stagecoach line, first; Steamboats; Time zones; Transportation, U.S. Department of; Turnpikes.

Public utilities

DEFINITION: Organizations that provide basic services, such as water, gas, and electricity, needed by all members of communities

SIGNIFICANCE: Without the basic services provided by public utilities, industrialization would not have been possible. The urbanization that accompanied the industrialization of the developed world required that basic services needed by residents be supplied collectively to all residences, and public utilities emerged to provide these services.

The most basic of public utilities is water. When most Americans lived in rural areas, they obtained the water they needed through the digging of wells and disposed of their wastes through the construction of cesspools on their property. Difficulties arose when industrialization brought large numbers of people together in a relatively small area, placing them in multiple dwelling units located in the immediate vicinity of the industrial activity. Although people initially used communal pumps, drawing water from a single, shallow well, as the number of users grew, people began to need more water than could be provided by a single well. Reliable water service was also needed to fight the numerous urban fires that occurred at that time. Wastes were often simply dumped on any unused ground and often migrated to the nearest streams.

NINETEENTH CENTURY BEGINNINGS

During the early nineteenth century, as American cities grew into communities with first tens of thousands of people and then hundreds of thousands of people living near one another, the old way of providing water to these residents ceased to be practical. At first, as in Boston at the beginning of the nineteenth century, entrepreneurs created networks of pipes, often made of wood, and buried them in the streets to deliver water to a single neighborhood. Service, however, was unreliable because the wooden pipes, especially those that were near the surface of the ground, froze during the winter.

The first serious attempt to solve the water problem occurred in Philadelphia, then the largest city in the United States. Benjamin Henry Latrobe and other civic-minded citizens put together a plan to draw water from the adjacent Schuylkill River and pump it, using water wheels as a source of power, up to a high point, from which gravity would secure its distribution through a series of pipes laid under the streets. After intense public discussion, this water system was built as a municipal system, and it served as a model for other cities that followed Philadelphia's example.

The far more grandiose system that supplied New York City with water (and still does) was the one that created the Croton Reservoir well north of the city and brought that water through an aqueduct to the city. The great difficulty lay in how to cross the rivers that surrounded Manhattan Island, and in the end, the problem was solved by the aqueduct that crossed the Harlem River and then made its way to storage reservoirs in the north part of the island. It also depended on buried pipes, but by this time the iron industry had developed the capacity to produce cast-iron pipes that could survive for years under the streets. The initial development of the Croton Reservoir occurred during the 1840's, again following intense public debate, and it also was municipally owned.

Boston immediately followed New York City's example. After considering various private proposals, city officials chose to adopt municipal ownership. After the country's three largest cities all chose the public ownership path, the pattern was set for the rest of the country. Although water was provided by private companies in some smaller towns, the rapid growth of urban centers dictated public ownership because only the government could generate the huge capital sums needed, through the sale of bonds. All systems depended on pipes laid under the streets, with individual dwellings tapping into the pipes.

GAS

Gas was the next service provided by public utilities, after some important technological developments. When the iron industry switched from wood to coal to provide the energy it needed, it was found that the coking process produced gas, called "manufactured" gas. Early in the nineteenth century, it was found in Europe (and not much later in the United States) that this gas could be collected and used to provide illumination "by gaslight," chiefly in the streets of the great cities that were growing so quickly.

In contrast to water, however, gas was provided overwhelmingly by private companies. The early pipes were sometimes made of wood (though they often leaked) or of discarded gun barrels. The first gas company organized in the United States was established in Baltimore in 1816. One emerged in 1825 in New York City, in Boston in 1829, in Louisville in 1832, and in New Orleans in 1835. Gas companies spread rapidly throughout the United States after the early companies demonstrated the feasibility of manufactured gas. Two communities created municipally owned gas systems: Philadelphia in 1836 and Fredonia in upstate New York in 1858, making use not of manufactured gas but of natural gas gathered from one of the many seeps in the area.

Not long after Edwin Drake struck oil and natural gas in Titusville, Pennsylvania, in 1859, natural gas became a rapidly growing resource often found in conjunction with crude oil. It had about twice the British thermal units (BTUs) of manufactured gas and was therefore useful for many more purposes. There were numerous sources of natural gas in the Appalachian region. Companies selling natural gas hastened to secure municipal franchises, and many cities had a multiplicity of gas companies. The city of Pittsburgh had six gas companies by the late 1880's. The entrepreneurs had only to sink a well into a gas-bearing fracture in the ground and then to build a network of pipes to residents ready to pay for the gas. Wherever people were congregated, the companies relatively quickly acquired a group of customers. Moreover, the distribution pipes, unlike those needed for water, were small, and by that time, the metal industry had learned to produce long lengths of pipe at moderate cost.

Once natural gas became readily available, it began to be used for purposes other than lighting. The earliest known case of industrial usage was that of the Great Western Iron Company in Pittsburgh in 1870-1871. Industrial use spread rapidly throughout Appalachia. In some of these areas, it began to be used for space heating and for cooking. Throughout the middle of the country, there were easily tapped local deposits of gas, as there also proved to be in California. In those parts of the country where there were no gas deposits, manufactured gas continued to be sold.

After 1900, the multiplicity of small gas distributors with municipal franchises began to be consolidated into larger companies, in many respects following the pattern in the oil industry set by John D. Rockefeller. This helped to create local monopolies that in turn evoked popular opposition and then a demand for regulation. Massachusetts was one of the first states to create a regulatory agency for the gas industry, the Board of Gas and Electric Commissioners, in 1885-1886, which in 1913 became the Public Service Commission. Many other states followed.

Although initially this and other regulatory bodies set up in other states had no power to regulate prices, this authority was in time acquired, as one of the reasons for their creation was to respond to consumer protests over gas prices. Creating this authority was at first made difficult by the lack of federal power to control rates. After the 1911 decision of the Supreme Court that broke up the Standard Oil Company, however, it was recognized that these firms had, in effect, a natural monopoly and that if the firms were not confined to a single state, it was essential for the federal government to provide regulation.

During the 1920's, the steel industry developed the ability to create large-diameter pipes, enabling long-distance pipelines to be laid to transport natural gas across many miles. The first long-distance gas pipeline was a 217-mile line laid between northern Louisiana and central Texas in 1925. The first 1,000-mile pipeline was laid in 1931 from Texas to Chicago. Subsequently, the country was covered by pipelines, which led to the division of the industry in terms of ownership into three parts: producers, who ran the gas wells; transporters, who ran the pipelines; and distributors, who handled the piping of gas to individual users, whether companies or households. Regulation was then divided between the federal government, which through the Federal Power Commission had the authority under the Natural Gas Act of 1938 to regulate pipeline rates, and the states, which through their public utility commissions regulated the local distributors. In 1977, the role of the Federal Power Commission was taken over by the Federal Energy Regulatory Commission (FERC), within the Department of Energy.

ELECTRICITY

The supremacy of gaslight as the preferred form of illumination was challenged and rapidly overtaken with the invention of the incandescent electric light bulb by Thomas Alva Edison in 1879. Initially supplied with a carbon filament in a glass enclosure from which all air had been evacuated, the incandescent bulb became what it remained for a century with the introduction of the longer-lasting tungsten filament. Edison recognized that the electric light bulb needed a power system to support it, and he incorporated the Edison Electric Illuminating Company in 1880 to build that power station in downtown New York City, on Pearl Street. He acquired a municipal franchise from the city, along with permission to bury the lines under the streets. Clearly, Edison saw the gaslight industry as his major competitor, and he was determined to go ahead with electric light only if he could provide electrical illumination at a lower cost than that charged for gaslight.

Because Edison used direct current in his first generating station, he was limited in the scope of its operation—the maximum distance direct-current electricity can be transmitted at a reasonable price is about one mile. Other inventors, notably William Stanley, believed that a system of transformers in the generating facility and the use of alternating current instead of direct current could overcome the distance limitations. With the financial encouragement of George Westinghouse, who built alternating-current generators at his manufacturing plants for railroad equipment in Pittsburgh, alternating-current generators and transformers made it possible to create central generating stations serving much larger geographic areas.

Westinghouse and the corporate inheritor of Edison's inventions, General Electric, took advantage of the new technology by creating many devices making use of electricity. In particular, they created electric motors that could easily replace steam engines, then the prevailing motive force in factories, and these motors spread with great rapidity throughout industry because of their adaptability. In 1900, 5 percent of the power used in industry was electrical, but by 1950, 80 percent of industrial power was supplied by electric motors.

Electric motors were essential to another major factor in the spread of electricity: trolleys. Although trolleys had existed before Edison's work, the cars were hauled by horses, and as the cities expanded, horses were not up to the required distances. However, electricity provided by overhead lines enabled trolleys to extend from the urban center to its outskirts and beyond. Trolley entrepreneurs saw that trolleys—because they moved a large number of users from the central city to the outskirts—were potentially a very profitable enterprise, made more so by the construction (often by the trolley companies) of amusement parks at the end of the line. Trolley companies found they could easily sell some of the electricity that ran on their lines to people living in the houses that sprang up along the lines.

Additional technological improvements were made to the central generating station courtesy of Samuel Insull, who started in the industry as Edison's assistant but soon moved on to Chicago, where he managed generating stations that he was later to build into a business empire. Insull introduced steam turbines to replace the old coal-fired steam generators, which proved spectacularly successful, reducing both the noise level and the cost of producing electricity. Others pioneered the use of waterpower to drive the turbines, and by the mid-twentieth century, really large electrification schemes depended on waterpower as their source of energy. One of the earliest generating stations to use waterpower was located at Niagara Falls.

From Edison's Pearl Street Station supplying direct-current electricity to businesses and a few homes in its immediate vicinity, the electric industry grew greatly, especially during the 1890's and the early twentieth century. It repeated the pattern of the gas industry, starting from a single generating station in one city and growing largely by consolidation, as single-city generating stations joined with others in their area. Because electricity, even more so than gas, involves heavy capital expenses at the outset but very little capital investment once the generators are in place and the lines to individual users have been built, there was a strong tendency for the central stations to be merged into ever-larger companies.

TRUSTS

Financing of expansion was easier when an existing company provided the start-up costs, and the industry soon, through amalgamations (including with natural gas distributors), had facilities all across the country. The building of high-voltage transmission lines encouraged consolidation. Some of the companies were part of trusts, and when trusts were found illegal by the Supreme Court, the industry turned to the holding company. Insull built his original holdings at Chicago Edison into Middle West Utilities and then into even larger corporate "pyramids," using the holding-company structure, in

UTILITIES IN THE UNITED STATES, 2002

Business Type	Number of Establishments	Revenue ($ millions)
Electric power generation, transmission, and distribution	9,394	325,028
Natural gas distribution	2,376	66,515
Water, sewage, and other systems	5,333	7,364
Utilities (total)	17,103	398,907

Source: Data from U.S. Census Bureau, *2002 Economic Census* (Washington, D.C.: Author, 2005)

Note: An establishment is a physical location where business is conducted and is not necessarily equivalent to a company or enterprise.

which a business could be purchased by owning just a small percentage of its stock. Before he was challenged in the courts, Insull controlled electric and gas companies with more than 4 million customers, selling them around one-eighth of all the gas and electricity sold in the United States.

Because these companies had no local competition, they were effectively natural monopolies. This enabled them to use monopoly pricing, which initially enriched them but led to political protest, seeking governmental control of their rates. The populist movement, which opposed the power of the trusts and holding companies to charge what they liked for the public service they rendered, got its first great boost from the progressive orator and politician Robert M. La Follette, who established a public service commission in Wisconsin with the power to regulate the rates charged consumers in the state. In the New Deal era, this kind of regulation was picked up by the Federal Power Commission, which set wholesale rates for utilities.

The Rural Customer

Although the New Deal broke up many of the private holding companies supplying electricity and gas to Americans, there were large parts of the population that did not receive electricity. These areas began to be served by the creation of monster hydro-electric systems powered by dams on the country's numerous rivers. The prototype was the Tennessee Valley Authority, one of Franklin D. Roosevelt's major objectives, legislated in the earliest months of his administration. On the West Coast, the Bonneville Power Authority and the Hoover Dam were created to supply most of the power generated in that part of the country.

Besides the big dams, the country needed a method of supplying electricity to rural customers, who lived too far apart to be profitable for a private business to reach. The Roosevelt administration filled this gap by creating rural electric cooperatives, which covered most of the parts of the country not served by the urban utilities. Their rates were heavily subsidized by the federal government, which supplied them with electricity from federally funded dams.

Nuclear Energy and Beyond

After World War II, another technological development boosted the creation of big systems: the de-velopment of nuclear power as a generating force. The large capital outlays that had characterized the industry from its beginnings became even greater when nuclear-generated electric power came on the scene during the 1960's and 1970's, for the capital needed to construct a nuclear plant was enormous. It became possible only when the government promised to provide liability coverage, and even this proved insufficient with the outbreak of the nuclear accident that occurred in 1979 at the Three Mile Island plant in Pennsylvania. As a result, private construction of nuclear plants in the United States came to a rapid halt, although overseas, construction continued (nuclear power generates most of France's electricity).

In the latter part of the twentieth century, the growth of companies to ever-larger sizes resumed, and globalization, the hallmark of the developed-world economy during the 1990's and into the twenty-first century, saw many national companies becoming part of international firms, often in effect holding companies on a global scale. Many of these were created in the wake of the antiregulatory policies that had become established in many governments.

Nancy M. Gordon

Further Reading

Castaneda, Christopher J. *Invisible Fuel: Manufactured and Natural Gas in America, 1800-2000.* New York: Twayne Publishers, 1999. Traces the development of the gas industry, from the start with manufactured gas through the extension of natural gas pipelines throughout the United States.

Edwards, Brian K. *The Economics of Hydroelectric Power.* Cheltenham, England: Edward Elgar, 2003. Looks at hydroelectric development from an environmental point of view.

Hausman, William J., Peter Hertner, and Mira Wilkins. *Global Electrification: Multinational Enterprise and International Finance in the History of Light and Power, 1878-2007.* New York: Cambridge University Press, 2008. Three specialists in the field of international business look particularly at the evolution of electrical utilities throughout the world, with special attention to international developments.

Lesser, Jonathan A., and Leonardo R. Giacchino. *Fundamentals of Energy Regulation.* Vienna, Va.: Public Utilities Reports, 2007. An extensive look at the regulation of energy, particularly gas and electricity, with attention to aspects such as cost measurement and allocation, market power, environmental regulations. Examines regulation as an economic concept.

Nye, David E. *Electrifying America: Social Meanings of a New Technology, 1880-1940.* Cambridge, Mass.: MIT Press, 1990. A good analysis of the process by which the United States became fully connected electrically. The author has a particular interest in technological history.

Peebles, Malcolm W. H. *Evolution of the Gas Industry.* New York: New York University Press, 1980. Covers the evolution of the gas industry in both the United States and western Europe.

Wasik, John F. *The Merchant of Power: Samuel Insull, Thomas Edison, and the Creation of the Modern Metropolis.* New York: Palgrave Macmillan, 2006. This story of Insull's climb to power covers the development of the power grid and the excesses of corporate power.

SEE ALSO: Colorado River water; Dams and aqueducts; Energy, U.S. Department of; Energy crisis of 1979; Enron bankruptcy; Government spending; Nuclear power industry; Telecommunications industry; Tennessee Valley Authority; Three Mile Island accident; Water resources.

Pullman Strike

THE EVENT: Strike held by Pullman Palace Car Company workers during the strained economic times of the Panic of 1893

DATE: May-July, 1894

PLACE: Chicago, Illinois

SIGNIFICANCE: The Pullman strikers not only received better wages as a result of the strike but also were successful in affecting economies in the majority of states throughout the union.

During the early 1880's, George Pullman, founder of Pullman Palace Car Company, constructed a town named Pullman for his workers. The amenities and seeming convenience of this town made the factory owner seem glorious in the eyes of his workers. However, when the Panic of 1893 negatively affected the nation's economic climate, life became brutal for Pullman's residents.

Magazine illustrations showing U.S. troops camped on the lake front (top) and freight cars and an engine wrecked by rioters at Kensington, near Pullman, in July, 1894. (Library of Congress)

Between July and November of 1893 alone, more than three-quarters of the Pullman workforce was laid off. For those who remained, work was harder but wages were no higher. On December 9, 1893, the workers struck, and although they had begun to unionize in early 1891, the number of unionized workers was not enough to make the strike effective. As a result, the December strike lasted only a few days.

In 1894, the economic situation worsened for Pullman workers. They continued paying high rents for their residences and inflated prices for goods, without a pay increase. When their attempts to obtain better wages failed, they struck on May 11, 1894. This strike is known as the Pullman Strike.

In between the short strike in December, 1893, and the large strike in May, a significant portion of the workers had joined the American Railway Union (ARU), a new union that had formed in the spring of 1894 under the leadership of Eugene V. Debs. Through the auspices of ARU, the strike literally stalled state economies across the United States. Pullman responded to the strike by leaving Chicago under the cover of night and moving to his summer home in the east.

Although Pullman refused to listen to the complaints of the workers, Debs and the ARU upped the ante by securing a boycott of all Pullman cars throughout the United States in late June, 1894. Because of the ubiquity of Pullman cars, this boycott stopped rail service throughout the midwestern states. In response to the boycott, railroad executives had nonunion railway workers attach U.S. mail-carrying-cars to trains that had been boycotted, thus forcing the federal government to intervene to se-cure mail delivery. In July, 1894, President Grover Cleveland sent approximately 12,000 U.S. troops to break the strike and ensure that mail would be delivered. Cleveland's actions ended the strike.

A. W. R. Hawkins

FURTHER READING

Burgen, Michael. *The Pullman Strike of 1894*. Minneapolis: Compass Point Books, 2008.

McMath, Robert C. *American Populism: A Social History, 1877-1898*. New York: Hill & Wang, 1993.

Summers, Mark Wahlgren. *The Gilded Age: Or, The Hazard of New Functions*. Upper Saddle River, N.J.: Prentice Hall, 1997.

SEE ALSO: Brotherhood of Sleeping Car Porters; Debs, Eugene V.; Labor history; Labor strikes; Panic of 1893; Postal Service, U.S.; Railroads; Randolph, A. Philip; Supreme Court and labor law.

R

Racketeer Influenced and Corrupt Organizations Act

THE LAW: Federal legislation enhancing the punishments for crimes committed as part of ongoing criminal organizations or enterprises

DATE: Enacted on October 15, 1970

SIGNIFICANCE: The RICO Act was designed to put an end to the enormous illegal profits enjoyed by the Mafia.

In the wake of Prohibition's repeal, organized crime families remained powerful by engaging in other forms of illegal trade, including narcotics and prostitution. Harry Anslinger, director of the Federal Bureau of Narcotics, was the first federal law-enforcement official to challenge the nation's drug rings, but he got no cooperation from Federal Bureau of Investigation (FBI) director J. Edgar Hoover. By 1950, organized crime family chiefs Joseph Bonanno, Joseph Profaci, Vincent Mangano, and Gaetano "Tommy" Gagliano ran their empires from behind the scenes with a free hand. Of the period's major Mafia bosses, only Frank Costello was known to the public.

Senator John L. McClellan, an Arkansas Democrat, chaired a Senate committee in 1957 to investigate organized crime. By 1970, with the help of Notre Dame law professor George Robert Blakey, McClellan had crafted the details of the Racketeer Influenced and Corrupt Organizations section of the Organized Crime Control Act (1970). Envisioned as a weapon against the Mafia, the broad provisions of the RICO Act enabled the courts to put in prison not only major mob chieftains but also the junk-bond dealer Michael Milken and other prominent figures from financial institutions. This broad use has prompted criticism from some lawyers and law professors, such as Harvard's Alan Dershowitz.

PROVISIONS

The RICO Act's primary target was the Mafia, which engaged in extortion, bribery, loan sharking, murder, drug trafficking, and prostitution. The Mafia's long practice of these crimes constituted a pattern that enabled prosecution of the so-called family godfathers. The act outlaws a broad range of illicit business activities, such as money laundering, acquiring or manipulating a business for racketeering purposes, and conspiring to do so.

In any RICO prosecution, a pattern of racketeering is identified by two features: relatedness and continuity. Relatedness emerges in a series of criminal actions that have the same purposes, results, participants, victims, or methods of commission. Continuity is established when a criminal act is repeated for a year or more. Before a RICO case can be made, it is necessary to prove that the individual crimes constituting the larger pattern of criminal activity were committed.

Prominent among the civil violations of the RICO Act are mail and wire fraud, bank fraud, and extortion; although the RICO Act was envisioned by Congress mainly as a weapon in criminal cases, since the 1980's the number of civil actions filed under the act has far exceeded the number of criminal filings. The RICO Act's civil remedies provision appears in section 1964(c):

> Any person injured in his business or property by reason of a violation of section 1962 of this chapter may sue therefore in any appropriate United States district court and shall recover threefold the damages he sustains and the cost of the suit, including reasonable attorney's fees.

SUCCESSES

The RICO Act remained unused against the Mafia until 1979, when two New York FBI agents, James Kossler and Jules Bonavolonta, were ordered by their boss, Neil Welch, to attend the lectures that Professor Blakey was giving at Cornell on defeating the Mafia. Blakey stressed wiretaps and the bugs allowed under Title 3 of the Omnibus Crime Control and Safe Streets Act of 1968, and the two agents realized these could be powerful tools against the Mafia, which was then realizing estimated annual illegal gains of $25 billion. The appointment in 1981 of Ronald Goldstock as head of New York State's Organized Crime Task Force led to the first infiltration of a Mafia family, and the attack on the families got a big boost from the appointment in 1983 of Rudy Giuliani as U.S. Attorney for the Southern District of New York.

Two Task Force agents achieved a coup when, in 1983, they planted a bug in the Jaguar in which Salvatore Avellino chauffeured Long Island's garbage boss, Antonio "Ducks" Corallo. This success was followed by bugging the hangouts of leaders in the Colombo, Gambino, and Genovese families. The information recorded by these devices was lethal for the mob, and in February, 1985, a federal grand jury in Manhattan handed down a fifteen-count indictment leading to the arrest of Anthony Salerno, Carmine Persico, Gennaro Langella, Antonio Corallo, Salvatore Santoro, Christopher Furnari, Ralph Scopo, and Anthony Indelicato. Giuliani chose an assistant, Michael Chertoff, as lead prosecutor, and on November 19, 1986, after six days of deliberations, the eight defendants were found guilty on all 151 charges. Indelicato was sentenced to forty years in prison; the others received sentences of one hundred years with no possibility of parole. The RICO Act's first major test was a success.

Other successes were to follow. The infamous John Gotti, head of the Gambino family, was tried unsuccessfully three times but was finally convicted in 1992 on racketeering and murder charges. He died in prison in 2002. After rebuilding the Bonanno family, Joseph "the Ear" Massino became the first New York boss to cooperate with the government and was convicted of RICO violations in 2004. One dramatic event clouded the history of RICO prosecutions: Federal judge Jack B. Weinstein overturned the convictions of two rogue detectives on the grounds that no continuing criminal enterprise had been proved at trial, because prosecutors had failed to prove continuity between crimes committed in New York and others in Las Vegas.

Frank Day

FURTHER READING

Barrett, Wayne. *Rudy.* New York: Basic Books, 2000. The story of Rudy Giuliani's success in fighting the mob in New York City using the RICO Act.

Blum, Howard. *How the FBI Broke the Mob.* New York: Simon & Schuster, 1993. Delves into the FBI investigation of the Colombo crime family, among others.

Bonavoluta, Jules, and Brian Duffy. *The Good Guys: How We Turned the FBI 'Round—and Finally Broke the Mob.* New York: Simon & Schuster, 1981. Bonavoluta was an early FBI convert to the importance of the RICO Act and a key player in federal mob investigations.

Raab, Selwyn. *Five Families: The Rise, Decline, and Resurgence of America's Most Powerful Mafia Families.* New York: St. Martin's Press, 2005. Smoothly written account of its subject in over seven hundred pages by a top investigative reporter.

SEE ALSO: Business crimes; Gambling industry; Identity theft; Justice, U.S. Department of; Organized crime; Prohibition.

Radio broadcasting industry

DEFINITION: Enterprises that produce and distribute original entertainment, news, and other audio content; create advertisements and secure advertising revenue; and transmit ads, original content, and preexisting content—such as music—by radio

SIGNIFICANCE: Radio broadcasts at once drew audiences to advertising and revolutionized entertainment in American households. When television supplanted radio as the nation's most popular entertainment media, radio nonetheless filled an important niche, offering Top 40 hits interspersed with disc jockey commentary and advertising. Political talk radio brought a new form of news entertainment during the late 1980's and early 1990's, and digital satellite radio initiated another shift in the twenty-first century.

The 1920's brought an enormous change in American entertainment. Suddenly, instead of having to go outside the home and buy expensive tickets to hear live performances of their favorite artists, people could tune in to broadcasts on their radios. Wireless radio broadcasts evolved from wireless telegraph broadcasts and could use two types of signal. Amplitude modulation (AM) signals varied the strength of the radio signal in relationship to the information being sent. Frequency modulation (FM) signals varied the frequency of the signal.

EARLY PROGRAMMING

Most early programs were broadcast using AM signals, and many early radios could pick up only AM signals. The first radio broadcast actually took place in 1906, when Reginald Aubrey Fessenden used a wireless telegraph station to broadcast a phonograph being played and a man singing. Lee De Forest took the process one step further, with the invention of the vacuum tube, which increased broadcast strength. He demonstrated its utility in 1910, and the popularity of this hobby grew.

In 1919, the Radio Corporation of America (RCA) was formed, to enable wireless radio communication between Great Britain and the United States. However, it quickly shifted its focus, using the idea of employee David Sarnoff to broadcast entertainment, and this quickly became its chief source of profits. The other big radio broadcaster in this era was Westinghouse.

Early radio listeners had to use headphones to hear a program, and musicians initially gave free live performances on the radio. Advertisers in this era relied on the prominent announcement of their names before programs to spread the word about their products. In 1921, RCA's Sarnoff created the first linked chain of nationwide stations. In that same year, the American Telephone and Telegraph (AT&T) began selling airtime to advertisers, who were then responsible for the content of their programs. It was this latter development that led to some of the most popular radio programs of the era.

By 1926, RCA and AT&T had merged their radio networks into the National Broadcasting Company (NBC), which had both a blue and a red line (named for the colors of their initial connecting cables). Competition came from William S. Paley's Co-lumbia Broadcasting System (CBS), and the Golden Age of radio began. Numerous smaller, unlicensed, stations sprang up, and competition was fierce. As competition between stations grew, sponsorship became more important to a program's survival.

In fact, had not Congress passed the Radio Act of 1927, there might have been an immediate industry crash, as competing signals gave listeners nothing but squelch and static. Most programs centered heavily on advertising, meaning sponsors profited from capturing and captivating listeners. They used music and comedy, interwoven with advertisements to promote their products. However, news, sports programs and special programming (such as presidential addresses) also retained their early popularity.

During the 1930's, the first soap operas (named because many of their sponsors were soap manufacturers) aired, and targeted advertising allowed marketers to reach out to homemakers who listened to the radio during the day. The actual programs aired in fifteen-minute increments each weekday, and each episode ended in a cliffhanger, so that listeners would tune in again the next day for more of the story (and more exposure to advertising). Products such as Jell-O gelatin and Cream of Wheat cereal became household names because listeners tuned into the programs their manufacturers sponsored.

During the 1930's, programs tended to be light-hearted efforts to cheer the country from the Great Depression or romantic dramas aimed at homemakers. Tobacco sales were helped by radio advertising. However, as the Depression lifted and the country headed into World War II, advertisers shifted as well, offering programs and advertisements filled with patriotic messages. Advertisers such as Quaker Oats expanded their popularity by reminding listeners that oatmeal was not rationed, as so many things were during the war.

As networks wanted more control of their own programming, radio would change its format so that multiple sponsors funded a single program, interspersing the sponsor's messages between segments of the show. Instead of concentrating all its advertising on one program or station, a sponsor could spread its advertisements over a whole day and many stations. Although initially unpopular, networks preferred this method, as it meant they did not have to rely on one sponsor or product for a show's popularity or success. They also retained better control of their shows.

ESTIMATED REVENUE AND EXPENSES FOR RADIO STATIONS, 2004-2005, IN MILLIONS OF DOLLARS

Year	Operating Revenue	Operating Expenses
2004	13,817	9,914
2005	13,713	10,150

Source: Data from the Statistical Abstract of the United States, 2008 (Washington, D.C.: Department of Commerce, Economics and Statistics Administration, Bureau of the Census, Data User Services Division, 2008)

TELEVISION BRINGS CHANGES

Radio's enormous popularity was not to endure. Toward the end of the war, a new broadcast medium, combining sound with live actors, moved into American living rooms: the television. Advertisers, quick to see the benefits of showing viewers pictures of their products, hurried to pour money into this new broadcast format, leaving radio sorely depleted by the early 1950's.

As advertising dollars flowed elsewhere, radio broadcasters scrambled to capture and retain audiences. Seeing their economic base abandoning them for television, radio broadcast corporations looked for something unique to draw people back. Ironically, these radio stations were often losing listeners to their own "children," as many local television stations were initially funded by radio stations.

From the beginning, public debate about the value of programming centered on advertisements, which were accused of being corrupting and demeaning. However, when advertisers withdrew their dollars, radio began to flounder. When it became apparent that television's popularity was not mere novelty, radio broadcasters began reinventing the medium.

Whereas, in their heyday, radio stations had presented everything from music shows to soap operas and children's programming, they now had to find a new focus. Television had effectively stolen the stars and audiences that made these programs work. Instead, radio discovered it could attract audiences with format programming. Although music programs (such as *The Grand Ole Opry*, which broadcast country music starting in 1925) had always been a part of radio, they now became its heart. Music stations bloomed, each offering a different musical genre aimed at a different demographic group.

Radio stations played popular music shows, hosted by disc jockeys (DJs) who gained their own followings. Early pioneers such as Martin Block and Al Jarvis had hosted *Make Believe Ballroom*, creating the concept of the DJ. During the early 1950's, those DJs became central to radio's continued success. During the 1950's and 1960's, the DJ sustained radio. Rock DJs, such as Alan Freed and Wolfman Jack (Robert Weston Smith) gave music commentary along with the songs they played, and their voices attracted listeners as much as their program content.

Music shows had another draw for radio corporations. Although programs with stars and casts were expensive to maintain, music programming with a single DJ was comparatively inexpensive, and fewer advertising dollars were needed to generate a profit. Local radio largely replaced the nationwide networks, as radios strove to maintain local audiences.

Where AM had previously been the preferred broadcast signal, FM began slowly growing in importance. Stations with a Top 40 format found the most success, playing the same popular songs from the given genre. AM signals broadcast farthest in the evening, which made that time radio's peak listening time. However, FM radio stations focused on mornings and commute times, when people either did not have access to a television or had no time to watch it.

REGULATORY CHANGES

Another factor preserving radio at this time was pioneered by the American Broadcasting Company (ABC), which split into four networks, allowing it to affiliate with four stations in one area, rather than just one. The company could then profit from all four stations in the area, instead of just one.

During the 1970's, FM evolved into an almost solely musical format, while AM shifted its attention to "talk" radio. The local programming that had proliferated during the 1950's gave way to stations that played the same songs and aired the same programs. Public radio, which offered more educational and unbiased content, gained some popularity, as it more closely resembled the old-time radio shows from the golden era of radio.

The same DJs who helped save radio were also widely condemned for pandering to the unintelligent. They often catered to a youthful audience, keeping their content light and concentrating largely on playing popular music. However, in all reality, few DJs had much freedom of expression. Most of them were managed strictly by their program directors, who controlled most of the content. DJs were just the on-air personalities fronting for the songs chosen by someone higher up.

Radio's other "villains," the advertisers, could dominate only a certain proportion of the airwaves until the Federal Communications Commission (FCC), in 1981, lifted the commercial load restrictions that had controlled how much advertising programming a station could carry.

Talk radio also grew in popularity, often drawing audiences to listen to extremely political content.

Until 1987, the Fairness Doctrine dictated that radio stations had to give both sides in any political side equal airtime, which led to them shying away from many political topics. However, the Fairness Doctrine was repealed in 1987.

As the 1990's began, listeners had a new reason to tune into commercial radio, as hosts such as Don Imus, Rush Limbaugh, and Howard Stern took formidable stands on political issues, ranted against and mocked those who disagreed, and invited famous guests to appear on their programs. Most important, however, talk radio invited listeners to call in with their perspectives. Thus, the average American could call and air an opinion on the radio. Its interactive nature inspired higher ratings, drawing new advertising dollars. It stayed on the air as its sponsors really made the stations profitable, and sponsors stuck with the talk-show hosts, who clearly drew listeners.

Newly formed satellite radio stations offered digital programming that mimicked the music and talk content of analog stations but without the commercials. Instead, listeners paid fees directly to satellite providers to receive the same stations nationwide, most of them commercial free. Although commercial stations still needed advertising dollars to succeed, the new digital channels were listener funded.

Thus, after an early heyday of only around thirty years, radio found itself eclipsed by television during the 1950's, forcing it to redefine itself as a source of Top 40 music hits. Talk radio grew in popularity during the late 1980's and early 1990's, when the Fairness Doctrine was repealed and stations could air biased political commentary without acknowledging the other side of the debate. Finally, digital satellite radio entered into competition with commercial radio, bringing still more changes to the industry, as advertisers struggled to find a niche within the new medium.

Jessie Bishop Powell

FURTHER READING

Douglas, Susan J. *Inventing American Broadcasting, 1899-1922*. Baltimore: Johns Hopkins University Press, 1987. Deep history of radio, analyzing the move from telegraph to sound broadcast. Focuses on the people and events required to make radio such a popular phenomenon beginning during the 1920's.

Finkelstein, Norman. *Sounds in the Air: The Golden Age of Radio*. New York: Scribner's, 1993. Discusses some of radio's most significant contributions to the entertainment industry, including humor, children's programming, soap operas, news programs, and, particularly, advertising.

Fisher, Marc. *Something in the Air: Radio, Rock, and the Revolution That Shaped a Generation*. New York: Random House, 2007. Explains how radio maintained popularity during the 1950's, after the advent of television, by pioneering the top 40 concepts and presenting revolutionary DJs like Alan Freed and Wolfman Jack.

Keith, Michael C. *Talking Radio: An Oral History of American Radio in the Television Age*. Armonk, N.Y.: M. E. Sharpe, 2000. Looks at radio broadcasting through the lens of its participants, interviewing figures ranging from Ray Bradbury to Studs Terkel to Casey Kasem.

Nachman, Gerald. *Raised on Radio*. New York: Pantheon, 1998. History of radio programs from the 1920's to the 1950's, looking at the various types of programs radio premiered. Includes discussion of several key performers from the era.

Smulyan, Susan. *Selling Radio: The Commercialization of American Broadcasting, 1920-1934*. Washington, D.C.: Smithsonian, 1994. Follows the growth of advertising programs, like *the Jell-O Show*, in which actors incorporated products into their performances.

Walker, Jesse. *Rebels on the Air: An Alternative History of Radio in America*. New York: New York University Press, 2001. Looks at some of radio's more radical elements and the ways radio has been used to promote revolutionary ideas in the United States.

SEE ALSO: Advertising industry; American Society of Composers, Authors, and Publishers; Electronics industry; Federal Communications Commission; Motion-picture industry; Music industry; National Broadcasting Company; Telecommunications industry; Television broadcasting industry.

Railroad strike of 1877

THE EVENT: Strike by U.S. railroad workers protesting wage cuts and poor working conditions
DATE: July 16-early August, 1877
PLACE: Major cities throughout the eastern and central United States
SIGNIFICANCE: Workers in many industries joined the railroaders in their strike, making this first nationwide strike one of the broadest general strikes in American labor history. Although the strikers initially gained much public sympathy, the widespread violence associated with the strike discredited the labor movement in the eyes of many Americans.

During the summer of 1877, the Baltimore and Ohio Railroad cut wages by 10 percent for all workers making more than $1 per day. A few months earlier, the Pennsylvania Railroad had made similar reductions. Railroad workers, many of whom were unorganized and represented by no union, were greatly concerned by these pay cuts and the general treatment of workers. A group in Baltimore, Maryland, organized a strike.

The strike began on July 16, 1877, at Camden Junction, near Baltimore, where brakemen and firemen refused to work. The following day, workers in Martinsburg, West Virginia, also walked off the job. The strike soon spread to nearly every major railroad center in the United States—only New England and the South were generally untouched. The railroads hired nonunion workers, but in many localities striking workers used mob action to prevent these "scabs" from operating the trains.

State militia forces were called out in many cities to restore order, but the militiamen often sympathized with the workers and were reluctant to employ force. The governor of West Virginia asked for federal troops, and President Rutherford B. Hayes sent the U.S. Army to restore order, marking the first such use of the U.S. military to put down a strike. Army troops were sent to cities in several states. The government argued that this use of force was necessary to protect the trains that carried the U.S. mail.

Throughout the United States, there were mass demonstrations, general strikes, and violence in support of the railroad workers. Railroad equipment was vandalized and burnt, and cargoes were

Magazine illustration shows the burning and sacking of freight trains (top), a mob outside James Bown & Son gunworks (center), and the burning of offices and machine shops in Pittsburgh. (Library of Congress)

looted. By the time the strike ended, about half of the railroad traffic in the United States had been disrupted. More than 100,000 workers had gone on strike. Countless numbers of the unemployed had joined in demonstrations and protests in sympathy with the strikers. More than one hundred people were killed in the nationwide violence, and more than one thousand were arrested. Although the railroads made few concessions to the workers, the widespread nature of the workers' resistance made it difficult to fire or discipline more than a small percentage of those involved in the strike.

Mark S. Joy

FURTHER READING

Bruce, Robert V. *1877: Year of Violence.* New ed. Chicago: Ivan R. Dee, 1989.

Stowell, David O. *Streets, Railroads, and the Great Strike of 1877.* Chicago: University of Chicago Press, 1999.

SEE ALSO: Labor history; Labor strikes; Panic of 1873; Postal Service, U.S.; Railroads; Transcontinental railroad.

Railroads

DEFINITION: Companies formed around a mode of transportation in which cars are drawn by locomotive or powered by motors on tracks formed by rails attached to ties on a roadbed

SIGNIFICANCE: Railroads were the form of transport that revolutionized American business. As one of the first big businesses in the United States, railroads had a positive effect on accounting, auditing, finance, management, and marketing practices. They also enabled other businesses to expand throughout the country.

The Baltimore and Ohio (B&O) Railroad, formed in 1827, and based on a British concept, was the earliest U.S. railroad. Although dozens of other railroads soon followed in the United States, it was the B&O that eventually became known as the "university" of railroad accounting and business operations. Many aspects of business management originated at the B&O. For a quarter of a century, the B&O was the source of all things good in railroading. Then, during the early 1850's, a new railroading environment led to the Illinois Central Railroad and the Mobile and Ohio (M&O) Railroad becoming important leaders. An analysis of the innovations of these three lines essentially covers most of the important aspects of the first half century of railroading, although admittedly the chief financial officer of the Louisville and Nashville Railroad, Albert Fink, made important managerial contributions near the end of this early period. The first half century of railroad operations was essentially a growth phase and was followed by a regulatory phase. The regulatory phase, highlighted by the creation of the Interstate Commerce Commission, was a period of controversy, as railroads alternately tried to help the regulators and to block their efforts by stifling certain rules and regulations.

CAPITALIZATION

What made railroads modern businesses was the capital requirements of these enterprises, which were far in excess of those of other contemporary businesses. This meant that external financing had to be sought to construct a railroad line. Although other businesses were owner-operated ventures that required no more than local bank loans, railroads required more funds than one person could risk because of the capital needed to construct a line. This created new issues of how to communicate with external investors regarding the performance of the railroad and how to monitor the railroad managers who were stewards of the company's assets. These so-called agency, or principal-agent, problems— regarding how to ensure that the workers and managers of a company work in the best interests of its investors—remain issues for modern-day companies.

Initially, there was a quasi-public nature about railroads. Governments played key roles in helping establish early rail lines. Besides providing support through the purchase and guarantee of securities, many state and local governments assisted individual railroads through land grants. Also, because railroads were often natural monopolies sanctioned by the state, their securities were viewed as akin to those of governments. In many cases, investors were not so much investing in the leadership of the railroad company but in the manufacturers, farmers, and consumers of the area in which the railroad operated. Thus, railroad securities were in some ways akin to government securities.

THE B&O

The B&O was formed in 1827 as merchants of Baltimore sought to preserve their city's commercial advantage as a seaport linked with the American interior. The city had risen to third in size in the United States because of the construction of the Cumberland Road, which bridged the Allegheny Mountains from Cumberland, Maryland, to the Ohio River Valley and on to the Mississippi River Valley of the Midwest. However, even with the Cumberland Road, travel by wagon was arduous, slow, and costly. The opening of the Erie Canal (which in effect connected the port of New York City with Lake Erie) in late 1825 threatened to ruin Baltimore's commercial role, as transport to the Ohio and Mississippi river valleys shifted to waterborne shipment

A B&O 5600 locomotive at the World's Fair in New York in 1939. (Library of Congress)

via canal, lake, and river through New York City. Freight prices dropped significantly and set off a boom in canal building by some cities and a search for alternative forms of transportation by others.

Because Baltimore did not have direct river access to the west, merchants of the city were willing to consider all ideas. Banker Philip E. Thomas had been corresponding with his brother, Evan, who was in England and was excited about "railed roads" there. Similarly George Brown, an investment banker, had been hearing from his brother, William, in Liverpool, about British railroads. So Thomas and Brown met over dinner and discussed the possibility of a railed road connecting Baltimore with the Ohio River. The two believed that the cost of construction of the railed road, even though it had to pass over mountains, would be less than the cost of the Chesapeake and Ohio Canal (the nearest competitive alternative), and the two felt that the railed road offered mechanical advantages, including that horse-drawn wagons could be pulled efficiently in a train on the smooth rails.

Merchants of Baltimore met and seized on the railed road idea. Investors quickly subscribed to thirty thousand shares of $100 stock, as virtually every citizen of Baltimore supported the enterprise. City of Baltimore and state of Maryland funds also were invested, as these entities received half ownership of the shares, making the B&O both a public and private entity. The incorporation act specified that the Maryland legislature would set freight and passenger rates and that the B&O would not pay taxes. An annual report issued by the corporation to its shareholders was required by the B&O corporate charter; however, the contents of the annual report were not specified.

TRACKING THE BUSINESS

The size and growth of the enterprise from the time of the initial public offering were significant. The railroad management quickly evolved into a separate professional class with only a small ownership interest but with expertise to run the operations. This early evolution would lead to agency relationships, which were significant in the development of accounting, auditing, finance, and business management. In accounting, the corporate annual report would evolve, becoming an essential financial communication device for management, describing the company's performance and its role as the steward of shareholder assets. These financial statements developed into the basic income statement, balance sheet, and early cash-flow report.

As they grew, the early railroads encountered new control problems involving how to deal with large volumes of business transactions occurring daily across long distances and with a multitude of employees handling cash or originating otherwise complex transactions. These employees ranged from ticket agents and freight agents at each station and depot to conductors on each train. Cash disbursements were the responsibilities of an ever-greater number of employees. Control over cash transactions would push accounting from the family-owned businesses' journal-ledger system of recording infrequent transactions to the development of techniques to ensure proper recording, transferring, safeguarding, depositing, and handling of cash. The railroads handled control problems by developing internal auditing and training accountants in legion. The accounting profession would become firmly established during the manufacturing revolution of the late nineteenth century.

Financial innovations were sparked by the railroads. The railroads raised large amounts of capital, requiring wider public sale of stock and bonds. This expanded the role of investment banking and the securities houses, which had previously been trading mostly government debt obligations. Railroad securities laid the foundation for industrial firms to issue stocks and bonds to the public half a century later. Innovations in the types of bonds issued were also a product of the railroads—as "mortgage" bonds, "interest" bonds, debentures, and a wide variety of other types of debt obligations evolved. Railroads also changed the practice of businesses' paying out profits as dividends to owners. Retention of profits became a major source of financing for the nineteenth century railroads. The early use of preferred stock can also be found at the B&O Railroad.

NET INCOME OF MAJOR U.S. RAILROADS, 1890-2005, IN MILLIONS OF DOLLARS

Year	Net Income
1890	106
1900	253
1910	583
1920	482
1930	578
1940	243
1950	855
1960	473
1970	126
1980	1,229
1990	1,977
2000	2,500
2005	4,917

Sources: Data from *Historical Statistics of the United States: Colonial Times to 1970* (Washington, D.C.: U.S. Department of Commerce, Bureau of the Census, 1975) and U.S. Census Bureau, *Statistical Abstract of the United States: 2008* (Washington, D.C.: Author, 2007)

Note: Major railroads are Class 1 railroads, defined as railroads with revenue of at least $348.8 million in 2006.

EFFICIENCY AND THE RAILROADS

Railroads created a new standard of precision of operations. To be successful, the railroad had to operate trains in a safe, efficient manner, which required a close coordination not widely practiced at the time. Operating from distant locations and running trains traveling at different speeds on one-way track in both directions required all employees to work by the same strict standards, from the establishment of a standard ("railroad") time system, to maintenance of the equipment and lines, and to strict adherence to procedure. Supervision was needed, and lines of authority were drawn. A hierarchy became established. Managers with special expertise evolved into a professional class who organized activities and made resource allocations. Railroad success depended on throughput: running the trains full and fast, and turning them around quickly. This concept was revolutionary in its day but became the essence of the Industrial Revolution, as high-volume plant utilization of fixed-cost facilities drove down cost per unit. Managing by accounting for costs of a department and other sub-units and by statistical factors, such as cost per freight-ton-mile, evolved with the railroads.

The railroads revolutionized the economy: Freight costs declined dramatically, and travel time between cities or regions of the country decreased from days to hours. The interior of the United States became open to farming as farmers' produce could be shipped to market and to merchants who in turn could sell goods to rural customers. The railroad saw the development of support industries and professions, including civil engineering, the coal industry, the steel industry, and the travel and vacation industry. Telegraph lines were first placed on the railroad rights of way, and the telegraph quickly became an essential way of communicating and coordinating train traffic.

QUALITY ANNUAL REPORTS

The B&O published excellent annual reports from its earliest years, primarily for the benefit of its existing investors, but it was the Illinois Central Railroad that perfected the annual report. From as early as the 1850's, the first years of its existence, the Illinois Central published annual reports that were aimed at both the general American public (that is, noninvestors) and the European capital markets (the majority investors). Admittedly, the Illinois

Central, because of the way it was founded, was a unique type of corporation, which had a greater responsibility to the general public than most corporations have; nevertheless, its reports provided a textbook example of reporting at its finest because the corporation's annual reports met the needs of both audiences.

The Illinois Central, sometimes called the Main Line of Mid-America, was the country's first cross-country railroad system, extending from Lake Michigan in the north to the Gulf of Mexico in the south. It also was the country's first land-grant railroad and thus an experiment in social economy. The transportation provided by the line was the intended product of a collaboration by northern senator Stephen Douglas of Illinois and southern senators Jefferson Davis of Mississippi and William R. King of Alabama, who joined forces to provide an unprecedented form of federal subsidy that could link agricultural markets and shipping points in the emerging population centers in the Midwest and South. The subsidy, in the form of federal land grants, was to shape the modernization of the American frontier. The country's rich interior land was almost worthless without access to markets, which railroads were to provide.

The land-grant legislation of September, 1850, marked the first time that public lands from the United States federal government were used to aid in the construction of a private rail line. It was to become a standard means by which the federal government subsidized railroads. Senator Douglas was the main supporter of the bill in Congress (with help in the House from Abraham Lincoln). An initial bill, limited to public lands in Illinois, was narrowly defeated in 1848. In 1850, Senators King and Davis amended the bill to extend the grants to the southern states. With this new source of support, the bill passed. A main argument in support of the legislation was that the federal land was worthless without a railroad, and no private railroad would build where there was no population to serve. If a portion of the land was given to the railroad, in checkerboard fashion, the remaining land still owned by the government would become more valuable. Thus, the sale of the land could be used to finance the railroad, which in turn would make both the railroad's and the government's land more valuable. In reality, the land grants were viewed by Congress not as subsidies but as investments in marketable land.

FINANCING THE ILLINOIS CENTRAL

The incorporators' plan for financing the Illinois Central was simple and, to insiders, most attractive. They anticipated using the land grant as security for a bond issue, the proceeds of which would pay for construction. Thereafter, the bonds could be paid off with proceeds from the sale of the lands, whose value was enhanced by the transport provided by the railroad. This would permit the incorporators to own the railroad and to operate it with minimal investment. In March, 1851, the Illinois Central board of directors held its first meeting and authorized a deposit of $200,000 with the state to guarantee good faith on behalf of the incorporators. The deposit came from the sale of stock to the thirteen incorporators. The incorporators wanted to keep their cash investments at a minimum. Bond sales were slow, particularly in Europe, where investors, especially in England, were wary of the state of Illinois because the state had missed interest payments on several loan agreements. However, by adding options to buy stock, large quantities of bonds were eventually (mid-1852) sold in both the United States and in Europe.

FRAUDS

Many frauds involving railroads occurred during the early years. In 1856, as the Mobile and Ohio Railroad was being built north, management problems occurred because the president and another officer speculated on acquiring land along the route. This conflict of interest between the officers and the railroad resulted in considerable controversy and the firing of officers involved in the land speculation. Noteworthy is the fact that an audit committee was designated by the board of directors to investigate the president. Fortunately, the M&O had a set of bylaws that mentioned ethical issues—a rare phenomenon at the time. Other small frauds took place at other railroads, but the king of railroad frauds involved the financing of the transcontinental railroad.

The Crédit Mobilier of America was the most widely publicized railroad fraud in history. A September 4, 1872, article in the powerful *New York Sun* accused Vice President Schuyler Colfax and other noted politicians of accepting stock in the Crédit Mobilier in exchange for their influence in Congress. Crédit Mobilier was the construction company that built the transcontinental railroad on behalf of the Union Pacific Railroad. The objective of the bribes was to be sure that there would be no interference from Congress that would delay federal money being funneled into railroad construction. To make the matter of taking bribes even worse, it was determined that one of the purposes of Crédit Mobilier, besides building the railroad, was to defraud the government by overcharging for construction of the tracks. Insiders at the Union Pacific Railroad had created the construction company to enable them to pay themselves millions of dollars to build the railroad. Thus, Crédit Mobilier was a scandal of gargantuan proportions even before it was connected to the acceptance of bribes by politicians.

The investigation disclosed that Colfax had received twenty shares of stock in Crédit Mobilier and dividends of $1,200 from that investment. Colfax asserted that he had never owned any stock that he had not purchased. Similarly, he claimed never to have received the supposed $1,200 in dividends. However, the House Judiciary Committee investigation determined that Colfax had indeed deposited $1,200 into his bank account just two days after the supposed dividend payment. After two weeks, Colfax explained that the deposit had been a campaign contribution from a friend who had since died. Even his strongest supporters doubted this story.

ICC AND OTHER REGULATION

The history of railroad regulation is a combination of social, cultural, and political phenomena, which together are justified by increased efficiency and lower prices for consumers. The early history of railroad regulation was state based, but in 1887, the federal government took over with the establishment of the Interstate Commerce Commission (ICC).

The Hepburn Act of 1906 gave the ICC the power to set maximum rates. More important, the ICC could view the railroads' financial records, which had to be prepared using a standardized accounting system. The Hepburn Act also expanded the ICC's authority to cover toll bridges, terminals, ferries, sleeping cars, express companies, and oil pipelines. Many scholars consider the Hepburn Act to be the most important piece of legislation regarding railroads in the first half of the twentieth century. Economists and historians have suggested that

the Hepburn Act may have crippled the railroads to such an extent and given so much advantage to shippers that a giant unregulated trucking industry—undreamed of in 1906—took away the railroad's freight business.

In 1968, the Pennsylvania Railroad and the New York Central Railroad merged to form the Penn Central Transportation Company (PC). Two years later, the PC, then the largest railroad in the United States, entered reorganization under the Bankruptcy Act. The bankruptcy led to the 1976 creation of Conrail. The PC's failure is illustrative of the problems of the railroad industry during the late 1960's. The PC was a victim of undesirable industry trends; the railroad industry was a sick industry. A big problem was that railroads were heavily regulated by the ICC and were still treated as if they had the transportation monopoly they had during the late nineteenth century. The railroad industry's freight market share decreased from 67 percent in 1947 to 40 percent in 1971, and government money was spent building highways and airports, while the railroads had to provide maintenance on their own track structure. Meanwhile, although the U.S. Postal Service diverted mail shipments from rail to both air and road, the ICC forced the railroads to continue operating money-losing passenger trains until the 1971 creation of Amtrak.

Basically, the railroad industry was impeded in its ability to compete by excessive regulation. Additional railroad bankruptcies in the Northeast led to the creation of a government-owned Conrail in 1976, and the government's response was to phase in deregulation of the industry. The bankruptcy of the PC was final proof that railroad regulation was not needed. The regulatory system for the transport industry lasted for nearly a century and was not forsaken until the passage of the Staggers Transportation Act of 1978. By this time, concerns about U.S. global competitiveness and the diminishment of efficiency because of market regulation induced Congress to support a new system based more on free competition among the railroads and rival modes of transportation.

Dale L. Flesher

FURTHER READING

Baskin, Jonathan Barron, and Paul J. Miranti, Jr. *A History of Corporate Finance.* New York: Cambridge University Press, 1997. The chapter on railroads provides a good background on nineteenth century railroad financing.

Cochran, Thomas C. *Railroad Leaders, 1845-1890.* Reprint. New York: Russell & Russell, 1965. A biographical look at the contributions of railroad managers.

Corliss, Carlton J. *Main Line of Mid-America: The Story of the Illinois Central.* New York: Creative Age Press, 1951. A great book written for the hundredth anniversary of the Illinois Central.

Cullen, E. *American Railway Accounting, A Bibliography.* Washington, D.C.: Railway Accounting Officers Association, 1926. This is a bibliography of books and articles on railroad management up through 1926.

Decker, Leslie E. *Railroads, Lands, and Politics: The Taxation of the Railroad Land Grants, 1864-1897.* Providence, R.I.: Brown University Press, 1964. Good book on the railroad land grants awarded to the Illinois Central and later railroads.

Dilts, James D. *The Great Road: The Building of the Baltimore and Ohio, the Nation's First Railroad, 1828-1853.* Stanford, Calif.: Stanford University Press, 1993. This is the premier volume on the history of the B&O.

Reynolds, Kirk, and Dave Oroszi. *Baltimore & Ohio Railroad.* Minneapolis: MBI Publications, 2008. A history of the railroad with many photographs.

SEE ALSO: Air transportation industry; Amtrak; Automotive industry; Highways; Railroad strike of 1877; Stagecoach line, first; Steamboats; Time zones; Transcontinental railroad; Transportation, U.S. Department of; Trucking industry.

Randolph, A. Philip

IDENTIFICATION: Trade union leader and civil rights activist

BORN: April 15, 1889; Crescent City, Florida

DIED: May 16, 1979; New York, New York

SIGNIFICANCE: As a leader in incorporating African Americans into the trade union movement and working to end discrimination in employment and segregation in the military, Randolph made major contributions toward integrating African Americans into the mainstream of the American economy.

A. Philip Randolph was the son of James William Randolph, an AME minister, and Elizabeth Robinson Randolph. He graduated as valedictorian of his class from Cookman Institute in 1907. In 1911, he moved to New York City, where he worked as an elevator operator, a porter, and a waiter. He also joined the Socialist Party and later became editor of the *Messenger,* the monthly publication of the Headwaiters and Sidewaiters Society of Greater New York.

In 1925, Randolph agreed to become the leader of the Brotherhood of Sleeping Car Porters (BSCP). For the next ten years, he led a campaign to organize the Pullman Car porters. In 1935, the BSCP became the exclusive bargaining agent of the Pullman porters, and in 1937, the Pullman Palace Car Company agreed to a contract with the BSCP, which was affiliated with the American Federation of Labor.

Randolph continued his efforts to end discrimination throughout his life. In 1941, he proposed a march on Washington after President Franklin D. Roosevelt refused to issue an executive order barring discrimination against African American workers in the defense industry. Roosevelt then issued the order. In 1947, Randolph called for the integration of the U.S. armed forces. A year later, President Harry S. Truman issued an executive order ending segregation in the military. In 1955, Randolph became a vice president of the AFL-CIO. He also served as founder and president of the Negro American Labor Council, president of the A. Philip Randolph Institute, and chair of the 1963 civil rights March on Washington. In 1964, he was awarded the Presidential Medal of Freedom by Lyndon B. Johnson in recognition of his accomplishments.

William V. Moore

SEE ALSO: Brotherhood of Sleeping Car Porters; Debs, Eugene V.; Labor history; Labor strikes; Pullman Strike; World War II.

Reader's Digest

IDENTIFICATION: Monthly general-interest magazine

DATE: Launched in February, 1922

SIGNIFICANCE: Based initially on the principle of condensing articles from other publications, *Reader's Digest* has become one of the most successful and enduring periodicals in U.S. business history. Its parent company, the Reader's Digest Association, not only publishes a wide variety of consumer magazines and books, but also is one of the largest direct marketers in the world.

Reader's Digest was the brainchild of DeWitt Wallace, the son of a college president. While recuperating from wounds sustained in World War I, Wallace developed a formula for condensing periodical articles that sought to preserve their substance, style, and significance. With the help of his equally enterprising wife, Lila Acheson Wallace, he launched the magazine during the 1920's, when Americans felt they had less time for reading as a result of competition from the radio, the cinema, and the automobile. Members of the public eagerly welcomed a magazine that digested information they believed might be useful. The articles were condensed to one-fourth their original length and distinctively packaged in a size (roughly 5 by 7 inches) that could be carried in a pocket and read whenever the opportunity arose. The earliest issues contained exactly thirty-one articles, one for each day of most months.

Over the years, the Wallaces shrewdly maintained their magazine's appearance while constantly making editorial improvements. Advertising was first accepted in 1955, and gradually more original articles were commissioned. The founding combination of light-hearted humor with serious-minded topics continued. Thanks to its publishing formula, the magazine's circulation climbed steadily, reaching a peak of 18 million domestically during the late 1970's, before dwindling to 10 million in 2008—still one of the top consumer magazines in both circulation and audience. A worldwide phenomenon, *Reader's Digest* is published in twenty-one languages and sold in more than sixty countries.

The Wallaces ran their business enterprise like a benevolent kingdom in which they not only controlled every detail but also endeavored to treat their subjects as trusted family members. They provided free buses from New York City to the company headquarters, built in Georgian style on eight acres in Chappaqua, New York. Cafeteria lunches were subsidized, and employees even received free peanut-butter sandwiches, which the Wallaces believed were healthy. The Wallaces sought no special privileges and eschewed exorbitant salaries, preferring to share their wealth with their employees and

The company headquarters in Chappaqua, New York. (Library of Congress)

their favored charities, sometimes giving away millions of dollars spontaneously.

When the Wallaces died during the 1980's, their enterprises were earning $80 million a year and were valued at $2 billion. Their successors focused on the company's core products: the magazine, condensed books, general books, recorded music, and a mailing list of 100 million customers. Other endeavors, such as educational software, were eliminated, as were many employee benefits. However, when the company went public for the first time in 1990, it began to diversify its holdings by acquiring several special-interest magazines and a network of book marketers. In March, 2007, the Reader's Digest Association was purchased for $2.4 billion by Ripplewood Holdings, a private-equity firm that holds investments in entertainment, financial services, manufacturing, and technology companies.

James I. Deutsch

FURTHER READING

Canning, Peter. *American Dreamers: The Wallaces and "Reader's Digest"—an Insider Story.* New York: Simon & Schuster, 1996.

Heidenry, John. *Theirs Was the Kingdom: Lila and DeWitt Wallace and the Story of the "Reader's Digest."* New York: W. W. Norton, 1993.

Schreiner, Samuel A., Jr. *The Condensed World of the "Reader's Digest."* New York: Stein & Day, 1977.

SEE ALSO: Advertising industry; *Barron's*; Book publishing; *Forbes*; *Fortune*; Magazine industry.

Real estate industry, commercial

DEFINITION: All privately owned nonresidential and agricultural real estate that is used for profit-making enterprises; includes such diverse property as apartment buildings, office buildings, industrial properties, medical centers, hotels, malls, and retail stores.

SIGNIFICANCE: As economic activity has grown more complex over time, commercial real estate has developed as a separate category from residential real estate. Although the numbers of commercial real estate properties are much smaller than those of residential properties, the total dollar value of commercial real estate property constitutes a substantial portion of the total real estate value in the United States.

Native Americans had only residential real estate, if their generally primitive housing can be described in such sophisticated terms. Early colonial real estate was residential in the sense that homes were built on agricultural land. When commercial or manufacturing structures were built, they usually included the residences of their owners. Inns and taverns included residential quarters for their owners, and store owners typically lived on the second floor above their businesses. As economic activity became more complex, a separation between residences and commercial property developed, primarily in urban areas.

By the nineteenth century, urban areas were already divided into commercial, manufacturing, and residential sections. By the twentieth century, these informal subdivisions were made permanent through zoning laws, which distinguished between various grades of manufacturing and commerce in several grades of commercial properties. Eventually even residential property zoning was used to indicate where high-density residences such as apartment houses could be located, in part to protect the owners of single-family housing from the traffic associated with such large developments.

The purchase and sale of commercial real estate are typically handled by specialized real estate agents who may work at firms specializing in commercial properties. By the twenty-first century, very complex real estate investment trusts with highly leveraged debt service were developed to handle the largest real estate projects.

Although all developed real estate parcels have certain fixed or hard costs, such as roads, sidewalks, lighting, utility lines, and sewers, commercial real estate typically requires much larger amounts of capital than that needed for residential real estate. This capital is typically raised through issuing stock or borrowing large amounts of money, frequently through the issuance of bonds. Financing for nearly all commercial real estate is so complex that separate divisions within commercial and investment banks are devoted solely to commercial operations.

Manufacturing installations can be so large and complex that zoning ordinances do not adequately cover them, and a separate regulatory regime has been created to deal with the environmental, transportation, communication, and utility aspects of their construction and operation.

Commercial and manufacturing real estate properties are generally so valuable that special assessments are imposed on them by local governments, and they can provide a substantial source of income for local governments, whether directly through taxes or indirectly through the added employment opportunities and business activity they bring to the community. So attractive are these business developments that local and state governments have shifted from taxing these properties heavily to offering tax forgiveness and exemption programs to encourage commercial real estate development in the hopes of adding jobs to their communities. Local governments then hope to cover the cost of infrastructure developments by gaining real estate tax revenue from the associated residential housing.

Richard L. Wilson

FURTHER READING

Shavell, Steven. *Foundations of Economic Analysis of Law.* Cambridge, Mass.: Harvard University Press, 2004.

Stoebuck, W. B., and Dale A. Whitman. *The Law of Property.* 3d ed. St. Paul, Minn.: West Group, 2000.

Waldron, Jeremy. *The Right to Private Property.* New York: Oxford University Press, 1988.

SEE ALSO: Housing and Urban Development, U.S. Department of; Real estate industry, residential; Retail trade industry; Small Business Administration; Supreme Court and land law; Trump, Donald; Zoning, commercial.

Real estate industry, residential

DEFINITION: Enterprises engaged in construction, sales, and financing of residences, including single-family homes, multiple-occupancy units, and manufactured homes

SIGNIFICANCE: Twenty-first century housing costs account for 30-50 percent of the typical American family budget, making housing the largest sector in the nation's consumer economy. Housing prices and availability strongly influence labor's costs to industry. Historically, both peaks and troughs in the housing market have created ripple effects influencing all aspects of the economy.

The modern residential real estate business in the United States rests on three legs: the contractor-developer, who oversees the planning and construction of multiple dwelling units; the realtor, who markets new and existing units to American families; and the lending industry, which provides capital both to the contractor-developer and to the home buyer. None of these entities operated to any significant extent before the U.S. Civil War. In colonial America and during the early decades of the republic, housing development was constrained by a general lack of capital and transportation systems, requiring most people to live within walking distance of work. In contrast to the situation in Europe, land and raw materials in the New World were cheap, so most free settlers lived in owner-occupied homes, ranging from the log cabin—for which the owner supplied all the labor and materials—through a simple frame house, to infrequent larger homes requiring much skilled craftsmanship and imported materials to complete. Even for these, the owner usually served as contractor.

The population was overwhelmingly rural—95 percent in 1790, 89 percent in 1840. In urban areas, combining the owner's residence with a store or workshop blurred the distinction between business and residential real estate. Real estate sales and loans associated with them were handled as a sideline by firms whose main source of income lay elsewhere—in the earliest days, with the maritime shipping industry, later with railroads.

The influx of large numbers of European immigrants during the 1840's created an urban housing crisis, especially in New York and Boston. Core areas became increasingly densely packed and squalid, while dependence on foot travel for transportation limited peripheral expansion. Owners of rural property on the outskirts of large cities found it more profitable to sell lots dedicated to middle-class, single-family housing than to allow a mixture of manufacturing and substandard shantytowns to grow up spontaneously in these borderlands.

Llewellyn Park, New Jersey, the first planned development in America, offered a parklike setting with all the trappings of a luxurious country estate, shared in common by upper-middle-class residents. Purchasers of lots agreed to multiple conditions ensuring uniform upscale development and became members of a self-governing homeowners' association. Although Llewellyn Park and other similar "Garden City" developments (Chestnut Hill, Pennsylvania; Garden City, New York) drew on contemporary utopian visions of ideal communities, they were decidedly business ventures catering to the dreams and aspirations of the well-to-do. A key feature of the Garden City was a ferry terminal or commuter rail station enabling businesspeople and professionals to commute to their jobs in the city.

Marketing single-family homes, built and furnished in a style beyond the means of the average working-class family, as the centerpiece of the American Dream dates from the middle of the nineteenth century. Andrew Jackson Downing's *Cottage Residences* (1841) and Catherine Beecher's *The American Woman's Home* (1869) equated domestic comfort with Christian virtue. Beecher (sister of Harriet Beecher Stowe, author of *Uncle Tom's Cabin*) referred to the idealized suburban home as "the home church of Jesus Christ." Neither Downing nor Beecher participated directly in real estate marketing, but their popular books set the tone for later promotional literature that elevated home ownership to the level of a patriotic and religious duty.

STREETCAR SUBURBS, 1880-1934

Urban development in the last quarter of the nineteenth century took advantage of improved local transportation and large amounts of capital generated by railroads. Streetcar suburbs attracted lower middle-class and skilled working-class families, and included a high proportion of rentals. The master developer bought farmland, subdivided it, and sold lots in small batches to entrepreneurs, who in turn contracted with builders. Standardized designs and materials reduced the need for skilled labor and brought down overall costs.

In Chicago, Samuel Eberley Gross, who billed his operations as the largest real estate business in the world, pioneered the comprehensive real estate development, acquiring land, creating the infrastructure, subdividing, financing the construction of thousands of standardized houses, and carrying mortgages for working-class families. Massive high-pressure sales campaigns attracted unsophisticated buyers. Riverside and Grossdale, the largest developments, proved of mixed benefit. Families attracted by the Why Pay Rent campaign and by illustrated brochures touting home ownership as the key to the American Dream discovered that ownership carried many unexpected costs.

During the Panic of 1893 and the subsequent depression, many homeowners experienced foreclosure, a phenomenon that became increasingly prevalent in the next century, as mortgages came to be the standard method of financing houses. Between 1900 and 1920, home ownership remained flat at about 46 percent of American families, while the percentage of homeowners having mortgages rose from 27 to 38 percent and aggregate mortgage debt rose sixfold, to $6 billion.

BOOM AND BUST

Real estate sales as a distinct profession emerged in the United States during the 1890's. Responding to a public perception that real estate and mortgage brokers were swindlers, brokers in major cities formed professional associations, membership in which guaranteed a buyer adherence to a code of ethics. Realtor associations regulated commissions, enforced exclusivity contracts, and provided local multiple listings that during the 1920's had evolved into a nationwide network. Lobbying efforts by the National Association of Realtors played a major role in shaping the housing legislation of the New Deal era so as to favor suburban sprawl.

During the economic downturn immediately following World War I, the National Association of Realtors launched a massive campaign touting home ownership as a patriotic duty. At the same time, Henry Ford's Model T (also known as the Tin Lizzy) made the average American much more mobile. The dream home of the 1920's was a Sears, Roebuck bungalow, assembled from precut, standardized components on a generous lot well outside the central city. Sears sold roughly seventy thousand houses mail order between 1908 and 1940. Local building supply houses sold many times that number. Savings and loan associations provided financing; however, most mortgages involved balloon payments and thus carried a high risk of default. Rapidly rising land prices led to much speculation.

The real estate market began to sour in 1926, beginning with the collapse of a housing bubble in Florida, and was already in serious trouble when the stock market crashed in 1929. By 1932, new housing starts had nearly ceased and communities were devastated by massive foreclosures. Congress responded with the National Housing Act of 1934, which established the Federal Housing Administration (FHA). Heavily influenced by the real estate industry, the act gave first priority to reviving the market for single-family homes and encouraging new construction.

The key to the FHA program was (and still is) mortgage insurance. The FHA establishes guidelines for buyer creditworthiness and property value, and collects an annual insurance premium from the buyer. In return, the lender is guaranteed a full return on its investment if the buyer defaults. The 1934 act also established a system of National Home Loan Banks, operating as cooperatives, to loan mortgage money to local banks and thrift institutions. This system worked remarkably well. By 1936, housing starts had nearly regained their 1925 level. FHA-backed mortgages and veterans' benefits underwrote explosive expansion of suburbia immediately following World War II.

Levittown, Pennsylvania, seen in this aerial view around 1959, was a typical suburban development. (Courtesy, NPS)

During the 1980's, average home prices in the same markets (Florida and California) that experienced the bubble of the 1920's reached levels the FHA would no longer insure. Lenders, counting on continued rapid escalation in property values, responded by issuing riskier and more costly mortgages and selling bundled mortgages to investors. Freed from the constraints imposed by the FHA, real estate markets in many parts of the country underwent exponential growth.

That growth came to an abrupt halt in 2007 with a wave of defaults and foreclosures and an investment community no longer willing to fund risky mortgages. As of mid-2008, the results of the meltdown of the subprime mortgage industry had spread to include a general tightening of consumer credit, rising unemployment, a fall in the stock market, and failure of a number of large financial institutions heavily invested in mortgages. Congress responded with the Foreclosure Prevention Act of 2008, which included, among other provisions, major changes to the hitherto successful FHA program.

MULTIPLE-FAMILY HOUSING

Although a majority (68.9 percent) of American households live in owner-occupied units—including single-family site-built homes, manufactured homes, and condominiums—a substantial minority are renters. The percentage of rental households stood at 53.5 in 1900, remained relatively constant until 1940, dropped below 40 percent by 1960 during the post-World War II building boom, and has declined slowly since.

From a market point-of-view, rental housing provides the investor with return both in rents and in property appreciation. For several decades, market conditions in most areas have not favored constructing new units for low- and moderate-income tenants. Increasingly, the most desirable apartments in core city areas are being renovated and sold as condominiums to urban professionals. New multiple-unit construction in suburbia also favors condominiums over rentals.

The U.S. Department of Housing and Urban Development (HUD), created in 1965, has attempted through subsidies and tax incentives to improve the stock and quality of rental housing in cities. The business of housing low-income renters has become dependent on these subsidies and is increasingly handled through state and local government and through nonprofits. There have been many scandals involving corporate diversion of HUD funds into development projects unconnected with the core mission of providing safe affordable housing to the urban poor.

MOBILE AND MANUFACTURED HOMES

Virtually unknown before World War II, mobile and manufactured homes have since become a fixture of the American housing market. During and immediately after World War II, a basic eight-by-twenty-foot sleeping unit on wheels, without plumbing, served as temporary housing for defense workers and returning veterans. During the 1950's, this evolved into a boxy twelve-by-forty-foot dwelling with kitchen and bath, technically mobile but usually permanently installed in a park or on rural land.

In 1976, when such dwellings were first included in national housing legislation, the term "manufactured home" replaced "mobile home."

During the early twenty-first century, Americans lived in 8.8 million manufactured homes, 8 percent of the nation's total housing units. These were concentrated in rural and low-income areas. The market for manufactured homes and the laws pertaining to them are a curious hybrid between real estate and motor vehicles. Older units indeed had many of the characteristics of motor vehicles, notably rapid depreciation that deprived this nominal form of home ownership of much of its long-term value. Newer manufactured homes, especially when installed on a foundation on land the buyer owns, differ rather little from lower-end site-built homes and retain their value if meticulously maintained. FHA-backed financing is available for manufactured homes. They are an important source of affordable housing, particularly in the South.

In many areas, land occupied by rental trailer parks came under pressure to be used for more lucrative developments. A tendency of local planners to welcome eradication of something regarded as an eyesore was tempered by growing recognition of the vital role manufactured-home parks play in housing lower-income workers and elderly people on limited fixed incomes.

Martha Sherwood

FURTHER READING

Duany, Andres, Elizabeth Plater, and Jeff Speck. *Suburban Nation: The Rise of Sprawl and the Decline of the American Dream*. New York: North Point Press, 2000. Contrasts the contrived development of suburbia with evolution of a village; critical of role of the FHA.

Fletcher, June. *House Poor: Pumped-Up Prices, Rising Rates, and Mortgages on Steroids*. New York: Collins, 2005. Principally concerned with runaway development in the preceding decade, declining affordability, and the shaky creative financing that fueled these trends.

Hayden, Dolores. *Building Suburbia: Green Fields and Urban Growth, 1820-2000*. New York: Pantheon Books, 2003. Thorough and well-documented account of real estate development including social and financial aspects; good coverage of the period before World War II.

Hornstein, Jeffrey M. *A Nation of Realtors: A Cultural History of the Twentieth Century American Middle Class*. Durham, N.C.: Duke University Press, 2005. Emphasizes the interaction between the real estate industry and the American political system. sociological in approach.

Wright, Russell O. *Chronology of Housing in the United States*. Jefferson, N.C.: McFarland, 2007. This time-wise look at American housing, from the arrival of the settlers to the twenty-first century, examines the transition from rural to urban life and issues such as sanitation, defense, and water supplies.

SEE ALSO: Housing and Urban Development, U.S. Department of; Land laws; Mortgage industry; Real estate industry, commercial.

Recession of 1937-1938

THE EVENT: Sharp economic downturn that was part of the Great Depression

DATE: September, 1937-June, 1938

PLACE: United States

SIGNIFICANCE: The recession demonstrated that the New Deal was having problems, and President Franklin D. Roosevelt blamed business for the economic downturn. His response was to attack business through the antitrust laws.

From the end of 1935 and into early 1936, President Franklin D. Roosevelt's New Deal was experiencing serious problems. The National Recovery Administration had been ruled unconstitutional by the U.S. Supreme Court's decision in *Schechter Poultry Corp. v. United States* (1935). The Agricultural Adjustment Act of 1933 was having problems with its use of scarcity economics, and eventually it would face an unfavorable court ruling. Even the relief programs, especially the Civil Works Administration (1933), were criticized, along with new innovations such as the Resettlement Administration (1935). Despite all this, however, Roosevelt ran in 1936 for reelection and won overwhelmingly against Alfred M. Landon. Businessmen generally backed Landon and even supported the Liberty League to stop Roosevelt's reelection, all to no avail. By the beginning of 1937, Roosevelt and the business community were on a collision course.

A series of events in 1937 caused the American economy to go into a recession which, simply put, was a depression within the Great Depression. Bearing in mind that Roosevelt had a real fear of inflation, it is not surprising that price increases were somewhat disturbing to him and his advisers. As prices rose, Roosevelt cut farm subsidies and relief programs. When the Federal Reserve raised the reserve requirement, it caused the economy to falter. Other strains on the economy included business inventory increases, the implementation of Social Security taxes, and Roosevelt's undistributed profits tax. The stock market decline in October made matters worse. It was the convergence of all these factors that brought the economy down. Industrial production dropped, national income fell, industrial stock averages plummeted nearly 50 percent, and unemployment rose.

Uncertain as to what had happened and why, Roosevelt and his advisers struggled to explain the recession. Some within the administration, such as Henry Morgenthau, Jr., thought that the lack of business confidence had contributed to the downturn and could prolong it. Others, such as Thomas Gardiner Corcoran and Benjamin V. Cohen, were not so sure. These advisers were very much against the concentration of economic power in business and wanted to break up the large corporations. Finally, still others, such as Marriner Eccles, thought that the tight money policy of the Federal Reserve had to be addressed. What really mattered is what the president thought. If actions speak louder than words, then it is clear that Roosevelt blamed business for the economic problems and agreed to launch an antitrust campaign, managed by Thurman Wesley Arnold, assistant attorney general in the Antitrust Department.

Although the antitrust campaign, which targeted price fixing and other monopolistic measures, may have caused problems for business, it was not the key to economic recovery. Rather, the Roosevelt New Deal inadvertently implemented Keynesian economics by increasing government spending to such an extent that the recession eventually ended by June, 1938.

In the end, the recession of 1937-1938 not only symbolized Roosevelt's growing antibusiness attitude but also demonstrated his moving closer and closer to Keynesianism, although he might not have realized it at the time. The consequent antitrust campaign definitely showed that business was not warmly regarded by Roosevelt.

Michael V. Namorato

FURTHER READING
Davis, Kenneth. *FDR: Into the Storm, 1937-1940.* New York: Random House, 1993.
Reagan, Patrick. *Designing a New America: The Origins of New Deal Planning, 1890-1943.* Amherst: University of Massachusetts Press, 1999.
Roose, Kenneth. *The Economics of Recession and Revival: An Interpretation of 1937-1938.* Hamden, Conn.: Archon Books, 1969.

SEE ALSO: Antitrust legislation; Business cycles; Great Depression; New Deal programs; Social Security system.

Rental industry

DEFINITION: Branch of the service sector of the economy that rents out vehicles, tools, furniture, properties, and many other products

SIGNIFICANCE: In a little more than sixty years, the American rental industry grew from a young market into a mature industry that in 2007 pumped hundreds of millions of dollars in revenues into the American economy.

Although the rental industry actually began after World War II, it was during the 1980's that conditions were ripe for its growth. President Ronald Reagan's tax-reform policies for eliminating tax investment credits and curtailing depreciation allowances for capital equipment provided companies with incentives to rent necessary equipment rather than lay out the purchase costs and then struggle to keep it operating. For years, rental companies had been mostly small, family-owned concerns, and they lacked the inventories to supply the demand in the 1980's. Rental houses that could raise the capital raced to invest in inventories and aggressively pursue industrial companies to supply the equipment they required on a short-term basis and for far less money than it would cost to buy the equipment outright.

Revenues from the equipment rental industry in 1984 reached $1.6 billion and climbed throughout the 1990's. In 1997, the number of independent

REVENUE FROM RENTAL BUSINESSES, 2000 AND 2005, IN MILLIONS OF DOLLARS

Type of Business	2000	2005
Commercial, industrial equipment rental and leasing	37,478	38,742
Passenger car rental and leasing	22,949	25,957
Truck, utility trailer, and RV rental and leasing	14,282	17,828
Video tape and disk rental	9,569	10,243
General rental center	3,636	3,791

Source: Data from the Statistical Abstract of the United States, 2008 (Washington, D.C.: Department of Commerce, Economics and Statistics Administration, Bureau of the Census, Data User Services Division, 2008)

rental agencies—many maintaining one or two stores—had reached 77 percent of the total rental agencies and the annual revenues increased to $18 billion. At this time, the thousands of separate businesses that had jostled for advantages began to merge into major rental companies. The growth of the rental industry had not peaked, as a great many industrial companies still wanted to discard the obligations of ownership and avoid the capital investment tax by renting rather than owning. The equipment rental industry, which began as a fledgling business during the 1980's, became a mature business during the early years of the twenty-first century, surviving slowdowns during the early 1990's and during the early twenty-first century but sustaining growth spurts during the late 1990's and after 2003. Amazingly, the industry even grew through the housing decline and into 2007. In 2007, revenues topped out at $36.5 billion.

The American Rental Association provides industry information to rental business owners, aids them with training employees and managing their business, and assists equipment manufacturers in locating rental agencies that need their products. The ARA breaks down the equipment rental business into three divisions: industrial and construction equipment; home-improvement or repair tools and lawn and garden implements; and apparatus for weddings or parties. The general tools for smaller do-it-yourself projects have led the market for the past decade, posting a profit of $8.5 billion for 2007. The party and special events market had revenues of $2.1 billion for 2007 and was predicted to be the strongest-performing market area of the forecast for 2007-2012.

CONSUMER PRODUCTS AND AUTOMOBILES

The consumer product rental industry, which includes digital versatile discs (DVDs), electronics, appliances, and home health equipment, generates annual revenues of $22 billion, with DVD rentals accounting for more than half the total. DVD rental stores, specifically Blockbuster, have experienced revenue losses because of online rentals, which feature convenience. Also entering the rental competition are no-return DVD's that degrade within a short period, therefore limiting their viewing time, and computer movie downloads that have limited accessibility.

The automobile rental industry, which began to grow after World War II, was connected from the beginning with the airline industry. Early rental agencies, such as Hertz and Avis, located their businesses at or near airports and advertised through the airlines. During the 1960's, a number of smaller family-owned car rental agencies arrived on the scene and provided strong competition for the older companies. Fledgling Enterprise Rent-a-Car led a trend to locate businesses in downtown neighborhoods and away from airports. During the 1980's, to improve sluggish new automobile sales, automobile manufacturers offered rental agencies new car reductions.

During the 1990's, as the automotive industry improved, the car rental industry began to struggle with extra costs. With the rise in fuel costs in 2007-2008, rental agencies found themselves struggling to meet the demand for fuel-efficient cars and hybrids, while customers struggled to pay gasoline prices that could double or triple the cost of renting a sport utility vehicle.

HOUSING

In rental housing, the vacation rental industry began during the 1970's as an offshoot of ski resorts and was assisted during the 1980's by the advent of the condominium time-share concept. In 1998, ResortQuest was formed by the merging of eleven companies that managed resort rentals and became the first nationwide vacation rental agency. Despite the travel setback following the terrorist attacks of September 11, 2001, the industry in 2004-2007 was in a strong growth cycle. The revenues for vacation rentals in 2007, according to some estimates, reached $63 billion, or about half the annual revenues for hotels. Some rental entrepreneurs see vacation rentals in direct competition with hotels and find that advertising online is a valuable tool for making customers aware of rental homes and condos as well as for debunking the myth that rental vacation houses and condos are much more expensive than hotels.

Although many rental homes in 2007-2008 were afflicted by record foreclosures and the immediate eviction of the occupants, foreclosures also affected the availability of low-cost housing. During this time period, the number of landlords defaulting on their mortgages increased. This led to foreclosed and abandoned rental properties, diminishing the number of units available to people and raising the rent on existing rental properties.

Mary Hurd

FURTHER READING

Ault, Suzanne. "Kiosks Nip Rental Biz." *Video Business*, December 18, 2006. Kiosk Operator, Redbox, co-owned by McDonalds, bites into traditional video rental revenues with one-dollar-a-night DVDs.

Bensinger, Ken. "Car Rental Companies Caught Short as Demand for Smaller Vehicles Soars." *Los Angeles Times*, July 14, 2008. Analyzes the pressures felt by car rental agencies from major carmakers in 2008 who have stopped selling new cars to rental companies at a discount, and who pay less to the rental agencies in the buy-back.

Krueger, Luke. *A Noble Function: How U-Haul Moved America.* Fort Lee, N.J.: Barricade Books, 2007. The story of U-Haul, a major moving truck rental company, from its beginnings.

Phillips, Kevin. *Bad Money: Reckless Finance, Failed Politics, and the Global Crisis of American Capitalism.* New York: Viking Adult, 2008. Discusses America's economic policies, mounting debt, mortgage and housing crisis, and rising fuel costs as indicators of a national crisis that foreshadows the end of America's dominance in the world market.

Retsinas, Nicholas, and Eric S. Belsky, eds. *Revisiting Rental Housing: Policies, Programs, and Priorities.* Washington, D.C.: Brookings Institute, 2008. Examines rental housing with respect to governmental policies, including subsidized housing.

SEE ALSO: Real estate industry, commercial; Real estate industry, residential; Retail trade industry; Video rental industry.

Restaurant industry

DEFINITION: Industry providing meals and refreshments in sit-down dining facilities and through take-out establishments

SIGNIFICANCE: Since the early twentieth century, the American restaurant industry has boomed and made a major contribution to the transformation of American culture. A significant part of the twenty-first century American economy, the industry is one of the leading employers of workers—particularly teenagers—in the private sector.

The huge American restaurant industry is largely a late twentieth century and early twenty-first century development. Before the mid-twentieth century, few American ate out frequently. During the nineteenth century, restaurants catered primarily to members of both the upper and the lower classes. High-class restaurants, such as Delmonico's, which opened in New York City in 1845, offered exquisite cuisine to the wealthy. Upscale hotels followed suit by adding fine dining establishments to serve their own guests. At the other end of the economic scale, members of the urban lower class, many of whose abodes lacked kitchens, patronized saloons and cheap "eating houses" that served only the most basic fare. Members of the middle class rarely dined out, unless they were traveling. In 1870, the general public was introduced to the first chain restaurants, the Harvey Houses, which were located by train stations. Other restaurant chains soon followed.

In 1921, White Castle became the first hamburger chain. Between 1923 and 1931, it opened one hundred of its restaurants throughout the United States. Over the ensuing years, the chain improved the nutritional content of its hamburgers and worked to develop standards that would ensure consistent quality. During the 1930's, White Castle became the first restaurant chain to sell food through takeout windows, and it began issuing coupons in newspapers to increase demand. As part of its 1930's marketing campaign, White Castle hired women as "Julia Joyce" hostesses, who gave women tours of the restaurants to show off their cleanliness. Visitors were also given 10-cent hamburgers to take home to promote the concept of carry-out service for families.

NATIONAL RESTAURANT ASSOCIATION

In 1919, the National Restaurant Association (NRA) was established in Kansas City, Missouri. It became a powerful advocate for the industry by lobbying and influencing legislation and providing education to restaurant operators. Over the years, the NRA has used national advertising campaigns to influence public buying habits. The NRA developed advertising campaigns to promote dining out with such slogans as Enjoy Life—Eat Out More Often and Take Her Out to Dinner at Least Once a Week. These campaigns helped popularize the concept of chain restaurants, as increasing numbers of middle-class Americans began dining out. Before World War II, the NRA estimated that American restaurants served about twenty million meals per day. After the war, the NRA reported that restaurants were serving sixty million meals a day.

LATE TWENTIETH CENTURY TRENDS

The advent of what would become known as the fast-food industry is generally dated to 1955, when Ray Kroc opened the first McDonald's franchise in Illinois. The first McDonald's restaurants were drive-ins with carhops. After Kroc took over McDonald's from its founders, he developed their assembly-line food-production system, eliminated carhops, and cut the cost of meals in half. The success of McDonald's production method soon inspired imitators, such as Burger King and Taco Bell. Meanwhile, the NRA began endorsing take-home meals that families could enjoy while watching television, one of the great technological innovations of the same era.

Between 1930 and 1960, restaurant chains proliferated, and during the 1960's, chains such as McDonald's, Kentucky Fried Chicken (later KFC), and Denny's began going public. Meanwhile, full-service restaurant chains were becoming major players. In 1968, Red Lobster was founded, followed by the Cheesecake Factory and Ruby Tuesday in 1972, Chili's in 1975, and Damon's in 1979. Starbucks coffee houses—which would become a twenty-first century sensation—began in 1971.

The 1970's also saw the advent of conglomerates, with Pizza Hut and Kentucky Fried Chicken being bought by PepsiCo, which also purchased Taco Bell in 1978. The trends of the 1970's continued into the 1980's and 1990's with restaurants being bought and sold like commodities. In 1997, PepsiCo spun off its fast-food restaurants to create Tricon Global Restaurants, which acquired Long John Silver's and

A Harvey House at the depot in the Atchison, Topeka and Santa Fe Railroad yard in Needles, California, in 1943. (Library of Congress)

A&W Restaurants and became Yum! Brands in 2002. In 1995, General Mills spun off Darden, a group of casual-dining chain restaurants, that began with Red Lobster and grew to also contain, as of 2008, Olive Garden, LongHorn Steakhouse, The Capital Grille, Bahama Breeze, and Seasons 52.

TWENTY-FIRST CENTURY TRENDS

The growth of the modern restaurant industry can be seen in NRA figures for total industry sales. In 1970, restaurants took in $42.8 billion. In 2008, they took in $558 billion—a thirteenfold increase in less than four decades. By 2008, Americans were spending 48 percent of their food dollars at restaurants, a figure nearly double that of four decades earlier. The 13.1 million workers employed by 945,000 American restaurants made the restaurant industry the largest private sector employer in the United States. Indeed, about 9 percent of all salaried persons in the American workforce are employed in food service industries.

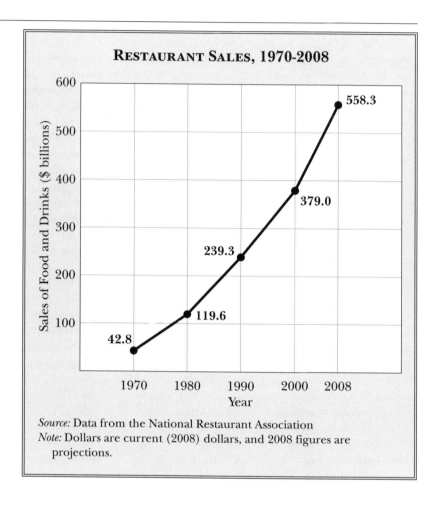

RESTAURANT SALES, 1970-2008

Source: Data from the National Restaurant Association
Note: Dollars are current (2008) dollars, and 2008 figures are projections.

Despite its remarkable growth, the restaurant industry encountered a number of problems during the first decade of the twenty-first century. Some of the major mergers and expansions were not working well. Examples included the merger of Wendy's and Tim Hortons (coffee and doughnut chain) and the McDonald's acquisition of the Donatos pizza chain. Other chains were encountering problems from overly rapid expansion. Examples included Boston Market, Bob Evans, and Starbucks. Bad publicity was also damaging the industry, thanks in large part to Eric Schlosser's 2001 book, *Fast Food Nation: The Dark Side of the All-American Meal*, and Morgan Spurlock's 2004 film documentary, *Super Size Me*, both of which blamed the fast-food industry for much of the nation's health and obesity problems.

In response, many restaurants added more healthful options to their menus. Government agencies also increased their regulatory oversight of the industry. In 2007, for example, New York City voted to ban transaturated fats in restaurant cooking. Although an NRA spokesperson countered that the city's ban was misguided and could be challenged legally, many chains such as Wendy's subsequently discontinued using transaturated fats in response to public pressures.

Marsha M. Huber

FURTHER READING

Anderson, Steven C., and Steven Steinhauser. *Restaurant Industry Operations Report 2004*. Washington, D.C.: National Restaurant Association, 2005. Annual industry report giving industry statistics based on market segment and sales volume.

Hogan, David. *Selling 'em by the Sack: White Castle and the Creation of American Food*. New York: New York University Press, 1999. History of the restaurant industry, focusing on the White Castle hamburger chain.

Jakle, John A., and Keith A. Sculle. *Fast Food: Roadside Restaurants in the Automobile Age*. Baltimore: Johns Hopkins University Press, 1999. Well-researched and illustrated study of the culture of the automobile and quick-service restaurants.

Love, John F. *McDonald's: Behind the Arches*. Rev. ed. New York: Bantam Books, 1995. Comprehensive chronicle of the rise of McDonald's, including behind-the-scenes stories. Illustrated. Index.

Mariani, John. *America Eats Out: An Illustrated History of Restaurants, Taverns, Coffee Shops, Speakeasies, and Other Establishments That Have Fed Us for 350 Years*. New York: William Morrow, 1991. Picturesque and anecdotal history of the restaurant industry.

Schlosser, Eric. *Fast Food Nation: The Dark Side of the All-American Meal*. New York: Houghton Mifflin, 2001. Strong critique of the fast-food industry and its health implications.

Spurlock, Morgan. *Don't Eat This Book: Fast Food and the Supersizing of America*. New York: G. P. Putnam's Sons, 2005. Humorous account of how the maker of the film *Super Size Me* lived solely on fast food for thirty days and the effect on his health.

SEE ALSO: Alcoholic beverage industry; Diners Club; Drive-through businesses; Fast-food restaurants; Food and Drug Administration; Food-processing industries; Hotel and motel industry; McDonald's restaurants; United Food and Commercial Workers; Vending machines.

Retail Clerks International Union. *See* United Food and Commercial Workers

Retail trade industry

DEFINITION: Enterprises that purchase products wholesale from their manufacturers or distributors and then sell them to consumers for a profit

SIGNIFICANCE: Retail trade plays a critical part in any economic system by linking producers and consumers. It also provides critical information on the value and price of goods.

In North America, Native American trade consisted of barter, since there was no money in circulation. Some tribes did use seashells or wampum as currency, but trade still resembled barter. Barter is inconvenient because of the difficulty of having items of the same value immediately ready for exchange whenever a product is needed. Still, barter survives even to the twenty-first century. The history of retail trade is one of increasing complexity alongside older forms of trade. The earliest North American colonists largely followed this pattern of barter, especially when trading with Native Americans. Still, because of their European origins, the colonists were aware of the usefulness of money as a medium for exchange and gradually introduced it into the New World.

Peddlers, whether traveling on foot, on horseback, or in wagons, were the next stage in the evolution of retail trade. Even in the most modern societies, some door-to-door sales continue to take place, as happens in the case of Girl Scout cookies, for example. Parallel with the development of peddlers was the institution of open-air markets and fairs in which goods can be exchanged through barter or the use of money. Such trade institutions survive into the modern world in the form of yard sales and flea markets.

STORES AND MAIL ORDER

Over time, the development of fixed retail sites became increasingly common, especially in towns and villages. In the smaller collections of human habitation, the most common form of fixed site retailing was the general store. As towns and villages evolved into cities, the fixed site general store developed into specialty retail stores. These specialty retail stores typically were divided between those that catered to women, such as grocery and clothing stores, and those that catered to men, such as lumber yards and heavy-equipment stores.

The general store did not disappear entirely, but it was gradually replaced by department stores in larger cities by the middle of the nineteenth century. Some of these reverted back to trade with both men and women as the size of the department stores increased dramatically. Earlier forms of retail trade did not disappear, but peddlers were often replaced by door-to-door salespeople for very specialized products.

By the end of the nineteenth century, catalog

sales had developed in which the door-to-door sales-person was, in effect, replaced by the mail carrier. The consumer would receive catalogs through the mail, would order supplies by mail, and would pay the mail carrier when he or she received the goods. The mail carrier replaced the peddler as the retail trade agent.

The mail carrier also acted as a key advertiser, supplementing the advertisements on fixed signs and in the newspapers. The retail trade has always depended on advertisements in the form of hand-bills, newspaper advertising, and mailers. By the twentieth century, first radio, then television, and still later, computers and the Internet transformed the nature of advertising. The combination of mod-ern retail outlets of all kinds and extensive advertise-ments led to what some call a consumer-oriented society. In this view, the nation's economic activ-ity depends on conspicuous consumption and planned obsolescence. From this perspective, the retail trade industry is an essential engine in the op-eration of the economy as a whole.

THE TWENTIETH CENTURY

Although some stores had always offered dis-counted merchandise, in the second half of the twentieth century, the urge for increased sales led to discount stores with a reputation for the lowest pos-sible prices. The Kresge department store led the way with a chain of stores called Kmart in 1962. Tar-get and Wal-Mart soon followed suit, with Wal-Mart eventually becoming the largest discount retail chain in the United States.

Although specialized retail outlets continued to exist, there was a return to an earlier general store concept but this time on a mammoth scale. Despite the breadth of products available in department stores during the mid-twentieth century, the 1980's saw the dawn of the age of the supercenters. The consumer was invited to shop at a massive store es-sentially containing a grocery store, drugstore, clothing store, appliance store, hardware store, fur-niture store, electronics store, photography studio, and automotive service center under a single roof.

The supercenters were pioneered in 1988 by Wal-Mart, which announced the goal of having a Wal-Mart supercenter within thirty miles of any signifi-cant population concentration in the United States. In the case of small towns, the Wal-Mart supercenter often replaced an entire downtown business district. This led to widespread complaints by small mer-chants that they were driven out of business by Wal-Mart's tremendous size and ability to purchase mer-chandise at prices far below what they could.

FRANCHISING

A franchise is defined as the right or license granted to a person or group of people to market another company's goods or services in a particu-lar territory. Implicit in this is the notion that the

---

RETAIL TRADE SALES BY KIND OF BUSINESS, 1995-2005, IN BILLIONS OF DOLLARS

Kind of Business	1995	2000	2005
Motor vehicle and parts dealers	580.8	797.6	888.3
Food and beverage stores	391.3	445.7	516.9
Gasoline stations	181.3	250.0	373.3
Building materials, garden equipment, and supply stores	164.8	229.3	327.4
Warehouse clubs and superstores	65.1	139.6	270.2
Department stores	210.9	239.9	220.5
Health and personal care stores	101.7	155.4	208.7
Clothing and clothing accessories	131.6	168.0	201.9
Electronic shopping and mail order houses	52.7	113.9	161.6
Sporting goods, hobby, book, and music stores	60.9	76.1	82.5

Source: Data from the Statistical Abstract of the United States, 2008 (Washington, D.C.: Department of Commerce, Economics and Statistics Administration, Bureau of the Census, Data User Services Division, 2008)

franchisee—the person receiving the franchise—follows the philosophy or mode of operation of the franchisor—the enterprise that has granted the franchise. The franchisor grants this right in return for a royalty fee and a percentage of the franchise's gross monthly sales. The franchisor provides intangibles such as training, advertising, and basic planning as well as the product or the machinery used to perform services. The franchisor enters into a contract with the franchisee for a specific time, usually from five to twenty years.

The franchisor is willing to do this because this business model allows for direct access to investment capital without giving up the control that the franchisor would lose if it tried to raise capital by selling stock. In some cases, franchising allows a franchisor to expand operations across the country and even across continents, where the franchisor would have a difficult time setting up business. For example, within the United States, often liquor licenses for restaurants or hotels can be acquired only by local operators, such as a franchisee. Through use of carefully worded contracts, the franchisor can operate a business far from its original location without the necessity of providing day-to-day supervision of the operations.

The franchisee benefits from being able to start a new business without having to develop a business plan for a product or service. The franchisee also benefits from whatever national or regional advertising has been done to promote the trademarked product or service. The franchisee also benefits from the training and supplies provided by the franchisor.

There are risks involved for both parties, but carefully worded contracts can minimize these problems. The franchisor suffers the danger that its trademark will be damaged by the improper or incompetent actions of the franchisee. The franchisee faces the danger of losing money expended on the business that cannot be recovered if the franchise is withdrawn.

The first franchise in the United States was granted during the 1850's by the sewing machine manufacturer, Isaac Merrit Singer. Also during this time, Western Union authorized others to use its telegraph system, while maintaining control. During the late nineteenth century, John Stith Pemberton began franchising a fountain drug, Coca-Cola. Believing that bottling his product had no future, he virtually gave away the bottling rights to Chattanooga, Tennessee, entrepreneurs, who made a fortune with their own bottling franchises.

Franchising for restaurants, motels, and fast-food enterprises began during the 1930's with A&W Root Beer. Howard Johnson began developing restaurant and motel franchises around 1935. Franchising expanded rapidly after World War II. As American consumers acquired the ability to travel widely, they showed a preference for trademarked enterprises because the products and services offered were familiar and of predictable quality. The McDonald's Corporation is one of the most successful fast-food enterprises.

COMPUTERIZED INVENTORY SYSTEMS

In addition to the new supercenter marketing concept, computerized inventory systems became available. Many retail chains began offering loyalty cards (also called rewards, points, or club cards), which the customer could use at checkout to obtain discounts on the official retail price. The stores offered discounts in return for being able to gather statistics on the kinds of products and brands that consumers were most likely to purchase. This increased retail chains' ability to determine what products to buy and in what quantities. This increased the stores' profit and allowed them to offer more competitive prices.

The most successful computerized concept developed so far has been that of Wal-Mart. Its computerized inventory system is so sophisticated that every time a customer goes through the checkout line in any Wal-Mart store, the bar code of the computerized system provides a record of the precise item the customer purchased. When sufficient quantities of products have been sold across the entire system, new quantities can be purchased. Because the purchases are recorded on an individual store basis, Wal-Mart can calculate how much to purchase and ship to each of its individual locations. This enables Wal-Mart to avoid the loss of sales because products were not available when customers wanted them and also to avoid the danger of overstocking items. Given the massive buying power of the Wal-Mart chain, this new computerized system has made Wal-Mart one of the most efficient retail chains in the world, earning record profits.

Although many characteristics of the retail trade industry have changed over the last few centuries, it continues to be true that the retail trade industry forms a critical link between producers and consumers and also provides critical information on products and prices for the entire economic system.

Richard L. Wilson

FURTHER READING

Benson, John, and Gareth Shaw, eds. *The Retailing Industry.* 3 vols. London: Macmillan, 1999. One of the most comprehensive examinations of retailing available.

Crossick, Geoffrey, and Serge Jaumain. *Cathedrals of Consumption.* Brookfield, Vt.: Ashgate, 1999. The architecture as an aspect of the retail industry is considered in this monograph.

Davis, Dorothy. *A History of Shopping.* Toronto: Toronto University Press, 1996. A general overview of retailing as shopping.

Dow, Louis A., and Fred Hendon. *Economics and Society.* Englewood Cliffs, N.J.: Prentice Hall, 1991. Strongly influenced by the free-market economics of Adam Smith, these coauthors look at economics in a societal context.

Willis, James. *Explorations in Microeconomics.* 5th ed. Redding, Calif.: North West, 2002. This mainstream text examines construction from a microeconomic perspective explaining the impact of retailing in the individual firm.

Wrigley, Neil. *Reading Retail: A Geographic Perspective on Retail and Consumption Spaces.* New York: Arnold, 2002. A theoretical perspective on the important issue of geographic location on retailing.

Wrigley, Neil, and Michelle Lowe. *Retailing, Consumption, and Capital: Towards the NEW Retail Geography.* London: Harlow, 1996. Economic and geographic theories are paramount in this study of retailing.

SEE ALSO: Catalog shopping; Christmas marketing; Credit card buying; Great Atlantic and Pacific Tea Company; Home Shopping Network; Montgomery Ward; Promotional holidays; Sears, Roebuck and Company; Thrift stores; Trading stamps; Wal-Mart; Warehouse and discount stores.

Retirement plans. *See* Pension and retirement plans

Revenue Act of 1913. *See* Underwood Tariff Act

Revolutionary War

THE EVENT: The American colonies' fight for and achieve independence from Great Britain
DATE: April 18, 1775-September 3, 1783
PLACE: Eastern North America
SIGNIFICANCE: The war established the United States as a sovereign nation, allowing it to set up its own system of taxation and trade. The newly formed nation became a strong competitor with European countries in the trade of goods as a result of its considerable natural resources.

In 1606, the London Company sponsored an expedition to Virginia; Jamestown was founded the next year. Thirteen years later, the *Mayflower* sailed to Cape Cod (now in Massachusetts). The Mayflower Compact was then created, and it established a form of local government whereby the colonists agreed generally to abide by the rule of the democracy, based on decisions that were for the general good of the colony. Other British colonies were set up in a similar manner over the next century.

The economies in the northern and southern colonies were dramatically different in the time period leading up to the Revolutionary War. In the South, the economy relied on plantations that were worked primarily by slave labor. Trading crops such as rice, corn, tobacco, sugar, and cotton with the British quickly became the backbone of the southern colonies' revenue, and they eventually sought to expand their trade to other countries in Europe and the West Indies.

In the northern colonies, wheat was the principal cash crop, while cattle, horses, and sugar were also essential to the colonies' trade with Europe and the West Indies. While large plantation owners had the lion's share of wealth in the South, merchants became the most influential group in the North, acquiring over half of the wealth in the region.

During the colonists' first century, major changes occurred to the government structure and economy of their home country, and Britain began to place restrictions on the economic freedoms that the burgeoning governments in the colonies were enjoying. Aware that the colonists had developed economic systems that were independent of Britain, a concern developed that the colonists could soon become competitors rather than resources. The Navigation Acts of 1651 and 1660 were passed, severely limiting the colonies' take in any traded goods and successfully weakening the independence that they had established. Britain also began to restrict the overall amount of the trade that the colonists could partake to detract from any competition the home country would receive from its own colonies. Although many of the causes that contributed to the Revolutionary War were yet to materialize, the economic independence that the British sought to halt might already have existed for too long, causing an eventual revolution to be inevitable.

CAUSES OF THE WAR

There are dozens, perhaps hundreds of events or situations that have been considered as causes of the Revolutionary War, but perhaps none of them is more important than the very nature of the people of the colonies. By the eighteenth century, some colonists were several generations removed from Britain and knew very little about the country that wanted to exercise control over them via their tax money and limitations on their trade. Thus, they began to resist British rule. The colonies had also grown considerably in over a century of development, and they no longer were threatened by the dangers from Native Americans, starvation, and disease that they had originally encountered. A growing perception in the colonies was that they were now capable of protecting themselves from intruders and did not need the protection or resources of Britain.

The colonists were also irritated over the effect that the tightening restrictions of the British had on their way of life. Many colonists believed that it would be nearly impossible for their economy to flourish if they were not able to govern themselves and their trade as they saw fit. This idea coincided with the strong belief that there should be no taxation without representation. In other words, taxes should not be placed on citizens unless they have a voice in the government levying the taxes. The colonists were beginning to perceive that their taxes were not being used on themselves, but rather to aid the lifestyle of Britain.

Although taxation was a central issue between the colonists and Britain, there were a number of events that took place that fueled the colonists' resentment of taxation. One of the major sources of tension was the colonists' anger at their treatment in the French and Indian War during the middle of the eighteenth century. The British and colonists eventually won the war after nearly a ten-year struggle and the brutalization of many colonists' homes and communities. The outcome of the war allowed the British to expand their territory, and they began to place heavy taxes on the colonists to pay for the war effort and the costs of maintaining their new land. This was met by heavy opposition from the colonists, many of whom were already in debt as a result of the war.

Other critical elements helped transform mere annoyance over taxes to rebellion. The Enlightenment movement was spreading ideology that was critical of government power and abuse, and it coincided with the advent of newspapers in the colonies that began to publicize the concept of revolution. The colonists also were able to watch Canadian provinces lose much of their local independence while they were being centralized, which engendered a resistant attitude to the possibility of similar centralization occurring in the American colonies.

CONDUCT OF THE WAR

As the 1770's began, there were already a series of ongoing skirmishes between colonists and British government officials. Most of these were conflicts between customs officials who were attempting to collect taxes and small groups of colonists. British military began to intercede in these skirmishes, and incidents such as the Boston Massacre further enraged the colonists. The British also passed a series of new acts that extended British taxes.

The British continued their military aggression, and on the night of April 18, 1775, Massachusetts militia men encountered British troops. They remained in a standoff, until an unauthorized shot was fired. Both sides then began to fire on each other and the Revolutionary War had begun.

The beginning of the Revolutionary War caused economic decline in the colonies. The colonists had difficulty organizing their economy to support a war effort, particularly because of the disjointed collection of states involved. The need for manpower led to a decrease in the merchandise and agricultural supplies necessary to acquire goods in trade, and this in turn decreased the success of the initial war effort. Adding to the colonists' troubles were the extreme hardships of the colonists not fighting in the war. Soldiers on both sides trampled the lands, and British soldiers commonly looted or seized colonists' houses. Despite financial assistance from Spain and France, the Continental Army often lacked food, clothes, ammunition, and cannons. Moreover, British ships blockaded the colonists' ports, which made it difficult and costly to import and export necessary goods.

The economic turmoil faced by colonists was amplified by the colonies' use of paper money and reluctance to levy taxes in order to finance the war effort. Confidence in the value of this money began to decrease, and many colonists were reluctant to sell goods in return for paper money from the Continental Army, which further deflated the value of the money. By 1780, the value of the paper money was as low as one-fortieth of what it had been before the war.

The first battles of the war were won by the British military, which had superior numbers, resources, ships, and experience in warfare. By the early 1780's, however, the British had reached a plateau in their war effort, and fatigue began to take its toll. American troops were becoming successful in nontraditional warfare, and their ranks could easily be replenished with local young men of fighting age and slaves offered freedom. The British had to wait for new arrivals and resources through ports that were now being blockaded by French ships. It was the British soldiers who now lacked food and were running low on ammunition and manpower, and the British people became weary of paying taxes to support what was increasingly seen as a losing effort.

A peace treaty was negotiated in France, where Benjamin Franklin represented the new American nation. By 1783, British forces and loyalists had left American borders, and major countries such as Russia, France, Germany, and Spain had all recognized the United States as a sovereign nation.

AFTERMATH

After the war, the United States began to draft a new constitution. The Articles of Confederation, the constitution that had been in effect during the

---

> ## MILITARY COST OF REVOLUTIONARY WAR, 1775-1783
>
> - In current year dollars = $101 million
> - In constant fiscal year (2008) dollars = $1,825 million
>
> *Source:* Data from Stephen Daggett, "CROS Report for Congress: Costs of Major U.S. Wars," Congressional Research Service, July 24, 2008

---

war, was perceived to lack sufficient provisions for central federal authority to enable the national government to oversee an entire nation. It lacked even the power necessary to tax states in the event of future wars. Thus, the U.S. Constitution was adopted in 1787, allowing greater strength to the federal government.

Despite their success in the war and newly established political order, the colonies witnessed their economic system suffer greatly long after the end of the war. They no longer enjoyed aid from the British, and their partnership with British merchants was largely diminished. Local merchants also had difficulty competing in price with imported European goods, causing many to shut down operation.

By the late 1780's, the United States' success in the trade of wheat and flour helped decrease its reliance on imported goods. The French Revolution and Napoleonic wars over the next decade would bring even greater demand for American products, representing an end to the country's economic woes and introducing it as a new power in international trade.

Brion Sever

FURTHER READING

Breen, T. H. *The Marketplace of Revolution: How Consumer Politics Shaped American Independence.* Oxford, England: Oxford University Press, 2004. Explicates some of the underlying complexities that ultimately led to the war between the colonies and the British. The book's greatest emphasis is placed on the development of the colonists as important international consumers and how this affected their relationship with the British.

Buel, Richard. *In Irons: Britain's Naval Supremacy and*

the American Revolutionary Economy. New Haven, Conn.: Yale University Press, 1998. Examines the impact of the British navy on the economies of both Britain and the colonies during the Revolutionary War.

Cook, Don. *The Long Fuse: How England Lost the American Colonies, 1760-1785.* New York: Atlantic Monthly Press, 1996. Details the causes of the Revolutionary War, with particular emphasis on some of the British government's actions that caused economic hardship to the colonists.

Ferguson, E. James. *The Power of the Purse: A History of American Public Finance, 1776-1790.* Chapel Hill: University of North Carolina Press, 1961. Analyzes economic issues surrounding the American colonies at the beginning of the Revolutionary War and into the early years of the newly formed country.

Middlekauff, Robert. *The Glorious Cause: The American Revolution,* 1763-1789. Oxford, England: Oxford University Press, 2007. Provides a comprehensive history of the Revolutionary War, including an analysis of the economic conditions that contributed to the war.

See also: Articles of Confederation; Boston Tea Party; Colonial economic systems; Constitution, U.S.; Depression of 1784; Navigation Acts; Royal Charters of North American colonies; Tea Act of 1773; War of 1812; Wars; Washington, George.

Rice industry

Definition: Enterprises that cultivate, harvest, process, and sell rice

Significance: The third most important cereal grain in the United States, after wheat and corn, rice is one of America's major food exports, as well as being used in quantity domestically.

Rice was originally domesticated in Southeast Asia and was then introduced into European cultures that settled what is now the United States in ancient times. Rice is a wetlands grass that requires substantial amounts of standing water to grow. As a result, it can be grown successfully only in areas with sufficient rainfall and irrigation. Most of the areas suitable for rice production in the United States are found in the South, where river deltas provide abundant water to keep rice fields (known as paddies) flooded.

The cultivation of rice in the American South predates the founding of the United States. A frequently related story holds that the original plantings were the result of a ship carrying rice from Madagascar being wrecked near Charleston, South Carolina. When the people of the colony there helped the sailors repair their ship, the captain left a small supply of seed rice as a token of his gratitude.

Early American rice production was generally accomplished entirely by hand, and it typically did not depend on irrigation. Rather, farmers planted rice in small patches in low-lying areas that would trap rainwater. If rainfalls proved inadequate, the crop might fail. As a result of this risky technique, successful crops were often called "providence rice." Rice was generally seen as a supplemental crop that could utilize ground unsuitable for the more usual crops of wheat and corn, rather than as a cash crop in its own right.

Progress in Production

By the turn of the twentieth century, improved cultivation techniques were being introduced even into the impoverished South. Deliberate irrigation was introduced, which made growing rice less risky. In addition, areas of rice cultivation began to move westward, away from the traditional Atlantic coastal regions to Louisiana, Texas, and California. In California, large numbers of Chinese and Japanese immigrants created a strong demand for their traditional rice-based cuisine. Anglo-Americans were also consuming increasing amounts of rice.

By the late twentieth century, rice production in the United States had become heavily commercialized and mechanized. High labor costs made it impractical to transplant rice plants from nursery fields into the fields from which they would be harvested, as was the normal practice in Asian countries. Instead, heavy machinery tilled and leveled the fields to the exact degree of slope necessary to hold the water in which the rice would grow. To avoid leaving ruts as a tractor-drawn planter or drill might do, seeding was often done by a low-flying airplane similar to a crop duster. Similarly, herbicides and insecticides were generally applied from the air.

At harvest time, the water would be pumped out of the paddy and the rice allowed to dry before being harvested. Because the ground was often still moist, combine harvesters used in rice production often would have rubber or steel tracks rather than wheels to reduce compaction.

THE GREEN REVOLUTION

American rice production benefited relatively early from the development of genetic science. Although scientific breeding of rice lagged behind that of corn and wheat, largely as a result of the historic impoverishment of the South after the U.S. Civil War, by the second half of the twentieth century scientists were examining how rice production might be increased by selective breeding. The original impetus for genetic improvement of rice was demand by American commercial rice producers. As humanitarian interests noticed the practicality of greatly increased rice yields, however, they realized that it would be possible to make these high-yielding rice strains available to impoverished countries. In theory, such "super rice" could banish hunger.

However, the realities proved somewhat less than the idealists had hoped. Much of the impressive yield enjoyed by American rice farmers using improved strains came from a synergy between the genetic strengths of the rice and the scientific application of artificial fertilizers that were generally unavailable to farmers in developing nations.

In addition, there were serious questions as to whether American commercial farming techniques were actually beneficial in the long term, even within the American context. For instance, rice was being grown for export in many areas only because of relatively cheap electric or gasoline-powered pumps that could transport water in quantity from rivers and aquifers (underground water-bearing structures), when in fact other, less water-demanding crops might have been better choices for the region. In addition, there was evidence that the use of intensive irrigation was leading to destructive salt deposits in rice fields. Finally, artificial fertilizers seemed increasingly dangerous to the environment, because when they washed out to sea, they contrib-

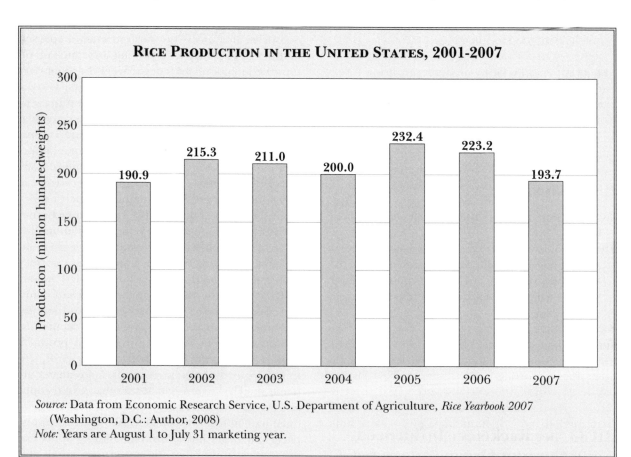

Source: Data from Economic Research Service, U.S. Department of Agriculture, *Rice Yearbook 2007* (Washington, D.C.: Author, 2008)

Note: Years are August 1 to July 31 marketing year.

uted to the growth of algal blooms that created vast oceanic "dead zones," in which fish could not survive.

Even in the twenty-first century, American rice production remained atypical as compared with that of other nations. While most rice-producing countries consumed their own harvests at home, as much as 60 percent of American rice crops were exported, either commercially or as part of food-assistance programs to impoverished countries. In addition, much of the rice used domestically was in highly processed forms, such as rice cakes and puffed rice breakfast cereals. However, there was a small but increasing demand for organically grown rice, which would generally be consumed as brown rice rather than in processed forms.

Leigh Husband Kimmel

FURTHER READING

Clay, Jason. *World Agriculture and the Environment.* Washington, D.C.: Island Press, 2004. Includes a study of the environmental effects of raising rice, both in the United States and abroad.

Hazell, P. R. B. *The Green Revolution Reconsidered: The Impact of High-Yielding Rice Varieties in South India.* Baltimore: Johns Hopkins University Press, 1991. Critical overview of factors causing rice varieties that produced well in American agriculture to fail to meet expectations in the developing world.

Midkiff, Ken. *Not A Drop to Drink: America's Water Crisis.* Novaro, Calif.: New World Library, 2007. Includes information on the problems involved in growing rice in Texas and California, where rice crops drain aquifers faster than they are replenished.

The New American Farmer: Profiles of Agricultural Innovation. 2d ed. Belleville, Md.: Sustainable Agriculture Network, 2000. Includes profile of a California farmer growing rice without intensive fertilizer use.

SEE ALSO: Agribusiness; Agriculture; Cereal crops; Colonial economic systems; Farm labor; Food-processing industries.

RICO. *See* Racketeer Influenced and Corrupt Organizations Act

Robber barons

DEFINITION: Derogatory, late nineteenth century term for extremely successful American business leaders who seized control of entire industries

SIGNIFICANCE: The robber barons transformed American business after the U.S. Civil War, helping found the modern, industrialized economy of the twentieth century. They developed techniques of organization and administration that led to the creation of expansive new industrial and financial enterprises. They revolutionized industrial production by pioneering a host of technological innovations, increasing output and lowering prices.

The term "robber baron" is synonymous with the highly successful U.S. business leaders of the later part of the nineteenth century. It is meant to conjure images of the predatory, feudal barons of the medieval period and was first used to describe the entrepreneurs, such as Jay Gould, who revolutionized the railroad industry through the ruthless takeover of smaller lines to create large, integrated track networks. Such men were viewed as villains or pirates who manipulated stock markets for their own financial gain.

As other avenues of American business grew to unprecedented proportions, the term was used to describe the captains of all types of American industry. These men amassed tremendous personal fortunes by developing huge business organizations through which they could control all aspects of their industries. The foremost examples of such robber barons are John D. Rockefeller and Andrew Carnegie. Rockefeller created the Standard Oil monolith by taking advantage of a lack of antitrust legislation. By 1880, Standard Oil was the largest and most powerful corporation in the nation. In 1884, it owned 77 percent of the refining capacity of the United States and marketed 85 percent of the country's petroleum products. A vertically integrated monopoly, the company eventually controlled oil products from the well to the consumer.

Carnegie Steel was also vertically integrated. Carnegie quickly discovered that immense profits could be made if he could control every stage of steel production. Ultimately, Carnegie Steel controlled all aspects of manufacturing from the mining of the ore to the sale of finished steel rails. Carnegie combined this level of control with harsh financial practices, such as paying very low employee wages, in order to slash consumer prices.

These men, along with others such as Philip Armour, Edward H. Harriman, J. P. Morgan, Gustavus Swift, and Cornelius Vanderbilt, with their colossal personal fortunes, became leaders of the new ruling class in American society. As such, they were often characterized as villainous scoundrels whose manipulations and ruthless business practices were responsible for the vast economic and social changes that industrialization brought the United States. These men were members of the last generation of American businessmen to operate in a relatively open and fluid environment that allowed unscrupulous practices and rewarded them with immense personal profit. The robber barons played this competitive game so well that they destroyed the system that created them, and American business leadership after them would be dominated by managers, corporate bureaucrats, and restrictive legislation.

Amanda J. Bahr-Evola

FURTHER READING

Josephson, Matthew. *The Robber Barons: The Great American Capitalists, 1861-1901.* San Diego, Calif.: Harcourt Brace, 1995.

Klein, Maury. "The Robber Barons." *American History Illustrated* 6, no.6 (1971): 12-22.

Morris, Charles R. *The Tycoons: How Andrew Carnegie, John D. Rockefeller, Jay Gould, and J. P. Morgan Invented the American Supereconomy.* New York: Holt Paperbacks, 2006.

SEE ALSO: Carnegie, Andrew; Gould, Jay; Morgan, J. P.; Muckraking journalism; Rockefeller, John D.; Vanderbilt, Cornelius.

Rockefeller, John D.

IDENTIFICATION: American businessman who created the Standard Oil Company
BORN: July 8, 1839; Richford, New York
DIED: May 23, 1937; Ormond Beach, Florida
SIGNIFICANCE: Rockefeller created a near monopoly of the oil industry with the Standard Oil Company and established the model for philanthropic foundations. Monopoly charges brought by the U.S. government and supported by a 1911 U.S. Supreme Court decision forced the breakup of Standard Oil.

John D. Rockefeller was born into a French Huguenot family that in the seventeenth century fled to Germany, where they changed the spelling of their last name from Roquefeuilles to Rockefeller. The Rockefellers emigrated to Philadelphia in 1723 and eventually settled in Richford in upstate New York. Rockefeller's father was frequently absent, and the family suffered both poverty and squalor. At the age of seven, John D. Rockefeller was already contributing to the family income. Under the puritanical upbringing of his mother, he learned the virtues of thrift, self-reliance, hard work, and enterprise. The young Rockefeller quickly established goals and pursued them to successful completion. His mother's altruism is usually given as the probable origin of Rockefeller's later philanthropy.

The militant evangelicalism of 1820's New York influenced Rockefeller to oppose smoking, dancing, playing cards or billiards, attending the theater, and doing business on Sunday. As a Christian soldier against temptation, Rockefeller was committed to personal self-improvement, the quest for perfection, and respect for women. His father's failure to provide an adequate income and his later legal difficulties forced the family to make periodic moves, finally settling near Cleveland, Ohio, where John D. Rockefeller was employed as a collection agent for a rental property. By this time, he had learned that in a rapidly industrializing America, one could run a business both in complete disregard and in violation of governmental rules without penalty.

As Cleveland was a major refining center in the United States, Rockefeller directed his business acumen to the oil industry. By 1870, he had created the Standard Oil Company of Ohio and skillfully eliminated his competition by working with the railroads to receive rebates, using predatory pricing to drive out competitors, conducting industrial espionage, bribing politicians, and making advantageous deals with oil producers, refiners, transporters, railroads, marketers, and bank directors. By 1900, Rockefeller controlled 90 percent of the oil industry and was regarded as America's first billionaire.

Rockefeller successfully escaped federal investigations until Theodore Roosevelt's assumption of the presidency. Roosevelt's progressive antitrust agenda and muckraker Ida Tarbell's hugely success-

John D. Rockefeller. (Library of Congress)

ful 1904 publication of *The History of the Standard Oil Company* tarnished both Rockefeller and his company. The Supreme Court decision in *Standard Oil Co. v. United States* (1911), ordered the breakup of the Standard Oil Company into thirty-four new companies under the 1890 Sherman Antitrust Act, because the company had illegally engaged in discrimination in its use of private tank cars, in its classification of and rules regarding shipment, and in setting public rates and secret railroad rates. Evidence showed that Standard Oil had set excessive prices where no competition existed, cut prices when there were competitors, and bought out competitors. Emerging from the breakup of the Standard Oil Company were twentieth century oil giants Exxon, Mobil, Chevron, Amoco, Arco, Conoco, Sohio, and Marathon Oil.

Rockefeller resigned as the head of the Standard Oil Company after the Supreme Court decision. Although he accepted the court verdict, it is doubtful that he forgot the drubbing his public image took. Rockefeller, never a man to reveal his true feelings, retired from the business world but proceeded to engage in philanthropic pursuits, establishing the model future charitable foundations would follow to both distribute and make money.

William A. Paquette

FURTHER READING

Chernow, Ron. *Titan: The Life of John D. Rockefeller, Sr.* New York: Random House, 1998.

Nevins, Allan. *John D. Rockefeller, Industrialist and Philanthropist.* Norwalk, Conn.: Easton Press, 1989.

Weinberg, Steve. *Taking on the Trust: The Epic Battle of Ida Tarbell and John D. Rockefeller.* New York: W. W. Norton, 2008.

SEE ALSO: Antitrust legislation; Business crimes; Getty, J. Paul; Muckraking journalism; Panic of 1907; Petroleum industry; Prohibition; Robber barons; Sherman Antitrust Act; Standard Oil Company.

Royal Charters of North American colonies

DEFINITION: Legal documents of incorporation issued by British monarchs that granted land to individuals or groups for colonization

SIGNIFICANCE: Initially, the royal charters provided support for early North American colonial farms and businesses, but later, monarchs used the charter's powers to impose taxes and regulations on the colonists, creating the impediments to colonial economic activity that laid the basis for the Revolutionary War.

England began colonizing North America about one hundred years after the Spanish began their colonization of the New World and decades after many other European nations started colonies. Although most European monarchs retained fairly tight political control over their colonies, the English and Dutch, in accordance with their commercial experience, allowed greater political freedom by using joint-stock companies and proprietary charters. For example, the original Jamestown settlement was based on a joint-stock company with British government approval.

Without charters of some kind, it would have been difficult for any colonization to take place. Initially, British monarchs did not object to joint-stock or proprietary charters as long as some colonization took place. Although the English explorers and colonists did not find much in the way of precious metals, they did prosper by growing tobacco, rice, and sugar. They also used the abundant New World forests for lumber—which had become scarce in England—to build ships.

King James II preferred a much more rapid development of the North American colonies and much tighter control. In some cases, he revoked earlier proprietary charters and required those colonies to accept royal charters. James saw a potential for profit from other economic activities. Colonial economic activity increased under this king, but the change to royal charters was one of the lesser charges that led to James's abdication in the Glorious Revolution.

King James II's successors did not govern the North American colonies harshly over the next eighty years, but eventually the British government came to view the cost of defending the North American colonies as too great to pay from existing revenues and imposed an increasing number of taxes and other punitive requirements on the colonies, which inhibited economic activity. Overall royal charters encouraged economic activity, but the punitive regulations in the eighteenth century were counterproductive. Whatever economic gains the British Crown got from royal charters were lost when its thirteen American colonies successfully rebelled and gained their independence. Economic activity was restrained by the perceived harshness of British rule, and business activity was often curtailed.

Richard L. Wilson

FURTHER READING

Canny, Nicholas. *The Origins of Empire: British Overseas Enterprise to the Close of the Seventeenth Century.* Vol. 1 in *The Oxford History of the British Empire.* New York: Oxford University Press, 2001.

Newman, Peter C. *Empire of the Bay.* Toronto: Madison Press Books, 1989.

Taylor, Alan. *American Colonies.* New York: Viking, 2001.

SEE ALSO: Colonial economic systems; Incorporation laws; Parliamentary Charter of 1763; Revolutionary War.

Rubber industry

DEFINITION: Enterprises that grow, harvest, process, market, and distribute rubber, as well as those that fashion it into products—primarily automobile tires—and market and distribute those products

SIGNIFICANCE: Were it not for the vulcanization of rubber and its subsequent development into tires, the automobile might never have become popular. Although there are other uses for rubber, it is the automobile tire that represents the main product of the industry—an industry dependent on resources originating in underdeveloped regions of the globe.

The name rubber came from the substance used to "rub" out pencil marks, but during the 1850's, the substance quickly developed into a raw material used in footwear and industry belting products. Most manufacturers of rubber products are, and have always been, in Europe and the United States, but the raw materials for these factories are grown in Southeast Asia and Africa. Rubber is obtained from the sap of a variety of plants, most commonly from what is known as the rubber tree. Approximately four hundred other plants, including common milkweed, contain the latex necessary to make rubber. However, most of these other plants contain such low levels of latex that commercial production using them would not be practical.

The rubber tree originated in South America and was unknown in Europe until Christopher Columbus returned with rubber balls used in Indian games. Raw rubber is not particularly useful, because it eventually rots, so it was not until Charles Goodyear obtained the patent on the vulcanization process in 1844 that rubber became anything more than a toy. The vulcanization process involves adding sulfur to raw rubber and then heating the mixture. L. Candee, a footwear manufacturing company in New Haven, Connecticut, was the first licensee of the Goodyear process.

Initially, all raw rubber came from wild trees in South America, but this source became inadequate by the late 1870's. Because of high prices and inconsistent quality, rubber manufacturers began raising rubber trees as domestic farm crops. Because rubber trees will grow only within about ten degrees of the equator, in climates where there is more than one hundred inches of rain annually, the obvious sites for plantations were in Southeast Asia and Africa. Virtually all contemporary rubber is grown in Malaysia, Singapore, India, Sri Lanka, and Nigeria.

With the invention of automobiles, tire manufacturing consumed a larger percentage of the rubber crop. The tire factories sprang up in various locations, but a large number were in Ohio (mostly around Akron), Massachusetts, and California. These three states produced nearly all of America's automobile tires during the 1920's.

Other components of the rubber industry include manufacturers of synthetic rubber and recyclers of rubber. Synthetic rubber gained importance during World War II, when the United States had its raw material supply from Asia cut off by the war. Ingredients of synthetic rubber include coal, grain, and petroleum. During the late twentieth century, rubber recyclers grew in importance. These companies acquire old, worn-out tires and reprocess them into new rubber, or use them as fuel.

The rubber industry has been at the foundation of the transportation industry for a century. Without rubber to cushion the ride, it is questionable whether automobiles would have ever achieved their present status.

Dale L. Flesher

The stockroom of a large automobile tire factory in Akron, Ohio, in 1917. (Library of Congress)

FURTHER READING

Korman, Richard. *The Goodyear Story: An Inventor's Obsession and Struggle for a Rubber Monopoly.* San Francisco, Calif.: Encounter Books, 2002.

Slack, Charles. *Noble Obsession: Charles Goodyear, Thomas Hancock, and the Race to Unlock the Greatest Industrial Secret of the Nineteenth Century.* New York: Hyperion, 2002.

Sull, Donald N., Richard S. Tedlow, and Richard S. Rosenbloom. *Managerial Commitments and Technological Change in the U.S. Tire Industry.* Boston: Harvard Business School, 1997.

SEE ALSO: Agribusiness; Agriculture, U.S. Department of; Automotive industry; Chemical industries; Trucking industry; World War II.

S

Sales taxes

DEFINITION: Consumption taxes on sales of products principally paid by end users but collected by sellers and forwarded to the government

SIGNIFICANCE: Sales taxes are a burden to businesses in the sense that they must be collected by the retailer, whose cost of collection must be considered as a cost of doing business. However, collecting these taxes may be preferred by businesses to paying the higher income or property taxes that would be necessary in their absence.

Sales taxes are a form of consumption tax. They are used in forty-five of the fifty states within the United States: Only New Hampshire, Delaware, Montana, Oregon, and Alaska have no sales tax, and Hawaii's sales tax is charged to businesses rather than directly to consumers. For the first 130 years of American history, state governments were small and relied on taxes on businesses or property for their revenue. The first state to use a sales tax was West Virginia in 1921. The number of states using a sales tax jumped during the Great Depression, and by 1940, some thirty states had a sales tax.

CONSUMPTION TAXES

Sales taxes are one of several kinds of consumption taxes used in the United States. Other consumption taxes are business or vendor taxes, luxury or consumer excise taxes, tariffs, and value-added taxes. Business or vendor taxes are used in many states. They are sometimes regarded as business privilege taxes, but because they can be passed on to the consumer in most cases, they are in fact a form of sales tax. Luxury, consumer excise, or excise taxes are also used with some frequency, but total revenue gain from such taxes tends to be small. Tariffs, especially revenue tariffs as opposed to protective tariffs, were imposed throughout the nineteenth century by the federal government, but they have been substantially reduced or eliminated as the United States attempted to promote international free trade.

Value-added taxes (VATs) are a major source of government revenue in Western Europe, Mexico, and in certain other countries around the globe. In Western Europe, the value-added tax requires all businesses to remit taxes on their total sales, although they can recoup the amount of the value-added tax that they pay to manufacturers and suppliers. This avoids cascading taxes and simplifies the government's job because it does not have to determine which items are taxable. Refunding the amount of the value-added tax paid to manufacturers by the final seller creates a paperwork problem for businesses in European countries, but it is generally believed that this paperwork is less onerous than the federal corporate and individual income taxes paid in the United States.

ADVANTAGES AND DISADVANTAGES

Although all taxes have some negative impact on total economic activity, taxes are clearly necessary if the government is going to provide the safe environment that makes it possible for businesses to avoid theft and destruction. The sales tax is a fair tax in the sense that the percentage of the tax paid at the point of purchase is uniform. A sales tax is difficult to avoid, is easy to calculate, and therefore has a high compliance rate. In the United States, the tax is paid only by the final purchaser, which avoids any cascading that might occur if the tax were imposed at several stages in the process of manufacture and sale. Because businessmen collect the tax and forward it to the state, it is highly attractive to state governments. State legislatures can exempt some industries from the application of the sales tax. Such exemptions are very widespread among the forty-five states that impose a sales tax, although granting exemptions makes the tax less fair.

One of the most important advantages of the sales tax is that it encourages saving rather than spending. While encouraging spending is important for the consumer part of the economy, most economists recognize that the United States has the lowest savings rates in the world. Therefore, the sales tax can be said to have a beneficial impact on the total economic strength of the nation, even if it limits consumer purchases that are important to some businesses.

The advantages and disadvantages of sales taxes need to be compared with those of income and property taxes, which are the chief alternatives to

State Sales Tax Rates as of January 1, 2008

State	Tax Rate (%)	Exemptions (Y = yes; N = no; %) Food	Prescription Drugs	Nonprescription Drugs	State	Tax Rate (%)	Exemptions (Y = yes; N = no; %) Food	Prescription Drugs	Nonprescription Drugs
Alabama	4	N	Y	N	Montana	none	none	none	none
Alaska	none	none	none	none	Nebraska	5.5	Y	Y	N
Arizona	5.6	Y	Y	N	Nevada	6.5	Y	Y	N
Arkansas	6	3	Y	N	New Hampshire	none	none	none	none
California	7.25	Y	Y	N	New Jersey	7	Y	Y	Y
Colorado	2.9	Y	Y	N	New Mexico	5	Y	Y	N
Connecticut	6	Y	Y	Y	New York	4	Y	Y	Y
Delaware	none	none	none	none	North Carolina	4.25	Y	Y	N
Florida	6	Y	Y	Y	North Dakota	5	Y	Y	N
Georgia	4	Y	Y	N	Ohio	5.5	Y	Y	N
Hawaii	4	N	Y	N	Oklahoma	4.5	N	Y	N
Idaho	6	N	Y	N	Oregon	none	none	none	none
Illinois	6.25	1	1	1	Pennsylvania	6	Y	Y	Y
Indiana	6	Y	Y	N	Rhode Island	7	Y	Y	Y
Iowa	5	Y	Y	N	South Carolina	6	Y	Y	N
Kansas	5.3	N	Y	N	South Dakota	4	N	Y	N
Kentucky	6	Y	Y	N	Tennessee	7	5.5	Y	N
Louisiana	4	Y	Y	N	Texas	6.25	Y	Y	Y
Maine	5	Y	Y	N	Utah	4.65	1.75	Y	N
Maryland	6	Y	Y	Y	Vermont	6	Y	Y	Y
Massachusetts	5	Y	Y	N	Virginia	5	2.5	Y	Y
Michigan	6	Y	Y	N	Washington	6.5	Y	Y	N
Minnesota	6.5	Y	Y	Y	West Virginia	6	4	Y	N
Mississippi	7	N	Y	N	Wisconsin	5	Y	Y	N
Missouri	4.225	1.225	Y	N	Wyoming	4	Y	Y	N
					District of Columbia	5.75	Y	Y	Y

Source: Data from Federation of Tax Administrators

Note: Tax rates for California and Virginia include a 1% statewide local tax. Scheduled changes for 2008 included increases in the state tax to 6% for Maryland and to 4.5% for North Carolina, and a decrease in the food tax rate to 3% for West Virginia. Food sales are subject to local sales taxes in Arkansas, Georgia, Louisiana, North Carolina, and Utah.

consumption taxes. Many economists favor income taxes, because income is required for any money to be available to pay the tax. Because an income tax can be proportional or progressive (with higher rates for higher incomes), an income tax can be viewed as the fairest tax. However, the process of calculating income is far more difficult than determining a sales price, and evasion is a very significant problem. Property taxes are problematic in that owning property, whether real or personal, is not the same as having cash. When property taxes are used to generate revenue, most local governments make exceptions for elderly, low-income property owners, who might be forced to sell their homes if they lack the money to pay the taxes. A number of economists also object to property taxes as taxes on accumulated wealth. In general, the federal government gains most of its revenue from income tax, states gain most of their revenue from sales taxes, and local governments receive most of their revenue from property taxes. When the system is viewed as a whole, it appears that the United States generally seeks a moderate outcome by using all three forms of taxes.

This chief objection to sales taxes is that they are regressive in their effect on low-income people because they are not proportional to income. High-income people can avoid paying sales taxes by simply curtailing their purchases—something low-income people cannot do—and therefore low-income people end up spending a higher percentage of their income on sales tax. Two qualifications to the regressive nature of sales taxes need to be recognized. First, some of the savings made by high-income people may ultimately be used to purchase goods that are subject to the sales tax. This has the effect of making the sales tax less regressive. Second, if the percentage of the tax is applied to the tax base (that is, purchased goods), then the sales tax is proportional, not regressive.

IMPACT

As a percentage of purchases, sales tax rates are not extremely high in the United States. In 2008, the highest state-based sales tax was in Tennessee, which has a 5.5 percent sales tax on groceries and a 7 percent tax on other items. Tennessee counties are allowed to add increments of 0.25 percent sales tax above the state levy up to a maximum of 2.75 percent total. Although the 9.25 percent sales tax in

force across most of Tennessee is the highest state-based sales tax, it is important to remember that Tennessee has no income tax. As of 2008, the highest sales tax paid in any jurisdiction in the United States was in Chicago, where the consumer must pay 10.25 percent when the state, county, and city sales taxes are combined, and the second highest sales tax was in Baton Rouge, Louisiana, where a 5 percent local rate is piggybacked on top of a 4 percent state rate. For purposes of comparison, it is useful to note that in a number of Western European countries and the value-added tax can be as high as 25 percent.

Generally speaking, the greatest burden on most businesses comes in the form of the requirement that they collect sales taxes, maintain careful records of the taxes collected, and forward them to the state. High-income individuals who own businesses are genuinely willing to pay for this expense because they believe they are paying less tax than they would if income taxes were used in place of sales. However, when sales tax rates differ between neighboring states, businesses in the state with higher rates lose an undetermined amount of sales to businesses in the neighboring state, particularly if the variation in tax rates is significant.

Richard L. Wilson

FURTHER READING

Baiman, Ron, Heather Boushey, and Dawn Saunders. *Political Economy and Contemporary Capitalism: Radical Perspectives on Economic Theory and Policy.* Armonk, N.Y.: M. E. Sharpe, 2000. This collection of essays examines economics and tax policy from a perspective sympathetic to socialism.

Brunori, David. *State Tax Policy: A Political Perspective.* 2d ed. Washington, D.C.: Urban Institute Press, 2005. Discusses state tax policies and includes a chapter on sales and use taxes.

Dow, Louis A., and Fred Hendon. *Economics and Society.* Englewood Cliffs, N.J.: Prentice Hall, 1991. These coauthors are strongly influenced by the free-market economics of Adam Smith and examine economics in a societal context.

Kurian, George T., ed. *A Historical Guide to the U.S. Government.* New York: Oxford University Press, 1998. A very useful guide to understanding the three branches of the federal government and the bureaucracy in a historical context.

Willis, James. *Explorations in Macroeconomics*. 5th ed. Redding, Calif.: North West, 2002. This mainstream text examines taxation from a macroeconomic perspective, explaining the impact of taxation on society.

SEE ALSO: Income tax, corporate; Income tax, personal; Internal Revenue Code; Retail trade industry; Taxation; Whiskey tax of 1791.

S&P's. *See* Standard & Poor's

Savings and loan associations

DEFINITION: Federally charted firms that accept deposits from the public and make loans, chiefly for home mortgages

SIGNFICANCE: Savings and loan associations are similar to banks but offer a somewhat narrower range of services because of government restrictions and their traditional emphasis on saving and lending money. Much of their lending is in the form of home mortgages, helping to finance businesses involved in construction and real estate.

Early savings and loan associations (S&Ls) were commonly called building and loan (B&L) associations. The first B&L was established in 1831, with a group of households pooling their savings so that a few members of the group could borrow money, primarily to buy a house. Most B&Ls were owned by the members, who received the profits and determined the management.

With urbanization, the number of B&Ls grew rapidly, until by 1890, they were operating in every state. During the 1880's, there was a boom in "national" B&Ls. These were for-profit organizations that offered high interest on savings, often by charging high fees and late-payment penalties. The depression of 1893 led to many failures among the "nationals," and they faded away.

In 1900, S&L assets totaled about $500 million, compared with $10 billion for commercial banks and $2.4 billion for mutual savings banks. There were about five thousand S&Ls, so their average size was about $100,000. Their mortgage loans were often made for periods of eight to twelve years—much longer than those from other lenders. S&L deposits (often called shares) might be payable on demand, but the institution could enforce a thirty-day waiting period.

In the boom conditions between 1900 and 1929, the middle class increasingly sought home ownership. By 1929, S&Ls held 22 percent of all home mortgages, and about 10 percent of the population were members of an S&L. The number increased from 6,600 in 1914 to 11,800 in 1924. By 1929, S&Ls had more than 12 million members. However, the $7.4 billion of S&L assets in 1929 was only slightly over 10 percent as large as the holdings of commercial banks.

THE GREAT DEPRESSION

Between 1929 and 1933, declining income and mass unemployment meant that many home buyers were unable to meet their mortgage obligations. Numerous S&Ls failed, and many more survived only by imposing severe restrictions on withdrawals. The flow of credit into new-home construction dried up.

The federal government moved gradually to provide relief. In July, 1932, Congress established the Federal Home Loan Banks to provide credit facilities for home-mortgage lenders. In June, 1933, Congress established the Home Owners Loan Corporation (HOLC). By the time the HOLC stopped lending in June, 1936, it had bought $768 million of mortgages from S&Ls. In June, 1934, Congress established the Federal Savings and Loan Insurance Corporation (FSLIC). Deposit accounts ("shares") were insured up to $5,000 per deposit. In June, 1934, Congress also created the Federal Housing Administration, which insured long-term amortized home mortgages, protecting lenders against default by borrowers.

The end of World War II in 1945 unleashed a huge boom in residential construction and mortgage lending. S&Ls provided much of the financing, aided by their ability to pay higher interest rates to depositors than commercial banks. Between 1945 and 1952, S&Ls increased their assets from $9 billion to $23 billion, an expansion of more than 150 percent, while commercial banks expanded by only about 20 percent. By 1965, S&Ls accounted for 26 percent of household savings and

NUMBER OF FDIC-INSURED SAVINGS INSTITUTIONS, UNITED STATES AND OTHER AREAS, 1984-2007

Year	Savings Institutions	Year	Savings Institutions
1984	3,418	1996	1,926
1985	3,626	1997	1,780
1986	3,577	1998	1,690
1987	3,622	1999	1,642
1988	3,437	2000	1,589
1989	3,087	2001	1,534
1990	2,815	2002	1,466
1991	2,561	2003	1,411
1992	2,390	2004	1,345
1993	2,262	2005	1,307
1994	2,152	2006	1,279
1995	2,030	2007	1,251

Source: Data from the Federal Deposit Insurance Corporation

provided 46 percent of single-family home loans. The number of S&Ls remained relatively constant from 1945 through 1965 at around six thousand, but many branches were added. Aggressive rate competition for savings led Congress in 1966 to impose rate ceilings on S&L accounts. Despite problems from rising interest rates, during the 1970's, total S&L assets continued to increase vigorously, rising from $176 billion in 1970 to $579 billion in 1979.

THE S&L CRISIS

The abrupt rise in interest rates during the late 1970's threatened the solvency of S&Ls, as assets declined in value, and depositors shifted funds to other savings media such as money market mutual funds. In response, Congress moved in 1980 to remove ceilings on deposit interest rates for banks and S&Ls. Then in 1982, the Garn-St. Germain Act increased the coverage of federal deposit insurance to $100,000 per account. (On October 3, 2008, this amount was increased to $250,000.) S&Ls were given greater discretion in types of savings media they could provide and greater latitude in lending. They were permitted to have up to 40 percent of their assets in commercial real estate loans, up to 30 percent in consumer lending, and up to 10 percent in commercial loans and leases.

Deregulation opened the way for S&Ls to take on greater risk in hopes of earning greater returns. Neither S&L management nor the regulatory authorities had enough experience to recognize signs of trouble. Because of decline in the market value of their mortgage assets, as many as half the S&Ls in the country were insolvent (had liabilities greater than assets) by the end of 1982.

In August, 1989, Congress undertook drastic measures toward the S&L industry in the Financial Institutions Reform, Recovery, and Enforcement Act (FIRREA). The law abolished both the Home Loan Bank Board and FSLIC, which had failed in their responsibilities. Regulation of S&Ls was lodged in the Office of Thrift Supervision under the U.S. Treasury Department. Deposit insurance for S&Ls was moved to the Federal Deposit Insurance Corporation. FIRREA also created the Resolution Trust Corporation (RTC). The RTC took over the assets of about 750 S&Ls and managed their sale, closing operations at the end of 1995. The ultimate cost to the government and taxpayers was roughly $150 billion. Many of the rules liberalizing asset choices were reversed. Capital requirements for S&Ls were increased from 3 to 8 percent.

The combined effect of deregulation and the crisis-bailout sequence greatly reduced the scale and scope of the S&L industry. By 2007, there were only about one thousand S&Ls, and their operations had become very similar to those of commercial banks.

Paul B. Trescott

FURTHER READING

Adams, James Ring. *The Big Fix: Inside the S&L Scandal.* New York: John Wiley & Sons, 1990. Emphasizes internal corruption, political ties, and fraud as the causes for S&L difficulties.

Barth, James R. *The Great Savings and Loan Debacle.* Washington, D.C.: American Enterprise Institute Press, 1991. Describes the problems that arose in the S&L industry and the personalities involved.

Black, William K. *The Best Way to Rob a Bank Is to Own One: How Corporate Executives and Politicians Looted the S&L Industry.* Austin: University of Texas Press, 2005. Account by the director of litigation for the Federal Home Loan Bank Board during the 1980's describes how some executives used a weak regulatory environment to perpetrate accounting fraud. Links the S&L crisis to business failures of the early twenty-first century.

Ewalt, Josephine H. *A Business Reborn: The Savings and Loan Story, 1930-1960*. Chicago: American Savings and Loan Institute Press, 1962. Industry-sponsored overview of its best years.

Mishkin, Frederic. *The Economics of Money, Banking, and Financial Markets*, 7th ed. New York: Pearson/Addison Wesley, 2007. All editions of this college text deal at length with the policy changes of the 1930's and the S&L crisis of the 1980's.

White, Lawrence J. *The S&L Debacle: Public Policy Lessons for Bank and Thrift Regulation*. New York: Oxford University Press, 1991. Excellent scholarly study of S&L problems analyzes the portfolio changes in the industry, showing that commercial, consumer, and land loans, not junk bonds, caused the asset value to fall, while regulatory problems allowed the S&Ls to weaken.

SEE ALSO: Bank failures; Banking; Construction industry; Credit unions; Deregulation of financial institutions; Federal Deposit Insurance Corporation; Financial crisis of 2008; Morris Plan banks; Mortgage industry; Real estate industry, residential; Supreme Court and banking law.

SBA. *See* Small Business Administration

Sears, Roebuck and Company

IDENTIFICATION: Retail department store
DATE: Founded in 1886
SIGNIFICANCE: As one of the pioneers of the mail-order retail industry and a leading retailer of the twentieth century, Sears, Roebuck introduced or popularized a number of innovative business practices in its efforts to adapt to changing markets.

During its early years, the Sears, Roebuck and Company sold only watches and other jewelry. However, its founders, R. W. Sears and Alvah C. Roebuck, quickly developed the company according to the mail-order retail model pioneered by Montgomery Ward, which used newly constructed railroad networks to ship a variety of goods at low cost to small towns and rural areas. Offering a steadily increasing variety of items in its annual catalogs, Sears, Roebuck provided cash-strapped Americans with an alternative to relatively expensive general stores and dry-goods merchants during the economic depression of the 1890's, outstripping the sales volume of other mail-order houses. By the early twentieth century, the company offered thousands of items, ranging from the most modest of household goods to automobiles and homes.

After assuming a dominant position among mail-order retailers serving rural markets, Sears, Roebuck began making inroads into urban retail markets, opening its first department store in Chicago in 1925. Several more stores in the Chicago area opened during the 1920's and early 1930's. Early Sears department stores proved successful, but they failed to match the market dominance of the company's mail-order business, because they were competing with numerous established urban retailers.

The proliferation of suburban neighborhoods in the United States following World War II led to a shrinkage of both urban and rural retail markets, forcing Sears, Roebuck to alter its business plan. In addition to opening a number of large anchor stores in suburban shopping malls during the postwar period, the company sought to solidify its hold on mail-order retailing by establishing catalog stores in small towns. In these stores, some large items such as appliances could be purchased in-store, and other items could be ordered from catalogs with the assistance of salespeople. The company also began producing its own merchandise under various brand names, including the popular Craftsman line of hand and power tools. These and other efforts at diversification allowed Sears, Roebuck to remain competitive during the economic changes of the second half of the twentieth century and to become the largest retailer in the United States, a position that it would retain until the early 1980's.

Sears, Roebuck also extended its diversification outside the retail sector, establishing the Allstate Insurance Company in 1931 and purchasing the Coldwell Banker real estate company in 1981. In the light of increasing consumer demand for revolving charge accounts, the company introduced the Discover credit card in 1985. In 2004, the Kmart discount chain purchased Sears, Roebuck and its various holdings. It continued to operate stores under both the Sears and Kmart brand names. Despite decreasing profits and a shrinking market share, Sears, Roebuck remained a powerful force in the global retail market during the early twenty-first century.

Michael H. Burchett

FURTHER READING

Katz, Donald R. *The Big Store: Inside the Crisis and Revolution at Sears.* New York: Penguin, 1988.

Martinez, Arthur C. *The Hard Road to the Softer Side: Lessons from the Transformation of Sears.* New York: Crown Business, 2001.

Worthy, James C. *Shaping an American Institution: Robert E. Wood and Sears, Roebuck.* Champaign: University of Illinois Press, 1984.

SEE ALSO: Catalog shopping; Credit card buying; Montgomery Ward; Retail trade industry; Wal-Mart.

A washer for sale at a Sears, Roebuck store in Syracuse, New York, in 1941. (Library of Congress)

SEC. *See* Securities and Exchange Commission

Second Bank of the United States. *See* Bank of the United States, Second

Secret Service, U.S.

IDENTIFICATION: Federal law-enforcement agency under the Department of Homeland Security

DATE: Established on April 14, 1865

SIGNIFICANCE: The U.S. Secret Service is one of the country's oldest federal law-enforcement agencies. Aside from its main task of protecting the president and other national and foreign officials, the service has played an integral part in investigating various types of business and financial crimes that threaten the country's economic well-being.

On April 14, 1865, during the administration of President Abraham Lincoln, the Secret Service was created under the auspices of the Department of the Treasury. Its main function at the time was to prevent Treasury notes and U.S. currencies from being counterfeited and disseminated.

For much of the nineteenth century, the American currency system had been in utter disarray and rife with corruption and illicit activity. At one point, each state had one or more versions of its own coin and paper currency. More than one-third of all paper currency in the United States during the mid-nineteenth century was estimated to be counterfeit.

In its first few decades of operation, the Secret Service shut down hundreds of counterfeiting operations throughout the United States. However, the Secret Service was also directed to look into many cases that fell outside its investigative realm. At various times, the presidents directed the Secret Service to investigate individuals involved in the Teapot Dome scandal, frauds committed by members of the government, and the activities of any U.S. citizen who posed a threat to the government and the people of the United States. The groups most frequently targeted by the Secret Service were those that exhibited antigovernment sentiment (for example, the Ku Klux Klan).

PROTECTION

Ironically, the same evening that President Lincoln authorized the creation of the Secret Service, he was assassinated at a theater in Washington, D.C., by John Wilkes Booth. This was the first time in U.S. history that a president was assassinated. The public was outraged and petitioned Congress to find a way to protect future presidents. It took Congress thirty-six more years to furnish this protection. During that period, two other U.S. presidents— James A. Garfield and William McKinley—were assassinated before the protection of presidents was added to the duties and responsibilities of the Secret Service. After the assassination of President McKinley in 1901, the U.S. Congress in 1906 created a federal law stating that the protection of the president of the United States was a distinct duty and responsibility of the Secret Service. In 1917, a verbal or written threat against a president or any members of the president's family became a federal offense. This law was later broadened to cover the vice president and any family members in 1951.

The protective role of the Secret Service has grown substantially since its inception. There are two divisions of Secret Service personnel who are responsible for various protective assignments. The first division is made up of special nonuniformed agents who act as personal bodyguards for various governmental dignitaries. These agents are specially trained and prepared for many years before being assigned to this duty. The second group is uniformed Secret Service officers who carry out their duties much like regular police officers. These uniformed officers, created in 1922 by President Warren G. Harding, are a visible presence charged with providing security at such places as the White House, the vice president's residence, all buildings in which presidential offices are located, all U.S. Treasury buildings, all foreign embassies in Wash-

The president's secret service men, probably in the 1920's or 1930's. (Library of Congress)

ington, D.C., and any other federal facilities throughout the United States deemed by the president to need further security.

INVESTIGATION

The primary investigative mission of the Secret Service continues to be counterfeiting and other financially related crimes. Since the early 1980's, Congress has expanded the investigative responsibilities of the Secret Service to include credit card fraud, crimes involving specific types of forgery, computer fraud, and any crimes related to various types of American financial institutions. After the September 11 terrorist attacks, the Secret Service was also mandated to investigate certain crimes related to domestic terrorism, especially incidents involving school violence and hate groups; certain cases of money laundering; and major identity-theft cases. The Secret Service is the only federal agency that has been delegated explicit federal investigative power over identity-theft cases.

ORGANIZATION

In 2003, the U.S. Secret Service became part of the Department of Homeland Security. As of 2008, the Secret Service had roughly 5,000 employees in various field offices both in the United States and overseas. Nearly 1,200 were uniformed officers assigned to protect various federal facilities affiliated with the president, vice president, 170 foreign embassies, and the Department of Homeland Security. Most of these facilities were in the greater metropolitan Washington, D.C., area. Close to 3,000 special agents were assigned to either investigative or protective duties in Washington, D.C., throughout the continental United States, and overseas. A special agent is trained in both protective and investigative functions and is expected to be able to perform the duties and responsibilities of both roles anytime and anywhere.

Paul M. Klenowski

FURTHER READING

Bullock, Jane, et al. *Introduction to Homeland Security.* Boston: Butterworth-Heineman, 2006. Provides a detailed look at the restructuring of many federal law-enforcement agencies, including the Secret Service.

Holden, Henry. *To Be a U.S. Secret Service Agent.* St. Paul, Minn.: Zenith Press, 2006. Offers insight into both the history and the recruitment and training of secret service agents.

Hulnick, Arthur S. *Keeping Us Safe: Secret Intelligence and Homeland Security.* Westport, Conn.: Praeger, 2004. Explains the new and expanded roles of many federal agencies, including the Secret Service, after the September 11 terrorist attacks.

Melanson, Philip. *The Secret Service: The Hidden History of an Enigmatic Agency.* Rev. ed. New York: Basic Books, 2005. The most complete and accurate look at the history of the U.S. Secret Service.

Petro, Joseph, with Jeffrey Robinson. *Standing Next to History: An Agent's Life Inside the Secret Service.* New York: Thomas Dunne, 2005. The real-life testimony of a former Secret Service agent, who often gives candid behind-the-scene accounts of his work.

SEE ALSO: Business crimes; Counterfeiting; Currency; Homeland Security, U.S. Department of; Identity theft; September 11 terrorist attacks; Treasury, U.S. Department of the.